A History of England

A History of England

FOURTH EDITION

Volume I
Prehistory–1714

Stuart E. Prall
Queens College and the Graduate School/University Center
City University of New York

David Harris Willson

HOLT, RINEHART AND WINSTON, INC.
Fort Worth Chicago San Francisco Philadelphia
Montreal Toronto London Syndey Tokyo

Publisher	Ted Buchholz
Developmental Editor	Martin Lewis
Acquisitions Editor	David Tatom
Project Editor	Steve Welch/Michele Tomiak
Production Manager	Tad Gaither
Art & Design Supervisor	John Ritland
Text Designer	Greg Draper
Cover Designer	Nancy Turner
Cover Illustration	James Tennison

Library of Congress Cataloging-in-Publication Data
Prall, Stuart E.
   A history of England / Stuart E. Prall, David Harris Willson.—4th ed.
     p.   cm.
   Rev. ed. of: A history of England / David Harris Willson. 3rd ed. c1984.
   Includes bibliographical references and index.
   ISBN 0-03-033424-1 (v. 1).—ISBN 0-03-033427-6 (v. 2)
   1. Great Britain—History. 2. England—Civilization.
I. Willson, David Harris, 1901- . II. Willson, David Harris,
1901-   History of England. III. Title.
DA30.W62 1991
942—dc20   90-43898
                                                                          rev. CIP

ISBN 0-03-033424-1

Copyright © 1991, 1984, 1972, 1967 by Holt, Rinehart and Winston, Inc.

All rights reserved. No part of this publication may be reproduced or transmitted in any form or by any means, electronic or mechanical, including photocopy, recording, or any information storage and retrieval system, without permission in writing from the publisher.

Requests for permission to make copies of any part of the work should be mailed to: Copyrights and Permissions Department, Holt, Rinehart and Winston, Inc., 6277 Sea Harbor Drive, Orlando, FL 32887

Address editorial correspondence to: 301 Commerce Street, Suite 3700, Fort Worth, TX 76102. *Address orders to:* 6277 Sea Harbor Drive, Orlando, FL 32887 1-800-782-4479, or 1-800-433-0001 (in Florida)

The paper used in this book was made from recycled paper.

Printed in the United States of America
   6 7 8 9   016   10 9 8 7 6 5

Holt, Rinehart and Winston, Inc.
The Dryden Press
Saunders College Publishing

Preface

This new edition of A History of England has been restructured in content and redesigned in format and appearance. The book continues to cover the whole span of English history, from the earliest settlers to the introduction of the Poll Tax and the fall of Margaret Thatcher. It is a combination of narrative and analysis, incorporating new research. There is much new narrative on the lives of ordinary people, women and men. The scholarly debates over the causes of the English Revolution have been brought up to date. The post-World War II era has been restructured and expanded.

The new material has provided the opportunity to introduce a time-line at the end of each chapter. This integrates the key events and persons in a chronological frame, helping the reader to see how the variety of topics—political, economic, social, military, literary, and religious—all flow along together from one period to another. The additional maps, combined with the time-lines, provide the reader with the tools to see the history in its full setting of time and place. The additional illustrations will turn names into familiar faces and give a greater immediacy to the study of the past.

Although much is new, the basic story of England's history is still true to the original text written by the late David Harris Willson. It has been my purpose from the outset to build upon the strengths in the original while expanding and updating the work. Many scholars made suggestions before the work began and many read the completed manuscript with great care. I have benefited greatly from their suggestions. Among those most closely involved were R.J.Q. Adams, Josef Altholz, Thom Armstrong, Jaquelin Collins, Clive Holmes, Mark Neuman, Johann P. Sommerville, and Malcom Thorp. I am grateful to them all.

Special thanks must go to Martin Lewis of Holt, Rinehart and Winston, whose inspiration, encouragement, and friendly and cheerful disposition were invaluable. My graduate assistant Guanrong Shen was of tremendous help in organizing and preparing the illustrations, maps, and charts. Many libraries and galleries provided photos and permissions. I am particularly grateful to Marcia L. Lein of Wide World Photos for helping me find my way through their vast collection of prints.

The new two-volume "split" edition is designed for those who break the course of study somewhere in the seventeenth century. Recognizing that many different dates are used to separate one semester from another, both volumes contain all the chapters on the seventeenth century.

This new edition has been a challenge. It has also been fun.

S. E. P.

Hewlett, New York

Contents

Preface	**v**
Tables and Maps	**xiii**

1 Early Peoples of Britain: Pre-Celtic, Celtic, and Roman — 1
Mountain and Plain — 1
Early Peoples in Britain — 5
The Celts — 9
Roman Britain — 12

2 The Anglo-Saxons — 20
The Invasion of Britain — 20
The Anglo-Saxons — 22
Conversion of the Anglo-Saxons — 23
The Origins of Political Unity — 27
King Alfred, 871–899 — 32
The Reconquest of the Danelaw — 35
The Height and the Decline of English Monarchy — 36
King Cnut, 1016–1035 — 37
Social Classes — 37
Anglo-Saxon Government — 41
The Achievement of the Anglo-Saxon Kings — 48

3 The Norman Conquest — 50
Normandy — 50
The Last English Kings — 53
The Norman Invasion — 55
Feudalism — 58
Norman Monarchy — 64
The Peasant, the Village, and the Manor — 68

The Domesday Book	70
William and the Church	70

4 From Normans to Angevins: William II, Henry I, Stephen, and Henry II — 74

William Rufus, 1087–1100	75
The Reign of Henry I, 1100–1135	76
King Stephen, 1135–1154	80
Henry II, 1154–1189, and the New Monarchy	83
The Legal Innovations of Henry II	84
Henry II and the Church	88
The Angevin Empire	91

5 Kings and Barons — 95

Richard I, 1189–1199	95
King John, 1199–1216	98
Henry III, 1216–1272	105

6 Society in the Twelfth and Thirteenth Centuries — 111

The Church	111
Architecture	120
The Intellectual Renaissance	122
Social and Economic Life	128

7 Edward I and Edward II: The Beginnings of Parliament — 137

Edward I, 1272–1307	137
The Government of Edward I	138
Edward and the Celtic Peoples	143
Edward I and France	149
Taxation	150
Edward's Last Years	152
Parliament	153
Edward II, 1307–1327	156

8 Edward III and Richard II: War and Plague — 159

Edward III, 1327–1377	160
Chivalry and War	160
Parliament in the Reign of Edward III	165
The Last Years of Edward III	168
Social and Economic Life	169
The Church	175
Richard II, 1377–1399	180
Literature and the Arts	182

9 Kingship in the Fifteenth Century — **187**
- Henry IV, 1399–1413 — 187
- Henry V, 1413–1422, and the War with France — 189
- Henry VI, 1422–1461 — 192
- The Collapse of Government under Henry VI — 197
- Edward IV, 1461–1483 — 199
- Richard III, 1483–1485 — 204

10 Henry VII: The Strengthening of Kingship — **209**
- Henry VII, 1485–1509 — 209
- Securing the Dynasty — 210
- The Strengthening of Kingship — 215
- Commercial Policy — 220
- The Expansion of Europe Overseas — 222

11 Henry VIII: The Break with Rome — **226**
- Henry VIII, 1509–1547: The Young King — 226
- The Great Cardinal — 229
- Background of the Break with Rome — 233
- The Reformation Parliament, 1529–1536 — 240
- The Dissolution of the Monasteries — 243
- The Church of England — 244
- The State — 245
- Henry's Last Years — 248

12 Edward VI and Mary: Religious and Economic Change — **250**
- Edward VI, 1547–1553, and the Return of Faction — 250
- Mary Tudor, 1553–1558, and the Catholic Reaction — 255
- Economic Tension — 259
- Inflation — 260
- The Cloth Trade — 261
- Agriculture — 262
- The End of the Boom — 266
- The Decline of the Guilds — 267
- The London Money Market — 268

13 Elizabeth I: The First Ten Years of the Reign — **270**
- The Queen — 270
- Initial Problems — 272
- Scotland and Mary, Queen of Scots — 278
- Economic Reform — 281
- The Catholics — 282
- The Puritans — 284

14 Elizabeth I: The Spanish Armada — 289
- Changes in the Alignment of Powers — 289
- The Beginning of Conflict — 290
- English Maritime Enterprise — 295
- The Spanish Armada — 302

15 Elizabethan England — 308
- The Spanish War, 1588–1603 — 308
- The East India Company — 311
- Gratuities and Faction — 312
- The Spirit of the Age — 314
- Literature — 315
- The Social Structure — 319
- London — 326
- The Court — 327
- The Privy Council — 328
- Parliament — 329

16 James I: The Prerogative Challenged — 333
- The British Solomon — 334
- The Religious Settlement — 337
- The Parliament of 1604–1610 — 340
- The Parliament of 1614 — 345
- Degeneration in Government — 345
- The Parliament of 1621 — 352
- James's Last Years — 353

17 The Reign of Charles I to 1642 — 355
- The New King, 1625–1649 — 355
- The Clash with the Commons — 356
- Charles's Personal Rule — 361
- The Bishops' Wars and the Short Parliament — 366
- The First Years of the Long Parliament — 368
- The Causes of the Civil War — 371

18 The Civil Wars and the Rule of the Saints — 374
- How the Country Was Divided — 374
- The Civil War, 1642–1646 — 375
- Presbyterians and Independents — 380
- The Commonwealth, 1649–1653 — 385
- The Barebones Parliament and the Instrument of Government — 389
- The Protectorate, 1653–1659 — 392
- Overseas Expansion — 394

Economic Change	398
The End of the Protectorate	401

19 Restoration and Revolution — 403
The Restoration	403
The Fall of Clarendon	408
The Cabal and the Secret Treaty of Dover	410
Danby, Political Parties, and Louis XIV	412
The Popish Plot	413
The Exclusion Struggle	413
James II, 1685–1688	415
The Glorious Revolution	417
Science and the Arts	421

20 William III and Anne — 426
William III, 1689–1702 and Mary II, 1689–1694	426
War with France	427
William and English Politics	431
The Partition Treaties	432
Queen Anne, 1702–1714	433

Suggestions for Further Reading — R–1

Index — R–13

Genealogical Tables

House of Lancaster	206
House of York	207
House of Tudor	224
House of Stuart	423
House of Hanover	442

Maps

Counties of England and Wales to 1974	facing page 1
Counties of England and Wales since 1974	3
Physical map of England and Wales Exe-Tees Line	5
The Civitates of Roman Britain	14
London: The Hub	16
Saxon kingdoms and Bretwaldaships 630–829	29
England in the seventh and eighth centuries	30
England, about 885	33
The Norman Conquest, 1066–1072	56
The French Dominions of Henry II	92
Medieval dioceses with monasteries and towns mentioned in the text	113
Scotland	147
English possessions in France in 1428	194
The Wars of the Roses: castles and battles 1450–1485	196
The Armada 1588	305
Ireland in the 16th century	310
Areas under royal control	376
India and the East Indies in the 17th century	398
The Atlantic Ocean 1660	399
The Indian Ocean 1660	399
The Netherlands 1700	436

A History of England

Counties of England and Wales to 1974.

Early Peoples of Britain: Pre-Celtic, Celtic, and Roman

The British Isles consist of two major islands—Britain and Ireland—and several smaller ones, among which is the Isle of Man. Of the two main islands, Britain is the larger. The island of Britain is composed of three distinct regions and cultures—England, Scotland, and Wales. England alone occupies about 56 percent of the area of Britain. Throughout recorded history an even larger portion of the British population was in England. The fact of the matter is that the history of Britain (and even of the British Isles) is the history of the dominant portion of the larger island. This book is about that one portion—England.

No one region of the United States has ever played as dominant a role in American history as England has played in the history of the United Kingdom, and, indeed, of the British Isles. The entire United Kingdom is equal in size to the state of Oregon. England alone is about the size of Alabama. The population of the United Kingdom is a quarter of that of the United States, crowded into an area the size of Oregon.

MOUNTAIN AND PLAIN

The island of Britain is divided by nature into two parts, the North and West, and the South and East. One is an area of high hills and mountains, the other an area of rolling plain. [The division may be marked by a line running from the southwestern to the northeastern part of the country.] Beginning at the mouth of the Exe River in modern Devon, the line runs northward to the Bristol Channel, skirts the mountains of Wales, turns northeast around the southern edge of the Pennine Hills, and reaches the North Sea at the mouth of the river Tees, which separates the modern counties of York and Durham.

To the north and west of the Exe-Tees line is a highland or mountainous zone that forms the remains of an ancient mountain chain and has three parts: the high moors of Devon, the mountains of Wales, and a very large area to the north, which includes much of Scotland and northern England. Through the ages this mountain chain has been worn by erosion and battered by storms from the Atlantic, so that its western coast is ragged and irregular, with deep glens and valleys between the mountain masses. Where agriculture is possible, the soil is thin and stony and the rock formation beneath is very hard, so that water from the Atlantic rains does not sink easily into the ground but runs off in swift unnavigable streams or keeps the earth in a water-logged condition. The area is cold and windy, and although it is of great natural beauty, with the green of the hills running to the water's edge, it is, in general, unsuitable for agriculture and uninviting for permanent settlement.

The country to the south and east of the Exe-Tees line is a gently undulating plain with large expanses of almost level ground. Most of it is less than 500 feet above sea level, and although there are some hills, they rarely reach a height of more than 1000 feet. The soil is normally fertile and productive, well suited either for pasture or for the cultivation of crops. There is a good deal of rain, but the climate is drier than in the highland zone, with more sunshine and less wind. Water sinks into the ground more easily. The temperature is moderate, without extremes of heat or cold. Life is easier and more comfortable than it is in the mountains. So long as Britain remained predominantly an agricultural country the lowland plain was the more prosperous, progressive, and thickly populated part of the island. But after the Industrial Revolution in the eighteenth century, population shifted to the area near the coal fields, which for the most part are north and west of the Exe-Tees line.

The water parting in Britain is far to the west. The western streams, flowing from the mountains toward the Atlantic or toward the Irish Sea, are swift and turbulent; but the eastern rivers flowing in the opposite direction are long, gentle, and slowly moving bodies of water on which small boats can travel for great distances. The Thames, of course, is the largest British river. It takes its rise far to the west and flows eastward through the southern part of the plain. To the north of the Thames Valley a number of smaller rivers, including the Ouse and the Welland, flow into the estuary known as the Wash; others, of which the longest is the Trent, join to form the Humber. Still farther to the north many streams—such as the Tees, the Tyne, and the Tweed—come down from the Pennine Hills in an easterly direction. The Severn River in the west is unique. Rising in the mountains of central Wales, it starts eastward, makes a half circle through western England, turns south, and enters the sea through the Bristol Channel. It is a natural and highly important waterway, navigable for long distances. Many cities have arisen upon its banks to form a thickly inhabited region in the western part of the country.

The lowland zone is broken by several chains of low hills. They appear to converge upon Salisbury Plain in the south-central portion of the country. One of these upland ridges, the South Downs, runs along the southern coast in Sussex and Hampshire.

Counties of England and Wales since 1974.

Another, the North Downs, follows a roughly parallel line farther to the east, skirting the southern edge of the Valley of the Thames. A third, the Chiltern Hills, stretches toward the southwest through the central portion of the plain; a fourth, known as the Cotswolds, is farther to the west near Wales. In prehistoric times, when most of Britain was covered by dense forest and there were large areas of marsh and fen, men walked on paths along the tops or sides of these chains of hills. One ancient path, known as the Icknield Way, began near the Wash and followed the Chilterns toward Salisbury Plain in the south. Another, the Harroway, running from Kent toward Salisbury, followed the North Downs for part of the distance. Invaders from the Continent, therefore, could quickly penetrate into the lowland zone. The Thames, the Ouse, and the Trent gave easy access to the interior, and the ancient pathways along the hills led directly into the heart of the country. As wave after wave of newcomers arrived in Britain, they took possession of the plain and drove the former inhabitants westward into the mountains. In the most important of these invasions, Anglo-Saxon tribes coming from Germany in the fifth and six centuries A.D. drove back the Celts into the mountains of Wales and Scotland and also into Ireland. Yet in truth the highland zone had already become a melting pot of earlier peoples.

Nor was it difficult for primitive men to cross the Channel. In modern times, of course, the Channel has become a protection against invasion; the sea has served England in the manner of a wall or as a moat defensive to a house. But the Channel became a barrier only when there were strong governments in England with armies and navies at their disposal to make invasion dangerous. In early times, when the coast was weakly defended or not defended at all, Britain was easy to invade. The passage by sea was short, and every little cove and inlet offered a safe landing place.

The inhabitants of the lowland and highland zones have differed from each other in medieval and modern times. This is largely a matter of race, since the plain has been occupied by Anglo-Saxons and the mountains by Celtic peoples. But it is possible that differences may be explained to some extent by geography. The mountaineers of Wales and Scotland have lived in poverty and isolation, cut off from contacts with the outside world. They have cherished their liberty and have resented interference from England. Conservative in temperament, they have been tenacious of old customs and old ways. New ideas and new movements coming into the highland zone of Britain have had to contend and compromise with ancient customs. The result has often been a blending of the two. In the lowland zone, where life is easier and more prosperous and where there are closer contacts with the Continent, changes have come about more readily. Yet in relation to the Continent, the whole country possesses some of the characteristics of the highland area. Movements from the Continent, such as the Italian Renaissance or the Reformation or the spirit of the French Revolution, have tended to come to Britain rather late and to have penetrated rather slowly. They have usually been altered and modified and have blended and assimilated with older traditions. The extent to which Britain is or is not fully European is a subject for debate among scholars and politicians on both sides of the English Channel.

Physical map of England and Wales: Exe-Tees Line.

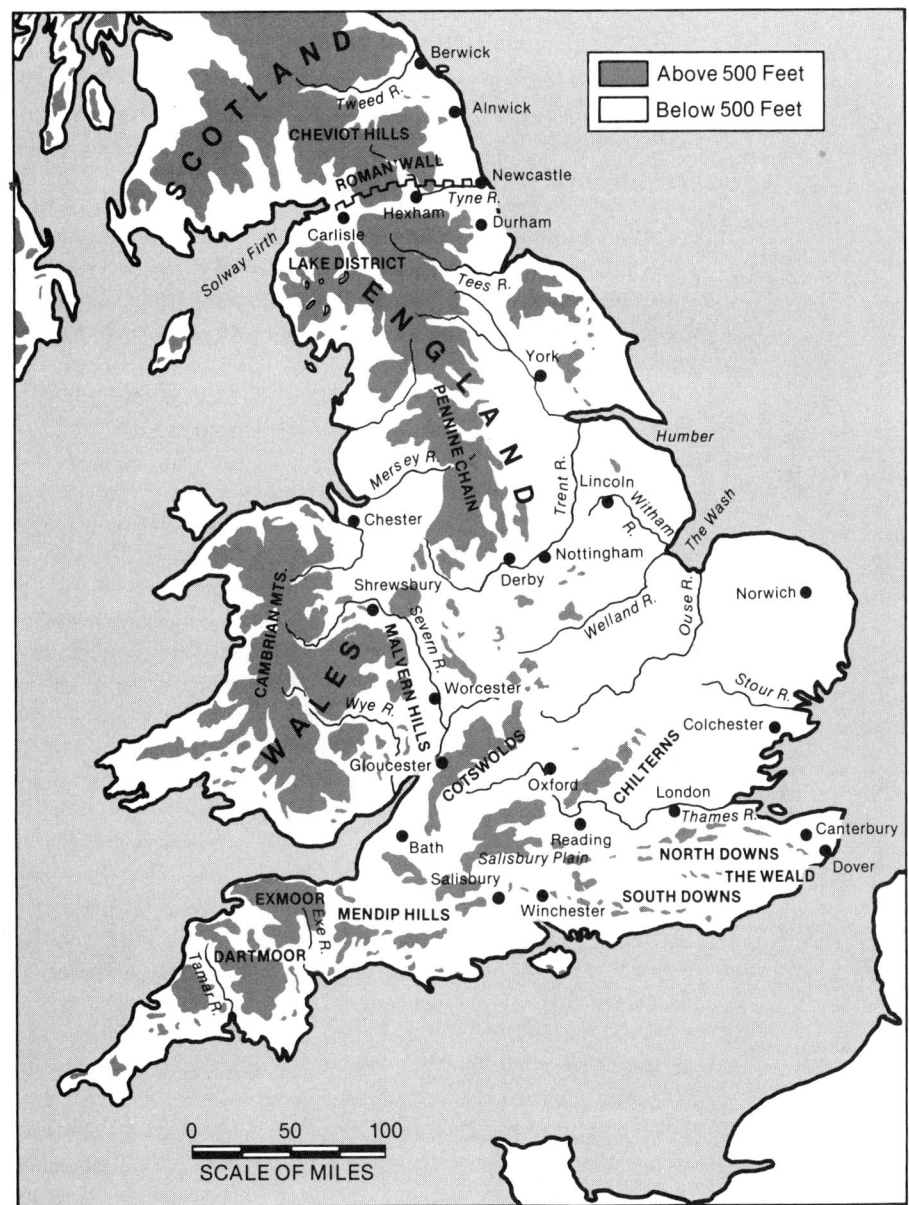

EARLY PEOPLES IN BRITAIN

The first human beings came to Britain by land perhaps half a million years ago, before there was an English Channel. We must think of the primitive men of the Stone age as retreating and advancing before ice sheets and glaciers, digging for the precious flints—those pieces of very hard stone they chipped to a point or to a cutting edge—fighting bears and hyenas, stalking the reindeer or the woolly mammoth or the wild horse or the boar in the primeval forest. While the men hunted and fished, the women gathered fruits and vegetables, nuts, edible roots, and shellfish.

About 3500 B.C. in the Neolithic or late stone age, a more civilized people appeared in Britain. They were a Mediterranean people whose culture was derived originally from the Middle East. They migrated north through Spain and France and crossed the Channel to southern and southwestern Britain, to Wales, to Yorkshire and Lincolnshire, to lowland Scotland, and to northeastern Ireland. They were short, dark, and slightly built, with long heads and delicate features. Archeologists have given them the rather clumsy name of the Windmill Hill people because of an excavation of their remains at Windmill Hill in Wiltshire.

The great contribution of the Windmill Hill people was a primitive agriculture. They introduced the fundamental change from a food-hunting to a food-producing society. They kept domestic animals—cattle of a fair size, sheep, pigs, and dogs. The women were skillful in making pottery, and, though there is no evidence of weaving in Britain at this time, it is probable that weaving was carried on. Agriculture was supplemented by hunting deer and small game. The men used bows and arrows tipped with finely cut pygmy flints. Larger and heavier flints were used for axes and picks; in fact, the search for flints became a specialized industry in which pits were sunk to a depth of fifty feet and miners crawled through underground shafts carrying little lamps, which were probably wicks floating in fat in small cups. The Windmill Hill people built encampments in which they and their animals could find protection, but there were also small villages and isolated houses.

The burial of the dead received much attention and was connected with magic and fertility cults and with worship of the earth as a life-giving mother. Bodies were placed in a crouching position in long pits or barrows and were covered with great piles of stones. Because of the leveling of time, these barrows today look like mere oblong mounds of rock. But when they were constructed they were often highly elaborate, sometimes with a large wooden facade at one end, sometimes with underground passages and subterranean burial chambers in which new bodies could be placed from time to time.

About the year 2500 B.C. Britain was invaded by a warlike people who are known as the Beaker folk because of the distinctive shape of their drinking vessels. They belonged to the Alpine peoples who inhabited the mountainous area of Europe stretching from the Balkans to the Pyrenees. The Beaker folk appear to have come from Spain in two wings or divisions. One wing moved north along the Atlantic coast until it reached the Channel Islands, where it crossed to southwestern Britain. A second and larger division expanded into eastern France and northern Italy, then turned north into central Europe, where it met and mingled to some extent with an even more warlike Nordic people to which archeologists have given the unprepossessing name of the Battle-Ax people. The Beaker folk then moved westward to the lower Rhine and from here crossed to many points along the eastern coast of Britain. Large numbers appear to have entered by the Wash and to have moved along the Icknield Way to Salisbury Plain. Larger and more powerfully built than the

Multiphase ring-ditch monument at Four Crosses, Powys. (Christopher Musson for Clowyd Powys Archaeological Trust)

Windmill Hill people, they quickly dispossessed the Windmill Hill people of their fields and cattle and probably the women.

We are now entering the early age of bronze. It is possible that the Beaker folk brought some bronze implements with them, but even before their coming there were smiths in Ireland and in the highland zone of Britain who were making copper axes, awls, and daggers. These copper instruments found a ready market among Beaker folk, although they also used flints for daggers, knives, arrowheads, and polished axes, and employed a stone ax-hammer borrowed from the Battle-Ax peoples on the Continent.

The Beaker folk were a restless pastoral people who preferred to follow their flocks and herds rather than engage in the harder labor of tilling the soil. Cereal crops played only a small part in their economy. They had a keen interest in trade. Glass, gold, and amber ornaments found in their graves point to trade with the Mediterranean, Ireland, and the Baltic. They wore both linen and woolen clothes, which they held together with buttons. The Beaker folk did not build tombs but buried their dead singly in small round barrows in which were placed the weapons and ornaments of the deceased, together with a bowl presumably containing some kind of drink. The grave was then piled high with stones until it resembled an inverted saucer.

The Beaker folk built majestic open-air temples. The most famous, though not the largest, is Stonehenge on Salisbury Plain. Here a space of level ground more than 300 feet across is surrounded by a circular ditch and bank. There is only one entrance which leads to the "temple" in the middle. This temple consists of two circles of huge stones fixed upright in the ground, one circle within the other. Inside these circles other stones form a kind of double horseshoe. The outer horseshoe is composed of five colossal trilithons, each a pair of huge rectangular stones standing upright with another stone resting upon them in the way a lintel rests over a doorway. The inner horseshoe is composed of "bluestones" known to have been brought from a place 200 miles away. At the center is a recumbent slab which forms an altar. As one stands before this slab looking toward the entrance, one faces the point at which the sun rises on the longest day of the year. Stonehenge and other stone circles show

Stonehenge. (Aerofilms, Ltd.)

that the Beaker folk believed in a sky-god, connected in some way with the sun, whom they worshiped in the open air. Stonehenge implies a large population, an ability to transport huge stones for many miles (probably by sea), and some sort of political and social organization.

For more than two hundred years both scholars and amateurs have sought the answer to the riddle of Stonehenge. That the Heel Stone's position was of both astronomical and religious significance is readily accepted. Every year at the summer solstice modern "Druids" make the pilgrimage to Salisbury Plain, much to the annoyance of those entrusted with its preservation. Whatever the intent of its builders over the centuries, it is still alive today.

The force of the invasions by the Beaker folk gradually spent itself; their culture lost its distinct individuality; their blood and traditions merged with those of more ancient peoples whose civilization tended to reappear. A period of change and diversity was followed by one of more uniform culture throughout the island. During the later period (roughly from 2000 to 1500 B.C.) the population increased and pushed into Ireland and into areas of Britain formerly unoccupied. The people were largely pastoral, though they grew some barley as well as wheat. Archeologists call them the Urn people because they cremated their dead and buried the ashes either in coffins or in funereal urns. The period is known as the middle age of bronze. The civilization of this era displayed a more distinctive British quality. Even though much attention is given to each of the several "invasions" of ancient Britain, all cultural changes did not spring from these invasions. There was throughout each period a twin process of development and of continuity.

THE CELTS

A new series of invasions began about the year 1000 B.C. From about this date until the opening of the Christian Era much of western Europe north of the Alps was dominated by a people known as the Celts. They occupied a huge area which included modern France, Belgium, southern and western Germany, Switzerland, and the western Alps. The Celts did not belong exclusively to one of the three distinct peoples of Europe (Nordic, Alpine, Mediterranean) but were a mixture of the first and second. They were descended in part from Battle-Ax people who came from the north of Europe and in part from Beaker folk who had been living in the upper Danube Valley and in the Alps. And they had in their veins a substratum of the blood of earlier peoples. Hence there was a strong family resemblance between them and the Beaker folk who had come to Britain almost a thousand years earlier and who in time had merged with older peoples to form what we have called the Urn societies of the middle age of bronze. The Celts in western Europe were under pressure from Teutonic tribes pressing down from the north and from Illyrian peoples invading Europe from the east. It is not surprising, therefore, that great numbers of Celts passed over to Britain in successive waves of invasion. They dominated the native peoples, merging with them but firmly establishing their own language and civilization.

It is thought that some Celtic refugees from the Continent may have come to Britain as early as the year 1000 B.C. New tools and weapons were developed—an ax with a socker into which a handle could be inserted, a bronze spearhead, and a double-edged sword which provided for the first time a slashing rather than a stabbing weapon.

About the middle of the eighth century B.C., the Celts invaded Britain in far greater numbers. This invasion was probably begun by Celts who had been living along the shores of the lakes of Switzerland. Attacked by Germanic tribes, these lake dwellers migrated to the west and crossed to Britain. In doing so they set other Celtic tribes in motion, so that the number of Celts who invaded Britain at this time was very large. They brought a renewed interest in agriculture. They had a light wooden plow drawn by two oxen. The plowshare cut a shallow furrow in the soil though it did not turn over the furrow. Wheat was grown in small enclosed fields, and cattle were bred in small enclosed pastures. The Celts of this period had superior weapons, both offensive and defensive, such as swords, spears, shields, and chest pieces for horses; they also possessed improved tools for carpenters and workers in bronze and silver, a well-designed sickle, and great bronze caldrons that were symbols of wealth and power.

There were further Celtic invasions of Britain in the fifth, in the third, and in the first century B.C. Coming into Europe from the eastern Mediterranean, the use of iron became known to the tribes in the central part of the Continent and gradually spread to the Celts living in the west. The first iron-using civilization north of the Alps is known as the Hallstatt culture. Hallstatt Celts (Iron Age A) invaded Britain in the sixth century, but the fifth century, when great numbers of Celts came to Britain, was the first true British iron age.

Meanwhile a new culture, the La Tène culture, was developing among the Celts in eastern France and southern Germany. Its rise was stimulated by Celtic trade with Italy and southern France. A principal import from the south was wine, for which the Celts developed a strong liking. Wine was brought north in bronze and pottery vessels decorated with Mediterranean designs, and the decorations as well as the contents of the vessels inspired Celtic craftsmen to develop patterns of their own. The Celts displayed a genius for linear design and for abstract art. The wild, uninhibited, and flamboyant tracery on Celtic pottery and weapons gave the La Tène culture a unique distinction. Hence it may be said that La Tène art owed its existence partly to Celtic thirst.

A table service of beautiful drinking vessels was the cherished possession of a wealthy aristocrat or warrior chieftain. It was these Celtic lords of war who invaded Britain in the third century B.C. (Iron Age B). They met with stiff resistance in southern Britain, so that this area did not develop a wholly La Tène culture. The invaders turned north into modern Norfolk and Suffolk, into Yorkshire and Lancashire, and into Scotland. Their culture followed an aristocratic pattern, with wealth and power concentrated in the hands of a few warrior chieftains. They dressed in long cloaks or tartans fastened at the shoulder with safety-pin brooches. There was a love of personal adornments such as bracelets and necklaces. Society was sufficiently sophisticated for the women to use rouge and hand mirrors and for the men to possess not only dice but loaded dice. Weapons became more elaborate; daggers with bronze hilts and iron blades, iron swords sheathed in bronze scabbards, and oval wooden shields decorated with tracery in bronze. Two-wheeled war chariots opened forward so that a warrior could dart along the shaft between the horses and rush out in front to attack his adversary. A combination of rich adornment and squalid living aroused the contempt of the Greeks and Romans for the barbarians.

The last Celtic invaders were the tribes of the Belgae (Iron Age C) who began coming to Britain about the year 75 B.C. They had been living in the area between the Rhine and the Seine rivers, under pressure from Germanic tribes to the north and from the Romans who were advancing into France from the Mediterranean. The Belgae—tall, fair-haired, and warlike—were Celts, but they contained a strong Germanic strain. They imposed themselves as a conquering aristocracy on the tribes of southeastern Britain, who hated them so bitterly that the cleavage between the Belgae and their neighbors was sharp. Their distinction lay in their mastery of the arts of daily life. They were skillful in weaving bright-colored tartans; they made pottery on a true potter's wheel; they developed useful crafts such as those of the carpenter, the blacksmith, and the boat maker. Their most important innovation in Britain was a heavy wooden plow drawn by eight oxen. It was equipped not only with an iron plowshare but also with an iron colter to slit the furrow and a moldboard to turn over the furrow. A plow such as this made agriculture possible in the river valleys where the soil, though fertile, was heavy clay which had defied the lighter plow of earlier times. The advanced agriculture of the Belgae, their knowledge of arts and crafts, their military prowess, their trade with the Continent, their coinage, and their political organization under strong tribal chieftains made southeastern Britain the best grain-producing portion of the island, the channel of trade, and the seat of political power.

The Belgae believed in goblins, elves, and spirits who dwelt in springs, rocks, and sacred groves. Many of these spirits were malignant and had to be propitiated by sacrifices, even of human beings. A priestly caste, known as the Druids, understood the mysteries of incantations and enchantments and committed to memory vast quantities of sacred verse. They combined the functions of priests, teachers, and magistrates; they could condemn a man to complete isolation from his fellows.

The Belgae maintained close connections with their kinsmen in France—or Gaul— where Julius Caesar in eight years of brilliant campaigning (58 to 51 B.C.) was pushing the Roman frontier northward. In 55 and again in 54 B.C. he crossed the Channel in the first Roman invasions of Britain. He knew that the Celts in Gaul were receiving aid from the Celts in Britain, and his incursions were therefore in the nature of punitive expeditions. He may have hoped for an easy conquest. Caesar's expeditions to Britain were failures. During his first invasion his fleet was damaged by a storm; the Celts, fighting in chariots, on horseback, and on foot, gave him some sharp encounters; and he returned to the Continent as soon as possible. In his second expedition he marched inland, stormed a Belgic hill fort near Canterbury, crossed the Thames near modern London, and after hard fighting obtained submission and a promise of tribute from the principal chieftains of southeastern Britain. But he returned to Gaul. Circumstances never permitted him to make a third attempt.

The Celts in Britain remained independent for almost another century. During that time the Belgic princes grew stronger and extended their territories westward. Their tribal centers, such as Winchester, Chichester, Verulamium (St. Albans), and Colchester, became small towns. Colchester was the capital of the greatest of the Belgic kings, Cunobelinus, the Cymbeline of Shakespeare's play, who ruled from about A.D. 10 to about 40. He possessed a mint and built docks for his extensive trade with Gaul, now a Roman province. Grain, tin, cattle, slaves, hunting dogs, and wild beasts for the shows in Rome were exported by the Celts in exchange for fine pottery, jewelry, and other luxuries. The Celts in eastern Britain were thus exposed to many Roman influences. But their civilization was very warlike and caused hatreds and divisions among the inhabitants of Britain.

ROMAN BRITAIN

In A.D. 43, almost a century after Caesar's invasions, Emperor Claudius dispatched a large army to make a thorough conquest of Britain. This invasion was a logical step in Roman imperial expansion and must be regarded as inevitable. The Romans, firmly established in Gaul, were well aware of conditions in Britain and may have hoped that a conquered Britain could export grain to Rome. The Roman legions, fanning out from the southeastern corner of the country, subdued the lowland plain within five years. They began at once to lay down the great military roads that radiated from London as a center. A short and violent revolt by the Celts in the year 60, led by Queen Boudicca, was quickly and harshly suppressed.

To deal with the fierce Celtic tribes in the mountainous areas to the west and north, however, was a far more difficult undertaking. There was fighting in Wales for some thirty years. Eventually the country was subdued and held in subjection. The Romans found it possible to withdraw their garrisons some time in the second century. But the Celts in Wales were not Romanized; they were merely held down by superior force. A conquest of Scotland proved to be not worth the cost. Agricola, who was Governor of Britain from 78 to 84, pushed north as far as modern Perthshire and inflicted a severe defeat upon the Celts, but the Scottish lowlands later were abandoned. The northern part of Roman Britain was made into a military zone defended by three legions, each of 3000 to 4000 men, one stationed at Chester to separate the Celts in Wales from those farther north, one at Carlisle to watch the tribes in southern Scotland, and one held in reserve at York. In 122 during the reign of the Emperor Hadrian, the Romans began the construction of a great wall, with forts and signal towers at fixed intervals, which ran for some seventy miles across the country from Solway Firth to the river Tyne. These arrangements were very expensive, but southern Britain, shielded by Hadrian's Wall and by an army of permanent occupation in the north, enjoyed a period of peace and prosperity, especially during the century from A.D. 200 to 300.

Roman Britain. Head-pot depicting woman, early third century A.D. (York, Yorkshire Museum)

Britain was part of the Roman Empire for almost 400 years, but for a number of reasons the permanent effects of the Roman occupation were small.

It was impossible to Romanize the northern military zone. Roman influences, coming into the north with the army, disappeared when the army was withdrawn. Some trade occurred between the army and the native population, and eventually the Romans followed a policy of recruiting soldiers from Celtic farms and villages. Yet Romanization in the north was superficial.

The impact of Rome was far greater in the south. Roman civilization was essentially an urban civilization. The country produced the food and other raw materials requisite for sustaining life and was a pleasant retreat for a short time, but for people to fulfill their potentialities they must live in a city. The Roman governors of Britain, therefore, set out to encourage urbanization, though they did so by example and not by force. They began by building four model Roman towns—Colchester, Lincoln, York, and Gloucester—with public buildings, amphitheaters, and baths, and filled them with Roman citizens, largely retired soldiers who had served their time in the legions. The government then encouraged the Celtic princes and aristocrats, who had ruled over tribes before the Roman conquest, to convert their tribal centers into cities. The Celtic nobles were soon imitating the model towns built by the Romans.

These tribal cities never flourished. In the first place, they were very small. We hear of one which covered only a hundred acres and contained no more than eighty

The Civitates *of Roman Britain.*

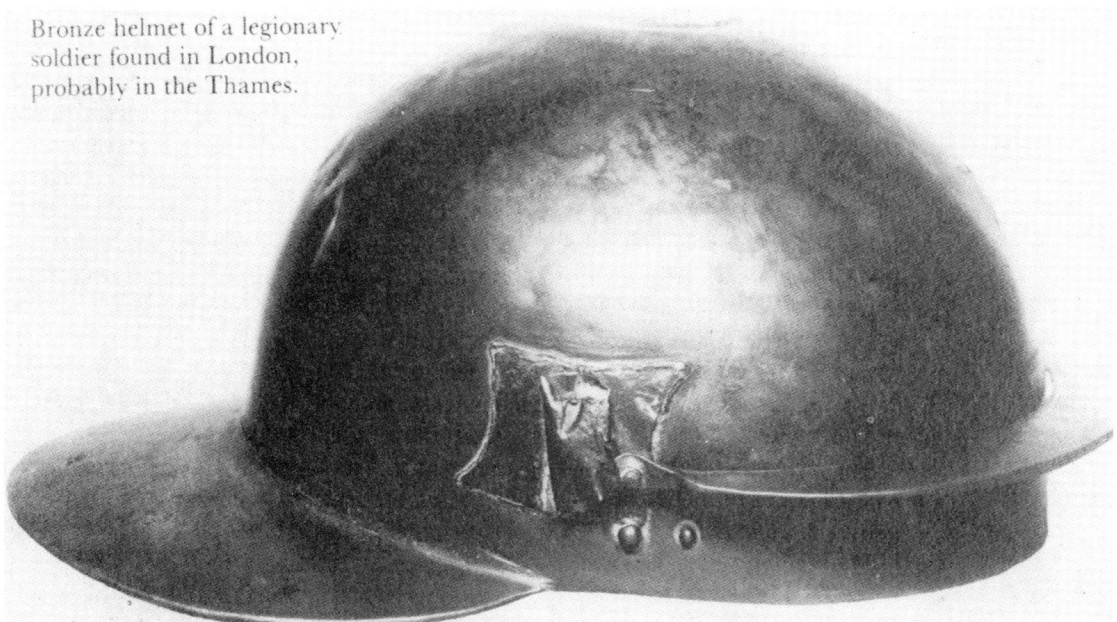

Bronze helmet of a legionary soldier found in London, probably in the Thames.

Bronze helmet of a legionary soldier. (London, British Museum)

houses. These towns were centers of local government and to some extent of industry and commerce. Economically, however, they were a drain upon the countryside. The goods and services they offered were not an adequate return for the food they consumed. At some time in the third century they began to decline. Trade diminished, public buildings fell into decay, finances were disordered, public life was paralyzed, the citizens lived in squalid and wretched conditions. The Roman model towns did better because they were administrative centers, but they did not grow. In a word, the urban life introduced by the Romans was too costly and too ambitious; a luxury the British economy could not sustain, it was an artificial and not a spontaneous development. Moreover, the position of cities throughout the empire was tending to decline. The emperors, who had lost interest in supporting town life as an end in itself, drained away the wealth of the cities in order to maintain the army in a state of high efficiency. The towns in Britain, affected by these wider developments, suffered accordingly.

Country life, on the other hand, grew in popularity. The wealthy class of Romano-Britons, finding town life precarious, burdensome, and highly taxed, built houses in the country known as villas. These were isolated farmhouses, some quite simple, but some very elaborate. Roman in architecture and in their mode of life, they were surrounded by large open fields cultivated by slaves or semiservile tenants. Here a

British aristocrat could lead a leisurely and cultivated life and could at the same time become more prosperous by the businesslike management of his estate. The villas were self-sufficing units which produced the food that found an eager market in the cities. They also became centers of specialized industries. Because their growth was spontaneous, and because the Celt at heart preferred rural to urban living, the villas displayed a staying power which the towns did not. Old pre-Roman Britain was beginning to reappear.

The bulk of the population lived in native villages which were not a part of the system of villas but quite distinct from it. These villages were primitive collections of huts scattered about without streets. The peasants grew wheat in small fields and kept domestic animals in a common pasture. They displayed few indications of Romanization. Their lives were more peaceful and ordered than in the days before the Roman conquest, but they did not increase in prosperity, nor were they greatly touched by Roman civilization.

During the first centuries of Roman rule there was a marked increase in British commerce and industry. The Romans made a determined attack upon the mineral resources of the country. Tin, copper, lead, iron, and coal were mined in large

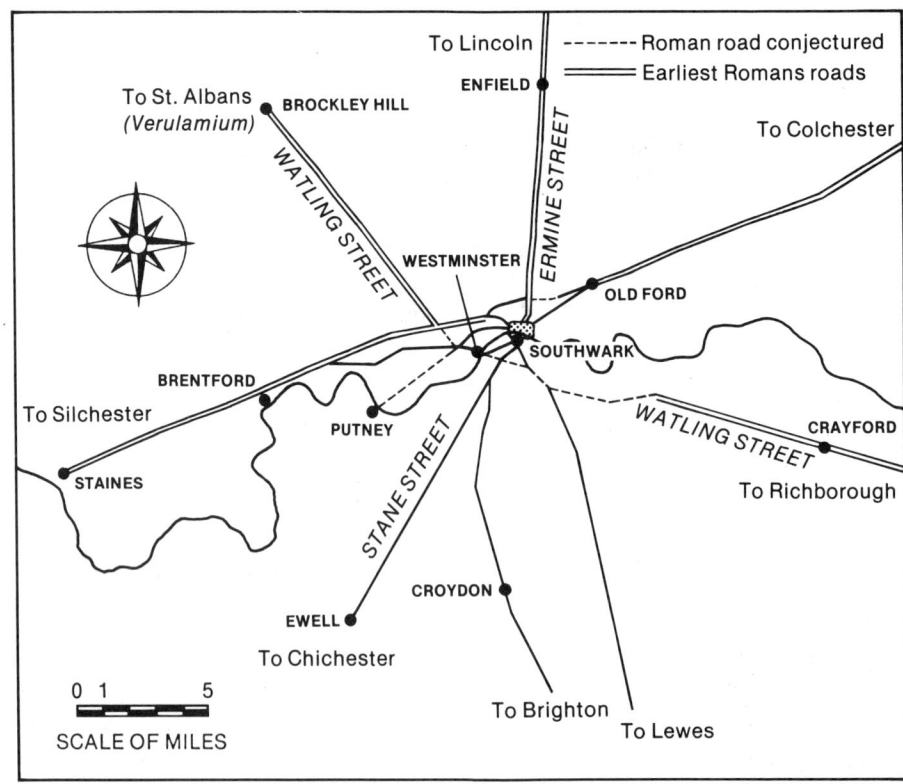

London: The Hub.

Insignia of the Roman civil governor. (Granger Collection)

quantities. Except for coal, these items formed important articles of export. British woolen cloth found a ready market in the Mediterranean. Other exports remained much as before—grain, cattle, hides, slaves, and hunting dogs. Imports consisted of wine, olive oil, fine pottery, glassware, and other luxuries. The Romans also stimulated industry. Bricks, glass, pottery, and woolen cloth were manufactured; stone and slate were quarried for building; iron and bronze work of high quality continued from an earlier period. Roman coinage and Roman roads aided both commerce and industry, but as Roman power and affluence declined, exports reverted more and more to raw materials, and imports were largely confined to military stores. The development of London as the center of roads and trade was of crucial importance. London could be reached by seagoing ships, and the Thames could be bridged to link northern and southern England. Since Roman times London has played a dominant role in the life of England, greater than that played by any other single city in any other European country. Recent archeological digs have revealed evidence of environmental pollution in Roman London. The Emperor Vespasion levied a tax on the tanning industry in order to reduce pollution.

The fourth century brought increasing signs that the Roman Empire was in decay and that the Roman position in Britain was in grave danger. New defenses had to be constructed against an enemy who came by sea. A navy was built, fortresses were erected in important harbors, and a special officer, known as the Count of the Saxon Shore, supervised the defenses of the coast. About the middle of the fourth century there were raids by the Picts from Scotland, who took to the sea and thus bypassed the Wall, and by Scots from Ireland. The military roads enabled Picts and Scots to penetrate to the southern parts of the island. In 367 there was a raid in which Picts, Scots, and Saxons descended simultaneously upon Britain. On more than one occasion, moreover, a Roman general or governor in Britain, such as Constantine the Great, aspired to become the Emperor at Rome and led his troops across the Channel to fight on the Continent. These troops did not normally return to Britain. Finally, early in the fifth century, when the empire was crumbling at home and the barbarians were at the very gates of Rome, the Romans recalled the remaining soldiers and officials from Britain, leaving the British to fend for themselves.

What, then, did the Romans leave that has had a lasting effect upon Britain? They left the roads which continued to be used for centuries and which marked outlines of communication that have not disappeared today. They left a tradition of urban life and a recognition of the favorable position of London as a center for commerce and administration. They also left Christianity, which had come to Britain along with various pagan cults and which was strong enough to survive the Roman collapse. However, "as a distinctive political and social structure the old Church had gone down with the old Romano-British world." (Salway, p. 739.) Beyond these things the Romans left very little. Roman civilization, which was to have so profound an influence upon medieval England, was brought in later by the Christian church and the Norman Conquest.

C H R O N O L O G Y

Early Peoples

c. 500,000 B.C.	First humans, hunters and fishers
c. 3500 B.C.	Neolithic (Late Stone) Age, Windmill Hill People
c. 2500 B.C.	Beaker Folk, Stonehenge
c. 1000 B.C.	Celtic refugees arrive

(continued on next page)

Chronology, continued

c. 800 B.C.	Celtic invasions
6th century B.C.	Hallstatt Celts; Iron Age A
3rd century B.C.	La Tène culture (Celtic); Iron Age B
2nd century B.C.	Belgae; Iron Age C
55 B.C.	Julius Caesar attempts conquest
A.D. 43	Roman Conquest; Emperor Claudius
A.D. 60	Queen Boudicca defeated by Romans
A.D. 78–84	Agricola governor of Britain
A.D. 122	Hadrian's Wall begun
A.D. 367	Picts, Scots, Saxons attack Britain
A.D. 450	Romans depart

The Anglo-Saxons

The history of Britain during the century and a half lying roughly between the years 450 and 600 is very obscure. Yet these years are of the utmost importance, for during this time Britain was invaded by Germanic tribes of Angles, Saxons, and Jutes who took possession of the lowland plain and made it their own. Joining them in attacks upon Britain were other Teutonic tribesmen, such as Frisians and Swabians. The Celts, though they resisted fiercely, were defeated. Some remained among their conquerors, but for the most part they, like earlier Celtic peoples, were driven westward into Devon and Cornwall, into Wales, or into a northwestern area known as Strathclyde. Some, with their bishops, went across to Gaul (Brittany). By the year 600 they were largely confined to the mountains of the west and north, leaving the plain in the hands of the invaders. Half of Britain had become England, the land of Angles; from that time forward the English have been predominantly of Anglo-Saxon blood, though tempered by Celtic and other peoples.

Written sources for the period of the invasions are extremely few. One tract was composed during the 540s by a Celtic monk named Gildas. The events described by Gildas are few, although he supplies hints that historians have found important. Two later works, Bede's *Ecclesiastical History of the English People*, completed in 731, and the *Anglo-Saxon Chronicle*, begun in the reign of King Alfred (871–899), contain materials drawn from earlier sources that were closer to the age of the invasions. From these major sources scholars have constructed a picture of the German invasions.

THE INVASION OF BRITAIN

The homeland of the Angles was Schleswig in southern Denmark; that of the Saxons was Holstein and the surrounding area in northern Germany. These peoples mingled and moved to the west until, just before their conquest in Britain, they occupied the coastal plain of northwest Germany between Denmark and the mouths of the Rhine. Under pressure from the Huns and the Avars, who were pushing into eastern Europe, the Angles and Saxons turned toward Britain, partly from necessity, partly from desire. For over a century they had been conducting piratical raids against its shores. They knew that the protection of Rome had been withdrawn and that the Celts were left to defend themselves as best they could. The Anglo-Saxons, moreover, were maritime peoples for whom passage by sea in long, open boats presented few difficulties.

During the half century after 450 great numbers of Angles and Saxons swarmed into Britain, drove back the Celts, and laid the foundations for later Anglo-Saxon kingdoms. There was a settlement on the coast of Sussex (South Saxons). Other bands of invaders followed the river systems of the Thames, the Wash, and the Humber. Along the lower Thames they settled on both sides of the river and established a colony to the north, Essex (East Saxons), which later became of some importance. Farther up the river other Saxons (the West Saxons) first occupied the area of modern Berkshire. Some of them may have come up the river, some may have landed on the southern coast and made their way northward to the Thames Valley, and some may have come in by the Wash and approached the river by following the Ouse and the Icknield Way. They then moved westward to establish the kingdom of Wessex in the regions known as Wiltshire, Somerset, Dorset, and Devon. Other groups of Angles and Saxons, entering by the Wash, settled in East Anglia (the land of the East Angles) or moved far inland to the vicinity of modern Lichfield, Repton, and Tamworth, which became the heart of the later kingdom of Mercia. The Humber River also offered easy access to the interior. Here two settlements were made: Deira, which was colonized very early and extended from the Humber to the Tees; and Bernicia, settled somewhat later, which stretched north of the Tees to the Firth of Forth and thus included a portion of modern Scotland. These two provinces of Deira and Bernicia were later to form the kingdom of Northumbria. Thus the foundations were laid for the seven Anglo-Saxon kingdoms known as the heptarchy: Kent, Sussex, Essex, Wessex, Mercia, East Anglia, and Northumbria.

About the year 500 the Anglo-Saxons suffered a severe defeat at the hands of a British general, Ambrosius Aurelianus, who stiffened the resistance of the Celts in western Britain and won an important victory at Mount Badon, which may have been on the upper Thames near modern Swindon. It has been suggested that he used cavalry effectively against the Saxons, who fought on foot. He forced them to settle down, consolidate their holdings, and abandon their course of easy plunder and destruction. It is on the basis of his achievements that there arose the legends of King Arthur, in which Ambrosius was made a king and his mounted soldiers converted into knights of the Round Table with all the glamour of medieval chivalry.

About the year 550 the Anglo-Saxon advance began once more. The West Saxons, pushing onward until they came to Bath and Gloucester, inflicted a severe defeat upon the Celts in the Battle of Dyrham in 577, a victory which carried the invaders to the Bristol Channel and separated the Celts in Wales from those in Cornwall and Devon. Somewhat later, between 613 and 616, the Angles defeated the Britons at Chester, thus dividing the Celts in Wales from those in Strathclyde. These battles marked the end of effective resistance by the Celts.

THE ANGLO-SAXONS

The Anglo-Saxons were what the Romans called barbarians when they invaded Britain. Living far to the north of Europe, they had missed the contacts with Rome which had moderated the savageness of the Germans along the Roman frontier. Their religion was that of Norse mythology; their political organization that of the tribal king or war leader surrounded by young warriors and older counselors. The Anglo-Saxon, tall, fair, red-haired, and blue-eyed, delighted in war. His poetry, sung by gleemen in the halls of the chieftains, recounted the deeds of mighty warriors and told of slaughter and bloodshed.[1] The Anglo-Saxon mother lulling her baby to sleep whispered in his ear that in time he would be a fighter who would redden the field with the blood of his victims. Gildas describes the fury of the Anglo-Saxon onslaught. He tells of the destruction of cities, the massacre of the inhabitants, and the devastation of the countryside. Those Britons who survived, says Gildas, became slaves or fled overseas or took refuge in the bleak western hills. The Roman civilization of Britain now disappeared; and the Romanized Celts who fled to the mountains adjusted perforce to the level of the cruder Celts with whom they were forced now to live.

The spearhead of the Anglo-Saxon invasion was the chieftain and his band of young warriors. It was known as the comitatus or group of companions. The chieftain must not be surpassed in bravery by his warriors, nor must they fall below the valor of their commander. To leave the battlefield alive after the chieftain had fallen was to earn lifelong shame and infamy. This ideal of mutual support and loyalty between the leader and his companions was a principal theme of Anglo-Saxon poetry. It was to be reflected in later times in the loyalty of a man to his feudal lord, in the loyalty of subjects to their king, in the loyalty of a man to his plighted word. The Anglo-Saxon warrior was not afraid of death; he believed that his fate would come at the appointed hour and that he could do nothing to avert his doom. He possessed a rough honesty, a kindliness toward his own people, and a crude sense of humor which expressed itself in practical jokes and in raucous horseplay. He loved to boast of his great deeds as he feasted in the timbered hall of his leader. The weapons of the chieftain consisted of a helmet, a shirt of ring mail, and a sword with fine decorations and inlaid jewels on the hilt. His men were not armed so well. They had spears and round wooden shields, but only a few had swords.

After the war leader and his warriors had cleared the way, they were followed by the mass of the freemen, who were farmers. These freemen appropriated the arable fields of the Celts. Slowly and painfully over the centuries they brought new land under cultivation and established the villages of medieval England. Below the freemen was a class of slaves, largely captives in war. This threefold division of society into noble or warrior, churl or freeman farmer, and thrall or slave is found among all the early Germanic peoples.

---

[1]*Beowulf,* the most famous of Anglo-Saxon poems, though of a much later date, recounts the deeds of a hero fighting monsters and dragons.

CONVERSION OF THE ANGLO-SAXONS

The Christian Missions

Two themes of central importance in Anglo-Saxon history are the conversion of the heathen invaders to Christianity and the movement of the kingdoms toward political unification. The two themes flow together and are closely related. The church was able to construct an organization common to all England at a time when political unity was still far in the future. A united church pointed the way toward a united kingdom. But the church could not obliterate local patriotism; its greatest work was to bring the warming, uplifting, and civilizing influences of Christianity to a heathen and barbaric folk.

Christianity came to the Anglo-Saxons in two distinct missions: one from the Celtic church in Ireland and Scotland, the other from the church in Rome. The Romanized Celts who had fled into Wales had taken Christianity with them, but the church in Wales made no effort to convert the Anglo-Saxons, who, in Celtic eyes, deserved nothing but damnation. Christianity's influence upon England came in a roundabout way, through Ireland and Scotland. Although Christianity had penetrated into Ireland in Roman times, the true founder of the Irish church was St. Patrick (c. 389–461). He was the son of a Romanized British official and was probably born near the modern city of Bristol. As a boy of fifteen, he was kidnapped by Irish pirates who took him to Ulster. Some years later he escaped, visited Italy, and studied in southern France. Consecrated a bishop in 432, he returned to Ireland to work among the heathen Irish for almost thirty years. He preached from coast to coast, made Latin the language of the Irish church, and brought the country into contact with Rome. The organization he established was episcopal, with the diocese coinciding with the boundaries of the tribe.

After St. Patrick's death his organization largely disappeared, and the church in Ireland was controlled by monasteries. Founded by kings or tribal chieftains and ruled by abbots who were normally members of the royal family, the monasteries, rather than the bishops' dioceses, became the units of ecclesiastical jurisdication. The bishops were reduced to a minor position. The Irish church, cut off from Rome by the barbarian invasions, developed other peculiarities. It differed from Rome in ritual, in the method of consecrating bishops, in the tonsure of the monks, and in the way in which the date of Easter was determined. Lacking any central organization, the church could maintain only a loose discipline, and monks were allowed to move from one monastery to another; even an abbot might abandon his charge to lead the life of a hermit. Irish Christianity inclined toward harsh asceticism. The monks lived in gaunt austerity in remote and desolate monasteries that were normally nothing more than groups of beehive huts surrounded by stockades for protection.

Nonetheless, Irish monasticism, especially in the century from 550 to 650, produced a most remarkable series of scholars, saints, and missionaries. Among them was St. Columba (c. 521–597), who, on the small island of Iona off the western coast of Scotland, founded a monastery which he used as a base for missionary work among the Celts on the mainland. It was from this monastery that Celtic Christianity later penetrated into the north of England and helped to convert the Anglo-Saxons.

In 597 a group of missionaries from Rome arrived in Kent. They had been sent by Pope Gregory the Great, who had entrusted the mission to Augustine, a Benedictine monk of the monastery of St. Andrew in Rome. Augustine and forty or so companions journeyed through Gaul, beset by fears of what might happen to them in England. However, they were kindly received by King Ethelbert of Kent (c. 560–616), who had always maintained close connections with Christian Gaul and who had married a Christian, the Frankish Princess Bertha. Her presence in Kent prepared the way for the conversion of her husband. He permitted them to preach and gave them an ancient British church near Canterbury. Somewhat later he accepted Christianity. In 601 Augustine became the first archbishop of Canterbury when Gregory sent him the pallium, or emblem of office, and empowered him to establish twelve bishoprics in southern England. He created only two, one at Rochester in western Kent, and one at London among the East Saxons, whose king was a nephew of Ethelbert. Another nephew, Redwald, the King of East Anglia, was persuaded by Ethelbert to accept baptism, though he did little more than erect a Christian altar in one of his heathen temples. Thus when Augustine died in 605 he had introduced Christianity into the three kingdoms of Kent, Essex, and East Anglia.

Augustine's accomplishments were rather limited. He failed to reach an agreement with the Celtic bishops in Wales. The Celtic bishops, connecting Augustine with the Anglo-Saxons, refused to submit to his authority. A great opportunity was thus lost. Acceptance of Christianity by the Anglo-Saxons was at this time a formal matter which made little difference in the lives of the people. After Ethelbert's death in 616 there was a strong pagan reaction in Kent.

Christianity was brought into Northumbria during the reign of King Edwin (616–632). Again a woman played an important part. In 625 Edwin married a daughter of Ethelbert of Kent. It was agreed that the bride should continue to practice her Christian faith, and she brought with her as chaplain a Bishop Paulinus. Shortly thereafter Edwin was baptized. Then followed a rapid though superficial conversion of the Northumbrians.

In 632 Edwin was defeated and slain. Christianity was overwhelmed by a pagan reaction, and Paulinus narrowly escaped with his life as he fled to southern England. This disaster was more than retrieved during the reigns of two Northumbrian kings, Oswald (633–641) and Oswy (641–670), brothers who had lived in exile at the Celtic monastery on Iona. As soon as Oswald was secure upon his throne he invited the monks at Iona to send missionaries to Northumbria. In 634 a group of monks under Aidan, a Scot, settled on the island of Lindisfarne off the Northumbrian coast. There followed a remarkable flowering of religious life in Northumbria. The Roman church of southern England also reappeared. One reason for the richness and depth of religious and scholarly achievement in Northumbria during the seventh and eighth centuries was the meeting and fusion of Celtic and Roman elements.

The two churches were not as hostile to each other as is often supposed, but since there were marked differences between them, the question arose which usage should predominate in Northumbria. The question was settled at the Council of

Whitby in 663, when King Oswy decided to support the Roman forms. This was an important decision, for it meant that the church could be organized along Roman lines and would not be divided between Roman and Celtic practices. It is probable that even if the Council of Whitby had never met, the usages of Rome would have gradually prevailed. The Celtic church, magnificent as were its achievements, depended too much upon the devotion of the individual. The episcopal organization of the Roman church offered greater strength and durability. This was widely recognized. The future belonged to Rome. By the year 700 Christianity had been adopted by all the Anglo-Saxon kingdoms.

Organization of the Church

The Council of Whitby opened the way for rapid organization of the Roman church in England and for the enforcement of its stronger discipline. This was the work of Theodore of Tarsus, an elderly Greek monk who was archbishop of Canterbury from 669 to 690. Theodore placed the church firmly upon an episcopal basis, added to the number of bishops, and increased and defined their powers. Bishops formed the very life of the early church. A bishop was required to travel incessantly, to baptize and confirm, to ordain deacons and priests, to preach, to teach, to visit monasteries. Theodore insisted that bishops regard the archbishop of Canterbury as their superior, that priests not leave their diocese without the consent of the bishop, nor monks their monasteries without the permission of the abbot. Theodore summoned ecclesiastical councils which legislated for the English church as a whole. He was called upon to rule on many points of morals and was celebrated for his system of penances and for his regulations concerning Christian marriage. He was formerly given credit for dividing the English dioceses into parishes, but it was only very slowly that the medieval parish—a village or a cluster of villages, with a resident priest—came into existence. In the age of Theodore the number of priests and the means for their support were quite inadequate for any such arrangement. Most of the early parishes were created by bishops to serve outlying portions of the diocese or by nobles and other wealthy persons who built churches on their lands and provided for the support of a priest. These nobles were apt to regard their churches as very much their own property. Hence arose the right of advowson, the right of a founder (and his descendants) to appoint the priest for the parish, subject to the bishop's approval. Theodore's church was a united church, owing allegiance to the archbishop of Canterbury; its bishops met in councils to discuss the needs of the church for all England; and its example of unity and centralization offered an ideal to the kings of the heptarchy.

Monasticism and Learning

The seventh and eighth centuries formed a brilliant period in English monastic life, especially in Northumbria. St. Hilda (614–680), a princess of the royal Northumbrian house, founded about 657 a famous monastery at Whitby of which she became abbess. This monastery was a school of literature and a training center for churchmen. Benedict Biscop, a Northumbrian noble, devoted his life to the founding and adornment of two monasteries, Wearmouth (674) and Jarrow (681). He made the long journey to Rome five times, returning with relics, vestments, stained glass, and, above all, a magnificent collection of books for his monastic foundations. Another Northumbrian noble, Bishop Wilfrid (634–710), a proud and difficult but most energetic prelate, who deliberately emphasized the pomp of Rome as against the humility of the Irish monks, strengthened discipline in the monasteries and built churches at York, Ripon, and Hexham. There were Irish monks at Iona and Melrose in Scotland, at Lindisfarne in Northumbria, and at Malmesbury in southern England. Thus the monastic ideal, drawn both from Ireland and from Rome, caught the imagination of the Anglo-Saxon people.

Irish and Roman inspiration combined to give the monasteries and schools of

St. Luke, Lindisfarne Gospels. (British Library, Cottonian MS, Nero D. iv., f. 137v)

England a high level of scholarship and culture. The Irish brought their learning to Lindisfarne, where the beautiful illuminated manuscript known as the Lindisfarne Gospels was written about the year 721. The Codex Amiatinus, a complete manuscript of the Vulgate Bible of St. Jerome, was copied at Wearmouth. Meanwhile, in the south, Theodore and Hadrian founded a school at Canterbury with a splendid library. Canterbury, Malmesbury, York, Wearmouth, and Jarrow were centers of learning and education at a time when the Continent was singularly devoid of scholarship.

The lovable and saintly Bede (c. 671–735), a scholar of European renown, was England's first historian. He was placed as a boy in the monastery of Jarrow in Northumbria and remained there all his life, "observing monastic discipline and always delighting in learning, teaching, and writing."[2] He knew the works of the early fathers of the church, wrote Latin with ease, and had some knowledge of Greek. His writings included commentaries on the Old and New Testaments, a life of St. Cuthbert, treatises on penmanship and chronology, and, above all, his *Ecclesiastical History of the English People.* It is a work of remarkable breadth. Bede conceives of all the English as belonging to one race, of the English church as part of the church universal, of events in England as a stage in world history. These themes are so skillfully fused that the book becomes not merely a history of the English church but of the formation of a people. Bede possesses the care and caution of the true historian, collecting and sifting his material conscientiously, telling where he obtained his information, and never filling the gaps with guesswork. He has a fine sense of chronology. It is he who introduced into England the practice of dating events from the year of the birth of Christ. This system of dating is not only simple and practical but places the central fact of Christianity at the heart of historical chronology. Bede wrote with simplicity, lucidity, and charm; his works abound in poetic figures and in vivid descriptions. His stories of saints and heroes are wonderfully fresh and natural. And all through his writings shines his love of God and man.

THE ORIGINS OF POLITICAL UNITY

The Bretwaldas

The political unification of the Anglo-Saxon kingdoms was a slow development which was not complete until the descendants of King Alfred ruled over all of England in the late tenth century. Unification, when it came, meant more than the conquest of one kingdom by another: It meant that the English felt themselves to be one people who of their own good will gave obedience and submission to one single ruler. From early times there had usually been one king strong enough to try to impose some sort of subjection upon his neighbors. An overking of this kind might try to make or unmake lesser kings, he might seek tribute from his dependencies, he might es-

---

[2] These are Bede's words.

tablish personal ties with subject princes on the honorable basis of master and man. The name given to such an overking was Bretwalda (Britain-ruler). Among the first were several who cannot have been more than mighty warriors against the Celts. King Ethelbert of Kent (c. 500–616), however, was a more important figure. His authority extended to Essex and to East Anglia, and Bede declares that it reached the Humber. During Ethelbert's reign Kent was the most civilized and probably the most populous of the kingdoms. He was the first Anglo-Saxon king to set down his laws in writing. As we have seen, he maintained close connections with the Franks and allowed Augustine to introduce Christianity.

At Ethelbert's death in 616, power passed to his warlike nephew, Redwald of East Anglia, who for perhaps a decade was the most powerful of the south English kings. Some years ago a wonderful treasure ship was excavated at Sutton Hoo near one of his residences. It contained weapons—swords, shields, and spearheads—and other objects of iron and bronze, beautifully and elaborately decorated. There were also fine textile materials. English craftsmanship in weaving and in work on iron and bronze had obviously reached a high level. A purse with a gold frame was found to contain about forty gold Frankish coins. Also found was a large number of silver objects—dishes, bowls, spoons, and ladles—which could hardly have been of Anglo-Saxon origin. Upon one bowl appears the monogram of a Roman emperor at Constantinople. The size and splendor of this collection are an indication that an East Anglian king in the seventh century was wealthier and more conversant with other parts of Europe than has been supposed. His authority disappeared with his death, and power passed in turn to the three kingdoms of Northumbria, Mercia, and Wessex.

During the greater part of the seventh century Northumbria was the strongest of the kingdoms. Bede gives King Edwin (616–632) the title of Bretwalda and describes him as the most powerful king that England had yet seen, overlord of most of the kingdoms south of the Humber, though Kent never submitted to him. He was followed by two kings of outstanding ability, Oswald (633–641) and Oswy (641–670). They did not have great power south of the Humber, where Mercia was growing too strong for them, but they were vigorous kings in Northumbria. Their reputation was so great that men in southern England looked to them for guidance and advice. Here was the ideal of political unity, though Northumbria never fulfilled the promise it appeared to offer. After Oswy's death in 670 the country was torn by rival claimants to the throne and sank into anarchy.

Northumbria's position of political leadership was taken by Mercia in the eighth century. The tribes in central England had been forced into a confederacy and their territories had been greatly enlarged in the seventh century by an able and warlike king, Penda (632–654). He was followed in the eighth century by two eminent rulers, Ethelbald (716–757) and Offa (757–796), who were much more than local kings. Ethelbald called himself King of the South English, and Offa used the style *Rex Anglorum.*

Offa incorporated Essex, Sussex, and probably East Anglia into Mercia in order to draw closer to the Continent and to bring London within his dominions. The first English king to have a foreign policy, he corresponded with Charlemagne and was

Saxon kingdoms and Bretwaldaships 630–829.

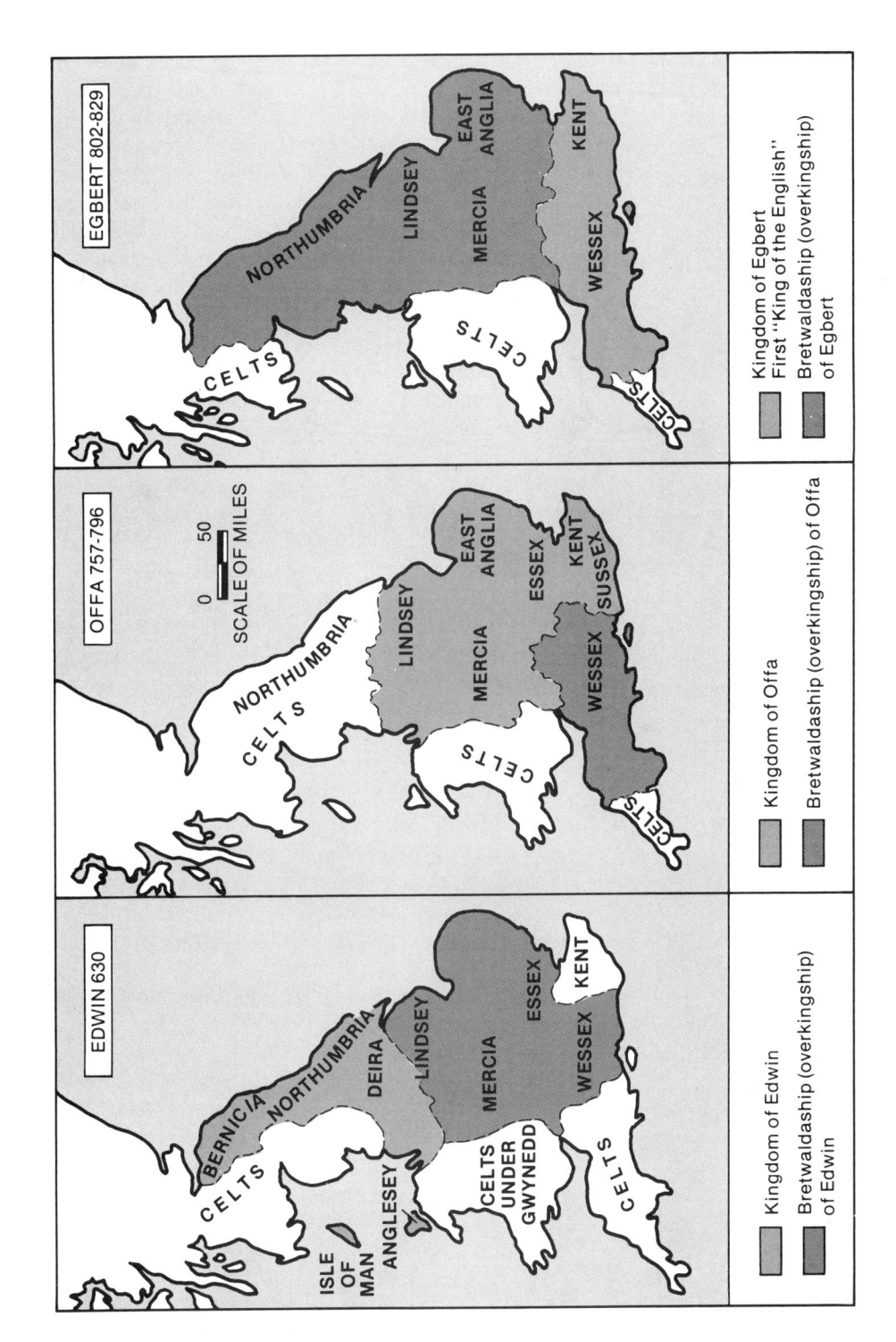

England in the seventh and eighth centuries.

interested in commerce and in the exportation of English woolen cloth. He built a great earthwork known as Offa's Dyke some 150 miles long to delineate his western frontier on the borders of Wales. His charters, written by professional clerks, indicate an efficient machinery of government and a systematic control over lesser kings. A document of his reign, called the Tribal Hidage, shows that his officials collected tribute in an organized way over a wide area. His code of laws, or dooms, now lost, was later referred to by King Alfred with respect. Offa exalted the church as a political ally, founded the abbey of St. Albans, and summoned important church councils. A papal mission was sent from Rome in 786 to incorporate England more fully into the church universal. In the next year Offa persuaded the Pope to create an archbishopric at Lichfield. But a third archbishopric, after Canterbury and York, was a step away from political unity, and it is fortunate that it lasted only until 803. Offa was followed by a series of incompetent kings whose weakness opened the way for the rise of Wessex under King Egbert.

Egbert, King of Wessex from 802 to 839, greatly advanced the position of his kingdom. Having inflicted a defeat upon the Mercians in 825 which ended their supremacy, he was quickly acknowledged as Bretwalda by Sussex, Kent, Essex, and East Anglia. At the same time he thoroughly subdued the Celts in Cornwall. He thus brought all of southern England under the sway of a single kingdom.

England was now to face a new and terrible danger, the invasion of the Danes, Norse barbarians from Scandinavia, before whose onslaught the civilization of Anglo-Saxon England, and, indeed, the civilization of all western Europe, seemed likely to disappear.

The Danes

The Danish incursions into England were part of a larger movement of the Scandinavian peoples who, making piracy a business, hurled their destructive raids against all the coasts of Europe. Coming by sea in their long, narrow boats, swiftly propelled by both sail and oar, these Viking marauders could land armies of several thousand warriors at unexpected places, could penetrate far up the rivers of England, France, Spain, and Italy, and could escape with their booty before resistance was organized. It was their practice to seize or build an armed camp near their ships, to round up the horses of the locality, and to make rapid inland raids until the terrified inhabitants paid them great sums to move away. The Northmen felt no compunction in sacking monasteries; around the year 800 they pillaged Lindisfarne, Jarrow, and Iona. They not only attacked western Europe but penetrated into modern Russia, connecting the Baltic and the Black seas. They dared to sail westward across the Atlantic until they discovered Iceland, Greenland, and North America.

It is not easy to explain the origins of this movement. In Norway it may have been due to overpopulation. In Denmark, as strong kings consolidated their position, they drove out rebels and rival princes who led great bands of fighting men abroad. It has been argued that Charlemagne opened the way for the Danes by destroying the sea power of the Frisians. Even so, there is an element of mystery about the origins of the Viking explosion. The Northmen were similar to the Anglo-Saxons of the fifth century: usually described as fierce, heathen warriors with a lust for pillage and slaughter. They were very cruel. Human sacrifices were offered to their gods, widows were burned on the funeral pyres of their husbands, prisoners were mutilated. Tall, blond, and blue-eyed, the Danish warriors were dandies in their barbaric way, delighting in scarlet cloaks, in brooches and bracelets, in finely decorated swords and daggers. They combed their yellow hair to a nicety. Their first raids were plundering expeditions, but in 850 a Danish army wintered in Kent; in 865 a great host landed in East Anglia prepared to stay for years, to plunder systematically, and to seize land for Danish settlement. In the next few years the Danes destroyed the kingdoms of Northumbria and East Anglia and had to be bought off by Mercia. In 870 they turned upon Wessex, the last of the old kingdoms that now remained a political and fighting unit.

KING ALFRED, 871–899

Alfred and the Danes

The Danes attacked Wessex just as King Alfred came to the throne. Alfred was the supreme hero of the Anglo-Saxons, a man of many gifts and of great versatility, a statesman and a scholar as well as a splendid general. But his great task was to fight the Danes. He could turn his attention to government and to the arts of peace only in the intervals between his Danish wars. These wars may be divided into three major campaigns. The first was in 871 and 872. The Danes, pressing into Wessex from their base at Reading on the Thames, were met with stiff resistance. Alfred knew, however, that he could not hope to defeat them at this time, and in 872 he paid them tribute on condition that they leave his kingdom. This payment, though humiliating, gave him five precious years in which to build his defenses.

The campaign of 876–878 was much more dangerous. Guthrum, the Viking leader, marched through Wessex to the south coast of Exeter. From there in the winter of 878 he made a surprise attack to the north, seized the royal manor of Chippenham, forced Alfred to take refuge in a swampy region around Athelney, and overran much of the kingdom. Yet in the spring Alfred was able to reassemble his army and to inflict a severe defeat upon the Danes at Edington. This victory was a turning point in the war. Guthrum agreed to leave Wessex and to accept Christianity. The battle at Edington led to other important developments. In 886 Alfred was able to take possession of London, which became a symbol of resistance and a token of hope that the Danes could be overcome. In the same year he made a treaty with Guthrum which fixed a boundary between Wessex and the Danelaw, as the Danish portion of England was called. The line ran from near London to the area of Chester, giving Alfred control of the western portion of Mercia. The possession of London and the treaty with Guthrum added to Alfred's stature as a national leader. His lordship was recognized by all who were free to acknowledge it, not because of his military power

England, about 885.

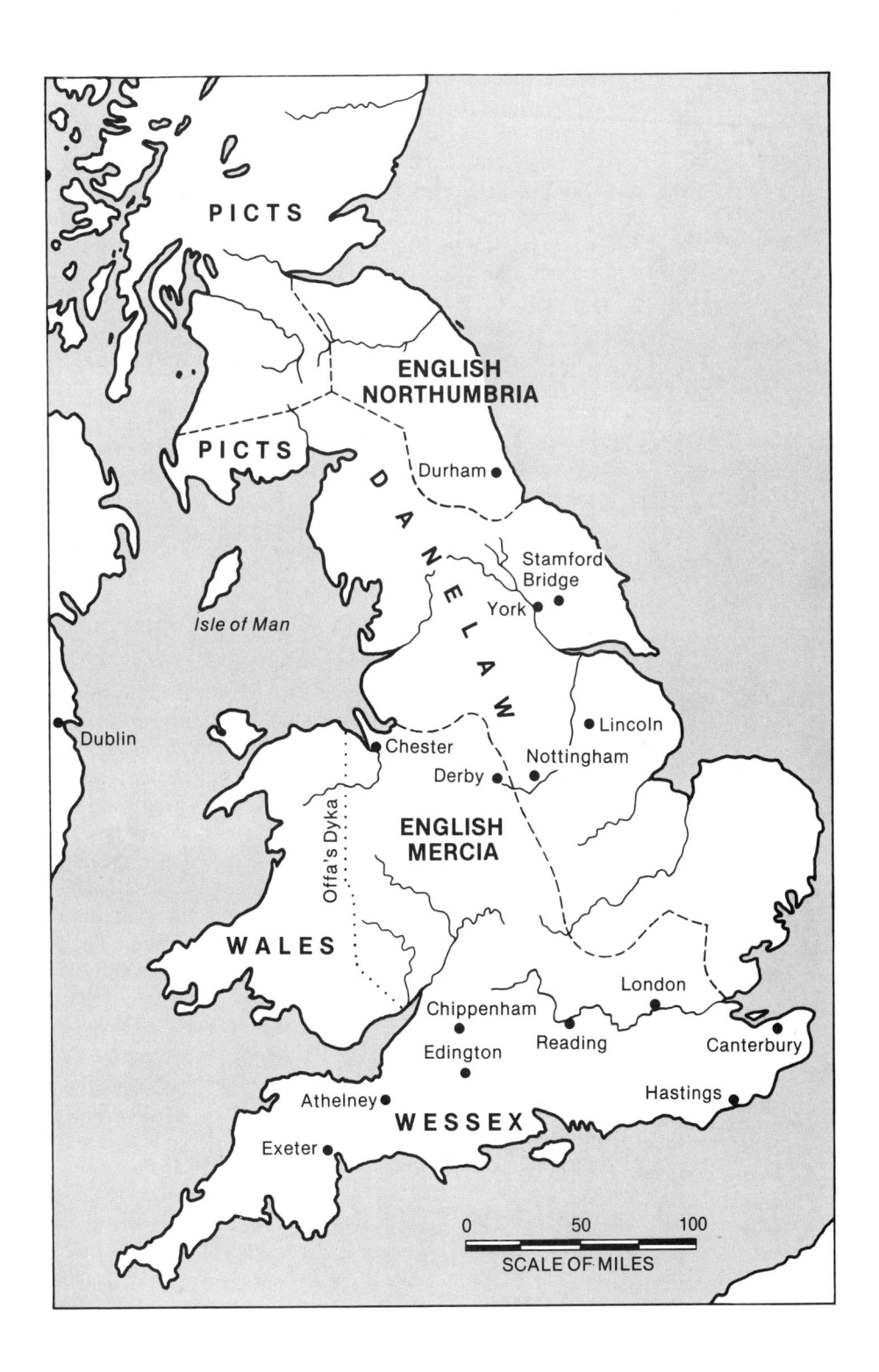

but because he stood forth as a national hero who represented the common interests of the English people. He was converting the kingship of Wessex into the kingship of all England.

Alfred had organized his military forces along new and successful lines. One of his problems had been the reluctance of the peasant militia, known as the fyrd, to remain under arms when the work of sowing and harvesting demanded attention at home. Alfred met this difficulty in two ways. He divided the fyrd into two parts: one to work in the fields, the other constantly ready for combat. Secondly, he encouraged the development of a military class, known as thegns, composed of nobles and wealthy landowners, who brought their retainers to battle and gave the army a core of experienced fighting men. Alfred also devised a system of fotresses which served as centers of defense and as places of refuge for the people in time of danger. These fortresses were garrisoned and kept in repair by men from the villages of the surrounding districts. Although his attempt to build a navy met with only moderate success, he so improved the defenses of England that resistance to the invaders was now possible.

The Work of Civilization

Alfred believed that kingship was a sacred trust to protect and to uplift the people; it was his aim not merely to beat back the Danes but to restore the civilization they had nearly destroyed. His efforts to this end reveal his deep religious piety, his interest in scholarship, and his artistic appreciation of the use of words and of the beauties of nature. It is good to stress the practical aspects of his work. His object was to reconstruct society, and there was a utilitarian side to all that he did. To combat the lawlessness that comes with every war, he issued a code of laws, drawn partly from the laws of Wessex but also from those of Kent and Mercia. His code stressed the protection of the weak against the strong; the sacredness of oaths, which played a large part in legal decisions; and the duty owed by a man to his lord. These lords were the thegns whose armed retainers added such strength to the army. Alfred watched the operation of the legal system and did what he could to improve its effectiveness.

It was Alfred's faith in education that is most astonishing. His thegns, he believed, must be trained to take part in government. For this purpose he gathered around him a small group of learned men and founded a palace school to which the aristocracy might send its sons. He set himself the task of translating into Anglo-Saxon a number of Latin books of instruction. With the aid of his scholarly companions he translated five such books. One was the *Pastoral Care* of Gregory the Great, a guide to the clergy in the performance of their duties. Another was Bede's *Ecclesiastical History*. The purpose of this translation was to give the English a sense of their origin and traditions. A similar purpose may have lain behind the *Anglo-Saxon Chronicle,* which was begun in Alfred's reign. In its original form the *Chronicle* commenced with Caesar's invasion of Britain, sketched Roman history to about 450, and thereafter traced the history of Anglo-Saxon England. The original manuscript ended in 892. But it was copied and distributed to various monastries and continued by the monks, who included local as well as national history, so that the surviving manuscripts, though much the same for the period before 892, differ greatly thereafter. Alfred also translated a history of the ancient world by Orosius, to which he added much material of his own. His last two translations, the *Consolation of Philosophy* by Boethius and part of the *Soliloquies* of St. Augustine, dealt with religious ideas. Thus Alfred gave his people a remarkable literature in their own tongue.

Alfred's personality and character drew men to him. His lovable qualities, his breadth of interest, his understanding of humanity, his simplicity, idealism, and deep Christian piety—all won him affection. "England's darling," as he was called in the Middle Ages, he is the one ruler of his country who is known as "the Great."

THE RECONQUEST OF THE DANELAW

During the half century after Alfred's death his son and daughter and his grandsons reconquered the Danish portions of England. A number of factors made this achievement possible. Invasions from Scandinavia temporarily abated. Moreover, the Danes, now settled for a generation in East Anglia, in eastern Mercia, and in southern Northumbria, were changing somewhat in character. They were, of course, different from the Anglo-Saxons, and they were not easily assimilated; having a strong sense of independence they retained their own legal and social customs. But at least they were now farmers rather than warriors. In England, as in the rest of Europe, they turned easily from piracy to legitimate trade. They accepted Christianity; there was intermarriage between the two peoples, and some English thegns, doubtless at the instance of the king, purchased estates within Danish areas. Finally, the reconquest was made possible by Alfred's military reforms, by the popular support he had inspired for his dynasty, and by the valiant leadership of his descendants.

His son Edward (899–924) and his daughter Ethelfleda, the famous "Lady of Mercia" who ruled that area from 911 to 918, embarked together upon a systematic reconquest of the Danelaw. They built fortresses at strategic points along the border, advanced into one Danish district after another, defeated the Danes in battle, and built new fortresses which they garrisoned with English settlers. By the year 918 Edward had carried the English frontier to the Humber "in one of the best sustained and most decisive campaigns in the whole of the dark ages." Edward's son Athelstan (924–939) captured York in 927. Ten years later he defeated a strong combination of Norsemen from Ireland and the Celts from Scotland and Strathclyde. Fighting continued in the north until 954, a date which marked the final conquest of Scandinavian England. On many counts Athelstan was a remarkable king.

THE HEIGHT AND THE DECLINE OF ENGLISH MONARCHY

To later generations the reign of Edgar the Peaceful (959–975) appeared to embody the highest achievement of Anglo-Saxon kingship. Edgar ruled without question over all England, he was accepted as overlord by the Celtic kings of northern Britain, he kept the kingdom secure from foreign attack, and he maintained a high standard of internal order. He placed his full authority behind a notable religious revival led by Dunstan, whom he made archibishop of Canterbury. King and archbishop worked in close harmony, and the re-establishment of monasticism, only now recovering from the Danish invasions, was the greatest achievement of his reign. He ceded lands in northern Northumbria to Kenneth II, King of Scots. He permitted the men of the Danelaw to continue their own legal and social customs. He allowed great authority to officials known as ealdormen who ruled over local districts.

A grave weakness of Anglo-Saxon kingship was the lack of any fixed rule of succession. This weakness became obvious at Edgar's death. He left two sons, one by each of his two marriages: Edward, a very young man, and Ethelred, a boy about ten years old. For reasons not altogether clear, certain nobles supported Ethelred for king rather than his brother, and for some months England was close to civil war. Many nobles, moreover, resented the large grants of land made to monasteries in Edgar's reign and hoped to acquire these lands for themselves. The atmosphere was one of discontent and selfishness. It was darkened further in 978 by the murder of King Edward under circumstances of treachery by members of Ethelred's faction.

Ethelred did not participate in the crime, but he never escaped its ill repute. Throughout his reign (978–1016) a deep suspicion existed between him and his nobles. He floundered from one policy to another and constantly appeared to be acting on bad advice; his nickname of Ethelred Unread or Unready was an ironic play upon his name which meant "noble counsel." With a weak king and treachery and suspicion among nobles, with many of the Danes in England only half loyal to the monarchy, and with oppression of the lower classes and a loss of morale among the people who had no confidence in their leaders, England fell an easy prey to renewed attacks by the Danes.

After ravaging wide areas in 991, the Danes obtained from Ethelred 22,000 pounds of gold and silver in return for their promise to depart. This was the first of many payments, known as Danegeld, by which Ethelred weakly bought peace. Danegeld, becoming a tax on land, imposed a crushing burden on the English peasantry. Between 997 and 1012 two large Danish armies remained in England for several years, draining away the wealth of the richest areas.

Then in 1013 the full strength of the Danish kingdom, directed by Swein, the King of Denmark, fell upon England in a fierce thrust at conquest. Advancing with precision and skill, Swein died in the moment of his triumph, but the war continued with his son Cnut fighting against the brave Edmund Ironside, the son of Ethelred. There were fierce battles, but when Edmund died in 1016 Cnut was acknowledged as King of all England. A rich and ancient kingdom had fallen to the Vikings because it was wanting in competent leadership.

KING CNUT, 1016–1035

Cnut was a successful ruler. His reign, though humiliating to English pride, was about the best that could be hoped for under the circumstances. Controlling the country easily because of its exhaustion, he was wise enough to respect English institutions and to stress the continuity of his government with the English government of the past. A code of laws issued late in his reign was largely derived from the laws of earlier English kings. The system of national administration, which had been developing in the tenth century, was also preserved. Royal charters and other documents of the type issued by Ethelred continued to be prepared by Cnut's writing staff.

Cnut saw the advantages of close alliance with the church. The church's sanction strengthened his hold upon the people; churchmen supplied him with his writing staff and recorded his reign with sympathy. He was the first Viking to be accepted by other rulers as a respectable Christian prince. The ordinary English regarded him as a conqueror, but as a conqueror who brought peace and growing prosperity, who enforced the law, honored the church, opened new markets for traders, and offered careers to the English.

The fact remained that Cnut was a foreign king with strong barbaric elements in his character. At first he ruled England as a conquered province, dividing it arbitrarily into four large areas, each ruled by a Dane or by an Englishman with close Danish connections. It was only at the end of his reign that Englishmen became his chief advisers. Cnut surrounded himself with a body of picked fighting men, known as his housecarls, who formed the core of his army. Their position was one of honor, privilege, and wealth. For their support and for the support of a navy Cnut imposed heavy taxation. There is evidence that a good deal of land passed from the hands of the English into the hands of Danes. Finally, his interest in Scandinavia remained strong, for he was King of Denmark and gained a temporary control of Norway and parts of Sweden.

At his death in 1035 he was succeeded as King of England by his two sons, Harold and Harthacnut, whose short and turbulent reigns were fortunately soon over. In 1042, Cnut's line having ended, the English turned back to the royal family of Wessex in the person of Edward, known as the Confessor because of his piety. The son of Ethelred and Emma of Normandy, he had grown up at the Norman court. He ruled until 1066, the date of the Norman Conquest.

SOCIAL CLASSES

In the first centuries of the Anglo-Saxon period society consisted of three distinct ranks—nobles, freemen, and slaves—but as time went on and as society became more sophisticated, these ranks were modified in various ways. Rich and powerful kings, who required an ever-increasing number of soldiers and officials, gave liberal rewards to men who served them well. As the number of nobles increased, a few became very wealthy, and many acquired rights of various kinds over the classes below them. The freemen, on the other hand, suffered a gradual decline, so that by the end of the period large numbers had ceased to be completely free, in an economic if not in a personal sense, and were bound to give labor and produce to the great man of their locality. The position of the slave, though always miserable, sometimes improved. By the time of the Norman Conquest, there were four classes in England: nobles, freemen, and slaves, as before, but in addition there was a large intermediate class which was neither slave nor free but something in between.

The Nobles

The earliest Anglo-Saxon nobles were athelings and eorls. The athelings were members of the royal family, and the eorls were also nobles by birth. Both groups, however, were gradually superseded by men who became nobles through service to the king. The new nobles were known as gesiths and later as thegns. Gesith meant "companion," and thegn had once meant "servant." But the companions and servants of the king were his warriors, his chamberlains, his officials. They were members of his household and helped him govern the country. He rewarded them with gifts of land, with privileges and immunities, and with valuable rights over the lower classes. The wergeld of a noble—the fine imposed upon anyone who killed him—was high (1200 shillings), six times as high as the wergeld of a freeman. By the tenth century, nobility was based upon wealth as well as upon service. A rich freeman might become a thegn, as might also a merchant who crossed three times to the Continent in his own ship.

A wealthy thegn owned large estates in various parts of the country, he and his family moving about from one estate to another. His house consisted of a timbered hall which served as a dining hall, as a center for the daily life of the household, and as the sleeping place of servants and retainers. The bedrooms of the noble and his family were separate from the hall and were sometimes in another building. The hall was furnished with tables and benches; mattresses and pillows lay on the floor to serve as beds; the walls were hung with curtains and tapestries. A noble and his guests feasted and drank in the hall, where the men boasted of their great deeds and listened to songs and to the music of the harp. A noble had many retainers—huntsmen, fowlers, messengers, domestic servants. He took pride in fine dogs and horses, in elaborate saddles and bridles, in handsomely decorated weapons, and in adornments of silver and gold. He dressed in trousers and in a long tunic falling to the knees, over which he might wear a silken mantle or a cloak of fur. His wife wore a tunic with a mantle over it, her tunic and mantle reaching to the ground and held in place by handsome brooches, often one on each shoulder. The noble woman had risen in legal status over the centuries from being treated as a minor to having a limited right to own property. She was still the subordinate of her husband, however, as long as he lived. A noble had to serve the king in war and to spend time at court, where he probably held some official position. He had to control his servants and retainers, for he was responsible for their good behavior; and he had to attend the local courts and take part in the work of local government and justice.

The Ceorls or Freemen

The ceorl, the farmer of Anglo-Saxon England,[3] was a freeman, the independent master of a peasant household. He had a wergeld of 200 shillings and could obtain redress in court for any assault upon his property. He paid dues to the church and a food rent to the king. The food rent was a fairly large amount of food which was due from a group of peasants once a year and was sufficient to feed the king and his court for twenty-four hours. The freeman attended the local court, served in the fyrd or militia, and had the obligation of repairing roads, bridges, and fortresses. He also had miscellaneous duties, such as supplying carts to carry the king's luggage.

The Anglo-Saxon ceorls, drawn together for protection and companionship, lived for the most part in small, compact villages and cultivated the surrounding fields as a cooperative enterprise. Their houses were no more than primitive huts of wood or of lath and plaster and contained one large room which housed the peasant family and perhaps the livestock as well, for people and beasts might sleep close together on a cold winter night. Smoke from the fire on an open hearth filled the hut (and at least kept down the fleas) before it escaped through the hole in the thatched roof. The village contained a mill and perhaps a church or the timbered hall of the great man of the area.

Beyond the village stretched large open fields without permanent fencing. There were normally two great fields, each cultivated in turn a year at a time, while the other lay fallow to regain its fertility. The fields were divided into long narrow strips, usually about 220 yards in length and about 16½ feet wide, stretching gracefully across the field in the shape of a huge elongated **S**. The strips were arranged in blocks, those in one block pointing in a different direction from those in another in order to obtain a natural drainage and to follow the contour of the land. There were shorter strips in queer-shaped blocks to fill out corners and irregularities in the open fields. A peasant's strips were scattered through the fields and interspersed with the strips of his neighbors. It was once thought that this scattering was due to a principle of equality by which each peasant secured some of the better and some of the poorer land in the open fields. The Anglo-Saxons, however, were practical farmers, not social theorists. Their problem was to wring a livelihood from the soil. They lived in fear of hunger, for a poor harvest might mean a famine. Faced with a common danger, they met it with a common effort. Very few peasants were rich enough to own the full team of eight oxen required to drag the heavy wooden plow. Cooperative farming was thus a practical method of agriculture, and cooperation presumably

---

[3]There were various ranks among the ceorls. Leats and geburs were freemen of lower status than the ceorl. The cotsetlan, or cottage dweller, was lower still. Geneats, on the other hand, who rode about an estate on various errands, performed more elevated tasks than the ceorl.

Agricultural laborers, c. 1025–50. (British Library, Cottonian MS, Claudius B. iv., f. 79v)

meant that the peasants had obtained their strip in rotation and not on the basis of any social theory.

In addition to the arable fields, a village required a pasture; a meadow for hay, which was highly prized; and a wasteland on the border of the forest where fuel could be gathered and pigs and geese allowed to roam. To keep the farm animals alive through the winter was a constant problem. Bees were valued for their honey, which was used for sweetening and for making mead.

Although compact villages and open fields were the normal units of agriculture, they were by no means universal. From very early times the land in Kent had been divided into much smaller fields enclosed by hedges or fences as in modern farming. The land in Wales and in the north and west of England was too hilly and rugged for agriculture in open fields. These areas were better suited for pasturing sheep and cattle, and solitary homesteads or shepherds' lonely huts were scattered over the countryside. Some grain was grown, however, for the making of bread.

The Decline of the Ceorl. The position of the ceorl tended to decline. For this there were many reasons. One was his economic insecurity. An illness, a wound, a run of poor harvests, a murrain among his cattle, an attack by robbers, a war between rival kingdoms, an incursion by the Danes—any of these might bring ruin to the peasant. It is not surprising that many ceorls, left destitute by disaster, placed themselves under the protection of a lord. They could give their land to a lord (receiving back from him its possession and use) in return for his promise of protection. They could offer him their labor on certain days each week or they could offer produce from their lands. It was sometimes the lord who took the initiative. A noble or a monastery, requiring laborers, might give peasants the right to use their lands in return for produce and labor.

A peasant's act in placing himself or his land under the lord's protection was known as commendation. It did not necessarily imply servility, for a distinction was made between personal and economic dependence. Yet he was likely to become increasingly bound by the obligations he had undertaken.

In certain ways the actions of the king hastened the decline of the freemen. The king rewarded his thegns not only with grants of land but with grants of royal rights. A thegn might be given the food rents or other services owed to the king by the peasants of a village. If the villagers after some disaster could not pay the food rents, they might be compelled to offer the thegn their labor or a part of the produce from their strips of land. The king, moreover, might grant the thegn judicial rights, the right to retain that portion of the fines levied in a local court which had formerly gone to the king, or the right to establish a new court and keep the fines it imposed. Kings were always troubled by the difficulty of bringing lawless persons into court, and they tried to solve the problem by commanding that every man must have a lord who was responsible for his appearance when that was desired. These practices opened the way for a lord to strengthen his hold upon a village community.

The Slaves. Slaves formed the lowest rank in society. Men became slaves in various ways. Some were captives taken in war, some were descendants of enslaved Celts, many were persons condemned to slavery as a punishment for crime or for inability to pay the fines levied upon them by the courts. The law gave slaves no protection. They had no wergeld. A man who killed a slave paid to the owner the slave's market value, which was roughly equivalent to that of eight oxen. Since slaves had no property in the eyes of the law, they could not be fined by the courts but were punished by flogging, by mutilation, or by death for serious crimes. The owner who maltreated or killed his slave was subject to the censures of the church but was not punished by public law.

In practice this harshness was somewhat mitigated. Custom and tradition gave certain rights to slaves. If they were laborers on the estates of their master, as most of them were, custom allowed them some share of the produce of the estate. The fact that they sometimes bought their freedom indicates that their right to acquire possessions was acknowledged. The church, frowning upon slavery, encouraged men to emancipate their slaves as an act of piety. Yet a freed slave was not fully free but remained subject in various ways to his former master. It was often to the owner's advantage to place strips of land at the slave's disposal in return for labor and produce; this practice meant that the position of the slave approached that of those former freemen who had sunk into the class of semiservile agricultural laborers.

ANGLO-SAXON GOVERNMENT

A study of Anglo-Saxon government is by necessity a study of government during the later Anglo-Saxon period from about the year 900 to the Norman Conquest in 1066. The earlier centuries are obscure, and many things can only be guessed at. But institutions developed rapidly, and new sources of information make them clearer, after Alfred's descendants came to rule all of England. It is possible to see that the Anglo-Saxons were building a system of government that was remarkably advanced. The central government contained the origins of later departments of state and employed ingenious devices of administration; the local government, with its many courts and officials, was to affect the whole course of English history.

Central Government: The King

The power and importance of the king, and the idea of what a king should be, constantly expanded during the Anglo-Saxon period. In the early days after the Germanic invasions England had contained many petty dynasties whose kings had been merely the leaders of bands of warriors. In the years after 900, however, kingship was vastly more than this. The king was the powerful and accepted ruler of all England; he wielded great authority and possessed a machinery of government through which his power could be exercised. The meaning of kingship grew as the number of kingdoms diminished and as kings ruled over wider areas. Alfred and his descendants, moreover, exalted kingship because they were national leaders against a common foe and because they inspired loyalty to the royal line of Wessex. They were sovereigns of international significance who were respected on the Continent.

English kingship also grew because of its close alliance with the church. Kings were taught that their first duty was to give the church honor and protection; in return for this protection churchmen cast about the king a halo of sanctity. Kingship acquired a religious significance. The king ruled by God's grace; he was the representative of God among a Christian folk. The church also gave Anglo-Saxon kings a vision of the exalted position and high responsibilities of the emperors of Rome. Hence the kings of the later Anglo-Saxon period regarded themselves as civil and religious rulers whose duty it was to protect the people and to promote the welfare of the country.

All public authority was derived from the king. He summoned and commanded the military forces of the kingdom in time of war. His favor gave men wealth and power. He appointed and removed officials. He also appointed leading churchmen—bishops, abbots, and priors. The choice of these prelates lay in theory with the monks of a monastic cathedral or of a monastery who, upon the death of a bishop or abbot, were empowered to elect a successor. But in practice the church, which owed so much to the king, accepted his candidates for high ecclesiastical office. The king summoned and dismissed the assembly of great men, known as the witan.

The king's authority may be illustrated by his laws and by the operation of the king's peace. His laws, which were issued after consultation with the witan, were national in scope and were aimed at the suppression of lawlessness and crime. The king's peace was based upon the notion that peace was attached to the house of every freeman. Fighting or violence by strangers in a man's house was a grievous offense which became infinitely more serious if the house was that of the king. But the king was mobile, constantly moving from one place to another, and hence his peace was brought temporarily to any area in which he happened to be. It extended itself gradually to places where he was present in theory, to the local courts, to roads and rivers, and to churches and monasteries. It was not until after the Norman Conquest, however, that the king's peace was thought to encompass the entire realm.

In the Anglo-Saxon period there was as yet no thought of a capital city. The central government was the household of the king and moved with him from place to place. It was essentially domestic, conducted by men who had once been the king's servants—his stewards, butlers, and chamberlains—and who were slowly developing into officers of the state.

Four divisions of the household were to become important administrative departments in later times. One was the chamber, the sleeping apartment of the king, his private retiring room, the heart of government and administration. A second was the wardrobe, an adjoining chamber, which contained not only the king's clothes but also his weapons, his jewels, his important documents, and his money. The money was kept in a treasure chest which traveled with him, though it is probable that at the end of the Anglo-Saxon period some treasure was left for safekeeping at the city of Winchester. Money came to the king from the profits of his estates; from rents; from fines levied in the local courts; from Danegeld, which developed into a tax on land; and from various miscellaneous sources. To handle these payments there must have been some kind of financial organization within the household, an organization which was to grow into the medieval treasury. Chamber, wardrobe, and treasury were in the hands of chamberlains who were acquiring administrative skills.

Then there was the chancery. This was the writing staff of the king, his secretarial department, where letters, charters, chirographs, and writs were prepared by a group of highly trained clerks. The first secretaries of the king had been the clergymen connected with the royal chapel. By the end of the Anglo-Saxon period they had developed into a body of skillful clerks; the chancery had become an ancient and sophisticated institution.

Charters were formal public documents by which the king made gifts of land or of privilege to monasteries or to nobles. Written in Latin, they were highly technical productions. The chirograph was a device to prevent the forgery of charters. A document was copied two or three times on the same piece of parchment; the copies were then cut apart in a saw-toothed line. Copies could later be authenticated by placing the irregular lines together and seeing whether they fitted properly. The writs were short informal letters of command or instruction from the king, written in English and addressed to local courts or magnates. An impression of the king's seal was attached to each writ, thus making it authentic. The writ, a most ingenious device, made efficient government possible and became the normal way in which medieval kings issued commands to their subordinates. Surrounded by a group of chamberlains and clerks, the king must have consulted with them upon problems of law and government. Here was the faint foreshadowing of a royal council.

A serious weakness in Anglo-Saxon government was the lack of any fixed principle of royal succession. Germanic tradition contained an element of election, but Roman practice pointed to heredity. Both principles seem to have been in operation among the Anglo-Saxons. Kings came from the royal family, and normally a son succeeded his father. But in times of crisis, as happened when Alfred came to the throne in 871, the strongest member of the royal family became king and the children of the former king were passed over. Sometimes a king settled the succession by will or by associating his successor with him in the work of government. In any case, the new king could not feel secure until he had obtained acceptance by the great men of the kingdom who were normally members of the witan. The action of the witan was not an election; rather, it was a formal recognition of the person to whom heredity, or merit, or special circumstances, or conquest pointed as the future leader. The vagueness surrounding the succession to the throne was at times a source of great danger.

An Anglo-Saxon king was limited in power by his coronation oath, a threefold promise given in the most solemn terms to defend the church, to punish crime and violence, and to temper his judgments with clemency and mercy. He was limited also by the ancient customs of the kingdom, which he could not violate with impunity. To some extent his power was restricted by the witan.

The Witan. The word "witan" or "witenagemot" meant an assembly of wise men and refers to meetings of the Anglo-Saxon king with the leading men of his kingdom. The witan was an ancient institution, for the early kingdoms had witans, but very little is known about it until the tenth century, when the successors of Alfred summoned witans composed of important persons from most of England. By that time the witan included members of the royal family and of the ancient nobility, bishops and abbots, the king's household officials, and his leading thegns. It reflected an aristocracy of birth, wisdom, and service. Its membership was never fixed, nor were the times or places of its meetings. These were determined by the king.

The work and functions of the witan were considerably vague. It acted as a court to try cases in which the king or the great men of the kingdom were interested, but its judicial work was not large, and it was not a court of appeal. It played a part in legislation, for the king did not issue laws until he had placed them before the witan; yet it was the king and his household officials who drew up the laws, and the witan was merely asked to express its approval. In the same way it witnessed the king's charters, thus giving its sanction to royal gifts of land and privilege. It was asked to approve other acts of the king.

The king was under no obligation to ask the consent or approval of the witan for his actions. Indeed, the witan never established its right to offer advice or to give its sanction. It never defined its position nor obtained a fixed place in the scheme of government. Yet in practice the king consulted it about most matters of importance. There were times when a minority, a weak king, or a national crisis gave the witan considerable power. But its membership, its procedure, and its functions were so vague and ill-defined that a strong king could control it much as he pleased.

Local Government: The Shire

Most of England in the later Anglo-Saxon period was divided into administrative districts known as shires. They originated in various ways. Some of them, as Essex, Sussex, and Kent, were ancient kingdoms that had been reduced in size and finally absorbed into Wessex. Norfolk and Suffolk represented a tribal division in the old kingdom of East Anglia. The shires of Wessex seem to have originally been areas around towns. Later, as the Danelaw was subdued, it was divided arbitrarily into shires.

The earliest official of the king in the shire was the ealdorman. It is likely that he was often of royal blood and was always a trusted member of the king's household, appointed to represent the king's authority in the shire. He assembled and commanded the fyrd, or local militia. He and the bishop presided at the meetings of the shire court. It was his duty to enforce the decisions of the court. He compelled the nobles of the shire to keep the peace and to restrain their retainers from acts of violence. Royal writs containing the commands of the king were addressed jointly to the ealdorman and to the bishop. The wergeld upon the life of the ealdorman was very high, and valuable lands were set aside for his support. He held a position of great profit, dignity, and social prestige.

As the Danelaw was conquered in the tenth century, the ealdorman increased in power and importance and was often placed in charge of several shires. He received a part of the fines levied in the courts and part of the tolls and customs paid by the towns. He was so great a noble that lesser thegns and freemen attached themselves to him as to their lord. Under Cnut the office became even more influential. The ealdorman, to whom the Danish title of earl was now given, ruled over such wide areas that all of England was controlled by a few great men.

As the position of ealdormen and earls expanded and as they were drawn into national politics, they became detached from the details of local government. The need arose for a new official who would be closer to the people and more devoted to the administration of a single shire. Such an official was the shire-reeve, or sheriff, who appeared about the middle of the tenth century. By the time of the Norman Conquest he had become the king's principal executive officer in all branches of local government. As the name implies, he was the king's reeve, that is, a royal servant charged with the protection of the crown's financial interests. He collected money owed to the king. Royal estates were under his supervision. When a large assessment such as Danegeld was imposed, it was the sheriff's duty to assess and collect the money. In the absence of the ealdorman he presided over the shire court along with the bishop. He proclaimed the laws and commandments of the king, led in the pursuit of criminals, and enforced the decisions of the court. He also summoned the fyrd, thus becoming important in both local and national defense.

His significance in the late Anglo-Saxon period lies partly in the fact that he was the agent of the king, to whom he was directly responsible. The symbol of royal power, he kept the king's authority before the eyes of thegns and freemen. These men had few direct dealings with the earl, but their dealings with the sheriff were constant. He was thus a bridge between the central and the local government.

The shire court, which assembled twice a year, was the shire in action, capable of exercising all the functions of local government. It carries out the commands sent to it by the king. It was a court of law for all kinds of cases. An ancient court, it had once been attended by all the freemen of the area, but in the later Anglo-Saxon period many freemen had dropped out, and the court was largely composed of the wealthier and more important persons of the shire. The duty of attendance became attached to certain pieces of land; men who held these lands owed service in the court. Although the court had grown more aristocratic and although the presiding officers were the ealdorman, the bishop, and the sheriff, it was, nonetheless, the assembled freemen who declared the law and who determined what the proof should be. The court was much used by the upper classes to confirm and publicize land titles.

The Hundred. In late Anglo-Saxon times the shires were divided into smaller judicial and administrative units known as hundreds. Although their origin is somewhat obscure, it is known that for a long time much of the work of local government had centered in the estates of the king. A royal estate served as the administrative core of the surrounding area and was under the supervision of a king's reeve or bailiff. These men did more and more work of a governmental nature, pursuing criminals, collecting money, and keeping order in their localities. It is possible that this small unit of government came to be called a hundred in the tenth century.

Whatever its origin, the hundred was a very active unit of local government. It contained a court over which an official known as a hundred reeve presided. He was responsible to the sheriff, who occasionally visited the hundred court. The court, meeting every four weeks, was the place attended by the ordinary freeman for all kinds of judicial, police, and commercial business.

The Borough. A survey of Anglo-Saxon local government must include not only the shire and the hundred but also the town or borough. The boroughs differed widely from each other; yet they possessed common characteristics that marked them sharply from the rest of the community. A borough, in the first place, was surrounded by a wall or by an earthen rampart which made it a fortress, a burgh, a defensible place. A borough also contained a market. It was thus a port, a place of trade; the king's official who governed it was the portreeve, for Anglo-Saxon boroughs remained under royal control. The wealthier merchants who lived in the boroughs were allowed to form guilds for the protection of their business interests and to develop rules and customs for the regulation of trade. Sometimes these customs were enforced by a borough court. If the borough followed certain rules, it might also obtain the right to coin money.

Not all the inhabitants of a borough were burgesses, though all were freemen. A burgess held his plot of land in the town by burgage tenure, for which he paid rent to the king. Because he paid in money and not in labor or produce, his position differed sharply from that of a peasant in the country. Yet the connections between the borough and the surrounding countryside were very close. Outside the town lay open fields, meadows, and woodland, in which each townsman had his share.

The question arises why some towns and villages developed into boroughs whereas others did not. The explanation has been offered that the boroughs began in the fortresses built by Anglo-Saxons and Danes in the ninth and tenth centuries. But some of these fortresses grew into boroughs, whereas others declined in prosperity. It was the economic factor that mattered: fortresses became boroughs only when their location, or their security, or some other advantage made them attractive as economic centers. Long before the boroughs of the ninth and tenth centuries, trade had developed between the Anglo-Saxons in southeastern England and the Franks in Gaul, a trade that stimulated such towns as London, Rochester, and Canterbury.

The Danish invasions, once their violence had subsided, brought a revival of commerce with the Low Countries, France, and even Italy. Some of the fortresses attracted merchants who were glad to obtain places of safe deposit for their goods and who made use of the portreeves or other responsible townsmen as witnesses in important business transactions. The king encouraged merchants to take up holdings in the boroughs. At the end of the Anglo-Saxon period London, Norwich, York, Lincoln, and Canterbury were important boroughs, and there were lesser ones in other places. London was by far the largest. It traded with most of the towns of western Europe and was the terminus of trade routes running across the Continent.

The Vill. The smallest unit of local government was the vill, or village. We assume that the men of a village met together to determine the calendar of the agricultural year in their cooperative enterprise of farming. The vill was also a small police unit. The difficulty Anglo-Saxon kings encountered in bringing people to court led them to demand that every man, unless he was a member of the upper class, should find a surety, that is, someone who would guarantee to produce him if he were wanted. One method was to arrange the peasantry in groups of ten, known as tithing groups, each headed by a tithing man. If one of the ten was wanted, it was the duty of the other nine to find him and bring him to court; failure to do so was severely punished. The Normans continued this practice, calling it frankpledge. In Anglo-Saxon times the tithing sometimes merged with the vill, so that the entire village was responsible for producing any of its inhabitants.

Legal Procedure. To modern eyes the law administered by the shire and the hundred courts may appear grossly barbaric. It must be remembered, however, that we are dealing with a primitive age in which law was only beginning to replace private vengeance and in which superstition mingled with a naïve belief that God would perform miracles to distinguish innocence from guilt. There was also an exaggerated reverence for oaths, based on the conviction that a man who swore falsely condemned his soul to eternal damnation.

A case in an Anglo-Saxon court proceeded somewhat as follows: The party who thought himself wronged appeared in court and made a formal accusation against his adversary. He then went to the house of the accused and, using a set formula of words, summoned him to come to court. Often the accused had no desire to comply. Various methods were devised to force his appearance, some of which have been mentioned. His kin, his lord, or his tithing group was responsible for his coming. In extreme cases he might be outlawed, which meant that his enemies were free to slay him if they were able to do so. But if both parties were in court, each took a solemn oath, the plaintiff repeating his accusation and the defendant making his denial. At this medial point in the trial the assembled freemen gave their judgment by determining which party should give proof and what the proof should be.

One method of proof was by oath-helpers, or compurgators. The value of an oath depended upon the social status of the oath-helper. The party making proof was told to find a set number of men who would swear that his oath was a good oath. If he produced the required number or value of oath-helpers he won his case. An oath was a very solemn thing, not to be made lightly, and a man of evil reputation might not be able to obtain oath-helpers. In cases of very serious crime the proof was sometimes by ordeal. This was an appeal to God to show by a miracle where guilt or innocence lay. The man undergoing the ordeal plunged his arm into boiling water or carried a piece of hot iron for several paces. If the wound healed quickly and well, he was considered innocent; if it did not, he was pronounced guilty. Or he might be bound and thrown into a body of water that had been blessed by a priest. It was thought that this water would not receive a guilty person. Hence, if a man floated he was guilty; if he sank he was innocent and was rescued, we may hope, before he proved his innocence by drowning. Many a guilty person, believing that the ordeal would reveal his guilt, preferred to confess or to make some compensation rather than undergo the ordeal. It is also very likely that some innocent persons confessed in order to avoid the agony of an ordeal.

Disputes over property were often settled by the testimony of witnesses. A man accused of stealing cattle, for instance, might prove his innocence by producing witnesses who would testify that they had been present when the cattle were purchased. The custom arose of summoning witnesses at almost every commercial transaction; hence if a man accused of theft could not offer witnesses of this kind he all but confessed his guilt.

Almost any crime was punishable by a fine. The murderer paid a very heavy fine, the wergeld, to the family of his victim. For a lesser offense, such as cutting off a man's finger, the defendant paid a fine known as a bot to the injured party and also an additional fine, the wite, which went to the king. The collection of these fines, often a difficult matter, was the obligation of the victorious party. He was supported by public opinion and was sometimes aided by the sheriff or the ealdorman. A weakness of the law was its formality. Every summons, every word in a trial, must be spoken in the proper formula; one slip of the tongue lost the case.

THE ACHIEVEMENT OF THE ANGLO-SAXON KINGS

The Anglo-Saxon kings, in the face of great difficulties, gave England territorial and political unity. For more than a century and a half before the Norman Conquest they labored to devise new methods of government. Basing local government upon the old institution of the folkmoot, they added vigor and authority to the shire and hundred courts and created officials through whom they could reach down to influence local affairs. Though it may have lagged behind local development, the central government contained the origins of various departments of state, ingenious devices of administration, and a strong tradition of monarchy. The Normans were to give these institutions new drive and energy, but they had little of their own either in political theory or in administrative practice that was as mature and sophisticated as the government of the Anglo-Saxons.

CHRONOLOGY

Anglo-Saxon England

410–442	Withdrawal of Roman legions
432	Patrick consecrated bishop
450–500	Arrival of Angles and Saxons
597	Augustine sent to Canterbury
616–632	Edwin of Northumbria, Bretwalda
663	Council of Whitby
721	Lindisfarne Gospels
731	Bede's *Ecclesiastical History of the English People*
8th and 9th centuries	Danish invasions
871–899	Alfred the Great, King of Wessex
1016–1035	King Cnut
1042–1066	Edward the Confessor
1066	Harold of Wessex, last English king of England

The Norman Conquest

The one date in English history that everybody knows is 1066; in that year William, Duke of Normandy, brought an army across the Channel, defeated the Anglo-Saxons at the Battle of Hastings, and was crowned as King of England in Westminster Abbey. The Norman Conquest was a turning point in English history. Sooner or later it affected every aspect of English life. A series of strong Norman kings molded English institutions to exalt the power of monarchy. The old Anglo-Saxon nobility disappeared, and a foreign French-speaking nobility took its place. The introduction of Norman feudalism created new social, military, and legal patterns which were to have a permanent effect. England was drawn closer to the Continent. Yet there were things the Normans had no wish to do and could not have done had they wished. Posing as the lawful heir of Edward the Confessor, William claimed all the rights and privileges that Edward had enjoyed and thus continued the traditions of Anglo-Saxon government. The framework of the shire and hundred courts and many principles of Anglo-Saxon law remained much as before. The life of the peasants, as they labored in the open fields, was substantially unchanged. There was great continuity with the past, and the civilization which gradually emerged was essentially an English civilization though deeply marked by Norman influences.

NORMANDY

Normandy was a duchy in Western France directly across the Channel from southern England. It centered in the broad valley of the lower Seine and extended westward to the border of Brittany. Its largest and most important city was Rouen. Other towns included Bec, the site of a famous monastery; Falaise, where William the Conqueror was born; and Caen, Bayeux, Coutances, and Avranches in the western portion of the duchy. Historians used to speak in glowing terms of Norman civilization and political genius. Normandy was called the most progressive and best-governed portion of France; the Conquest was said to have brought a higher culture to England. Historians today do not hold these views. The truth is that the materials for the history of pre-Conquest Normandy were very meager; our knowledge is slight; and what we know leaves the impression that the Normans were a fierce, violent, grasping, and warlike race, less literate and less civilized than the Anglo-Saxons whom they conquered.

Normandy may be regarded as a kind of French Danelaw. Pirates from Denmark had ravaged France in the ninth century in the same way that they had ravaged England. In 841 they sacked Rouen, and four years later they sacked Paris. In 885–886, when they reappeared at Paris with a force estimated by contemporaries at 700 ships and 40,000 warriors, the French King Charles the Fat saved the city by paying them 700 pounds of silver and by giving them permission to pillage the country farther up the Seine. Thus Charles the Fat attempted to buy peace as Ethelred the Unready attempted to buy it in England. But the Danes returned and began to make permanent settlements in Normandy.

During the century and a half between 911 and 1066 the Vikings in Normandy adopted the religion, the language, the methods of warfare, and the social customs of France, though we do not know much about how the transformation took place. By the time of the Conquest there was little to distinguish them from other Frenchmen. Their relations with the king at Paris brought the feudalism of northern France into Normandy. The duke held his duchy from the king in return for military service, that is, in return for supplying the king with a body of fully equipped knights when called upon to do so; and the Norman nobles held their lands from the duke upon similar terms. At this time a knight was no more than a soldier trained to fight on horseback. In the turbulent conditions of life in Normandy every noble of importance maintained a group of knights in his household. He could normally perform his duty to the duke by leading these knights to battle at the duke's command. By 1066 the feudal process had gone a step further: Norman nobles were granting estates to some of their knights in return for the military service the knights performed.

The military pre-eminence of the Normans rested on their skill as knights and as castle builders. They did not originate these methods of warfare; they merely borrowed them. But they became specialists in war, and they were able to employ their crude wooden castles as bases for extensive cavalry operations. Knights and castles, however, could be used to defy ducal authority. No duke before William had been able to prevent the nobles from building castles at their pleasure. Even William, although he inspired great dread, could not end private warfare among the Norman barons. The population of the duchy was increasing. There were large numbers of warriors—younger sons, unattached knights, knights dissatisfied with their small holdings—who were ready for warlike adventure. William was shrewd enough to use this potential power for his own advantage rather than allow it to turn against him or to slip away into enterprises which brought him no profit.

Although the Normans became great warriors, they were slow in developing a well-governed state. Prior to the Conquest there was no Norman system of administration which could function when the duke was weak or incompetent. The moment his authority faltered, the duchy sank into anarchy, and its history became a dreary tale of private war, murder, pillage, and revolt. The Normans had no written law to bring with them to England. There was a ducal household modeled upon that of France, but there was no chancery worthy of the name. Charters and writs, few and irregular, could not bear comparision with the impressive series of documents issued by the Anglo-Saxon kings. The duke had a court composed in theory of his feudal barons. It met infrequently, however, and consisted largely of his household officials, his kinsmen, and his special friends. One of its members wrote that he had never known the court to differ from the duke. In comparison with the Anglo-Saxon witan it was rudimentary. One local official was known as the vicomte, not unlike the English sheriff, though large portions of the duchy were not entrusted to vicomtes but to William's kinsmen.

Both William and his greater barons founded monasteries and maintained them with rich gifts. Yet Norman enthusiasm for the church was rather recent; learned monks, such as Lanfranc and Anselm who made Norman monasteries famous, were importations from Italy. Over the church as a whole William exercised complete domination, appointing bishops and abbots, controlling church councils, and resisting the pretentions of the papacy to greater power. Normandy in 1066 was still a state in the making. The fact that William became duke despite his illegitimate birth was an indication that ordinary rules of church and of law could be defied.

Duke William

Historians have often overrated William and have endowed him with a political genius he probably did not possess. But he was certainly one of the strong men of history. Grasping, masterful, and suspicious, he was as ruthless in imposing his will as he was unscrupulous in his methods. He was devout in a superstitious way, but he allowed religion to place no restraint upon his conduct. After the Conquest the English were chiefly impressed by his implacable severity against all opposition.

William was born in 1027, the bastard son of Duke Robert the Magnificent by Arlette, a peasant girl, whom the duke had kidnapped and carried off to his castle at Falaise. In 1035, when William was eight years old, his father died on a pilgrimage to Jerusalem and William was proclaimed duke. But ducal authority was at a low ebb, and for the next twelve years William lived among disorder, revolts, and assassinations. He had four guardians in succession, all of whom met violent deaths. Disorder reached a climax in 1047, when most of western Normandy revolted. William was forced to make a perilous journey by night through the lands of his enemies. He was fortunate in retaining the allegiance of the eastern portion of his duchy and in having the support of his lord, King Henry I of France, who won for him the Battle of Val-ès-Dunes near Caen, where the rebel barons were crushed.

In the years that followed, William increased and consolidated his power by every means at his disposal. He effectively eliminated rebellious barons by cutting off their heads. He formed an alliance with the count of Flanders, whose daughter Matilda he married in 1053, although the marriage brought him into conflict both with the church and with the king of France. The king invaded Normandy but was defeated in battles at Mortemer (1054) and Varaville (1058), battles which rendered William virtually independent of his lord. He waged war with the county of Anjou and seized the district of Maine, which lay between Anjou and Normandy. Reminded of his illegitimacy by the town of Alencon, William captured the town and cut off the hands and feet of thirty-two of the leading citizens. Thus by war, diplomacy, trickery, and savage intimidation he increased his strength. In 1066 he was ready for fresh aggression.

THE LAST ENGLISH KINGS

It is natural to view the reigns of the last two English kings, Edward the Confessor (1042–1066) and Harold (January to September 1066) from the vantage point of the Norman Conquest. The death of Cnut was followed by the short and shameful reigns of his two sons. They were both dead by 1042, and the witan turned back to the descendants of Alfred, selecting Edward, the son of Ethelred the Unready by his second wife, Emma, who was a sister of the Norman Duke Richard II. Edward was thus half Norman, and he grew up in Normandy. Later known as the Confessor, he was a pious man, conscientious and well-intentioned, but weak and incapable as a ruler. He had been educated by Norman monks, and at heart he remained a monk all his life. Although he did not entirely forfeit the powers or neglect the duties of kingship, he disliked affairs of state, preferring a life of contemplation dedicated to his private devotions, to his almsgiving, and to the building of Westminster Abbey. He surrounded himself with Normans, made French the language of the court, and formed ties with Normandy which, in view of William's ambitions, were very dangerous to England. Edward complicated matters in another way: On the eve of his marriage he took a vow of chastity and hence produced no heir. The problem of the succession disturbed his reign and played into William's hands in 1066.

It often is said that England was endangered during Edward's reign by the excessive power of a few great earls. But Cnut had easily controlled the earls, and Edward could have done the same. It was his weakness which tempted them to take an unusually prominent part in national affairs. So colorless and incompetent a king was certain to cause dissensions unless a great noble became the power behind the throne. And if Edward invited strife and invasion by his refusal to beget an heir, why should not an English earl become his successor instead of a usurper from abroad? These circumstances more than justify the policies of Godwin, Earl of Wessex, and his son Harold. However aggressive and ambitious, these two were not bent upon destroying monarchy. Their aim was to preserve it, to secure the throne for themselves at Edward's death, and thus to prevent foreign invasion.

From a simple thegn in Sussex, Godwin had risen to become the greatest and wealthiest noble in England. His advancement was due to the closeness of his connection with Cnut and to his marriage into the Danish royal house. Having supported Edward's succession in 1042, he naturally demanded his reward. His family grew ever richer and more important. His daughter became Edward's queen, his son Swein secured an earldom in the Severn Valley, his son Harold became earl of East Anglia, a nephew Beorn obtained an earldom north of London, while Godwin himself remained earl of Wessex. Edward's reaction was to draw closer to his French and Norman friends, some of whom were most unworthy.

In 1051 a clash occurred between Edward and Godwin which proved to be a turning point in the reign. Anti-Norman sentiment was now strong in England, and Godwin showed his sympathy with it, first by an unsuccessful attempt to prevent the elevation of a Norman, Robert of Jumièges, to the archbishopric of Canterbury, and secondly by a quarrel with a visiting Norman, Eustace of Boulogne, the king's brother-in-law. Angered by this quarrel, Edward displayed unaccustomed energy, collected an army, and prepared to march against Godwin. Had Godwin been merely a rebel, he would have resisted. As it was, he submitted to a royal sentence of banishment and went into exile in Flanders. Edward employed his triumph to give Godwin's estates to greedy Normans and to welcome a visit from Duke William, whom he apparently named as his successor. In 1052 Godwin and his family felt strong enough to return. He and his sons were welcomed by the people, Robert of Jumièges fled to Normandy, and the king perforce restored Godwin and his family to their former estates and dignities. Smarting under this humiliation, Edward lost what little interest he had in government and withdrew more completely than ever to his private devotions.

Godwin died in 1053 and his son Harold succeeded to his influence. The great fact in English history during the next twelve years was the steady rise of Harold to a position of preeminence. He was a remarkable man, valiant and expert in war, wise, cautious, and conciliatory in time of peace. He strengthened his popularity by a successful war against the Welsh and he increased the prosperity of the country. At the same time he advanced his family until he and his three brothers controlled all the earldoms except that of Mercia. "No subject of the English Crown had ever been at once so powerful in relation to other noblemen and so great a figure in the country at large."

Harold's position was weakened in 1065 when Northumbria revolted from the harsh rule of his brother Tostig. Harold allowed the Northumbrians to expel Tostig, who fled abroad to become his brother's evil genius. Meanwhile Edward was dying, and the problem of the succession had to be solved. No one in England put forward a claim for William of Normandy, who was regarded as "essentially a Dane and a Dane of bastard origin." The choice lay between Harold and a descendant of the old English line, Edgar the Atheling, a sickly boy who had grown up in exile. For twelve years Harold had been the protector and all but the ruler of the country. The witan selected him as a matter of course; for the next nine months he was the king of England.

THE NORMAN INVASION

William prepared for an invasion of England by propaganda and diplomacy as well as by gathering an army. He insisted that Edward the Confessor had named him as his heir and that Harold, having fallen into his hands in 1064, had bound himself by an oath which concerned the succession. The terms of the oath are unknown, but presumably Harold broke them by accepting the crown of England. William also sought the support of the papacy. He posed in Rome as a true son of the church, desirous of freeing England from a perjured king and from an uncanonical archbishop. This archbishop, an Englishman named Stigand, had been appointed without papal approval after Robert of Jumièges had fled from the country. In the eyes of the papacy, hostile to lay interference in the affairs of the church, Stigand's elevation appeared highly reprehensible. Hence it was decided in Rome that William should be supported. The Pope sent him a consecrated banner, thus lending his aggression an appearance of holiness. Papal approval was of advantage to William in raising an army. He had the support of the Norman barons, but their resources were insufficient for an enterprise of this magnitude, and William had to attract adventurers from other parts of Europe. Some served for pay, others for hope of booty. It was a mark of William's high quality as a commander that he gave his miscellaneous host some coherence and discipline.

William's army cannot have been larger than five or six thousand men. Perhaps half were knights; the remainder were infantrymen, archers, and crossbowmen. The leaders wore shirts of ring mail, as Norse chieftains had worn for centuries, which now extended to the knee and divided in the middle to permit riding. Most of the knights, however, possessed only a leather garment of the same shape sewn over with metal rings. Helmets were made with a protective front piece for the nose. Their shields were not round but shaped like kites to protect the soldier's body and a portion of his leg when on horseback. Their weapons consisted of a sword and short spear. A horse, leather boots, bridle, saddle, stirrups, and spurs completed their equipment. Having passed through a long period of training in the household of a great baron, these soldiers utilized the most efficient fighting methods known.

The English forces, on the other hand, though large in number, or in potential number, were poorly organized, slow to mobilize, and almost impossible to keep in the field over an extended period. The English had neglected the new techniques of war which had developed on the Continent. Their army consisted of three elements—the housecarls of the king and other great lords; the thegns and their retainers; and the militia of freemen known as the fyrd. The housecarls were professional soldiers, superb fighting men, trained, disciplined, and ready for instant combat, but they were too few to act unaided in extensive operations, and so were used as the core of larger armies. The thegns and their retainers were essential in any important campaign, but their mobilization might be a long-drawn-out affair. Finally, there was the fyrd. By 1066 the fyrd appears to have been less a national militia than a smaller body of selected men with some training and equipment for war. The thegns and housecarls wore shirts of ring mail but fought on foot in a formation of

The Norman Conquest, 1066–1072.

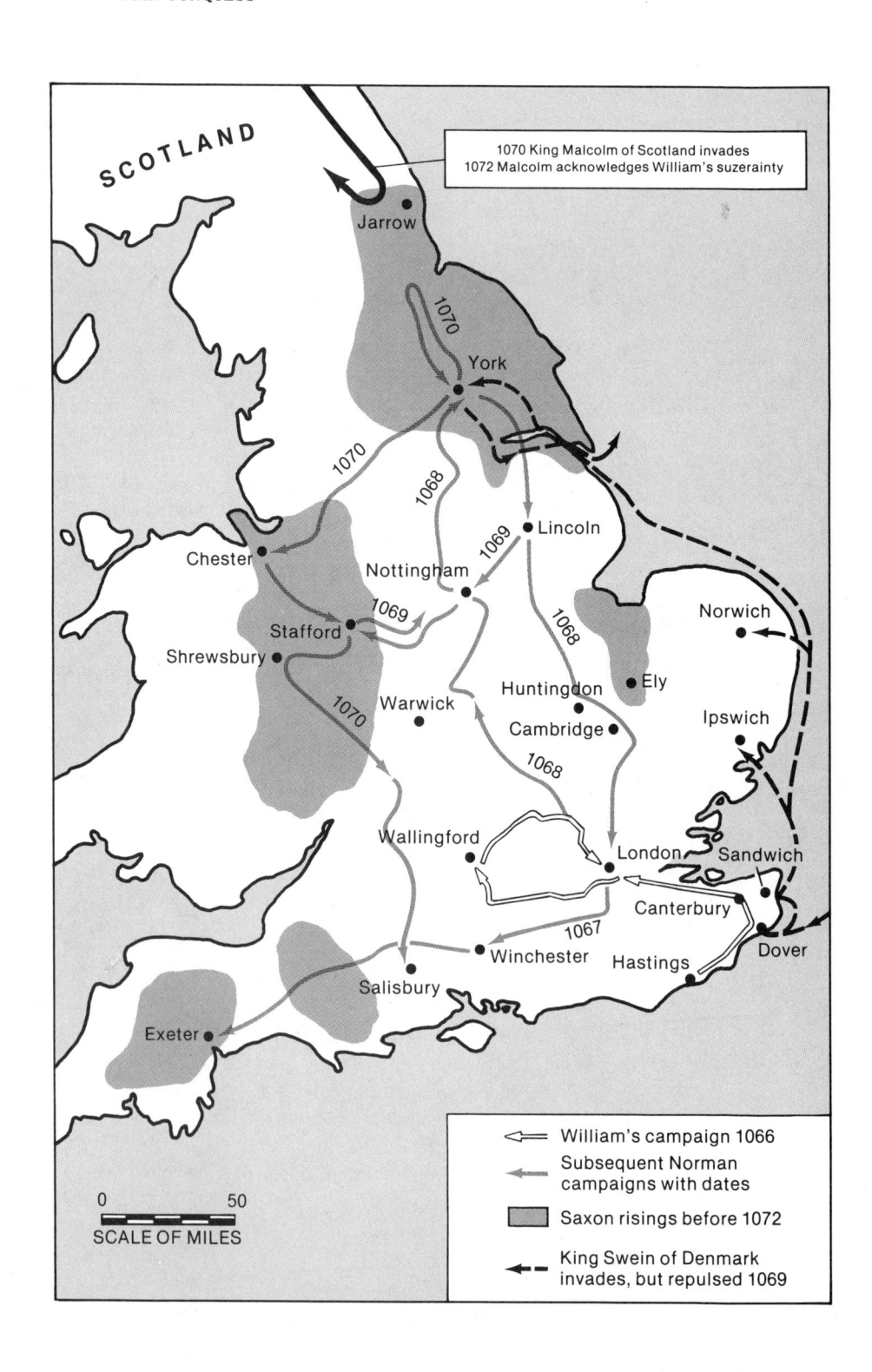

massed infantry. Forming a wall with their round shields, they depended on the Danish battle-ax of their forefathers, having done little to develop their skill in archery. Although his army's methods were out of date and lacking in mobility and striking power, Harold was confident that he could prevent William from landing. He might well have done so had not circumstances combined to give William every advantage.

In the first place William was fortunate because for the moment he could leave Normandy without fear of attack by its neighbors. A timely windstorm also proved favorable. Had it come earlier, Harold would have been ready on the English coast. Had it come later, William might not have been able to hold his motley host together. His greatest good fortune lay in the fact that Harold was suddenly caught in a cruel dilemma. His exiled brother Tostig had persuaded a famous warrior, Harold Hardrada, King of Norway, to try his fortunes in England. In September 1066 a Norwegian fleet of some 300 ships sailed up the Humber, defeated the local English levies, and captured York.

Harold of England, thus faced with the predicament of two simultaneous invasions, tried to meet them by a series of forced marches. Hastening northward, he fell upon the Norwegians at Stamford Bridge near York, defeated them soundly, and killed both Tostig and Harold Hardrada. Only a remnant of the Norweigian host made its

The Bayeux Tapestry. The Battle of Hastings, showing Norman and Anglo-Saxon arms. (Musée de Reine, Bayeux, France)

escape. Stamford Bridge was a great English victory, but three days afterward William landed unopposed on the southern shore. Harold made a hasty pacification in the north and within two weeks was facing William at Hastings. But the English soldiers were tired, and Harold made the error of advancing against a dangerous foe before his forces had reached their full strength. He took his position on the crest of a low hill which fell off sharply on each side and was approached in front by a gentle slope. The hill was narrow and the English were crowded. Yet they withstood the charges of the Norman knights for many hours. It was only when the Normans pretended to retreat that some of the English broke their ranks and pursued, to be cut down by the Normans, who turned upon them. Between the charges of cavalry William used his archers to good effect. Slowly the pressure of mounted knight and unmounted archer wore down the English. By night the Normans had won, and Harold and his brave housecarls lay dead upon the field.

William then advanced to London, devastating the country and terrorizing its people along the way. Many Anglo-Saxons of wealth and position, accepting the inevitable, made their submission; William was soon recognized as king by most of England south of the Humber. Yet it was some five years before the English were completely subdued. There were revolts along the Welsh border, in Exeter, and in Northumbria. William determined to teach the north a lesson. He carried fire and sword through the northern shires, devastating an area of a thousand square miles. He destroyed every inhabited place between York and Durham, burned farm implements and stores of food, and reduced the inhabitants to starvation. The destruction extended to Staffordshire, Derbyshire, and the vicinity of Chester. Thereafter there was little resistance save by the popular hero Hereward the Wake, who held out for some time in the fens around Ely.

Many dangers remained for William. He still needed an army, not only to crush native revolts and curb his restless followers, but also to prevent invasion from Scandinavia and to protect Normandy. To secure such a massive and permanent army he introduced the system of Norman feudalism.

FEUDALISM

Feudalism is a term used to describe certain institutions which emerged in western Europe in the seventh and eighth centuries and which developed rapidly in the two centuries that followed. These institutions appeared because rulers were so constantly engaged in war and so limited in their machinery of government that they could not protect the people at a time when Europe was under deadly attack by Saracens, Slavs, Magyars, and Norsemen. Feudalism was a means by which society placed itself on a permanent war footing and obtained some small amount of local government and local security.

Historians have disagreed as to whether or not feudalism was introduced into England by William the Conqueror. Some scholars note that all the ingredients, if not the vocabulary, were already in place before 1066. Others stress the "revolution" worked by William; The personalizing or privatizing of relationships and jurisdictions had already emerged, however the legal entity known as the "fief" was undoubtedly new to England. New or old, feudalism was firmly established in England after 1066.[1]

Feudalism consisted of three basic elements. The first was personal. A baron who received English lands from William bound himself in the most sacred and solemn way to become William's man, his vassal, and to give him loyalty, service, and good counsel. The baron performed an act of homage and swore an oath of fealty, pledging himself to be William's faithful follower. William in turn promised protection to his vassal. This protection was not only military, but legal. William held a feudal court which the baron had to attend and in which he could seek redress for any wrong done to him by another baron. This bond of lord and vassal, which we have seen foreshadowed in the comitatus, was made as sacred and as unbreakable as possible, for it held society together. And yet it was a contract. If the vassal failed to perform his duty and service, his lands were forfeited. If the king broke the contract by injustice or tyranny, the vassal could in extreme cases renounce his fealty in a declaration called a defiance. In practice the defiance was extremely rare, for it did the baron little good unless he could defend himself by successful revolt.

A second element of feudalism was the land granted by the king to a vassal in return for military service. The vassal was a tenant in chief because he received his land directly from the king; the land was held by feudal or military tenure and was called the fief. William had vast quantities of land, for he confiscated the estates not only of Harold and his brothers but of all the English who fought at Hastings or who later rose in rebellion. Indeed, there was the implicit claim that William was the proprietor of England and that all land belonged to him. He made arrangements with about 180 of his barons, lay and ecclesiastical, granting estates to each in return for the service of a stipulated number of knights, calculated for convenience in multiples of five. A few of the greatest barons owed sixty or seventy knights, and in general the feudal burden was much heavier than it had been in Normandy for an equivalent amount of land. These knights equipped for battle were brought to the feudal host and were obligated to serve for forty days a year, that is, for the summer campaign.

It was absolutely essential that a baron supply the knights he owed. So vital was this obligation that various safeguards, known as the feudal incidents, protected the king or feudal suzerain in case the knights were not forthcoming. The incidents, as they developed in Anglo-Norman feudalism, were somewhat as follows.

Relief. The estate held by a baron in military tenure was in practice hereditary. But in theory it was not, for death ended the contract, and when a baron died the king might legally take back the land. What happened was that the heir paid the king a sum of money known as relief and was then invested with his father's estates. The king demanded that the fief be held together and that one person by responsible for the knights due from it. Hence there arose the principle of primogeniture by which the fief descended to the eldest son and to him alone.[2] Primogeniture was a measure of

---

[1] It should be emphasized that feudalism differed in various parts of western Europe.
[2] The principle of primogeniture was not firmly established in England until about 1200.

the insistence with which the king demanded knights' service from a fief at the earliest possible moment.

Primer Seizin. The king might seize and hold the property until relief was paid.

Wardship. If the heir was a child and thus unable to fulfill the military obligations of the fief, the king might take possession of the estate and manage it for his own profit until the heir came of age.

Marriage. Should the fief descend to a woman, the king was in danger of losing the military service owed him. The heiress might marry someone who could not perform this service, or she might marry an enemy of the king and transfer her wealth to him. Hence the king reserved the right to select a husband for an heiress, though the husband must not be her inferior in rank.

Escheat. If the vassal's family became extinct, or if the vassal suffered a long imprisonment for some grave offense, the fief reverted or escheated to the king, who regained complete control over it.

Fine on Alienation. A vassal wishing to sell or alienate a portion of his fief could not do so without the king's consent and would normally pay a fine for the privilege of alienation.

Forfeiture. A vassal who failed to perform his military service, or who broke his agreement with the king in some other way, was tried in the king's feudal court and, if found guilty, forfeited his lands, which then reverted to the king.

These feudal incidents not only assured the king that knights' service would be forthcoming from a fief but also underscored the fact that the fief was not a gift but a conditional grant of land in which the king retained many rights. They provided occasional opportunities for the king to obtain revenue from the fief. In addition, the king could ask for the feudal aids, sums of money payable by a vassal when the king was in financial need. There was at first a good deal of uncertainty about the aids, but during the twelfth century they became payable on three occasions only: when the king knighted his eldest son, which might be an occasion of great splendor and expense; when he arranged the marriage of his eldest daughter and had to supply a dowry; and when he was captured in war and held for ransom.

The third element of feudalism was private jurisdiction. The barons who obtained estates from William also obtained the right to hold courts for the men living on their lands. These courts were of various kinds. A court known as the manorial court existed for the unfree peasants on each estate. A feudal court was held for the vassals of a lord who had granted (or subinfeudated) a portion of his lands to his knights or to other persons in return for military service. The private courts for the freemen of the area were usually the old Anglo-Saxon hundred courts that the Norman barons took over either through a grant from the king or through quiet usurpation. It was this element of private jurisdiction that gave feudalism its governmental aspect. The enforcement of law was left in private hands in a way no modern state would permit.

These feudal principles become clearer in light of the events following the Conquest. William granted fiefs, as we have seen, to about 180 of his barons, who were pledged to supply a large army of at least 4000 knights. The number of knights required from each fief was determined by the king, whose assessments seemed arbitrary since he was often ignorant of the value of the lands involved. Some of the fiefs were clustered around the sixty or so castles William built, and the knights served in rotation on garrison duty when they were not needed in the field. Such an arrangement was called a castellaria. In a few dangerous border districts—such as Chester, Shrewsbury, Hereford, Durham, and Kent—palatine earldoms were established in which an earl governed a compact block of territory with extraordinary powers.

Most of the great fiefs were composed of estates scattered throughout the kingdom. Henry de Ferrers, Earl of Derby, held lands in fourteen counties. This scattering of estates has sometimes been attributed to policy, but it was probably due to the piecemeal nature of the Conquest and to the way in which Anglo-Saxon nobles had held lands in various parts of the kingdom. The result was to lessen the military power of the Norman barons and to give them an interest in the country as a whole rather than in any one locality. The estates making up a great fief were known collectively as an honor, which was administered as a unit from the principal castle of the baron. It has its officials, its council, its feudal court, its exchequer; its organization and management were modeled upon the administration of the king. William held the greatest of honors, the honor of England.

Having obtained a fief, a Norman baron speedily took possession. The Anglo-Saxon nobles who survived the Conquest disappeared into poverty or exile; when William died in 1087 scarcely more than one percent of the land remained in the hands of those who had held it before 1066. William insisted that the Normans hold their lands with all the rights and obligations of the former owners. For this reason the Normans adopted the fiction that the Anglo-Saxon nobles had been their ancestors. Occasionally a Norman married the Anglo-Saxon heiress of the lands he had obtained from the king. To hold the people in subjection required military strength; the Norman baron, using the forced labor of the peasants, at once built a castle. This was done by digging a circular ditch and by throwing the earth into a great mound in the middle which was called the motte. On the top of the motte was built the castle, known as the keep or donjon, a crude timbered structure surrounded by a wooden stockade. The ditch was filled with water. Beyond it and below the castle was a courtyard or bailey which contained stables and outbuildings. It was protected like the castle with a stockade and was connected with the motte by a drawbridge that could be raised in time of danger. From the crude timbered castles, not replaced by stone for another century, the Norman barons and their knights rode to hold the countryside in subjection.

Every baron, lay and ecclesiastical, maintained a number of knights in his household. Knights were essential, not only to fulfill a baron's obligation to the king and to hold down the native population, but also to garrison castles and to escort the baron and his family as they traveled from one estate to another. The barons began very shortly to grant lands to some of their knights in return for military service. This process was known as subinfeudation, and the knight who obtained a fief became the king's subvassal. Knights were most anxious to be enfeoffed in this way. Without an estate they were apt to remain crude fighting men all their lives. The Anglo-Saxons saw no reason to regard them with respect; in fact, the Anglo-Saxon word *cniht* meant servant or retainer. But if a knight could obtain a fief he might rise in the social

Motte and bailey castle, Great Berkhamstead, Hertford. The motte is seen beyond the bailey. (Aerofilms, Ltd.)

scale. Some knights secured lands through the honor of their lord; they attended his feudal court, and perhaps acted as his officials. They held as much land as some of the smaller tenants in chief, and were even referred to as barons. They might receive fiefs from several lords, having one—their liege lord—to whom they owed loyalty above all others. This process, by which a great baron held land from the king and then subinfeudated part of it to knights or lesser barons (who might repeat the process to knights below them), created in time the elaborate hierarchy of the landed classes in medieval England.

In the reign of Henry I (1100–1135) there arose a practice of paying money to the king in lieu of military service. This payment, known as scutage or shield money, was often of advantage to both parties. A baron might be old or ill; and although there were warrior-bishops who loved to take part in battle—William's brother Bishop Odo swung a great club at the Battle of Hastings because cannon law forbade him to shed blood by the sword—many churchmen preferred to pay scutage in place of knights' service. The king welcomed scutage because he had much fighting to do on the

Continent, where he could easily hire knights. In the long run scutage had important results. The smaller barons became less warlike and more devoted to the management of their estates; men could assume the obligations of a fief although they did not intend to fight; and a baron could grant a fraction of a knight's fee, which was the amount of land necessary to support a knight.

A few general comments may be made at this point. In the first place, it is clear that feudal institutions concerned only the nobility. The mass of the people, peasants and townsmen and even merchants of some wealth, had no part in the feudal system. The obligations of the peasants as they worked in the fields were regulated by ancient custom; the land could change hands, from Anglo-Saxon to Norman, without altering the dues and services of the peasants. Secondly, feudalism under the strong Norman kings was not disruptive. Rather, it strengthened the monarchy, held society together, and made possible the performance of public functions which otherwise would not have been carried out at all. The Norman nobles exhibited a tightly knit cohesion and solidarity unknown before the Conquest. Yet, the feudal structure was far more flexible than can be indicated in a short description. Every bargain between William and his tenants in chief, and between these tenants and their vassals, was a separate agreement which might differ from all others. Many of William's barons came from places other than Normandy and introduced feudal customs they had known in their homelands.

Feudalism as a military institution was strictly male. Women were accounted for only within the legal system, with regard to property rights. In the absence of male heirs, daughters could inherit fiefs, but an arranged marriage suitable to the interests of the lord was assumed. The new husband became the new vassal, because only he could perform the required military service. Widows of lords/vassals had a dower right to a third of the husband's estate for the rest of their unmarried lives. The funding for the widow's dower was originally supplied by her father when he paid a dowery to the groom or groom's father. Since a widow's dower rights often depleted the estate, now in the hands of her son, widows sometimes re-married or else went to a nunnery. In all, feudalism engendered a decline in the rights of women. Whereas in Anglo-Saxon times women could be willed property on equal terms with men, primogenture and the military fief ended this tradition.

This change in the role of women in feudal society can also be attributed to concomitant church reforms. The vast reforms accompanying the pontificate of Gregory VII put a great stress upon clerical celebacy, and brought a far more restrictive view of women's natural functions. The separation of sexes on the clerical level led to a further restriction of activities acceptable to women among the laity.

Finally, the question arises: Had feudalism developed in Anglo-Saxon England? Certainly feudal elements existed in Anglo-Saxon society. There was the personal loyalty of a man to his lord. There was the element of land, although royal grants were in the nature of gifts and were not conditional upon military service. A thegn fought for the king, not because he held land, but because the status of a thegn implied military activity. Private jurisdiction existed, but it was a rare delegation of royal authority, not a right which accompanied the holding of land. These elements were never fused into a system. They remained vague, casual, and haphazard until feudalism converted them into a precise and definite scheme. The feudal fief, land held directly for knights' service, did not exist; its introduction was perhaps the greatest innovation of the Conquest. Other reasons exist why feudalism did not fully develop in pre-Conquest England. A line of strong kings had led the nation to victory over the Danes. Monarchy acquired great prestige and won the loyal affection of the people. Anglo-Saxon kings did not have to bribe their nobles with lavish grants of land. The reconquest of the Danelaw made it possible for kings to organize local government and to retain control over it. Finally, because both Danes and Anglo-Saxons fought on foot, England was not threatened with mounted attacks, and the cost of war could be kept comparatively low.

NORMAN MONARCHY

The King

William the Conqueror and his sons increased the strength of the monarchy and actively participated in the work of government. They had the advantage of ruling a kingdom in which the foundations of the state had been firmly laid. Anglo-Saxon kings had given England a political and territorial unity quite unknown in France. The royal household contained the beginnings of various departments—chamber, wardrobe, treasury, and chancery. The Danegeld was a tax levied on a national scale, and in the king's chamber were officials experienced in the administration of finance. The chancery possessed its staff of skilled clerks, charters, writs, and a royal seal. The local courts of the shire and of the hundred had vigorous traditions; the sheriff was a royal official bridging local and central governments.

William wisely decided to accept the past, to rule as the heir of Edward the Confessor, and to preserve Anglo-Saxon law and institutions. In the first years after the Conquest he had the ideal of an Anglo-Norman state in which he would be served by men of both nations. This proved impossible, and in the end William made more changes than he intended. Yet his borrowings were numerous. It seems probable that the writing staff of the Confessor's chancery passed into the service of the Conqueror. William's first writs were in the English tradition and in Anglo-Saxon. It was only after some years that their style became French and their language Latin. The Anglo-Saxon writ was quickly adopted. The Danegeld tax delighted William; he not only retained it but increased it threefold. Finding the sheriffs highly useful, he greatly increased their authority.

But while William assumed the rights and prerogatives of Anglo-Saxon kings, he also acquired new rights as the supreme lord of many vassals. It was this combination of the sovereignty of the Anglo-Saxon monarch and the suzerainty of the feudal overlord which exalted the position of the Norman kings. They claimed both the allegiance due from the people to an Anglo-Saxon king and the fealty due from feudal vassals to their lord. The fryd was retained, though their military strength was based upon the feudal host. Anglo-Saxon sources of revenue became even more productive, and at the same time the kings exacted feudal aids and incidents from their barons. While preserving the popular justice of the shire and hundred courts, Norman kings also introduced the rules of feudal justice. They strengthened the Anglo-Saxon doctrine that a king duly crowned and anointed ceased to be merely a layman and acquired a divine and holy character. He was God's vicar, deriving his authority from the Almighty; he possessed a miraculous power to heal the disease known as the scrofula, a swelling of the lymphatic glands. William did all that he could to exploit this sacrosanct position of kingship.

The Great Council

King William, says the *Anglo-Saxon Chronicle,* "wore his crown three times every year, as often as he was in England; at Easter he wore it at Winchester; at Whitsuntide at Westminster; at Midwinter at Gloucester; and then were with him all the rich men over all England, archbishops and suffragan bishops, abbots and earls, thegns and knights." These were the great social occasions of the year, replete with solemn ritual and pageantry, when the barons of the king met to do homage. High Mass was sung by one of the archbishops; the crown was placed upon William's head; liturgical laudes glorifying God, but also glorifying William by implication, were chanted before him. Pomp and circumstance were followed by feasting and revelry, and in conclusion William discussed matters of state with his barons.

This assembly, though known by different names, may be called the *Magnum Concilium* or the King's Great Council. It did not differ much in appearance from the Anglo-Saxon witan and it was sometimes called the witan by contemporaries. But there were fundamental differences between the two. The Great Council was a feudal body. It was the duty of a feudal suzerain to summon his tenants in chief to attend his court, and it was both the duty and the privilege of the tenants to be present. The basis of attendance was the possession of a fief held directly from the king. But William continued the prerogative of the Anglo-Saxon king to summon anyone he pleased. He included his household officials, his barons who held fiefs only in Normandy, foreign guests and envoys, and visiting dignitaries of the church. On one occasion in 1086 he summoned a very large assembly on Salisbury Plain, where all the barons, great and small, as well as their vassals, swore an oath of fealty to William as their paramount lord. Normally the small tenants in chief did not attend, and the assembly consisted of fifty to seventy-five of the richest and greatest barons. A formal summons was not generally issued for the three great sessions of the year, but only for lesser meetings.

The principal function of the Great Council was to act as a court of feudal law. In 1075 it tried a baron for rebellion, found him guilty, and sentenced him to life imprisonment. Later in 1096 one baron in the council accused another of taking part in a revolt. The issue was decided by the Norman ordeal of battle. This ordeal, like those of the Anglo-Saxons, was an appeal to God to show which party was in the right. Plaintiff and defendant fought in mortal combat before the court, to the joy of the spectators; the victor was assumed to have won because his plea was just. When the unfortunate baron accused in 1096 was defeated, the King ordered that his eyes be put out and that he be castrated. The Great Council also tried cases of a nonfeudal nature, such as a dispute in 1070 between two bishops over certain lands, a case in which the council turned to the evidence of Anglo-Saxon charters.

Apart from its legal work, the functions of the Great Council were vague. It witnessed charters issued by the king and gave formal approval to many of his actions. It gave him advice on such matters as he chose to place before it. He sometimes turned to it for support in his relations with foreign powers or in his domestic policy. Opposition to his wishes, however, was extremely rare; he constantly acted without consulting the Great Council, and one must assume that it was no great check upon his power. Rather, it was a means of sounding out baronial opinion, for even the strong Norman kings would have been foolish to entirely ignore the wishes of their vassals.

The Small Council

The Great Council was only in occasional session, and the daily work of government was carried on by the king with the assistance of members of his household and of those barons who happened to be in attendance. Officers of the household supplied the professional skill required to carry on the work of central administration, and yet their duties were a strange mixture of official business and care for the domestic life of the king. A list of these officials dates from about 1135 and is headed by the chancellor, the chief of the royal chaplains, who presided over a staff of clerks and was responsible for the secretarial work of the government. Then comes the steward, who had charge of the hall and the arrangements for preparing and serving food; the chamberlain, who presided over the royal bedchamber and the king's wardrobe; the treasurer; the butler, with his staff of cellarers and cupbearers; the constable, who managed the stables and outdoor activities; and the marshal, who maintained order in the court. Other members of the household were frequently away from court on various administrative tasks throughout the country. In addition, a number of the greater barons seem to have been with William a good deal; and as he traveled around the kingdom he was attended by the barons of the area through which he was passing. Hence he always had officials and advisers with him. They formed what may be called the *Curia Regis,* or the king's small council.

The work of the small council should not be differentiated from that of the Great Council, for both bodies did much the same sort of business. When the Great Council met, the small council merged with it and became its heart and core. Questions of major importance were reserved for the larger body. But the members of the small council advised with the king, witnessed charters, corresponded with local officials, and frequently acted as a court of law.

We must picture William as constantly on the move, his court an armed camp, traveling from place to place, suppressing revolts, receiving oaths of fealty, deciding disputes, consuming the feasts prepared for his visits, hunting in the forests, governing as he went. His household traveled with him. In the darkness before dawn, with a great clatter and commotion, the royal documents of state, the king's moneybags, his bed, his wardrobe, his arms and weapons, the pots and pans of the kitchen, the holy objects of the chapel, were all loaded on pack horses or placed in carts, as the royal cavalcade began its lumbering journey across the country.

Local Government

The Norman Conquest brought about important changes in local government. And yet old customs and old ways of doing things, the ancient folkright of the people, remained essentially unaltered. The courts of the shire and of the hundred continued to meet and to enforce Anglo-Saxon law. The peasant was still required to serve in the fyrd, to take part in the hue and cry, and to come to the hundred court to be assigned to a tithing group—a practice the Normans referred to as frankpledge. The Anglo-Saxon village retained its essential unity. The substructure of peasant society was not fundamentally altered.

The shire court was strengthened as a result of the Conquest. It became the means by which Norman kings controlled local government and imposed their will upon all parts of the country. They thought it worthwhile to compel the people to attend the shire courts as in the past and thus to keep open a means by which the king and his subjects could have some contact with each other. William the Conqueror made great use of the sheriff, giving him large powers, so that the sheriff was more potent in the century following the Conquest than ever before or since. William's sheriffs were important barons holding large estates in their shires and were men whom William trusted. They presided in the shire courts and heard royal pleas or cases in which the king had an interest. Twice a year they visited the hundred courts in what was known as the sheriff's tourn. On these visits they checked attendance at the court, they saw that persons wanted by the court were present, and they supervised frankpledge. The sheriff helped with the hue and cry, apprehended criminals, enforced the decisions of the courts, and was responsible for law and order. He also called out the fyrd and acted as custodian of royal estates and castles. Highly important in finance, he collected various fines, taxes, and miscellaneous revenues from courts, lands, and boroughs. Much of this money he disbursed locally; the rest he sent to the king. He gave hospitality and protection to itinerant officials and to the royal court when it visited his shire. In general, the sheriff executed the commands of the king sent to him in royal writs.

So powerful did the sheriffs become that they posed problems for the government. There was danger that the office might become hereditary and that sheriffs might turn into great feudal magnates who could challenge the king's authority. But this was prevented. William II appointed a humbler type of sheriff who had no great standing in his locality or who had served as a minor official in the royal household. The sheriff was curbed by resident justices and later by the necessity of making semiannual reports of his finances to the exchequer. Nonetheless he had many opportunities to oppress the people. Irregularities were winked at as long as the offender was loyal and generous with donations. The problem of the unscrupulous sheriff continued for centuries.

The hundred courts were depressed by the Conquest. They lost business to the shire courts and to new courts which came in with feudalism. It was the right of a feudal lord to hold a court on each of his estates to which the peasants brought their disputes and in which they were punished for petty offenses. Lords, moreover, held feudal courts for their vassals. These feudal courts were important on the great fiefs, though jurisdication of this type dwindled as time went on. But the Norman lords had exercised broad rights of justice on the Continent and expected to do the same in England. Many great fiefs contained several hundred courts which were overtaken by Norman barons, with or without a proper royal charter. Such courts lost their public character and became private courts. Although attended by the same men, the lord's steward now presided and the profits of justice went to the baron, not to the king. If the baron could also obtain the coveted right to supervise frankpledge, he might exclude the sheriff altogether from his private court. By the end of the thirteenth century, when Edward I tried to reverse this process, perhaps half of the hundred courts in England had passed into private hands.

THE PEASANT, THE VILLAGE, AND THE MANOR

The peasants were less affected by the Conquest than was the Anglo-Saxon nobility, but they were sharply depressed in prosperity and in legal status. They suffered in a material way from the destruction of property wrought by William the Conqueror in suppressing rebellions. They suffered from his policy of setting aside large tracts of land as royal forests. A village situated in these forest areas lived under a harsh and repressive code of forest regulations. Many an Anglo-Saxon freeman, moreover, his lands confiscated without compensation and given to a Norman, was compelled to become a laborer bound to the soil formerly his.

The peasants also suffered in legal status. The class of Anglo-Saxon peasants, as we know, was very heterogeneous: freemen at the top and slaves at the bottom, and in between great numbers of men economically dependent upon a lord and yet free in the eyes of the law. Thousands of peasants, though economically unfree, had some tincture of freedom about them. This combination of freedom and unfreedom in the same individual was incomprehensible to the Normans. Finding the legal status of such persons difficult to define, the Normans lumped them all together either as villeins (who had some rights in the land) or as cotters (who had two parts: a small number of freemen at the top; a huge mass of unfree serfs below. Slaves did not fit into feudal society. They were classed as the lowest rank of unfree serfs, though this slight rise in status brought them no material benefit.

The daily life of most peasants went on much as before. The traditions of the past, though disrupted, remained unbroken. Agricultural prosperity slowly revived. The peasant was much more aware of the condition of his crops or the weather than of the legal distinctions (or lack of them) imposed by Norman conquerors.

In Anglo-Saxon times the unit of agriculture and the lowest unit of local government had been the village. What the Normans were to call the *manor* had already begun to emerge as well. The manor may be defined as an estate under a single lord which was farmed and administered as an agricultural entity. A piece of property with an established value, it was thought of as consisting of two parts. The first was the lord's demesne, that is, his portion of the arable land, consisting either of strips scattered among the peasants or of a solid block of strips near the castle or manor house. In the economy of the manor the cultivation of the lord's demesne was paramount.

The second part of the manor comprised the arable strips of the peasants. The peasants held their land by servile tenure. They were legally bound to work the soil and could be returned by force if they ran away. They owed the lord two or three day's labor each week upon the demesne, a portion of the produce of their own strips, and attendance at the manor court. Additionally, peasants owed fines such as the heriot, a death duty of their best farm animal payable when a peasant died and his son took over the holding, and the merchet, a fine imposed if the peasant's daughter married outside the manor, depriving the lord of a worker. Since women labored with the men in haymaking, weeding, mowing, driving oxen, and road building, a price had to be paid for their departure. In many ways the villein was at the lord's disposal.

Historians once erroneously thought the village and the manor were identical in area and that all over England the Normans quickly molded the first into the second. It is now known that villages and manors had distinctive differences, and that manors did not become universal after 1066. It was merely a part of the rural scene. The manor was a unit of property, tenure, and feudal jurisdiction. The village, on the other hand, was a piece of land which could be splintered into a number of manors. In Norman England some villages were divided among several manors, and some manors contained more than one village. The two were rarely identical. There were lords who had surrendered parts of their demesne to other lords, freemen and even villeins who acquired land on more than one manor, villages of freemen who had no lord, manors without a lord's demesne, and manors without villeins or villein services. The manor, moreover, did not develop in the far north, nor along the Welsh border, nor in Kent. It was not the universal pattern in the northern Midlands nor in East Anglia. The area in which it occurred most frequently was the south and the southern Midlands. Thus the old picture of England as divided neatly into a great number of manors, each coinciding with an Anglo-Saxon village, is greatly simplified. The rural organization of England was much more complex than has been supposed, and the manor was far from universal.

Citizens continued to think of the village as the essential unit of the countryside. The kings did the same, for while they did not interfere with the internal affairs of the manor, they regarded the village as a unit of taxation, administration, and police. Deeply rooted in the traditions of the people, the village proved to be more permanent than the artificial division of the manor.

THE DOMESDAY BOOK

There is no clearer proof of William's power than the great survey of England he carried through in 1086. In that year he sent out officials to travel in four circuits through all of England south of the Tyne. They were instructed to visit each hundred and to summon the sheriff, the Norman barons and their vassals, the freemen who attended the hundred court, and the priest, the reeve, and six villeins from each village. These men, put under oath to tell the truth, were asked a long list of questions concerning every manor:

> how the manor is called, who held it in the time of King Edward, who holds it now, how many hides there are, how many ploughs in demesne, how many men, how many villeins, how many cotters, how many serfs, how many freemen, how many sokemen, how much woods, how much meadow, how many pastures, how many mills, how many fish-ponds, how much has been added or taken away, how much it was worth altogether and how much now, and how much each freeman or sokeman had or has there. All this information is given three times over: namely, in the time of King Edward, when King William gave it out, and how it is now—and whether more can be had from it than is being had.

This mass of information was arranged in feudal groupings under the tenants in chief and the fiefs of each locality and was then compiled by the King's clerks in the various volumes of what is known as the Domesday Book. Such a detailed inquiry exists for no other country during the Middle Ages. Historians have wondered what prompted William to launch such a project. One theory is that the Domesday Book was to form the basis for increased taxation. But it is possible that William may merely have wished to know in detail the extent and value of his great conquest. He may have planned to impose a more rigid feudal pattern upon what the Normans regarded as the chaos of Anglo-Saxon rights, jurisdictions, and social classes.

WILLIAM AND THE CHURCH

Norman monks, writing after the Conquest, spoke of the Anglo-Saxon church as in great need of reform. But if the church in England contained abuses, so did the church on the Continent. To understand William's policy one must take a broader look at the church throughout all Europe.

Three matters in particular worried men who had the interests of the church at heart: lay appointment to church office, simony, and the marriage of the clergy. For many centuries the church, seeking the protection of temporal rulers, had permitted them to exercise a large control over ecclesiastical appointments. Anglo-Saxon kings had named bishops and abbots, as had the dukes in Normandy. But lay appointments had inherent dangers, which increased with the development of feudalism.

In a feudal society bishops and abbots played a double role. They were feudal tenants in chief holding large fiefs from the king; they were the king's advisers and administrators, often deeply involved in matters of state. But they were also high officials of the church upon whom its welfare depended. If the king appointed a bishop who could fulfill his obligations as a feudal vassal, there was no assurance that this bishop would serve the church in a spiritual way. And if the church appointed a bishop well qualified for holy office, there was no guarantee that such a bishop could perform his feudal duties to the satisfaction of the king. This dilemma caused bitter quarrels between church and state until in 1170 an archbishop of Canterbury lay murdered in his own cathedral. Although such a combination of priest and warrior was possible in the eleventh century, this double role of the higher clergy sometimes became grotesque and dangerous.

As feudalism developed, appointments to many offices in the church fell into the hands of nobles who sometimes regarded ecclesiastical office as a marketable commodity that could be sold to the highest bidder. Hence began the abuse of simony—giving or receiving money in return for office in the church. Many churchmen were also disturbed by the large number of married clergy, for it was believed that only a celibate priesthood, which had renounced the world and the ties of family life, could devote its attention exclusively to the work of the church.

During the tenth and early eleventh centuries a movement for church reform began in various places—in the monastery of Cluny in Burgundy, in Lorraine, and in Italy. Pope Gregory VII (1073–1085), formerly the monk Hildebrand, was a product of the reform movement and the principles of his program were somewhat as follows. (1) Papal authority must be supreme within the church, that is, the clergy were to obey the commands of the pope without question. (2) The clergy must regard itself as a class apart from the rest of society, renouncing all worldly ties. The symbol of this great denial was the celibacy of the priesthood. (3) The church must be independent of lay control. It should select its own officials, refusing those chosen by kings or barons. (4) The pope, as the successor to St. Peter, must be superior to all lay rulers and temporal sovereigns. Gregory's determination to dominate the world in order to bring it to salvation was certain to produce a crisis between church and state.

William was ready to reform the church in England, strengthen its administration, and endow it generously, but he had been master of the church in Normandy and he was determined to be its master in England. He idealized a strong and orderly government; an independent church would make strong monarchy impossible. He insisted, therefore, upon the older tradition of kingly control. He appointed bishops and abbots in the English church. When in 1080 Gregory demanded that William surrender England to the papacy and receive it back as a feudal fief, thus becoming the pope's vassal, William sent a prompt refusal. Furthermore, he laid down certain rules regarding his relations with Rome: No pope should be recognized in England without his consent. No papal letters should be received without his knowledge. No bishop should leave the country and no tenant in chief should be excommunicated without his permission. William also exercised a veto over the legislation of ecclesiastical councils meeting in England. He thus retained control of the English church despite the lofty claims now voiced in Rome. Gregory, preoccupied with affairs on the Continent and knowing that William was eager for reform, did not retaliate.

William's principal adviser in ecclesiastical affairs was Lanfranc, the Archbishop of Canterbury, who worked closely with the king and supported his policy toward the papacy. A remarkable man, Lanfrac had studied and practiced law before turning to theology. He had previously been associated with the monastery at Bec in Normandy and later with the abbot at Caen. As an Italian he brought to his work in England a wider knowledge of the world than was possessed by most churchmen there.

His aim was to make the church in England conform with continental practice. To clear the way for change, he and William gradually removed Anglo-Saxon bishops and abbots, replacing them with Normans. Lanfranc also established his supremacy over the archbishop of York. He then summoned a series of church councils to enact important legislation. Bishops were instructed to strengthen their control over parish priests, to hold diocesan synods for the discipline of the lower clergy, and to visit and investigate local churches. A priest could not leave his diocese without the permission of the bishop. Diocesan centers, often located in rural areas in Anglo-Saxon times, were transferred to large towns from which the bishop could govern more efficiently.

Despite pressure from Rome, Lanfranc refrained from violent action against the number of married clergy in England. Instead, he obtained a decree permitting clergymen already married to remain so, while all new candidates for the priesthood would take vows of celibacy. Lanfranc did no more than assert a principle, for marriage continued among the clergy. Similarly, the evil of simony was forbidden though certainly not ended by the Normans, who strengthened the organization and discipline of the church without greatly improving its morals.

Although William and Lanfranc resisted the pretentions of the papacy, each of them in turn took steps to strengthen papal power. About 1072 William decreed that ecclesiastical cases should not be heard in the hundred courts but reserved for church courts presided over by bishops. As a result, the bishops gradually ceased to attend the shire courts, and a sharp division arose between lay and ecclesiastical jurisdiction. In the twelfth century the church courts claimed many cases which William had not originally intended to give them. Throughout the Middle Ages the separate courts of the church formed a powerful means of extending Roman influence.

In preparing himself for his work as archbishop, Lanfranc made a thorough study of canon law and later drew up a summary of the law of the church. Still, cannon law exalted the position of the papacy and encouraged churchmen to look to the pope rather than to the king as the source of ecclesiastical authority.

CHRONOLOGY

The Norman Conquest

1066	Battle of Hastings; William I 1066–1087
1066	Feudalism; manorialism
1070	Lanfranc, Archbishop of Canterbury
1072	Church courts established
1086	Domesday Book

4 From Normans to Angevins: William II, Henry I, Stephen, and Henry II

William the Conqueror had three sons, among whom, as he lay on his deathbed, he divided his great possessions. To Robert, the eldest, he bequeathed the duchy of Normandy; to William, the kingdom of England; to Henry, the youngest, he left 5000 pounds of silver. Of these three sons, Robert was the least disagreeable. Though brave, generous, and good-natured, he was weak in character, self-indulgent, and without purpose or determination. Under his wretched government Normandy sank rapidly into anarchy and chaos. William, King of England from 1087 to 1100, had a short and stocky build and so fiery a face that he was nicknamed Rufus. An excellent soldier, he was generous and loyal to his army—but there his virtues ended. One spiteful chronicler wrote that every night William went to bed a worse man than he had been in the morning, and every morning he arose a worse man than the night before. Cynical, violent, avaricious, licentious, and utterly untrustworthy, he was the Norman baron at his worst. His primary policy was to extract money from his people, who fled at his approach. Henry, who ruled England from 1100 to 1135 had many of the same qualities: he too was stern and ruthless, cruel and grasping, but with several redeeming qualities as well. Patient, orderly, and industrious, Henry was a prudent king who had his father's capacity for government. In fact, the machinery of government developed rapidly during his reign and was operating smoothly when he died.

In a confused series of wars the three brothers quarrelled with each other over their inheritance. In 1094 Robert secured the alliance of King Philip of France, who greatly feared William as a neighbor. But Philip was so lazy and self-indulgent that he was little help. Tiring perhaps of his own misgovernment, Robert took the Cross in 1096 and departed for the Holy Land on the First Crusade. Having no money with which to finance his enterprise, he pawned his duchy to William for three years for

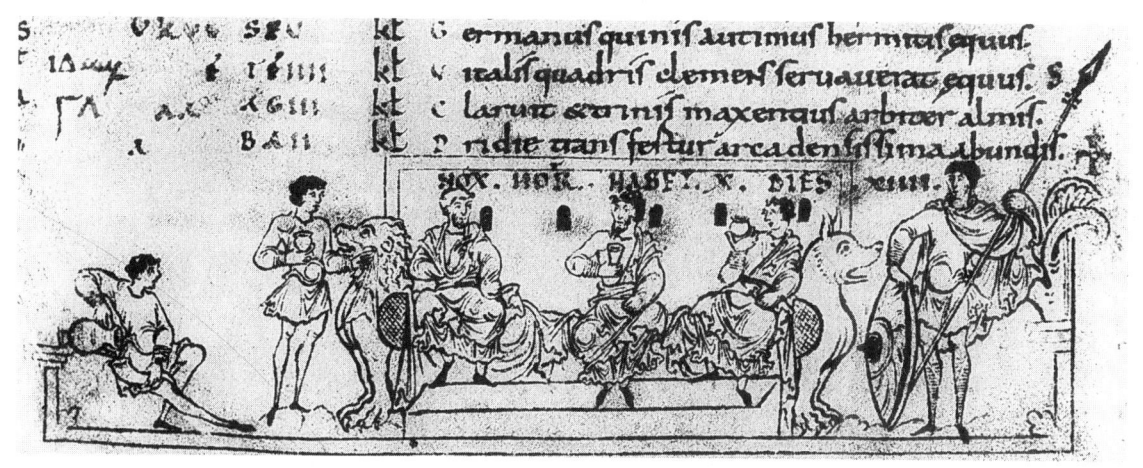

Banquet in the Norman King's Hall. (Marburg/AR NY 1185731)

10,000 marks of silver.[1] William then ruled both England and Normandy until his death in 1100, when Robert, returning with an enhanced reputation acquired in the Holy Land and with a wealthy bride acquired in southern Italy, regained possession of his duchy.

WILLIAM RUFUS, 1087–1100

In England William Rufus and his minister, Rannulf Flambard, had employed all the powers of the Crown to extract money from the people. The shire courts were encouraged to levy fines and confiscations. The feudal incidents were enforced with ruthless savagery. The relief demanded from heirs was so exorbitant that it equaled the value of their inheritance. Heiresses and widows of tenants in chief married whomever would pay the highest price for them. Escheats and forfeitures were harshly extorted; new and heavy aids were demanded frequently. Thus the rules of law—both of the popular courts and the feudal court of the king—were employed to obtain money. Similar methods were applied to the church. When high offices in the church fell vacant, William claimed a kind of ecclesiastical wardship and appropriated the revenues of a bishopric or monastery until a new appointment was made. It was thus to his advantage to keep the office vacant as long as possible; at the time of his death he was holding the lands of three vacant bishoprics and eleven monasteries. Newly appointed bishops and abbots had to pay great sums as relief; nonfeudal aids were demanded from the church. It is little wonder that the clergy looked to the papacy and not to the king for leadership in ecclesiastical affairs.

[1] A mark was two thirds of a pound.

THE REIGN OF HENRY I, 1100–1135

On August 2, 1100, on a hunting expedition in the New Forest in Hampshire, William Rufus was struck by an arrow and killed. Though unproved, allegations were made of a plot involving his brother Henry, whose actions appear premeditated. On the day that William was killed, Henry galloped to Winchester and seized the royal treasure despite the protests of its keepers. On the following day he was approved as king by a mere handful of barons. And on August 5, just three days after the shooting, he was crowned by the bishop of London, in a ceremony normally performed by one of the archbishops. Such hasty progress toward the throne was an indication that his position was precarious. He knew that Robert's claim was better than his, and unfortunately he had sworn fealty to Robert as his liege lord; thus his seizure of the throne exposed him to the charge of perjury. Moreover, the barons in England, smarting from the exactions of William Rufus, were in a discontented mood.

Henry therefore sought to win support not only from the barons but from the nation as a whole. He imprisoned Rannulf Flambard, William's instrument of extortion. He then recalled Anselm, the Archbishop of Canterbury, who had quarreled with William and was living in exile on the Continent. In his coronation charter Henry made sweeping promises of better government: "I henceforth remove all the bad customs through which the kingdom of England has been unjustly oppressed." In the future, the charter declared, lands were not to be taken from vacated estates of bishoprics or monasteries. Heirs were not forced to buy back their fathers' lands but would pay a "just and legitimate relief." The right to control the marriage of heiresses was to be exercised with moderation, and widows were not to be forced into marriage against their will. Oppressive exactions and other abuses were to be abolished.

Historians have sometimes made Henry's charter appear more important than it really was. It was not an admission by the Crown of any contract between king and barons in the feudal structure, nor that his contract placed limitations upon the king. The charter was issued by the king to all his subjects in a bid for general support, with no guarantee that its promises would be kept. As soon as he felt secure Henry disregarded his promises shamelessly. Nonetheless, they were remembered a century later when the barons extracted Magna Carta from King John.

To ingratiate himself further with the native English, Henry married Edith, a descendant of the Anglo-Saxon kings of Wessex. The marriage symbolized the eventual demise of Norman exploitation and Henry's wish to unite Englishmen and Normans as a homogeneous people. "By intermarriage and by every other means in his power," wrote a chronicler, "he bound the two peoples into a firm union." In about 1170 it was said that one could not distinguish the one from the other.

In spite of Henry's conciliatory policy, there was a rebellion against him at the end of his first year as king. A group of barons who held lands on both sides of the Channel, believing they had more to gain from the weak rule of Robert than from the strong rule of Henry, persuaded Robert to invade England. Landing at Portsmouth in

August 1101, he began a march toward London, joined by only a few barons. He became alarmed, accepted Henry's offer of an annual subsidy of £2000 in return for a renunciation of the English throne, and returned rather tamely to Normandy. Henry severely punished the barons who had revolted against him, though realizing that such plotting would never cease until he was master of both England and Normandy. Laying his plans with care and finding allies on the borders of Normandy, Henry led three expeditions against his brother. Their culmination was the Battle of Tinchebrai, September 28, 1106, forty years to the day after the landing of William the Conqueror in 1066. Robert was defeated and spent the rest of his days as a prisoner. Transferred from castle to castle, he lived another twenty-eight miserable years, dying at Cardiff in Wales in 1134, an old man of eighty, only a few months before the death of Henry. England and Normandy were thus reunited under one ruler.

As duke of Normandy, Henry became deeply involved in wars and diplomacy on the Continent. His primary interests lay in continental affairs, and his experiments in English government and finance reflect this fact. The French king Louis VI (or Louis the Fat, 1108–1137) was beginning a policy which was to continue for centuries and by which the kings of France slowly extended their authority over the great French fiefs until they were rulers of the entire country. On three occasions Louis began hostilities against Henry but never seriously threatened Henry's hold on Normandy. Spending nearly half his time on the Continent, Henry was forced to develop a system of government for England that would function in his absence and help to carry the cost of his continental wars.

The Justiciar

To meet the need for a government without a resident sovereign, Henry devised a new office, that of justiciar. The justiciar was the head of the administration, the king's most trusted minister, his viceroy or deputy with power to issue writs and to govern the country when the king was in Normandy. The first justiciar was Roger, bishop of Salisbury. Once an obscure priest in Normandy, Roger had first attracted Henry's attention, it was said, by the rapidity with which he had conducted Mass one morning when Henry was eager to go hunting. He became Henry's steward, then his chancellor, and finally his justiciar. Roger expanded the functions of government and improved their procedure. He was the most important of a number of officials whom Henry raised from obscurity and rewarded liberally with wealth and privilege. It was an indication of Henry's strength that he could thus dispense with feudal barons as ministers, and develop an official aristocracy of service.

The king's small council was composed of these new bureaucrats, his household officials, and those barons who happened to be in attendance. When the king left the country he was apt to take his household officers with him, so that administration in England centered in the justiciar. The justiciar's court, sometimes called the king's court of the exchequer, handled every phase of government—financial, judicial, administrative—and formed the pivot of the entire administration.

The Early Exchequer

The early exchequer was famous in Henry's reign for its financial sessions. Twice a year, at Easter and at Michaelmas in the autumn, sheriffs and other officials who collected money appeared before it to render an account of their finances. There were two parts to the exchequer as Roger developed it: the lower exchequer or treasury, where the sheriffs paid their collected sums and had the coins tested for weight and purity; and the upper exchequer of account or of audit. Here a large table was covered with a black cloth on which large squares were marked as on a huge checker board. Each column of squares indicated a denomination of money: *d.* (pence), *s.* (shillings), £ (pounds), £20, £100, £1000, and £10,000. At the head of the table sat the justiciar, flanked by the chancellor and other officials from the household. At the side of the table to the right of the justiciar sat the treasurer and clerks who entered the sums of money involved on long narrow strips of parchment known as the pipe rolls. On the opposite side of the table, to the left of the justiciar, was a calculator, who moved the counters from square to square, and a master of the writing office, who attended to any necessary correspondence.

Facing this formidable company, at the end of the table opposite the justiciar, appeared the sheriff. The sums of money for which he was responsible were read from the pipe roll, and counters were pushed into place to indicate the amounts he owed. The sums he had paid into the lower exchequer were then indicated by moving other counters thus revealing discrepancies and any amounts still due. It must be remembered that the exchequer, while an ingenious device, used Roman, not arabic, numerals, so that the simplest calculations in arithmetic—such as addition—were all but impossible. Zero had no symbol in the Roman system and so was represented by a blank square on the table. The exchequer thus made accounting visual. After the accounting was complete, the sheriff received a stick on which notches were cut to indicate how much was paid and how much was still due. The stick was then split into two parts, the sheriff retaining one and the exchequer the other. It is interesting to note that a pile of dried out tally sticks caught fire in 1834 and burned down the Houses of Parliament. The Houses were rebuilt by Sir Charles Barry in the 1840s.

The Sheriff

Appearance before the exchequer must have been a sobering experience but one greatly needed by the sheriffs of Henry's reign. William the Conqueror had commonly appointed powerful barons as sheriffs then allowed them great freedom. William Rufus, however, had sought to curb the sheriffs, and Henry continued this policy. Appointments were made from his trusted officials; sheriffs served for one year only and were required to render their accounts in the exchequer every six months. They were forbidden to summon meetings of the local courts in an arbitrary way. As in the reign of William Rufus, resident justices were appointed to curtail the sheriffs' power. Henry also continued a practice which had begun in Anglo-Saxon times. It was not uncommon for the king to send out special commissioners or justices to the local courts to preside over cases in which he had a special interest. These itinerant justices (or justices in eyre) were made a normal part of the machinery of government and law. When they presided in a local court, that court became a king's court, its authority based not on Anglo-Saxon custom but on the king's writ. This development was to have great significance for the future.

The techniques of government steadily advanced during the reign of Henry I. Yet Henry's achievement had limitations. Feudal fines and exactions were strained in favor of the Crown; government was based upon fear and severity; and Henry remained largely a feudal monarch whose principal concern was to hold the barons in subjection. A strong assertion of baronial independence was almost certain to come in the reign of Henry's successor.

Henry I and the Church

During the pontificate of Hildebrand (Gregory VII, 1073–1085) the church had embarked on a program of reform, independence from lay control, and papal supremacy over kings and emperors. One of the many difficulties this program brought about between church and state concerned the appointment of bishops. The bishop played the double role of church offical presiding over the administration of a diocese, and feudal baron holding a great fief. It had been the practice of England and elsewhere for a bishop, having been elected by a cathedral chapter, to do homage to the king for his lands and then to be invested by the king in his holy office through the formal presentation of a ring and staff as symbols of pastoral authority. This practice, known as lay investiture, gave the king control over the appointment of bishops. It was challenged by Anselm, the archbishop of Canterbury, who refused to do homage to Henry for his lands. Anselm, an Italitan of good family, was a saint and a scholar, gentle and peace loving, but adamant in defense of principle. Without great experience or breadth of view, he did not recognize that the king might have a case in the clash of church and state. Henry stood his ground, demanding that Anselm do homage. This conflict, though conducted in a dignified way, continued for several years and became very awkward for both.

At length a compromise suggested by Ivo, bishop of Chartres, was reached. By it the king surrendered the right to perform a lay investiture, while bishops continued to do homage for their lands. This was a triumph for the church in that the king lost all semblance of divine authority in appointing churchmen. Yet in a practical way it was the king who won. He could not be forced to accept the church's candidates, for he could refuse to receive their homage, and he was able to ensure in all cases that homage to him preceded consecration to holy office. Thus bishops and abbots continued to be men whom the king approved.

Two other issues between the church and the king arose in Henry's reign. One concerned appeals from the king's courts in England to the papal courts in Rome. So long as these appeals concerned disputes within the church there could be little objection to them. But if cases involving temporal matters were appealed from

English to Roman courts, the king's position as the source of law might be severely damaged. There was no decision on this matter in Henry's reign and the problem was left for the future. A second dispute concerned papal legates, envoys sent out by the papacy to solve local problems of the church. Hildebrand had begun to grant them the full authority to act as though the pope himself were present, which obviously threatened royal power. After a long controversy it was agreed the pope should have a permanent representative in England but that this representative should be the archbishop of Canterbury. Thus Henry controlled the church, though his control was not as complete as his father's.

The Succession

Henry was troubled for many years by the problem of the succession. William, his son and heir, had been drowned while crossing the Channel in 1120. The young noble and a group of companions, all more or less intoxicated, had set sail with an equally intoxicated crew, struck a rock, and perished. This tragedy left the king with only one legitimate child, his daughter Matilda. In 1114 she married the German emperor Henry V, but upon his death in 1125 she had returned to England. On two occasions her father obtained from the barons an oath, most reluctantly given, to accept her as their future queen. In 1127 he arranged her marriage to Geoffrey, the heir to the county of Anjou. In 1133 Matilda bore him a son, who was to become Henry II. Although Norman hatred of Anjou was bitter, Henry hoped this marriage would prevent an attack from Anjou upon Normandy and would provide his daughter with a warlike and powerful husband. Nonetheless, when Henry died in 1135, most Englishmen were highly doubtful whether Matilda should be made their queen. The mere notion of a woman ruler was novel and distasteful.

KING STEPHEN, 1135–1154

Since Matilda appeared so dubious a choice, it is not surprising that the English turned to a more likely candidate. This was Count Stephen of Blois, whose mother, Adela, was a daughter of William the Conqueror. Stephen had many advantages. He had been a great favorite of his uncle, Henry I, who had enfeoffed him with large estates on both sides of the Channel. He was also very popular with the barons in England and boasted high connections in the English church. His brother, Henry of Blois, bishop of Winchester, persuaded other churchmen to support him and helped to induce the Pope to recognize him as king of England. The sanction of the papacy was a great advantage to Stephen, for it virtually absolved the barons from the oaths they had sworn to accept Matilda. High officials, such as Roger of Salisbury, eager to have the kingship settled, accepted Stephen as the candidate in possession, for upon Henry's death Stephen had hastily crossed to England, had been chosen king by the citizens of London in a highly doubtful manner, had seized the treasury at Winchester, and had been crowned, all, said a chronicler, "as in the twinkling of an eye."

Thus Stephen began his reign in a strong position. That he soon lost his prestige and allowed the country to sink into feudal anarchy was due to his weakness of character and to his limited concept of kingship. In some ways he was an attractive man. He was a great warrior who delighted in the newly popular yet dangerous tournaments (in which knights rode about over a delimited area and fought anyone whom they happened to meet). He was chivalrous, kindly, and recklessly generous. But he was also a simple-minded king with little plan or policy. When two of his royal castles were seized by barons and Stephen failed to respond, unlawful seizure of property was soon rampant. Thus Stephen failed to keep law and order, both at home and abroad. In 1137 he went to Normandy, which was under attack by Geoffrey of Anjou, but very shortly he concluded an unfavorable treaty with Geoffrey. An attack on England from Scotland was followed by the grant of a large area to the king of Scots. There were other flaws in Stephen's policy. He was almost entirely a feudal king who thought only in terms of feudal custom and law. The barons similarly debased allegiance to the king as a public duty to the mere fulfillment of their feudal obligations. Stephen also made the error of trying to win support by a policy of concession. Royal authority diminished quickly as lands and privileges were given away. The policy of concession, once began, had to be continued, and in the end the barons rebelled if they did not obtain whatever they demanded.

Stephen's folly reached its height in dealing with the church, for he first made great concessions and then lost the church's support through a quarrel with Roger, Bishop of Salisbury. He had allowed the church a large extension of its jurisdiction. In separating lay and ecclesiastical courts, William the Conqueror had intended no more than that the church should handle its own cases. A clergyman committing a lay offense was still to be tried in the lay courts. But under Stephen the church obtained the right to try all cases involving clergymen and all those involving ecclesiastical property. The church also secured jurisdiction over cases concerning marriage and the probate of wills. In addition it obtained the right to appoint bishops and abbots and to hold ecclesiastical councils without the royal consent. The consessions were so sweeping that never again in medieval times was the church of England controlled by the Crown.

Having thus allowed the church to exalt itself, Stephen proceeded to quarrel with it. At the time of his accession, the administration of the government was in the hands of Roger of Salisbury and his rich and powerful relatives. There were bishops who held many castles and large bodies of retainers they moved about like great lords. Stephen became jealous of them, perhaps with some reason. In 1139 he arrested them on a trivial pretext, subjected them to needless humiliations, and seized their wealth. This foolish action disrupted the administration and deeply offended the church.

Matilda, watching events from the Continent, decided that the time had come to assert her rights. She landed in England in the autumn of 1139, accompanied by her half brother, Earl Robert of Gloucester, an able and resolute man who held great estates in Western England.[2] He and Matilda soon dominated the west and awaited a time to strike at Stephen. Their opportunity came in 1141 when Stephen was facing a rebellion. Joining forces with the rebels, Robert defeated and captured Stephen in a battle at Lincoln. For the moment Stephen's government collapsed, and Matilda was recognized as queen. Her triumph, however, was short-lived. Her tactlessness and arrogance were so offensive that she was expelled from London by the angry citizens. Stephen's forces rallied, defeated Matilda, and captured Earl Robert, who was exchanged for the king in 1141. The fighting diminished but dragged on until 1148, when Matilda departed for France, leaving Stephen in possession of England. In 1153 he made the Treaty of Wallingford with Henry, Matilda's son, who had come to England to battle for her rights. By this treaty Stephen was to remain on the throne until his death but was then to be succeeded by Henry. Stephen died, old and disillusioned, in the following year.

The Extent of the Anarchy

Because Stephen's reign often is referred to as the anarchy, the question arises how far this name was justified and what lessons it taught. The period was certainly a time of widespread misery and suffering. Not only was there a civil war but also great lawlessness among the barons, who strengthened their castles, fought private wars, and tyrannized their own localities. The civil war was fought largely in the west and did not affect many parts of the country. Plundering was local, and the bloody careers of men like Geoffrey de Mandeville were usually short. Many barons, interested in their estates, had no desire for anarchy and agreed not to attack one another. Moreover, there is evidence that the machinery of law and order was not entirely destroyed but continued to function in a halting way. It is significant that Stephen appears to have had a fair supply of money, an indication that he cultivated the towns, gave some protection to trade, and collected some revenues through the exchequer. Bad as conditions were, they were probably not as bad as the horrified chroniclers would have us believe. Perhaps the worst result was the tendency toward lawlessness and disregard for the rights of property.

The lessons of Stephen's reign were obvious. It was clear that strong and effective government bestowed inestimable benefits upon the nation, whereas the lack of such government brought chaos, misery, and war. It was equally clear that the only hope of good government lay in the monarchy. Only a king could govern well, but he must be more than a feudal suzerain. He must be a sovereign, using his prerogative power to protect the nation as a whole. He must be a strong personality. Government was still a personal institution which would not function without the guiding hand of a powerful ruler. An oppressive king was better than a weak one, and one great tyrant on the throne was less to be feared than hundreds of petty tyrants in every hilltop castle. Finally, the anarchy showed the danger of allowing a person to ascend the throne after some kind of dubious election. While Stephen had stressed election,

---

[2]Robert of Gloucester was an illegitimate son of Henry I.

Matilda had stood on hereditary right, and thereafter royal birthright was seldom ignored.

The same principle, moreover, came to be applied to the lands held by the barons. The Norman kings had acted as though all the land of England belonged to them and barons were their mere tenants. This royal claim of ultimate ownership explains the arbitrary way in which the kings had exacted the feudal aids and incidents. Indeed, much of the trouble of Stephen's reign arose from the insecurity of tenure felt by the barons. But now the doctrine that all land belonged to the king was abandoned; the new king, Henry II, fully recognized the right of a feudal heir to succeed to the lands held by his father.

HENRY II, 1154–1189, AND THE NEW MONARCHY

Whether England could recover from the anarchy depended upon the strength and character of the young man who became king at Stephen's death in 1154. It was England's supreme good fortune that Henry II was one of the greatest of her kings. His wonderful sense of law and order, his interest in intellectual and cultural things, his boundless energy and keen intelligence enabled him to understand and to adopt the new theoretical and practical foundations of kingship that were being established in Europe in the twelfth century. The older, theocratic concept of a king as a holy and sacred ruler who derived his authority from God's grace was changing to the concept of a king as legislator. This idea was inspired by the revival of interest in Roman law and the intellectual awakening of the twelfth century and was derived directly from the rediscovery of the *Corpus Juris Civilis,* the compendium of Roman law compiled by Emperor Justinian in the sixth century. Kingship, of course, remained sacred, but the concept of a king as legislator brought a wealth of new meaning to his office.

Roman law, and the study of the principles that lay behind the law, exalted the role of kingship and taught the necessity of an organized legal system applied in a uniform way throughout the kingdom. Government was placed upon a higher plane than that of a crude suppression of the feudal barons.

Employing his prerogative freely, Henry improved and strengthened the law in England, devised new legal procedures, expanded the legal activity of the Crown, fought the lawlessness following Stephen's reign, and protected the rights of property.

Early Reforms

Henry's reforms were not begun during the first decade of his reign, for other matters required immediate attention. The first task was to impose order in place of anarchy and to restore the machinery of government. As soon as Henry was crowned on December 19, 1154, he ordered the mercenary troops—especially the "Flemish wolves"—of Stephen and Matilda out of the country. He resumed the royal castles and Crown lands Stephen had recklessly given away, he suppressed most of the earldoms Stephen had created, and he destroyed the strongholds of unruly barons. Most of Stephen's supporters yielded to him, some fled, and a few resisted. Indeed, the majority of the barons, weary of plunder and civil war, gladly cooperated with him. There was no rival candidate for the Crown around whom opposition could gather. Henry selected his ministers from both parties. Nigel, Bishop of Ely, treasurer in the reign of Henry I, was restored to his former position; Thomas Becket became chancellor. These two men had supported the Angevin side. But Henry's justiciars, Robert, Earl of Leicester, and Richard de Lucy, had belonged to Stephen's party. The work of pacification was done so quickly and thoroughly that Henry was able to visit the Continent in 1156.

Henry seized an opportunity in 1166 to impose a new assessment of the feudal obligations of his tenants in chief. He asked them to declare the number of knights they were pledged to supply to him, and the number they had actually enfeoffed. The result of this inquiry, preserved in documents known as the *Cartae Baronum,* showed, as Henry was aware, that some tenants had enfeoffed fewer knights than they owed, whereas others had enfeoffed many more. He thereupon decreed that tenants with fewer enfeoffed knights than they were bound to supply must continue to send their ancient quota, and that those with more knights than were necessary must in future supply the full number they had enfeoffed. There was naturally much objection, but Henry carried his point. He also insisted that all subvassals do homage to him as to their liege lord, thus subordinating feudal homage to the older concept of universal allegiance to the king. In 1181 he breathed new life into the fyrd by regulations concerning the military equipment that each member must possess. He also made arrangements with certain ports on the southern coast, the Cinque Ports, to supply him with ships in time of war. By these measures Henry showed that he wished his military strength to rest not only upon the feudal host but also upon the whole body of freemen.

In 1170 Henry carried through a wide and ambitious investigation of local government. This inquiry, called the Inquest of Sheriffs, included a scrutiny of many other local officials—bailiffs and stewards of great nobles, royal foresters, and certain minor officials of the church. The king had been receiving complaints that the sheriffs were again becoming oppressive and that local officials were defrauding not only the people but also the central government. Dividing the country into circuits, Henry dispatched commissioners to collect information. The result was a salutary suppression of corrupt practices. Most of the sheriffs were dismissed, their places taken by royal officials. The new sheriffs were industrious and dependable bureaucrats, closely responsible to the king. They were gradually given a host of administrative duties and became the local agents of the Crown in the new rash of legal reforms.

THE LEGAL INNOVATIONS OF HENRY II

The legal reforms of Henry II, which constitute the glory of his reign, may be summarized as the development of a central court of administration and justice resident at Westminster, the reorganization and expansion of the system of itinerant justices to enforce the king's law in local areas, and the introduction of new principles and methods of justice which greatly improved its quality.

Henry's problem, like that of his grandfather, was to create an administration which would continue to function while he was abroad. Hence it was not the Great Council of the tenants in chief which developed, nor even the small council of those who attended the king in his travels. It was the court of the justiciar—known as the exchequer—which grew and matured in Henry's reign. The exchequer contained highly trained clerks, skillful administrators, and judges or justices learned in the law. It was at once a financial bureau, a chancery with a busy staff of clerks, a place where decisions could be quickly made, and, above all, a court of law. As yet there was no great differentiation of function; administrators were judges and judges administrators. The business of government, however, was growing rapidly, and more and more legal work arose in which the king was interested. The problems of crime and violence inherited from Stephen's reign had to be faced. Moreover, many ancient Anglo-Saxon methods of justice were out of date.

The Common Law

Henry and his justices struck out in new directions, using some parts of Anglo-Saxon and Norman law, borrowing from Roman law and from the law of the church, devising new practices to meet new needs, until king and justices began to create a new law with a body of decisions from which precedents and legal principles could emerge. This was the origin of the English common law. The king's court was soon dispensing a type of justice that was superior to the justice of the local courts. Men wished to have their cases tried by the king's judges. They were willing to pay for this privilege by buying the proper writ, for such a purchase—which was commanded by the king—came to be the normal way in which a case was begun. So great was the demand for the king's justice that in 1178 Henry set aside five judges at Westminster solely to hear pleas.

The Itinerant Justices

The court at Westminster normally tried only large cases involving important persons and large amounts of property. But the number of cases was increasing rapidly, and Henry made the great decision to place his justice at the disposal of freemen and lesser barons by improving the system of itinerant justices. Former kings had sent out officials to preside over cases in which the Crown had an interest. Henry developed the journeys or iters of the itinerant justices into an efficient and indispensable organ of government. The kingdom was divided into circuits; and the highest officials of the Crown—justiciars, chancellors, archbishops of Canterbury—traveled through the counties, bringing the justice of the king to smaller litigants throughout the kingdom. A county court, when the justices were present, became for the moment a royal court and the same legal methods were employed as at Westminster. In this way the law became a common law—common to all England.

The itinerant justices also did a vast amount of work that was not judicial. They performed an ever-increasing number of administrative duties, inquiring into any matter in which the king might be interested, until half the county seemed to be attending to the business of the Crown. A general iter, as it was called, became a dreaded experience for the people.

New Principles

One of the most important new practices introduced by Henry involved the prosecution of felony cases. Serious crimes were made an offense against the king because they broke the king's peace; their trials should not be left to the local courts but brought into the courts of the king before the itinerant justices. The conception of felony, that is, of a crime that was particularly base and degrading, had come in with the Normans, as had the practice of escheating to the Crown the property of a convicted felon. Henry therefore had a number of inducements to transfer the trial of criminals from the local to the royal courts.

Another principle of no less importance was that the king, as the fountain of justice, was responsible for the protection of property and might intervene in the proceedings of the hundred or shire courts or the feudal or private courts of the nobles to ensure that cases concerning property were justly handled. Such intervention was carried out through royal writs. Henry issued what were known as writs of right, which were letters addressed to persons responsible for local justice, commanding them to see that justice was done and warning them that they must account for any negligence. Henry also issued the writ praecipe, which had the effect of lifting a case from a local court and transferring it to the court of the king. Finally, Henry made use of the jury in both criminal and civil cases.[3]

The Criminal Jury. At the beginning of Henry's reign a criminal trial was begun, as in Anglo-Saxon times, by an accusation. The injured party, or his relative or lord, must appear in court and make a formal charge against the accused. The court might order proof by the ancient methods of ordeal or compurgation. The Normans had introduced the duel or ordeal by battle. If the court permitted this method of proof, the accuser and the accused fought each other to the death. Should their weapons break, they must continue the fray with their bodies and if the vanquished party survived he was mutilated or hanged for his crime or else heavily fined for his false accusation. These duels, though infrequent and usually avoided, were as obviously barbaric as the Anglo-Saxon ordeal. A new procedure was clearly needed.

Reform came in Henry's famous Assize (or decree) of Clarendon in 1166, which placed the responsibility for accusing criminals upon the local community. Twelve responsible men from every hundred and four from every vill had to appear before the sheriff and later before the justices in the county court to declare upon oath the names of persons in the neighborhood believed to be robbers, thieves, murderers, or the protectors of such persons. This was the jury of accusation, the ancestor of

---

[3] A civil case was a dispute over property, usually over land, in which no crime had been committed. In Henry's reign, however, disputes over land often involved violence, such as the seizure of property without a court judgment.

the modern grand jury. When the justices arrived it was the duty of the sheriff to produce the persons suspected.

The normal method of proof employed by the justices was the Anglo-Saxon ordeal of cold water. The accused was bound and lowered into a body of water which had been sanctified by a priest. It was thought that water sanctified in this way would not receive a guilty person, and hence if a man floated he was guilty, if he sank he was innocent. Punishment was swift and terrible: a man found guilty at the ordeal had his right foot cut off and must abjure the realm. In 1176 Henry added forgery and arson to the list of felonies and decreed that if a man failed at the ordeal he should lose his right hand as well as his right foot. Mutilation was not the only method of punishment. After the iter of 1166, when the justices tried cases in London and Middlesex, the sheriffs reported in the exchequer the cost of thirty-four ordeals, five duels, fourteen mutilations, and fourteen hangings. The trials of men suspected of felonies were known as the pleas of the Crown.

The origin of the accusing jury is a matter of dispute among historians. The usual opinion is that the jury was of continental origin. It is known that in the later Roman Empire men were put on oath to tell the truth and then were asked to assess the value of land. This use of the jury, it is thought, passed from Rome to the Franks, to the Normans, and so was brought to England at the time of the Conquest. In the Domesday survey of 1086 William's commissioners employed juries to assess the value of property. A jury of this type has no connection with a trial; it is thought that Henry's innovation was to bring the jury into court and use it in the accusation of criminals.

Some historians, however, believe that the accusing jury was of Anglo-Saxon origin. They point to a decree by Ethelred the Unready about 997 in which it was ordered that twelve leading thegns in the courts of the Danelaw should be sworn to tell the truth and should then give information about criminals. After this single decree, no more is heard of such juries, but historians who support an Anglo-Saxon origin of the jury believe they continued. In the hundred and shire courts, it is held, men were constantly employed in the apprehension and punishment of criminals, and many persons must have been tried without an accusation by an injured party. It is likely that "small groups, as groups, were being compelled to voice suspicions, tell tales, inform against the criminals." According to this interpretation Henry's innovation was to raise the accusing jury from the obscurity of local procedure and employ it in courts where it appeared at once in the public records.

Henry clearly did not like the ordeal of cold water as a method of proof. Nonetheless, it continued until a council of the church decreed in 1215 that priests should take no part in ordeals. This decree deprived the ordeal of its justification as a judgment of God. It straightway disappeared, and a second jury, known as the petty jury, was used to determine the question of innocence or guilt. The ending of ordeals in 1215, therefore, resulted in England and the Continent taking separate legal directions. The Continental jurisdictions relied upon the recently rediscovered Roman law of Justinian as a substitute for the Germanic ordeals. The English criminal courts adopted the common law system that had already developed for civil procedures in the royal courts. The Continent was to be greatly influenced by the Roman system of inquisitorial justice, while England was to use its own adversarial system. The petty jury would play a crucial role in this process.

The Civil Jury. In civil cases, which involved disputes over land or other property, Henry opened the royal courts to all freemen and again made use of the jury. His reforms began with what are known as the petty assizes, court actions which offered a temporary rather than a permanent settlement but which had the enormous advantage of prompt redress of wrong. The most important was the assize of *novel disseisin*, that is, recent dispossession. The assize offered speedy justice for the man who had been ejected from his property without a judgment in court. Such a person could buy a writ of *novel disseisin*, which ordered the sheriff to bring a jury before the itinerant justices. The jury was simply asked whether the purchaser of the writ had been dispossessed of property without a court judgment. If the answer was yes, he was placed once more in possession.

There were other petty assizes, though for the most part they were popular variations of the same theme. These were preliminary in nature, however, and did not settle the question of ownership or best right. Such disputes were normally tried in the feudal courts of the barons and were determined by the ordeal of battle. Henry began to intervene in various ways until, by a procedure known as the grand assize, of which the probable date is 1179, he laid down certain principles: anyone who wished to challenge a freeman's title to his land must open the case by the purchase of a writ; a freeman so challenged could transfer the case from a feudal court (where it would be tried by the ordeal of battle) to the court of the king; the freeman, by the purchase of the proper writ, could then have the case tried by a jury. The grand assize was not swift like the petty assizes. It was a solemn affair tried before the court at Westminster. All the parties to the suit and the jury as well might have to travel a long distance. But the grand assize was hailed as a measure of the highest equity, for it enabled a freeman to avoid the hazards of combat and to have his case tried by a jury. By these wise and salutary measures Henry protected the possession of property, offered jury trial in cases of best right, extended the scope of royal justice, and decreased the number of cases that came before the feudal courts.

HENRY II AND THE CHURCH

A clash of some kind between the king and the church was inevitable in Henry's reign. Under Stephen, as we have seen, the church had obtained new privileges and independence. A strong king like Henry II was certain to resist the pretentions of the clergy and to seek to regain the control exercised by his predecessors. He saw, moreover, that the church sheltered abuses which hindered his program of legal reform. The unnecessary violence of his clash with the church was due to the determined and uncompromising stand of Thomas Becket, the Archbishop of Canterbury.

Becket's character is not easy to analyze. He was born into a middle-class family in London, was given a sound education, and became attached to the household of

Archbishop Theobald. His exceptional ability as a diplomat and man of business brought him rapid promotion. At Henry's ascension he obtained the high office of chancellor; and as chancellor from 1154 to 1162 he involved himself ardently in the administrative work of the government, supporting the interests of the king against those of the church. He appeared the worldly courtier, handsomely dressed, fond of hunting, the jovial companion of the king. Then suddenly, upon his appointment as archbishop in 1162, he became the unbending churchman, ostentatiously ascetic, the upholder of the most extreme claims of clerical independence and of papal supremacy. Seeing the church as supreme and infallible, Becket had completely accepted the roles of church and state as defined in the Hildebrandine reforms of the eleventh century. It is difficult to explain his sudden change of view. Sobered by the significance of his new office, he may perhaps have experienced a religious conversion. Or there may have been some psychological twist to his character. He may have been an actor who played to the full every role he undertook. In any case, as archbishop he quarreled with the king at once, opposing him on matters in which no principle appeared to be involved. At the same time Henry heard of a number of ugly crimes committed by clerks in minor orders who were able to escape with light sentences in the church courts.

Angered by these events Henry issued the Constitutions of Clarendon in 1164. This document was a careful and accurate statement of the "ancient customs," that is, of the rules and practices which had governed the relations of the church and the state under William the Conqueror and his sons. According to those rules, as the document pointed out, cases concerning advowson and debt, disputes as to whether lands were held by ecclesiastical or lay tenure, should be tried in the lay courts. Clerks convicted of a crime should be punished in the same way as laymen who had committed the same offense. Laymen should not be prosecuted in the church courts on the basis of rumor but only upon accusation by an individual or by a jury. Other clauses repeated rules laid down by William the Conqueror: without the king's consent no clergyman should leave the country, no cases could be appealed to Rome, and no official or tenant in chief could be excommunicated. The compromise of the reign of Henry I concerning investiture should stand.

Although the Constitutions of Clarendon were moderate in tone, they proved to be a cardinal error. The position of the church had altered since the days of William I. The papacy had been exalted, papal government highly organized, canon law expanded and matured. The church could not ignore these developments. Hence both the Pope and the English bishops, although they disapproved of Becket's conduct, were forced to oppose the "ancient customs." Henry had acted too quickly and played into Becket's hands.

Becket eventually rejected all the "ancient customs." The clash between him and Henry, however, centered upon the trial and punishment of criminous clerks. It should be remembered that an enormous number of persons had some slight connection with the church and that below the ranks of respectable and beneficed clergymen were many clerks in minor orders, some without occupation and a few disreputable. The church courts did not shed blood. They might unfrock a clerk, that is, deprive him of the right to exercise his office in the church, or they might imprison him. Even for serious crimes the church courts did little more than impose a sentence of fine and penance. They failed to inflict the harsh punishments that were needed to maintain order in a violent age. Henry did not claim the right to try criminous clerks. He asked that the accusation be made and the offense be proved in a lay court, that the culprit then be tried in the church court in the presence of a royal representative, and that if found guilty he be unfrocked and returned to the lay court for punishment. Becket refused these arrangements. The entire process of trial and punishment of clerks, he held, must lie in the church courts.

The quarrel of king and archbishop became increasingly bitter and acrimonious, as Henry tried to ruin his adversary. In 1164 Becket fled to the Continent, where he kept the quarrel alive through a voluminous correspondence. Six years later in 1170 Henry offered Becket a hollow reconciliation and permitted his return to England.

The murder of Archbishop Thomas Becket as shown in a twelfth-century manuscript. (British Library, Harleian MS 5102, f. 32)

But Becket immediately excommunicated certain bishops who had crowned the king's son, an act normally reserved for the archbishop. It was at this new affront that Henry uttered the fatal words, "Will no one rid me of this troublesome priest?" A few days later four of his knights murdered the archbishop in the cathedral at Canterbury.

Few events in the Middle Ages shocked Europe as profoundly as did the murder of Becket. The head of the church in England had been struck down by the king. Here was a tragedy made to order for all who supported the pretensions of Rome. The people at large were also deeply affected. The cult of St. Thomas Becket flourished mightily; visits to the shrine of the holy blissful martyr at Canterbury became the most popular of English pilgrimages.

After the initial outcry of indignation had subsided, Henry was able to make his peace with Rome. He conceded two important points. Surrendering his claim to try clerks for felonies, he allowed the church courts full jurisdiction over them. For the many offenses below the rank of felony, however, the clergy were to be tried in the lay courts, where they had no special privilege. A second concession made by Henry was a promise not to obstruct appeals to Rome, a point in which the Pope felt much more interest than in the trial of criminous clerks. Appeals to Rome of all sorts of cases had been growing steadily, and the number now continued to increase. In other respects Henry was able to stand his ground. He continued to control the appointment of bishops and abbots. He continued to enjoy the revenues of vacant sees; no excommunication of his tenants in chief or his high officials and no visits to England by papal legates were to be permitted without his approval. The church courts tried cases concerning wills and marriages, ecclesiastical property, and offenses against morality. But the lay courts retained jurisdiction over advowson, over debts and contracts, and over misdeeds of the clergy below the rank of felony.

THE ANGEVIN EMPIRE

One must think of Henry as a great French noble whose primary interests lay in his continental possessions. For every year that he spent in England he spent two abroad. He was already an international figure in 1154, when he obtained the English throne at the age of twenty-one. He had inherited Anjou, Maine, and Touraine from Geoffrey, his father, who had died in 1151. From his mother, Matilda, he had inherited Normandy. In 1152 by a sudden turn of fortune he had acquired the right to rule over vast new territories. This had come about through his marriage to Eleanor, the heiress of Aquitaine, the greatest fief of southern France. Eleanor had formerly been the wife of the French king Louis VII. But Louis and Eleanor were far from congenial. Louis was a pious man, obsequious toward the church, rigid in his conduct, and rather simple-minded in policy. Eleanor was young and beautiful, proud and high-spirited, representing the full-blooded and vivacious temper of the south. She scorned a husband indifferent to love, and the two were divorced in March 1152.

In May of the same year she married Henry, thus transferring to him her enormous possessions of Aquitaine, Poitou, and Auvergne. Before he became king of England Henry controlled half of France. Thereafter he was master of an empire which extended from Scotland to the Pyrenees, far more extensive than the shorn lands of his overlord, the king of France. But Henry's possessions did not form a unit in any way. They differed in interests, in laws, and in language; allegiance to him was the one strong bond of union. Henry was constantly on the move, often traveling at great speed. His people saw more of him than might be supposed and his enemies were constantly confounded by his sudden appearances.

The French Dominions of Henry II.

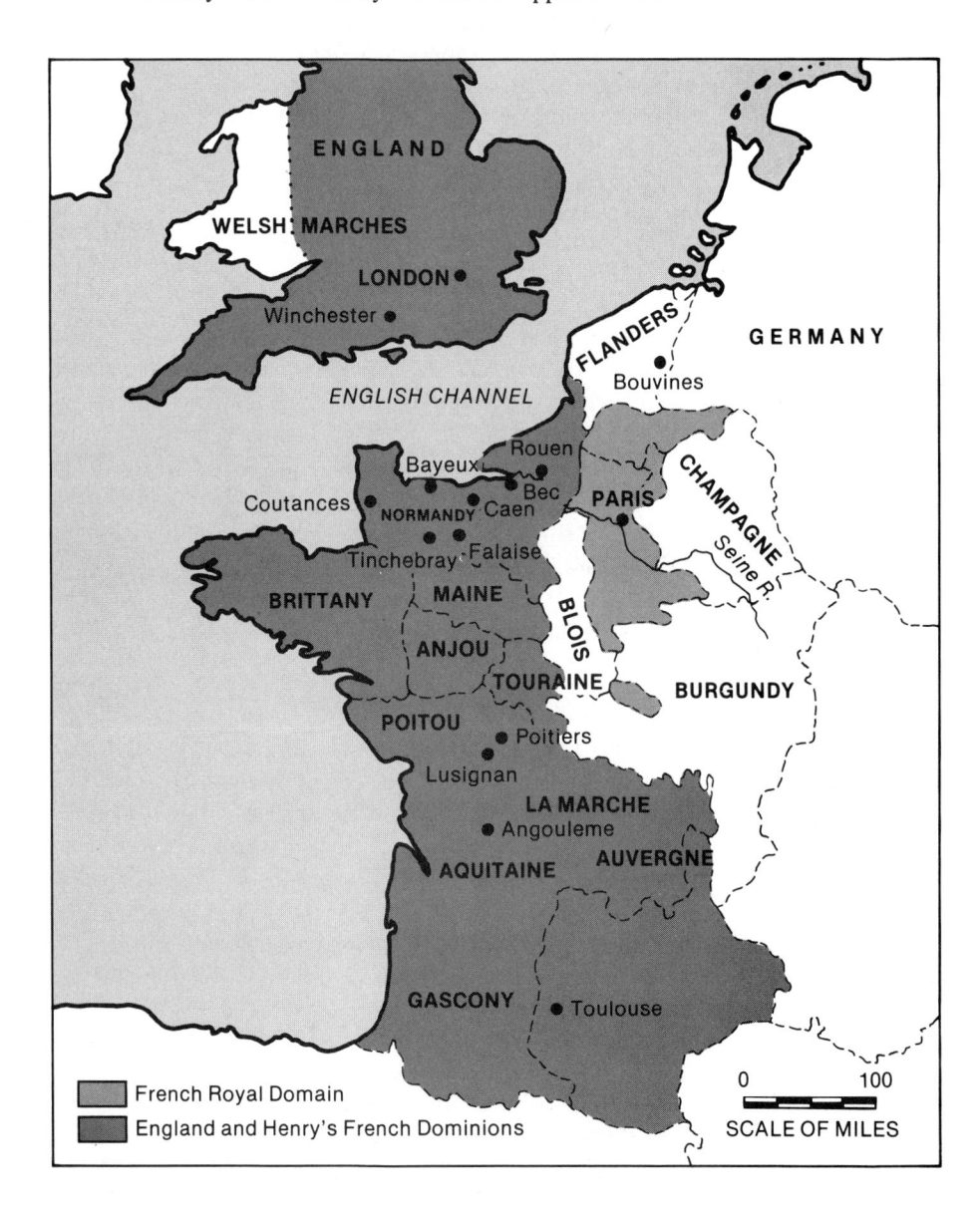

During the first years of his reign his object was to consolidate his empire. He made several expeditions against the Welsh; he forced the Scots to cede territory they held in northern England and later he obtained the homage of William, the Scottish king; he also visited Ireland and received the submission of most of the Irish kings. By diplomacy and by the marriages of his children (some of whom were wed while they were infants), he obtained the Vexin, an area on the Seine, and gained control of Brittany. The possession of Aquitaine brought him wider contacts—with Spain, with the German emperor Frederick Barbarossa, and more distantly with Italy. He forced the Count of Toulouse to do him homage. But his dream of power in Italy, and perhaps in the empire also, never materialized, for he was drawn from his ambitions by the serious rebellion of 1173–1174.

Henry, it was said, could rule every household but his own. His four sons grew up discontented and hostile toward him, without respect or loyalty, and in the end they ruined his policy. Henry was partly to blame. As a parent he was indulgent and yet masterful, he gave his sons titles but little money or power, he sent them to represent him in various parts of his dominions but expected them to be as obedient as paid officials. Henry, the eldest, was a handsome young man, but impious and treacherous. Richard, the second son, grew to be a mighty warrior but without a sense of government and with a morbid hatred of his father. Geoffrey, the third, was a brainless plunderer. The career of John, the fourth son, speaks for itself, as shall be seen. The three older brothers were eager to revolt against their father. In this they were encouraged by their mother, Eleanor, who no longer lived with the king. She held her court at Poitiers in her own lands in France, where she presided over a motley society of knights and troubadours who exalted knightly love, war, and the cult of chivalry. Eleanor's fame as an attractive woman was expressed in a German student song:

> Were the world all mine
> From the sea to the Rhine
> I'd give it all
> If so be the Queen of England
> Lay in my arms.

Henry's sons also were encouraged in revolt by Louis VII of France. The great rebellion of 1173–1174, which included risings in England, Normandy, Brittany, and Aquitaine, was managed—or, rather, mismanaged—by Louis. It was the far-flung nature of the revolt that made it dangerous. But Henry was supported by the church, by his great officials, by the smaller tenants in the country, and by the towns. His sons were too young to lead so extensive an enterprise, and there was little overall planning. Hence the revolt was put down, as it had arisen, in piecemeal fashion. Louis was driven back to Paris, an invasion of England from Flanders was defeated, and Eleanor was captured while masquerading in male attire. The king of Scots, while invading from the north, also was captured. Henry forgave his sons and increased their revenues. But he destroyed the castles of the barons who had revolted against him and he kept his wife under restraint for the rest of his life. His sons revolted again in 1183, a rebellion in which the young Henry died while fighting both his father and his brother Richard. Another uprising tore the family in 1186; and in 1189 Richard and John joined the French king Philip Augustus in war against their father. This was Henry's last campaign. When he heard that John, his favorite son, had joined the rebels, he lost heart. Turning his face to the wall and "muttering 'Shame, shame on a conquered king,' he passed sullenly away."

CHRONOLOGY

The Norman Kings

1087–1100	William Rufus
1100–1135	Henry I; Coronation Charter; Exchequer
1106	England conquers Normandy
1107	Investiture Compromise; St. Anselm
1135	Matilda denied the throne
1135–1154	Stephen; Civil war; "the anarchy"
1154–1189	Henry II; Angevin Empire: Eleanor of Aquitaine
1162	Thomas Becket, Archbishop of Canterbury
1164	Constitutions of Clarendon
1160s–1170s	Common law writs begun
1170	Becket murdered

5

Kings and Barons

The splendid machinery of government developed by Henry II was so firmly and soundly established that it continued to function during the reigns of his irresponsible sons. It survived the absence of Richard and the avarice of John. Indeed, during these reigns the authority of the Crown increased, and the Angevin monarchy, immensely powerful under Henry II, became more powerful than ever. It was obviously freeing itself from old restraints imposed in the past by custom, feudal law, and the influence of the church. How far was royal authority to go? Was the king to become an irresponsible despot? Should powers and perogatives—beneficial in the hands of a good king—be left at the disposal of an evil one? And if a bad king was to be curbed, how was it to be done? The reign of Richard illustrated the growth of royal power; the reign of John drove home the lesson that disastrous things might happen if the power fell into the hands of a tyrant. Hence the small number of people who thought in terms of politics—that is, some of the barons and a few members of the upper clergy—began to consider carefully the proper relation of the Crown to the baronage and to the law and the proper relation of the barons to the growing machinery of government. It is in the light of these problems that we must study Magna Carta, the first major check upon the growth of royal absolutism.

RICHARD I, 1189–1199

Richard was more highly regarded by his contemporaries than he is by posterity. Although he neglected England, he played a great part in continental affairs. Everywhere he went, in Europe or in the Holy Land, he was revered as a powerful crusader who had done brave deeds beyond the seas. Above all else he was a soldier feared by his enemies for his great physical strength and skill in arms. With a fine eye for tactics in battle and campaign strategy, Richard was regarded as a superb general. Fond of music and poetry, he was an exrtravagant patron of the troubadours of southern France. Although he deceived his father, Richard respected those who had fought faithfully on his father's side. He was born in England but has been called the least English of her kings. Despising the arts of peace Richard did not take the trouble to understand the problems of English government. He spent only five months of his reign in England, regarding that country merely as a source of financial support for his many wars.

When he ascended the throne in 1189 he was pledged to take part in the Third Crusade and devoted himself to the task of raising money for his great enterprise. In addition to tapping the usual sources of revenue, he sold places in the government to the highest bidder. "Everything was for sale," wrote a contemporary, "powers, lordships, earldoms, shrievalties, castles, towns, and manors." "I would sell London," Richard remarked, "if I could find a suitable purchaser." His provisions for the government of England during his absence showed little wisdom. He divided authority between two justiciars: Hugh de Puiset, the princely bishop of Durham, and William Longchamp, a faithful servant but a foreigner of humble origin who was inclined to be tactless and highhanded. Longchamp first drove Hugh de Puiset from office and then was superseded by a new justiciar, Walter of Coutances, Archbishop of Rouen. There was thus much friction in England. John, the king's younger

"Elephant Standing," bestiary, Latin, twelfth century, by Philip, Canon of Lincoln. (John Pierpont Morgan Library, M81f, 23)

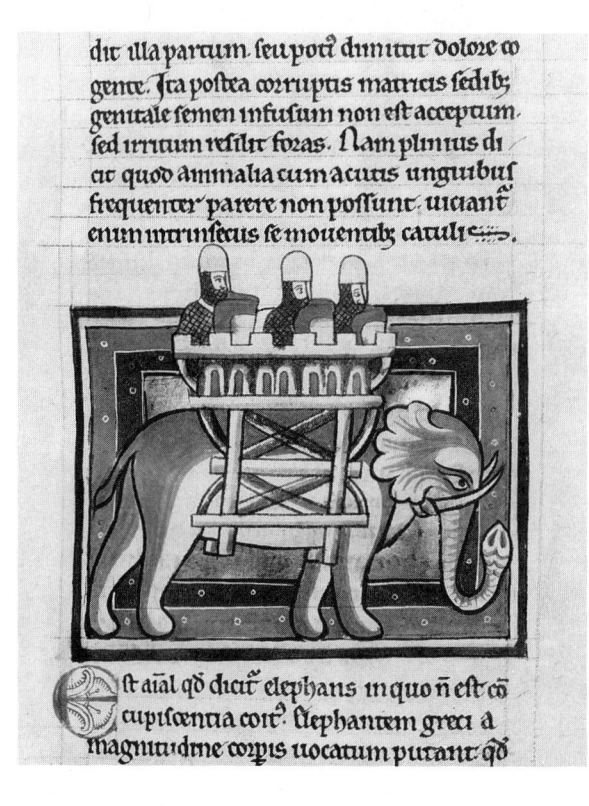

brother, caused endless trouble. Richard had given him large estates, a rich wife—Isabel of Gloucester—and a dominion of six counties over which he ruled as an independent prince. Nonetheless, when Richard was captured on his way home from the Holy Land, his greedy brother seized the English throne. Rebuffed at home, John crossed to France and was recognized as king of England by the French king, Philip Augustus, who had been Richard's enemy. But the appointment in 1193 of a new and able justiciar, Hubert Walter, and Richard's release in 1194 exposed John as a traitor and reversed the ugly situation.

The Third Crusade

The Third Crusade took place after disasters had befallen Christian arms in the Holy Land. It was not a century since Pope Urban II had first appealed to the military aristocracy of Europe to reconquer Jerusalem from the hands of the Muslims. His appeal had met with tremendous enthusiasm. A number of crusading armies had converged upon Constantinople in 1097, to the dismay of Emperor Alexius Comnenus, who had hurried the crusaders forward on the long and dangerous march across Asia Minor to the Holy Land. Ignorant of local conditions, the crusaders had been parched with thirst because they neglected to take water bottles and had suffered from dysentery because they were careless about their diet. Nevertheless, by sheer bravery, brute force, and a sublime assurance of victory, they defeated the Turks at Antioch, marched southward to capture Jerusalem in 1099, and set up a Latin kingdom with Jerusalem as its center. Most of the crusaders then returned to Europe.

By the last quarter of the twelfth century, the Muslims, who had formerly been divided among themselves, were united under Saladin, a remarkable man who was king of both Egypt and Syria. Partly to hold his people together, he preached a war against the Christians, overran much of the Holy Land, and captured the cities of Acre and Jerusalem in 1187. These disasters furnished the impetus for the Third Crusade.

Richard left England in December 1189 but remained in France until the following summer. He then embarked on the Mediterranean and coasted leisurely along the Italian shore until he came to Sicily, where he became involved in local politics. There he had to face the animosity of Philip Augustus of France, who had also taken the Cross. The two kings, having spent the winter of 1190–1191 in constant bickering, sailed for the Holy Land with deep bitterness toward one another. Richard stopped on his way to conquer Cyprus and arrived before the wall of Acre in June 1191. Within a few months the crusaders captured the city; and later took Jaffa. Upon two occasions Richard brought his troops within sight of Jerusalem, but Jerusalem never was captured. In July 1191 Philip returned to France, where he continued his former intrigues against the Angevin empire. Richard remained in the Holy Land for another year, but realizing he could accomplish little without large reinforcements, he sailed home in October 1192.

Fearing that Philip was plotting to prevent his return, Richard made his way up the

Adriatic Sea to Vienna, where he was captured by Leopold, Duke of Austria, and then handed over to the German emperor Henry VI as a prisoner. Such treatment of a crusader was an indication that the religious zeal of the crusading movement had degenerated badly. Henry demanded an enormous ransom of £100,000, a sum equal to five years' revenue in England. It is a tribute to the efficiency of the exchequer and to the prosperity of the country that a substantial portion was raised and sent to Germany. Richard returned to England in 1194, only to demand more money for a war against Philip in France. To this war he devoted the last five years of his life. In alliance with his former captor, Henry VI, he greatly challenged Philip. Philip might have lost his kingdom had he not been relieved by Henry's death in 1197 and by Richard's in 1199. Richard died from a skirmish wound inflicted by one of his own vassals.

Meanwhile in England, despite the king's absence and the enormous drain upon finance, the government in Hubert Walter's hands continued to function normally. To ensure that the king's financial rights were fully exploited, he sent out itinerant justices in 1194 to make a strict and searching inquiry into the whole fabric of local government. The records of this inquiry reveal the existence of a new official, the coroner, who investigated crimes as soon as they were committed and brought suspected persons before the justices from London. In 1198 Hubert Walter attempted to introduce a new land tax known as a carucage, but the scheme was not fully developed. In the same year there was a proposal that the tenants in chief, instead of performing their normal military service, should supply funds sufficient to maintain a force of 300 knights under constant arms on the Continent. When the barons became suspicious, the plan was dropped.

KING JOHN, 1199–1216

Richard was succeeded by his brother, John, traditionally pictured as a monster of iniquity who deliberately chose the path of evil and took pleasure in following it. In recent years, however, historians have regarded him more favorably, stressing his ability, industry, and interest in government and administration. The truth is that John was a highly complicated person of many contradictions. His private morals were admittedly lacking: he was cruel, vindictive, and treacherous. His sense of fun was ghoulish and sadistic. Twisting the rights of the Crown to his own advantage, he provoked the rebellion that resulted in Magna Carta. So profoundly was he mistrusted by his contemporaries that they were never allayed; such suspicion largely explains the hostility between John and most of his barons. Yet as a public official John had much to his credit. He was energetic and active, constantly moving about the country to supervise its government. He was genuinely interested in the administration of justice. If a case touched his own interests, he was apt to be partial and extortionate; otherwise he acted with fairness and honesty, dealing swiftly with those who broke the peace. He also was interested in the functioning of the exchequer, which he sometimes attended in person, and he was not entirely unsympathetic toward the work of the church. As a diplomat he was shrewd and clever[1] yet often unstable. He would follow a policy for a time with great energy; yet he seemed incapable of sustained effort. His apologists have pointed out that he faced strong opponents: Philip Augustus, the wily king of France; Innocent III, the most potent of medieval popes; and the English barons just as they were becoming politically self-conscious. In each of these struggles John was defeated. Sustaining one frustration after another, he became increasingly bitter and suspicious

Fastidious about his personal appearance, and something of a dandy, he wore fine clothes and jewelry. He liked royal splendor and enjoyed a good table.

The Loss of Normandy, 1199–1206

The first years of John's reign were occupied in a struggle with Philip of France, in which the Angevin empire collapsed and Normandy was lost to England. Philip easily found pretexts for war in the heated dispute over Richard's successor. England and Normandy readily accepted John, but the nobles of Aquitaine did homage to John's mother, Eleanor. Brittany, Anjou, Maine, and Touraine acknowledged Arthur, the twelve-year-old son of John's deceased brother Geoffrey and Constance of Brittany. The young boy's mother sought the protection of Philip, who thus was able to champion Arthur against John. In the year 1200 John recognized Philip as his overlord for the Angevin lands in France, made certain territorial concessions, and paid the large relief of 20,000 marks. In return, John became Richard's heir and did homage for his French lands, while Arthur became his vassal as duke of Brittany.

John, however, quickly gave Philip a new pretext for beginning hostilities. A dispute had arisen between the families of Angoulême and Lusignan in Poitou over an area known as La Marche. The families made peace when Hugh de Lusignan was betrothed to Isabel of Angoulême, a handsome young girl of fourteen. At this point John intervened. He allied himself with Angoulême, married Isabel,[2] and seized certain lands of the house of Lusignan. Hugh appealed to Philip as his supreme lord, and John was summoned to Philip's feudal court in Paris. Failing to appear, John eventually was sentenced to the loss of all his French possessions, and war began in earnest in 1202. In August, John achieved one of his few triumphs by capturing Arthur and a number of prominent persons of Poitou. This victory, which might have aided John greatly, turned instead to loss when Arthur disappeared. His fate is unknown, but it is assumed that he was put to death by John. Rebellion broke out against John in Brittany and indignation against him swept through France.

A general debacle followed in which John's possessions in northern France quickly slipped from his grasp. Normandy was lost by 1204; by 1206, Anjou, Touraine, and Brittany were also lost. Aquitaine, including Poitou, remained in English hands for

---

[1] During the reigns of John and his son, Henry III, there was an advance in the keeping of public records. Historians are able to examine the government in this period in far greater depth than can be done for any other European monarchy.
[2] John had secured an annulment of his marriage to his childless first wife, Isabel of Gloucester.

Eleanor relinquished her rights to her son. Philip's position was far stronger this time, whereas John had suffered an enormous loss of prestige. Suspicion and blame further divided John and his English barons. Moreover, those barons who elected to retain their English estates and to forfeit their French ones, when forced to choose, now thought solely in terms of their English possessions.

John and Innocent III

John refused to believe that his continental possessions were irretrievably lost. But from 1206 to 1213 he was so preoccupied by a quarrel with Pope Innocent III that he could do little in France. This quarrel, the most violent clash of church and state in England during the whole of the Middle Ages, began in a disputed election to the archbishopric of Canterbury, left vacant at the death of Hubert Walter in 1205. By canon law the right of election lay with the monks of the cathedral chapter at Canterbury. But John was determined to replace Walter with another royal official. The bishops of the province, wishing to share in the election, sided with the king. Fearing to lose their privilege, some of the monks secretly elected one of their own number and sent him to Rome to obtain the Pope's approval. When John heard of this move he came to Canterbury in great wrath and induced the monks to elect his candidate, who also journeyed to Rome. Confronted by these rivals, Innocent determined to take matters into his own hands. He was a most aggressive prelate, determined to exalt the papacy above all temporal rulers. He therefore quashed both elections, ruled that the right of election lay solely in the hands of the monks, and induced those at Rome to select Stephen Langton, a learned and able Englishman and newly appointed cardinal.

Innocent was asserting new and unprecedented powers. Had John acquiesced he might well have lost all control of episcopal elections in England; it is not surprising then that he refused to accept Stephen Langton. In reply Innocent placed England under an interdict. This papal weapon closed all the churches in the kingdom and withheld from the people the normal services of the clergy. Only baptism and confession for the dying were allowed. In 1209 John was excommunicated. In great bitterness he began a systematic spoliation of the church, appropriating large amounts of church property and diverting ecclesiastical revenues to the sum of £100,000. Many bishops and abbots fled the country, and monks in some monasteries were dispersed. Yet England remained quiet until 1212 when there were indications that the barons might revolt; Philip was preparing to invade England. In 1213 John suddenly submitted to Rome, agreeing to receive Stephen Langton as archbishop, recall the exiled clergy, and recompense the church for the losses it had suffered. He further consented to hold England as a feudal fief from Innocent, to whom he agreed to pay an annual tribute of 1000 marks. Thus John was thoroughly worsted in his quarrel with the papacy. Yet his submission was eminently wise, for the Pope now became his protector. Philip could not invade England without quarreling with Rome, and a new alliance against France became possible.

"The Virgin Appears to St. Thomas of Canterbury," psalter, thirteenth century, Canterbury. (John Pierpont Morgan Library, M756 f.10r)

John's Defeat in France, 1214

For some time John had been building an alliance against France. It consisted of England, Germany under Otto IV, Flanders, and lesser principalities in the Low Countries. Otto and the count of Flanders were to attack France from the northeast; John was to operate from Poitou and to push northward toward Paris. The plan was sound, and Philip was in great danger. John landed at La Rochelle in 1214 with some initial success. But he was checked on the Loire because the nobles of Poitou under his command refused to fight against Philip, their supreme lord; John fled back to La Rochelle. This disaster enabled Philip to operate in the north without fear for his southern flank. He met the armies of Otto and of the count of Flanders at the village of Bouvines one hot afternoon in July. Philip was completely victorious, the leaders of the coalition against him being either captured or dispersed in flight. Bouvines was one of the few medieval battles which decided great issues: it left Philip supreme in France and in Flanders, it ended Otto's rule in Germany, and it forced John to return dismally to England, defeated once again.

Magna Carta

John's wars, though unsuccessful, were extremely expensive. The age was one of inflation, especially in soldier's wages. Partly because the English barons were reluctant to fight overseas, John relied heavily on mercenaries—knights; men-at-arms, both mounted and unmounted; foreign crossbowmen; and foreign mercenaries who were sometimes mere gangs of freebooters. They were all expensive, as were the construction and the repair of castles. Richard had spent thousands of pounds on his beloved Château Gaillard on the Seine. Siege engines, such as stone throwers, were now so improved that the stoutest castle was certain to be badly mauled in a siege and to require frequent repair. John also poured out money in building his alliances against France. He lived in a costly fashion. In the exchequer he had an effective means of extorting money, and he depleted his subjects with a frequency that infuriated the barons. There were, of course, other abuses in his government: he distorted his feudal rights to his own advantage; his justice could be highly arbitrary; he employed dishonest persons as sheriffs and as other local officials; he used the law of the forests to increase his revenues; and he demanded hostages from the barons and then treated his prisoners with great cruelty. Such abuses resulted in deep suspicion and bitter hatred between John and the nobles.

Even before John's disastrous expedition to Poitou in 1214, a number of barons had met at St. Paul's Cathedral in London to discuss means of curbing the King's bad government. It was recalled that Henry I had issued a charter renouncing abuses, and it was proposed that some kind of charter might be extracted from John. When John returned from the Continent, defeated and shattered in prestige, and demanded further taxes, there was an explosion. A number of barons formed a coalition, pledged themselves to act together, renounced their allegiance in a formal defiance, occupied London, and compelled the king to set his seal to Magna Carta in the summer of 1215. It should not be assumed that all the barons thought or acted alike. Some were moved only by personal grievances. Others believed that all would be well if the king abided by feudal law. Only the more enlightened barons saw that the problem went beyond feudalism, that the issue was the preservation of good government under an evil king. Many of the older barons feared a civil war, whereas those demanding the charter were young and impetuous. Stephen Langton, the new archbishop, strove for peace, but revolt took place against his advice.

In later centuries Magna Carta was to become a quarantee of good government and a symbol of English liberty. It was to be praised and glorified and appealed to again and again. But succeeding generations, as they looked back at Magna Carta, usually construed it to their own interests with interpretations the document could not bear. The barons of 1215 would have been bewildered indeed to learn they were the true founders of Parliament or of democracy, or the original advocates of no taxation without representation, or of the right of all to be tried by jury. These points were simply not in the charter.

Magna Carta was drawn up by feudal barons, whose self-interests were naturally predominant. A large part of the charter, therefore, was devoted to the workings of feudalism with the object of preventing the king from abusing his feudal rights, many of which were dangerously vague and in need of definition. There were many articles dealing with the incidents of relief, wardship, and marriage, with sums of money set down in precise terms. The king was not to have relief if he had already enjoyed the incident of wardship. The lands of a ward were to be maintained and returned to him when he came of age, in as good condition as they had been when the wardship began. A ward was not to be married to a person whose rank was inferior to his. A widow was to be allowed her dower (the lands she had brought to her husband) and was not to be compelled to remarry against her will.

Other articles protected the rights of inheritance of a deceased baron's heirs and prohibited the arbitrary seizure of his chattels to pay debts he owed the Crown. Magna Carta also included other articles about debts, for even a great lord might be forced to borrow money in order to meet his obligations to the exchequer. Such articles relating to the rights of townsmen show that the newly emerging merchant class must be reckoned with by both sides at Runnymede. A famous article declared that the king might levy the three ordinary aids allowed by feudal custom but could not collect other aids without the consent of the barons. This consent must be obtained in the feudal council of the tenants in chief. It is possible that this arrangement was inserted by the king's negotiators, for the barons would hardly erect machinery by which they could be taxed. The barons suppressed the writ praecipe, which transferred cases from feudal to royal courts. The charter was thus a statement of feudal custom with safeguards against royal abuse.

Had Magna Carta dealt strictly with the details of feudalism it would have lost significance as feudalism passed away. But it also emphasized the principle of a feudal contract between the king and his tenants in chief. This principle—that the barons could resist if the king broke the contract—was one with great future applications.

The charter went beyond feudalism in a number of other ways as well. In the first place, the charter protested the arbitrary use of the system of law and government which had arisen during the twelfth century, especially during the reign of Henry II. The barons wished to preserve this system but they also understood its strength and terrible potential in the hands of an evil king: it could itself become a tyranny. John had refused to issue certain writs, suspended courts and withheld justice, seized property arbitrarily, and inflicted punishment without trial. The charter declared that these abuses were to cease. There were to be frequent visits of the itinerant justices to try the petty assizes. The writ *de odio et atia,* which protected a man from false accusation, was to be issued free of charge. Justice was not to be sold, refused, nor delayed. Common pleas were to be held in some fixed place, so that litigants would know where their cases could be tried. Article 39 declared: "No free man may be arrested or imprisoned or disseised or outlawed or exiled, or in any way brought to ruin, nor shall we go against him nor send others in pursuit of him, save by the legal judgment of his peers or by the law of the land." This article meant that a man must be tried by due process of law before he could be punished. The barons would be tried by their "peers," and others according to the "law of the land." The charter did not define the law of the land, but it stated that there was a law, that there were recognized legal procedures, and that these must be followed.

In demanding that the king not misuse the machinery of government, the barons were standing upon the feudal contract, for they were saying that the king could not alter the law, punish his vassals, nor take their money without consulting his tenants in chief. Another principle arose from the church. Many of the higher clergy believed that the duty of the king was to establish a government of law and morality which upheld as far as possible the moral law ordained by God and revealed in the Scriptures. If the king failed in his moral duty he became a tyrant and must forfeit all authority and power. The idea of the feudal contract, the protest against arbitrary government, and the thinking of the church all pointed to the fundamental principle that even the king must obey the law.

The charter also transcended feudalism by granting benefits to classes other than the nobility. The first article declared that the English church should be free, that is, free from the control of the king and free to obey the papacy. The privileges of London and of other boroughs were confirmed. Foreign merchants should enter England freely with exemption from arbitrary tolls. Justice was guaranteed to Welshmen who had lost their property or who were held as hostages. Tenants in chief should pass on to their vassals the benefits they had received from the king. Even the peasants profited from an article declaring that they must not be amerced so heavily as to lose their means of livelihood. There were also articles of a general nature which benefited the nation as a whole: dishonest officials should be dismissed, arbitrary exactions ended, and the forest areas curtailed. The legal reforms of Henry II, including many uses of the jury, were confirmed. We must not read too much into these concessions, most of which profited the barons indirectly. Yet the fact that other classes besides the barons gained advantage indicates that the charter was more than a feudal document.

The charter also passed beyond feudalism in its attempt to devise machinery by which the king could be forced to keep his promises. A representative council of twenty-five barons was established to watch John's government and to bring to his attention any infringement of the charter. If the infringement was not corrected, the twenty-five barons should organize and lead an armed revolt against the king. This provision was crude because it legalized civil war, but the barons had few alternatives. The attempt to control the king, as a step toward limited monarchy, was of great significance for the future. Moreover, it gave opposition a lawful place in the scheme of government. Basing their actions upon the feudal contract, the barons could now resist the Crown without incurring the stigma of treason.

The agreement between John and the barons embodied in the Great Charter lasted only about two months. John had no difficulty in persuading Innocent III to denounce the charter and to free him from his promises. He summoned mercenary troops from the Continent and prepared for war. The barons on their side invoked the article legalizing rebellion and invited Louis, the son of Philip Augustus, to come to England as their king. Louis soon held London and the southeastern portion of the country while John held the north and west. Then, in October 1216, John suddenly died. It can at least be said of him that he was not a nonentity: few monarchs have left so strong a mark on England. His vices were the vices of the Angevins in exaggerated form; his virtues were also their virtues, though in him they appeared in pale reflection.

HENRY III, 1216–1272

The Early Years of the Reign, 1216–1232

Friction between the king and the barons continued throughout the long reign of Henry III. The source of the problem was a king who wished to rule in a personal way but lacked the capacity to do so. Yet the fundamental issue of forcing the king to meet his responsibilities remained.

John's son, Henry III, was only nine years old when he came to the throne. For the first time since the Conquest the king was a minor. The country was divided by civil war, and a foreign invader, Louis of France, was in possession of important sections of the kingdom. But the young king was a disarming figure. His adherents wisely selected a regent, William Marshal, Earl of Pembroke, to rule in his place. Marshal was a fine warrior-statesman, a man of great strength of character, of blunt, rough honesty, and of long experience in government. He was able to end the civil war and to begin the task of bringing order out of chaos. Defeated by a rather lucky chance, Louis agreed to leave the country, though he obtained excellent terms. John's death removed the greatest cause of conflict, and with both John and Louis out of the way, the rebel barons returned to their allegiance. The king's party was surprisingly successful.

After Marshal's death in 1219, Hubert de Burgh, the justiciar, was able to make himself supreme. He was the last of the justiciars to rule as though they were kings. There was much less need for such an office now that Normandy had been lost and the king was not apt to spend long periods abroad. He did good work in restoring order, but he was self-seeking and rather arbitrary, and he might well have been driven from office had he not had the constant support of Archbishop Stephen Langton. Eventually Henry tired of de Burgh, who lost his position in 1232 after a long period of power.

Henry's Personal Rule, 1232–1258

In 1232 the king was twenty-five years old. He had been kept in tutelage much longer than was normal, but once he obtained control of affairs he showed himself determined to rule and to continue the autocratic power of his predecessors. He easily gathered the reins of authority into his own hands. During the minority a few great barons had worked along with high officials in the daily tasks of administration. Although the Great Council of all the tenants in chief did not meet frequently, the barons at least felt they were being consulted and that they were joined with professional administrators in what may be called a government by council. But there was no tradition for such a government. The tradition was that of a strong king who could seek advice where he pleased. Henry acted without consulting the barons, insisting upon freedom in selecting his officials.

Unfortunately, he was thoroughly incompetent as a ruler. He was a religious man, chaste and pious in his private life. He was also artistic, a person of finely cultivated taste, with a passion for building and decorating churches and for collecting beautiful objects. Like Edward the Confessor, whom he greatly admired, Henry devoted much attention to the building of Westmister Abbey. But in affairs of state he was weak, foolish, extravagant, and thoroughly exasperating. He could be petty and obstinate, and he was quite ready to deceive when he found himself in a tight corner.

Henry longed to regain the provinces in France lost by his father. In two expeditions against France he displayed complete incompetence, and in 1259 he concluded a treaty with Louis IX in which he acknowledged the loss of English possessions in northern France and did homage for Aquitaine and Gascony in the south. He also made the mistake of showing favor to large numbers of Frenchmen and Italians who came flocking to the English court. Their refined manners and obsequious flattery pleased the king greatly; he gave them money, lands, and offices. A number of Frenchmen from Poitou were introduced into the government by Peter des Roches, the bishop of Winchester, who became important after the fall of Hubert de Burgh. Moreover, Henry's wife, Eleanor of Provence, and his mother, Isabel of Angoulême, had many kinsmen. The majority were mere adventurers, yet they crowded into England and were rewarded by the king.

Henry's close relations with the papacy also brought in Italians. The king displayed a surprising subservience to Rome, humbly believing that he had owed his throne to the support of the papacy during his minority. Unfortunately his reign coincided with a period in which the pope was in great need of money, for if the papacy was to become a universal ecclesiastical state, a monarchy on a European scale, its financial requirements were necessarily enormous. Means must be found to support a host of officials at Rome and a network of legates, diplomats, and tax collectors throughout Christendom. Demands for money from the church in England became constant and merciless. Not only were the clergy heavily taxed; there were unprecedented applications for such things as a year's income from vacant churches, a monk's share from every monastery, and two prebends (stipends of members of cathedral chapters) from each diocese. There were also appointments by Rome to offices and livings in the church in England; English bishops were instructed to find parishes for Italians who often continued to live abroad. There was naturally a storm of protest. Lay patrons lost their rights of advowson; and clergymen, their opportunities of advancement. Henry, however, was sympathetic toward the papal policy, and his remonstrances were halfhearted. His unsuccessful expeditions to France, his welcome to aliens who came to England, his acquiescence in the exorbitant financial demands of Rome—all gave the impression that he was weak and incompetent.

A program of reform gradually took shape among the baronial leaders. They asked, in the first place, that Magna Carta be reissued again, as it had been on various occasions. They also asked that they should be consulted about the problems of government. This was sound feudal doctrine, for a feudal suzerain was supposed to summon his tenants in chief in meetings of the Great Council and to talk with them concerning affairs of state. Thus the barons, regarding themselves as the natural counselors of the king, refused to be ignored. Further, they sought to obtain some control over the machinery of government, especially over the appointment of the great ministers of state, the treasurer, the chancellor, and sometimes the justiciar. The Exchequer and the Chancery were now distinct departments separate from the rest of the government. Their officials were powerful and, the barons thought, too independent. If they could be brought under baronial surveillance, the power of the Crown to rule irresponsibly would be much diminished.

It was only in times of great crisis that the barons attempted to control the royal household. This also had grown in importance because Henry II, finding the exchequer and the chancery too cumbersome to transact quickly the personal affairs of the king, had developed a miniature exchequer and secretariat in the chamber, that is, in the king's sleeping apartment. Under Henry III a similar development took place in the wardrobe, the apartment where the king kept his clothes and armor. Certain revenues were paid into the wardrobe, which was not under the control of the Exchequer.

It should not be thought that the barons were seeking to build a new constitution, but were rather protecting what they considered to be their ancient rights. As amateurs in government they suspected the expert and disliked the trained official. And yet in opposing the king they easily assumed that they were speaking for the nation and that they represented a constituency with which the king should cooperate.

The Provisions of Oxford, 1258

Henry's financial difficulties came to a head in 1258. In prolonged negotiations with the papacy in 1254–1255 Henry had foolishly accepted the crown of Sicily for Edmond, his second son. The Pope was at war with Sicily at the time and did not control that territory. Yet Henry agreed to pay all past and future expenses of the papal campaign and thus made himself responsible for financing a distant war over which he had no control. The papal forces made little headway, the venture was hopeless by 1257, and Henry was responsible for the huge debt incurred by Rome. At the same time he was overwhelmed by other expenses. A campaign in France and a war in Wales had to be paid for, Westminster Abbey was unfinished, and a hard winter in 1257–1258 rendered extraordinary taxation impossible. When the barons, exasperated by the folly of the Sicilian adventure, demanded sweeping reforms in 1258, the king had no alternative but surrender.

The demands of the barons were incorporated in a famous memorandum, known as the Provisions of Oxford. A council of fifteen persons, almost entirely barons, some selected from supporters of the king and some from his opponents, was placed in virtual control of the government. The council was to advise the king on all matters of policy, so that he could make no important decision without its knowledge and consent. It was to appoint the treasurer, the chancellor, and the justiciar, who were made responsible to it. The provisions also included administrative reforms and gave the council control over local officials.

It is interesting to compare this document with Magna Carta, which was concerned with feudalism. The Provisions of Oxford show that the barons were less interested in the details of feudalism than in the machinery of government and that they accepted that machinery as a matter of course. They wished to capture it but they also wished to continue its operation. Distrusting the king, they put the kingship in commission by transferring royal authority to the council of fifteen. But the work of government was done by a larger group. The justiciar, though not one of the council, almost certainly sat with it. Prominent judges and heads of departments worked with it in close cooperation. Thus the council relied upon the experience of ministers of state, employing their technical skill and their close acquaintance with the details of government.

The Provisions of Oxford remained in force until 1262. At first the important magnates who had created the new government displayed remarkable unanimity, introducing reforms and allowing local knights to draw up lists of grievances. But government by council was a novel idea, and the barons, looking at events from the standpoint of their own class, resented demands that they reform the management of their own estates. They began to quarrel among themselves. In 1259 the Lord Edward, Henry's son, emerged as a person of importance and formed a small royal party. He allied with Simon de Montfort, a more radical leader, until Henry broke up the combination, reasserted himself, and began to undermine the Provisions of Oxford. Civil war broke out in 1264 with Edward commanding the king's forces, and Simon de Montfort leading the opposition. At the Battle of Lewes, in Sussex, Simon defeated Edward, captured the king, and found himself in control of the government.

Simon de Montfort, 1264–1265

Historians have often glorified Simon de Montfort as though he were an apostle of liberty and one of the great architects of Parliament. As a matter of fact, he was neither. He was a French feudal baron who looked upon the world from the point of view of his class. But he was an unusually able, clear-headed, and confident man, an advocate of reform, and one of the first statesmen to see that a middle element, below the baronage but above the peasants, was beginning to emerge in English society. In great need of support, he courted this middle element.

He was not considered a foreigner by the English nobility. When he had come to England in 1231, Henry welcomed him warmly, gave him lands which had been held by Simon's father, made him an earl, and bestowed upon him the king's sister in marriage. For a time Henry had sent him to rule Gascony. When Henry became dissatisfied with Simon's administration, however, he recalled him and forced him to submit to a trial in which the king himself attacked Simon bitterly. There could be no friendship between the two men after this. The discontented nobles gathered around Simon as much because he was the king's brother-in-law as because he was a strong man and an advocate of reform. After the Battle of Lewes he held dictatorial power, but he did not wish to be a dictator. He thought it possible to return to the Provisions of Oxford, for he was quite aware that government of the ordinary kind was out of the question. A magnate in his position, with the king in captivity and the barons divided, could hardly hope to remain in power long. Simon, with two close associates, ruled in the king's name. They selected a council of nine members whose functions were somewhat similar to those of the earlier council of fifteen.

To strengthen this highly precarious experiment in government, Simon turned for support to the middle elements of English society. During the thirteenth century the meetings of the Great Council of the barons were beginning to be known as Parliaments. The early history of the English Parliament will be considered in a later chapter, but it may be said that the king, for his own convenience, sometimes summoned groups of smaller landowners called knights of the shire to meet with him at the same time as his tenants in chief in the Great Council. Simon de Montfort continued and extended this practice. To a parliament in 1264 he summoned not only the barons and high churchmen who were his adherents but also knights from each shire. In 1265 he summoned not only knights from the shires but also burgesses from a selected number of towns. He was not trying to construct a new institution. He merely saw that the support of smaller landowners and of prosperous townsmen was worth obtaining and that a parliament was a place where important business could be transacted.

Simon's position was weakened in 1265. He lost the support of one of his most powerful adherents, the earl of Gloucester, who turned against his government. At about the same time the Lord Edward escaped, joined Gloucester, and gathered an army. Together they defeated and slew Simon at the Battle of Evesham, Worcestershire. The king was released from captivity and resumed control of the government, though actual power was exercised not by Henry but by his son, the Lord Edward.

To all appearances the barons had accomplished very little by their attempts to control the king. The full force of monarchy was quickly reestablished after Simon's death, and Edward was to prove a king who asserted his full authority of kingship. The oligarchical rule of a small group of barons was not the answer to the problem of an irresponsible sovereign. There were, however, certain accomplishments. A number of the reforms desired by the barons were continued and became a permanent part of the administration. There was now an established principle that affairs of state should be discussed in meetings of the Great Council or in Parliament. Indeed, a broader concept emerged that the king should consult his subjects when their rights were involved and that he should seek cooperation with all the groups and interests among the ruling classes. Finally, the barons had set a precedent of great importance when they attempted to curb the power of the king without destroying the machinery of government.

CHRONOLOGY

Rebellions and Reforms

1189–1199	Richard the Lion-hearted
1189–1192	The Third Crusade
1199–1216	John
1206–	Loss of Normandy
1206–1213	Struggle with Innocent III; Stephen Langton
1215–	Revolt of the barons; Magna Carta
1216–1272	Henry III
1258–1265	Baronial Revolt
1258–	Provisions of Oxford
1264–1265	Simon de Montfort; defeated at Evesham

6 Society in the Twelfth and Thirteenth Centuries

THE CHURCH

It is probable that the Christian Church had a greater hold upon the minds of people in the Middle Ages than at any time before or since. Its primary function was to lead them to salvation. There were certain acts and ceremonies, known as the sacraments—baptism, confirmation, penance, the Holy Eucharist or Mass, extreme unction, marriage, ordination of the priesthood—through which God's grace was imparted by the church to the people. These rites and holy mysteries, with their hope of salvation, exerted an incalculable influence over the people. But the church touched human lives in countless other ways. The parish church in a small village was a social as well as a religious center; the village market might be held in the churchyard, and social life revolved around the festivals of the Christian year. Vivid religious scenes were portrayed on the inner walls of the parish church. Cathedrals in the cities embodied the majesty of the church. The church courts dealt not only with heresy, but with perjury, moral offenses and matrimonial cases, and the probate of wills and settlements of property. And while Christianity thus touched the people on every hand, it was itself growing more humane. The mercy, the love, the tender compassion of Christ, his life on earth, and his sufferings upon the cross received new emphasis. There was an increase in the cult of the Virgin Mary, who represented the human aspect of Christ and who could intercede with her Son in behalf of frail humanity.

The church was highly complex, containing great varieties of wealth, function, and social division. It contained deacons and subdeacons, with limited knowledge and responsibility, as well as sophisticated philosophers of great breadth and subtlety of learning. The parish priest often farmed the glebe belonging to his church whereas the aristocratic clergy controlled great estates and held high office in the service of the crown. Great numbers of men and women, seeking respite from the world, lived in religious monasteries and nunneries. In the thirteenth century the Franciscan and Dominican friars appeared in England and were eagerly supported. Men sometimes lived in solitude, as hermits and anchorites, devoting themselves to religious contemplation.

The Organization of the Church

Archbishops, bishops, and parish priests formed the three principal ranks of the secular clergy. The bishop ruled over an area known as a diocese. He alone could perform the sacrament of confirmation and ordain men to the priesthood. Although lay patrons nominated priests to livings, the bishop held a veto; it was his duty to prevent unsuitable appointments and to secure an adequate stipend for a newly installed priest. The bishop dedicated altars and consecrated churches, disciplined the clergy of the diocese, and either in person or by deputy inspected the parishes within his diocese and corrected irregularities. The bishop visited monasteries in the same way. It was his duty to summon annual synods of the principal clergy of the diocese.

The administrative center of a diocese was normally the most important town of the area. Here the bishop had his palace and his cathedral. A formal body of disciplined clergy connected with each cathedral was known as the cathedral chapter. By a system peculiar to England, a number of the cathedrals, such as Canterbury and Durham, were the churches of Benedictine abbeys, their chapters being composed of monks who conducted the daily services. Other cathedral chapters were made up of canons, who were secular priests. The head of the chapter was the dean. He was assisted by the precentor, who was responsible for the daily liturgy; the chancellor, who might also be the master of the cathedral school; the treasurer; and the resident and nonresident canons. Some canonries in the secular cathedrals had prebends, or incomes without duties attached to them; these places were sought by the king as rewards for his servants and by the pope for officials at Rome, who might never come to England. During the twelfth century cathedral chapters became invested with the right to elect the bishop (though not without advice from the king) and with the administration of the diocese during a vacancy. The chapter, managing its own endowments, generally acquired considerable independence from the bishop. Thus situations arose in which a bishop might have little jurisdiction over his cathedral or over the chapter attached to it.

The bishop therefore developed his own household of clerks and officials quite apart from the dean and chapter. For a long time the bishop worked informally, assisted by a small, though sometimes brilliant, group of clerks. A change took place early in the thirteenth century when the administrative and legal activities of a bishopric greatly expanded. Episcopal registers appeared, containing a record of all the bishop's activities, and a group of officials emerged who did much of his formal work. The most important officials were the registrar, who presided in the bishop's court, and the vicar-general, who was the bishop's deputy in administration. These

THE CHURCH   113

Medieval dioceses with monasteries and towns mentioned in the text.

offices were sometimes combined in one person, known as the chancellor. Certain functions, however, could only be performed by a person with the rank of bishop. Hence a suffragan bishop was sometimes appointed. He was no more than a temporary assistant to the bishop, holding a title without a see or else with an inaccessible see in Ireland. Below these officials were archdeacons and rural deans. The archdeacon, who held an ecclesiastical court in a subdivision of the diocese, made visitations in the parishes under his jurisdiction, summoned offenders to his court, and imposed fines for moral and ecclesiastical offenses. He was a highly unpopular official. The rural dean or archpriest exercised similar, though very restricted, powers over small areas. The archdeacon, like the cathedral chapter, acquired some independence from the authority of the bishop. A bishopric contained a good many islands, such as exempt monasteries and churches belonging to other dioceses, in which the bishop could not exert authority.

Dioceses differed greatly in size and endowments. The dioceses of York and Lincoln were enormous, while those of Ely and Rochester were very small. Canterbury, York, Winchester, Ely, and Durham possessed princely endowments; others, such as the Welsh bishoprics, were poverty-stricken. Like other magnates, the bishops were expected to live in a lavish way, with large staffs of officials and household servants. A few men of humble origin attained bishoprics, but the bishops were normally drawn from the monasteries, the universities, or the officials of the Crown. Many of them were men of distinction in scholarship or in royal administration. The thirteenth century was fortunate in having a number of outstanding bishops, such as St. Edmund of Abingdon, St. Richard Wych, and Robert Grosseteste, bishop of Lincoln and the first chancellor of Oxford University. The provinces of Canterbury and York were unequal in size. The archbishop of Canterbury presided over eighteen bishoprics, including four in Wales while the archbishop of York held only three. The archbishop acted as bishop in his own diocese and exercised jurisdiction over the other bishops of his province. Under an aggressive archbishop this jurisdiction could be very real, but normally an archbishop did not attempt a close control over his bishops. The archbishop of Canterbury was so occupied with business at the court of the king that he paid little attention to the affairs of Canterbury, and even less to those of other bishoprics.

A rural parish usually covered the area of a small village of perhaps three hundred to four hundred people. The priest was often of peasant origin and lived much like other peasants except with certain advantages and sacred duties. He had been educated, at least minimally, at a monastic school or in the household of a bishop. He probably lived in a better house than the other peasants and held more land in the open fields. But on weekdays he was often a farmer who tilled the glebe of the parish, and occasionally performed villein services for the lord of the manor. He derived his income from the glebe and from tithes paid in agricultural produce by his parishioners. But an ecclesiastical living was regarded as a piece of property; hence the right to appoint a priest (advowson) and to dispose of the income of a parish might pass from the lord of the manor to a monastery or to a cathedral or perhaps to the king. When this happened, or when the rector of a parish was permitted to be nonresident, part of the parish income was normally used to supply a vicar, who performed the necessary duties of the parish church. These arrangements could lead to serious abuses. At the time of the Norman Conquest many parish priests were married, and even in the thirteenth century the celibacy of the clergy was far from universal, despite the insistence of the church.

The Monasteries

During the century following the Norman Conquest there was a remarkable revival of monasticism in England. William the Conqueror and his barons founded many monasteries; Stephen's reign, despite the anarchy, was a time of many new foundations. At the time of Stephen's death in 1154 the number of monastic houses had risen to nearly 300. An impulse of reform came first from a famous monastery founded at Cluny in French Burgundy in 910 and later from new orders which established themselves in England. Many of the leading churchpeople of the time, including both Lanfranc and Anselm, were monks. The psychology of the founders was sometimes curious. The rough barons of Stephen's reign first plundered the countryside and then established religious houses with the proceeds, but the movement's universal support derived from its strong appeal to men of the twelfth century. The monastic ideal of rejection of the world, of devotion to religion in the regulated life of the cloister, caught the imagination of the people. To say that a man was converted to religion did not mean that he had become a Christian but that he had become a monk. The movement declined somewhat in the thirteenth century, for it was almost impossible for monasteries to maintain their high ideals while becoming wealthy from royal endowments. Nevertheless, the monks continued to be important in the life of the nation, quite apart from their wealth and prestige.

Monastic life rested primarily upon the teachings of St. Benedict (c. 480–c. 544). This Italian monk, disliking the fanaticism of early monks and hermits in Egypt and Syria, devised a famous rule by which religious men could live a communal life together in austerity and self-restraint without undue excesses. Upon entering a Benedictine abbey a novice took the usual vows of poverty, chastity, and obedience. He also took a vow of stability, that is, he swore to remain in the monastery until his death. There were both common sense and humanity in St. Benedict's rule. It gave great authority to the abbot and left many details to his discretion. The vow of stability brought permanence to monastic life. The rule also provided that monks should spend several hours each day in manual labor. This gave their lives variety and made the monastery self-supporting at least to the extent that it could refuse corrupting gifts.

Though it remained the basis of monastic regulations, the rule of St. Benedict had been revised and modified in various ways by the twelfth century. The ritual of the daily services became more elaborate so that the monks spent a larger part of their time in church. There was greater attention to scholarship, in which St. Benedict had had little interest. The monks became the custodians of learning. Copying and illuminating manuscripts, they also kept chronicles, and taught in monastic schools. St. Benedict's injunction to labor in the fields was abandoned; it became the practice

Monks singing daily services, fifteenth century. (British Library, King Henry VI's Psalter, Cottonian MS Domitian A. xvii, f.122v)

for a monastery to enlist a number of lay brothers to cultivate the monastic lands. These were peasants of a religious cast of mind who took vows of poverty, chastity, and obedience but were too ignorant to sing the services.

St. Benedict set down detailed instructions for the services, or offices, to be performed each day. These services, known as the *Opus Dei,* "the Work of God," formed the center of monastic life, and nothing was allowed to interfere with them. They consisted of singing psalms, saying responses, and reading lessons from the Scriptures. The first, Matins, was performed at two in the morning and was followed immediately by a second, Lauds. The monks then retired to their dormitory, to which the church was accessible by a stairway, and slept until six, when they arose for a series of services and Masses which continued until about half past eight. There followed a meeting in the chapter house, where the business affairs of the abbey were discussed. The monks then read and worked in the fields until the midday meal. In the afternoon they read and worked again (for the Cistercians did not follow other orders in abandoning manual labor). Supper was followed by two more services, Vespers and Compline, before the monks retired.

Apart from the church, the life of a monastery centered in and around the cloisters. A cloister was an enclosed walk or arcade, perhaps twenty feet wide, forming a square around an open lawn or garden. The cloisters gave access to almost every part of the monastery. It was in the cloisters that the monks spent hours reading and teaching.

Most of the monastic foundations in England were Benedictine houses. They included some very large and prominent houses, such as St. Albans, Bury St. Edmunds, Glastonbury, and St. Mary's, York. Of the new orders, the most influential was the order of Cistercians, which originated in 1098 at the monastery of Citeaux in the desolate forest area of Burgundy near Dijon. It was one of the frequent attempts to regain the simplicity envisaged by St. Benedict. The monks lived in great austerity, following the rule to the letter: without "coats, capes, worsted cloth, hoods, pants, combs, counterpanes, and bedclothes," without fine food in the refectory or anything else contrary to the rule. Their first foundation in England was at Waverley in Surrey in 1129, but their most famous houses were in the desolate north, at Rievaulx, Fountains, and Kirkstall in the solitary dales of Yorkshire. They founded so many daughter houses that their monasteries can be arranged in a kind of family tree. They owned huge flocks of sheep and became wealthy through the sale of wool. An even stricter order was that of the Carthusians, who followed a very early and pre-Benedictine form of monasticism in which the monks lived alone in cells, each monk preparing his own food and saying the daily offices to himself. The first Carthusian house in England was Witham Abbey in Somerset, founded in 1179. Its first prior was Hugh of Avalon, a Burgundian who became bishop of Lincoln and was a personal friend of Henry II. But the order was too severe to be popular and only a handful of Carthusian monasteries existed in England. The Gilbertines were an English order of pious women, founded about 1131.

So strong was the monastic ideal that groups of priests serving large churches or forming cathedral chapters felt the urge to live according to a rule. These priests, known as regular canons, followed the rule of St. Augustine (354–430), which was more elastic than the rule of St. Benedict. During the twelfth century more than a hundred houses of Augustinian, or Austin, canons were established in England.

In the thirteenth century there was a decline in the idealism and influence of the monasteries, which no longer supplied the religious and intellectual leadership they had in the past. Although some new houses were established, the great age of founding monasteries was over, and although they continued to be supported reasonably well by gifts and endowments, many benefactors turned their attentions elsewhere. It is true that a baron or other wealthy person often inherited an interest in a particular house and was ready to assist it as occasion offered. Some of the larger Benedictine and Cistercian abbeys profited greatly from the high farming of the thirteenth century. The Benedictine houses were inspected by their own order as well as by the bishops. They also sent representatives to central assemblies known as chapters, which acquired powers of government over the order.

But the monasteries were by now wealthy and well-established institutions, and it was not easy to maintain the spirit of the Benedictine rule. Monastic life became more comfortable. Glass windows, clocks, and softer beds were introduced. The monks became more interested in good living; they ate meat, which was forbidden by the rule. They also paid greater attention to the management of their property. It was only to be expected that a vigorous abbot would watch over the monastic estates and manage them in a businesslike way. A worldly spirit was creeping into monastic life, though this is a matter difficult to judge, and every monastery differed to some extent from every other. Nonetheless, it seems clear that the monasteries, though a stable and traditional element in society, had lost much of their early religious fervor.

The Friars

The friars, who represented the last great movement of reform in the medieval church, were perhaps the most vital element in English religious life during the thirteenth century. They first appeared in 1221, when a body of Dominicans, or Friars of the Order of Preachers, arrived in England. The order had been founded by St. Dominic (1170–1221), a Spanish priest who had been combating the heresy that had arisen in northern Spain and in southern France. Reflecting on the needs of the church, he conceived of an order of well-educated and skillful preachers who, living in poverty, could move among the people, correcting the deficiencies of the lower clergy in teaching and preaching and strengthening the orthodoxy of the church by attacking heretical doctrines. The Dominicans therefore laid great stress on the education of their members. They established at once a convent at Oxford for the training of young friars. They were fortunate in obtaining the assistance of Robert Grosseteste, later bishop of Lincoln, who became deeply interested in the order.

A second group of friars, the Order of the Friars Minor, the Franciscans, came to England in 1224. Their founder was St. Francis of Assisi (1181–1226), one of the most memorable figures of the Middle Ages. The son of a prosperous Italian merchant, he experienced a conversion as a young man, renounced his inheritance, and lived in complete poverty, begging for his daily bread as he traveled about preaching and doing good works among the poor. His message to his followers was the message of Jesus to his disciples—to renounce the world and to live among the destitute. In 1210 St. Francis obtained from Innocent III a somewhat hesitant approval of his band as a new order in the church. Later, under the supervision of the papacy, the order was given a necessary organization, much to the sorrow of its founder.

The Dominicans and the Franciscans, though differing in purpose, had much in common and tended to grow very much alike. Their members took the usual vows of poverty, chastity, and obedience. They lived by a rule, though not a monastic rule, for the friars mingled with the people. By the end of the century each of the orders had established about fifty houses in England. Almost from the first, the Franciscans

Hospital. (Giraudon/Art Resource)

recognized the importance of education and scholarship, though St. Francis had not done so. Like the Dominicans, they established a convent at Oxford which attracted a group of eminent scholars. Robert Grosseteste, although he was not a friar, agreed to lecture on theology. Other distinguished thinkers at the Franciscan convent were Adam Marsh, John Pecham, who was later archbishop of Canterbury, and Roger Bacon.

The friars made a great appeal to the people of the time. They were the evangelists of the Middle Ages, living among the poor in the towns, attending the sick and destitute, and preaching to classes neglected by the church. They were far better educated than the parish priest, and they spiced their sermons with wit and humor as well as eloquence.

In the fourteenth century the orders declined, not because of their wealth, for they had comparatively little, but because of the excessive privileges and immunities given to them by the papacy. They could use the parish churches, celebrate Mass, hear confession, and impose penance, and they were greatly sought after by the laity to perform the normal functions of the clergy. Yet they were responsible only to their own superiors, who in turn were responsible only to the pope. In competition with the priests for the attention of the public and with the monks for gifts and endowments, they were normally on very bad terms with both. Their begging became a nuisance; at the end of the fourteenth century Geoffrey Chaucer had little good to say of them.

ARCHITECTURE

The Normans began a great age of English architecture. Their architectural style—the Norman or the Anglo-Norman Romanesque—appeared about 1090 and continued to be used until about 1175. During that period cathedrals and large monastic churches were built or rebuilt at Durham, Tewkesbury, Winchester, Canterbury, Old Sarum, Chichester, Ely, Norwich, Bath, and elsewhere. Despite rebuilding in later centuries, many fine examples of Norman architecture may still be seen; they illustrate the distinctive features of this style. These cathedrals were of enormous size, twice the length of the Saxon cathedral at North Elmham in Norfolk, which measured 140 feet. As a matter of fact, the tendency to build large churches existed all over Europe, chiefly because of the increasing pomp and ceremony of the liturgy. But English cathedrals were large even for the era of their construction. In addition to size, they gave the impression of strength and solidity, ideas conveyed by their massive piers or pillars carrying heavy rounded arches, their large lantern towers above the middle of the church, and their thick and heavy walls.

Cathedrals were built in the shape of a cross, with the upper portion of the cross pointing toward the east. The lower portion was represented by the nave, which was the main body of the church. The fine proportions, great impressiveness, and massive strength of these Norman naves are still evident today. The transepts, large projections built to the north and south, represented the arms of the cross. It was above the intersection of nave and transepts that the central tower was erected. To the east of the transepts was the choir, which formed the upper portion of the cross and was the place where the clergy assembled to sing the daily services. Smaller than the nave, the choir contained stalls or carved wooden seats for the clergy; at the eastern end was the high altar. Along both sides of the nave and choir ran a wide aisle separated from the central part of the church by an arcade of piers or pillars. At Durham, where some of the best Norman work has survived, the arcade consisted of alternating round piers and clustered columns; the piers were ornamented with bold spiral or zig-zag patterns and the rounded arches with running motifs of various designs. Above the piers was the triforium, a small gallery close to the wall, decorated with arches and small columns. Above this was the clerestory, a portion of the wall pierced by narrow windows. Sometimes the aisles ended at the east of the church in small rounded apses which were used as chapels; sometimes they were continued and joined together in a semicircle behind the choir. In later ages the apses often disappeared and were replaced by a square east end. A notable feature at Durham was the stone vaulting carried by cross-ribs to form the interior of the roof. This style of vaulting made the clerestory possible; the weight of a stone barrel-vault required solid walls.

Late in the twelfth century Romanesque architecture gave way to the Gothic or Early English style. Gothic architecture, as it had been developing in France, was first brought to England by the Cistercian monks who came from Burgundy and built their English abbeys in the style they had known at home. About the same time the monks at Canterbury engaged a Frenchman, William of Sens, to rebuild the choir. Like the Cistercians he employed the Gothic style he had known in his own country. The style at Canterbury was soon followed in other English cathedrals, as at Wells

Gothic or early English architecture. Salisbury Cathedral. (A. F. Kersting)

and Lincoln, which were being built in the last decade of the twelfth century and were almost entirely Gothic. These churches, together with Salisbury and Westminster Abbey, formed the greatest monuments of Early English architecture. Salisbury was completed within thirty or forty years after it was begun in 1220 and thus possessed great unity of design and purity of style. Westminster Abbey, upon which Henry III lavished care and money, was more elaborate than the others. A happy blending of French and English influences, with a beautifully proportioned nave and with handsomely sculptured stone, it brought new richness and splendor to English architecture.

An obvious feature of Early English architecture was the pointed arch, which appeared in many shapes and sizes and culminated in the lofty arches of the vaulting supported by columns rising from the floor. These columns, massive at first, became in time more slender and graceful and often were adorned by clusters of Purbeck marble shafts. Strengthened by buttresses on the outside of the building, the columns supported the roof, relieving the walls of much dead weight and making larger windows possible. Stained glass and tracery in geometrical patterns were used in the windows; and their larger size increased the amount of light, which combined with pointed arches and slender columns to give the cathedral an airy grace and chaste aesthetic beauty. Simple, austere, and restrained, these cathedrals were finely built though not extravagant. They relied upon symbolism rather than upon exact copies of natural objects, and they achieved a synthesis of the arts by subordinating them to religious purposes and to structural needs.

THE INTELLECTUAL RENAISSANCE

In the twelfth and thirteenth centuries a remarkable awakening of intellectual life took place in Europe. Learned men among the upper clergy moved easily among the schools of western Europe, while students followed famous teachers from place to place. The universal language of these cosmopolitan scholars was Latin. In the opening years of the twelfth century Archbishop Anselm was the most eminent scholar in England. As priors of the monastery of Bec in Normandy, both he and Lanfranc had made that monastery a center of learning. Later Anselm gathered a group of pupils around him at Canterbury. But this group was small, and Anselm was to be the last of the great monastic teachers. The monastic schools, whose primary purpose was the training of monks to take part in the daily services, produced great scholars only as a kind of by-product. By the middle of the twelfth century these schools had fallen into eclipse; educational leadership had moved from the regular to the secular clergy, from the monastic schools to those connected with cathedrals. But although the cathedral schools in England were advancing in reputation, it was fashionable for English students to complete their education at the more famous schools on the Continent.

The Classics

The intellectual awakening that began in the eleventh century centered in the cathedral schools of northern France at Laon, Paris, Chartres, Tours, and Orléans. Its first expression was an intense interest in the classical literature of Rome. Most of the Latin authors known today were studied in the eleventh century, not merely as models of literary grace, but as a means of understanding the thought and culture of Roman antiquity. This classical education produced excellent results: students trained in the French schools developed broad cultural interests and great literary skill.

The most distinguished Englishman among them was John of Salisbury. For some twelve years he continued his education, studying first under the famous Abelard at Paris and then at Chartres, the home of classical scholarship. Between 1154 and 1161 John of Salisbury was a member of the household of Archbishop Theobald at Canterbury, acting as his secretary and writing many of his letters. Theobald sent him to Rome on various missions of which John has left lively descriptions. At Rome he was a friend of Nicholas Breakspear, an English cardinal who, as Adrian IV, became the only English pope. While John was living at Canterbury he wrote a long treatise on political theory and a shorter one on logic, both dedicated to Thomas Becket. After Theobald's death John entered Becket's household, defended him in his quarrel with Henry II, and later wrote his biography. John spent the remainder of his life as bishop of Chartres.

Another scholar connected with the household of Archbishop Theobald was Peter of Blois, the author of numerous letters. Literary men often found employment at the court of Henry II. Walter Map, a Welshman who had studied at Paris, was highly regarded by Henry and served him as ambassador and itinerant justice. Map wrote a witty and penetrating account of Henry's court. Gerald of Wales, also a former student at Paris and a friend of the King, wrote books on Wales and Ireland and a treatise on the education of princes in which he made some caustic comments on Henry and his sons. An author of a very different type was Geoffrey of Monmouth, whose history of the early kings of Britain was a collection of Celtic tales which supplied later writers with material for legends of King Arthur. These men illustrate the breadth of twelfth-century culture, its love of belles-lettres, and also Henry's appreciation of literary talent.

Philosophy and Theology

About the middle of the twelfth century, interest in classical literature was overwhelmed by a greater interest in philosophy and theology. John of Salisbury and other literary men complained that young students neglected the classics to hurry on to the study of theology and law, the utilitarian subjects of the day. The new interest in philosophy and theology developed into a type of learning known as scholasticism, an attempt to apply reason and deductive logic to the study of theology and to seek the solution of theological questions through logical argumentation. The most famous exponent of this method in the twelfth century was Abelard (d. 1142), a brilliant thinker and teacher who attracted hundreds of students to Paris. In his book *Sic et Non (Yes and No)* Abelard showed that the Bible and the writings of the early church fathers contained many contradictions, and he sought the truth through the application of reason. He aroused the hostility of conservative churchmen, among them Anselm, the formulator of the ontological proof of the existence of God, who feared that he was placing reason above faith and dogma and whose view was well expressed by Anselm's famous aphorism, "Believe that you may understand." Faith must be placed before reason, dogma before knowledge. Abelard, on the other hand, would have said, "Understand that you may believe." The difference was fundamental. Abelard fascinated the younger generation of churchmen as much as he horrified the old. But he had no thought of challenging faith, and the controversy developed into efforts to reconcile faith and reason and to achieve a synthesis that would satisfy the demands of both.

Behind these arguments and largely responsible for them was the gradual recovery of the works of Aristotle (384–322 B.C.), the Greek philosopher who held that knowledge must begin with the collection of facts and that only after facts had been assembled and assimilated could a philosophy of life or an understanding of truth be constructed. Before the twelfth century only a small portion of Aristotle's works was known in western Europe. The rest of his writings, however, were recovered during the twelfth century and made available to scholars in the thirteenth.

Eastern Science

A knowledge of Greek was almost unknown among the scholars of western Europe. Hence the writings of Aristotle and other Greek philosophers and scientists had to be translated into Latin before they were generally accessible. There was some translation directly into Latin from Greek, but a much larger portion of the writings of the Greeks made their way into western Europe through the Arabs who had studied Greek civilization, translated Greek texts into Arabic, and, especially in mathematics and medicine, further developed Greek thought. It was by contact with Arab sources in Spain, Sicily and southern Italy, and Asia Minor that Western scholars learned of Eastern science and brought back a knowledge of it. In this diffusion of Arabic learning Englishmen played an important part.

One of the first was Adelard of Bath (c.1099–c.1150). He traveled widely, in Greece, Asia Minor, Sicily and southern Italy, and perhaps in Spain, and translated into Latin a number of Arab texts on philosophic and scientific subjects, of which the most important was Euclid's work on geometry. A translation of Ptolemy's *Almagest,* the standard work on ancient astronomy, also is attributed to Adelard. It is probable that he was employed in England by Henry I as an official in the Exchequer and that his knowledge of Greek and Arabic mathematics helped to develop its technique. To catch the attention of young Henry Plantagenet, later Henry II, Adelard wrote a treatise on falconry, the first of its kind in western Europe. He is a remarkable link between Christian and Muslim learning and between the scientist and the person of letters.

His contemporary, Robert of Chester, an even more elusive figure, studied in northern Spain and was commissioned by the abbot of Cluny to make a translation of the Koran. His chief interests being mathematical, he translated an Arabic work on algebra which introduced that subject to western Europe. It may have been Robert's work that first brought Arabic numerals to the West, though centuries passed before their use became general. Daniel of Morley, another Englishman, interested in astrology, studied in Toledo in the last quarter of the twelfth century. In the thirteenth century Michael the Scot also worked at Toledo, translated Aristotle's treatise on animals, and became a famous astrologer. Robert Grosseteste though a bishop of Lincoln, theologian, and lecturer at Oxford, found time to study mathematics and to experiment with lenses. His preeminent student was scientist Roger Bacon. An independent and original thinker, though something of an intellectual snob, Bacon criticized scholastic dependence upon argument and called, instead, for experimentation.

Law

Interest in Roman antiquity in the twelfth century included a study of the Roman law, which in turn produced a notable advance in the development of the canon law of the church. The two systems were somewhat alike, for the church had borrowed freely from Roman law. During the twelfth century, Italian scholars made a thorough investigation of the code of Roman law compiled by Emperor Justinian; they wrote elaborate commentaries or glosses upon it. The canon law, which had been in a state of great confusion, was drawn into systematic form in a famous work, the *Decretum,* written by the monk Gratian about the year 1140. This textbook of canon law, arranged by subject and easy to use, greatly promoted knowledge of the canon law and increased the activity of the ecclesiastical courts.

The development of canon and Roman law naturally had its effect on England. Archbishop Theobald, seeing the increase of litigation in the church courts, made every effort to promote legal studies. The clerks of his household, including Thomas Becket, discussed and argued points of law; Becket himself went abroad to study law at Bologna and at Auxerre. One can see in this activity at Canterbury the background of Becket's clash with Henry II. To obtain professional assistance and to train the clergy, Theobald brought to England an Italian jurist, Vacarius, who taught Roman law at Canterbury and may have taught it later at Oxford. The study of Roman law, although it led to no profitable profession in England and was frowned upon by the church, was very popular at Oxford, where a thriving school of law developed.

But England had a law of its own, the common law. This law was affected by the spirit and logic of the Roman law, not by its substance. A famous legal work of the twelfth century, *Treatise on the Laws and Customs of England,* normally attributed to the lay justiciar Rannulf Glanville, confined itself to the law administered in King's courts. Glanville had a smattering of Roman law, but this did no more than lead him to arrange his book in a logical and systematic form. The greatest book of law produced in England during the Middle Ages was Henry de Bracton's treatise, *Concerning the Laws and Customs of England,* written largely between 1250 and 1258. Bracton, a justice of the King's Bench, spent his life in the royal courts. He compiled a notebook containing digests of some two thousand cases; his treatise was based upon them and upon his long experience as a justice. He was familiar with Roman and canon law. He drew from them an understanding of what a law book should be, how it should be organized, and how the principles of law should be set forth. While Bracton understood the rules of Roman and canon law as they applied to English law, his book, like Glanville's, described only English common law as it was administered in the royal courts.

History

The intellectual revival affected the writing of history. Historical writing now contained far greater detail than in the past and exhibited a broader view, a more critical judgment of the value of evidence, and a higher literary quality. Two monastic chroniclers of the twelfth century—William of Malmesbury and William of Newburgh—were men who may be termed historians. Not all historians were monks. Henry of Huntingdon was an archdeacon, Ralph de Diceto was dean of St. Paul's, and Roger of Hoveden was an itinerant justice in the reign of Henry II. In the thirteenth century there were two monks at St. Albans who carried the writing of history to a high level of achievement. Roger of Wendover expanded the range and detail of the monastery's chronicle and wrote in a lively style. Matthew Paris, who continued the chronicle from 1235 to 1259, was a man of wide knowledge, keen intelligence, and frank truthfulness. A person of some eminence with many important connections including King Henry III, Paris was well informed about public events and quite independent in his judgments.

The Rise of Universities

The rise of universities in the twelfth and thirteenth centuries was the result of the new interest in learning in western Europe; there was now a greater body of knowledge to teach to many more eager students. Universities grew slowly and imperceptibly. The earliest in time was the university of Salerno in southern Italy, where a school of medicine existed in the eleventh century. But Salerno remained a medical university and contributed little to the growth of university institutions, which grew more fully at Bologna. Though Bologna was chiefly famous as a school of law, it had become a many-sided institution by the middle of the twelfth century, with a charter of privileges from the emperor and a student body of several hundred from many parts of Europe. The students formed a guild as a protection against exorbitant landlords and against teachers who accepted student fees but failed to perform their duties properly. At Paris the university sprang from the cathedral school of Notre Dame.

Paris was an excellent geographical location and possessed a brilliant teacher in Abelard, who made it a center for philosophic and theological studies. The professors formed a guild in order to exclude teachers who did not have the M.A. degree. This degree was only conferred after difficult examinations and was in effect a license to teach. The university at Paris clashed with the bishop, who wished to retain his ancient right to grant such licenses. But the pope sided with the university and decreed in 1231 that if the faculty granted the license it could not be vetoed by the bishop.

In the thirteenth century a university had distinct characteristics. It contained a cosmopolitan student body drawn from a number of countries; it was a *studium generale,* a general resort of students. This was the term generally employed, for the word *universitas* meant the total membership of any guild and might apply equally to guilds of carpenters or to guilds of students and masters. The faculty of a university was of some size and distinction, its members holding the degree of M.A. Furthermore, a university contained at least one of the higher faculties of law, medicine, or theology. And finally, the university had obtained from kings or from the papacy a charter conferring upon it various immunities and privileges of self-government.

The first universities were merely groups of teachers and students without university buildings. The students found lodgings where they could; the lectures were given in rented halls. In an age without printing, textbooks were impossibly expensive, and the normal method of instruction was for students to attend lectures, take careful notes, and memorize them. At the end of three or four years a student qualified for the A.B. degree by taking examinations or by engaging in public disputations. There was almost no discipline in the early universities; and the students, who matriculated at an early age (thirteen to sixteen), indulged in a good deal of drinking, brawling, and bad company. They were constantly short of money. They probably did not come from noble families or from the peasantry, but from the middle classes of gentry and townspeople.

A number of schools of distinction existed in England in the second half of the twelfth century. Northampton, Exeter, Lincoln, and Winchester possessed schools that might have grown into universities, but for one reason or another they did not do so, and the first English university developed at Oxford. About the year 1167 Henry II, engaged in his quarrel with Becket, ordered all the English students at Paris to return to England. A number of them presumably came to Oxford, for from about this time the Oxford schools developed steadily into a *studium generale.* In 1209, however, a serious incident occurred when one of the students killed a woman. The townspeople arrested several of his fellow lodgers and hanged two of them. Lectures were at once suspended, and students and faculties dispersed, not to reassemble for some five years. In 1214 the citizens were forced to accept humiliating terms which provided, among other things, that the students were subject to the jurisdiction of the bishop of Lincoln or his representative, the chancellor of the university. Power gradually passed into the hands of the chancellor who held a court in which cases involving students were tried. By the end of the thirteenth century Oxford was one of the leading centers of learning in Europe, its body of masters and students numbering about 1500. Cambridge, which was smaller, grew more slowly.

A unique feature of English universities was the system of colleges which developed in both institutions. Originally designed to be hostels where students could lodge under supervision, the colleges became so important in themselves that they nearly overshadowed the university.

SOCIAL AND ECONOMIC LIFE

Population and Wealth

During the twelfth and thirteenth centuries England became populous and wealthy. In very round estimations, the population rose from about 1.5 million to about 3 million persons. This was a startling increase, and not entirely explainable. Life in the Middle Ages was hazardous and insecure at best. Population, however, has a tendency to rise unless it is diminished by plague or famine. There was no plague in England during this period; and the rise of a money economy lessened the danger of famine, for families with a little money were no longer dependent upon the food they had grown. Increasing wealth enabled the upper classes to improve their conditions of living and thus to raise larger families, but the standard of life among the poor remained low and primitive. A growing population required greater amounts of food, the price of agricultural products mounted steadily, people farmed their lands intensively and brought new land under cultivation. Fens were drained, forests cleared, wastelands brought under the plow. Old villages expanded and subdivided and new ones appeared. The prudent management of estates had become a carefully fostered skill. Small boroughs and towns, and with them the number of fairs and markets, grew larger. There was also a notable increase in foreign trade with the Baltic, with Flanders, with Gascony, and with the Mediterranean.

The Magnates and High Farming

A large part of the new wealth was in the hands of a few men at the top of society—twelve to fifteen earls, twenty to thirty baronial families of considerable means, bishops, and abbots of large monasteries. These were the magnates, the great men of the kingdom. Below them a much larger number of knights and country gentlemen also shared in the rising prosperity.

The pressure of a large population upon the soil placed the great landowner in a highly advantageous position. He was an agricultural millionaire who could lease his land at a high rent or farm it himself at a good profit. He probably used the manors surrounding his castle to supply his table, while his more distant manors produced grain, meat, or wool that could be sold. The greatest magnates held vast amounts of land. Their manors were sometimes divided into geographical groups. Gilbert de Clare, earl of Gloucester, held at the end of the thirteenth century one group of manors in South Wales, another in Dorset, and a third in East Anglia.

An estate of this size required an elaborate system of management. Accounts must be kept, rents collected, the unpaid labor of the villeins exploited, and the dishonesty of the reeves, who were skillful at cheating their masters, guarded against. One method of protection was to estimate in advance the revenues that might be expected from every source, and then to watch closely how income agreed with these estimates. A magnate normally had a steward who was responsible for the whole of the estate, in addition to a bailiff in charge of each manor. A reeve, who was a kind of foreman for the peasants, was elected by them once a year and supervised their labor on the demesne. Receivers collected money and auditors checked accounts. To supplement the work of villeins and casual hired laborers, some estates maintained a permanent staff of workers, such as plowmen and shepherds. A constant effort was made to enlarge the size of the estate by purchase or reclamation. Landowners specialized in a single crop, or in cattle for meat or milk, or, more often, in raising sheep. Some lords and monasteries owned flocks that numbered ten or twelve thousand. Attempts were made to discover the type of grain best suited for cultivation in various kinds of soil, cattle were moved from one pasture to another as grasses matured, and small fields were enclosed by hedges to promote better farming. Marl and loam served as fertilizers. The use of horses in place of oxen increased the efficiency of agriculture. A system of three instead of two open fields was sometimes adopted, so that only a third of the land lay fallow each year. High farming of this kind could only be conducted on large estates, of which there were many in the thirteenth century. Castles, manor houses, abbeys, and cathedrals dominated the countryside, each drawing support from the agriculture of a large surrounding area.

A baron drew revenue not only from his estates but also from the offices he held at the court of the king and from royal gifts of land and money. He could hardly hope to prosper unless he enjoyed the good will of the monarch. When an heir inherited an estate, for example, he was required to pay relief. The sums demanded were very large, but a favored noble might hope to have his payments reduced or perhaps forgiven entirely. The idea arose that the king owed his barons an income commensurate with their social position, and the court was thus regarded as a source of personal wealth.

Although a baron might have had a large income, he also had heavy expenses in maintaining a castle and elaborate household. The wooden castles of the eleventh century had been superseded in the twelfth by large stone keeps. These were strong high towers, circular or rectangular in shape, dark, crowded, and uncomfortable. In the thirteenth century a baron built a more sumptuous house that centered in a great hall, with the private apartments of the baron at one end and the kitchen at the other. The house was surrounded by a strong wall, known as a curtain wall, with battlements and towers upon it. These battlements became very elaborate, the space enclosed by the wall contained a number of buildings, and the whole attained a considerable magnificence. The household of a baron included a steward to supervise the establishment, a clerk to keep accounts, a chaplain, and many domestic servants. The baron had a council of his important adherents—his relatives, friends, lawyers, and officials—to advise him on matters of business.

A baron had to have a large and extravagant retinue of knights and followers to escort him when he traveled about the country, and to enhance his prestige in court.

He was expected to dispense a lavish hospitality and to be generous in gifts and favors. This magnificence reached its height in the fourteenth century. The best entertainment that a baron could devise was a tournament. These costly shows consisted of jousts between pairs of knights who fought according to set rules, with prizes awarded the victors and hospitality provided for all in attendance.

Feudal relations remained important between the king and his tenants in chief, but below this level feudal bonds had loosened or ended, especially after subinfeudation was prohibited in the reign of Edward I. A wealthy magnate, wishing to increase the number of his followers, sometimes made indentures with knights, country gentlemen, lawyers, chaplains, or even minstrels or cooks, to become his retainers in return for lands or money. These contracts were business arrangements quite outside the feudal structure. The services to be rendered were specified and varied, as was the length of the agreement. While the principal purpose of such contracts was obviously for display, they offered a magnate opportunity to aid his friends and kinsmen. Though very costly, they enabled a baron to raise a small army quickly, and thus added to his prestige in politics and society.

Knights and country gentlemen formed a lesser nobility, later known as gentry. Holding small estates of one or two manors, they were far below the great barons in wealth and power. Their primary interest was the management of their property. Knights, however, were still warriors trained to fight on horseback. They had received knighthood through an elaborate and costly ceremony, and were surprisingly few in number. In war they served as retainers in the retinue of the king or of a great magnate, or else commanded bodies of mercenary troops.

The Peasants

The life of the peasants altered less during the twelfth and thirteenth centuries than did the life of the upper classes. A peasant's status and obligations remained much the same as they had been in the years following the Norman Conquest. Such changes as occurred were due to the value of labor services in a time of agricultural prosperity and to the increase in the quantity and use of money, which deeply affected rural life.

The village was likely to be larger than in the past. The houses stretched along a single street or were arranged around a village green. Some cottages had a framework of wooden crucks, that is, of curved timbers which stood upright in the ground but bent together and met at the apex of the roof, where they were fastened to a pole that ran from one set of crucks to the next. A house of this type could be lengthened to form several rooms, though there were rarely more than two. The walls between the crucks were made either of hardened mud or timber. Beyond the village stretched the open fields, the meadow, the pasture, and the waste.

The basic division among the peasants was that between the freeman and the villein. The freeman was the virtual owner of his land. There was a feudal touch about his tenure, for he performed an act of homage to the lord of the manor and paid relief when he entered upon his holding. However, the rents and services he owed did not approach the value of the land, and so were not rents in the modern sense of

Open fields at Laxton, Nottinghamshire. (Aerofilms, Ltd.)

the word. By paying a fee he could obtain permission to sell his land, and in general he was much less at the lord's disposal than was the unfree villein. As the use of money increased, a class of lease-holders appeared who normally paid a rent commensurate to the true value of the land.

By far the largest number of peasants were unfree villeins who held land by servile tenure. Bound to the soil, they could not marry or leave the manor without the lord's consent. They owed him week work, that is, two or three days' work each week upon the demesne without compensation; and boon work, which meant extra labor at the busy times of plowing and harvesting. In addition, the villein owed substantial payments in kind, in animals and produce, at stated dates during the year. The villein must also attend the manorial court, which tried petty criminal offenses and any civil suits in which the peasant became involved. For serious crime he was tried in the courts of the king, but he could not bring civil suits into those courts. The normal holding of a villein was called a virgate and amounted roughly to thirty acres. Cotters, the lowest class of villeins living near the subsistence level, held perhaps five or ten acres and performed lighter services.

The villein lived in poverty, performed backbreaking labor, and was subject to galling restrictions. Because of the high price of agricultural products the lords wanted as much labor as possible, and there was a tendency for labor services to be carefully defined and strictly enforced. In a quarrel with his lord the villein was at a great disadvantage in the manorial court, though records indicate there were peasants who stood up for their rights. Yet there is reason to believe that the villein's lot was not as hard as the laws of villeinage might suggest. Week work was not as burdensome as it sounds. A villein with several sons need only send one to work on the demesne, and presumably that son was not the most efficient worker in the family. The villein's rights were protected by the custom of the manor and by the fact that a lord, dependent upon the labor of his villeins, could not afford to treat them harshly. Moreover, the rise of a money economy enabled a thrifty peasant to purchase land and to buy relief from some of the services he owed his lord. This process is known as commutation. Such relief did not make the villein a freeman, but it was a step in that direction. Commutation, which had begun in the twelfth century, diminished in the thirteenth because the lord required labor. Nonetheless, lords found that hired labor was more efficient and agreeable than unpaid workers.

Commerce

Commerce developed to a remarkable degree in medieval England. On the local level, weekly or monthly markets were held in towns when the country people came in to sell their produce and buy manufactured goods. The right to hold a market was acquired by a town or village from a local lord or sometimes from the king. It was a prized possession, for tolls were levied upon all who sold at the markets. Far more elaborate were the annual fairs held by a lord or a high churchman under a royal grant. These fairs attracted merchants from all over the country and sometimes from abroad. At the largest fairs a good deal of wholesale as well as retail business was carried on. Famous fairs were held at St. Ives (Huntingdonshire), Northampton, Stamford, and Boston. St. Giles's Fair at Winchester and Stourbridge Fair near Cambridge were international in scope. The dates for holding them were staggered so that merchants could travel from one to another. Courts, known in England as courts of piepoudre,[1] settled disputes on the spot according to the law merchant, a code of rules that had grown up among traders. By the thirteenth century much business was conducted outside the fairs by English merchants who had settled in the larger towns and seaports. These merchants played a large role in foreign trade, attracting many foreign merchants to England. It is evident that foreign commerce existed on a large scale, that commodities traveled over long distances, and that trade was concerned not merely with the import of luxuries but with the exchange of basic goods.

The largest single article of import was wine from Gascony in southern France. Most of this trade was carried in French ships, for the amount of English shipping was small. In exchange for wine the French bought English grain, fish, and coarsely woven woolen cloth. The economies of England and Gascony complemented each other nicely, and the trade was highly important to both areas.

Except for woolen cloth, English exports consisted almost entirely of raw materials: tin, lead, a little coal, grain, fish, salted meats, sheepskins (including fleece), leather, and, above all, wool. Wool, the basic article of English foreign commerce, was produced in enormous quantities. The poorest peasants possessed a few sheep,

[1] From the French *pied poudre,* meaning that men came into the court informally with dusty shoes.

SOCIAL AND ECONOMIC LIFE 133

Agricultural scenes, fourteenth century. (British Library, the Luttrell Psalter Additional MS 42,130, Historical Pictures Service, Chicago)

WEEDING.

REAPING

TYING UP SHEAVES

CARTING CORN
C. A.D. 1340.
Loutrell Psalter.

but the monasteries of Yorkshire and Lincolnshire, such as the Cistercian abbeys of Fountains and Rievaulx, owned huge flocks and acted as agents to collect wool from smaller producers to sell directly to Italian merchants. At the end of the thirteenth century England was exporting about 32,000 sacks of wool a year, which amounted to nearly 6000 tons.

This extraordinary expansion of trade was due to the foreign merchants, who bought about two thirds of the wool exported from the country. The merchants of the Hanseatic League, a commercial alliance of north German cities which dominated the trade of the Baltic Sea, had secured many privileges in England. They had their own guildhall in London and were exempt from paying duty on cloth. They exported wool, cloth, and tin, and brought in timber and furs from the Baltic and fine cloth from Flanders. Flemish merchants exported English wool, which came back in the form of cloth from Flanders. The Italian merchants were the most important, representing large firms in northern Italy, where industry, commerce, finance, and banking were more advanced than anywhere else in Europe. They had come to England originally as papal tax collectors. These taxes were paid in produce as well as in money, and the Italians became accustomed to handling English wool. They had large cash balances in the country and formed connections with English religious houses. They not only bought great quantities of wool, but served as bankers, supplying capital and credit and teaching Englishmen the techniques of finance and international trade. They imported wines, fruit, raisins and currants, as well as the luxuries of the East—Oriental rugs, silks, muslins and other fine cloth, spices, and precious stones. The Italian merchants were held in high regard by the king, who protected them, granted them many privileges, borrowed heavily from them, and eventually ruined their position in England when he failed to repay his loans.

Industry

In the twelfth and thirteenth centuries England was essentially a producer of raw materials. Industry, lagging behind commerce, was primitive in comparison with industrial development in Flanders or Italy. Some industries were carried on in rural areas. Coal, tin, and iron were mined in considerable quantity; some weaving of woolen cloth was done in the country, for a good deal of the manufacture could be performed in a peasant's cottage; the making of iron had to be carried on near forests which supplied charcoal for fuel. But the towns, of course, were the industrial centers. An established artisan who owned a house manufactured articles of common use—shoes, candles, or clothing—in a back room or shed and displayed them for sale in another room opening onto the street.

Merchants or craftsmen formed themselves into guilds to protect their interests and monopolize particular trades. In many towns an organization known as the guild merchant was composed of all those who offered goods for sale. Its purpose was to control the trade of the town. Merchants from other towns were subjected to many restrictions. They must pay tolls, they were forbidden to deal in certain articles, and they must conduct wholesale business only with members of the guild merchant. The guilds settled disputes among their members and attempted to protect them in other towns. They were also fraternal and charitable societies. Their meetings, held for conducting business, were social occasions with much feasting and drinking; to "drink the guild merchant" was to attend an assembly of the fraternity. The guilds assumed responsibility for members in sickness and old age, attended their funerals, and supported the widows and orphans of those who died in poverty. But their principal purpose was always to protect their economic interests in a highly exclusive and monopolistic spirit.

As industry became more complex in the larger towns, guilds known as craft guilds were formed of artisans engaged in a single craft. In the middle of the fourteenth century the more important guilds in London were listed as the "grocers, mercers, fishmongers, drapers, goldsmiths, woolmongers, vintners, saddlers, tailors, cordwainers, butchers, and ironmongers." These guilds were similar in many ways to the guilds merchant but were more exclusively interested in industry. They set standards for the quality of the goods produced, regulated holidays and hours of work, and fixed prices and wages to some extent.

The desire to ensure high standards of competence in trade and industry led to a system of apprenticeship. In return for a sum of money from the parents of the apprentice, the master agreed to support him and to teach him the mysteries of his craft. When his seven-year apprenticeship was over, the student was eligible to become a master and could open a shop of his own. Before the end of the thirteenth century, however, many apprentices discovered that they could not set themselves up in business, having worked without wages for seven years. The capital required for such a venture had increased, the trade could support only a limited number of masters, and the masters had no wish to admit new members. Many apprentices, unable to become masters, remained as employees working for wages. They were known as journeymen, and in the fourteenth century they formed guilds of their own. Like the guild merchant, the craft guilds were fraternal and charitable societies. It was the masters who ran the guilds. As time went on, the guilds became more aristocratic, dominated by the richer masters who almost always controlled the government of the town.

The Towns

By the end of the thirteenth century there were more than 100 towns or boroughs in England.[2] The towns differed greatly in size, importance, and the amount of their independence from their lords or from the king. London, with a population of between 25,000 and 40,000, was by far the largest. The population of Bristol was about 17,000, that of Norwich about 13,000, that of York about 10,000. Many towns were little places of perhaps 2000 or 3000 inhabitants. They were small struggling communities in an alien world of barons, castles, and monasteries. Nonetheless, the towns were becoming an important element in medieval society. A village became a borough when the lord permitted its inhabitants to hold their land by burgage tenure, which allowed them to pay rent in place of the normal obligations of the manor. As the towns grew in size and importance they became self-conscious communities with

---

[2]A town was called a city only when it contained a cathedral and was thus the administrative center of a diocese.

a corporate spirit, and their increased wealth permitted them to bargain with their lord or with the king for charters granting them varying degrees of self-government and independence.

These charters began in the eleventh century, and eventually most towns of any consequence held charters from the king. They never became free cities, as did some of the towns in Germany and Italy, for the government of the king was too strong and all-pervasive. Towns generally wished to collect the rents, tolls, taxes, and court fines it owed the Crown and to pay the king in a lump sum in order to free it from interference by the sheriff in its internal affairs. For the same reason, towns wished to receive and execute the king's writs, and to hold courts. Seeking freedom from tolls imposed by other towns and districts, towns wanted to hold markets or fairs and to levy tolls on merchandise sold within their borders. Finally, they wished to establish guilds and to elect their own officials. Only the more important and wealthy towns could hope to obtain all or most of these privileges, and there was great diversity.

The government of the towns differed widely. In a simple form of government the burgesses met in the borough court and elected a mayor. Burgesses paid taxes and owned property in a way similar to members of the guild merchant. In larger boroughs the mayor was assisted by a council, the councilors being known as aldermen. By the close of the thirteenth century many towns had lost their democratic features and were governed by oligarchies over which the burgesses had little control. The aldermen remained in office for long—even lifelong—terms, choosing new aldermen as vacancies occurred in their membership and electing one of their own number as mayor.

CHRONOLOGY

Norman and Gothic

1090–	Norman style architecture used
1142–	Peter Abelard, *Sic et Non;* Anselm disagrees
1167 and after	Oxford University founded; followed by Cambridge
1179–	First Carthusian monastery, Witham Abbey
1221–	First Dominican Friars in England
1224–	First Franciscan Friars in England
Late 12th century	Gothic architecture appears
12th and 13th centuries	Commercial and urban revivals; increasing agricultural productivity; increase in population

7. Edward I and Edward II: The Beginnings of Parliament

EDWARD I, 1272–1307

Edward I, who ascended the throne in 1272, was determined to assert his rights as sovereign and to fully exercise his powers of kingship. Although aggressive and sometimes unscrupulous, Edward was dominated by a concept of the community of the realm and of the common good. This concept assumed that the kingdom was a corporate society, that there was a body politic, that government should be conducted for the general welfare, and that this welfare transcended the advantage of individuals or of social classes. The king, Edward believed, should act as judge and legislator, exerting his full powers of kingship to promote the public good. Yet, as subjects had certain protected rights, a king should consult with learned counselors when those rights were in question.

Edward was not an innovator like Henry II; he was, however, an organizer and administrator who desired order, efficiency, and a smoothly running government. During the first half of his reign he made prolonged and careful inquiries into many aspects of government. These inquiries formed the most thorough process of stocktaking since the days of William the Conqueror. On the basis of his findings Edward reconstructed the administration of the government and of the law, partly by statutes, partly by informal instructions to his ministers. His reign was a period of legal definition. He did not aim to make new law but to restate the old with gaps, errors, and inconsistencies removed. His statutes concerned a wide variety of subjects: the duties and powers of officials, the feudal rights of the magnates, the militia and the police, the merchants, the land law, the civil and criminal law, legal procedure, and the reform of organs of government. At the same time he pursued a spirited foreign policy in defense of his rights in Wales, Scotland, and France; he hoped to unite the nations of Europe in a new crusade.

For many years Edward ruled successfully, yet after 1293 he became entangled in protracted wars which proved to be more costly than the resources of the Crown could support. Such financial straits aroused the discontent of the magnates, and in later years led to rapid development in methods of taxation and in the growth of Parliament.

Edward's character is not easy to understand. An active man, both physically and mentally, Edward responded to every situation with vigor and determination. He was a majestic figure, tall, erect, lithe, and athletic, fulfilling the medieval ideal of what a king should be. As a crusader and warrior who hated to be crossed, Edward loved tournaments and hunting, fiercely defended his frontiers, and made foreign conquests. He spoke with firmness and clarity. Conventional yet industrious in government, he lavished care upon his statutes and administration. And yet there was a cold and unsympathetic quality about him, perhaps due to the legal cast of his mind. If the law was on his side, he was apt to exact his pound of flesh. He endangered his conquest of Wales and destroyed his hopes of success in Scotland by the rigidity with which he stood upon what he considered his legal rights. He was easily moved to anger and hated to be crossed. A conventional man, he lacked imagination and humanity, and a slothful strain in his character suggests that his resolution and energy were not entirely natural but sprang from a sense of duty and obligation.

THE GOVERNMENT OF EDWARD I

Edward governed in close collaboration with his principal advisers. They were his great officials, such as the chancellor and the treasurer, the heads of lesser departments, the judges, the "king's clerks" who saw him daily and wrote his letters, and a few knights and magnates who took part in the central administration. Most of them, drawn from the middle class, were bureaucrats who spent their lives as royal officials and grew old in the king's service. Some who rose to high positions were recruited from the lower ranks of the king's service, from the households of barons and churchmen, or were recommended to the king by patrons. A closely knit society of clerics and laymen, a self-conscious elite in the personnel of royal administration, they moved from department to department doing all kinds of business.

The barons did not relish the growth of this bureaucracy, but Edward selected his officials as he pleased. His best-loved servant for the first sixteen years of his reign was the chancellor, Robert Burnell, who became a major figure in the government and a clearinghouse for all kinds of public affairs. A shrewd and competent man of business with a fine mind but with probably no great education, he had entered Edward's household in 1254 and had served him in many capacities. He rose to be chancellor, bishop of Bath and Wells, and the king's closest adviser. He and others like him served Edward well.

There were four principal parts of the administrative side of the government: the Chancery, the Exchequer, the Household, and the Council. The Chancery was the secretarial department where charters, writs, and formal letters were prepared by a staff of skillful clerks. The chancellor was the keeper of the Great Seal used to authenticate documents. He was usually a churchman, sometimes the archbishop of Canterbury, though the pope denied that office to Burnell, who was more businessman than cleric. The Exchequer received and issued money, scrutinized the semiannual accounts of sheriffs and other local officials, and kept the pipe rolls. It was presided over by the treasurer, its important officials were known as the barons of the Exchequer, and it was staffed by a large number of clerks. Both departments were now old and venerable, and they had gone out of court, that is, they were separate departments distinct from the Household and the Council. They were stationary at Westminster. It would be a mistake to think that they were removed from the central administration. The chancellor and the treasurer were important councilors and familiar figures in the Household. Burnell was no less a trusted servant of the king because he did much of his work in his own department.

Nonetheless, the procedures of the Chancery and the Exchequer had become somewhat formal, routine, and cumbersome. Edward felt a loss of efficiency when he was on a journey or a campaign while the chancellor or the treasurer remained in London. He therefore followed the practice of earlier kings in developing the Household, which normally traveled with him. Its staff was large, with perhaps fifty officials. Within the Household wherever he went he had his private apartments or chamber, the inner sanctum of government. In the chamber, protected by ushers who guarded the doors, Edward talked in private with his intimate friends and advisers and made those countless decisions which did not require consultation with the whole Council. The principal steward of the Household was a layman, usually a knight of high social position, who was close to the king and was an important figure at court.

The portion of the Household which developed most fully in Edward's reign was the wardrobe. It had its treasurer or keeper, its controller, its cofferer, and many clerks. There was a privy seal in the wardrobe, a small royal seal the king kept with him. It was employed to authenticate letters dispatched from the Household and to send instructions to the chancellor concerning the use of the Great Seal at Westminster. Various revenues, diverted from the Exchequer, were brought directly to the wardrobe, which became the organ of government Edward used to finance his wars. Thus miniature secretarial and financial departments were created within the wardrobe independent of the Chancery and the Exchequer. The barons did not like this development, for they thought it made the king too independent, and in the reign of Edward II they found occasion to end the wardrobe's expansion.

The most vital organ of administration was the king's Council.[1] It consisted of his principal ministers, his judges, his most trusted clerks, and a select few of the magnates. The Council dealt with all kinds of business. Here the king consulted with

---

[1] In discussing the century following the Norman Conquest, the term "small council" has been used to refer to the group of officials in constant attendance upon the king, and the term "Great Council" to refer to a meeting of the tenants in chief. In the thirteenth century the smaller group was called the Council and the larger group was coming to be known as Parliament.

his advisers in a more formal way than in the chamber, and here he made important decisions. His close association with his councilors, including his judges, gave firmness and confidence to his policy, for he felt that he was not acting alone. The Council did a great deal of administrative work. It dealt with matters that were unusual or extraordinary or did not fall within the competence of established departments, which often referred difficult points to the Council.

Above all, the Council was a court. It tried cases that fell outside the jurisdiction of other courts, or that other courts could not determine, or that the king referred to the Council because his interests were involved. The Council reviewed cases from the lower courts on writs of error, though the notion of appeal played little part in medieval common law. There was an element of equity in the Council's legal decisions, for the Council was close to the king and felt no obligation to adhere strictly to the common law. It framed new writs and interpreted the meaning of royal charters. Cases of unusual importance or difficulty were brought before it, for it was regarded as higher than other courts. And sometimes, when a case was of a public nature and affected the whole community, it was taken to the assembly of the king's tenants in chief of which the Council was a part. This Great Council, now called Parliament, was the highest court of all.

The Law

Edward and his judges were influenced by a famous book, *Concerning the Laws and Customs of England,* which had been written about the middle of the thirteenth century by Henry de Bracton, the greatest of English medieval jurists. Bracton had been a judge under Henry III, and his book was a description of the daily operation of the law in the king's courts. He showed how the common law had grown from the accumulation of decisions in the royal courts and how principles of law could be deduced from particular cases. Bracton set forth the doctrine that the king must not govern by caprice but by the rules of the law. The king, said Bracton, was not under man but under God and under the law, for it was the law that made him king. The king was the fountain of justice. All jurisdiction in private or local hands, though protected by charters or by long usage, was derived ultimately from the Crown.

The growth of the common law during the thirteenth century had steadily strengthened the principles set forth by Bracton. As the itinerant justices had carried the common law throughout the kingdom they had undermined the ancient jurisdiction of the hundred and the shire courts and had reduced the scope of the private courts of barons and great churchmen. Royal justice was on its way to supremacy. Yet when Edward came to the throne there were many areas, known as franchises or liberties, in which jurisdiction was in private hands, especially in the north and west. The most conspicuous example was the county palatine of the bishop of Durham, where the bishop had his own justices, sheriffs, and chancery, and where he exercised a jurisdiction within his liberty similar to that of the king in other parts of the realm. Franchises were held by many lords in the Welsh marches, by the church of Ely, and by the abbot of Bury St. Edmunds, while lesser lords had restricted rights over what had once been hundred courts.

In the reign of Henry III the government had occasionally issued writs of quo warranto, demanding to know by what warrant a lord exercised his rights of private jurisdiction. The principle of these writs was carried much further in the Statute of Gloucester (1278) in which Edward declared that all holders of private jurisdiction must prove their warrant before the king's justices. A few of the barons possessed royal charters which justified their rights, but most of them did not. They strongly resented the king's action. Edward therefore offered a compromise by which he confirmed jurisdictions that had been exercised without interruption since the accession of Richard I in 1189. As a result of the quo warranto proceedings Edward did not annul many franchises, but he curbed their expansion and established the principles that private jurisdictions were delegations from the Crown and that the Crown could interfere in them if it saw reason. Franchises grew less and less important as time passed.

Edward also attempted to adjust the law relating to land held by feudal tenure. Feudal relations remained important as a set of fiscal rights, but as land was subinfeudated again and again over the years, the arrangements concerning it grew highly complicated, and the tenants in chief had difficulty in obtaining the feudal incidents due them. They complained to the king that they were losing their rights, and Edward knew that he was losing in the same way. His legislation was an effort to protect himself and his tenants in chief in this respect.

The Statute of Mortmain (1279) prohibited a vassal from giving land to the church without his lord's consent. The difficulty here was that a gift of land by a vassal to the church deprived the lord of most of the feudal incidents because the church never married, had children, or died; hence the land was held by a dead hand (mortmain) so far as the grantor's lord was concerned. As a matter of fact, grants to the church continued, for Edward was soon selling the right to break the statute.

In 1285 Edward issued the Second Statute of Westminster which, among other provisions, regulated the rights of both parties when a lord sought to recover land from a tenant who was not fulfilling his feudal obligations. The most important clause in the statute, the clause beginning with the words *De Donis Conditionalibus*, established the principle of entailed estates. An entailed estate was one which could descend from one generation to the next only under the conditions set forth in the original grant. The grant normally required that the entire estate should pass as a whole from father to eldest son. The effect was to hold the estate together, to make it heritable as an undivided unit, and to strengthen the principle of primogeniture.

In the Statute of Quia Emptores (1290) Edward prohibited further subinfeudation. Henceforth, if A granted (or sold) land to B, B did not become the vassal of A but of A's lord. Only the king could now make a man his feudal vassal. The unforeseen result of this statute was that feudal relations declined in importance. Land became an article of commerce to be bought and sold at the pleasure of the owner. These statutes indicate that although feudalism was passing away it left a deep and permanent stamp upon the land law of England.

The Machinery of Justice

Edward improved the machinery of justice in the courts at Westminster and in the work of the itinerant justices. At Westminster, as we have seen, the highest tribunals of justice were the king in Council and those solemn assemblies known as Parliaments. Below them were three central courts of common law which had developed during the thirteenth century. By Edward's reign these courts had separated or were separating from the rest of the government. One was the Court of Exchequer. From an early date the Exchequer had found that collection of money from the king's debtors had involved some legal business. So swift and efficient had been the methods of the Exchequer in collecting these debts that private creditors had wished to have their debts collected by the same tribunal. Thus the Exchequer began to try cases between private litigants involving debts and the collection of damages. During the thirteenth century the Court of Exchequer separated from the financial Exchequer. It had its own roll and its own judges, who were known as Barons of the Exchequer.

A second court was the Court of Common Pleas. The faint foreshadowings of this court may be seen in 1178, when Henry II had set aside five justices to remain at Westminster to hear pleas. Magna Carta (Article 17) had decreed that common pleas were to be held in some fixed place. During the thirteenth century this court also separated from the Council and acquired a roll and judges of its own. It dealt with civil cases, that is, disputes over property. The third court of common law was the Court of the King's Bench. It may be discerned in Edward's reign though it had not yet separated from the Council. It was closer to the king than the other two courts because it tried criminal cases (the pleas of the Crown) in which the king as guardian of the peace had a special interest.

Edward increased the efficiency of the central law courts by designating certain periods of time each year, known as the law terms, when the courts were all to be in session. Four law terms were established: Hilary term, which lasted for a month or six weeks early in the year; Easter term, later in the spring; Trinity term, in the summer; and Michaelmas term, which was the longest of the four and might continue for some ten weeks in the course of the autumn. The itinerant justices were normally sent out on circuit during the intervals between the terms. Circuits were arranged so that the justices visited each locality once a year. In the past the justices had been burdened with very heavy commissions and had been required to do all sorts of administrative and judicial work; hence their stay in each locality had been prolonged and tedious. A whole village had once taken to the woods at their approach. In place of these general iters in which many kinds of business were transacted, Edward sent out the justices with limited commissions. They normally tried one class of cases only. This made their circuits more rapid and efficient, and the general iter came to an end. Lawyers were attached to the courts visited by the itinerant justices, so that litigants could obtain legal counsel if they so desired. Thus the whole machinery of justice was made to function with more order and precision.

The reign of Edward I marked a definite break in the history of the common law. During the century from about 1150 to about 1250 the law had been flexible and growing rapidly. New law developed from the decisions of the justices and from new writs issued by the chancellor. The result was rapid legal development but also some confusion. It was Edward's achievement, by his statutes, to give the law order and organization, but he also made it more rigid. Judge-made law is flexible; statue law is fixed and timeless. Statutes blocked the growth of unenacted law. This process of ending the law's flexibility had begun under Henry III. The barons, suspicious of the king, had opposed the issue of new writs by the chancellor, because new writs made new law. The Provisions of Oxford stated that new writs were to be issued only with the consent of both king and Council (which was to be baronial). Under Edward I the principle was growing that new law could be made only with the consent of Parliament. Rigidity also was increased by a new type of judge and by the rise of a legal profession. Both judges and lawyers were specialists. They knew the common law but cared little about other forms of knowledge, and the study of Roman law was neglected. The common law ceased to grow amid a general feeling that it was nearly complete. The way was opened for the eventual rise of a system of equity and the court of chancery.

EDWARD AND THE CELTIC PEOPLES

As England grew stronger and more wealthy in the thirteenth century she was certain to extend her influence into the Celtic lands of Wales, Scotland, and Ireland. It is not surprising that during the Middle Ages this process reached its height in the reign of an aggressive king like Edward I, who subdued the Welsh, fought the Scots in futile wars that altered the course of Anglo-Scottish history, and increased royal power in Ireland.

Wales

In the thirteenth century the Welsh were still a pastoral people living in a primitive state. Matters of marriage and legitimacy were taken rather lightly. They had no towns. The peasants built temporary huts out of tree boughs as they followed their cattle from one pasture ground to another. The only area where grain was grown in any quantity was on the island of Anglesey. The people were divided into tribes ruled by chieftains, who lived high in the mountains and counted their wealth in terms of cattle. Constantly warring, the tribes fought by rushing down the mountainside in a wild, disordered charge sounding war horns and flinging themselves upon their foes. If the first savage rush was repulsed, the attackers turned and fled. Bards and minstrels, with vivid imaginations and great musical skill, sang rather dolefully of the glories and wealth of ancient warriors and kings.

Shortly after the Norman Conquest, a number of Norman barons had pushed into central Wales, where they built castles, carved out baronies, and imposed servile obligations upon the peasants. Many of the Welsh had fled to their tribal chieftains in the hills and from there raided and fought the Norman intruders. Although the barons in the marches of Wales were feudal vassals of England, the king's writ held no authority in their lands; the barons ruled as though little kings. As such, they represented Norman expansion rather than the spreading influence of English monarchy.

In the thirteenth century there was a Welsh revival under the Llywelyn princes of Gwynedd, an area in North Wales centering upon the mountainous district of Snowdon. Llywelyn ap Gruffydd, Prince of Wales, had conquered a large principality in the northern and central parts of the country, some of it taken from the marcher lords. Recognized by Henry III in 1267, it was independent in all but name, though nominally held as a feudal fief from the King of England. Llywelyn might have kept it had he not acted with great arrogance and indiscretion toward Edward. He refused to do homage when Edward came to the throne, making the excuse that his brother David, an exile in England, was plotting against him. In 1275 he arranged a marriage with Eleanor, a daughter of Simon de Montfort, but she was captured by the English as she sailed from France to Wales. This episode brought about war in 1277. In a masterly campaign assisted by many marcher lords, Edward invaded Wales with a large army, closed in upon Llywelyn as he hid in the fastnesses of Snowdon, and starved him into submission. By the Treaty of Conway late in 1277 Llywelyn surrendered the lands he had taken from the marcher barons. Paying a large indemnity, he did homage as Edward demanded. He then was permitted to marry Eleanor and to retain the title of Prince of Wales.

The Treaty of Conway lasted for a little more than four years, but there was bitter litigation over the lands to be returned to the marcher lords. Llywelyn accused Edward and his judges of bad faith, and in 1282 a revolt broke out in Wales. It was begun by David, Llywelyn's brother, but Llywelyn quickly joined it. Once more Edward invaded the country. At first the Welsh met with some success but very shortly they were discouraged by the death of Llywelyn, who was killed almost by chance, and the capture of David. The revolt was over in 1283. The Statute of Rhuddlan in the following year annexed Llywelyn's principality to the Crown of England.

Edward's infant son was presented at Caernarvon Castle and designated "Prince of Wales." The title is still conferred upon the eldest son of a reigning monarch, signifying him as the male heir to the throne.

The principality was divided into shires, English criminal law was introduced, and the country was administered by the justices of North and South Wales. Edward built a series of magnificent castles to ensure his conquest. These castles—the majestic ruins of which are still standing—were constructed at a time when the art of castle building had reached its height. They were elaborate, strong, and very expensive. The most important were Conway, Harlech, Rhuddlan, Beaumaris, and Caernarvon. The portions of Wales outside the principality remained, through the rest of the Middle Ages, in the hands of the marcher lords, whose semi-independent status Edward dared not disturb. The Welsh were conquered, though their assimilation with England was only beginning.

Beaumaris Castle, Anglesey, built by Edward I. Note the double wall and flanking towers. (Aerofilms, Ltd.)

Scotland

In contrast to the success of Edward's wars in Wales, his wars against the Scots formed the greatest blunder of his reign. Not only did he fail to conquer Scotland; he aroused among the Scots a hatred of England that was to last for centuries.

The kingdom of Scotland had been created by the gradual union of four distinct peoples: Picts, Scots, Britons, and Angles. The Picts were the original Celtic inhabitants; the Scots came from Ireland, largely in the fifth century, and occupied the area of modern Argyllshire; a little later the Angles in Northumbria extended that kingdom northward to the Firth of Forth, thus including a portion of what is now modern Scotland; the final element, the Britons, were Celts who had been pushed westward into Strathclyde by the Angles of Northumbria. The process of unification began in the year 843, when Kenneth MacAlpin, king of Scots, subdued the Picts and added Pict-land to Scot-land. Scotland was deeply affected by the Viking invasions. Settling first in the Shetland and Orkney Islands, the Norsemen moved down the western coast of Scotland, separating the Scots from their old connections with Ireland. Meanwhile, Danish invaders destroyed the Anglo-Saxon kingdom of Northumbria; eventually the northern portion of Northumbria was united with Scotland. This all-important part of Scotland, extending from the Cheviot Hills to the Firth of Forth and centering upon the rock-fortress of Edinburgh, was inhabited by Angles, who added a Germanic element to the Scottish people. After the Norman Conquest other Anglo-Saxons fled northward to escape the fury of William the Conqueror. Meanwhile the kings of Scotland acquired domination over the Britons in northern Strathclyde.

In the centuries between the Norman Conquest and the reign of Edward I, English and Norman influences penetrated into the Lowlands of Scotland, while Celtic and tribal life shrank back into the Highlands. This process began in the reign of King Malcolm III (1058–1093), who had spent his boyhood at the court of Edward the Confessor. His second wife, the saintly and strong-minded Margaret, was a Saxon princess. She strengthened the use of the Anglo-Saxon tongue in Scotland and introduced reforms in the Scottish church, bringing it in line with the church in England and on the Continent. Her son, David I (1124–1153), transformed Scotland into a feudal kingdom. He too had lived in England. He saw the vast superiority of the Norman knight fighting on horseback over the wild rush of the Celts as they flung themselves with spear and claymore upon their foes. He therefore invited English and Norman barons, including the families of Balliol and Bruce, to come to Scotland and to accept fiefs from him as his feudal vassals. The Normans built castles in Scotland and enforced servile obligations upon the peasantry, but as in England they also built churches and monasteries. David introduced into Scotland many English and Norman institutions of law and government. Thus in the twelfth and thirteenth centuries a feudal kingdom, though not a strong one, arose in the Scottish Lowlands. Turning its back on the Celtic Highlands, it looked to England and maintained fairly cordial relations with that country.

This era of Anglo-Scottish amity came to an end in the reign of Edward I. In 1286 the Scottish king, Alexander III, was killed when his horse fell over a sea cliff. His only heir was his little granddaughter, Margaret, a child of about three who was living in Norway. Her mother, Alexander's daughter, had married the king of Norway but was now dead. In 1290 the Scots and Edward I arranged a treaty by which the "Fair Maid of Norway" was to be brought home to be married to Edward's son, the future Edward II. The Scots inserted clauses in the treaty guaranteeing their independence. Had the treaty taken effect the two countries, each with its own institutions, would have remained separate kingdoms under the same king.

Unhappily, the little "Maid of Norway" died on the voyage to Scotland, leaving the Scottish throne in dispute. Nine claimants arose, including John Balliol and Robert Bruce; the number soon swelled to thirteen. Fearing a prolonged civil war, some of the Scots suggested that Edward be asked for aid and counsel. Seeing an opportunity to advance his interests, Edward summoned the Scottish barons to meet him at Norham on the English side of the border, where he declared that he would do justice among the many claimants to the Scottish throne but that he would do so as the feudal lord of the kings of Scotland. This claim was highly doubtful. It was true that some Scottish kings had been vassals of the Norman kings of England, but in 1189 Richard I, willing to turn any right into cash, had freed the kings of Scotland from this obligation; henceforth they had done homage only for lands they held in England. Nine of the Scottish claimants, however, accepted Edward's terms, each hoping to ingratiate himself with the king and thus obtain the Scottish throne.

Scotland.

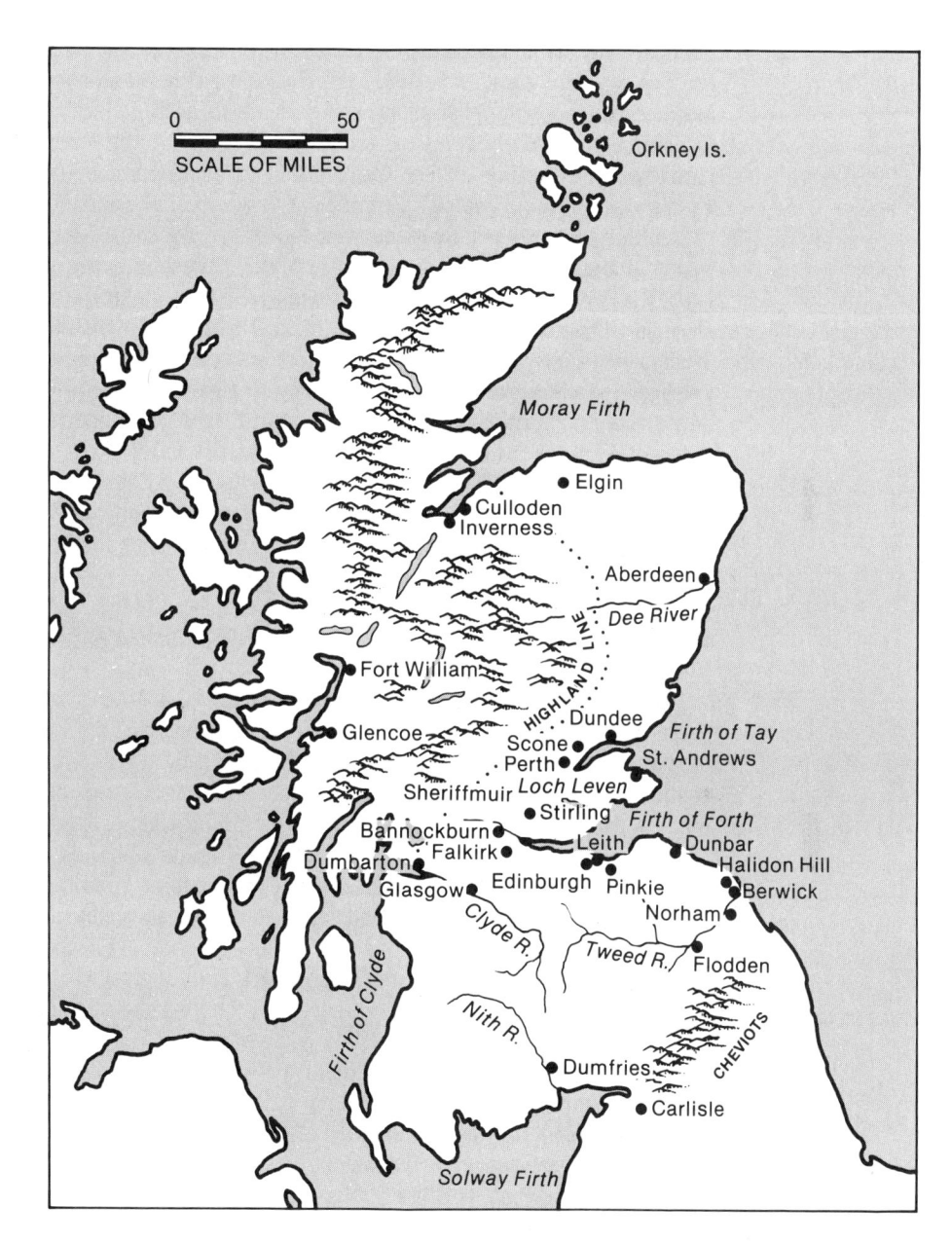

Edward's decision, which was quite justifiable, went in favor of John Balliol, who was crowned in 1292 and did homage to Edward as his lord. Edward soon showed his determination to exercise fully his rights as feudal suzerain. He accepted appeals from Scottish courts, summoned Balliol to England as a feudal vassal, and demanded military service for a campaign in Gascony. Such opposition arose in Scotland that Balliol was forced to refuse Edward's demands. The Scots allied themselves with the

French, with whom Edward went to war in 1294. In 1296 he marched north to punish the Scots. Their army was defeated, Balliol was forced to abdicate and was thrust aside. Making a triumphal progress as far north as Elgin, Edward brought back to England the Stone of Scone and sacred relics from the abbey at Holyrood. He held a parliament at Berwick, where the Scottish barons did homage to him as their king. English garrisons occupied the principal fortresses of Scotland.

But this conquest of Scotland was too easy to endure. Edward had aroused in Scotland a spirit not often found in the Middle Ages—a spirit of democratic patriotism. The revolt that broke out in 1297 was not led by the nobility, many of whom held lands in England and had no wish to quarrel with the English king. The leader was William Wallace, a member of the gentry, under whose inspiration scattered risings swelled into a national revolt. Defeating an English force at Stirling, Wallace began to harry the northern counties of England. Edward came north again in 1298 and defeated Wallace at the Battle of Falkirk, which ended Wallace's effective career. As resistance continued English armies entered Scotland almost yearly. In 1303–1304 Edward subdued the country for a second time; captured Wallace, who died a traitor's death; and took up the reins of government once more. Another revolt took place in 1306 under a new leader, Robert Bruce, the grandson of the claimant of 1290. Defeated in his first encounters, Bruce resorted to guerrilla tactics in which he was making progress when Edward died in 1307 as he led an army northward for the last time.

His death left the struggle more equal, for Edward II was a man of small capacity. With the aid of Sir James Douglas, Bruce established himself as King Robert I, destroyed his personal enemies, raided England, and gradually captured the Scottish castles in English hands. Edward II occupied at home quarreling with magnates, made a supreme effort in 1314 to relieve Stirling Castle. Invading Scotland with a large army he pushed on to Stirling. Not far from its walls, on the field of Bannockburn, his army found itself caught on a narrow strip of ground flanked on both sides by marshes. His cavalry, trapped and helpless, was unable to maneuver and his archers could not fan out to harass the Scots. The homely Scottish sheltrons, bodies of massed spearsmen, thrust the English back upon themselves. The battle became a rout and the rout a disaster, the worst defeat for English arms in all the Middle Ages.

Bannockburn gave the Scots their independence. During the rest of the Middle Ages English kings became too involved in France to return to the conquest of Scotland. But the Scots paid a heavy price for their freedom. Warfare along the border exposed the wealthiest part of Scotland to devastating raids. The French alliance brought far more harm than benefit. Scotland remained a lawless, backward, and poverty-stricken land, its nobles quarrelsome, its church corrupt, its economy primitive, and its government weak and inefficient.

Ireland

At the beginning of Edward's reign, Ireland, like Wales, was a half-conquered country. There were really three Irelands. The English Pale, a narrow coastal strip behind Dublin and Drogheda, was settled by Englishmen in the twelfth century and had adopted the English law and language. The Pale was governed from Dublin, where there was a justiciar who represented English authority, with an Exchequer and a Chancery on the English model. But the Pale was small. The western and northern half of the island was almost purely Celtic. There were tribal chieftains as in Wales, a pastoral people who counted their wealth in cattle, constant intertribal wars, cattle rustling as a national preoccupation, minstrelsy, and only primitive agriculture.

Between the Pale and this Celtic world was a middle zone which blended the frontiers and characteristics of the others. It had been conquered, or partially conquered, in the twelfth century by Norman barons, much like those who had pressed into central Wales. Indeed, many of these barons came from the Welsh marches and were partly Welsh in blood. Led by "Strongbow" Richard de Clare, Earl of Pembroke, they had defeated the Irish in various areas, had erected baronies, and had built castles according to Norman custom. Although their descendants in Edward's reign owed allegiance to the distant king of England, the Anglo-Irish barons did about as they pleased. Surrounded by a Celtic atmosphere and isolated from England, in time they resembled Irish chieftains rather than the barons of England.

Edward made efforts to increase his influence in Ireland by extending the Pale, introducing a parliament at Dublin on the English model, and increasing the commerce of a few coastal towns such as Dublin, Cork, and Waterford. By neglecting to actually visit that country, however, the king accomplished little. After Bannockburn, Edward Bruce, the brother of the Scottish king, invaded Ireland through Ulster, rousing the Celtic Irish and some of the Anglo-Irish barons against English rule, and carrying fire and sword to the very walls of Dublin. English power in Ireland suffered greatly from this incursion and declined during the fourteenth century. The Pale became a little island of English life in an alien Celtic world. The only king of England who visited Ireland during the rest of the Middle Ages was Richard II, but his authority crumbled at home and his Irish policy collapsed. The English conquest of Ireland began again in modern times.

EDWARD I AND FRANCE

The first twenty years of Edward's reign were remarkably successful. His reorganization of government and law, his famous statutes, his conquest of Wales, his early successes in Scotland, and his able diplomacy on the Continent—all belong to this period. About the year 1293, however, there was change for the worse. Revolts occurred in Wales in 1294 and 1295 that required immediate attention. The war with Scotland, begun in 1296, continued intermittently for the rest of the reign. And above all, Edward became involved in war with France. Military operations on the Continent against such a powerful kingdom as France were more costly and difficult than were the wars in Britain. Edward's expenses soared far beyond the resources at his disposal. His constant demands for taxation aroused bitter opposition at home.

From the Norman Conquest to the middle of the fifteenth century—a span of almost 400 years—the kings of England held large possessions in France. This fact was the fundamental cause of the many wars between the two countries. As the kings of France extended their power over the great French fiefs and as France developed a sense of nationality, the constant ambition of French rulers was to drive out the English. And yet no English king could relinquish his holdings on the Continent without incurring disfavor and disgrace at home. An important step in Anglo-French relations had been taken in a treaty between Henry III and Louis IX in 1259. Henry abandoned all claim to Normandy, Maine, Anjou, and Poitou. In return he was confirmed in his title of duke of Aquitaine and in his lordship of Gascony as a fief from the king of France. In addition Henry was promised certain territories to the north and east of Gascony which had once belonged to Henry II and Eleanor of Aquitaine but had later been lost to France. He never obtained possession of these territories, and in a later treaty in 1279 Edward wisely agreed to accept part of them and to relinquish his claim to the rest. For many years his relations with France were not unfriendly.

Then in 1293 the French king, Philip IV (1285–1314), determined to undermine the English position in Gascony by asserting his authority as supreme lord of that area. Taking his cue from Edward's actions in Scotland, Philip encouraged appeals to his feudal court from Edward's vassals in Gascony and summoned Edward to appear in Paris. Edward refused the summons and made grandiose plans for an attack upon France in 1294. A large army was collected in England; and alliances were concluded with Philip's enemies, the count of Flanders, the duke of Brabant, and Adolf of Nassau, the king of Germany. Simultaneous assaults were to be made upon France from Gascony, Flanders, and the Rhine. His plans were thwarted when troubles arose in Wales and Scotland. Edward did not leave England for Flanders until 1297. By that time Adolf had made peace with Philip, and Edward was having great difficulty in raising money in England. His expedition to Flanders, on which he had spent vast sums, ended tamely in a truce with Philip after a brief campaign. After years of negotiations a peace was made in 1303 on the basis of the *status quo* before the war. Edward had successfully defended his rights in France, though at a high price.

TAXATION

For the campaigns in Britain and abroad the king required great armies and the money to maintain them. Edward could summon the feudal host of his tenants in chief, but they were growing less effective as a fighting force, demanding swifter payment and displaying great reluctance to fight on the Continent. Although Edward could also call upon the whole militia to serve as infantry, he instead perfected a system of commissions of array addressed to the local gentry, requiring them to raise a limited number of men on the basis of a quota from each shire and borough. At first the militia served without pay, though by the end of the reign the custom of wages had begun. Since the king required a much larger army than these methods could supply, he began to raise troops by making contracts with nobles or with military leaders to supply him with soldiers of various kinds at set wages. These mercenary troops were efficient but costly.

The old feudal forms of royal income were falling into decay, and new methods of taxation were obviously necessary. One innovation of the thirteenth century was a tax on income and movable goods, levied upon clergymen as well as laymen. Cathedrals, monasteries, and rectors of parishes, for example, might be asked to pay a tenth of the assessed value of their annual incomes. The assessments were low but through them the king obtained large sums of money. Landowners in the shires and burgesses in the towns paid a percentage (a sixth, a tenth, a fifteenth, or a thirtieth) of their movable property and income, Assessments were made by local juries under the supervision of sheriffs and royal officials, and the standard tax of the later Middle Ages became a fifteenth of personal property in the shires and a tenth in the towns.

Because in theory this tax was voluntary feudal aid it was necessary to obtain the consent of the classes to be taxed. This could be done in various ways. During much of the thirteenth century the clergy consented to taxation in diocesan synods. In Edward's reign, however, the clergy developed a body known as convocation, a kind of ecclesiastical parliament, one for each archbishopric, and it was in convocation that churchmen granted taxes. It was customary for the clergy not to consent to taxation without the approval of the pope; this gave them a certain protection. For some time laymen granted taxes in various bodies. In 1283 consent was given in provincial assemblies of knights and clergy. In 1297 the barons and the knights consented to the levy of an eighth. By the end of the century the normal place where laymen granted taxes was Parliament.

Customs duties upon exports and imports, enacted in the twelfth century, had remained unorganized until Edward's reign. In 1275 he obtained from Parliament an export duty of 6s. 8d. upon every sack of wool, which became a standard levy and was termed the Ancient Custom. During the financial pinch of the 1290s Edward made arrangements with the merchants to impose a much heavier duty of £2 on every sack, and although this duty was abolished in 1297, the king later arranged with foreign merchants to levy heavy duties, known as the New Custom, upon wool and other articles. Customs duties became the largest single source of income of the later medieval kings.

The decade of the 1290s also began with the confiscation of all Jewish property, followed by the expulsion of all Jews from the kingdom. The Jewish community had first settled in England after the Conquest and had grown to 2,500 in number by 1290. Barred from taking Christian oaths of homage and allegiance as vassals, the Jewish business community had been recognized as having rights of debt settlement by the Magna Carta. Otherwise, they were completely at the king's mercy, with a status equivalent to that of resident aliens. With minor exceptions, the Jew was absent in England until Jews were readmitted by Oliver Cromwell in the mid-seventeenth century.

EDWARD'S LAST YEARS

The last years of Edward's reign were ones of strain and conflict. He felt that he had been betrayed by the Scots and defrauded by the French. As his mood hardened into a grim determination to maintain his rights as he understood them, he became grasping and extortionate, which resulted in trouble in Parliament and suspicion on the part of the barons. Between 1294 and 1297 efforts were made to raise money by various levies: the New Custom on wool, the high taxes obtained from Parliament in 1294, 1295, and 1296, and by the heavy contributions required of the church. A crisis arose when even more money was demanded in 1297. Robert Winchelsea, the archbishop of Canterbury, was determined to protect the interests of the church. When Pope Boniface VIII issued the bull *Clericis Laicos* in 1296, which stated firmly that no ruler should tax the clergy without papal consent, Winchelsea led the clergy in refusing further payments. It was only when Boniface modified the bull to say that churchpeople could grant money to the king in emergencies and could judge for themselves when emergencies existed that Winchelsea withdrew his opposition to a clerical grant in 1297.

There was also trouble with the barons, who were irritated by the constant demands for money, by an attempt of Edward to enforce knighthood upon all landowners whose estates were worth £20 a year, and by a command that some of them should fight in Gascony while the king was in Flanders. The barons prevented the collection of a tax Edward had obtained from a small assembly of accommodating nobles. Edward was driven to summon a full assembly of barons and knights, to annul the grant already made, and to obtain a new one by making a solemn confirmation of Magna Carta and the Charter of the Forest. An important clause was added to the effect that no tax should be levied in the future without the consent of the whole community of the realm and for the common benefit of the kingdom. The Confirmation of the Charters was later to be regarded as a major landmark on the long road toward parliamentary and constitutional monarchy.

The controversy between king and barons continued after 1297. Magna Carta and the Charter of the Forest were again confirmed in 1299; twenty new articles were added in the Parliament of 1300. These articles declared that the king's rights in the forests should be investigated, that purveyance should be restricted, and that legal actions should be begun by writs under the great Seal and not under the privy seal.[2] Again in 1301 the charters were confirmed. The barons made an unsuccessful attempt to force the resignation of the treasurer, Walter Langton, bishop of Lichfield. Thus Edward's reign, which began with an increase in royal power and prerogative, ended with their curtailment.

[2] Purveyance was the right of the king to live off the country as he traveled about.

PARLIAMENT

The origin of Parliament is to be found in the Great Council, the fuedal court of the king, which was attended by his tenants in chief—archbishops, bishops, abbots, priors, earls, and greater barons. Attendance was part of their feudal duty: the king could summon them whenever he pleased. The Great Council was not a large body of all the tenants in chief great and small; it was a small select assembly of wealthy and powerful persons, great magnates, lay and ecclesiastical. In theory the obligation of attendance fell equally upon all tenants in chief, but in practice the lesser tenants of the king did not come to the meetings of his court and were not expected to do so. They did not receive individual summons, as did the great barons, but were summoned in general terms through the sheriff. This they regarded as permission to stay away. By the thirteenth century they had become small landowners—knights or gentry—more interested in the management of their estates and in local affairs. They had dropped out of the baronial class. The greater barons, however, had not yet hardened into a fixed caste. Among them were men whose status was not yet established. The king arbitrarily summoned the barons to Great Council meetings, and his choice of members could be capricious.

About the middle of the thirteenth century the meetings of the Great Council began to be called parliaments. The word "parliament" at this time meant merely a parley, a talking together, a meeting at which there was conference or debate. It was an occasion, not an institution, and there were other meetings of entirely different kinds which also were referred to as parliaments. Meetings of the Great Council, of a parliament, were occasions when the king met with the great men of the kingdom to discuss matters of high importance and to transact various kinds of business. These meetings were encouraged by the thirteenth-century concept of the community of the realm. A good king, it was held, should seek the cooperation of his magnates; and the noblest type of government was to be found in a harmony of king and barons ruling together. The barons who attended these meetings thought of themselves as representing the nation as a whole, as speaking for the community of the realm, and they sometimes referred to themselves as though they were that community. Their decisions were binding upon the community as a whole.

The heart and center of medieval parliaments were the king and his small council of judges and administrators. Parliament, which as the Great Council, had always been a court, was thus well equipped for judicial work. It was the high court of Parliament, the supreme court of the kingdom, where cases of great importance or cases which touched the public interest were brought for trial. Grievances were aired and wrongs righted in Parliament. Great numbers of petitions from persons high and low begging for legal action were submitted to Parliament; as early as 1278 a procedure arose by which these petitions were sorted and cases of small importance assigned to the ordinary courts.

Parliament had many other uses. Edward I promulgated his statutes there. Although these statutes were drawn by the king's officials, they often were inspired by complaints made in Parliament or else sought to rectify defects in the law that had

"A Parliament of Edward I." (First published November 1, 1724, by L. Herbert, 29 Great Russell Street, Bloomsbury. British Museum)

become apparent as a result of Parliament's deliberations. Parliament discussed political problems, gave approval to royal policy, and supplied information upon which better government could be based. It consented to taxation. The king, it was held, could not alter the law or levy extraordinary taxes without the consent of the magnates.

During the course of the thirteenth century the king began to summon representatives from the middle classes to meet with him and with the barons in Parliament. The growth of this practice was slow and intermittent; one must not think that it happened quickly or that the king was doing more than acting for his own convenience. The middle classes in the counties were the knights and country gentlemen whose ancestors had obtained their lands as small tenants in chief or as vassals of the greater barons. By the thirteenth century these knights and gentry had become less warlike and more interested in the management of their property. They were substantial people who were constantly used by the Crown in the work of local government, as sheriffs and coroners, as men who supplied information to royal agents sent out to make inquiries, and in these capacities they frequently represented the local community. The idea of representation was far older than Parliament. The middle class also included the wealthier burgesses in the towns, men who controlled the guilds, who governed the boroughs as mayors and aldermen, and who in the thirteenth century were acquiring moderate riches. They often represented their towns in negotiations with royal officials and in many other ways. The middle classes thus were experienced in government and familiar with the idea of representation.

When the king wished to investigate local conditions, he normally sent out his itinerant justices to travel from place to place and to make inquiries. But he sometimes found it more convenient to summon representatives of various localities to meet with his officials at some central place. These meetings in essence were concentrations of juries. The king, however, might find it more convenient to summon representatives from localities to assemble before him and his officials or magnates and to give the information there. In 1227 the sheriffs were directed to obtain the election of four knights in every county court to meet with the king and the Great Council. These knights were to report complaints against the sheriffs. Two knights were elected in each county in 1254 to meet with the Great Council at Westminster and to determine upon an aid to be sent to the king in Gascony. In both 1264 and 1265, as we have seen, Simon de Montfort summoned knights from the shires to meet with the barons in Parliament, and to the second of these assemblies he also summoned burgesses from certain towns. His Parliaments, it is true, were revolutionary assemblies, for the king was under restraint and Simon was trying to rally support for his dubious government.

During the next thirty years there were concentrations of many kinds. Most of them were meetings of the magnates alone. One, at least, contained representatives of the lower clergy but neither knights nor burgesses. On another occasion some knights and burgesses were instructed to meet at York while others met at Northampton. In 1283 a Parliament at Shrewsbury conducted certain business and then divided—the barons remained where they were to pass judgment upon Prince David of Wales, while the burgesses went to Acton Burnell to discuss matters of trade. It is obvious that Edward occasionally summoned knights and burgesses merely because their presence helped him accomplish his goals. In 1295, however, under pressing need for money he summoned a Parliament which contained many elements—bishops, abbots, heads of religious orders, knights, burgesses, and representatives of the lower clergy. This was the largest of medieval Parliaments.[3]

In these early assemblies, in which the role of the representative element was very slight, knights and burgesses were not an essential part. They stood deferentially at the rear of the chamber, sometimes as mere observers. They might be asked to grant taxes but were then dismissed, while the barons remained in session to transact other busness. In 1297, however, in the Confirmation of the Charters, an additional clause laid down the principle that taxes should be granted by the whole community of the realm and not merely by the class to be taxed. Thus representative elements were emerging as normal members of Parliament, though they had not been so regarded through the thirteenth century.

---

[3] It is often called the Model Parliament, though there was nothing model about it except that it contained all the classes found in later medieval Parliaments.

EDWARD II, 1307–1327

The reign of Edward II was an unhappy interlude of strife, bitter personal hatreds, and occasional civil wars, with constant quarrels between king and magnates. Edward II may be pitied for the nearly insoluble problems left to him by his father and for his tragic and humiliating fate. Weak and unambitious, he was ignorant of the business of government, incapable as a leader in war, and lacking in the dignity and high dedication required of a king. He liked the unkingly amusements of common young men, such as amateur theatricals, rowing, driving, digging, and thatching houses. His fondness for unsuitable companions was an ill omen, for it meant that he turned to "evil counselors" instead of working with the barons who in their own estimation were the natural and legitimate advisers of the Crown.[4] There was deep suspicion between him and the magnates from the very beginning of the reign. This suspicion has been explained as a baronial reaction against the strong rule of Edward I, but it was certainly increased by the new king's character. The magnates probably knew enough about him as Prince of Wales to suspect his inadequacy and constantly sought to check his power as king. They introduced an unusual clause into his coronation oath by which he pledged himself to observe such laws as should be determined by the communality of the realm.

Edward quickly justified these apprehensions. He recalled to England a young Gascon knight, Peter de Gaveston, who had been exiled earlier because of his questionable influence over Edward as Prince of Wales. Gaveston was an able man, but tactless and insolent toward the barons, who disliked him cordially. The leader of the opposition was the king's cousin Thomas, Earl of Lancaster, the holder of five earldoms, a magnate of enormous wealth and influence, with a vast retinue that could be swelled into an army at a moment's notice. As early as 1310 Lancaster and other magnates forced the king to appoint a committee of twenty-one barons to prepare a series of ordinances for the better government of the realm. These ordinances of 1311 were reminiscent of the Provisions of Oxford of 1258. They stipulated that Gaveston and an unpopular Italian banker be banished, that the chief officials of the royal Household be appointed only with the consent of the magnates in Parliament, that the king not go to war without baronial approval, that heavy duties laid by Edward I upon exported wool be abolished, and that money not be brought to the wardrobe without passing through the Exchequer. But though these ordinances were a vigorous statement of baronial grievances, there was no provision for their enforcement, and they remained an expression of opinion rather than a frame of government. Gaveston went into exile but returned before the end of the year. In 1312 the barons were in open revolt. Gaveston was seized by one of his many enemies and beheaded. A war was avoided only when Edward submitted to further restrictions. Though for some years Lancaster shared royal power with him, he

---

[4]"Evil counselors" was a conventional term used by antiroyalist magnates whenever they disapproved of the men close to the king.

never won the king's friendship or confidence and was lacking in energy and constructive talent. In 1318 a middle party arose at court. Its aim was to protect the king from dependence on favorites as well as to protect him from an overpowerful subject such as Lancaster, whose influence began to diminish.

It was not long before one of the middle party, Hugh Despenser, began to dominate the king as Gaveston had done previously, and to build a personal ascendancy at court. Even more objectionable, he soon had many enemies among the marcher lords of Wales, where he was increasing his possessions, and among the northern lords who followed Thomas of Lancaster. In 1322 the king displayed unusual energy, collected an army, and defeated Lancaster at the Battle of Boroughbridge in Yorkshire. Lancaster was executed, and the ordinances of 1311 were formally revoked in Parliament. For some years Edward and Despenser controlled the government. Despenser established a number of reforms in the royal Household, but more arrogant and grasping than before, he aroused a host of enemies, two of whom were very dangerous. One was Roger Mortimer of Wigmore, a marcher lord, who was imprisoned but escaped and fled to France. The other was Edward's queen, Isabella, a sister of the French king, Charles IV. In 1325 Isabella was sent to France to negotiate with her brother concerning the affairs of Gascony. She remained there and joined forces with Roger Mortimer in Paris and became his mistress. She persuaded her husband to send their son, the young Prince Edward, a boy of twelve, to France to do homage to Charles IV for Gascony. With the prince in her hands, she and Mortimer arranged a marriage for him with Philippa, a daughter of the count of Hainault. Using the dowry to buy arms, they invaded England in 1326. Edward, defeated, was forced to abdicate in 1327 and was murdered shortly theraftter. So ended his tragic career.

Parliament in the Reign of Edward II

Although limitations upon Edward's power were imposed in meetings of Parliament, it is clear that the magnates formed the driving force and that the role of the knights and burgesses was largely passive. When the barons in 1311 asked for frequent parliaments, they were thinking of aristocratic assemblies of their own class. Yet knights and burgesses were present in Parliament in almost every year of Edward's reign and at moments of crisis in 1311, 1322, and 1327. When Edward's deposition was determined, a deputation representing various elements in Parliament waited upon him at Kenilworth and extorted some kind of abdication. Moreover, knights and burgesses, now recognized as normal members of Parliament, consented to every tax that was levied during the reign. The Statute of York in 1322 declared that matters of importance should be treated in Parliament with the assent not only of the magnates but also of the community of the realm.

CHRONOLOGY

LAWS AND STATUTES

1272–1307	Edward I
1278	Statute of Gloucester, *Quo Warranto*
1279	Statute of Mortmain
1284	Conquest of Wales
1285	Second Statute of Westminster, *De Donis Conditionalibus*
1290	Statute of *Quia Emptores;* expulsion of the Jews
1296	Bull of *Clericis Laicos*
1297	Confirmation of the Charters
1307–1327	Edward II
1311	Ordinances of 1311
1314	Battle of Bannockburn
1322	Statute of York
1327	Deposition and murder of Edward II

8. Edward III and Richard II: War and Plague

The fourteenth century had characteristics of its own which distinguished it from earlier and later periods. It was, in the first place, a very warlike century. Although feudalism had subsided, the upper classes still eagerly engaged in war, seeking financial profit as well as honor and renown. They gladly followed Edward III in a great war with France, the first part of the Hundred Years' War. A modern spirit of nationalism arose and England found unity and strength in the brutal game of plundering the French, but later in the century military success was followed by military failure. Richard II, a peaceable king, was faced by the opposition of powerful and discontented barons, critical parliaments, and a disillusioned people.

The fourteenth century was profoundly influenced by the plague. This dread disease, which dramatically reduced the population, created an atmosphere of alarm and a sense of crisis. Social and economic conflict arose as a reduced labor force demanded better wages and freedom from the bonds of serfdom. Commerce and industry appeared to suffer less than agriculture, for it was during this period that England ceased to be merely a producer of raw wool and became a manufacturer of woolen cloth. Some merchants prospered greatly. There was a gradual rise in the standard of living. And thus, although the nobles were still very grand and powerful, and some attained great wealth, the gulf between them and the middle classes was less than it had been in earlier centuries. For many reasons the influence of the clergy declined in the fourteenth century, and a strong anticlerical sentiment arose. Finally, it was in this period that English emerged as a literary language, although French was favored by the nobility and Latin remained the language of the church.

EDWARD III, 1327–1377

The Minority

The deposition and murder of Edward II in 1327 was followed by a period in which his widow, Queen Isabella and her paramour, Roger Mortimer, dominated the government. In October 1330, the young king, Edward III, who was just under eighteen years of age, carried through a palace revolution. Assuming control of the government, Edward ruled for almost half a century.

Edward's Character

The chroniclers of Edward's reign lavished praise on him, but modern historians, until very recently, have tended to judge him rather harshly. A soldier, his lifework was the war in France. To promote the war, he allowed the magnates unprecedented influence in the government, made concessions to Parliament, and sacrificed the interests of the church, of sound administration, and of the trading classes. He squandered the resources of the Crown, leaving an empty exchequer and many problems to his successor. Earlier historians have accused him of sacrificing the future for the present, of waging an aggressive war which was doomed to ultimate failure, and of neglecting the problems arising from social and economic change.

Recent writers, however, have drawn a more favorable picture of Edward. He was keenly aware that his father's tragic demise stemmed from quarrels with the barons. Determined to avoid that error, he cultivated the good will of the magnates and sought to resolve old feuds and hostilities. These policies succeeded admirably. Edward surrounded himself with a group of young and warlike barons who sympathized with him, admired him, and remained loyal to him even in his declining years. The same may be said of his five sons. Edward's relations with his nobles were closer and happier than were those of any other medieval king in England. He won the loyalty of his people and the affection of his magnates, he raised his dynasty from the degradation of Edward II's reign and he ruled in a moderate and conciliatory way, carefully avoiding clashes with the church, Parliament, or the nobility.

CHIVALRY AND WAR

Edward was a majestic figure as he sat in state surrounded by his noble queen and five tall sons. An extravagant and cheerful man, he loved the pomp and pageantry of war and chivalry. He delighted in palaces, costly feasts, and elaborate tournaments. These jousts between two knights, fought according to rules, were still dangerous yet not as deadly as the old tournaments of Norman times. They were held in an open field called the lists, not unlike a modern football field, surrounded by galleries for spectators. The ladies of the court, who attended the tournaments, added a note of romance and refinement to jousting by turning it into a means of winning honor for one's lady.

Chivalry—a social and moral code of knightly behavior—laid stress on bravery, honor, virtue, courtesy, and on devotion to the service of a lady as her attendant and champion. It was set forth in tales romanticizing King Arthur and his Round Table and in those taken from the classics and given a medieval setting. Edward added to the cult of chivalry and used it to his own advantage by creating the famous Order of the Garter about 1348.

Ironically, however, this code of chivalry had little relation to daily life, for women were often beaten and maltreated, and their position in society was low. The marriage of an heiress was a matter of business and diplomacy. A great noble regarded his sisters and daughters as so many pawns in the game of marriage alliances with other noble houses; even the king sought marriages for his sons with the great heiresses of the kingdom. This had the unfortunate result in later years that almost any revolt against the Crown could find leaders who were related to the royal family, but in Edward's reign there was no such danger; concentration of wealth in the hands of the king's sons supported their dignity and added strength to their father's regime. Heiresses often were married as children. Courtly love, moreover, with its devotion to the service of a lady, often meant that a knight fought for the honor of one lady but happened to be married to another. Hence courtly love could easily lead to adultery.

Careful marriages, the king's generosity, and the profits of the wars in France sometimes combined to bring enormous estates into the hands of a few magnates. As in the thirteenth century, these men lived in great ostentation, maintaining sumptuous households, dispensing a lavish hospitality, and adding to their dignity and power by an ever-increasing number of dependents and retainers. And yet, the income from agriculture was declining, and the magnates soon exploited the profits that could be derived from war. The most lucrative form of plunder was the ransom demanded by the English from prisoners of war, for every captured Frenchman had his price and noble captives yielded enormous sums. Holding both the king of France and the king of Scotland as prisoners, Edward obtained a ransom of half a million pounds from the first and a hundred thousand marks from the second. It is small wonder that the war was popular. The common soldier drew excellent wages, and commanders might make a fortune.

The English armies that fought in France were raised in various ways. We have seen that the old feudal host was falling into decay, and it was fully understood in Edward's time that the only way to build an efficient and disciplined army was to pay for it. Even the greatest commanders—the Black Prince, for example—drew wages at a daily rate. The king made contracts or indentures with nobles or with celebrated captains to supply him with fixed numbers of fighting men. Indentures were of various kinds, and those made with lesser commanders were fairly simple. Edward Montagu, for instance, agreed to serve in Brittany in 1341 for forty days and to supply six knights, twenty men-at-arms (who may have been light horsemen), twelve armed men, and twelve archers.

But agreements with great nobles were much more elaborate, covering such details as the cost of transportation, wages, length of service, compensation for lost horses, and the division of ransom money. A noble might make up his quota of soldiers from his own household, from his retainers, or from subcontracts. Edward I, as we have seen, had organized a system of commissioners of array in order to obtain soldiers from the militia. The commissioners were local gentry who surveyed the men available for duty and selected the best to serve for wages with the king. There was no need to exert pressure: a peasant could obtain better wages as a soldier than as an agricultural laborer. More volunteers came forward than could be used.

The commanders were drawn from the aristocracy and from the class of nonnoble knights. Great nobles sat in council with the king to determine general strategy. A select rank of knights, known as bannerets, who were skillful captains and men of some wealth, commanded troops, garrisoned castles, and conducted other operations in the field. Below them were the knights bachelors, less wealthy than bannerets but men of standing and experience. Knights wore costly and elaborate armor made of plate, now so heavy that shields disappeared. They were armed with sword, lance, and dagger. Each knight was supplied with three or four warhorses, for although the knight fought on foot, horses were essential in the raids in France and were used to pursue the enemy.

Below the knights were various kinds of men-at-arms: lightly armored horsemen who carried the same weapons as the knights and foot soldiers and foot archers armed with short swords, knives, and bows and arrows. The foot archer soon was replaced by the mounted archer, who combined mobility with great firepower. He used a six-foot bow, a Welsh weapon developed in England, where archery had become the great national sport. Drawn with the whole strength of the archer's body, it could send an arrow through chain mail; a good bowman could shoot ten or twelve arrows a minute. The longbow was a magnificent defensive weapon against the charge of French feudal knights, for it sent a deadly shower of arrows among them and maddened the horses. The archer fought on foot. Normally, the English formed a line, with groups of various types of soldiers interspersed with each other, to resist advancing cavalry, and so long as the French were foolish enough to charge in the old disorderly fashion, as they did at Crécy, Poitiers, and much later at Agincourt, they were defeated by the English defense.

One other part of the English army should be mentioned. Among the foot soldiers were many Welshmen, armed only with long knives and daggers. When the French knights were thrown from their horses, these Welsh troopers darted forward to slit the throats of the fallen Frenchmen, for a knife could be thrust between the plates of armor. This was not fighting according to the rules of chivalry: it was the deadly business of slaughtering the foe.

Edward's First Campaigns

Edward's first campaigns were fought against the Scots. These early campaigns led to nothing and were abandoned. In 1337 excuses for fighting France were not hard to find: the French had been assisting the Scots; the English were conspiring with the cloth-manufacturing towns of Flanders against the French; the French king, Philip VI, announced the annexation of Gascony; and Edward laid claim to the French crown through his mother, Isabella, a daughter of King Philip IV. These causes of conflict might well have led to hostilities. But one suspects that Edward and his magnates, inspired by high spirits and material greed, were ready to employ any excuse that served their turn.

Edward's first campaigns against France were planned upon a magnificent scale. Alliances were concluded with various rulers in the Low Countries and along the Rhine, including the German emperor Lewis IV; the wool trade was manipulated to increase royal revenue and to force the count of Flanders to turn against the French; and finally, plans were made to invade France through the Netherlands. Edward crossed to Flanders in 1338 but found that his allies were far from eager for war; meanwhile he was spending great sums of money. Throughout the years 1339 and 1340 he was able to do no more than conduct two small campaigns which ended tamely in a truce. His principal success was a naval victory over a French fleet at Sluys. In 1340 he returned to England, angry and disillusioned. His money was gone before he and his expensive allies had struck a serious blow at the enemy.

The Hundred Years' War, 1337–1361

Thereafter Edward turned to a new pattern of warfare which proved to be highly successful: to cross directly to France and raid the country's interior. These inexpensive raids did not need costly allies, and the mobile English armies found they could plunder whatever supplies they needed. The raids began in 1341 in the duchy of Brittany, where a disputed succession enabled the English to support one candidate while the French supported another. In 1342 Edward overran much of Brittany, which became an important base for English operations. In 1345 raids were made into France from Brittany and Gascony.

The next few years brought brilliant victories. In 1346 Edward crossed to Normandy with an army of some 10,000 men, of whom 7000 were archers. Sacking the city of Caen, he moved northward to the area of Ponthieu and the river Somme. On August 26, at the village of Crécy, he was met by a large French army. The French knights charged the English line, riding over their own crossbowmen in their eagerness, but falling in bloody defeat under a hail of English arrows. Crécy pointed to the passing of the feudal knight, who could thus be conquered by the fire of plebeian archers and the knives of Welsh peasants. Other victories followed. In the same year, 1346, the Scots were defeated at the Battle of Neville's Cross near Durham, and the Scottish king, David II, was taken prisoner. In 1347 the English defeated the French in Brittany and after a long siege captured the city of Calais which remained an English outpost in France for more than two centuries. A long pause in the Hundred Years' War was due to the Black Death, a plague which devastated both England and France, disrupting trade and the collection of taxes.

War began once more in 1355, when two large English expeditions crossed to the Continent. One of them, commanded by the king, operated from Calais but accom-

Battle of Crecy. (Giraudon/Art Resource)

plished nothing of moment. The other, led by the Black Prince,[1] penetrated from Bordeaux into Gascony and Toulouse. In 1356, as the Black Prince was marching toward the city of Tours, he was met at Poitiers by a huge French army commanded by John, the chivalrous but inept King of France. Again the French knights charged the English line and again they were completely defeated. Large numbers of the French nobility, including the French king, were taken prisoners and were brought to England to be held for ransom.

By now Edward's resources were exhausted and he was ready to make peace. Conditions in France were miserable. The Black Death raged without mercy, the government was disrupted by the absence of the king, great stretches of the countryside lay waste, the wretched peasants rose in revolt, free companies of English soldiers roamed about the country, plundering as they went. In 1359 the Black Prince led an army in a great circle around Paris. Negotiations for peace, opened in 1360, led to the Treaty of Bretigny in the following year. Gascony and large adjacent areas including Poitou and, in the north, Ponthieu and Calais passed to Edward in full sovereignty. King John's ransom was fixed at £500,000. In return

---

[1]Edward, the Black Prince, was the eldest son of Edward III. Duke of Cornwall and Prince of Wales, he developed into one of the finest soldiers of the age. He was never king, for he died a few months before his father.

Edward renounced his claim to the French throne and restored certain lands and fortresses outside the area covered by the treaty. In 1362, however, the treaty was modified at Calais. Edward's renunciation was to become effective only under certain conditions which were not likely to be fulfilled, and the way was left open for future claims by English sovereigns. The French honored the terms of the treaty, making English influence in France greater than it had been since the days of Henry II.

PARLIAMENT IN THE REIGN OF EDWARD III

Although the magnates prospered financially from war with France, the knights and burgesses assembled in Parliament were less enthusiastic, for their part was the unromantic one of paying the bill. Yet the King's constant need for money gave Parliament, and especially the Commons, an opportunity to develop rapidly. It was in this reign that Parliament assumed its historic structure of Lords and Commons and began, though in a tentative way, to acquire some of its basic powers.

Forty-eight Parliaments met during Edward's reign of fifty years, and to every one of them he summoned the classes which had composed the Model Parliament of 1295: the upper clergy, the magnates and greater barons, proctors representing the lower clergy, knights from the shires, and burgesses from the towns. He also summoned a few of his great officers, councilors, and judges; these men still formed the heart and core of Parliament, guiding its activities and guarding the interests of the Crown. Some Parliaments continued to sit after the knights and burgesses had been dismissed, but none of them met without the presence of the Commons, whose members were fully accepted as an essential part of Parliament.

Parliament was composed of various classes. The upper clergy, or spiritual lords, consisted of twenty-one bishops and archbishops and a group of abbots and priors. The number of abbots and priors differed from time to time. Edward I had summoned seventy in 1295, but the number declined during the fourteenth century until it became established at twenty-seven in 1364. The magnates, or temporal lords, consisted of dukes, marquises, earls, and barons.[2] In the thirteenth century the only duke had been the king (who was duke of Aquitaine), but Edward III conferred dukedoms on four of his five sons; later in the century six other dukes were created. The title of marquis first was conferred in 1385 by Richard II. At the end of Edward's reign there were about fourteen earls. These nobles were summoned as a matter of course. The number of barons called to Parliament, however, varied greatly—from ninety in 1321 to thirty in 1346. Sometimes both a father and his son were summoned together, sometimes a son in place of his father, sometimes a man in the right of his wife. Occasionally a knight banneret was summoned. A clearly delimited nobility, with an exclusive right to be summoned to Parliament, did not exist in the fourteenth century. But the tendency was in this direction, for the lords now considered themselves a class apart and above all others. They were the peers of the realm, a

---

[2]The title of viscount, a rank between that of earl and baron, was not introduced until the fifteenth century.

unique and superior caste. After Richard II began to create peers by letters patent in 1387, the list of nobles summoned to Parliament gradually hardened into a fixed class of peers. Only then could one speak of a House of Lords.

Each of the members mentioned above received individual summonses to Parliament. But the representatives of the lower clergy were summoned indirectly through the bishops, and the knights and burgesses through the sheriffs. The lower clergy gradually ceased to attend. When a Parliament was called, the sheriff of each of thirty-seven counties (Chester and Durham were not represented) received a writ directing him to cause two knights to be elected in the shire court, two citizens in every city, and two burgesses in every borough. Some cities and boroughs, however, hoping to escape expense, managed to evade the command of the sheriff and did not return members.

Though little is known about these elections, it is certain they were neither popular nor democratic. Often the sheriff or some local magnate, or the two working together, proposed names in the shire court; these names were accepted by acclamation, and the election was over. Undoubtedly the sheriff exercised great influence, and a local lord with a body of retainers might easily sway the electors. The writ called for knights as members, but the number of knights was insufficient,[3] and so various other members were recruited. They might be sons of nobles, knights, country gentlemen, well-to-do farmers, retainers of local magnates, or persons interested in trade. The members' assets or contributions were usually a combination of personal wealth, some prior experience in government, and a knowledge of local conditions.

The elections in the boroughs, though varying in practice from town to town, were essentially controlled by the wealthy merchants and industrialists who dominated the guilds and town governments. Members from the boroughs were lawyers, capitalists, merchants, or smaller business persons; but even in the Middle Ages members of the gentry class were sometimes returned by neighboring towns. The tendency was toward the election of members of the gentry rather than fellow burgers, resident or nonresident. The number of towns that sent members varied somewhat, averaging between seventy and eighty-three in the reigns of Edward III and Richard II.

The most important developments of the fourteenth century were the division of Parliament into two parts, the Lords and the Commons, the latter formed from the union of the knights and burgesses. The lords naturally acted together as an aristocracy, receiving individual summonses and holding land directly from the king; the lower clergy dropped out; and the vital question remained whether the knights would join with the lords or else unite with the burgesses. In some early parliaments the knights met with the lords to decide upon taxation, but as the aristocracy hardened into the peerage the knights found themselves excluded. Knights and burgesses bore the heaviest burden of taxation, and had a common interest in resisting demands for money. They also discovered that the grievances and abuses they wished redressed were of the same general nature. By 1339 knights and

---

[3] A sheriff once reported that there was only one knight in his shire and that he was "languidus et impotens ad laborundum." May McKisack, *The Fourteenth Century 1307–1399*, p. 188n.

burgesses were more unified in action, and so formed a single body. This union had great significance. Without it the burgesses would have remained in a position of permanent subordination, but acting together, knight and burgess had some hope of defending their interests against the king and a powerful aristocracy.

Sessions of Parliament were short, lasting normally only two or three weeks. Lords and Commons met together in the Parliament chamber at the opening of a Parliament, as they do today, and heard an oration from one of the councilors explaining the reasons for the meeting. Petitions, addressed to the king and his Council, not to Parliament, were then presented. The Parliament divided for deliberation, the Lords remaining in the Parliament chamber while the Commons met elsewhere, normally in the chapter house or the refectory of Westminster Abbey.

The work of Parliament may be divided into deliberation, action on taxation, judicial work, and legislation. Edward III used Parliament as a clearinghouse for discussion, laying important questions before the Lords and the Commons. The Lords gave advice, which might or might not be followed. The Commons, however, were hesitant in offering opinions. Hence unless their interests were directly affected, they were rather noncommittal. Their great victory was in the field of taxation. By 1340 the principle was established that taxes could be levied only with the consent of Lords and Commons; by the end of the century it was recognized that proposals for grants of money must originate in the Commons. Control of taxation gave the Commons power to bargain with the king for the redress of grievances, which normally preceded the voting of supply.

Judicial work was largely the function of the Lords, who continued, as in the thirteenth century, to form the high court of Parliament, the highest court in the land. But the judicial work of the Lords was declining. Many cases could be settled in the three central law courts, and in the fourteenth century there came a new court, the court of chancery, which based its decisions upon equity rather than upon the strict letter of the law. The court of chancery could handle many of the unusual cases formerly brought before the Lords. Moreover, the legal work in the Lords was done largely by the judges who were summoned to Parliament, but as the Lords made the peerage more rigid and exclusive, they resented the presence of these judges, who were normally not peers. This attitude naturally tended to discourage the legal work of the judges in Parliament. In one aspect of judicial work the Commons played an important part. In 1376 we find the first case of impeachment. In this procedure the Commons, acting as a body, places accusations against corrupt officials before the Lords. The Lords then acted as a court to try the ministers in question. Impeachment gave the Commons power, not to control the selection of ministers, but to attack those who broke the law.

The Commons also gained some share in legislation, though their achievements were limited. As soon as Parliament met, as we have seen, it received petitions of various kinds; these were addressed to the king and his Council with a request for action or redress. Such petitions might be sponsored by individual members, but it shortly occurred to the Commons that there would be advantage in pooling their petitions and their pressures upon the Crown. Thus arose the common petition backed by the whole body of the Commons. If the Lords assented and if the king accepted the petition, it could be thrown into the form of a statute and become the law of the land. "The common petition is thus the root of the house of commons as a separate legislative assembly." The king, however, possessed various methods of rendering these petitions ineffective, even though he had accepted them. The wording of the statute might be quite different from the wording of the petition, with vital matters altered or omitted. The statute might remain a dead letter for lack of provision for its enforcement or because the king blocked its execution. In 1341 Edward attempted to annul a statute as contrary to his prerogative. But the next Parliament formally repealed the statute in question, and no other attempts were made to void a statute by royal pronouncement. In the fourteenth century the Commons never wholly succeeded in preventing evasions and omissions in the form of statutes.

It is obvious, nonetheless, that the Commons made great gains in the fourteenth century: they debated matters laid before them by the Crown, they gained the great victory of control of taxation, they devised the procedure of impeachment, and they obtained some share in legislation. A Speaker of the Commons appears in 1376. It is true that the early Speakers were agents of the king and the magnates rather than of the Commons, and that the Commons often opposed the Crown when they were assured of the backing of some of the magnates. While the influence of the Commons must not be exaggerated, their progress in the fourteenth century was impressive.

THE LAST YEARS OF EDWARD III

During the 1360s Edward enjoyed the rewards of successful war. He made few requests to Parliament, his financial needs satisfied by the ransom of the French king John. English politics were tranquil until the war was renewed in 1369 when the situation altered radically. The years between 1369 and 1382 were filled with stress and turmoil both at home and abroad. Owing to a remarkable resurgence of royal power in France, the victory belonged to the French from the onset.

The war began when the French nobles in Gascony revolted from English rule, assisted by Charles V (1364–1380). English countermoves were feeble. Edward, too old to fight, was sinking into his dotage. The Black Prince was ill. An English expedition based upon Calais in 1370 was a failure, and a march by John of Gaunt, the king's third son, from Calais to Bordeaux, was spectacular rather than important. Moreover, the English had to fight Castile as well as France. In 1367 Castile had been invaded by the Black Prince in support of King Pedro the Cruel, who had been driven from the Castilian throne by a French candidate. Pedro was restored, but only for a short time. Thereafter Castile allied with France, and the English in Gascony had an enemy on both flanks. The Castilian navy, joining that of France, defeated an English fleet in 1372, won control of the Channel, and helped to raid the English coast. English conquests in France were quickly lost, so that when Edward III died in 1377 the English held no more than the city of Calais, a narrow strip around

Bordeaux, and scattered harbors along the coast of Brittany. Events in England must be viewed against this background of defeat.

There was also a decline in morale at the English court. After the death of Queen Philippa in 1369 Edward fell under the influence of an unscrupulous mistress, Alice Perrers. She and William Latimer, the chamberlain, dominated the court. They were protected by John of Gaunt, duke of Lancaster and the most influential son of the king. The corruption at court and the mismanagement of the war caused an explosion in the Good Parliament of 1376. Sir Peter de la Mare, the Speaker of the Commons, with the secret support of certain magnates, attacked the court party and brought charges before the Lords. This was the first use of impeachment. Latimer and Richard Lyons, a financier, were condemned; Alice Perrers was driven from court.

The Good Parliament inaugurated a period of political crisis which lasted for some years, but in itself it accomplished very little. Alice Perrers and Latimer were soon back at court once more. Edward III died in 1377. Despite the military glory of his prime, his reign ended on a note of gloom, defeat, and corruption.

SOCIAL AND ECONOMIC LIFE

The Black Death

In August 1348 the bubonic plague, or Black Death, suddenly appeared in England. Its germs were carried by the fleas on black rats that came into the country on ships from abroad. The first outbreak of the plague was of intense ferocity, for the people had no immunity and persons living close to the margin of subsistence fell victims to the disease. Returning in 1361, the plague caused high mortality among children born since 1348; there were other visitations in 1368 and 1375. Thereafter the plague subsided in the rural areas but remained endemic in London and other towns, where it could become active at any time and could spread along lines of communication into the country. It remained in England for more than 300 years.

The plague caused a sharp and sudden drop in population. The best estimates place the population of England (exclusive of Wales, Scotland, and Ireland) at about 1.1 million in 1086, about 3.7 million in 1348, about 2.2 million in 1377, and not much more than that by 1450. The startling fact about these figures is the amazing drop between 1348 and 1377. It may be that the number of people in overcrowded England already was beginning to decline before the coming of the Black Death. There were floods and famines in the years between 1315 and 1317. Certainly the plague caused a high mortality. In some monasteries the monks all but disappeared (it is thought that half the clergy in England fell victims to the pestilence); numerous villages were left deserted. After the first visitation widows and widowers remarried quickly and produced as many children as before; but because of the high mortality among young people, this population increase was not maintained later in the century.

"The Black Death at Tournai, 1349." (Gilles le Muisit's "Annales" 1352, MS 13076–77, fol. 24v. Bibliothèque Royale de Belgique, Brussels. Giraudon/Art Resource)

Agriculture

The Black Death had its most striking effect on the rural economy. The laborers available could not keep pace with the amount of land under cultivation, so that casual labor was employed at wages that doubled within a decade. Relations between lord and peasant were quickly altered. Successful farming in the thirteenth century had relied upon a scarcity of land, a large population, and a great demand for food—conditions that had forced the peasants to remain on their holdings and accept the burdens of serfdom. A villein now found he could easily escape to another manor, where employment would be offered with no questions asked. In such an age of declining population, when the demand for food was less, the profits of agriculture shrank. High farming, which had already been slipping before 1348, came to an end.

Landowners complained bitterly of the shortage of labor and the increase of wages demanded. In 1351 they obtained the Statute of Laborers, which fixed wages at the rates before the plague, declared that all landless men must accept work when it was offered to them, and prohibited peasants from moving from one manor to another. For a time the statute had some effect, but in the long run it was useless, for wages continued to rise and employers had to pay them. There was also a scarcity of tenants. As few manors were without vacant holdings, the yield was less and income from the land declined. Yet while agricultural products no longer fetched high prices, the cost of luxuries and manufactured goods increased.

Faced with these difficulties, the lord of a manor had several options: he might treat his villeins with severity, holding them to their old obligations, denying them concessions, even forcing them to take up land they did not want. Increasingly restless under such treatment, the villeins sought new opportunities to enrich themselves in the changing conditions of rural life. Chafing bitterly at the restraints of serfdom and keenly aware of their value in a labor shortage, they conspired to refuse their former services. The tempo of resistance quickened until it exploded in the Peasants' Revolt in 1381.

A second course open to the lord was to abandon cultivation of the demesne and instead lease it to peasant farmers. This process was common during the second half of the fourteenth century. The new leaseholders might be freemen, villeins, or adventurers from outside the manor who energetically grasped this opportunity to prosper and to rise in the world. Some of them became big farmers with large estates. Within a few generations they sometimes were inheriting the position of the manorial lords and pushing their way into the gentry. Great differences in wealth soon developed between the prosperous peasant who acquired land and the landless agricultural laborer who still worked for a daily wage. To offset this imbalance, laborer's wages would rise in the later Middle Ages.

A third course open to the lord was to transform the demesne into a sheep pasture and sell the wool for a high price. This was a common solution in the fifteenth and sixteenth centuries. Or the demesne could be made into a deer park, which added to the dignity of the lord and provided his table with venison. In any case his income from his lands declined. He became a landlord living on rents rather than a country gentleman cultivating his own estates.

The Peasants' Revolt

In 1381 the peasants rose in revolt, angered by a series of poll taxes imposed by Parliament between 1377 and 1381. These taxes—attempts to shift part of the burden of taxation on the peasantry—were clumsily drafted, harshly collected and greatly resented. It was soon apparent, however, that the rising had other more fundamental causes. The rebels were not desperate or starving men; they were peasants who held land, who were getting on in the world, and who found the burdens and irritations of villeinage intolerable. Their goal was to put an end to villeinage and to lower the rent for land. There was also an element of social revolt against the class distinctions of the time. John Ball, a priest who played a large part in the rising, preached radical sermons declaring that all men should be equal, that lordship should be abolished, and that land should be taken away from the aristocracy and upper clergy and distributed among the poor. Ball used a text that became famous:

> When Adam delf, and Eve span,
> Wo was thenne a gentilman?

Thus the desire for material gain combined with radical theories of social equality.

Rising in Essex and Kent, the peasants moved toward London, burning manor houses, destroying manorial records containing evidence of their villeinage, and murdering unpopular landlords as they went. The government seemed helpless. The rebels entered London without opposition, sacking and burning a number of buildings and killing unpopular officials, including the archbishop of Canterbury. They demanded an interview with the king. With great bravery Richard II granted this request, and two astonishing meetings took place between him and the peasants: one at Mile End to the east of the city, the other at Smithfield, just north of the city wall. At Mile End the peasants demanded the abolition of villeinage and an annual rent for land of not more than *4d.* an acre. The king promised to grant all their requests, and many of the peasants from Essex returned homeward, naïvely believing that their new rights would be permanent.

The next day there was a much more dangerous meeting at Smithfield between the king, attended by a few councilors, and the peasants from Kent led by Wat Tyler. A man of vigor and determination, Tyler repeated the demands of the previous day but added new ones. There was to be no law save the police regulations of Edward I—this was a protest against the Statute of Laborers. There was to be no lordship save that of the king, no bishopric save one, all other men should be equal, and the lands of lords and clergy should be divided among the peasantry. When Richard approved these radical changes a dispute arose between Tyler and the mayor of London, who was with the king. Tyler was suddenly pulled from his horse and slain.

On the left, Richard II meets Wat Tyler. The picture shows the slaying of Tyler. On the right, Richard addresses the mob. (British Library, Royal MS 18E. i.f.175)

A great cry arose from the peasants, who might well have attacked the king. With great presence of mind Richard rode forward declaring that he would be their captain. He led them away from the city and ordered them to disperse. Strangely enough, they obeyed, perhaps believing they had accomplished their purpose. Within a month the peasants were suppressed, the promises of the king were withdrawn, and the revolt was over.

In the end the revolt accomplished nothing. The economic forces of the time continued to operate as before. Landowners were faced with low prices for agricultural products, low rents, rising wages, declining villein services, and vacant tenements. Since the peasants would not accept land on the old terms, a new type of land tenure appeared, known as copyhold, by which the tenant was free from villein services and paid rent for his holdings. The agreement between lord and peasant was inscribed on the manor roll, and the peasant was given a copy. Land held in this way passed from father to son upon the payment of a fee. Thus the new tenant was a freeman holding his land by what was virtually a perpetual lease.

The rise of tenure by copyhold replaced villeins with free tenants. Moreover, when a villein family died out it could not be replaced by other villeins. Many villeins ran away to the towns or to other manors, where their villeinage was forgotten. When a lord rented his demesne he could dispense with villein services. Thus villeinage practically disappeared by 1485.

The Towns

The clash of interest between lord and peasant was paralleled to some extent by conflicts in the towns. A shortage of labor existed in industry as well as in agriculture, and workers saw the opportunity to improve their position. Journeymen formed guilds of their own to bargain with employers; artisans founded organizations which, under the guise of religious guilds, were aimed at economic objectives. Conflicts arose in various forms. Struggles began between the masters of the guilds and their employees. Since the masters controlled the government of the towns, there were also quarrels between the town corporation and the citizens. In some cases the larger merchants defended their position by opposing both the citizens and the industrial guilds. Ill will developed between the larger and smaller masters. On the whole, the wealthy classes held their own more successfully in the towns than in the country because commerce was less affected than was agriculture by the Black Death. The suppression of troublesome guilds and their members caused discontent among workers in the early fifteenth century; many left the towns and carried weaving and other industries into the rural districts.

Commerce and Industry

Changes in commerce and industry were as remarkable as those in agriculture. When the fourteenth century opened, England was essentially an exporter of raw materials, of which wool continued to be by far the most important. The wool trade prospered the most when government interfered the least with the natural forces of commercial enterprise. The king sought control, however, not merely for the lucrative revenues collected in customs and loans, but for the trade's diplomatic power against foreign countries. The larger exporters, in turn, desired to monopolize the trade. A compromise was reached in the idea of a staple, or town, usually on the Continent, decreed by the king as a special center of English trade. English exporters took their goods to the staple, with special privileges secured from local rulers. The first compulsory staple, to which exporters were required to take their merchandise, was set up at St.-Omer in Flanders in 1314. At the beginning of the Hundred Years' War Edward III established staples at Antwerp and later at Bruges. The plan was popular with large exporters but distrusted by the growers and smaller merchants, who suspected the staple was used to hold down the price of wool in England. The Commons obtained a statute in 1353 to establish staples in various English towns, but this arrangement failed. In 1363 the staple was established at Calais, where it remained, except for brief intervals, for nearly 200 years.

Supervision at Calais was entrusted to a company of twenty-six English merchants, known as the merchants of the staple. They monopolized the export of English wool[4] and laid down rules for its sale in Calais and for the conduct of English and foreign merchants. The company itself did not trade. It established conditions and standards under which the members of the company could buy and sell, each merchant taking his own profit or loss. Though the export of wool remained an essential part of the economy, the volume of trade declined after the establishment of the staple at Calais. Strict control did not foster expansion.

The principal reason for this decline of trade, however, was the great increase in the manufacture of woolen cloth in England during the second half of the fourteenth century. By a remarkable industrial development England began to export manufactured articles as well as raw wool. It is not easy to explain this fundamental change. Edward III induced some foreign weavers to migrate to England, but their coming can hardly explain so great a development. More vital was the fact that while the king laid heavy duties on the export of wool, he was less strict with exported woolen cloth. Weavers in Flanders complained that they paid as much for raw wool at Calais as other merchants paid for manufactured cloth. Thus the English manufacturer had a great advantage.

The industry in England, moreover, was freer from regulation by guilds and municipalities than was the older weaving industry on the Continent. The decline in agriculture may well have spurred peasants and landowners to take advantage of opportunities offered by manufacturing. And finally, in the last quarter of the fourteenth century, English merchants were aggressive in seeking new markets for English cloth in western Germany, the Baltic, the Netherlands, and the Mediterranean countries. Thus the value of wool exports through Calais came to equal the value of exported woolen cloth. Though in the fifteenth century the English were driven from the Baltic by the Hanseatic League and, though the Mediterranean

---

[4]Italian merchants were permitted to buy wool in England and to export it directly to Italy.

market was dominated by the Italians, the Dutch market for English cloth steadily increased. The export of wool, meanwhile, continued to decline.

Another important economic trend soon became apparent. The clothing industry, initially centered in towns such as York, Norwich, and Coventry began to move in the late fourteenth and early fifteenth centuries into rural areas. As the guilds became increasingly aristocratic many journeymen and small masters grew disillusioned and were willing to move into the country if they could find employment. Conditions in rural areas favored the small wool grower and manufacturer, who found a ready labor force among peasants eager to turn from agriculture to weaving.

Probably the principal cause of this rapid industrial development was the introduction of water power in the process of fulling or cleaning the cloth. Fulling mills required swift streams of pure water, which were found in hilly rural districts. Important cloth-making areas developed in the southern Cotswolds in Gloucestershire, in western Wiltshire, in the valley of the Stour River in Suffolk and Essex, and in the western part of Yorkshire. As the industry grew the merchant clothier became important. These merchants bought wool from the grower then distributed it among spinners, weavers, fullers, and so on, until the cloth was finished and ready for market. The merchant clothiers were sometimes wealthy capitalists who employed hundreds of workers. During the fifteenth century this rural industry continued to expand, thus overshadowing the larger clothing centers and diminishing the export of raw wool through Calais.

THE CHURCH

In the second half of the fourteenth century three famous writers—William Langland the moralist, John Wycliffe the philosopher, and Geoffrey Chaucer the poet—were all highly critical of the clergy. Langland's puritanical piety was shocked by the worldliness of the upper clergy, while Wycliffe challenged the whole position of the church and Chaucer exposed its weaknesses with courtly satire. At the same time a strong anticlerical sentiment in Parliament prompted the Commons to insist that the church pay its full share of taxation and to suggest that the lands of the monasteries be confiscated by the Crown.

Parliament was also critical of appointments, known as provisions, made by the papacy to places in the English church. The church had been endowed, it was held, for the spiritual benefit of Englishmen, and its patronage should not be used for the convenience of the papacy. In 1343 Edward III sent the pope a strong letter of protest. Aliens appointed to benefices in England, he said, did not know their congregations, did not speak the English tongue, and often did not live in England. The result was a decline in devotion. From 1309 to 1377 the popes resided not in Rome but in Avignon in southern France. During these years, when most of the popes and cardinals were Frenchmen, the English believed that any money going to Avignon lent support to the kings of France, with whom England was at war.

Some famous antipapal statutes were passed at this time. Two Statutes of Provisors (1351, 1390) dealt with Roman appointments to places in the church in England. By the first act the King could expel a person so appointed and fill the vacancy himself. The second imposed heavy penalties upon those who accepted benefices at papal hands or helped others to obtain them; no sentence imposed by Rome in retaliation was to be brought into England. Three Statutes of Praemunire (1353, 1365, and 1393), which forbade appeals from English courts to foreign ones, were obviously aimed at cases concerning provisions. The first act was not directed against all appeals abroad but only those which attempted to reverse decisions made in the king's courts. The statute of 1393 went much further, declaring that no citations to Rome, no letters of excommunication, and no bulls concerning provisions should be brought into England. The Roman curia was forbidden to deal with cases concerning English benefices. Yet, as we shall see, these statutes remained largely a dead letter, used by the kings as diplomatic weapons, but not enforced in any systematic way. The exploits of Henry VIII, however, would later make them notoriously famous.

Despite the anticlericalism of the fourteenth century, the English were a religious

"Teacher and Pupils," c. 1335–40. (Bodleian MS 264 fol. 123v. Bodleian Library, Oxford)

people. Traditional Catholicism retained its hold, and the normal apparatus of the church was taken as a matter of course. The friars' loss of prestige resulted from excessive begging and thinly-disguised demands for additional church support. The fourteenth-century friar was contrasted unfavorably with St. Francis, who was still a living memory. Yet the number of religious guilds, chantries, and pilgrimages testified to the strength of orthodox Catholicism. The heresies of Wycliffe were repudiated.

Why, then, was there such an eruption of anticlerical sentiment, especially in the years from 1371 to 1384? The truth was that both the king and the pope wished to exploit the English church. The king wished to obtain clerical offices for his servants so that they would draw their incomes from the church and not from the royal exchequer. The pope tried to increase the income of cardinals and other important churchmen by providing them with cathedral offices—canonries, prebends, and archdeaconries. It was here and not at the parish level that the pope made appointments, for he seldom interfered with private rights of advowson. Both king and pope wished to tax the English clergy. The king had the advantage, for he could exert pressure upon the English church, and the Commons would not tolerate papal taxation of the clergy. In the quarrels of king and pope the English Parliament sided wholeheartedly with the Crown.

Throughout the hostilities, however, neither party wished for a serious split. The popes understood the benefits of friendship with the English kings, who in turn found the popes and cardinals useful in their diplomacy. Hence king and pope often worked together, with compromises and adjustments. When the pope was asked to pay part of the ransom for the French King John, some of the money was raised from the English clergy with the assistance of the king of England. Although both king and pope had rights in the selection of English bishops, it was normally the former who got his way; in return he was inclined to allow the papacy to make provisions for lesser places. There was a remarkable agreement of this kind between Richard II and the pope in 1398. Hence royal denunciations of papal provisions often were made for effect; but Parliament opposed papal taxation in order to make the clergy's money available for the king and thus lighten the burden on the laity.

There were other reasons for the anticlericalism of the time. The church in the fourteenth century was not animated by great religious zeal. There was no movement of reform, such as the monastic revival in the eleventh and twelfth centuries or the rise of the friars in the thirteenth, to sharpen religious enthusiasm. The spiritual leadership of former ages was lacking. A parish church or cathedral office was regarded as a piece of property to be sought and exploited rather than as a means of serving God. The churchmen portrayed in Chaucer's *Canterbury Tales* were in no way meant to inspire deep veneration or devout respect.

The church was not as wealthy as it appeared. In the twelfth and thirteenth centuries it had been the master of such vast wealth that it could hold its own with kings and magnates, but it had lost heavily as land values sank in the fourteenth century and the income from agriculture declined. The church could not recoup its fortunes, as did the nobility, by going to war. Although the greater monasteries

Pilgrims leaving Canterbury. The walls of the city are seen in the background. (British Library, Royal MS 18D.ii, f.148)

recovered from the shock of the Black Death, many smaller ones and nunneries as well were in financial difficulties. If a monastery leased its demesne, it lost control of its own lands; monks living on rents appeared less useful than those who actively managed their property. Monasteries, which were heavily taxed, had other financial burdens. Their hospitality offered to travelers imposed a heavy drain.

Many parish priests lived in poverty. John Ball, who figured prominently in the Peasants' Revolt, was a poor priest who would gladly have seen the upper clergy renounce their comfortable livings. In the long run this decline in the wealth of the church was certain to bring a decline in influence. Yet the clergy were often regarded with jealousy for their landed property and for the conspicuous wealth of a few great churchmen.

The prestige of the pope as the head of the universal Church also declined during this period. Very early in the century a conflict arose between Philip IV of France and Boniface VIII, an arrogant and lofty pope who was so badly defeated in the quarrel that he died of chagrin in 1303. Two years later Philip persuaded the cardinals to elect a French pope, Clement V, who eventually established a new papal capital at Avignon in Provence just on the frontier of France. For almost seventy years the popes remained at Avignon and formed damaging associations with the French monarchy. This association damaged their position as international leaders. In 1378 another scandal befell the papacy when a disputed election led one pope to live in Rome and another at Avignon. The Great Schism, as it was called, continued until 1417 and did much harm to the unity of the church.

Meanwhile in England, anticlericalism was given a theological justification by a group of writers and thinkers at Oxford. Of these writers the most important, though perhaps not the ablest, was John Wycliffe. A man of intellectual power but of rather narrow sympathies, he dominated thought at Oxford in his own generation. He entered the royal service early in the 1370s and played a prominent role in politics, especially when he interceded for John of Gaunt in quarrels with the bishops over taxation.

With a strong bias against ecclesiastical authority, Wycliffe's views became increasingly heretical. He held that no lordship, lay or clerical, was justified unless the lord was a good man in a state of grace. A sinful person had no right to authority or property, and if a churchman abused his property the secular power might deprive him of it. This doctrine, which was subversive of all ecclesiastical authority, was condemned by the pope in 1377. Wycliffe also developed the radical concept of the true church as the community of believers and not the hierarchy of ecclesiastical dignitaries. Though not heretical in itself, this view led to assertions by Wycliffe that popes and cardinals could err, that they were not necessary for the government of the church, and that a worldly pope was a heretic who deserved deposition. Finally, Wycliffe struck at the heart of Catholic orthodoxy by denying the doctrine of transubstantiation, the belief that in the Mass the bread and wine became Christ's body and blood. Wycliffe stressed the Scriptures as the source of truth, sufficient in themselves both as a revelation of Christ and as a guide to conduct.

These views gave strength to John of Gaunt's anticlerical policy; he protected Wycliffe for some years, but the English bishops were thoroughly alarmed. Wycliffe's doctrines were condemned in 1381; in the next year the church's machinery for punishing heretics again was strengthened, and a persecution was begun. In 1401 a statute provided that heretics be burned at the stake. Nevertheless, Wycliffe's views persisted and were advanced by a number of followers who became known as Lollards. This group was responsible for the completion of one of Wycliffe's special projects after his death in 1384—an English translation of the Latin Vulgate Bible. A few Lollards were to be found at Oxford and even among the gentry, but most of them were obscure, unlicensed preachers. It is difficult to know whether these preachers were merely critical of the church or whether they represented a serious heretical movement. Wycliffe's connection with them is also uncertain. He collected a group of followers at Oxford, though they were largely dispersed by pressure from the church.

RICHARD II, 1377–1399

Upon the death of Edward III in 1377 the throne passed to his grandson, Richard II, a boy of ten and the son of the Black Prince. One of the problems of the time was the tremendous power and political influence wielded by a few wealthy magnates. Chief among these magnates were the young king's uncles. Edward, the Black Prince, and Lionel, duke of Clarence, were dead, but three other sons of Edward III remained: John of Gaunt, Duke of Lancaster; Edmund Langley, Duke of York; and Thomas of Woodstock, soon to be duke of Gloucester. Other magnates were the powerful earls of Arundel, Warwick, and Nottingham. The war with France was going badly and, to continue, would require funds from the Commons, who were reluctant to contribute to unsuccessful expeditions. Behind the problem of finance loomed social and economic questions and a restless sense of impending crisis. The Peasants' Revolt took place in 1381.

A council of regency was established to rule during the king's minority. It was composed of various parties, but the most influential councilor was John of Gaunt. He had great prestige and power as the eldest living son of Edward III and as the owner of the estates of the duchy of Lancaster. The king's mother, Joan of Kent, also proved powerful and influential at court until her death in 1385. As the young king grew to manhood his character became increasingly important.

Richard has been a favorite theme of dramatists, who have sometimes portrayed him as half-mad. He was in fact emotional, unstable, and unpredictable, but also a highly intelligent person. A refined and sensitive king, Richard regarded the nobles as crude and brutal. He excluded them from his friendship and built his own circle of friends and favorites. The magnates, however, regarding themselves as the natural advisers of the Crown, resented Richard's favorites and thought that his innovations in manners—such as the use of pocket handkerchiefs—were effeminate. Given to melancholy and introspection, he brooded over any injury done him, awaiting the hour for revenge. He could thus be vindictive in dealing with his foes. He resented the control of his uncles, and in fact disliked any interference with his actions, either from the magnates or from Parliament.

Richard's reign may be divided into three parts, though the same themes run through them all. As he grew to early manhood, he surrounded himself with a group of courtiers and officials who shared his tastes and opinions. The most important were Michael de la Pole, the son of a famous merchant, who became chancellor and earl of Suffolk, and Robert de Vere, Earl of Oxford, whom Richard created a marquis and later a duke. The magnates regarded these promotions with aversion, but Richard kept his friends and quarreled with John of Gaunt and other nobles. Two explosions resulted. One took place in 1386, when Parliament, inspired by the magnates, demanded the removal of Suffolk from the chancellorship, impeached him, and condemned him to prison. A council was set up to advise the king. It included Thomas of Woodstock, Richard's most hated uncle, and Arundel, his most bitter foe. In 1387 Richard restored Suffolk to favor and prepared for civil war. In the next year, however, Suffolk accepted the summons of the so-called Merciless Parliament, and a

Richard II visits Ireland. (Giraudon/Art Resource)

second explosion resulted. It struck down most of the king's friends. Suffolk and Oxford were driven into exile, others were imprisoned, and a few were executed. The magnates did not employ the procedure of impeachment: they merely accused or appealed Richard's party of treason before the Lords in Parliament. Hence the leading magnates were known as the Lords Appellant. They included Woodstock, Henry Bolingbroke (son of John of Gaunt), Arundel, Warwick, and Nottingham. Threatened with deposition, Richard could only give way.

The second portion of Richard's reign extended from 1388 to 1397. It was a relatively quiet time in which the king appeared to accept the domination of the Lords Appellant. He remained on good terms with John of Gaunt and with Henry Bolingbroke, but there were indications of Richard's deep resentment. In 1389 he declared himself of age and announced that he was free to rule as he pleased. He showed his hatred of Arundel by striking him when Arundel insultingly arrived late at the funeral of Richard's beloved queen, Anne of Bohemia in 1394. He quietly built a party at court, more moderate and less objectionable than the court circle in previous years. Suddenly in 1397 Richard lashed out at his foes. Woodstock, Arundel, and Warwick were arrested and appealed in Parliament just as they had appealed the king's friends in 1388. Arundel was executed, Warwick was banished, and Woodstock was murdered shortly after his arrest. Archbishop Courtenay also was banished; in the next year both Bolingbroke and Nottingham followed him into exile. Thus Richard took vengeance upon the Lords Appellant by striking down the most important men of the kingdom.

From 1397 to 1399 the king high-handedly sought to free himself from the control of Parliament. In 1399, at the death of John Gaunt, Richard seized the estates of the duchy of Lancaster, which should have descended to Gaunt's son, Henry Bolingbroke. It was this act which brought about Richard's downfall. Within a year Bolingbroke invaded England. Finding himself without support, Richard was forced to surrender. Some form of abdication was extorted from him and was presented to Parliament. Bolingbroke then arose and claimed the vacant throne. Since he had a large army behind him, no one objected, and he became king. Shortly afterward there was a failed plot by Richard's friends to restore him to power. At this Richard disappeared, miserably done to death in prison.

LITERATURE AND THE ARTS

Richard II had made his court a center of artistic achievement; hence it is fitting to conclude an account of his reign with a word about literature and the arts in the second half of the fourteenth century. The most important literary development was the replacing of French by English as the language of the upper classes. Henceforth, except for the Latin of the clergy, English was the spoken tongue of all the people. Writing in English had never entirely disappeared during the centuries since the Norman Conquest. This writing had dealt with religious and devotional themes, with denunciations of sin, and with legends and Bible stories. It had often taken the form of translations from French or Latin works. English literature continued into the early fourteenth century; but it was crude and parochial in comparison with the classics in Latin and the brilliant literary achievements of the French in the twelfth and thirteenth centuries.

In the years following 1350, however, writing in English greatly increased, partly in revulsion against all things French. Wycliffe, as we have seen, did some of his writing in English and sponsored an English translation of the Latin Vulgate Bible, a project completed in the 1390s. This was the first translation of the entire Bible into the vernacular. John of Trevisa, a scholar at Oxford, translated books on history and science. *The Travels of Sir John Mandeville,* a translation from the French, recounted the fabulous and exotic adventures of a fictitious English knight on a pilgrimage to Jerusalem. Also written in English were the miracle plays. These dramatic representations of episodes from the Scriptures were performed by members of the craft guilds in the principal towns. Of four famous cycles of miracle plays—those of Chester, York, Coventry, and Wakefield—the first three were developed at this time. Moreover, some English poetry appeared in the north of England. Three of these poems, *Pearl, Patience,* and *Purity,* contained the usual medieval moralizing. A fourth, *Sir Gawain and the Green Knight,* was an Arthurian romance of great imaginative power. Thus writing in the vernacular was increasing rapidly.

The three most important writers of the time were William Langland, John Gower, and—by far the greatest—Geoffrey Chaucer. Langland, the author of *Piers Plowman,* was a poor cleric in minor orders but a man of genius and of some learning. Much of his poem was a satire upon the weakness of the church. A seeker after truth, Langland was bitterly disillusioned with the theologians, friars, and wealthy prelates at the top of the hierarchy. The unrhymed alliterative verse of the somber poem seems archaic, but there are passages of fervent strength and beauty.

John Gower, by contrast, was a cultivated gentleman of wealth and leisure. A stylist interested in the correctness of his verses, he wrote with clarity and ease in French, Latin, and English. His first long poem, in French, was a denunciation of sin. But though a moralist, he had no sympathy with the poor. In a second poem, in Latin, he expressed the horror and detestation aroused in the minds of the upper classes by the Peasants' Revolt. In the same poem he criticized King Richard II with some severity, urging him to emulate his noble father, the Black Prince. Nonetheless, he tells us, the king was kind to him and urged him to compose something more palatable to royalty. It is possible that the king advised him to write in English, which he did in his *Confessio Amantis,* a collection of about a hundred tales intended to entertain as well as instruct the reader.

Few poets have led such an active life in the world of men and of business as did Geoffrey Chaucer. The son of a wine merchant, he became comptroller of the petty customs at the port of London. Through his position as page to nobility and as valet and esquire to Edward III, as well as through his marriage to a lady of the court, he was connected with fashionable society. He served as a soldier in two campaigns in France, in one of which he was captured and had to be ransomed; he was sent on embassies to France and Italy. Chaucer's political positions included justice of the peace, member of Parliament, clerk of the king's works (buildings belonging to the Crown) and deputy-forester in a royal forest. But Chaucer was also an ardent reader, who came home from a long day's work to spend the evenings with his books. Besides all this, he was one of England's greatest poets.

Chaucer's literary contributions made up for what had been lacking since Anglo-Saxon times—creative writing in the vernacular comparable to anything produced on the Continent. He did so, not by returning to archaic verse forms, but by studying and learning from continental models. In his early poems—*The Book of the Duchess, The House of Fame,* and *The Parliament of Fowls*—there was too much French influence. But the genius of the poet was maturing. In his *Troilus and Criseide* he transformed Boccaccio's sensuous tale into a series of subtle character studies. Chaucer's masterpiece was the *Canterbury Tales,* written between 1387 and his death in 1400. This was a collection of stories told by members of a company of pilgrims as they journeyed from London to Canterbury; the storytellers were described in the famous *Prologue,* one of the finest bits of social history in English literature.

Chaucer's greatness lay in his sympathetic understanding of all humanity, in his tolerance, humor, and gentle satire, in his poetic gifts, and his powers of description and of vivid imagery. Above all, though their patterns of speech reveal a world long ago, he made his characters live for all time.

In architecture two principal developments took place during the fourteenth century. First, the Early English style, which was simple, austere, and restrained, with great reliance upon symbolism, developed into the more elaborate and luxuriant Decorated Gothic. This new style was dominant from about 1275 to about 1350. It was made possible by greater technical skill in engineering and building and in carving in stone and alabaster. A greater interest in the world of nature called for more realism and exactness in copying natural forms.

Columns became stronger and more slender, walls and roofs lighter in weight though more firmly constructed. It was now possible to enlarge windows and place them in the aisles rather than in the clerestory. Huge windows often were constructed in the east or west end of the church. The tracery in the windows ceased to be geometrical and became flowing, flamboyant, and curvilinear, with freedom for the play of colored glass and intricate design. Artistic sculpture produced fine carvings of leaves, flowers, animals, and human figures as well as small arches, pinnacles, and canopies surrounding a tomb. Sometimes the result was such a riot of exuberant decoration, as in the tomb of Edward II at Gloucester, that the tomb itself was all but hidden. There was a fondness for the ogival arch, which, curving outward and then inward and rising to a point, was sophisticated and decorative, though structurally weak. Brightly colored paint was used freely on tombs, effigies, and pictured walls. The vaulting also became more elaborate. Cross-ribs of stone had always been used to help support the roof, but now other ribs were introduced to cover the vault with complicated designs. Finally, architectural devices were employed to soften the divisions and enhance the unity between parts of the cathedral.

Many of the embellishments of the Decorated style were works of art. And yet, over all, something was lost. The restraint of the thirteenth century degenerated into ostentation, into prettiness, and into decoration for its own sake quite apart from any religious purpose.

A second development in architecture was the emergence in the mid-fourteenth century of the Perpendicular style. Although this style dominated English architecture through the remainder of the Middle Ages, it was almost entirely confined to England. The reasons for its appearance are not wholly clear. It may have stemmed from a desire, as in literature, to repudiate French influence. While the Decorated Gothic became increasingly ornate in France, English Perpendicular architecture conveyed an impression of somber and pious austerity symbolic of English thought in the later Middle Ages. Moreover, building in the Perpendicular style was comparatively cheap. Parts could be prepared in standardized units before they were set in place. And since contracts were made with master masons at prearranged prices, it was to the mason's interest to build as cheaply as he could within the terms of the contract.

The perpendicular style of architecture. Fan vaulting in the nave, Kings College Chapel, Cambridge. (A. F. Kersting)

Distinctive features of the Perpendicular style included splendid fan vaulting as in the Ante-chapel at King's College, Cambridge and in St. George's Chapel at Windsor. Its characteristic enormous windows are seen at York Minster. Increased height of the columns and clerestory in the nave, with the triforium shrinking to a strip of paneling, and a constant emphasis upon vertical lines all point to this peculiarly English style.

Art took many other forms in the second half of the fourteenth century. Fine halls, such as Westminster Hall, were constructed with elaborate wooden roofs. English embroidery, used to decorate ceremonial robes, was famous for its elaborate designs and bright colors. In the same way the illumination of manuscripts with elegant initial letters and with drawings of leaves, animals (especially rabbits), and human figures, was brought to a high state of perfection in the monasteries and in the shops of professionals. Sculpture in stone and alabaster, wall paintings in churches and manor houses, stained glass, effigies in stone or cast in bronze—all indicated that Richard's reign attained a high level of artistic achievement.

CHRONOLOGY

War and Plague

1327–1377	Edward III
1337	Hundred Years' War begins
1339	Knights and burgesses act together in Parliament
1340	Battle of Sluys
1346	Battle of Crécy
1348	Black Death (Bubonic Plague)
1351	Statute of Laborers
1351 and 1390	Statutes of Provisors
1353, 1365, and 1393	Statutes of Praemunire
1356	Battle of Poitiers; French king captured, held for ransom
1360	Treaty of Bretigny
1363	Staple at Calais
1370–1390	John Wycliffe; Bible in English
1376	Good Parliament; Impeachments; office of Speaker of House of Commons established
1377–1399	Richard II
1381	Peasants' Revolt
1387–1400	Chaucer's *Canterbury Tales*
1388	Merciless Parliament; Lords Appellant
1399	Death of John of Gaunt; overthrow of Richard II

9

Kingship in the Fifteenth Century

HENRY IV, 1399–1413

Henry Bolingbroke, England's first Lancastrian king, had engineered the deposition of Richard II in 1399 and secured the Crown as Henry IV. Like his father, John of Gaunt, Duke of Lancaster, Henry was a regal figure, accustomed to riches and magnificence, with the lofty and impressive bearing of a prince. He was an able and energetic man of much independence of character. Although he could be both impulsive and obstinate, the harsh experiences of his youth and exile had taught him caution, determination, and self-restraint. He longed for military glory, having exhibited great skill in jousting as a youth, but he was frustrated all his life by poor health. Mental strain was apt to prostrate him physically. At one time the king appeared so pale and white that it was rumored he had contracted leprosy. He was a studious man, passionately fond of music.

Under more agreeable conditions Henry might have proved a highly effective sovereign, but his reign was not as successful as the great coup by which he obtained the throne. He never escaped the fact that he was a usurper. Richard II, being childless, had named as his heirs the descendants of his uncle Lionel, Duke of Clarence (the second son of Edward III). These descendants belonged to the family of Mortimer, headed by the earl of March, and as such had a substantial claim to the throne. Hence the circumstances of Henry's accession offered a standing excuse for rebellion against him. Although he was cautious and conciliatory with his opposition, his reign was troubled and his position insecure.

The king's first difficulties arose in Wales, where much sympathy was felt for Richard II. Their fear of exploitation by both the English government and the marcher lords was easily fanned into rebellion by Owen Glendower,[1] a Welsh

---

[1] The Welsh name was Owain Glyn Dwr.

landowner. The revolt, spreading throughout all Wales, proved very difficult to extinguish. It became much more dangerous in 1402, when Glendower was joined by discontented factions in England. He had captured Sir Edmund Mortimer, the uncle of the earl of March, and Mortimer expected that Henry would ransom him. When Henry declined to do so Mortimer joined Glendower.

Meanwhile the king found that he had irritated the Percy family, who held large territories in the north of England. The head of the family was Henry Percy, Earl of Northumberland, whose son Henry, nicknamed Hotspur, has been made famous by Shakespeare. Although members of the Percy family had been among the king's most valuable supporters in the revolt of 1399, they were now rebellious. Perhaps they thought that, having helped to make one king, they could make another more to their liking. Henry owed them money for their services as wardens of the marches facing Scotland. What's more, when Hotspur defeated the Scots at Homildon Hill in 1402, the king demanded that the Scottish prisoners be surrendered to him for ransom. Hotspur was also Mortimer's brother-in-law. When the Percys suddenly joined Glendower, the king promptly gathered an army and defeated and killed Hotspur at the Battle of Shrewsbury in 1403. Glendower, however, continued to receive aid from Northumberland and obtained some assistance from France. By 1410 his rebellion was complete and, though he departed for the mountains, Glendower's disappearance and expected return became legendary. He had caused Henry great anxiety but had left his own country shattered.

Throughout the Welsh revolt Henry was also greatly troubled by France. Richard II's widow, Isabella, was the daughter of the French king, Charles VI, and the revolt in 1399 had thus involved the deposition of a French princess. Henry had hoped to keep Isabella in England with an arranged marriage to his eldest son, thus continuing the peace with Paris. But the French demanded a return of Isabella's dowry, and in the end Henry sent her back to her family at great expense.

Henry soon discovered that in the return of Isabella he had merely lost a trump card, for relations with France grew worse. Taking the initiative, the French harried the southern coast of England, burning Plymouth in 1403 and landing on the Isle of Wight in the following year. They sent aid to Glendower and even threatened to attack Calais. Such aggressions disrupted trade in the Channel and annoyed the English merchants. The magnates, wishing for plundering expeditions against France in the old manner, regarded the king's policy as tame, but Henry had no thought of war. He had no money for such a large undertaking and no wish to push the French into greater hostility. Danger from France subsided after 1407.

Henry had been accustomed to great private riches, but as king he found that his finances were difficult and that demands of all kinds kept him short of funds. His poverty put him at the mercy of the Commons, who tightened their hold on taxation, criticized his defense of the southern coast, and demanded that he curtail his expenses. They appointed councils to supervise his administration, so that he "was constitutionally unable to control any part of the machinery of government without the consent of a council whose nomination had been imposed upon him." It was in Henry's time that the Commons reached the height of their influence during the Middle Ages. Historians used to speak of a "Lancastrian constitution" as though the

Commons were attempting to build a system of parliamentary control, but this myth has been discarded. This was simply a period in which the monarchy was weak and in which the Commons naturally took advantage of that weakness.

Toward the end of the reign Henry also had difficulties with family members, especially with his son Henry, Prince of Wales. Though still very young, the prince was masterful and ambitious and appeared eager to take his father's place. He quarreled with his father over policy, resisted the king's efforts to inquire into Lollardry at Oxford University, opposed his father's chancellor, and supported one faction in France while his father favored another. While it is possible that their differences stemmed from an honest clash of policy, the prince was certainly pushing and impatient. Twice he came to London with troops as though he meant to take over the government by force.

Another branch of the royal family was becoming prominent. John, Henry, and Thomas Beaufort—the king's half brothers—were the sons of John of Gaunt and Katherine Swynford, Gaunt's mistress and later his third wife. The sons had been legitimized by Parliament in 1397. John, Earl of Somerset, became chamberlain and captain of Calais but died in 1410. Henry, Bishop of Winchester and later a cardinal, was a brilliant though scheming man who was to play a great part in politics for many years. Thomas, Earl of Dorset, who served for a time as chancellor, was a noble of fine character, willing to occupy high office without using it for his own advantage. The Beauforts appear to have allied with the prince, though the details are obscure.

Henry IV died in 1413, a disillusioned man broken in spirit and neurotically fearful about his physical condition.

HENRY V (1413–1422) AND THE WAR WITH FRANCE

Henry V, the warlike king who renewed the long conflict with France, was highly praised by his contemporaries as the leader who restored glory to England after the tame and humiliating inaction of Henry IV. Shakespeare portrayed him as the happy warrior; and Winston Chruchill recounted the triumphs of Henry's French campaigns. Henry was a tough young soldier with a gift for leadership and a sense of discipline. He had grown up in the Welsh wars against Owen Glendower, and when he was crowned at the age of twenty-five Henry had been commanding troops for more than a decade. A formidable foe, Henry could demolish the arguments of his opponents with a keen and passionate logic. He was self-righteously certain that God would give him justice against the wicked French, who in 1361 had conquered the areas ceded to England at Bretigny. He treated the French with great severity, as though he were God's avenging angel. But although his character was not attractive, his achievements should not be underestimated. Like Edward III, he won the confidence of the aristocratic classes; all the great English magnates followed him to the French wars. Once more the nation was united in patriotic endeavor against a foreign foe. Having solidified England's power, he would have been king of France if he had lived a little longer.

Henry's ambition to conquer France once and for all, to create a dual monarchy in

Battle scene, fifteenth century. (British Library, Cottonian MS, Julius E, iv, Art 6, f. 20v)

which the same king ruled in London and in Paris, was an impossible one. It gravely miscalculated the temper of France, placed an unbearable strain on the monarchy in England, and condemned both countries to war and suffering. And thus, although Henry's hold on his kingdom was stronger than his father's had been, his reign added no lasting stability or permanence to the kingship. His triumphs were ephemeral, his projects were risky, and his uncertain adventures were largely ill-advised. In the later Middle Ages the inducement of immediate gain by aggressive war was obviously more potent than the sober consideration of consequences.

Henry was very fortunate in the timing of his attack on France. The revival of French power begun in the 1360s was now at an end, and France was highly vulnerable. Elderly King Charles VI was subject to fits of insanity. Moreover, there was a bitter feud between two factions of the royal family. One was led by John the Fearless, Duke of Burgundy and son of Philip the Bold, who had made Burgundy into a powerful duchy, including large districts in the Netherlands. His strength lay to the east and north of France. The other faction, the Orleanists or Armagnacs, were the followers of the duke of Orleans, a brother of the king. In 1407 Orleans had been murdered by the Burgundians, and this crime so deepened the feud that the two sides were at daggers' points. Both had appealed to England for help in the later

Siege of a coastal town, fifteenth century. (British Library, Royal MS 14E.iv, f. 23)

years of Henry IV, who had sympathized with the Orleanists, but Henry V, then Prince of Wales, had pursued his own policy of friendship with the Burgundians. As soon as he became king he claimed the French throne as well, together with the territories ceded to England at Bretigny. The Orleanists at Paris tried to restrain him by various concessions, but he quickly prepared for war.

In 1415 he landed with a well-equipped army at Harfleur in Normandy, took the town after a month's siege, and began a long march through Normandy to Calais. Not far from Calais he was met by a large French army at Agincourt. The French knights expected to overwhelm the English line of defense by sheer numbers, but they were instead caught on a narrow front with English archers on both flanks, and slaughtered like sheep in a terrible defeat. The battle brought Henry great prestige and large sums of money from ransoms but no great political advantage. Changing his strategy, he invaded Normandy again in 1417 and began a systematic conquest of the principal towns in order to obtain a permanent hold on some portion of France. It was advantageous that the Burgundians were also attacking Paris, which they captured in 1418 along with the French king. France was now divided among three parties: the

Burgundians in the north, the Orleanists in the area south of the Loire River, and Henry's forces in Normandy.

It seemed possible that the Orleanists and Burgundians would join forces until 1419, when an Orleanist murdered the duke of Burgundy, and the rift between the factions widened hopelessly. The new duke of Burgundy, Philip the Good, quickly allied with Henry, making possible the Treaty of Troyes, which was concluded in 1420. This famous treaty provided that Henry become the king of France upon the death of Charles VI and that meanwhile as regent he should marry Charles's daughter Catherine. Although Charles's son, the dauphin, was disinherited, southern France remained loyal to him and refused to accept the treaty. Determined to crush the dauphin's party, Henry continued the struggle. He contracted dysentery in a campaign in 1422 and died at thirty-five.

HENRY VI, 1422–1461

The Minority

The sudden removal of the dominant personality of Henry V was one of the decisive facts in the history of the Lancastrian dynasty. As Henry's heir was merely nine months old, England was faced with a long minority and a dangerous vacuum in the supreme place of monarchy. There was bitter conflict among councilors and nobles, and great dispute over the task of governing large areas of France. Most unfortunately, the vacuum in leadership continued after Henry VI came of age. He proved to be a pious, gentle, well-intentioned recluse, utterly incapable in war and politics. Thoroughly dominated by his councilors, uncles, and his wife, Henry was subject in his last years to fits of insanity. He lived to see his great inheritance crumble, his finances decay, his crown tossed about among usurpers, and his magnates engaged in civil war. His reign represents the nadir of medieval kingship.

For many years the government was dominated by three uncles of the king, ruling with the support and guidance of a council nominated in Parliament. The most respected of these men was John, Duke of Bedford, a brother of Henry V. A skillful soldier and an able administrator, his task was the government of France under the Treaty of Troyes. For some years he maintained and even extended English power, but his constant trips abroad prevented him from playing a dominant role in English politics. A second brother of Henry V was Humphrey, Duke of Gloucester. Gloucester was a glamorous patron of the arts, who occasionally won a following among the merchants and people at large. But he was rash and unstable as a politician and pursued policies at variance with those of Bedford and other councilors. He was mistrusted by almost everyone in authority. Henry V had intended that he should have a large share in governing England, and in 1422 Gloucester sought to be named as regent. The magnates in Parliament, refusing to give him such power, made him protector and defender of the realm—but only when Bedford was in France. Parliament, moreover, established a nominated council. Gloucester became "chief of the king's Council," but was not to act without its consent. Dissatisfied with this arrangement, he proved to be very troublesome.

Gloucester was also constantly at odds with the king's great-uncle, Henry Beaufort, Bishop of Winchester. Beaufort was important in politics for an unusually long period—from 1404, when for a time he held the office of Chancellor, to his death in 1447. He was extremely wealthy, drawing riches not only from his bishopric but also from his position as a trustee of the duchy of Lancaster. His large loans to the government helped to save it from financial collapse. His great wealth and political savvy were more than a match for Gloucester. On more than one occasion Bedford was summoned home to settle their disputes. Beaufort's faction gradually became supreme, dominating the king and the Council during the 1440s. It included John and Edmund, Dukes of Somerset, William de la Pole, Earl of Suffolk, and Queen Margaret of Anjou, whom the king married in 1445.

The War in France, 1422–1453

English success in the Hundred Years' War continued for some years after the death of Henry V. Henry VI succeeded Charles VI as king of France, and most of the northern part of France was ruled from Rouen by the English duke of Bedford acting as regent. Bedford maintained a close alliance with Duke Philip of Burgundy, whose sister he married, though the alliance was strained by the antics of Humphrey, Duke of Gloucester, who indulged in a personal feud against Burgundy. English possessions were consolidated and extended, Bedford won an important victory at Verneuil in 1424, and many English magnates and lesser captains gained renown in France. This was a time of success and enrichment for the English nobility, at the expense of the people of northern France, who were subjected to many hardships.

The period of English triumph, however, came to an end in 1429 with the appearance of Joan of Arc. In one of the miraculous stories of history this saintly peasant girl persuaded the dauphin that victory was within his reach and gave him new hope and determination. She was permitted to accompany the army and to share in planning its strategy. Riding with the vanguard in full armor, accompanied by a body of priests, she inspired the troops with religious and patriotic fervor. The English were besieging the city of Orléans, the door to southern France. They were quickly driven north, and the dauphin was consecrated as King Charles VII. Although Joan was captured by the Burgundians, sold to the English, and burned at the stake for heresy in 1431, and although the young Henry VI was brought to Paris and crowned in the same year, success was now on the side of the French. The deaths of Bedford and of the Burgundian alliance was a blow to the English cause. The duke thereupon made peace with Charles VII and recognized him as king of France.

The new English commander, Richard, Duke of York, made little headway against the French, who took the initiative both in Normandy and in Gascony in the south. It was felt in England that the war must end and a truce was arranged in 1444, largely through the earl of Suffolk. In the next year the marriage of Henry to Margaret of Anjou opened the way to peace, then Charles resumed the war in 1449 and expelled

English possessions in France in 1428.

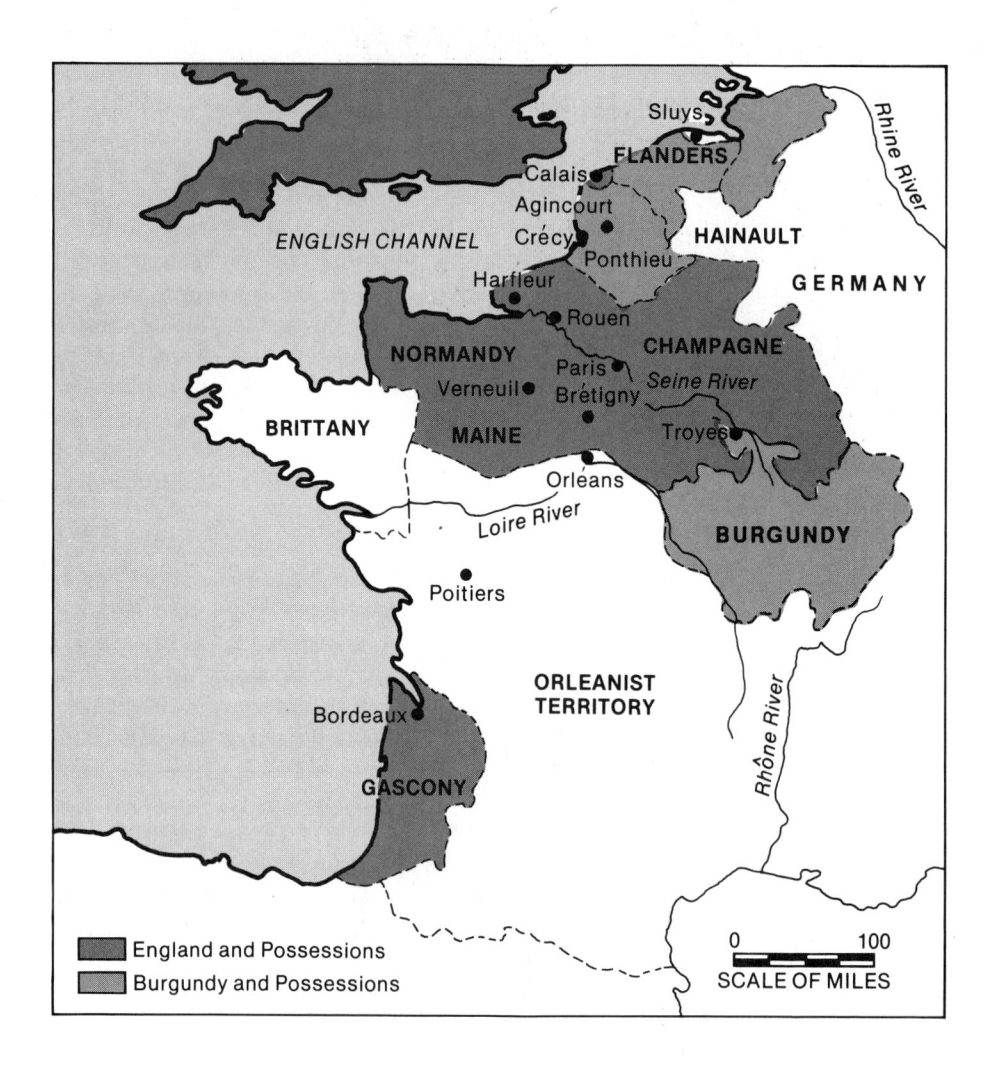

the English from Gascony in 1453. With Calais its only French territory, England's dream of conquering France was at an end. The victory of the French was due to superior military tactics and to the centralized government established by Charles VII. The overall decline in English morale and degeneration in English monarchy also proved advantageous to the French.

The Wars of the Roses, 1455–1471

The degeneration in the English monarchy led to a period of civil wars in England known as the Wars of the Roses. Henry's government weakened steadily under the impact of military defeat, corruption, poverty, and increasing disorder throughout the country. An ineffective king who simply retired from the scene to let affairs take their course, he permitted dangerous rivalries and animosities among the nobles. Such a rivalry arose between the Beauforts, who were members of the House of Lancaster, and the Yorkists, another branch of the royal family. There was no great issue at stake between them. The Yorkists were discontented magnates who felt themselves excluded from power in a weak and corrupt court. There was, however, a cause for personal dislike. After Bedford's death in 1435, Richard, Duke of York, had been appointed supreme commander in France but later had been superseded by the Beaufort dukes of Somerset and had been forced to yield his authority. Smarting under this humiliation, Richard was naturally critical of their foreign failures and domestic administration.

It was this rivalry that erupted into the Wars of the Roses. The wars occurred at a time when the nobles were no longer expending their energies in France and apt to cause trouble in England. Moreover, all through the fifteenth century there was uncertainty about the succession to the throne. This uncertainty stemmed from the revolution in 1399, when the Lancastrians had seized power. Richard of York's claim was substantial. On his mother's side, through the line of the Mortimers, he was descended from Lionel, Duke of Clarence, the second son of Edward III. His father was the son of Edmund Langley, Duke of York, Edward's fourth son.[2] Richard was also the wealthiest magnate in the kingdom. Hence, when Henry VI proved a failure, there was an alternate claimant about whom discontent could rally.

The period of the Wars of the Roses was a time of trouble and disorder with only occasional battles between rival magnates, and long intervals of peace. The life of the nation was less disturbed than one might suppose. However, because the wars came at a time when the government was near collapse, they made that collapse more complete. The name given the wars is also misleading, for although the white rose was the emblem of the Yorkists, the red rose was not a badge of the Lancastrians but of the Tudors, who did not come to the throne until 1485.

Widespread hostility arose against the Beauforts in 1450. In that year the earl of Suffolk, a member of the Beaufort faction, who had arranged the king's marriage by making concessions to France, was impeached in Parliament, exiled, and murdered while crossing the Channel. In the same year there was a rising in Kent known as Jack Cade's Rebellion. Unlike the Peasants' Revolt of 1381, it consisted of small landowners and respectable members of the middle classes, and its aims were political rather than economic. Actually, it was a protest against corrupt officials, a lack of justice, the supposed treachery in the loss of France, the interference of great lords in parliamentary elections, and against the Statute of Laborers. These Yorkist allies purposed to drive the Beaufort faction from power and then introduce reforms, but after murdering several London courtiers they soon were suppressed.

The significance of the revolt lay in its disclosure of deep and widespread dissatisfaction with the government. In two Parliaments between 1450 and 1454 Edmund Beaufort, Duke of Somerset, was hotly denounced by the Yorkists. Mounting hostilities between the parties finally erupted into battle at St. Albans in 1455. Somerset was killed and for a time the Lancastrians retained control of the govern-

---

[2] See the genealogical table on page 207.

The Wars of the Roses: castles and battles 1450–1485.

ment. In 1460 the earl of Warwick invaded England from Calais with a Yorkist army, occupied London, and defeated the Lancastrians at Northampton. Richard now claimed the throne. However, he was killed in a battle at Wakefield in Yorkshire; it was his son Edward who obtained the crown in 1461. The Lancastrians were defeated once more at Towton near York. Margaret and Henry VI fled to Scotland.

THE COLLAPSE OF GOVERNMENT UNDER HENRY VI

The reign of Henry VI was more than a time of weak government and of civil war between factions of the nobles; it was a period in which the whole structure of medieval government nearly collapsed, beginning with the old system of taxation. Taxes, as they had developed in the thirteenth and fourteenth centuries, consisted of lay subsidies and customs duties voted in Parliament and of clerical subsidies voted in Convocation. These taxes continued through the reign of Henry V. Henry's victories in France stirred his country's patriotism and he was able to obtain large grants from the Commons. Henry VI was not so fortunate, for in his reign the Commons strongly resisted taxation.

A number of reasons account for the lack of generosity on the part of the Commons. It was discouraging to appropriate funds for a war that was being lost. During the 1420s the cost of war and government in France had been met to a considerable extent by plunder and by levies on the French, especially in Normandy, but as these sources dried up the full burden was thrust upon the English Exchequer. The Commons suspected that affairs in France were being mishandled and that courtiers were intercepting funds intended for military operations. It was known that Cardinal Beaufort and other creditors of the king were enjoying large profits, and that Suffolk and the queen were making contributions in order to build their faction. Such a government was in no position to persuade the Commons for money.

Even more important was the fact that the fifteenth century was a period of recession, arrested development, and declining national income. There was also a shrinkage in agricultural trade. Many towns suffered, including Norwich, Nottingham, Northampton, and Leicester, but London, Southampton, and Bristol remained prosperous. It is probable that the rapid growth of the clothing industry in the second half of the fourteenth century leveled off and even declined in the fifteenth century. Many districts, therefore, could not maintain the old level of taxation. Poverty was both a cause and a standing excuse for refusal to grant taxes.

Grants of money by convocation were also diminishing. In the time of Wycliffe and John of Gaunt the church had resisted the principle that its subsidies should parallel those of the Commons. By the reign of Henry VI the church had won, and its contributions were less than those of a century before. The Crown, of course, had other sources of revenue, the steadiest and most reliable of which was the duty on exported wool. But these revenues, burdened with exemptions and assignments that greatly reduced their yield, were also declining. The Crown owned estates in Wales, Cornwall, Cheshire, Yorkshire, and elsewhere, though they were often mismanaged. Other miscellaneous revenues were collected, often coming from old feudal rights. Had there been no war, the monarchy might have been self-supporting, but now the Crown resorted to constant borrowing, and dubious devices to make ends meet. This "pauper government" ruled with the consent of its wealthier subjects, who were given economic favors and inducements to lend the king their money. Before the Wars of the Roses the Crown's finances had already fallen into a state of pitiful dilapidation.

The medieval conception of the community of the realm, in which the king consulted with the ruling classes in Parliament, had come to an end. Parliament, especially the Commons, having developed greatly in the time of Edward III, now occupied a place of surprising importance in the reigns of Richard II and Henry IV. It is, of course, suspected that the Commons were frequently prompted to action by the magnates. About 1430, however, Parliaments were summoned less frequently than in the past, and no longer held a central place in the government. This decline took place partly because no government sector was functioning properly, and because the issues involved in the Wars of the Roses concerned the relations between king and nobles. Sometimes Parliament became caught up in the struggle, acting as an agent of the faction in power. A principal cause of Parliament's diminished influence was the king's inability to obtain additional funds.

The period of Parliament's greatest influence in the late fourteenth and early fifteenth centuries was also a time of much government by council. During the reigns of Richard II and Henry IV, councils were nominated in Parliament to remain with the king and control his actions. The Good Parliament of 1376, having impeached several royal ministers, set up a council in the vain hope of preventing a recurrence of old evils. A council established in 1386 represented an attempt by the magnates to check the actions of Richard II. This development reached its climax in the reign of Henry IV, when in 1404 and again in 1406 continual councils were named in Parliament to supervise the government. Such councils disappeared in the reign of Henry V, but the minority of Henry VI necessitated a council of regency which served until the 1440s, when power fell into the hands of the Beaufort faction. The effectiveness of these nominated councils varied greatly as circumstances altered, but there were periods in which they exercised considerable authority. They came to an end in the upheavals of the mid-fifteenth century.

A third indication of government degeneration was the increasing amount of corruption among officials, who exploited their positions to increase their own wealth and power and to obtain places for their friends and retainers. Government was becoming a spoils system in which the interests of the Crown were neglected or forgotten. The earl of Warwick, for example, was captain of Calais in the last years of Henry VI, from whom he held his commission. He refused to surrender his position at the command of the king, made Calais a Yorkist center, and in 1460, using Calais as a base, he invaded England.

Finally, the Crown could not maintain law and order. Apart from the battles of Lancaster and York, there was much disorder and violence throughout the country. This violence erupted into petty wars between great landed families, as when members of the Percy and Neville families battled at Stamford Bridge in 1453. Many lords not only had retainers who could supply them with troops but maintained small armies of men-at-arms who wore the distinctive badge or livery of their master. This practice was known as livery and maintenance or "Bastard Feudalism." Maintenance meant that a lord attempted to secure governmental offices for his followers, and defended them if they fell afoul of the law. The term "Bastard Feudalism," implying illegitimacy, indicates that something was out of order. Earlier feudalism was based upon land tenure and represented an attempt to secure public order. The new system was based upon the purchase of services, and signaled the collapse of public order. It was not uncommon for a lord to come to court with a body of armed men when one of his dependents was on trial. Such action was disruptive of all impartial justice. Sheriffs and justices of the peace[3] were intimidated, jurors were bribed, and even the itinerant justices from London were defied. The men-at-arms who followed a magnate were often ruffians, terrorizing their localities, committing violent crimes, and engaging in brawls and riots that could become small battles. It was impossible for a poor man to obtain justice against the rich and powerful, and such an attempt might be dangerous. Thus the machinery of justice was paralyzed by the weakness of the Crown.

EDWARD IV, 1461–1483

The First Decade of the Reign

The first ten years of the reign of Edward IV were largely a continuation of wars and disputes. The Lancastrians were strong in the northern part of the country, and Queen Margaret was seeking aid from her kinsman, Louis XI of France. In 1464 a break occurred between Edward and his strongest supporter, Richard Neville, Earl of Warwick, known as the Kingmaker. Preoccupied with suppressing Lancastrian centers of opposition the two had allowed their relations to falter. Warwick held great authority in military affairs, was given a general supervision of the north, and led a number of expeditions against castles still in Lancastrian hands. The rift began when Edward secretly married Elizabeth Woodville, a beautiful widow whose connections were Lancastrian. Warwick considered the marriage unsuitable and was angered at its secrecy. He discovered, moreover, that numerous Woodvilles were now obtaining offices and places at court.

Foreign policy was also hotly debated. France and Burgundy were hostilely competing for alliance with England. Warwick favored an agreement with Louix XI, who had dropped his early support of Queen Margaret. But Edward turned to Burgundy, intending to protect the market for English cloth in the Netherlands, which was controlled by Burgundy. In 1467 he concluded an alliance with Burgundy

---

[3]Justices of the peace were country gentlemen who at first were appointed to assist the itinerant justices. In time they were commissioned to try a variety of cases.

A walled garden in a town, late fifteenth century. (British Library, Additional MS 19720, f.214)

and arranged for the marriage of his sister, Margaret, with Duke Charles the Bold. Tensions between Edward and Warwick increased.

In 1470 Warwick changed sides, joined the Lancastrians, and began a revolt. Edward, caught off guard without an army, fled to the Netherlands. For a moment Warwick was master of the kingdom. King Henry VI, was then brought from the Tower (he had been captured by Edward in 1465), and Warwick ruled in his name. Edward struck back quickly. Gathering forces in Burgundy and the Netherlands, he returned to England in 1471, defeated and slew Warwick at the Battle of Barnet, and captured Henry VI, who was put to death in the Tower a few months later. At the Battle of Tewkesbury in western England Edward defeated and captured Queen Margaret and killed her son Edward, the Prince of Wales. The direct line of the Lancastrian dynasty was now extinct; Warwick the Kingmaker was no more. For the remainder of his reign Edward occupied the throne in relative security.

Edward is described as a tall, fine-looking man, large but well proportioned, with a quick wit, high spirits, and a retentive memory. He was quite unconventional, with little sense of class distinctions, genial and affable to everyone. Such familiarity was often ill-advised, as his proneness to sexual pursuits led him to connections that were felt to be below his royal dignity. Behind these traits of good fellowship and dissipation, however, were other qualities that made him a successful king. He was a strong soldier with a facility for determined action and with the ability to extricate himself from danger. An excellent businessman, Edward was keenly interested in economic questions. In fact, he paid such careful attention to the management of his finances that he died a wealthy man. An able administrator who improved the efficiency and honesty of the government, he restored law and order to the best of his ability. It was during his reign that the power of the monarchy began to revive.

The Government of Edward IV

Edward's achievement in creating a strong monarchy and peaceful countryside was remarkable, and, though he left much work for his successors, the Tudor kings, he laid foundations upon which they were able to build. About the middle of the fifteenth century the population began to slowly increase. Land resumed its former value and the profits of agriculture revived. Commerce also became more prosperous before Edward's reign was over, thus increasing his revenues from customs duties. The people, moreover, were tired of strife and welcomed a king who would promote law and order.

His principal success was improving the finances of the Crown. this was accomplished largely in two ways, both basically quite simple. The first was the abandonment of the war in France. This in itself transformed the whole financial picture, for it had always been the cost of the war that had drained the king's coffers. Edward

Herstomonceaux Castle, Sussex, fifteenth century. Built for comfort as well as defense. (Copyright Country Life)

escaped from the vicious old circle in which the king had first wrung money from a reluctant House of Commons and then spent it on a war that enriched the nobles but impoverished the Crown and drove the king back to the Commons for further funds. On one occasion Edward did secure from the Commons a grant for a campaign in France. Having done so, he allowed himself to be bought off by the French king, who offered him a pension in return for peace. Edward never fought a battle in France.

The second foundation of his financial plan was his steady accumulation of land. In the fourteenth century the amount of land in the hands of the king had been relatively small, and estates coming to the Crown through escheats and forfeitures had been freely granted to courtiers and to the nobility. But the Commons became critical of the king's liberality and in 1404 suggested that he examine the grants made over the last forty years with a view toward resuming the lands that had been given away. To resume lands once they had been granted was an impossible procedure that would have alienated half the aristocracy; yet the Commons insisted that it be attempted.

Edward acquired lands in various ways. Some old Crown lands came into his possession when he became king. To these he added three of the largest inheritances of the later Middle Ages. One was the property of the Yorkists, which came to him from his father. Another was the duchy of Lancaster. This had been added to the lands of the Crown, though it was administered separately, when Henry Bolingbroke, Duke of Lancaster, became Henry IV. The duchy was seized by Edward after his defeat of the Lancastrians. A third group of estates, the very extensive property of Warwick the Kingmaker, was confiscated following Warwick's revolt. There were additional confiscations from the king's brother George, Duke of Clarence, and from other rebel lords.

Edward's policy toward the lands of the Crown was very different from that of earlier rulers. The lands were now retained, increased at every opportunity, and managed with great care. While magnates employed a number of officials who were experts in the management of landed property, the king's land had not been handled in this way. The Exchequer was a department of receipt, not of supervision. It audited the money that was brought to it but did not go into the country to ensure the king was collecting all that was due. Edward, however, placed his lands in the custody of professionals who applied the careful scrutiny given to private estates. These officials were usually members of the royal household; the money they collected was brought to the chamber, which again became a financial department as it had been some centuries before; and the Exchequer was bypassed. The vast estates of the Crown, scattered throughout the country, now represented the king's capital, his endowment, and his accumulated wealth, which brought him substantial revenues and independence from Parliament.

Other sources of income included customs duties, the pension from France, fines levied in the courts, occasional grants from Parliament and from convocation, forced loans, and benevolences. A forced loan was what the name implies: a loan to the king made under some pressure and normally repaid. A benevolence, however, was a gift. The king became skillful in extracting benevolences from wealthy men. Edward

Little Sodbury, Gloucestershire. A fifteenth-century manor house. (Copyright Country Life)

lived in some state and magnificence, for he rightly believed that a show of wealth and power added to the authority of the Crown.

Edward made his government more effective by centralizing power in the hands of his personally selected councilors and household officials. These royal servants were industrious, efficient, loyal, and reasonably honest. As the king's agents, they drew their authority from him, were completely at his command, and could be dismissed at any time. Edward was free from conciliar and parliamentary control.

Edward attempted to make his authority felt in all parts of the realm. He showed an interest in local affairs and selected household officials who had had a share in local government and who maintained their former connections with local officers. On two occasions Edward accompanied his itinerant justices as they made their circuits. To enforce the law in disturbed districts he gave judicial authority to magnates and local councils. There was a small council to administer the royal principality in Wales, and to this council Edward issued a commission to supervise the four English counties of Shropshire, Hereford, Worcester, and Gloucester. He entrusted judicial power in the north to his brother Richard, Duke of Gloucester, and to the earl of Northumberland. Later, when he became king, Richard continued this experiment by establishing a Council in the North Parts.

Richard III. (From Sir George Buck, The History of the Life and Reign of Richard the Third, *London, 1647. Department of Special Collections, Wilson Library, University of Minnesota)*

Royaulte me Lie

The true Portraiture of Richard Plantagenest, of England and of France King Lord of Ireland the third King Richard

RICHARD III, 1483–1485

That Edward had only made a beginning in the suppression of lawlessness is evident from the short and bloody reign of his brother Richard, Duke of Gloucester, who became Richard III. This king was not the complete villain that legend and Shakespeare have made him. An intense, reserved, and silent man, Richard had a serious, even puritanical, side to his character. He had always been completely loyal to his brother, though he might well have sided with his tutor, Warwick the Kingmaker. With a prominent part in the Wars of the Roses Warwick had commanded the right wing of Edward's army at the crucial Battle of Barnet. Edward had trusted him with great authority in the north of England. He fully intended to continue and improve the government established by his brother. At Edward's death, however, he was suddenly faced with a choice either of seizing power (which he could justly claim as his) or of allowing it to slip away. He not only seized it but did so with great violence; and having started upon the course of killing off his adversaries could not turn back. His reign of fear and terror resulted in numerous rebellions, and in 1485 Edward lost his life.

The heir to the throne at the death of Edward IV in 1483 was his young son, a boy of twelve, who figures in English history as Edward V although he never ruled. His mother, the queen, was Elizabeth Woodville, whose relatives filled many of the highest offices, sharing power with a handful of other intimate associates of the late king. The Woodvilles naturally wished to remain in control. Apparently they planned to have Edward crowned at once, to establish a regency with the Queen Mother as regent, and to rule through a council composed of their faction. Richard, meanwhile, resided in the northern part of the kingdom where his power lay. He was the strongest man in the country, and if he could win a few allies among the older nobility he could easily drive the Woodvilles from court. He discovered, moreover, that his brother had made a will naming him as protector of the king and kingdom. Thus the issue was clearly drawn between the two factions. Richard came down from the north and struck quickly. Acting with Henry Stafford, Duke of Buckingham, he seized the king and his escort of Woodvilles as they were on their way to London for the coronation. This violent deed caused consternation among the Woodvilles at court. Some of them fled abroad; the queen entered sanctuary at Westminster. Coming to London, Richard easily persuaded the Council to accept him as protector.

Here the matter might have ended, had Richard remained protector and had the Woodvilles disappeared into obscurity. But the atmosphere was filled with rumors of plots and intrigues, and Richard became suspicious of certain councilors, especially William Lord Hastings, the former chamberlain of Edward IV. At a meeting of the Council Richard suddenly accused Hastings of treason and had him immediately executed. This fatal crime led directly to Richard's seizure of the throne. Summoning Parliament, Richard declared that the marriage of Edward IV and Elizabeth Woodville had been illegal, that Edward V was therefore illegitimate, and that he, Richard, was the rightful successor to his brother. No one was powerful enough to object, and Richard assumed the crown at once. All these events took place within three months of the death of Edward IV. A number of Woodvilles were now executed, and Edward V and his younger brother, a boy of ten, were imprisoned in the Tower. Shortly thereafter they mysteriously disappeared. One can only say that they disappeared while Richard was on the throne, and that he never addressed the rumors of their murder. The story of the "princes in the Tower" has fascinated readers ever since, resulting in many theories and potential villains. Richard III had the opportunity for wrongdoing, and certainly had the motive.

Richard's reign was very short. A revolt in 1483 by the duke of Buckingham in favor of Henry Tudor, a Lancastrian, was suppressed, but in 1485 Henry succeeded and Richard was slain at the Battle of Bosworth Field. The Yorkist attempt to reconstruct the government on a basis of law and order failed in Richard's reign. Yet the Yorkist monarchy, at least under Edward IV, foreshadowed and helped make possible the success of the Tudors.

HOUSE OF LANCASTER

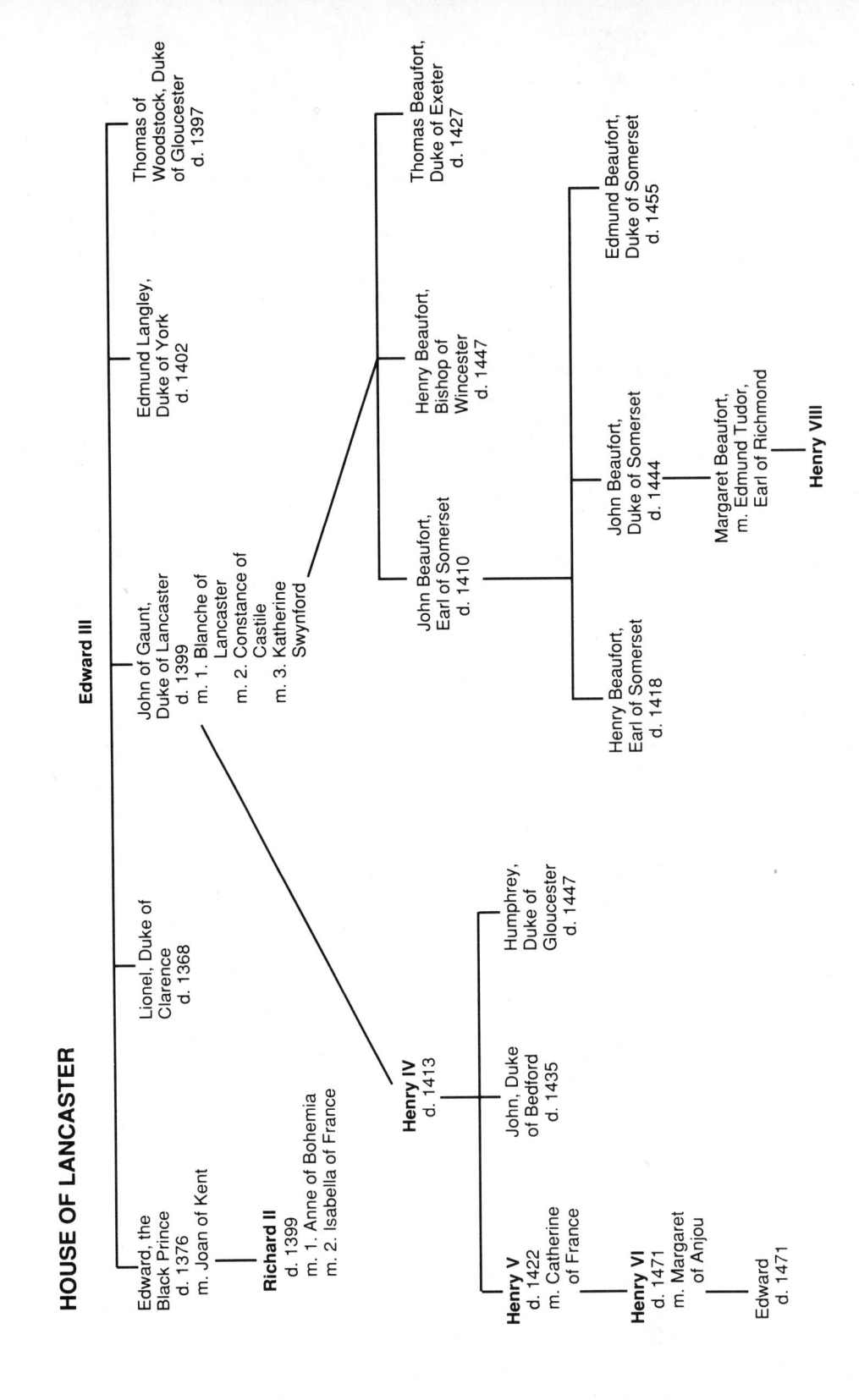

Edward III

- Edward, the Black Prince
  d. 1376
  m. Joan of Kent
  - **Richard II**
    d. 1399
    m. 1. Anne of Bohemia
    m. 2. Isabella of France
- Lionel, Duke of Clarence
  d. 1368
- John of Gaunt, Duke of Lancaster
  d. 1399
  m. 1. Blanche of Lancaster
  m. 2. Constance of Castile
  m. 3. Katherine Swynford
  - **Henry IV**
    d. 1413
    - **Henry V**
      d. 1422
      m. Catherine of France
      - **Henry VI**
        d. 1471
        m. Margaret of Anjou
        - Edward
          d. 1471
    - John, Duke of Bedford
      d. 1435
    - Humphrey, Duke of Gloucester
      d. 1447
  - John Beaufort, Earl of Somerset
    d. 1410
    - Henry Beaufort, Earl of Somerset
      d. 1418
    - John Beaufort, Duke of Somerset
      d. 1444
      - Margaret Beaufort, m. Edmund Tudor, Earl of Richmond
        - **Henry VIII**
    - Edmund Beaufort, Duke of Somerset
      d. 1455
  - Henry Beaufort, Bishop of Wincester
    d. 1447
  - Thomas Beaufort, Duke of Exeter
    d. 1427
- Edmund Langley, Duke of York
  d. 1402
- Thomas of Woodstock, Duke of Gloucester
  d. 1397

HOUSE OF YORK

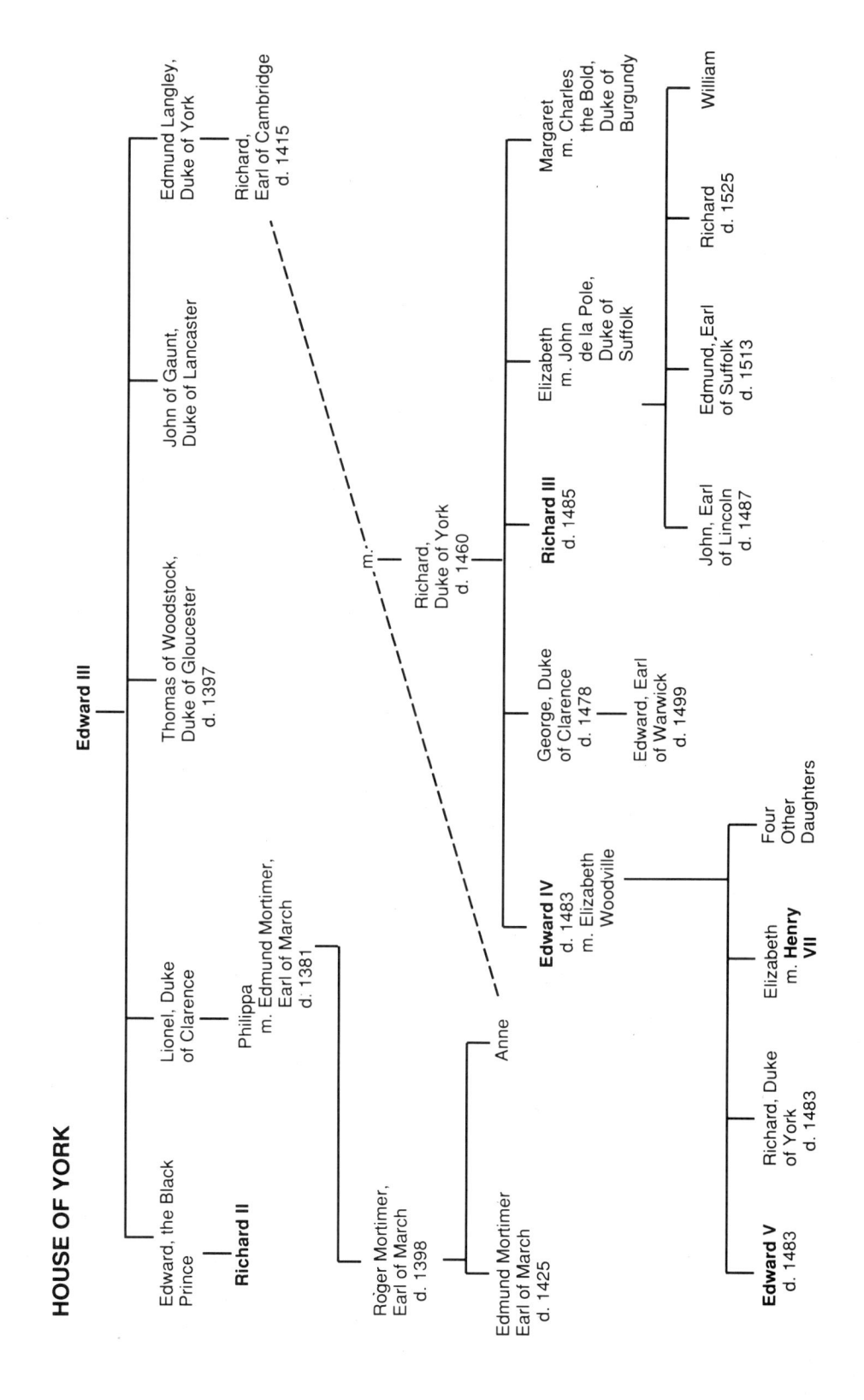

Edward III
- Edward, the Black Prince
  - **Richard II**
- Lionel, Duke of Clarence
  - Philippa m. Edmund Mortimer, Earl of March d. 1381
    - Roger Mortimer, Earl of March d. 1398
      - Edmund Mortimer, Earl of March d. 1425
      - Anne m. Richard, Earl of Cambridge
- John of Gaunt, Duke of Lancaster
- Thomas of Woodstock, Duke of Gloucester d. 1397
- Edmund Langley, Duke of York
  - Richard, Earl of Cambridge d. 1415
    - Richard, Duke of York d. 1460
      - Edward IV d. 1483 m. Elizabeth Woodville
        - Edward V d. 1483
        - Richard, Duke of York d. 1483
        - Elizabeth m. **Henry VII**
        - Four Other Daughters
      - George, Duke of Clarence d. 1478
        - Edward, Earl of Warwick d. 1499
      - **Richard III** d. 1485
      - Margaret m. Charles the Bold, Duke of Burgundy
      - Elizabeth m. John de la Pole, Duke of Suffolk
        - John, Earl of Lincoln d. 1487
        - Edmund, Earl of Suffolk d. 1513
        - Richard d. 1525
        - William

CHRONOLOGY

Lancaster and York

1399–1413	Henry IV, first Lancastrian king
1399–1410	Rebellions of Harry Hotspur and Owen Glendower
1413–1422	Henry V
1415	Battle of Agincourt
1420	Treaty of Troyes
1422–1461	Henry VI
1429–31	Joan of Arc leads French rebellion
1450	Jack Cade's Rebellion
1453	English expelled from Gascony; end of Hundred Years' War
1455–71	Wars of the Roses
1461	Battle of Towton; Yorkist seizure of the throne; Warwick the Kingmaker
1461–83	Edward IV
1470	Henry VI restored; Warwick the Kingmaker
1471	Battles of Barnet and Tewkesbury; Edward IV restored
1483	Edward V
1483–85	Richard III; death of "princes in the Tower"
1485	Battle of Bosworth Field; Tudor seizure of the throne

10

Henry VII: The Strengthening of Kingship

HENRY VII, 1485–1509

Henry was only twenty-eight when he came to the throne, but had already shown himself to be a good soldier and a man of action who could strike hard blows at his enemies. "His dealing in terms of perils and dangers," wrote a contemporary, "was cold and sober with great hardiness." Yet he was far removed from the medieval warrior, such as Richard I or Edward III. He was essentially a man of peace and business, practical, shrewd, calculating, and successful. He saw that England required an end to the civil wars once and for all. For this reason, after he was secure upon the throne, his policy was one of mercy in order to heal the wounds of the past. But his was the cold-blooded mercy of a man whose emotions were under firm control. To self-restraint he added high intelligence, inflexible resolution, and hard common sense. He was most industrious. He labored long at the tasks of government, with an infinite capacity for detail, as is apparent from his careful scrutiny of expenditure. He was "incomparably the best business man to sit upon the English throne, . . . the most uniformly successful of English kings, and a millionaire into the bargain." Henry was determined to be a king in every sense of the word. "He was of an high mind, and loved his own will and his own way, as one that revered himself and would reign indeed . . . not admitting any near or full approach either to his power or to his secrets. He was a prince sad [grave], serious, and full of thoughts and secret observations; and full of notes and memorials of his own hand, especially touching persons; as whom to employ, whom to reward, whom to inquire of, whom to beware of; keeping as it were a journal of his thoughts." This hard, industrious, self-contained, and prudent statesman was the founder of the Tuder character.

SECURING THE DYNASTY

Henry's Claim to the Throne

Henry won the Battle of Bosworth by hard fighting and slew his enemy, Richard III. Richard's naked corpse was carelessly flung over a horse's back and taken to an obscure grave. The crown, which Richard had worn into battle, was found under a hawthorn bush and placed on Henry's head while his soldiers shouted their acclamation. But Henry was a king only by conquest. During the quarter century ending in 1485 the Crown had been lost and won by violence on several occasions; and to the people the Battle of Bosworth must have appeared nothing more than a return to the endless Wars of the Roses. No one could know that Henry was to prove one of the wisest and most successful of English rulers and was to establish a dynasty which would last more than a hundred years.

His claim to the throne by inheritance was weak indeed. Through his father he had no claim at all. His grandfather, Owen Tudor, was a gentleman from Wales, clerk of the wardrobe in the household of Catherine of France, the widow of Henry V. But Owen Tudor, with the audacity characteristic of his family, commended himself so successfully to Catherine that she accepted him as her husband. When this presumptuous marriage became known, Owen Tudor was summoned before the Council, was twice imprisoned and twice escaped. Later he fought on the side of the Lancastrians, was captured by the Yorkists, and executed. He had two sons by Catherine, Edmund and Jasper Tudor, who were thus half brothers to Henry VI. Henry treated them kindly, and in return for their loyal support he created Edmund, Earl of Richmond and Jasper, Earl of Pembroke. This good fortune, however, gave Edmund, the father of Henry VII, no royal claim to pass on to his son. What claim Henry possessed came through his mother, Margaret Beaufort, daughter of John Beaufort, Duke of Somerset, a descendant of John of Gaunt. This descent came through John of Gaunt's third wife, Katherine Swynford. She had been Gaunt's mistress before she became his wife, and her children had been born out of wedlock. Parliament legitimized them in 1397, but in 1407 Henry IV declared them debarred from the succession.[1]

These were the obvious weaknesses in Henry's title, quite apart from the fact that in 1485 members of the Yorkist royal family were still alive. Indeed, Henry had been important solely because his claim was the best the Lancastrians could put forward and because he had long been the hope of that party. His youth had been spent in adversity. Born in Wales in 1457, he was a posthumous child, his father, Edmund, having died at the age of twenty-six before his son's birth; his mother at the time was but fourteen. Jasper Tudor, Henry's uncle, gave protection to mother and child. In 1471, when the Yorkists appeared triumphant, Jasper took Henry to Brittany, where he lived for many years, an exile and sometimes a semiprisoner. Later Henry went to Paris and was befriended by the French king, Charles VIII. In Paris Lancastrians and Yorkist dissenters gathered around him. But he might well have been

---

[1] See genealogical tables on pages 206–207.

Henry VII, artist unknown. (National Portrait Gallery, London)

assassinated by Richard's agents (fear of whom doubtless prompted him to make a bid for the Crown). Or he might well have remained an exile for life had not Richard's bloody rule in England produced the far-flung conspiracy which brought Henry to the throne.

The Elimination of Rivals

Henry was well aware that though he had won the throne with comparative ease he could keep it only with difficulty. Yorkist claimants were still alive, their followers embittered by the confiscation of lands and by the loss of office which followed Bosworth; Ireland was Yorkist in sympathy; and Henry had enemies on the Continent eager to support Yorkist plots. For twelve years he had to face dangerous conspiracies. During those years he showed his capacity for kingship merely by remaining king.

His first task was to eliminate his Yorkist rivals. Richard III, very fortunately, was childless and had smoothed Henry's way by the crime of which he was probably guilty—the murder in the Tower of the two young sons of Edward IV. But Edward left five daughters and five nephews. The daughters were disposed of easily. The eldest, Elizabeth, became Henry's queen. Their marriage had formed part of the agreement between Lancastrian and Yorkist plotters before Henry's invasion of England, and Henry fully intended to carry it through. But he did not marry Elizabeth at once: undue haste would imply that he owed his crown to his wife. He waited until his first Parliament, which, having been carefully coached, requested him to marry the Princess Elizabeth. This he graciously consented to do. The marriage took place in January 1486; in September of the same year Elizabeth gave birth to a son who received the Welsh name of Arthur. Thus the houses of York and Lancaster were united. The fact that Henry's son combined the claims of both greatly strengthened his dynasty. Three of the queen's sisters were married to men whom Henry believed he could trust, though one of them, Lord William Courtenay, later fell under suspicion and was imprisoned in the Tower. The fifth sister became a nun.

The nephews of Edward IV remained to be dealt with. One was Edward, Earl of Warwick, a lad of ten who in 1485 was placed in the Tower, where he remained—the innocent center of Yorkist plots—until he was executed in 1499. Another was a restless young noble, John de la Pole, Earl of Lincoln, whom Richard III had designated as his heir. It was inevitable that Lincoln would plot against Henry. He was probably implicated in a minor conspiracy in 1486 and certainly in a major one in the following year.

The second of these conspiracies originated in the mind of a priest of Yorkist sympathies who taught one of his pupils—a gentle boy named Lambert Simnel—to impersonate Edward, the young earl of Warwick, the prisoner in the Tower. It was easy for the Yorkists to spread false rumors that Warwick had escaped, which persisted even though Henry brought the earl from the Tower and paraded him through the streets of London. Lincoln and other Yorkists took up Simnel's cause. They knew he was an impostor and would doubtless have pushed him aside once he had served their turn. They took him to Ireland, where he was well received. Lincoln raised an army of 6000 Irish troops and obtained 2000 German mercenaries from the Netherlands, sent by that archenemy of the Tudors, Margaret, the dowager duchess of Burgundy and sister of Edward IV. Lincoln and Simnell landed in Lancashire in 1487. But the English, sick of civil war, showed them little sympathy, and at the grimly contested Battle of Stoke in Yorkshire Henry defeated the rebels. Lincoln was slain and Simnel captured. Pretending to hold the revolt in derision, Henry made Simnel a scullion in the royal kitchen and had him wait at table on other Yorkist prisoners. The rising, however, was no jest; it was dangerous while it lasted.

Some years later Henry was threatened by another pretender, Perkin Warbeck, who proved to be far more troublesome than Lambert Simnel. Warbeck, a native of Flanders, was first heard of in Ireland in 1491. He pretended to be Richard, son of Edward IV, the younger of the two little princes murdered in the Tower. Actually, he was the servant of a Breton merchant. A youth of charm and intelligence, he played his impudent part with some skill, but he lacked the toughness of character needed to achieve success. He was dangerous because he was supported by the Yorkists, by Henry's enemies abroad, and by some of the king's officials at home. From Ireland, where he was backed by the earls of Desmond and Kildare, Warbeck went to France and was well received by Charles VIII, then at war with Henry. But the treaty which ended the war in 1492 contained a clause expelling Warbeck from France, and he made his way to the Netherlands. There he was supported by the dowager duchess of Burgundy, Emperor Maximilian, Maximilian's son, Philip, and Yorkists from England. There were arrests and executions at home when Henry discovered a cell of the conspiracy in his own household.

In 1495 Warbeck led an expedition against England, but his men were driven back when they landed in Kent (Warbeck himself prudently remained on his ship), and the little fleet sailed on to Ireland and then to Scotland. King James IV of Scotland received him kindly and arranged a marriage for him with the daughter of a Scottish earl. Warbeck stayed in Scotland until 1497, but he accomplished nothing beyond a few border raids. The savagery of these raids, it was said, rather sickened his unwarlike nature. In 1497, when an uprising occurred in Cornwall, Warbeck thought his opportunity had come. He sailed from Scotland, only to arrive in Cornwall after the revolt had been crushed; an invasion of England from Scotland was turned back; and no aid came from the Continent, where Henry's diplomacy had robbed Warbeck of support. The impostor was captured, placed at first in easy custody, then imprisoned in the Tower and executed in 1499. At this time the earl of Warwick also was executed. Although the circumstances are obscure, it was obviously thought that conspiracies were rampant.

Thus ended two of Edward's nephews, Warwick and John de la Pole, Earl of Lincoln, who had fallen in the Simnel rising. Lincoln had three younger brothers. Two of them, after further intrigues, died in the Tower. The third entered the French army and was killed at the Battle of Pavia in Italy in 1525. So ended the de la Poles, and the danger of Yorkist revolt died with them.

Foreign Relations

It might be supposed that Henry, faced with grave problems at home, would have little share in the diplomacy and wars of Europe. Yet as long as Yorkist pretenders received aid from abroad, Henry was forced in his own defense to take part in the complicated affairs of the Continent. He was eager, moreover, to gain recognition for his dynasty and to form an alliance with a strong continental power. Such an alliance would aid him against his enemies, increase his prestige, and benefit English merchants trading abroad.

Henry VII was bound to France by ties of gratitude, for he had lived in Paris before his invasion of England and had been aided in that enterprise by the French king, Charles VIII (1483–1498), but circumstances induced him to ally with Spain. He found that hostility to France was very strong in England and that English possession of Calais was a constant irritant to the French. Charles VIII, moreover, opposed England in an attempt to absorb the independent duchy of Brittany. When Francis

II, Duke of Brittany, died in 1488, leaving only a twelve-year-old daughter, Anne, Charles claimed her wardship. When this was refused he sent an army against her. In the same year a band of volunteers sailed from England to the defense of Brittany, but they were slain almost to a man, and passions against France ran high in England.

Thus drawn into hostility toward France, Henry in 1489 concluded the Treaty of Medina del Campo with Spain. In some respects Henry obtained what he wanted. His son Arthur was to be married to Catherine, daughter of Ferdinand and Isabella, when the children should reach marriageable age. The dowry was to be large; Catherine was to be sent to England with jewels and other furnishings befitting a princess. Neither Spain nor England was to harbor the rebels of the other. English merchants were to enjoy valuable concessions in Spain. But other clauses in the treaty indicated that Henry was the weaker party and was paying a high price for the alliance. The treaty bound him to go to war with France. Spain desired two French provinces in the Pyrenees—Roussillon and Cerdagne. If Spain secured them, she could, by the terms of the treaty, withdraw from the war, but Henry could withdraw only if France ceded Normandy and Aquitaine to him, which was quite impossible. Henry, in other words, had to fight until Spain got what she wanted.

Meanwhile the situation in France altered rapidly in 1491 and 1492. Although Henry was sending aid to Brittany, the French were winning the war, but suddenly in 1491 the young duchess agreed to marry her adversary and become the Queen of France. The absorption of Brittany into France could not be prevented and yet Henry was pledged to war. In 1492, having obtained funds from Parliament, he crossed to France with an army. Again the situation altered. Charles VIII cherished ambitions to conquer Italy, where he had a claim to Milan and where internal rivalries invited French aggression, but he could not begin an Italian campaign while Spain threatened his southern frontier and while an English army remained in northern France. He therefore made a hasty peace with Spain, ceding to her the coveted provinces in the Pyrenees. With Henry he concluded the Treaty of Etaples, in which he excluded the pretender Perkin Warbeck from France and paid Henry a handsome sum of money to return to England. Realizing his good fortune, Henry accepted these terms most gladly. He had fulfilled the terms of his agreement with Spain, and he could now make an honorable peace with France. He had obtained funds from Parliament to begin the war, and he now obtained funds from France to end it. If his sudden return to England after a very short campaign appeared disappointingly tame to his soldiers, no one could doubt the wisdom of his action.

In 1502 a heavy blow fell on him. His son Arthur had married Catherine in 1501, but within six months the young prince was dead and Catherine was a widow. The patient diplomacy of many years appeared to be shattered. Beginning once more, Henry concluded an agreement with Spain in 1503 by which Catherine should remain in England (along with her dowry) and should in due course marry Henry's second son, the future Henry VIII. This marriage, which did not take place until 1509, was to alter the course of English history. In 1503 Henry VII became a widower. There had been affection and fidelity between him and his queen, but he began at once to seek another wife. Secure upon his throne, he apparently wished to play a greater role on the Continent, and he regarded his unmarried state as a diplomatic advantage not to be lost. He alarmed the Spaniards by suggesting that he marry Catherine, his son's widow. He considered other ladies, among them Joanna, another daughter of Ferdinand and Isabella. Although Henry was ready to ignore the princess's insanity, these unsavory negotiations came to nothing. The king, now old and toothless at 53, remained unwed.

Scotland and Ireland

Scotland and Ireland were connected with the king's foreign policy. Since the Battle of Bannockburn in 1314 the Scots had been independent; yet they were convinced that England would attempt to conquer them if possible. They therefore continued their alliance with France, though it brought them little good; there was constant raiding and fighting along the border; James IV, as we have seen, invaded England in support of Perkin Warbeck. But Henry was too wise to be swayed by a blind hatred of the Scots. In 1499 he proposed a marriage between his daughter Margaret and James IV. The marriage, which took place in 1503, produced only a temporary improvement in Anglo-Scottish relations.

By the beginning of the Tudor period the English Pale in Ireland had shrunk to a small coastal area around Dublin and Drogheda. Its nobility and gentry were largely of English or Norman descent. Some of them maintained English traditions, but others were as Irish as the Irish themselves. Beyond the Pale the country was controlled by tribal chieftains, either purely Irish like the O'Neills in Ulster or Norman-Irish like the Burkes of Connaught. These chieftains ignored the English government altogether.

The Pale was ruled by a lord deputy appointed in England, usually from the Anglo-Irish nobility. The earl of Kildare, lord deputy at the beginning of Henry's reign, was of this class. Like most of the nobility in the Pale, he was Yorkist in sympathy and supported Lambert Simnel. Henry thereupon removed him and in 1494 sent over an Englishman, Sir Edward Poynings, as deputy. Poynings summoned a Parliament at Drogheda and secured a number of famous acts. One of them declared that henceforth no Parliament could meet in Ireland until its proposed agenda had been approved by the English king and Council. Another act provided that all English statutes existing in 1494 should apply in Ireland and England alike.

THE STRENGTHENING OF KINGSHIP

Bad government and the decay of law and order in the fifteenth century had been due to the weakness of the kings and not to any fundamental defect in the constitution or in the people. Henry VII had no standing army; the armed guard with which he surrounded himself was more for display than for any military purpose. It might protect him from assassination but it could not repress disorder on a large scale. Henry relied upon the ancient duty of every male citizen to serve in the militia when need arose. The leaders of the militia were the nobility and the more prominent gentry; Henry's problem was to preserve the military value of the militia, led as it was by nobles, without allowing the nobles' power to get out of hand. His method was to punish unlawful recruiting of retainers, but in emergencies to issue commissions of array to nobles and gentry whom he could trust.

In essence Henry relied upon the good will of the people. The middle classes—gentry, merchants, and craftsmen, those below the peerage but above the peasantry—were ready and eager to support a king who could repress disorder and preserve the peace. It was the gentry who counted most and whose support Henry knew he must cultivate. The merchants, whose aid was also sought by the king, were still few and their importance can easily be exaggerated. It would be an error to think that Henry wooed any class or classes above all others. His method was to exalt the monarchy as something to be revered by all. Kingship had been cheapened in various ways, and it was his policy to place it on a new plane of eminence. His court was brilliant, and he spent large sums on ceremonial occasions to increase the splendor and magnificence of monarchy. He built a beautiful chapel in Westminster Abbey and made it the home of the Order of the Bath.

The king, the symbol of the state, was exalted far above the greatest of his subjects. This could be done more easily because the older nobility had been weakened by the wars and disasters of the fifteenth century. Nobles too closely related to the royal family gradually were liquidated. Henry did not oppose the nobles as such. He opposed lawless and troublesome persons of any class. His followers were ambitious to enter the ranks of the peerage, and he gradually created new nobles who owed their promotion to him and who were well aware of their allegiance. They were despised by the older nobility; hence their protection lay in the exalted position of an all-powerful king, the sole fountain of honor, who could ennoble anyone he so pleased.

Henry selected his councilors as he pleased and expected loyal service from them all. Tudor kingship became strong and independent. He created loyalty by removing rivals to the throne, he ruled with moderation and drove no class to despair, and he greatly exalted the royal prerogative, that reservoir of undefined rights and powers by which the king could act in emergencies and rule for the public good. Henry's policies were national and he expected support from all classes. If the middle classes derived the greatest benefit from his rule they did so because they stood to gain the most from the kind of government he provided.

Law and Order

Henry knew that law and order must be restored and maintained and that for this purpose the government must be strengthened at all levels. The central core of administration consisted of the king and his Council. The Council was large and somewhat nebulous—about 150 men took the councilor's oath during his reign to serve as the king's civil servants, his bureaucrats and administrators. Henry did a good deal of governing in informal interviews, and he could summon any councilors whom he wished to consult. There was some differentiation of function. We hear of a legal council to advise the king in matters of law. There was a court of requests, to which poor men might bring petitions, and also the Council in the Star Chamber. An inner circle of some twenty to thirty councilors close to the king were the most important in government. They were his principal administrators, controlling and supervising details of government throughout the entire kingdom. Selected for their ability, loyalty, and efficiency, they rose in the king's service by merit and hard work. Henry gave them great power because they were wholly dependent on him and represented his will in action. The Tudor period is sometimes called the age of government by council.

Henry's Council did a large amount of judicial work. For this purpose it met in the Star Chamber, a room in the council building decorated with stars in the ceiling. The Star Chamber in Henry's reign was not separate from the rest of the Council. It was merely the place where councilors met to transact judicial business, work chiefly connected with the problem of law and order. Any man could bring complaints to the king and Council; persons who had suffered wrong through local disturbances were encouraged to petition the Council for redress. Cases could also be begun with an accusation by the king's attorney general. The Council heard complaints of riot, which meant almost any breach of the peace; of brawls and bloody affrays; of illegal assemblies, which were the normal precursors of violence; of bribery and intimidation of jurors and sheriffs; and of corruption and misconduct by local officials. The Council also heard cases of the poor against the rich—cases subject to misrule in the local courts because of the "great might" of one party and the "great unmight" of the other.

The Council in the Star Chamber developed a swift and effective procedure. It did not use the jury, which had failed so often to do justice in the local courts. It put men under oath and forced them to answer questions that might incriminate them. Procedure consisted of an accusation, an answer by the accused, the collection of evidence, and the hearing of witnesses. This material was written down, and on the basis of these written documents the councilors reached their decision. Punishments consisted of fines, confiscation of property, and imprisonment. The Council in the Star Chamber did not deal with treason and never inflicted the death penalty. It did not have a law of its own but rather enforced the common law and made it work. The councilors in the Star Chamber were powerful because they represented the king. They could not be intimidated, bribed, or defied, and they could act impartially in dealing with powerful offenders. The Star Chamber did its work well. It was a boon to the people in the early Tudor period and remained a popular and busy court for more than a century.

Henry also strengthened local government. The Council in the Star Chamber might curb the overmighty subject, but numbers of lesser offenders disturbed the peace and had to be dealt with locally. The wars of the fiteenth century had created a spirit of violence. People were quick to challenge their adversaries, to draw their daggers, and to come to blows. Henry enacted a number of laws dealing with local law and order. It became illegal to hunt in disguise, for this practice led to murders and assaults. Women could not be taken from their homes without their own consent. No man could have retainers who were tenants of the king. Other laws struck at the perjury and corruption so frequent among fifteenth-century jurors. A sheriff might be punished for empaneling a juror who was obviously unfit for his task. In general, the duties of local officials were defined more clearly. In 1504 the laws concerning livery and maintenance were drawn into a code.

It was enforcement, not new law, that was required. Henry did not restore the sheriff to his ancient importance, for the sheriff had acquired a bad name in the fifteenth century. Instead, Henry made increasing use of the justices of the peace. These justices of the peace were country gentlemen who, as we have seen, had been employed in the later Middle Ages to assist the itinerant justices and to try minor cases in the local courts. The judicial work of the justices of the peace had expanded in the fifteenth century and continued to increase under the Tudors until the justices could deal with a large number of offenses. Henry watched the justices carefully, appointed them for one year at a time, and usually included some of his councilors in the commission. Justices were quickly reproved for any neglect of duty. To be dropped from the commission of the peace was a sharp setback for a country gentleman, the more so because Henry regarded service in the capacity of justice as a kind of apprenticeship to be completed successfully before a man could hope for higher office. The justices, on the whole, did their work well; the problem of local law and order was being solved.

Finance

Henry further strengthened his government by improving his finances. He has been called a miser, but unfairly so, for he did not hesitate to spend money on things he deemed essential. A vital aspect of kingship was involved. Many English kings in the later Middle Ages had been weak because they had grown poor. They had allowed the resources of the Crown to be drained away by war and by other causes which had enriched a few great nobles but had impoverished the Crown. It was the Yorkist Edward IV who first reversed this trend and set about the necessary task of making the Crown independent by making it wealthy. In the sixteenth century money was more essential than ever because an increasing number of services had to be paid for in cash; a poverty-stricken king was in a hopeless position. For Henry, therefore, the accumulation of wealth was absolutely necessary if he wished to be strong and independent. Doubtless he enjoyed the process, but he had no choice. In 1485 he had been poor, owing money to his backers in France and Brittany.

The kingship, once gained, had many financial resources. Henry exploited them to the full, husbanded his wealth, and left a handsome treasure to his son. The revenues of the Crown were derived from what may be called ordinary and extraordinary sources. Ordinary sources—Crown lands, the customs, feudal rights, the profits of justice—provided income which belonged to the king by law. They were his by legal right. Extraordinary sources consisted of grants by Parliament and of such things as loans and benevolences. It was the theory of the time that under normal conditions the king should live of his own, that is, from his ordinary revenues. Only some great crisis or emergency, such as a war, entitled him to seek funds in extraordinary ways. Henry accepted this theory. He did not wish to incur the unpopularity that was certain to arise if he demanded large grants of money from Parliament. He asked Parliament for taxes in time of war, but as his financial position improved he held fewer Parliaments, preferring to enlarge and cultivate his ordinary sources of income.

Of the four principal sources of ordinary revenue, Crown lands were the most important in Henry's reign. Like Edward IV, he systematically increased the landed property of the Crown. He naturally took possession of the estates belonging to the Yorkist kings; and his first Parliament allowed him to resume all the lands held by the Lancastrian King Henry VI in 1455. He was thus the inheritor of both Yorkist and Lancastrian estates. By dating the commencement of his reign on the day before the Battle of Bosworth, he was able to confiscate the lands of all who had fought against him in that battle; later conspiracies and revolts were followed by further confiscations. The lands acquired in these ways were managed with business skill and produced an ever-increasing revenue.

The customs duties formed a second source of income. The amounts that could legally be collected had hardened into a fixed schedule, known as tonnage and poundage, which Parliament gave to the king for life. Henry could increase his income slightly by placing a higher valuation on goods which were taxed at rates proportionate to their estimated value. But there were only two ways in which the customs could be made to produce substantially larger sums: to increase the volume of foreign trade, in which Henry had some success; or to reduce smuggling, in which he made little progress. Indeed, the customs never produced the revenue they should have done at this time.

Income also came from the profits of justice. Some money was obtained from the sale of writs and from miscellaneous fees charged by the courts. A far more lucrative source of income consisted of fines and amercements levied by the courts as punishment for many kinds of offenses. The Star Chamber, as we have seen, inflicted heavy fines. Revolts and conspiracies also were punished by fines; and such fines, large and small, were imposed for all sorts of misdemeanors. From the great noble who paid heavily for keeping too many retainers to the petty merchant who smuggled a few woolen cloths out of the kingdom, fines formed the normal punishment. Many fines were so heavy that the offender could pay them only over a number of years. Toward the end of the reign, when Henry felt secure, he was not above accepting money in return for promises of royal favor to litigants in the courts.

Henry further increased his revenues through a systematic enforcement of his feudal rights. In the confusion of the fifteenth century these rights had often been lost to the Crown, but Henry revived them and made them highly valuable. In 1504 he obtained money from Parliament in lieu of a feudal aid for knighting Arthur, his eldest son, though Arthur was dead; and for marrying Margaret, his eldest daughter, though her marriage had taken place sometime before. Such feudal incidents as wardship, relief, and escheat, if carefully exacted, could bring in large sums of money. It was to the interest of tenants to coneal the occurrence of these incidents where they could; therefore, Henry set up greatly unpopular commissions of inquiry to establish his claims. There was, indeed, a pitiless quality about Henry's financial policy, and his agents, such as the notorious Richard Empson and Edmund Dudley, were cordially hated. Henry became impatient with the antiquated methods of the Exchequer. Reviving a practice of medieval kings, he formed an office of finance in his household. Income was diverted from the Exchequer to the Chamber; and his treasurers of the Chamber, Sir Thomas Lovell and later Sir John Heron, became the principal financial officers of the Crown. Henry himself checked and initialed most of their accounts.

COMMERCIAL POLICY

As good a businessman as Henry VII was certain to have great interest in foreign commerce. By enriching the merchants Henry enriched himself through increased customs duties, and at the same time he won the gratitude of the business classes. Henry's efforts to increase England's foreign commerce, however, must not be erected into a system. While he did what he could as circumstances permitted, there were many things he could not do, and Henry was often forced to subordinate trade to the necessities of foreign policy. The great bulk of English exports still consisted of wool and woolen cloth. The export of raw wool, however, had declined until, in 1485, the amount sent abroad was only about 10,000 sacks per year, scarcely one third of the figure for the 1340s.

On the other hand, woolen cloth was exported in very large quantities (perhaps 50,000 cloths a year) at the beginning of the Tudor period. Until about 1450 this cloth had been shipped from a number of English ports to various towns along the Atlantic seaboard of Europe. English merchants had pushed aggressively into the Baltic Sea and into western Germany where they met the bitter hostility of the Hanseatic League of North German trading towns. There followed almost a century of strife, a war in 1468, and a treaty in 1474 by which the English were largely excluded from the Baltic. Meanwhile merchants trading to Gascony and Spain found their business ruined by the Hundred Years' War and other disturbances. Exporters of English cloth therefore tended to crowd into the Netherlands, the one great market that remained, and to confine their trade to Antwerp, where they had acquired privileges during the fifteenth century.

The merchants of London, who had opened the trade to Antwerp, resisted the intrusion of merchants from other parts of the kingdom. The Londoners drew together, at first in a loose organization of traders who belonged to various London companies. In 1486 they became the Fellowship of the Merchant Adventurers of London and set out to monopolize the cloth trade to Antwerp by making the entrance fees to their society so high that merchants from the rest of the country could not afford to enter. A bitter wrangle ensued. In 1497 an act of Parliament forced a settlement on the London Adventurers by which they were compelled to reduce their entrance fees and to admit other English merchants into their society. This may appear as a sharp defeat but actually the arrangement of 1497 implied the right of the Londoners to control admission to the trade to Antwerp and to impose conditions on those who wished to engage in it. Gradually the Merchant Adventurers developed into a powerful corporation, intimately connected with the state and enjoying the monopoly of a highly desirable trade.

They benefited greatly from a treaty made by Henry with the Netherlands in 1496. For some years he had been at odds with the government in Flanders over its support of Perkin Warbeck. In 1493 he had forbidden all trade between England and the Netherlands and had moved the staple of the Merchant Adventurers to Calais. This had been a heavy blow to merchants on both sides of the Channel, but the Flemings had felt it more keenly than the English. In 1496 they yielded, withdrew their support from Perkin Warbeck, and agreed to a commercial treaty known as the *Intercursus Magnus.* This treaty accepted the principle of freedom of trade between England and the Netherlands, established a schedule of customs duties, granted mutual fishing rights, and proposed joint action against pirates. The Merchant Adventurers returned to Antwerp under favorable conditions.

Ten years later in 1506 Henry employed a devious trick to obtain even better terms. While voyaging to Spain, Archduke Philip, ruler of the Netherlands, was shipwrecked on the English coast in heavy weather. Henry brought him to London and treated him with great courtesy, but before he left England Philip was induced to sign a new commercial treaty. The name given this treaty in the Netherlands, the *Intercursus Malus,* is an indication of its one-sided character. English merchants, paying only the customs established in 1496, were to be free from all local tolls in Flanders and were permitted to engage in retail trade throughout the country. This placed them in a more favorable position than that of native Flemish merchants. It is no wonder that as soon as he was out of England Philip repudiated the treaty; Henry consented to its modification in 1507.

The Merchant Adventurers prospered in Henry's reign. Their prosperity increased the demand for wool in England and encouraged the expansion of the cloth-making industry, with important economic results. In addition to the staplers and the Merchant Adventurers there were unincorporated English merchants trading to Spain, southern France, and Ireland. Although their principal objective was political alliance, Henry's treaties with Spain improved conditions for English merchants doing business with that country. The trade with southern France, consisting of imports of wine from Bordeaux and of woad (used in dyeing) from Toulouse, was conducted largely in French ships. Henry attempted to transfer this commerce to English shipping and offered bounties for ships built in England. He secured a Navigation Act declaring that the trade to southern France must be conducted with English ships. He found, however, that the act could not be enforced. The volume of English shipping was too small to meet the needs of foreign trade, and a large portion of English commerce still had to be carried in vessels belonging to foreigners.

Two important branches of English trade were almost entirely in foreign hands. The Hanseatic League of German trading towns along the coasts of the Baltic Sea and in northwestern Germany was perhaps the most influential mercantile organization of the Middle Ages. It was a power in international affairs and controlled large quantities of shipping. The merchants of the Hansa were in a strong position in England. Although they had a large establishment in London known as the Steelyard, where merchants from dozens of Baltic towns displayed and sold their wares and bought in exchange large quantities of wool and woolen cloth, they excluded English merchants from the Baltic and monopolized trade to that important area. Henry would have gladly curtailed the excessive privileges of the Hanseatic League in England. He punished the Hansa merchants severely when he caught them abusing their rights, he obtained their permission for Englishmen to trade to Iceland, and he made a treaty with the King of Denmark in 1490 by which he hoped to obtain access to the Baltic for English shipping, though the Hansa was able to prevent the fulfillment of the treaty. Yet Henry was cautious in dealing with the Hanseatic

League. Its sea power could be dangerous to him. The Hansa merchants flourished in England during his reign.

Henry was more successful in dealing with the Venetians. At the beginning of the reign the Venetians monopolized trade between England and the Mediterranean. Once every year a fleet of their galleys came through the Strait of Gibraltar and made its way to Antwerp, trading at various points along the route. Stopping at Southampton and London the Venetians did a large volume of business. Despite the Venetian monopoly some English merchants were beginning to find their way into the Mediterranean, trading in Crete and in Chios, where choice wines could be obtained. Irritated by this traffic, the Venetians exercised their control in Crete by imposing new and larger customs upon English goods. In retaliation Henry increased the customs to be paid by the Venetians trading in England. He also concluded a treaty with Florence that made Pisa, its seaport, the sole distributing center for English wool in the Mediterranean. The staple at Piza was short-lived, but it served its turn. The Venetians gave way, and English voyages to Crete and Chios continued.

THE EXPANSION OF EUROPE OVERSEAS

The success of Henry's commercial policy lessened his interest in the wonderful voyages of oceanic discovery that were taking place during his reign. These epic voyages are a mark of cleavage between medieval and modern times and spring directly from Europe's interest in Oriental trade. For centuries the merchants of Italy had traded in the Near East, bringing to Europe the spices, dyes, and fragrant woods, the jewels, silks, tapestries, and rugs of Asia. But European merchants could go no farther than the eastern shores of the Mediterranean, for there they met the hostile world of Arabs and Turks through which they could not penetrate.

The path to the Orient was closed, and if Europeans were to reach the East they must do so by sea. The first European nation to accomplish this feat was Portugal. Led by the vision of Prince Henry the navigator (1394–1460), Portuguese seamen began to work their way south along the western coast of Africa. In 1487 Bartholomew Diaz reached the Cape of Good Hope; ten years later Vasco da Gama sailed around the Cape and up the eastern coast of Africa until he found pilots who took him to India. The Portuguese quickly established themselves along the western coast of India with their capital at Goa, broke Muslim sea power in the Indian Ocean, seized Ormuz at the mouth of the Persian Gulf, and pushed farther east to the Malay Archipelago—Java, Sumatra, and the smaller islands where the best spices were found. The trade from Asia to Europe was diverted from the old routes and began to flow around Africa. Lisbon grew rich while the Italian cities declined, and Portugal enjoyed a brief period of wealth and greatness.

Meanwhile another voyage was made, perhaps less difficult than that of Vasco da Gama, yet exceedingly important as a great act of faith. Christopher Columbus believed he could reach Cathay by sailing west. In 1492 he made his famous voyage across the unknown Atlantic, discovered the West Indies, and sent to the Indians a formal letter from Ferdinand and Isabella addressed to the Great Khan. The Spanish soon established themselves in the larger islands. From Cuba as a base Cortez conquered Mexico between 1519 and 1522; and in 1535 Pizarro sailed from the western side of the Isthmus of Panama to the conquest of Peru. This era of oceanic discovery reached its climax when Magellan, a Portuguese sailing in the service of Spain, passed through the strait that bears his name and crossed the Pacific in a heroic voyage lasting a hundred days.

The Voyages of John Cabot

Englishmen were slow to take part in this movement of world expansion. They had been cut off from the Mediterranean, that center of scientific geography and navigation, and the old trades with France and the Netherlands had been so profitable as to discourage adventure in new directions. However, a memorable voyage from England in Henry's reign resulted in the discovery of North America. Seamen from the English city of Bristol, voyaging to Iceland for whales, must have heard of the Norse discoveries in America about the year 1000. Bristol merchants traded to Portugal and knew of the Portuguese voyages along the African coast. There were some voyages from Bristol into the Atlantic during the fifteenth century, though the evidence is vague. There was a tradition at the time regarding an unknown island in the Atlantic, somewhere to the west of Ireland.

About 1490 an Italian seaman names John Cabot came to Bristol. Not much is known about him, for his name seldom appears in the records of the time and in later years his son, Sebastian Cabot, claimed credit for the voyages made by his father. Yet John Cabot may have been a greater voyager than Columbus, with a more lucid mind and a sounder concept of geography. A native of Genoa, he became a citizen of Venice and traded in Egypt as a Venetian merchant. He read the accounts of Marco Polo and was a student of geography, skilled in maps and globes as well as in practical seamanship. Like Columbus he hoped to reach China by sailing across the Atlantic. He came to Bristol after he had been refused support in Spain and Portugal. But why did he select Bristol? He may have known of Bristol's interest in the Atlantic. He wished to make his westward voyage in northern latitudes so that the distance from Europe to Asia would be shorter than sailing farther to the south. He believed that the coast of Asia sloped in a southwesterly direction, making the north coast closest to Europe. Cabot's arrival in Bristol brought together a number of maritime traditions: the Norse discoveries, the voyages of Bristol seamen, the science of Italy, Italian trade in the Near East, and the Portuguese voyages along West Africa.

Henry VII showed an interest in the project, giving Cabot a monopoly of trade with any lands he might discover and naming Bristol as the only port through which that trade should pass. But he gave Cabot no ships. Bristol supplied him with only one tiny craft, the *Mathew,* and a crew of eighteen men. In this little vessel Cabot crossed the Atlantic in the summer of 1497, reaching the coast of America at an unknown point, probably more on the mainland than on Newfoundland. The season was advanced, however, and he returned to England without attempting to sail south along the American coast. He believed that he had reached Asia and announced that

HOUSE OF TUDOR

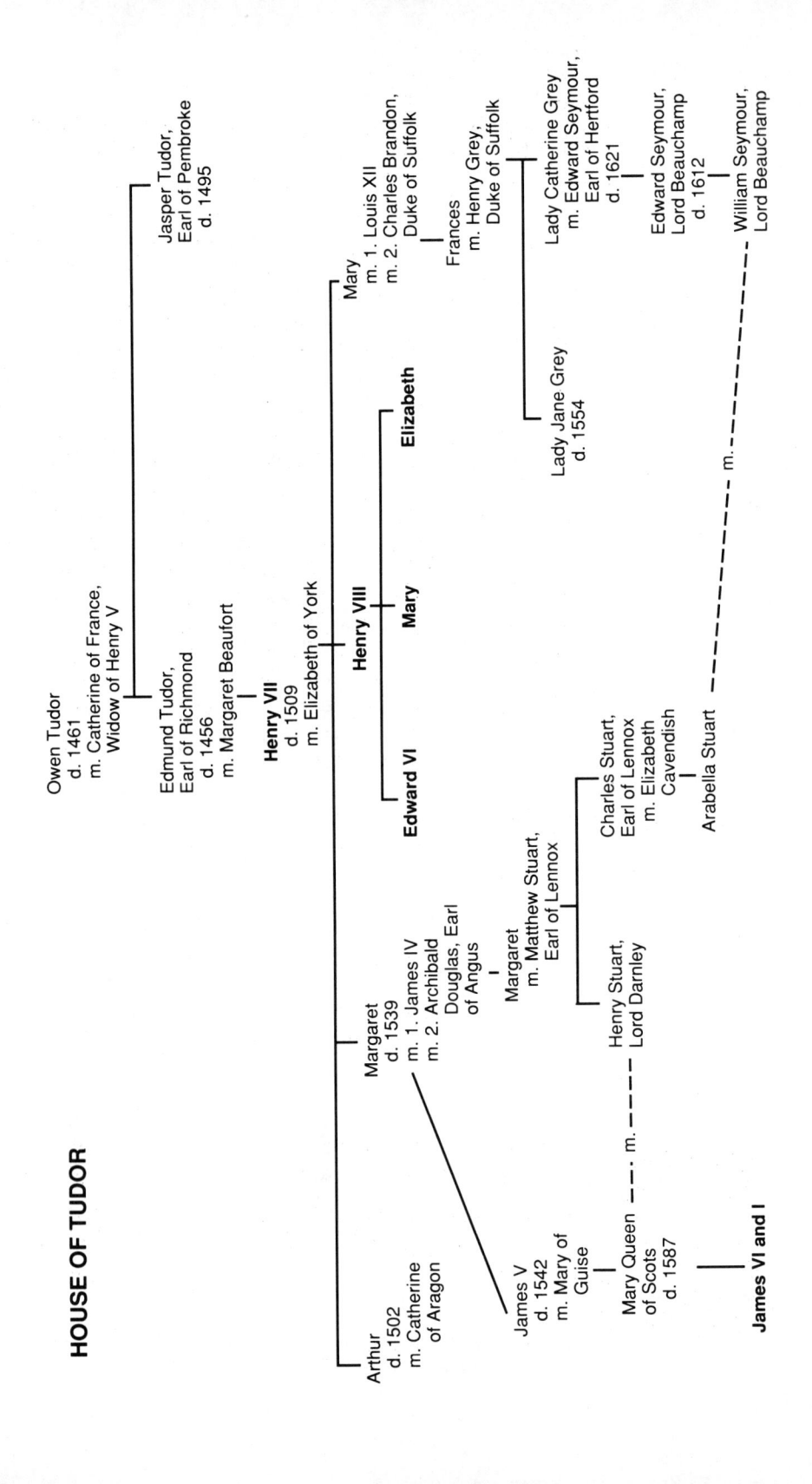

Owen Tudor
d. 1461
m. Catherine of France, Widow of Henry V
┬
├── **Jasper Tudor**, Earl of Pembroke, d. 1495
└── **Edmund Tudor**, Earl of Richmond, d. 1456
     m. Margaret Beaufort
     │
     Henry VII d. 1509
     m. Elizabeth of York
     │
     ├── **Arthur** d. 1502, m. Catherine of Aragon
     ├── **Margaret** d. 1539
     │   m. 1. James IV
     │   m. 2. Archibald Douglas, Earl of Angus
     │   ├── **James V** d. 1542, m. Mary of Guise
     │   │   │
     │   │   **Mary Queen of Scots** d. 1587 — m ---
     │   │   │
     │   └── **Margaret** m. Matthew Stuart, Earl of Lennox
     │   │
     │   **Henry Stuart, Lord Darnley** — m ---
     │   │
     │   **Charles Stuart**, Earl of Lennox
     │   m. Elizabeth Cavendish
     │   │
     │   **Arabella Stuart** ----------- m ----------
     │   │
     │   (from Mary Queen of Scots + Lord Darnley:)   │
     │   **James VI and I**   │
     │   │
     ├── **Henry VIII**   │
     │   ├── **Edward VI**   │
     │   ├── **Mary**   │
     │   └── **Elizabeth**   │
     │   │
     └── **Mary**   │
           m. 1. Louis XII   │
           m. 2. Charles Brandon, Duke of Suffolk   │
           │   │
           Frances m. Henry Grey, Duke of Suffolk   │
           ├── **Lady Jane Grey** d. 1554   │
           └── **Lady Catherine Grey**   │
                 m. Edward Seymour, Earl of Hertford, d. 1621
                 │
                 Edward Seymour, Lord Beauchamp, d. 1612
                 │
                 William Seymour, Lord Beauchamp ------

224

he had done so. Great excitement prevailed in both London and Bristol. Cabot secured five ships for a second voyage in 1498. But here his story fades into anticlimax, for he never returned from his second voyage. Perhaps some of his ships did return. If so, they brought no lading from the Orient, and the merchants who had financed the voyage must have lost both their money and their enthusiasm. For three quarters of a century there were few English voyages to the mainland of North America. Gradually it became evident that Cabot had not reached Asia but had discovered a new continent which barred the way to the East. At that time it could be exploited in only one way. Cabot had noticed the great quantities of fish in the waters south of Newfoundland, and fishermen of many nations soon came to this area. Such is the honorable story of John Cabot. It was he who discovered North America at the close of the fifteenth century, and he had done so in an English ship.

Henry VII died in 1509 and was buried in the beautiful chapel he had added to Westminster Abbey. Though not a spectacular or showy king, Henry established his dynasty on a firm foundation, gave England peace, prosperity, and good government, left rich funds in his treasury, and won the loyalty if not the love of his people.

CHRONOLOGY

The First Tudor

1485–1509	Henry VII; founder of Tudor Dynasty
1486	Merchant Adventurers of London organized
1487	Lambert Simnel defeated; earl of Lincoln (Yorkist) killed
1489	Treaty of Medina del Campo; Catherine of Aragon
1494	Poynings' Law for Ireland
1496	*Intercursus Magnus*
1497	John Cabot discovers North America
1499	Perkin Warbeck and earl of Warwick (Yorkist) executed
1502	Death of Prince Arthur; Catherine of Aragon widowed
1503	Catherine betrothed to Henry; Princess Margaret married to James IV of Scotland
1504	Laws against livery and maintenance

11

Henry VIII: The Break with Rome

HENRY VIII, 1509–1547: THE YOUNG KING

The death of Henry VII was not greatly lamented. England turned gladly to the colorful and attractive young prince who now ascended the throne. Henry VIII, not quite eighteen at the time of his father's death, appeared to contemporaries as a prince from a fairy tale: handsome, lively, intelligent, rich, with great endowments of nature and every courtly grace. He was also a fine athlete, a skillful rider and huntsman, an excellent archer and tennis player. "It is the prettiest thing in the world to see him play," wrote a foreign ambassador, "his fair skin glowing through a shirt of the finest texture." He enjoyed the company of learned men and had been carefully educated in the new learning of the Renaissance; he spoke Latin, French, and Spanish. A student of theology, he wrote *Assertio Septem Sacramentorum,* an attack on Martin Luther, for which the Pope conferred on him the title of Defender of the Faith. As a musician Henry composed songs he set to music and sang to his own accompaniment.

It was natural enough that in the first flush of youth Henry should devote himself largely to pleasure, to music, to hunting, to endless pageants and tournaments, and to the easy task of spending his father's money. His good humor, glamour, and openhanded expenditures captured the imaginaton of the people and brought him a popularity he never lost, but his time of youthful pleasure lasted too long. During the first twenty years of his reign one looks in vain for any noble purpose or notable achievement. Henry spurned the drudgery of close application to business and left the details of government to his minister, Cardinal Wolsey. Instead of building the state, as his father had done, the young Henry turned to the empty honor and glory of diplomacy and war (that sport of kings) and to the excitement of struggle for power on the Continent.

He soon displayed those darker traits for which he is best known: he was both unscrupulous and cruel. In a desire to win popularity he brought fictitious charges of treason against two of his father's ministers—Empson and Dudley—and hustled them off to execution. These men had been extortionate, but were also loyal servants of the old king. Henry combined supreme self-confidence with supreme selfishness. He had, of course, been born to the purple and had not had to struggle as Henry VII had done. The father clawed his way to achievement; the son was flattered and lionized from the cradle until he believed that his own will and his own way were the will and way of heaven. The father had sacrificed lives to clear the succession; the son continued to sacrifice lives but clouded the succession by his interest in mistresses, though these connections produced only one son, the illegitimate duke of Richmond.

Henry's Early Wars

Henry's reign fell within a period of intense rivalry between the Valois kings of France and the Hapsburg rulers of Spain and Austria, much of whose fighting was done in Italy. These wars, confused and endless, have little meaning for English history. They began when the French king, Charles VIII, attracted by the wealth and disunity of Italy, invaded that country in 1494 in the vain hope of adding it to the dominions of France. Despite his failure, his example was followed by other French kings—Louis XII (1498–1515) and Francis I (1515–1547).

At nearly the same time, Ferdinand of Spain was succeeded by his grandson, Charles V[1] (1516–1556), Archduke of the Netherlands. Through a remarkable series of marriages, Charles inherited the Netherlands and other portions of the old Burgundian duchy, the Hapsburg lands in and around Austria, together with Spain and the Spanish possessions of Naples, Sicily, and Sardinia, as well as all the Spanish colonies in the New World. In 1519 he became holy Roman emperor. He was not a brilliant man, but he possessed common sense, industry, patience, and determination.

Between these two rulers stood Henry VIII, the weakest of the three, yet hopeful of using their rivalry to give England a dominant place in the affairs of the Continent.

During the first twenty years of his reign Henry fought two wars with France (1512–1514 and 1522–1526) and one with Spain (1528–1529). In 1511 the papacy, Spain, and Venice formed what they termed the Holy League to drive the French from northern Italy. Invited to join the League, Henry made war on France. The war was based on no true English interest and was confused and meaningless from the onset. In 1512 Henry sent an army under the Marquis of Dorset to cooperate with Ferdinand in southern France, but it soon became evident that Ferdinand was using the English to facilitate his conquest of a part of Navarre, which was shortly in his hands. Thereupon he withdrew from the war. The English troops, in miserable condition from neglect and dysentery, ignored their commander and came home without permission. A more complete fiasco could hardly be imagined. Boiling with

---

[1]Charles I of Spain; Charles V as Holy Roman Emperor

rage against both France and Spain, Henry collected an army and crossed to Calais in 1513. Defeating the French in a brilliant cavalry action known as the Battle of the Spurs, Henry captured the French town of Thérouanne and the fortress of Tournai and returned to England in a blaze of empty glory.

A much more important victory had been won during Henry's absence. The Scots, very hostile to England, maintained the "Auld Alliance" with France, and Henry had to assume that there would be fighting in the north while he was abroad. The defense of England was placed in the hands of the earl of Surrey, an able general who led an army northward just in time to meet the Scottish King, James IV, as he crossed the border in August 1513. The Scots at first occupied a strong defensive position on Flodden Hill, a spur of the Cheviots, but James IV allowed himself to be enticed onto more level ground. Both wings of his army were defeated, and the English closed upon the Scottish center, where the king, surrounded by the flower of the Scottish nobility, fought fiercely against a solid ring of foes.

In time the king was slain, and the broken remnant of his defenders escaped under cover of darkness. Flodden was no disgrace for Scotland, for it was bravely fought. But it was a national disaster. Thirteen earls, fourteen lords, one archbishop, one bishop, two abbots, and scores of knights and gentlemen fell with their king. For the moment Scotland was crushed. The new king, James V, was a child. The regent, Queen Margaret, was Henry's sister.

Deserted by Spain, Henry determined to make terms with France. With Wolsey's aid he concluded a peace in 1514 which allowed him to retain Tournai and provided for the marriage of his younger sister, Mary, to Louis XII. The marriage was short-lived. It took place in July 1514; but Louis, an old man at fifty-two, was unequal to the social whirl demanded by his lively queen and was dead within a year. Henry wished his sister to marry her husband's successor, Francis I, but the lady had other views and secretly married Henry's ambassador to France, Charles Brandon, Duke of Suffolk, on whom she had looked with favor before her marriage to Louis. Timidly the couple returned to England. Wolsey, meeting them at Dover, assured them dolefully that they would both be executed. But Henry, having extracted a fine from Suffolk, pardoned his favorite sister and allowed the pair to live quietly in the country.

France and Spain were again at war in 1520, each seeking the alliance of England. In the course of these negotiations there was a friendly meeting between Henry and Francis on French soil near Calais at the so-called Field of the Cloth of Gold, where each king sought to outdo the other in vigorous sports competitions and royal magnificence. Nevertheless, in the next year Henry allied with Spain and in 1522 began a second war with France. This war brought him no showy triumphs, for two large and very costly expeditions against France accomplished nothing. The inevitable war against the Scots amounted to no more than some fierce border raids. It was Emperor Charles who startled Europe by inflicting a crushing defeat on Francis at Pavia in Italy in 1525.

So abject was Francis' plight that Henry shifted his policy and attempted to restore the balance of power by joining France in a war against Spain in 1528–1529. This war was disastrous for Henry in a number of ways. To England's great economic loss it disturbed the cloth trade at Antwerp. The fighting, chiefly in Italy, resulted only in additional defeats for France. The Battle of Pavia and the astonishing sack of Rome in 1527 by Charles's mutinous troops left the Pope a prisoner in Charles's hands. It was at this unfortunate juncture that Henry sought a divorce from Catherine of Aragon, who was Charles's aunt. Only the pope could decide upon the divorce, but he was now in the power of Charles, the enemy of the king of England.

Meanwhile Henry was gravely embarrassed financially. The first war with France had exhausted the treasure of Henry VII. The second was financed in part by a benevolence, or forced gift, imposed on the well-to-do in 1522, and in part by a parliamentary grant in 1523 which was obtained only after a sharp struggle. When a demand was made for a second benevolence—while Wolsey's agents still were collecting the first—and when the second benevolence was applied to the poor as well as to the rich, murmurs of discontent broke into an uproar. The money could not be collected; indeed, the peasants of Kent, East Anglia, and Lincolnshire were on the verge of revolt. The government was forced to withdraw its demand and to abandon a projected campaign in France. The wars of the 1520s brought Henry close to bankruptcy. In no time had Henry VII's treasure been exhausted and his fiscal prudence thrown to the winds.

THE GREAT CARDINAL

The first French war had shown Henry the great administrative talents of his minister, Thomas Wolsey who, under the king, ruled England for almost twenty years. He rose from humble origins, for his father was a butcher and cattle dealer of Ipswich in Suffolk. Displaying great promise as a youth, Wolsey took his B.A. at Oxford when he was fifteen and entered the church as the normal road to a career. In 1507 he became a chaplain to Henry VII, who employed him as a diplomat and rewarded him with the deanery of Lincoln. Under Henry VIII he rose rapidly. A member of the Council in 1509, he became successively bishop of Tournai in France, bishop of Lincoln, and archbishop of York in 1514. In the next year he induced the pope to create him a cardinal. It was also in 1515 that he became lord chancellor and served as the king's principal minister—dominant in government, law, and diplomacy. He owed his advancement to his splendid intellectual gifts, to his tremendous industry and drive, and to his devotion to the interests of the king. So long as he retained Henry's favor he held the reality of power.

Wolsey was a vain, arrogant, and showy man. Perhaps because he had risen from obscurity to prominence, he held the most lofty views of his own importance and gloried in extravagant display of wealth and luxury; he reveled in magnificent houses, of which the grandest was his palace at Hampton Court, and in sumptuous banquets, at which he ate and drank immoderately. He paid great attention to his dress and personal adornment. When he came from his private chambers to hear cases at Westminster Hall, he was "apparelled all in red, in the habit of a cardinal." The Great Seal of England and his cardinal's hat were borne before him by a noble or a gentleman. He was surrounded by footmen who carried gilded battle axes or crosses of silver; and his mule was trapped in crimson velvet with silver stirrups. There was policy in this display, for authority was increased by a show of pomp and circumstance, but there was also great vulgarity. The rotund cardinal, basking in self-glorificaton and reveling in the good things of the world, was gross and fleshy.

His manner of life was so extravagent that he was constantly seeking means of increasing his revenues. A shameless pluralist, he always held at least one bishopric in addition to the archbishopric of York; he was abbot of the monastery of St. Albans, which was quite improper for a secular priest; and he was not above accepting bribes and extorting money by threats of his displeasure. His fees from the many courts he headed, his revenues from sees to which foreigners had been appointed as bishops, his gifts from continental rulers and from people at home who sought his favor—all taken together may have swelled his income to perhaps £50,000 a year at a time when one fifth of that sum would have made him the richest man in England aside from the king.

Wolsey as an Administrator

As an administrator Wolsey was arrogant and highhanded, unable to translate his ability and drive into any great accomplishment. He did not have to make many changes in the details of administration, for Henry VII had left them running in orderly efficiency. Finance continued to be conducted through the Chamber; the one important innovation was the appointment of two general surveyors to audit the accounts and to administer revenues from Crown lands. Henry VII had done this work himself, but his son could not be bothered. Wolsey destroyed the inner group of councilors who had surrounded the old king and quickly stood forth as the one all-important minister of state. Through his offices and his dependents he controlled the Great Seal, the privy seal, and the signet,[2] thus dominating a large portion of the administration. His policy in general was a continuation of the work of Henry VII—to strengthen the Crown, to centralize its power, to exalt the sovereign—and thereby to exalt himself. But although he was the effective ruler of the country, so that contemporaries overestimated his power, he was always the servant and the king the master. He held his vast authority because it was Henry's pleasure that he do so.

As a financial minister Wolsey was weak. He did not understand the importance of trade, and he was surprisingly blind to the economic forces of the time, as he showed by his efforts to stop the enclosing of land. He destroyed some illegal enclosures, but he did not relieve the agrarian problem from which enclosing arose and he antagonized the landed classes, which were the natural supporters of the Crown. He was unable to create new sources of revenue, merely looking about desperately for money, obtaining it where and how he could. His efforts in the 1520s were, as we have seen, unsuccessful. His methods increased the exasperation of the aristocracy and gentry, which were the classes represented in Parliament. Wolsey never learned to manage the House of Commons but approached it with arrogance and contempt.

[2] The signet was a small royal seal, often inserted in a ring, which the king kept with him in the custody of his secretary.

By reducing their role to one of merely granting money, he infuriated the members and thereby reduced the government's chances of obtaining funds. His enemies multiplied in the 1520s when he enforced economies at court which in turn reduced the pensions and perquisites of many courtiers.

Wolsey and the Courts

Wolsey's best work was done in the field of justice, where again he carried forward the policy of Henry VII. The country was far more law-abiding than in the fifteenth century, but the old spirit of violence and personal revenge was as strong as ever. Wolsey was determined that the overmighty subject be taught to obey the law, that the royal courts be respected, and that there be one course of justice for rich and poor alike. His determination may have been more resolute because the upper classes never accepted him as one of themselves. The chancellorship gave Wolsey power over the whole system of justice, and he employed this power to the full. He made great use of the Star Chamber, of which the chancellor was the presiding judge. The Star Chamber had been rather inactive during the early years of Henry VIII, but Wolsey revived it, lent it his great authority, and used it freely to punish riots, brawls, and disorders of every kind. He removed cases of perjury, forgery, and libel away from the courts of the church and transferred them to the Star Chamber. Above all, he transformed the Star Chamber from a court used primarily by the Crown into a popular tribunal to which large numbers of people brought their cases. The Star Chamber, with its dignity enhanced and its jurisdiction broadened, became a normal part of the judicial system.

Wolsey also strengthened the court of chancery, which was a court of equity for civil suits for such matters as trusts, wills, contracts, and disputes over property. Developed in the fourteenth and fifteenth centuries in response to the rigidity of the common law, the court of chancery decided cases on their merits rather than on technicalities. Wolsey made the court more efficient, more expeditious, and better able to enforce its decisions. He transformed it, as he had done the Star Chamber, into a normal part of the legal structure of the kingdom. He also revived the court of requests, which was a kind of poor man's court of chancery, where wrongs against the weak and needy could be heard upon petition. Wolsey also drew other cases within his jurisdiction by appointing commissioners to hear individual cases and by assigning cases in the northern parts of the country and in Wales to the local councils in those areas. Many cases were thus taken from the common-law courts and brought within the jurisdiction of courts connected with the Council.

It has been said that the very existence of the common law was in danger during the Tudor period because of rival courts set up by the Crown. While this danger was never great, it was most threatening in the period of Wolsey's power. Wolsey discovered, however, that the volume of business brought to the conciliar courts was greater than could be handled. He had invited the people to bring their cases to him, and the response was more than he had expected. In 1528 he transferred a mass of minor cases from the Star Chamber to the courts of common law, thus admitting the necessity of these courts. Nonetheless, his encroachments upon the juristiction of the common-law courts were sufficient to enrage the common lawyers, who saw their business decline before the highhanded aggressiveness of the chancellor. Wolsey thus added the lawyers to the ranks of his enemies.

Wolsey and the Church

Wolsey ruled the church as autocratically as he ruled the state. His policy was twofold: he wished to dominate the church, for his temper was domineering, and at the same time he wished to introduce reforms. He talked of reforming the monastic orders, of tightening discipline among the secular clergy, of improving their education, of creating new bishoprics, and of making war on many abuses. But he spent more time and energy in acquiring the powers necessary to inaugurate a policy of reform than on the reforms themselves. He was peculiarly unsuited to play the role of reformer, for he was guilty of almost every abuse from which the church was suffering. How could the greatest of all pluralists, the greediest of all money grabbers, the priest who obtained livings for his illegitimate (and very youthful) son tell other clerics to mend their ways? His reforms, therefore, amounted to very little. He investigated and dissolved a few small monasteries. He established a number of new lectureships at Oxford and founded an Oxford college (which survives as Christ Church) for the training of priests. The school he set up in his native Ipswich to feed the college at Oxford disappeared when he fell from power. But this was about all; domination over the church was closer to his heart than its reform.

Since the provinces of York and Canterbury were independent of each other, Wolsey as archbishop of York had no authority over the church in England as a whole. His hope of becoming archbishop of Canterbury was thwarted by the unusual longevity of Archbishop Warham. Wolsey therefore induced the pope to appoint him *legatus a latere,* an office which made him papal viceroy in England. During their visitations *legati* superseded all local ecclesiastical authorities. This appointment enabled Wolsey to override Warham and to control the province of Canterbury as well as that of York. Thereupon he subjected the church in England to a despotism such as it had never known before. Papal supremacy, which in the past had been mild and far distant, was now severe and close at hand. Wolsey allowed long vacancies to occur between the death of one bishop and the appointment of the next, so that in the interim he might appropriate their revenues. He encouraged the appointment of foreigners as bishops on condition that he receive a part of their income and he even forced some English bishops to hold their bishoprics on similar terms. Convocations met less frequently and the scope of their work was curtailed. Drawing cases from episcopal courts into his court as legate, Wolsey extracted larger fees than customary. He frequently interfered with the ordinary administration of abbots and bishops. The church in England had never been so impotent in managing its own affairs.

Wolsey's domination was disastrous for the church in England. His greatly augmented power over the church was based on papal power; hence the English upper clergy, united in hatred of him, came to look askance upon the source from which his authority was derived. Under Wolsey's is direction and command, papal supremacy became evil. Supremacy of the king could hardly be worse. Thus the bishops did not oppose Henry's later encroachments as ardently as they might have done had Wolsey never existed. Wolsey, moreover, had so weakened and undermined the position and influence of the bishops that they could not hope to withstand the king in the struggle that was to come.

BACKGROUND OF THE BREAK WITH ROME

The King's Great Matter

Early in 1527 the king became concerned about the validity of his marriage to Catherine of Aragon, who was his brother's widow. A union of this kind was prohibited by canon law; and a verse in the Scriptures (Leviticus 20:21)[3] declared that a man who married his brother's widow should be childless. At the time of the marriage, however, the Pope granted a dispensation and all appeared to be well. The marriage at first was a happy one. Henry was eighteen, his bride twenty-four; for many years, despite an occasional peccadillo, the king treated his wife with respect and affection. But a curse seemed to lie on Henry's children. One after another they died at birth or in early infancy; the one normal and healthy child who survived was a daughter, the Princess Mary. The sad death of his children turned the king's mind to the ominous verse in Leviticus. Perhaps he was being punished by God for his uncanonical marriage. Perhaps the pope had exceeded his powers in granting the dispensation. Henry became convinced that his marriage was a sin, these whisperings of conscience being strongly fortified by other considerations.

Henry was, in the first place, greatly worried about the succession, which rested on the life of one young girl. Without the assurance of a strong and lasting dynasty there could be no permanent peace; the anarchy and civil wars of the fifteenth century could easily return. Henry had complicated the succession by an irresponsible affair with one of the queen's ladies in waiting, Elizabeth Blount, who became the mother of his illegitimate son, Henry Fitzroy, Duke of Richmond. Henry showered honors and offices upon this boy, obviously with the possibility in mind of making him his heir, but Catherine was certain to fight for the rights of her daughter. If this daughter succeeded to the throne, there would be grave dangers ahead. There had only been one ruling queen of England—Matilda in the twelfth century—an unhappy precedent. It was not at all certain that a female ruler could inspire the awe and exact the obedience a male sovereign could command. Her marriage would raise grave difficulties. If she married a foreigner (as Mary was to do), the door would be open for undue influence on English affairs by a foreign power. If she married an Englishman, she would arouse the jealousy of others. Henry's longing for a legitimate male heir was shared by the people, although most of them were shocked and angered by

---

[3] "And if a man shall take his brother's wife, it is an unclean thing: he hath uncovered his brother's nakedness; they shall be childless."

Henry VIII, after Hans Holbein. (National Portrait Gallery, London)

Henry's sordid efforts to discard Catherine and to obtain a wife who could bear him children; nevertheless, they acquiesced in Henry's actions because they understood the importance of a male heir to the throne.

There was also another consideration. Sometime between 1525 and 1527 the king fell in love with a lady at court, Anne Boleyn, the daughter of a diplomat, Sir Thomas Boleyn. Catherine at forty was no longer attractive physically; it is not surprising that Henry in his middle thirties became infatuated (as his love letters show) with a lively young woman of twenty or a little less. Thus as Henry questioned the validity of his marriage the need for a male heir grew more insistent; Anne Boleyn offered a tempting solution to the problem if Catherine could be eliminated.

It was soon apparent, however, that to obtain a divorce would be extremely difficult. One obstacle was Catherine's righteous indignation at the wrong to which she was subjected; innocent, proud, queenly—the object of universal sympathy and

Catherine of Aragon, artist unknown. (National Portrait Gallery, London)

respect—she stood her ground against her husband. The question could be settled only by the pope. What Henry wanted was a papal pronouncement that the dispensation of 1509 was in error, that the marriage to Catherine had been invalid from the beginning, and that the king was therefore in an unmarried state, free to take a wife whenever he chose. Clement VII, though he naturally disliked his role, would probably have found a solution. Wolsey had already seen a loophole in the law and seems to have passed on the information to Rome. Wolsey knew how to strengthen Henry's weak legal case, but Henry no longer trusted him. Perhaps Henry was obstinate and was determined to do it his own way or not at all. In any case Clement dared not offend Charles in order to please Henry.

At Wolsey's failed attempt to free the pope by making war on Spain in alliance with France (1528–1529) Clement still hoped for some unforeseen escape from his dilemma. Meanwhile, as Wolsey's failure became obvious, an angry king took affairs into his own hands, stripped the cardinal of his offices, allowed him to die in disgrace, and, within the space of seven stormy years (1529–1536), severed the ancient bonds between the church in England and the church in Rome. Within these seven years an enormous amount of history was concentrated. The revolution thus effected in church and state has shaped the course of English history from that day to this.

Condition of the Church

To understand how Henry was able to bring about these momentous changes we must look at the church in the early sixteenth century and at the way in which it was regarded by the people. In doing so, however, one must not assume that a reformation was inevitable or even likely. There is little doubt that in the later Middle Ages the church had been drawn away from its ideals, that it contained many weaknesses, and that reform was overdue. Clergymen in the early Tudor period were no longer accorded the respect and affection that had been given them in the past. The church as an institution still was venerated and the English were quite orthodox, but anticlericalism was widespread. The besetting sin of the upper clergy, as often before, was worldliness. Bishops, archdeacons, abbots, holders of rich livings, often born, like Wolsey, in the middle class and advanced because of their drive and ability, were apt to be sophisticated businessmen rather than spiritual leaders. Many were taken from the service of the church and employed by the Crown as lawyers, administrators, councilors, and diplomats. They accumulated offices and livings in the church; they practiced nonresidence, nepotism, and simony; their wealth and ostentation were resented by the lower clergy and by the people at large.

Great numbers of clerks in minor orders engaged in all sorts of secular occupations while claiming the immunities of the clergy. The parish priest, normally of peasant stock, was often a small farmer, cultivating the glebe of the parish church. His poverty tempted him to exact his tithes and perquisites with unbecoming zeal; moreover, he often lacked the education, the material means, and the social standing to command respect.

Monasticism, which had never recovered from the Black Death, was in decay in the early sixteenth century. Although there were notable exceptions, the bulk of the monasteries had lost their early fervor. They differed greatly from each other in wealth, population, and spiritual life. Some maintained the high ideals and traditions of the past, but many—chiefly small houses—had degenerated hopelessly and had little justification for existence. Between these extremes were many large and medium-sized houses, sometimes with more than adequate incomes in relation to the number of inmates, where there was much worldliness as well as a decline in devotion and, occasionally, graver abuses. The monasteries, on the whole, were harmless and tolerable, yet they had ceased to be of value to the community. Their hospitality had declined, as had their spiritual life and intellectual vigor. They no longer evoked the devotion of the people or appeared to justify the wealth with which they had been endowed by the piety of a more zealous age.

The church was a very expensive institution. Clerics serving the Crown were rewarded by appointments to ecclesiastical office and thus drew their incomes from the church, so that actually their money came from the people. The high fees charged by the clergy for baptisms, marriages, and burials, the fines and charges levied by the ecclesiastical courts, even the normal collection of tithes for the support of the parish priest—all were beginning to arouse a growing resentment. The church, it appeared, was wealthy; yet it must forever be taking money from ordinary folk. Resentment increased when the money went to Rome, for Rome was regarded as a corrupt and luxurious city, draining away the wealth of poorer and more wholesome communities. Men wondered whether the services of the church were being paid for at too dear a rate.

The history of the papacy in the later Middle Ages tended to lower it in popular estimation. For almost seventy years (1309–1377) the popes resided in the city of Avignon on the southern frontier of France, a period during which most of the popes and cardinals were Frenchmen and the papacy was virtually subordinate to the French government. There followed the Great Schism (1378–1417) when, to the scandal of western Christendom, there was one pope in Rome and another in Avignon. The schism was ended only with great difficulty. In the subsequent long struggle for supremacy between the popes and a series of church councils the popes were triumphant, but meanwhile, fearful lest they lose control of the papal lands in Italy, they became deeply involved in Italian politics. They had many reasons for doing so, but the loss was greater than the gain. By the end of the fifteenth century the popes were regarded by many Englishmen as Italian princes rather than as the spiritual leaders of Christendom.

The King and the Church

We have seen how often in the Middle Ages the double allegiance of the clergy—to the pope and to the king—had caused trouble between the church and the English government. For a moment in the fourteenth century it seemed as though these quarrels would come to a climax. But a break was avoided, largely for two reasons. In the first place, since the English were orthodox, their criticism of the papacy was political, not religious. At the same time, the "heretical" views of Wycliffe and the Lollards had survived and had come to the surface occasionally. Secondly, a new harmony arose at the end of the fourteenth century between the popes and the English kings. The Lancastrian rulers were in need of papal support, and the popes of the time of the Great Schism lacked the authority to combat antipapal legislation in England. The kings, wishing to reward their servants with bishoprics, found that the popes were willing to concur in the necessary appointments. Papal provisions to lesser benefices in England tended to diminish, and there were few quarrels in the century preceding Henry's divorce.

But Tudor despotism, with its exaltation of kingship and its emphasis on the power of the Crown, was likely to revive old disputes with the church. The king tended to regard the church as a barrier to good government. Anyone connected with the church, even when the connection was tenuous, could claim benefit of clergy, that is, the right to be tried by the courts of the church. The culprit did not fall afoul of the king's courts until he had committed a second crime. As a matter of fact, benefit of clergy was being curtailed before Henry's break with Rome. By an act of 1491 clerks convicted in the church courts were to be burned in the hand, so that, if they later came before the king's courts, the judges would know they had already been convicted. An act of 1512 deprived clerks of benefit of clergy unless they had taken major orders. The right of sanctuary by which a criminal fleeing from justice could claim asylum in a church or churchyard or in an ecclesiastical liberty was another hindrance to royal justice. It, too, was being whittled away and would disappear in the 1530s.

Sanctuary and benefit of clergy were illustrations of the dual allegiance of churchmen. Henry told the Commons in 1532: "We thought that the clergy of our realm had been our subjects wholly; but now we have well perceived that they be but half our subjects—yea, and scarce our subjects. For all the prelates at their consecration make an oath to the pope clean contrary to the oath they make to us, so that they seem his subjects and not ours." Tudor despotism demanded that every person in the realm should owe the king an undivided allegiance and that the clash of jurisdictions should end in the complete victory of the Crown. This was Henry's view, and on the whole the people agreed with him.

In summary it may be said that Henry quarreled with the pope at a time when the church was weakened by abuses, when its cost bore heavily on the people, when the papacy had fallen into scandals which lowered its prestige, and when the new monarchy of the Tudors would tolerate no rival to its authority in England. The English Reformation was quite different from that on the Continent. There was no Reformation in embryo waiting to be born. The English Reformation came from on high, although the ground below was ready for the seeds once sown. Had Henry not sought a divorce, an English Reformation at that time would have been most unlikely.

The English Humanists

The early Tudor period was a time of great intellectual activity. New colleges were founded at Oxford and Cambridge, the old curriculum of the universities was called into question, such aristocrats as Lady Margaret Beaufort, the mother of Henry VII, and William Blount, Lord Mountjoy, the friend of Henry VIII, became patrons of learning. A group of brilliant scholars at the universities and at court, known as the English humanists, represented the impact upon England of both the literary and artistic Renaissance that originated in Italy and the more religious humanism that developed in Germany and the Netherlands. The Renaissance, which began in Italy in the fourteenth century as a renewed interest in the literature and culture of ancient Greece and Rome, was a reaction against scholasticism. Italian scholars, or humanists, did not break with the idea of authority but found their authority in pre-Christian pagan authors. The classics opened new fields of study and provided a bolder and freer spirit of criticism and inquiry than could be found in medieval schoolmen. The humanists thought of the world, not as a dreary desert in which men sought painfully to save their own souls, but as an interesting and beautiful place, to be studied, understood, and enjoyed for its own sake. Gradually the Renaissance flowered into new activity in every form of intellectual, artistic, and practical life—in literature, scholarship, science, painting and sculpture, political thought, geographical discovery, and business and finance. Here was the beginning of the modern world.

Secular in tone, the Italian Renaissance sought the satisfaction of aesthetic tastes and intellectual curiosity and absorbed the pagan philosophy inherent in classical literature. But as the Renaissance passed into northern Europe it changed somewhat in character. In the north there was a deeper piety and greater preoccupation with religion. The northern humanists remained Christian. They turned with zest to the study of classical authors, but they were also concerned with Christian antiquity, that is, with the Bible and with the writings of the fathers of the church in the first centuries of the Christian era. They wished to study these Christian sources in the original texts, and for this they had to know Greek and Hebrew as well as Latin.

The humanists in England were of the northern Christian type, combining a devotion to classical studies with a deep religious feeling. They were critical of the abuses they saw in the church but had no thought of breaking away. The new learning, they believed, was to reform and refresh the church, not to destroy it.

An early humanist was William Grocyn, a famous Greek scholar who studied in Italy, was intimate with many learned men, and lectured in Greek at Oxford. Another was William Linacre, who combined the study of Greek with the practice of medicine. Like Grocyn he visited Italy and taught for a time at Oxford. He then came to court as the tutor of the king's children and as one of the physicians of Henry VIII. He helped found the College of Physicians in 1518. His fame among his contemporaries, however, rested on his Grecian studies and on his translations from Greek into Latin. John Colet, another humanist, was dean of St. Paul's Cathedral in London and the founder of St. Paul's school for boys (where the Greek scholar William Lily was the first headmaster). Colet was a more ardent reformer than Grocyn or Linacre. So sharply did he denounce abuses in the church that on one occasion he was cited for heresy before the church courts. Like later reformers, he preached a return to the purity and simplicity of early Christianity.

The most inspiring of the English humanists was Sir Thomas More. As a student at Oxford under Grocyn and Linacre he became so absorbed in the new learning that his father, a barrister, took him out of the university and set him to reading law in London. More studied law with avidity, built up an excellent practice, and was later drawn into the service of Henry VIII, who made him lord chancellor after the fall of Wolsey. More devoted his leisure to humanistic studies and made his household famous for its cultured atmosphere and learned guests. Beneath his love of letters and his brilliant wit lay a deep religious feeling, a devotion to principle, and an unshakable courage. As the king moved toward separation from Rome, More voiced his disapproval and retired to private life, not to be let alone. When he refused the oaths required by Henry's legislation, he was imprisoned and executed, a martyr to the older faith. His most famous work was his *Utopia* in which, under the guise of describing an imaginary community, he criticized the abuses of his day. All the English humanists paid deep respect to Erasmus, the greatest scholar of the age, who made long visits to England and lectured for a time at Cambridge.

Did the humanists prepare the way for the break with Rome? Historians in the past

Sir Thomas More, after Hans Holbein. (National Portrait Gallery, London)

have held they did. Recent scholars, however, have denied this, asserting that the humanists were loyal to the papacy and did nothing to cause or lead to the English Reformation. They were, of course, a small group of intellectuals confined to the universities and to the court. Henry's break with Rome was political in nature, not religious, and it came only when the crown had taken the lead. Nonetheless, the humanists penned their criticisms of the church in books which, in an age when books were few, must have had some impact. It can at least be said that the humanists swelled the chorus of criticism and supplied arguments for those who wished a break.

THE REFORMATION PARLIAMENT, 1529–1536

The famous Parliament which Henry summoned in 1529 passed a large amount of complicated and highly important legislation. This legislation can be divided for convenience into four groups of acts. Such a division will help to explain the course of events, for at the beginning of the Parliament neither its members nor the king himself had any notion how far they were to travel. The first group of acts was initiated by the Commons and not by the Crown. Allowing anticlericalism to take its course, Henry permitted the Commons to debate what the members pleased, and they passed at once a number of bills against abuses in the church. A Probate Act and a Mortuaries Act in 1529 reduced and regulated the fees that could be charged by the church courts for probating wills and by the clergy for conducting burials. A Pluralities Act of the same year declared that a clergyman who held a living worth £8 a year must resign it if he accepted a second benefice. Benefit of clergy, already restricted, was further curtailed in 1531, as was also the right of sanctuary. Henry hoped to frighten the pope by these statutes, but the pope, more afraid of the king of Spain than of the king of England, stood firm.

A second group of acts deprived the English clergy of independence and forced them into complete subordination to the Crown. Henry knew that if he were to make headway against Rome he had to control his own clergy and must silence Convocation, which had displayed some opposition to his policies. He therefore took the astonishing course of accusing the entire body of the English clergy of having broken the Statute of Praemunire. This statute dealt with appeals from English courts to the papal curia, but its language was so vague that almost any business with Rome could be brought within its compass. The accusation was clearly absurd.

Yet public opinion was all against the church; the clergy were thoroughly frightened. The Convocations of Canterbury and York obtained a pardon only by paying fines of £100,000 and £18,000, respectively, and by making a submission to the king. This submission, Henry asked, should recognize him as "sole protector and supreme head of the Church and clergy in England"; but Convocation managed to substitute the words "singular protector, only and supreme lord, and as far as the law of Christ allows, even supreme head." In 1532 Henry obtained an even humbler surrender. Convocation granted him the right to review all its past canons or ordinances and to abrogate those he disliked, and it was further agreed that all future canons must receive his approval before they became effective. These concessions were embodied in an Act for the Submission of the Clergy in 1534. Henry did not bother to review the canons. His victory was achieved: he had been accepted by the church as its supreme legislator in place of the pope. The independence of the clergy was ended.

To understand a third group of statutes we must look for a moment at a new minister who was becoming important. This was Thomas Cromwell. Of humble birth—his father having been a blacksmith and a fuller in London—Cromwell had travelled the Continent as soldier, lawyer, land agent, and merchant. During the 1520s he was in Wolsey's service. Then, after Wolsey's fall, he caught the king's attention by his skill in managing the House of Commons in the interest of the Crown. He was soon on his way to high office, becoming Secretary by 1534.

Cromwell has often been denounced as the king's evil genius, the cunning and unscrupulous agent of royalty in destroying the ancient church. Cold and ruthless he certainly was, but he had great ability; he possessed a remarkable gift for penetrating to the heart of a problem, seeing his objective clearly, and driving at it with remorseless and single-minded purpose. He knew where he was going when other councilors floundered. His mind was secular, and he was strongly anticlerical. Cromwell's great purpose was to increase the power and wealth of the king while maintaining his position as the king's chief minister. He saw that the way to achieve these ends was to exclude the papacy completely from England and to seize the wealth of the church for his royal master. During the crucial years of the Reformation Parliament the king usually followed Cromwell's counsel.

A series of statutes now aimed directly at the powers of the pope in England. In 1532 an Act in Conditional Restraint of Annates declared that annates and other fees due Rome from the English clergy might be withheld at the discretion of the king. Here was the most obvious pressure to obtain the divorce, but the Pope remained adamant. Hence the payments were withheld; and in 1534, when a break with Rome had become inevitable, an Act in Absolute Restraint of Annates ended these payments altogether. The act of 1532 had withheld them on the ground that they were extortionate, but another statute in 1534 lamely explained that they were still to be paid, though from now on the money should go to the king. These acts also provided for the selection of bishops and archbishops in England by the king alone. Cathedral chapters in the past, when about to make an election, had received advice from both king and pope. The law now required that only the king should give advice and that his nominee should be elected automatically.

Late in 1532, Anne Boleyn, timing her surrender nicely, ceased to resist the king's advances. Catherine was removed from Whitehall, Anne was installed in her place, and she and Henry were secretly married in January 1533. Anne was soon pregnant, and fast action was required if her child was to be legitimate. There followed the most crucial act of the Reformation Parliament: a statute forbidding appeals from English courts to any courts abroad in spiritual suits. The act provided that the final court of appeal in ecclesiastical cases should be the court of the archbishop of Canterbury, or, in cases which concerned the king, the upper house of Convocation. Shortly thereafter the archbishop's court declared that the marriage to Catherine was null and void. Anne Boleyn's child, born in September, was legitimate in English common law. To the king's chagrin it proved to be a girl, the future Queen Elizabeth. In 1534 the Act of Appeals was amended. The king, if he wished, could appeal a case to a new court, the Court of Delegates, which was to consist of commissioners appointed by the Crown in Chancery. The outcome of an appeal taken to the Court of Delegates could be prophesied with some assurance.

A fourth and final series of statutes was designed to construct a new ecclesiastical framework in place of that which had been demolished. The Act for the Submission of the Clergy, already mentioned, gave Henry the right to control the clergy and thereby to build a church anew. An Act of Supremacy in 1534 acknowledged the king as the supreme head of the English Church on earth, with all the titles, honors, jurisdiction, and powers inherent in that position. He was to be accepted as supreme head by the people, who could be required to take an oath supporting the principles of the act. The royal power to reform errors and heresies within the church also was acknowledged. An Act of Succession declared that the succession to the throne lay in the children of Henry and Anne Boleyn. Their marriage was not to be criticized, and again there was an oath accepting the principle of the act. It was the refusal of this oath which brought about the executions of Sir Thomas More and Bishop Fisher of Rochester, according to the provisions of the Treasons Act of 1534. The Ten Articles (1536) and the Six Articles (1539) were attempts to define the doctrines of the church.

THE DISSOLUTION OF THE MONASTERIES

Kings had often cast envious eyes at the wealth of the monasteries. It is not surprising that Cromwell, wishing to make his master rich, should have advised the spoliation of the church over which Henry was gaining mastery. The methods employed in the great dissolution were crass and hypocritical. Appointed vicar-general in 1535, Cromwell was given power to visit and investigate the religious foundations in England; during the next six months his agents, an unscrupulous crew, dashed from one monastery to another, paying far greater attention to cataloging the wealth of the monks than inquiring into their morals. This was a visitation to end, not to mend, the monasteries, beginning with the smaller houses. An act of 1536 dissolved all monasteries with an income of less than £200 a year. Some 300 small

The Vyne, Hampshire. A manor house of patterned brick built in the reign of Henry VIII. (Copyright Country Life)

monasteries, nunneries, and convents were dissolved, their lands and other possessions passing into the hands of the king. The larger foundations soon discovered that their turn would come. Within the next three years many of them, hoping to secure favorable terms, made voluntary surrenders by which they placed themselves at the king's mercy. They were thereupon dissolved. The end came in 1539, when an act of that year dissolved those that remained. All told, some 800 houses, including friaries, disappeared.

The dissolution of the monasteries leads us to the social and economic results of the Reformation, which will be discussed in the next chapter. Here only a few points need be mentioned. An important form of religious life ceased to exist. Monks and nuns became unknown in England for many centuries. The transition to Protestantism was simplified and made more abrupt, for the monks had been a bulwark of the Roman Catholic Church and might have retarded changes. Great destruction of buildings and churches followed, with the loss of objects of medieval art, books, and manuscripts, for Henry allowed the monastic libraries to be scattered. The monks who had belonged to the richer monasteries did not fare badly, provided with pensions or livings in parish churches. The nuns and friars whose houses were less prosperous were not treated so well, and some of them received nothing. A few royal ministers, including Cromwell, a few court favorites, and some local supporters of the king, were given large estates. But as long as Cromwell lived the great bulk of the monastic lands was retained by the Crown. After his death in 1540 perhaps two thirds of these lands were sold, often in a very unbusinesslike way. For the most part they passed into the hands of the nobility and gentry, often laying the foundation for the rise of new families.

It has been argued that Henry should have kept the land as a permanent endowment for the Crown, but there was shrewdness in allowing it to enrich the upper classes. During the Middle Ages there had always been an ecclesiastical majority in the House of Lords. Abbots, priors, and bishops could outvote the temporal peers. But now the abbots and priors were gone, and, though the bishops remained, the lay peers in that chamber formed a majority they have since retained. Henry did little to redeem his pledge that he would put the wealth of the monasteries to better uses than in the past. It is true that he created six new bishoprics, which were badly needed. But next to nothing was done to relieve the poverty of the lower clergy, or to found schools or colleges, or to assist the poor. Most of the money from monastic lands went into a very costly war which Henry waged against France in the last years of his reign.

THE CHURCH OF ENGLAND

The significance of the changes made in the church may be gathered from the preamble to the Act of Appeals in 1533. This preamble contained a ringing declaration that England was an empire, that is, a free and sovereign state, owing no allegiance whatever to any foreign prince. The empire of England, the preamble continued, was governed by a ruler who was supreme head in matters spiritual and king in matters temporal, possessing "plenary, whole, and entire power, preeminence, authority, prerogative, and jurisdiction" over the people of his realm; and the people, both clergy and laity, owed him a natural and humble obedience. These powers came to him, not from any earthly source, but from "the goodness and sufferance of Almighty God."

The pope thus was excluded, and Henry assumed all the powers which the papacy had formerly exercised in England. He could administer the church, discipline its clergy, control its laws through Convocation, tax it and dip into its revenues, appoint its officers and dignitaries, and supervise its courts. Holding that his supremacy came directly from God, Henry returned in theory to the position of the Anglo-Saxon kings, who combined temporal authority with spiritual attributes. The king was not a priest and did not perform priestly functions. Nonetheless, he possessed a sacred quality, he was both *rex* and *sacerdos,* and he could determine doctrine and regulate ritual. This definition of the king's supremacy broke sharply with the doctrine of the pope as supreme pontiff. Henry was establishing a new church. The church *in* England was becoming the Church *of* England.

The people as a whole accepted these changes with surprising tranquility. A few brave men, such as More and Fisher, resisted them to the death; a rebellion in the north in 1536 known as the Pilgrimage of Grace looked dangerous initially, but in the end amounted to little. Henry's alterations in the church were accepted probably for two reasons. One was the genuine hostility to Rome and the willingness to support the king. Secondly, the dogma and ritual of the church remained virtually unchanged. The Mass was performed as it always had been, ancient creeds and ceremonies remained, and the ordinary person attending the parish church saw only minor changes from the past. Pilgrimages and prayers to saints were suppressed and shrines were demolished, but when Parliament defined dogma in the Six Articles in 1539 the faith of the church remained Catholic. Transubstantiation was confirmed, communion in one kind remained, the Mass and auricular confession continued, private Masses were justified, and clerical marriage remained illegal. But if Henry thought that the church would continue in this condition, without the intrusion of Protestant doctrine, he was quite mistaken, for such doctrines surfaced rapidly after his death. Indeed, he himself paved the way. In 1539 a Bible translated into English was placed in every church, and thus the Scriptures became available in English to the entire nation.

THE STATE

The preamble of the Act of Appeals acknowledged that the temporal power of the king was as ample as his supremacy over the church. Henry stood high above his subjects: he inspired confidence in his capacity to govern; he was able to cast his plans into forms which were acceptable to the people; and he embodied national aspirations. The new sovereign state, over which he ruled and of which he was the symbol, was regarded as all-powerful. Its interests transcended the interests of individuals, corporations, and ancient institutions. The king's power was indeed real, and his mastery and leadership were acknowledged. Yet while Henry built his absolutism, he also supplied the limitation to that absolutism. He had revolutionized the church through parliamentary statute; and he had shown that he was most potent when he was King-in-Parliament, that is, when king, lords, and Commons united in making law. He thus acknowledged that the House of Commons was an integral part of the state, a partner of the Crown in legislation. Had he not been able to control the Commons, his views might have been less enlightened.

The king and Cromwell may be said to have invented the art of parliamentary management. The task was not difficult, for Parliament was still a primitive institution: the Lords were largely Tudor creations; and the Commons were far more deferential and compliant than they became later in the century. The Commons contained a number of royal officials, including those members of the King's Council who were not peers and who now sought election to Parliament. These men could speak in favor of royal measures and could carry with them something of royal authority. The speaker in a house still without rigid procedure could help greatly in parliamentary management. Cromwell used his influence with county magnates and town corporations to return members favorable to royal policy. Above all, he carefully drafted the great statutes which brought about the break with Rome. Thus the Commons were given a program to debate and were not left to their own devices.

It is the paradox of Tudor history that under this treatment the Commons made rapid advances. They were given a thorough schooling in the art of legislation, for the statutes of Henry's reign equaled in bulk the statutes of all the medieval kings. The self-respect and self-confidence of the Commons were increased by Henry's attitude. Ready to persuade rather than coerce, he tolerated occasional criticism of his policy. The Commons obtained some control over their own members and something of the aspect of a court in punishing offenders against their privileges. We must not, of course, be too charmed by Henry's methods. He was an awesome figure, inspiring some terror, and much of Cromwell's manipulation was very crude. But at least the Commons knew they were worth manipulating.

A number of administrative reforms strengthened the government. One was the development of the Privy Council. In the large and loosely organized Council of Henry VII there had been an inner ring of councilors close to the ruler. This group had disappeared during Wolsey's ascendancy, for Wolsey, allowing no rivals, had preferred to make the Star Chamber the center of the Council. After his fall, however, the Star Chamber was less prominent, and an inner ring of councilors reappeared. Cromwell developed this group and used it, though he kept it well under control. It became known as the Privy Council. The distinction between it and the Star Chamber was clearly visible by 1540. The Star Chamber was judicial; the Privy Council was political, advisory, and administrative.

Composed of fifteen to twenty of the king's principal ministers, most of them holding high office, the Privy Council watched over the entire administration of the kingdom. It kept in close touch with local officials, whom it directed and controlled by constant correspondence about roads and bridges, religious laws, disturbances of the peace, inns and alehouses, the care of the poor, and economic conditions and economic quarrels. It concerned itself with naval and military administration, with the royal household, with English ambassadors abroad, and Ireland, Wales, and the Channel Islands. It took a paternal interest in the nobility, settling disputes and dividing estates among heirs. The Privy Council was the king in action, ubiquitous in its watchfulness, and flexible in its capacity to deal with any problem which affected the interest of the state. Much of its work had a judicial implication, for the Tudors did not distinguish sharply between the administrative and the judicial functions of its servants.

The dissolution of the monasteries involved a great deal of financial administration for which the Chamber, as developed by Henry VII, proved inadequate. Cromwell therefore took revenue away from the Chamber and set up six separate institutions which acted both as courts and as financial departments. The Exchequer administered revenues coming from the customs and from parliamentary grants. The duchy of Lancaster handled the lands belonging to it. A court of general surveyors dealt with the land acquired by Henry VII, while a body known as the court of augmentations controlled the lands taken from the monasteries. A court of first fruits and tenths collected revenues coming from the church; a court of wards and liveries handled the feudal revenues of the Crown.

Cromwell held the office of the king's principal secretary, and in his hands this office became the most important in the state. The secretary was developed into the chief executive minister of the Crown, responsible for the direction of both foreign and domestic policy. Much of later administrative history was merely the growth of this office and the subdivision of its work among a number of secretaries.

During the Middle Ages numerous bits of territory scattered through the kingdom were known as franchises or liberties, which in one way or another retained semi-independent rights. There had been many such franchises in the north, in Wales, and in the Welsh marches which had been the source of great trouble during the fifteenth century. When a statute of 1536 swept them away, the king's government became supreme for the first time throughout the entire kingdom. It was this statute which ended the county palatine of Durham; a natural sequel was the establishment in 1537 of a permanent Council of the North. This Council, composed of royal officials with both judicial and administrative powers, governed the five northern counties as a branch office of the Council in London. There had been temporary councils in the north since the reign of Edward IV, but now a strong and permanent one was set up to quiet those "peccant parts." Cromwell gave new strength and vigor to the council in Wales established by Edward IV. Moreover, a famous statute in 1536 (expanded in 1543) incorporated the whole of Wales with England. The old lordships of the Welsh marches were dissolved, some annexed to existing shires, the others divided into five new counties. Justices of the peace were appointed, and the Welsh counties and boroughs were to return twenty-four members to the House of Commons. Thus the law and administration of England were extended to Wales in this first act of union.

HENRY'S LAST YEARS

In his last years Henry was a most unpleasant figure, bloated and sickly in body—so corpulent that a little derrick had to be arranged to lift him from bed—cynical, suspicious, and cruel, though still vigorous in mind. The charming young prince was gone; a sour, coarse, and ill-tempered old man had taken his place. The problem of the succession continued to haunt him. His matrimonial vicissitudes became so complicated that they give a touch of the ridiculous to the story of a most regal figure. In 1536 Anne Boleyn, having failed to produce a male heir and having disillusioned the king in other ways, was condemned to death and executed. The next day Henry married his third wife, Jane Seymour, a pale and gentle lady, who died in 1537 a few days after she gave birth to a son, the future Edward VI. Henry at length had a male heir, though the heir was likely to be under age at the time of his father's death. In 1540 Henry married Anne of Cleves. This marriage was a move in the game of diplomacy, for Cromwell was seeking an alliance with the Protestant states of Germany. Anne, however, was not the most beautiful of princesses. Henry married her with a sigh and then, resolving there were things he could not do for England, arranged a separation which enabled her to live in quiet affluence—intent on her needlework—until her death in 1557. Cromwell paid the price for his error, fell from power, and was executed under a bill of attainder. Catherine Howard, the king's fifth wife, was married to him in 1540 and was executed for her youthful indiscretions in 1542; Catherine Parr, whom Henry married in 1543, proved an excellent nurse for her irascible old husband and managed to survive him. The reign ended in gloom and degeneration. One should think of Henry, not in his old age, but in the vigor of his prime when he showed himself a ruler of ability, a fine parliamentarian, and a king who carried his people with him through revolutionary change.

It has always been difficult to see the real Henry VIII amid the many myths and legends. It has been difficult to determine just what his relations were with Wolsey and Thomas Cromwell. He was notorious over his relationships with women; yet he had more wives than mistresses, which was not often the case among kings. A rare combination of the medieval and the modern, Henry consumed vast financial resources in an impossible attempt to conquer France; he also reorganized and built a more efficient administration in both Church and State. The old king died still a Catholic, but he bequeathed his heir a Protestant Council of State. England's Harry has never ceased to be an object of interest, if not awe, for succeeding generations.

CHRONOLOGY

Reign of Henry VIII

1509–47	Henry VIII
1509	Henry married Catherine of Aragon
1520	Field of the Cloth of Gold
1525	Battle of Pavia
1527	Henry seeks divorce
1529	Fall of Wolsey; Thomas More lord chancellor; Reformation Parliament meets
1532	Submission of the Clergy in Convocation
1533	Henry married Anne Boleyn; Act in Restraint of Appeals; Elizabeth born
1534	Act in Absolute Restraint of Annates; Act for Submission of the Clergy; Act of Supremacy; Act of Succession; Treasons Act
1535	Thomas More executed
1536	Anne Boleyn executed
1536–39	Dissolution of the Monasteries
1539	Act of Six Aritcles
1540	Thomas Cromwell executed

12 Edward VI and Mary: Religious and Economic Change

EDWARD VI, 1547–1553, AND THE RETURN OF FACTION

The paramount political fact of Edward's reign was that the king was but a child. Edward was nine years old when he ascended the throne and only fifteen when he died of tuberculosis. From the moment of his birth he was surrounded by an elaborate household with all the trappings of royalty. Fully assuming the role of king, Edward was inclined to assume a cold and rather imperious attitude toward his councilors. With little enthusiasm for sports, he was much more interested in his books and questions of theology. His sympathies were Protestant. Though Edward was an intelligent boy who seemed to grasp the significance of religious and political problems, he was too young to impose his own will and was controlled by the men around him.

This situation struck at the essence of Tudor government. Henry VIII had vastly increased the powers of the king, he had been a most regal figure before whom his councilors trembled, and he had fashioned a state which depended upon the presence of a strong ruler at the helm. Now suddenly that strength was gone; power at the center was followed by a vacuum. The result was a return to faction, to quarrels and intrigues among ambitious councilors, and to instability, weakness, and corruption in government. Yet because Tudor government had been built so well it could not be easily overthrown; England escaped a return to the chaos of the fifteenth century and survived the dangerous crisis of Edward's minority.

The Lord Protector Somerset, 1547–1549

Henry had attempted to devise a government that would function after his death. His will provided, not for a regent, but for a council of regency. A council of this kind, however, could be effective only if it acted as a unit, which was found to be impossible, and only if it provided leadership, a function for which Henry had given it no training. His Council had existed merely to do his bidding. His plan for Edward's reign collapsed at once. The clique in power, composed of nobles and politicians who hoped for the spoils of office, carried out a *coup d'état* by which Henry's will was set aside. Edward Seymour, Earl of Hertford, became duke of Somerset and assumed the office of Lord Protector and governor of the young king. Somerset was a logical person to step into preeminence, for he was a soldier, he had been a favorite of Henry, he was the brother of Henry's third wife, Jane Seymour, and hence the uncle of Edward VI. But there was another councilor, John Dudley, Viscount Lisle and later duke of Northumberland, who might have been made protector. Failing in this, he became a bitter rival of Somerset; the struggle of these two men fills much of the annals of the reign.

Somerset, who was much the more attractive, was something of a liberal and an idealist, though he was ambitious, rather arrogant in manner, and ready to enrich himself as he saw opportunity. His good intentions could never express themselves in practical policy. Believing that leniency was better than terror, he relaxed the restraints of Henry's rule, but as a result he opened the way for unscrupulous politicians to turn liberty into license. With a generous sympathy for the poor, he attempted to relieve their sufferings, thus incurring the hostility of the prosperous middle classes. Like Henry, he hoped to eliminate French influence in Scotland and to draw the two countries together by a marriage between Edward and Mary, Queen of Scots, then a child about four years old. But Henry, unable to come to terms with the Scots, had made war upon them. Somerset did the same when he invaded Scotland and won the useless Battle of Pinkie Clough near Edinburgh in 1547. His actions drove the Scots closer to France. Within a few years they sent their little queen to Paris to be educated as the future wife of the dauphin, later King Francis II. French influence in Scotland increased and remained a problem for years to come. Nor did Somerset's Protestant reforms win him popularity. As a statesman he must be considered a failure.

Northumberland in Power, 1549–1553

Somerset's followers became restive, and it was not difficult for Northumberland to intrigue against him. Following a revolt in 1549, known as Kett's Rebellion,[1] which was thought to have been caused by Somerset's sympathies for the lower classes, a cabal of councilors led by Northumberland forced the protector out of office and sent him to the Tower. He was released in the following year. For a short time there was some cooperation between him and Northumberland, but soon their rivalry became more deadly than ever. In December 1551 Somerset, accused of plotting against Northumberland and the king, was tried for treason and executed early in 1552. Northumberland secured the first place in the Council though he was never lord protector. He returned to Henry's policy of force and ruthlessness, but did not make the government popular or strong. He was an unscrupulous adventurer, the new

[1] See pages 265–266.

statesman at its worst, without pity or moral restraint, a gambler playing for high stakes in the dangerous game of politics.

His fall came suddenly. For some time he had strengthened his position by cultivating the good will of the king, but he discovered in 1553 that the young king was dying. If Edward was succeeded by his sister Mary, the Catholic daughter of Catherine of Aragon, Northumberland knew his ruin would follow. He devised a daring plot by which he proposed to alter the succession. He arranged a marriage between his fourth son, Guildford Dudley, and Lady Jane Grey, a granddaughter of Mary Tudor, the sister of Henry VIII. Mary Tudor had married Charles Brandon, Duke of Suffolk; her daughter Frances was the mother of Lady Jane Grey. Other marriages were arranged to win supporters; councilors and judges were browbeaten into acquiescence. But the plot failed, for at Edward's death the country stood for Mary, the rightful queen. She displayed her courage by escaping from Northumberland's power into the county of Suffolk, where supporters quickly gathered round her. The plot collapsed and Northumberland was executed. The pathetic victim of his machinations was Lady Jane Grey, an attractive, learned, and completely innocent young lady, imprisoned with her husband at the time of the plot and executed in 1554 when Mary was faced with a dangerous rebellion.

Radical Protestantism

It was in the reign of Edward that the Church of England became definitely Protestant. Henry's alterations had been political and constitutional, and he had not made radical changes in the doctrine or ceremonies of the medieval church. In Edward's reign there was a sudden turn to the left; the Church of England became more radically Protestant than at any other time in its history. The abruptness of this shift comes as something of a shock. How can it be explained?

Henry's break with Rome had been the first step toward Protestantism, but his heavy hand had prevented the introduction of Protestant doctrine. Somerset, however, permitted much more freedom of debate. There followed a period of intense theological discussion and of rapid entry into England of religious ideas from the Continent. Henry himself had paved the way for new ideas by placing an English translation of the Bible in every parish church.

A surprising number of continental reformers came to England at this time. Some were exiles from persecution, some were invited by Somerset or by Archbishop Cranmer. The learned Italian Peter Martyr, a former Augustinian monk, arrived in 1547 and became a professor of divinity at Oxford in 1549. In that year Cranmer invited another famous reformer, Martin Bucer, an Alsatian, who was made professor of divinity at Cambridge, and who brought with him Paul Fagius, a Hebrew scholar. Others included John à Lasco, or Laski, a Pole; Vallerandus Pollamus, a former minister at Strasbourg; and Francisco de Enzinas, a Spaniard.

These men and others brought many variations of continental Protestant thought. Essentially, however, their doctrines were those of Martin Luther: justification by faith (the belief that one obtains salvation through faith that God will save you);

reliance on the Bible as the sole source of religious truth; sanctity of conscience as the supreme guide to moral conduct. Discussion in England centered upon the Eucharist, the sacrament of the Lord's Supper. Transubstantiation, the Catholic doctrine that the elements of bread and wine actually become the body and blood of Christ, was rejected by the Protestants, but they could not agree upon what to put in its place. Peter Martyr wrote from Oxford that there was contention about the Eucharist in every corner of the land and that even in the Council there was great disputing among the bishops and other members.

Thomas Cranmer, Archbishop of Canterbury, was of great importance in these discussions. He was a scholar, not a man of action, and in the reign of Henry VIII he had appeared to follow rather too tamely the dictates of his master. His theological views developed slowly, but they steadily became more Protestant. He was in close touch with the reformers on the Continent and with the continental visitors in England, though his beliefs were less extreme than theirs and he constantly sought a compromise which would be accepted by most of his countrymen. Somerset and Northumberland accepted a policy of reform out of political rather than religious

Thomas Cranmer, Archbishop of Canterbury, by G. Fliccius. (National Portrait Gallery, London)

motives. Somerset appears to have had some sympathy with Protestantism, but he hoped to win popularity by a Protestant policy and he feared that Catholics might plot in favor of Princess Mary, the king's sister. He knew that his followers hoped to enrich themselves by the continued spoliation of the church, which was carried out in the name of reform. Northumberland was without religious interest or scruple. He feared Princess Mary even more than Somerset had, he planned to pillage the church, and he found it expedient in politics to side with the reformers.

Shortly after Somerset became protector the government issued a set of injunctions addressed to both clergy and laity. The clergy was urged to attack the Roman Catholic Church from the pulpit, while the laity were warned against Roman images, candlesticks, and religious paintings on the walls of churches. Both clergy and laity responded with zeal, and mobs destroyed sacred objects in churches and desecrated shrines. Stressing the Scriptures as the only source of religious truth, the injunctions commanded the clergy to study the Bible and teach it to the people. Parts of the service were to be said or sung in English: the Epistles and Gospels and Cranmer's beautiful translation of the Litany. His book of homilies or short sermons, which taught justification by faith, was recommended.

A Parliament summoned in 1547 passed a number of important acts. Laws concerning heresy and Henry's act of Six Articles were repealed. Another act provided that bishops be appointed by letters patent, as were other officers of state. This was followed by an act dissolving the chantries and confiscating the religious endowments of guilds, fraternities, and colleges on the plea that they encouraged "vain opinion of purgatory," for the chantry priests sang Masses for the souls of the founders. The avowed purpose of the act was to provide endowments for education, but in reality the money went largely to unworthy courtiers; education suffered greatly from the weakening or destruction of schools and colleges, though some of the old foundations were spared and a few new grammar schools were begun. The act was sheer spoliation, and little can be said in its defense.

Another Parliament, meeting in 1548 and 1549, passed the first Act of Uniformity. Freedom of religious expression had degenerated into chaos, so that it became necessary to bring order and uniformity into divine worship. For some time a commission had been at work on a prayer book which could be made common throughout the kingdom. The new prayer book was largely the work of Cranmer, who headed the commission. Its tone was conservative, since it was for the most part a translation of the Latin service of the Catholic Church, but the fact that it was in English, so that the congregation could understand what was being said, was a step away from Rome. This prayer book—one of the most lovely expressions of devotion in the English language—displayed Cranmer's power of writing beautiful prose. It was imposed upon all churches. Priests who made use of any other service were subject to severe penalties, but the laity were not compelled to attend divine service. Finally, an act of this Parliament permitted priests to marry. Such were the more important religious changes during Somerset's regime. They represented cautious and moderate reform.

Northumberland's legislation was more drastic. An act of 1550 required that service books not authorized by the Act of Uniformity be destroyed. Another act appointed a commission to reform the canon law; a new commission was appointed to revise the Prayer Book. A second prayer book, again the work of Cranmer and more radical than the first, was embodied in a second Act of Uniformity in 1552. The act swept away much Catholic ritual, eliminated minor officials of the ancient church, and referred to the priest as a minister and to the altar as a table. Transubstantiation was denied. The people were to receive the Communion (both bread and wine) in a kneeling position, but the Prayer Book made clear that this did not imply an adoration of the elements. A general confession, spoken by the congregation, took the place of private confession to a priest; the sacrament of baptism and the vestments worn by the clergy were made more simple; attendance at church on Sundays and Holy Days was now required of the laity. Meanwhile Catholics were removed from the Council and from the bench of bishops. Cranmer listed the doctrines of the church in Forty-two Articles which he naïvely hoped would be accepted by everyone. The new prayer book was in force only about eight months and may never have penetrated to some parts of the country.

Protestant beliefs and practices which came into the church during this period included justification by faith and the appeal to conscience, denial of transubstantiation, communion in both kinds, simplification of ritual, the service in English, the acceptance of the Bible as the sole repository of religious truth, the dissolution of the chantries, and the marriage of the priesthood.

MARY TUDOR (1553–1558) AND THE CATHOLIC REACTION

There was no doubt that Mary exercised a profound influence on the course of English history. She checked the headlong rush toward radical Protestantism and drove England in the opposite direction, thus preparing the way for the religious compromise of the reign of Queen Elizabeth. Nevertheless, the results of Mary's policies were the opposite of what she hoped. Her militant Catholicism implanted in her people a hatred and suspicion of Rome which was to last for centuries. Her marriage to Philip of Spain resulted in English hostility to all things Spanish. Finally, her reign tested the machinery of government set up by her father. Events were to show what that machinery could do when it was directed by a vigorous personality—and what it could not.

The queen had many Tudor traits—pride, courage, ability, fixity of purpose, ruthlessness, and strength of will—but in Mary such potential strengths were her downfall. Until she was about fifteen she had been a favorite of her father and the heiress presumptive to his throne. Then came divorce and disgrace for her mother, the taint of illegitimacy for herself, and the slurring attacks on the church she loved. Close to her mother, she shared her Spanish sympathies and had her stern Spanish piety; hence she felt very deeply her mother's shame. Mary became warped and bitter. She hated the Reformation which had brought such humiliations on her. The Catholic religion was her one solace and she became a religious fanatic. Loving her people, she was determined, if ever it was within her power, to save their souls by

Mary Tudor, by Antonio Moro. (Museo del Prado, Madrid)

bringing them back to the Church of Rome. According to her lights, her policy was noble. It was self-sacrificing, for she was ready to risk her throne in its behalf; it was honest, for she acted with complete sincerity. Yet she lacked patriotism and the ability to identify herself with her country. She could be gentle and forgiving in dealing with political offenders, but her determination in matters of religion was implacable; it brought tragedy on herself and grief to her kingdom.

Mary was in a strong position during the first months of her reign. The support accorded to her against Northumberland had been spontaneous and widespread. It was natural that Northumberland's followers be turned out of office, as they were. She was then able to appoint Catholic ministers and to liberate and restore the Catholic bishops who had been imprisoned in Edward's reign. Stephen Gardiner, bishop of Winchester, became lord chancellor and the queen's principal adviser until the arrival of Cardinal Pole from Rome in 1554. Declaring herself a Roman Catholic, Mary encouraged priests to celebrate the Mass, which now reappeared throughout the country. The continental reformers, so influential under Edward, were told to leave the country. They were followed by a considerable number of Englishmen who preferred exile to life under a Catholic queen. These Marian exiles, as they were called, were to be of great importance. Settling in various Protestant centers in Germany and Switzerland, where they grew more radical with the years, they were to bring their doctrines back to England in the first years of Queen Elizabeth.

Mary's first Parliament carried through part of her program with surprising alacrity. It annulled the divorce of Henry and Catherine of Aragon, thus removing all question of the legitimacy of Catherine's daughter. Proceeding further, Parliament swept away the statutes of Edward VI concerning religion. The church was brought back to where it had been at the death of Henry VIII. On the other hand, there were things this Parliament would not do. It refused to touch the royal supremacy over the church or to revive papal power. The Erastian nature of the English Reformation—that is, the subordination of the church to the control of the state—was too firmly fixed to be easily altered. Parliament also refused to restore the monastic lands which had passed into the hands of the laity. It declined to impose any penalty upon those who did not attend the Mass. Moreover, Parliament was giving the queen a lesson regarding its position and power under the constitution. It knew very well what she wanted, but it decided what should be granted and what should be denied. Mary might well have heeded this warning. She might have seen that public opinion, as displayed in Parliament, was ready to return to the church of Henry VIII and to the Mass as practiced in the last years of his reign. It was unwilling, however, to restore papal supremacy, to force people to attend church, or to touch the monastic lands. Finally, Parliament showed itself suspicious of a Spanish marriage by petitioning the queen to marry one of her own subjects.

The Spanish Marriage

The warnings were disregarded. Within a year Mary married Philip of Spain, son of Emperor Charles V, and brought England once more within the fold of the Roman Catholic Church. The marriage of a queen, in any age when women were subject to their husbands, was a difficult matter; but Mary, like her father, felt a compelling necessity for an heir. If she had none, the throne would go to her sister, Elizabeth, the daughter of the hated Anne Boleyn. Catholics regarded Elizabeth as illegitimate; if she became queen, the future of Catholicism looked dim. It was natural for Mary to turn to Spain for a husband. She was half Spanish by blood and more than half by sympathy. An alliance with the Hapsburgs, the most powerful rulers in Europe, appealed to her pride; their devotion to the Catholic Church appealed to her religious sympathies. Philip, when he arrived, seemed more than satisfactory, and Mary fell in love with him. He was twenty-seven; she was thirty-eight, austere, strait-laced, and very plain. Her love was not returned, so a new sorrow entered her life. The marriage took place at Winchester in July 1554.

The terms of the marriage treaty were quite favorable to England. Philip and Mary were named as joint sovereigns and Philip was to have the title of King. Mary was to appoint her ministers of state, who were to be English. England's foreign commitments remained as before, and the country was not to be drawn into Spain's many wars on the Continent. A child born of the marriage should be Philip's heir in the Netherlands and in Burgundy, as well as Mary's heir in England; Philip, if Mary died without children, should have no claim upon the English throne.

Despite these favorable terms the English were violently opposed to the marriage. The Spanish ruler, Charles V, aimed at the domination of the Continent. It could hardly be expected that Philip would abandon his father's ambition; hence England, despite the treaty, might well be used to advance the march of Spanish imperialism. England might become a dependency of Spain, ruled by a foreigner, and exploited for Spanish purposes. Thus the work of Henry VIII might be undone. The marriage not only posed a formidable threat to English independence but aroused the Englishman's traditional dislike and suspicion of foreigners. Although nationalism in England in the sixteenth century was very strong, it was still crude and unreasonable, and it was deeply offended by the prospect of a foreign king. The possibility that an English ruler might one day control the Netherlands was rendered less attractive by the decline of Antwerp as a market of English cloth.

More than one violent protest was made when the marriage treaty was concluded in January 1554. Wyatt's Rebellion was highly dangerous because Kent was so close to the capital and because there was much sympathy for it in London. As Wyatt advanced from Rochester with a small army, troops were sent against him, but they changed sides and joined his cause. The Privy Council was in panic, but Mary, showing her courage by remaining in London, was able to rally the citizens in her defense. The rebellion collapsed, but it was a clear indication that England wished to have no Spanish king.

The Return to Rome

Philip and Mary returned to Rome in November following their marriage in July 1554. Mary succeeded in obtaining a House of Commons which was more amenable to her will than its predecessor had been. It petitioned her to restore papal supremacy by returning the Church of England to the Catholic fold. This was done on the arrival in England of Reginald Pole, a cardinal and *legatus a latere* from Rome. He was an aristocratic Englishman, a descendant of the Yorkist kings, whose devotion to the Catholic Church had forced him into exile in the reign of Henry VIII. A power in Rome, he was almost elected pope in 1549. On November 25, 1554, upon the intercession of the king and queen, he absolved England from the sin of schism and received her into the Roman Church. But the church and Mary had to pay a price. Before Parliament sanctioned Pole's coming, it passed an act which safeguarded, carefully and completely, the retention of the monastic lands by those holding them, who were to continue to enjoy them "without scruple of conscience, . . . without impeachment or trouble by pretence of any General Council, canons, or ecclesiastical law, and clear from all dangers of the canons of the Church." A complete return to the old order was thus impossible.

The Parliament of 1554, however, passed other legislation which Mary desired. It repealed in a great sweep all the ecclesiastical statutes of Henry's reign after 1528, thus undoing the English Reformation, at least on paper; it restored old laws against heresy and reestablished the former jurisdiction of the church courts. This opened the way for the persecution which now began. Mary and Cardinal Pole believed that a few executions would terrify the people into universal acceptance of Catholicism, but they were wrong. The blood of martyrs is the life of the church; and the dauntless men and women who suffered the torture of being burned at the stake gave strength and inspiration to other Protestants to remain true to their religion.

Before the close of Mary's reign some three hundred persons had been put to death. About a third of them were clergymen, some sixty were women. Neither the upper classes nor the peasantry provided many martyrs. It was the common folk of the industrial towns, especially in the southeastern portion of the country, the artisans and small tradesmen, who suffered steadfastly for their faith. Among the clerics were some famous victims: Cranmer, the archbishop; Hooper, "the father of nonconformity"; Ridley, the radical bishop of London; Latimer, the fearless preacher. "Be of good comfort," said Latimer to Ridley, as they died together, "we shall this day light a candle, by God's grace, in England, as I trust shall never be put out." This was a true prophecy. The burnings of Mary's reign, though insignificant in comparison with those on the Continent, were unparalleled in English history. They sank deeply into the minds of the people and created a fierce hatred of Roman Catholicism as well as the Protestant spirit which Mary had sought to extinguish.

Despite the safeguards of the marriage treaty, it was only to be expected that Philip would attempt to align England with Spain in her constant wars against France. When new hostilities broke out in 1557, he persuaded Mary to bring England into the conflict as Spain's ally. This was bad enough, but there was worse trouble to come, for Spanish imperialism in Italy aroused the hostility of Pope Paul IV, who allied with France and excommunicated Philip. Mary was thus in a cruel dilemma: her two great loyalties, to the pope and to her husband, were in open conflict. The war went very badly. The English people did not support it financially, nor did the English soldiers display much fighting spirit. As a result the French captured Calais in January 1558. Its loss did England little harm; in fact, the kingdom was relieved of a burden, but Calais was a symbol of achievement and of the victories of the Hundred Years' War. The supine way in which it was surrendered was a national disgrace and Mary felt the shame keenly. At her death, she said, the word "Calais" would be found written on her heart. The queen was in a tragic plight. Deserted by her husband, who spent his time in Spain, deprived of the hope of motherhood, faced by the animosity of her people, tainted with bloody persecution, oppressed by a terrible sense of failure, she sank into a state of melancholia which all but deranged her mind. On 17 November 1558, this broken, misguided, and melancholy figure passed away, leaving her country impoverished, torn, and defeated.

ECONOMIC TENSION

Although the Tudor period was an age of vigorous economic growth and increasing wealth and prosperity, the middle years of the century were years of economic crisis which, as it swelled to a climax and then slowly receded, affected a large part of the century and pointed the way to economic and social change. It caused great suffering among the lower classes. Preachers and reformers protested loudly that the times were out of joint, for economic forces had the effect of adding to the wealth of those who were already wealthy and further depressing those who were already depressed.

INFLATION

A fundamental cause of economic dislocation in the Tudor period was the constant inflationary rise in prices. For perhaps a century and a half in the later Middle Ages the level of prices had been steady or declining. Between 1500 and 1540, however, prices increased by some fifty percent; during the next twenty years they more than doubled; after 1560 they were perhaps five times what they had been when the Tudor period began. Contemporaries were bewildered by this phenomenon. They continued to think, as people had done in the Middle Ages, that every commodity had a just price determined by natural law. In the same way money had a just value, which was equal to the worth of the bullion it contained. If, then, goods had a just price and money a just value, the price level should remain constant unless wicked persons tampered with it for their own ends. Men could understand that in a time of dearth or famine, when goods were scarce while the amount of money remained the same, prices would rise. But it was only late in the century that they grasped the fact that prices would also rise if the amount of goods remained relatively steady while the money supply increased. This is what was happening in the Tudor period. Inflation did not come from the greed of particular men, or from shortages of goods, for the age in general was a time of abundance; it sprang from a sharp increase in the amount of minted bullion.

The serious lack of bullion in the later Middle Ages had produced a determined effort to extract more silver from old mines in Germany and Bohemia. The amount of silver coin on the Continent increased, and it is there, perhaps, that the rise in prices began. The impact was quickly felt in England because of the cloth trade with the Netherlands. The rapidity with which Henry VIII squandered his father's treasure may have added to the amount of money in circulation. Gold and silver objects taken from the monasteries were turned into coin; moreover, the increased business activity resulting from this dissolution had an effect similar to an increase in money, for if money circulates rapidly it adds to the effective amount of coin.

The fantastic rise in prices during the last years of Henry VIII and the first years of Edward VI, however, was the result of a reckless debasement of the coinage. There had been a minor debasement in 1526, but the worst once came between 1544 and 1551, when Henry found himself close to bankruptcy because of his wars with France and when Somerset, lord protector under Edward VI, debased the coinage still further. English money was lowered in both weight and quality until it contained only about one-sixth the amount of silver as it had in 1485. The Crown made a large profit, perhaps half a million pounds, though this advantage disappeared with the rise in the cost of all government purchases. The people suffered cruelly. Retailers would not accept the new coins as the equivalent of the old, and prices shot up in an appalling way.

In 1551 the government, seeing its error, began to stabilize the coinage. In that year Northumberland, having followed Somerset in power, devalued the "little shilling" to half its face value and began to issue new shillings containing a larger amount of silver. The coinage improved, and by 1560, in the reign of Elizabeth, money had regained its old proportion of bullion. Prices, however, continued to rise. Europe was now feeling the impact of the vast quantities of bullion brought by Spain from the mines of Mexico and Peru.

Inflations and depressions can quickly inspire the search for scapegoats, if not causes, among the people who suffer. For the people of Tudor England all the problems could be explained by the fall of Adam and Eve and the evils consequent upon that event. It is evidence of the beginnings of sound economic thinking that the government quickly identified as causes the flood of bullion and the debasement of the coinage. Some action could be taken to counteract the flood of money whereas little could be done about the sinfulness of humankind. From a twentieth-century perspective, it could be said that England was beginning to show signs of a dramatic economic growth. The fact that money now circulated at a faster rate could portend an expanding economy.

THE CLOTH TRADE

In the first half of the century the manufacture and export of woolen cloth was greatly stimulated by inflation. The export trade, as we have seen, was largely in the hands of the Merchant Adventurers,[2] who channeled the cloth through London to the great market at Antwerp. Fine English broadcloth sold well on the Continent, but the demand for coarse cheap cloth, known as kersey, seemed insatiable. English merchants had the advantage of selling in a market where the rise of prices was even greater than at home, and the export trade to Antwerp, which grew rapidly, received a fresh and violent impetus from Henry's debasement of the coinage. A pound sterling which was exchanged for thirty-two Flemish shillings in 1522 brought only thirteen shillings four pence in 1551. Foreign buyers could thus obtain English cloth at a cheap rate, and the trade at Antwerp rose to such enormous heights that the whole English economy became distorted. One analyst has estimated that half the population of England was engaged in one way or another in supplying the demand for English cloth abroad.

Industry

The manufacture of woolen cloth experienced a rapid and continual expansion. It was carried on both in the towns and in the country. The urban workers, trained by apprenticeship and controlled by the regulations of the guilds, were superior crafts-

[2]See pages 220–222.

men who produced the finest cloth. But the industry in the towns was closely organized and restricted along medieval lines, was not elastic, and could not easily expand. The rural industry, on the other hand, was free from tradition, was younger and more pliable, and could be altered and expanded to meet the requirements of the market. Moreover, it produced the cheaper cloths, the kerseys, which sold so well in Antwerp. Hence it was the rural branch of the industry which developed in the early Tudor period. Spinners, weavers, and fullers multiplied in clothmaking areas, and many villages became semi-industrial centers.

This rapid expansion seems to have resulted in some decline in the quality of the cloth produced. On the other hand, the industry became better organized and the flow of production more efficient. One difficulty in the domestic system of manufacture in the rural areas was a lack of coordination among its many units. The weaver might have to wait for his yarn and the fuller for his cloth; there was much carrying of goods from one worker to another. The industry in the country was only made possible by the merchant clothier, who bought the raw wool, put it out to be spun, woven, and finished by his workmen, paid them rates, collected the finished product, and sent it on to a larger merchant or exporter. In the expanding economy of the early Tudor period the clothier developed greatly and sometimes became very wealthy.

AGRICULTURE

Agriculture as well as industry felt the effects of inflation and of increased demand for English cloth abroad. The medieval manor, with its lord and peasants, its open fields divided into age-old strips, its lord's demesne, its common pasture, common meadow, and common waste or woodland, was still the unit of agriculture in the grain-producing portions of England. The peasant had obtained his freedom in various ways, but by whatever tenure he held his land, whether by free socage or by copyhold or customary tenure or by a shorter lease, he paid some sort of rent to the lord of the manor. The owner of an estate was thus a landlord, deriving his income from rents, from fines paid by the peasants upon entry to their lands, from the profits of the manorial court. These payments were determined by custom and were relatively fixed, but the man with a fixed income in a time of inflation found himself in difficulties. His costs went up, his visits to London became more expensive, and his standard of living was undermined. He might easily be dragged from riches to poverty. In order to escape ruin he must in some way extract a larger income from his land.

What then did landlords do? It is obvious that many lords did nothing, either from conservative pride in the old way of life, or from kindly sympathy for their peasants, or from sheer inertia; in the majority of manors there was no change. But other landlords, desperate for cash, broke away from the restrictions of custom and seized upon any measures which offered hope of larger incomes. Such a lord might raise rents whenever opportunity served—when leases expired or when a peasant

Thomas Paycocke's House, Great Coggeshall, Essex. Paycocke was a wealthy merchant clothier. (Copyright Country Life)

entered upon the land held by his father; if a peasant could not pay he was evicted and another peasant was found who could. There appears to have been a general rise in rents about the middle of the century. Or a landlord might rent his demesne to a farmer, who thus obtained control over a considerable portion of the estate. The farmer, paying a sizable rent, was then under pressure to increase his income from the land.

Finally, an enterprising owner might take the management of his estate into his own hands and share directly in the profits to be derived from selling agricultural products in a rising market. Such a landlord might improve old methods of husbandry. If he could manage his transportation problem he might join in the national industry of supplying London with food. He might dig for coal or other minerals on his property or take part in some local industrial enterprise. Or more frequently, he might raise sheep and thus profit from the incessant and rising demand for wool. The number of sheep in England had been rising steadily since the middle of the fifteenth century. The amount of land under pasture steadily increased, reaching a peak between 1540 and 1555. But at the end of the fifteenth century the human population of the country also began to rise. There were more mouths to feed, and a contest ensued between the amount of land to be devoted to pasture and the amount to be kept in crops. The landlord who profited from the high price of wool was apt to clash with the peasant who derived his living from crops raised on the arable fields.

Enclosures

The extension of pasturage for sheep led to enclosures. An enclosure was a solid block of land carved out from some portion of the manor and surrounded by a hedge or fence so that domestic animals could not leave or enter. There had been some enclosing in the later Middle Ages by the peasants. An upper class of peasants had emerged, more prosperous than their neighbors, who had acquired land and had sometimes surrounded their holdings by a hedge. One positive aspect of the Tudor period was that these peasants often thrived, became yeomen, and sometimes made their way into the lower ranks of the gentry.

Most Tudor enclosures, however, were carried out by bigger men than peasants. The process often began with the enclosure of the demesne, sometimes for raising food for the manor house, sometimes for ostentation in making a deer park, more frequently for raising sheep. The peasant might lose heavily by the enclosing of the demesne. The interests of the manor were cut in two, the lord wishing to raise sheep; the peasant, crops. The peasant could no longer graze his animals on the demesne after the harvest had been gathered. And if the lord departed for London, the peasant and his family lost casual employment as servants in the great house of the village. A second step was to enclose the village waste or pasture or meadow. This type of enclosing was bitterly resented, for it left the peasant without pasture for his animals. Finally, the lord or successful farmer might rid himself of the peasants altogether and turn the open fields of the village into great sheep runs. The results were deserted villages, evicted peasants, and increased vagabondage.

One must not exaggerate the amount of enclosing that took place. Only a small fraction of the open fields was enclosed during the Tudor period; even in counties where the movement was strong it is probable that less than a third of the arable land was enclosed. There was some enclosing for improved cultivation of the soil and some was carried out by the peasants themselves. It is true that peasants were evicted at times in a highhanded way, and that some of them, being simple folk, suffered wrong without asserting their rights. But most peasants fought for what was theirs, and for the most part found that the courts would defend them.

A peasant owning his land could not be deprived of it against his will. Customary tenants and copyholders held land by a kind of perpetual lease renewable by one generation after another upon the payment of a fine. The agreement between lord and peasant was enscribed on the manor roll. Copyholders possessed a copy of this enrollment whereas the customary tenant did not. What really mattered was less the possession of the copy than the exact terms on which the land was held. If these terms were clear and precise and if a peasant could pass his lands to his son upon payment of a fixed amount, he was relatively safe. If the terms were vague, if the peasant held only a life interest in the land, or if the sum payable by his son could be arbitrarily increased, the peasant was in a dangerous position. He was better off, however, than the tenant at will, who held land merely at the lord's pleasure and could be evicted at any moment. A peasant who lost his holding was in a pitiable condition. He and his family drifted away to the towns, or swelled the ranks of vagabonds and beggars, or settled as unwelcome squatters on the wastelands of unenclosed manors. A small amount of enclosing could inflict a great deal of suffering upon the poor.

Into this millstream of inflation, debasement, enclosures, and artificially stimulated foreign trade, Henry VIII flung the lands he had taken from the monasteries. To meet the cost of the French war, much of this land was unloaded on the market for the going price. There were about a thousand buyers, some of whom purchased land as a longterm investment, some of whom were London speculators who sold as soon as they could make a profit. Often the land changed hands a number of times; indeed, a brisk land market existed for many years. This process probably stimulated enclosing. A new owner, perhaps a businessman, regarding his purchase partly as an investment and lacking the kindly sympathies of a man who had known a locality from childhood, was doubtless inclined to reap a profit where he could. In the long run, however, most of the monastic lands made their way into the hands of the nobility and even more into the hands of the gentry, who probably dealt with their new tenants much as they had dealt with the old. The old hunger of the age did not always arise from a desire for profit. Many a wealthy merchant, lawyer, and official was ambitious to found a county family, which first required the acquisition of an estate. The urge to own property in the country, to break into the magic circle of the gentry, to display one's wealth by building a fine country house, and to enjoy the pleasures of rural life made the ownership of land attractive and raised its price.

Kett's Rebellion, 1549

The Protector Somerset permitted more freedom of speech and of the press than had been allowed in Henry's reign; a sudden outburst of indignation at the economic ills of the time and a bitter denunciation of enclosing were to be expected. Writers such as Henry Brinkelow and Robert Crowley (who printed an edition of *Piers Ploughman*), preachers such as Hugh Latimer and Thomas Lever, and politicians such as John Hales lashed at the greed and materialism of the age and depicted the sufferings of the lower classes in vivid colors. These reformers declared that people must have consideration for the general welfare—for the commonweal—and must not be allowed to do as they pleased, even with their own, if doing so brought distress upon other people.

In 1548 John Hales, who had the support of Somerset, obtained two measures which might have brought some relief to the poor. One was a subsidy bill by which the government was to surrender purveyance—the right of the king to live off the country as he traveled about—and in exchange should levy a small tax on sheep and wool used in manufacturing cloth, and a heavier tax on each broadcloth exported from the kingdom. The object of the act was to discourage concentration of the economy on the manufacture and export of cloth. Hales's second measure was the appointment of a commission to investigate the extent of enclosures, both as a warning to landlords that their actions were being watched and as a promise to the poor that some relief was at hand. But the commission's work was obstructed by the upper classes who refused to supply needed information, and by the peasants who, excited by the hope the measure offered, broke into a series of revolts.

For some years there had been local riots against enclosing. In 1548 these riots swelled into an uprising of the peasants through much of southern England. In Cornwall and Devon the rebellion was partly a protest against the religious radicalism of Edward's reign. This part of the revolt, as it moved eastward, was stopped at Exeter and was crushed by government troops. More serious was a remarkable rebellion in Norfolk led by Robert Kett in 1549. In this "sitdown strike" the peasants of Norfolk gathered in great numbers outside the city of Norwich and simply stayed there, setting up a kind of communistic state with governors, councils, and law courts. They were surprisingly orderly and religious, and they used the new Prayer Book recently issued by the government. It is difficult to explain their inertia. It may be that Kett, knowing that Somerset had much sympathy with the poor, believed he would support the uprising. Or Kett may have considered himself an unofficial agent of the state who had assumed unbidden the task of teaching a lesson to the gentry of East Anglia. If Kett had such thoughts he was in error. The peasants were slaughtered by royal troops, the rebellion was made an excuse to turn Somerset out of power, and under Northumberland a reaction took place against Somerset's liberal policy.

THE END OF THE BOOM

IN 1551 Northumberland called down the shilling to half its face value. This action had an immediate effect on the English market for cloth at Antwerp. Devaluation of the English shilling meant that foreign buyers must pay twice as much for English cloth as before. The Antwerp market came crashing down and the great boom ended forever. In the 1560s the Netherlands revolted against Spain; in these wars Antwerp was so thoroughly devastated that it never recovered its old position. In England the results were depression in the cloth industry and much suffering among the craftsmen. The clothier fell upon evil days. It is in the glut of unsold cloth and in the decline of the market at Antwerp that we find the origin of a new and determined effort to open new trades and markets overseas for the sale of English goods. Enclosing subsided, though it did not disappear, and some pasture land was again used for crops.

The Merchant Adventurers, having lost their staple at Antwerp, sought some other city on the Continent to make the headquarters of their trade. They settled at

Middelburg in Zeeland. Seeing their trade decline, they sought a tighter monopoly of what remained to them. They obtained government action against the merchants of the Hansa. The Merchant Adventurers also turned against those members of their society who were not Londoners and drove them from the association. In 1564 the Merchant Adventurers obtained a new charter which gave them a virtual monopoly of the export of cloth to the Continent. Suffering greatly from interlopers who invaded their monopoly and disturbed their closely regulated commerce, their goal now was to retain what they had.

THE DECLINE OF THE GUILDS

A few additional points may be made concerning the economic history of the time. Of these the most crucial was the rapid decline of the guilds. The guilds in the later Middle Ages, as we have seen,[3] had lost the unity of their membership. It had become impossible for most apprentices to become masters. Instead, they became journeymen who worked for wages; and the journeymen, finding that they had little to gain from the old guilds, had formed guilds of their own or else migrated into rural areas in search of freer conditions. The old conception of master and apprentice had been transformed into the modern relationship of employer and employee. A division between the richer and the poorer masters also appeared. The wealthier ones, usually those engaged in selling, had obtained control of the guild organization as well as control of the government of the towns in which they resided.

Similar forces operated in the Tudor period. The exodus to the country continued. New industries, such as the refining of sugar and the manufacture of glass, grew up in rural areas away from guild restrictions, and many industries using wood or coal as fuel migrated to regions where those fuels could be obtained. There was a great deal of mining, not only of coal, lead, iron, and copper, but of zinc (for brass cannon), saltpeter (for gunpowder), and alum (for dyeing).

The gulf between richer and poorer masters widened. In the fifteenth century livery companies began to appear. These were guilds in which a small group of masters secured for themselves a status superior to the others. To be "of the livery," a master must pay a heavy fee and purchase an expensive livery to be worn on state occasions. These liverymen were capitalists inside the guilds who controlled the guild organization and who monopolized—or tried to monopolize—the sale of the articles the guild produced. Liverymen were becoming merchants who sold the goods made by craftsmen of the guilds. Because the livery controlled its own membership, it could require that only persons with capital be admitted. Smaller masters, though they employed apprentices and journeymen, sold their goods to liverymen and lost contact with the customer.

Other companies appeared, composed of merchants who had nothing to do with manufacture. Although they took their name from some trade—they were grocers,

[3]See pages 134–135.

mercers, vintners, or haberdashers—these companies were composed of merchants who secured charters allowing them to sell a particular article. They claimed the sole right of selling at retail and tried to exclude the smaller masters from retail business. There was little left of the old guild organization.

The guilds also suffered from an ever-increasing regulation of economic life by the state. While it is true that some statutes and other actions of the government at times protected the guilds, the general tendency was in the opposite direction. The Privy Council devoted an enormous amount of time to the regulation of industry; and many statutes dealt with the true making of this or that manufacture. Two acts of 1504 undermined the position of the guilds: they could not make new rules concerning industry without obtaining the consent of the government and they could not forbid their members from appealing to the national courts in trades disputes. In 1547 Parliament dissolved the chantries, which were small endowed churches or chapels, but the act was so worded that it also swept away other religious foundations, including endowments held by the guilds for religious and social purposes. Some guilds never recovered from this heavy financial loss. The Statute of Artificers of 1563, a great industrial code, gave power to the justices of the peace to control local prices, wages, and hours of labor, thus superseding much guild regulation. By the end of the century the guilds no longer staged their mystery plays, partly because of their poverty, partly because professional actors in London were beginning to make tours into the provinces. In some towns the guilds survived only by combining into a single organization.

THE LONDON MONEY MARKET

An important money market developed in London, as is illustrated by the career of Lionel Cranfield. Cranfield quickly made his fortune as a member of the Mercers Company and the Merchant Adventurers, exporting fine English cloth to Holland and coarser kerseys to Stade in northern Germany. His imports consisted largely of expensive Italian fabrics and other luxuries to be sold to the fashionable world at court. With the money accumulated in trade, Cranfield moved into the position of a capitalist with wealthy associates in the city and with influential friends at court. He speculated in the collection of the customs, in Crown lands, and in the exploitation of economic privileges bestowed by the queen on her courtiers. With other moneyed men in the city he helped raise loans for the government. He also acted as a banker, accepting private funds on deposit and paying them out on demand; he was entrusted with money to be put out at interest; and he made loans to needy aristocrats on the security of their estates (which sometimes fell into his hands). He was the hard, shrewd, moneyed man of the city, with a hand in countless deals. In the reign of James I he became a favorite courtier and was a leading example of the later custom of accumulating wealth before going into service. More traditional at the time was the exploitation of one's royal service to make money.

THE LONDON MONEY MARKET

Sir Thomas Gresham's Royal Exchange (London's first shopping center), by Franciscus Hogenberg, 1569. (British Museum)

CHRONOLOGY

The Little Tudors

1547–1553	Edward VI
1547–49	Lord Protector Somerset
1549	Cranmer's first **Book of Common Prayer;** Kett's Rebellion
1549–53	Northumberland rules king and kingdom
1551	Devaluation of the currency; collapse of Antwerp market
1552	Cranmer's second **Book of Common Prayer**
1553	Edward VI dead; Lady Jane Grey executed
1553–58	Mary I
1553	Henrician Church restored
1554	Marriage of Mary and Philip II; Wyatt's Rebellion; Catholic Church restored
1556	Cranmer burned at stake
1558	Loss of Calais

13 Elizabeth I: The First Ten Years of the Reign

THE QUEEN

Queen Elizabeth I is famous for her political genius, for the brilliant success of her reign, and for the loyalty she evoked in the hearts of her people. She shaped her country's destiny. She came to the throne at twenty-five, an attractive young woman, tall, well-built, vigorous in mind and body, with an olive complexion and reddish-gold hair. Her traits of character were not the qualities of sweetness and gentleness but the ones of pride, strength, aggressiveness, self-confidence, and courage. There was an imperious quality about her reminiscent of her father. Like him she was determined to rule. She held lofty views of her royal prerogatives, and she could stand her ground against councilors, Parliament, and people.

She was an excellent conversationalist, alternating gracious affability with tart reproof, kindly approbation with biting criticism; she could win, she could baffle, and she could deceive. A story is told of an audience with an ambassador from Poland who boastfully advised her that for her own good she should ally with his master. The ambassador spoke in Latin. In reply, Elizabeth poured forth a torrent of Latin invective which amazed the court and deflated the ambassador. Elizabeth was highly educated; besides Latin, she spoke French and Italian. Even after she was queen she read Latin and Greek with her old tutor, Roger Ascham. It was her practice after a stormy interview to retire to her chamber and regain her serenity by reading Latin verse. As an administrator she possessed a grasp of reality. She was industrious, willing to spend time on the details of government, very careful of her money, and a fine judge of character. Her boldness was tempered by prudence, and she hated to make decisions which could not later be revoked. As a diplomat she was shrewd, deceitful, and wily, quite able to hold her own with other sovereigns.

Like her father, she was vain, with a keen awareness of physical appearance both

Queen Elizabeth I, artist unknown. (National Portrait Gallery, London)

in herself and in others. She enjoyed the company and admiration of handsome men. Her courtiers had to pretend they were smitten by her charms long after those charms had withered. During the first months of her reign, when the popularity of the Tudor dynasty was at a low ebb, she set out to win the hearts of the people. By every grace and art of an attractive young woman, mingling mildness with majesty, she sought popular support by courting her subjects, a courtship she continued throughout her reign. Nor was it mere acting. She possessed a broad and genuine humanity, a lively sympathy with the joys and sorrows, the hopes and prejudices of her people. She loved England, she identified herself with her country, she gloried in being "mere English."

Her youth had taught her that intelligence, not emotion, must guide her conduct. When she was only fifteen she had had a short love affair, unsavory but harmless, with Thomas Seymour, brother of the lord protector Somerset. Seymour had sought to advance himself by intriguing to marry her. Suddenly he had been arrested and executed for his folly and some discredit had been thrown upon Elizabeth. The episode was a lesson in the dangers that scandal could bring. During the reign of Mary Tudor, Elizabeth had been the unwitting pawn in every conspiracy against the throne; she had been sent to the Tower under suspicion of complicity in Wyatt's Rebellion; a false step might have cost her her life. From these experiences she emerged self-reliant, cautious, and self-controlled, but hard, suspicious, and rather lacking in magnanimity.

INITIAL PROBLEMS

Relations with Foreign States

At the accession of Elizabeth the country was faced by problems of the most serious kind. Conditions abroad were very dangerous. England was still at war with France, though the fighting was over and Calais was lost. France, the national enemy, possessed a great advantage in the Franco-Scottish alliance. In 1548 the Scots had sent their little queen, Mary, who was only five, to France, where she was educated to marry Francis, the eldest son of the French king, Henry II. The marriage took place in 1558. Mary was a descendant of Henry VII;[1] in Catholic eyes she was the rightful queen of England, for Catholics regarded Elizabeth as illegitimate. As soon as Elizabeth ascended the throne, the French proclaimed Mary the queen of England. Her mother, Mary of Guise, who was regent in Scotland, ruled that country in the French interest. Hence a French army aimed at the invasion of England could easily land in Scotland. The French king, said an Englishman, "bestrides the realm, having one foot in Calais and the other in Scotland." England was almost defenseless—its forts decayed, its finances disordered, its army demoralized, its navy worthless. One hope lay in the fact that Philip of Spain, in his hostility to France, would not allow that country to conquer England. Elizabeth judged rightly that should France try to invade England Philip would defend her in order to protect himself. So sure of this was she that when Philip made her a condescending offer of marriage she had the fortitude to decline. When Spain and England on the one hand and France on the other made peace at Le Cateau-Cambrésis in 1559, one section of the treaty provided for Philip's marriage to a daughter of the King of France. If Catholic Spain and Catholic France became allies, the prospects of a Protestant England were dim indeed.

A Woman Ruler

At home many problems centered in the person of the queen. That a woman could rule successfully was a novel idea; that an unmarried woman could do so was unthinkable. Just before Elizabeth ascended the throne, John Knox in Scotland had

---

[1] See genealogical table, page 224.

written a denunciation of female rulers, *The First Blast of the Trumpet against the Monstrous Regiment of Women.* "It is more than a monster in nature," he wrote, "that a woman should reign and bear empire above men." This war whoop had been directed against Mary of Guise; and Knox was abashed, though he would not apologize, when Elizabeth became queen. He merely expressed the view of his contemporaries, who wondered whether Elizabeth could obtain the obedience of her councilors and courtiers.

She had reconstructed her Privy Council, retaining eleven of Mary's ministers and adding seven new ones, thus wisely reducing the Council to about half its former size. Her most important appointment was that of her secretary, Sir William Cecil, later Lord Burghley. Cecil's lucid mind and grasp of realities, his sagacity, his industry and attention to detail, and his utter loyalty made him a perfect minister. The trust between him and the queen was to grow with time, and he was to remain her principal adviser for forty years. Yet even Cecil was at first inclined to think that young women follow the counsel of their masculine elders. Elizabeth rarely attended the meetings of her Council. She feared that in the give-and-take of discussion she might be overruled; her practice was to have problems debated in the Council and its

William Cecil, Lord Burghley, probably by Marcus Ghearaerts. (National Portrait Gallery, London)

advice brought to her, so that she could accept or reject that advice as she pleased. Much of her governing was done in private interviews with one or two of her ministers, but she soon established her authority. Shortly after her accession the Spanish ambassador wrote that she was "incomparably more feared than her sister, and gives her orders and has her way as absolutely as her father did." This was no small achievement for a young woman of twenty-five.

Then there was the court, a giant household of some fifteen hundred persons, including all ranks of society from nobles and statesmen to the servants in the kitchen. The court was the center both of government and of fashion; it was the symbol of royalty, the place to which all men looked who hoped for a career in the service of the state. Elizabeth must maintain its splendor and high spirits to attract men to it, to keep the nobility amused, and to impress the envoys of foreign lands. She must win the loyalty of her courtiers, since from them she selected officials and ministers. She must pacify the quarrels of proud nobles and jealous bureaucrats and must restrain her many servants within the bounds of decency and decorum. And all had to be done at a reasonable charge. Elizabeth controlled the court through her masterful personality as well as her unique ability to create the atmosphere of a fairy idyll in which all men pretended to be in love with her and to serve her as the mistress of their hearts. The comedy was artificial and tended to false flattery, but it served its turn.

Other problems concerned the queen's marriage and the succession. Elizabeth was the last of the children of Henry VIII; if she died without issue the throne would go to a collateral line. The Scottish claim was represented by Mary of Scotland. But Mary's succession, which would have been backed by France and by the Catholic north of England, would almost certainly have provoked a civil war. In his will Henry VIII had passed over the Scottish line and had vested the succession, in case his children died without issue, in the descendants of his younger sister Mary, who had married Charles Brandon, Duke of Suffolk. The Suffolk claim was represented in Elizabeth's reign by Lady Catherine Grey and later by her son, Edward Seymour, Lord Beauchamp. But Catherine's secret marriage, of dubious legality, enraged Elizabeth and all but excluded both Lady Catherine and her son from the succession.

It was assumed by everyone that Elizabeth would marry. Her protestations that she was content to remain a virgin produced at first polite approval and then downright annoyance. She had many suitors, most of them foreigners who never came to England. But she was determined not to marry without seeing what she was getting; and she feared that a husband who was a foreigner might influence policy in behalf of his own country, as Philip of Spain had done in the reign of Mary Tudor. Hence her many negotiations for marriage were no more than moves in the game of diplomacy.

Early in the reign she was fascinated by one of her courtiers, Robert Dudley, son of the duke of Northumberland who had ruled England in Edward's reign. Dudley was a handsome and dashing soldier, an accomplished courtier, and a good conversationalist, though actually a man of no great ability. The court was filled with rumors of an impending match. But the thought of Dudley as the queen's husband horrified councilors and courtiers. Moreover, he was already married; and when his wife, Amy Robsart, fell down the steps at her country house and broke her neck, there were ugly suspicions of murder. Had Elizabeth married Dudley under these circumstances she would have risked her throne. Her intelligence fought with her emotions, and her intelligence won. Dudley remained the master of the horse and became earl of Leicester, a friend and favorite of the queen, but nothing more. It is not unlikely that in rejecting him she rejected marriage. For thirty years the English lived in dread that her sudden death would be followed by chaos.

The Settlement of Religion

Religion was another vital problem. Within a few years the country had experienced three ecclesiastical settlements: the Anglo-Catholicism of Henry, who had repudiated the pope but had retained the Mass; the radical Protestantism of Edward; and the return to Rome under Mary. Elizabeth was not a religious person. She had none of Mary's fanatical zeal and had no wish to make windows into men's souls. Like the *politiques* in France, she regarded peace as more important than a solution of the religious quarrel. What she wanted was unity—a settlement which the bulk of the people would accept and which would diminish the danger of internal strife. Her approach was conservative. She believed that the Crown had the right to impose a religious settlement; she liked decorum, form, and order in the church as well as in everything else; she would have preferred a return to conditions as her father had left them. But such a return was impossible; her choice lay between Catholicism and the Protestantism of Edward.

Without a doubt she weighed the advantages of retaining a moderate Catholic Church purged of Mary's fanatical fury. Such a solution not only would have eased her relations with continental states but would have enabled her to keep the church much as it was without the turmoil of a new upheaval. But the adoption of Catholicism would have been an appeasement of Catholic Europe. Elizabeth's courage—her faith in herself and in her people—dictated a bolder course. Her pride revolted at the thought of acknowledging papal supremacy. She knew that large numbers of her subjects were bitterly opposed to Rome and that this opposition would be strengthened by the return of the five hundred or so English Protestants who had gone into exile in Mary's reign. Many were gentry and many were clergymen; they would be leaders of English religious thought for years to come. On the Continent they had been deeply influenced by the doctrines of John Calvin; they returned to England more radically Protestant than when they had left. Moreover, the Protestants at home who had supported Elizabeth during Mary's reign and who hailed her now as their hope and deliverer were strongly anti-Catholic. Should she reward their loyalty by deserting them? Elizabeth chose to be Protestant. But she wished to move in that direction slowly, so as not to alienate Philip of Spain before she was well seated on her throne.

Her religious settlement was made in her first Parliament in 1559, one which was thoroughly Protestant. A dozen of the Marian exiles were influential members, and at least a fourth of the Commons were eager for radical change. Slowly Elizabeth was coerced into a more Protestant settlement than she desired. Her wish seems to have been that Parliament should pass an act of supremacy restoring the legislation of Henry VIII, but that the Mass should be retained, at least for the present. The Commons, on the other hand, desired not only an act of supremacy but also a Protestant form of worship, to be embodied in a new act of uniformity by which the Mass should be abolished. There was a struggle, but Elizabeth eventually accepted both supremacy and uniformity. Thus the settlement was one dictated in part by the lay politicians in the House of Commons.

The Act of Supremacy of 1559 restored the laws of Henry VIII separating the English Church from Rome. There were certain alterations. The queen assumed the title of Supreme Governor of the Church, not that of Supreme Head. This change of title, although meaningless in practice, was a concession to Catholics, who regarded the pope as the only head of the church, and also a concession to those radical Protestants who held that the church had no earthly head but only Christ. The new act, like that of Henry, contained an oath; a person taking the oath swore that he believed in the principles of the act. Henry's oath, however, could be forced upon anyone; refusal had often meant death. Elizebeth's oath could be required only of officeholders, and the penalty for refusal was no more than loss of office.

The Act of Uniformity provided for a new prayer book to be used by the clergy in divine worship throughout the kingdom. Although it was based on the second and more Protestant prayer book of Edward VI, modifications rendered it more conservative than Edward's. Certain words in the service of Holy Communion implied a belief in the doctrine of transubstantiation, whereas other words appeared to reject that doctrine. Thus more than one interpretation was possible. Attendance of the people at church on Sundays and holy days was compulsory, but the penalty for absence was merely a fine of one shilling. These acts were followed by royal injunctions which permitted clergymen to marry, prescribed the clerical vestments to be worn in church, decided the position of the altar, and governed the conduct of the people during divine worship.

Although the church was in Catholic hands at Elizabeth's accession, the transfer to Protestantism was accomplished with surprising ease. Cardinal Pole, by a strange oversight, had left five bishoprics vacant at the end of Mary's reign; his death added a sixth. Four more Catholic bishops died within a year. There were thus ten vacancies in an episcopal bench of twenty-six; and these ten bishoprics, as the Spanish ambassador wrote gloomily, "would now be given to as many ministers of Lucifer." The remaining Catholic bishops, with one exception, refused the Oath of Supremacy and were deprived of office. Their opposition was only to be expected. What is surprising is that the majority of parish priests accepted Elizabeth's church and remained within it. Those who refused numbered somewhere from two hundred up to one thousand. Whatever the truth, it is clear that Elizabeth's church began its existence with a serious shortage of parish priests—a source of just criticism for years to come.

The Treaty of Edinburgh

A crisis arose in 1559 as a result of the Scottish Reformation. The Reformation in Scotland differed entirely from that in England. It was not a movement led from above by an autocratic ruler such as Henry VIII, but a revolt from below against a Catholic government. From the first it contained an antimonarchical and republican element; it was more violent than in England, more uncompromising, and more complete. Its tone was set by John Knox, that thundering Scottish Elijah who hated the Catholic Mass more than an army of foreign foes and who filled his followers with a horror of all things Roman.

In the 1550s the movement to reform became more formidable. It was led by a group of nobles, the Lords of the Congregation, but it drew its strength from the towns, from the lairds or gentry, and from a handful of clergymen, of whom John Knox was the most important. Knox had joined the insurgents and was captured and sent to France, where for a time he was a galley slave. After a stay in England he made a shattering return to Scotland in 1559. A sermon at Perth was followed by a riot in which the church was demolished. Knox was not a pleasant man. He was narrow, hard, rough, and uncompromising, but also a great leader, a fighter, and a powerful preacher. Of boundless energy and courage, he "neither flattered nor feared any flesh."

Scottish Protestantism was strengthened by Scottish national feeling. Since 1554 the country had been ruled by Mary of Guise, a Frenchwoman and mother of Mary, Queen of Scots. With French advisers and French troops, Mary of Guise had been making Scotland a mere dependency of France. Opposition was bitter. The Scots, having fought for centuries to remain independent of England, had no mind to become a French satellite. Their old ally was becoming their tyrant. Mary of Guise, moreover, had conducted a vigorous campaign against Protestantism. Hence patriotism merged with religious zeal in hostility to her regime. A rebellion broke out in 1559, but it became obvious that the Scottish Protestants could not defeat the government without assistance. Mary of Guise, backed by French troops, was too strong for them. Before the summer of 1559 was over they appealed to Elizabeth for aid.

Elizabeth was faced with a difficult decision. She hated rebels and she disliked religious radicals; yet the Scottish Protestants were both. As for Knox, who had blown the trumpet against female rulers, no one dared to mention him in her presence. The French court was very anti-English. Henry II died in July and was succeeded by his son, Francis II, a boy of fifteen whose wife, Mary, Queen of Scots, was now queen of France. Her ambitious uncles, the duke of Guise and the cardinal of Lorraine, dominated the court. If Elizabeth sent assistance to the Scots she threw down a challenge to France that might result in a general war. If she did nothing she tightened French control in Scotland and increased the Franco-Scottish-Catholic threat at her northern border. If, on the other hand, the Scottish Protestants with her assistance could drive out the French, her position would be vastly improved. A friendly Protestant government could perhaps be set up in Scotland in place of a hostile Catholic one. Bold intervention was thus supported by strong arguments, and Elizabeth followed this course.

At first she sent aid secretly while shamelessly denying her actions. Money and arms were dispatched to the north in the summer of 1559. In January 1560, an English fleet entered the Firth of Forth, destroyed French shipping, and prevented the landing of war supplies from France. An English army entered Scotland and advanced against the French fortress at Leith. The response from France was surprisingly weak. The Guises, who had just crushed a conspiracy against them, had their hands full at home. Two French fleets dispatched to Scotland were driven back by heavy weather with great loss. And in Scotland Mary of Guise was at the point of death. The French, therefore, instead of fighting further, sent a delegation to negotiate for peace.

The important Treaty of Edinburgh, which followed in 1560, provided that both French and English troops be withdrawn from Scotland; that Scotland be governed by twelve Scottish nobles, six to be named by Mary and six by the Scots themselves; and that France recognize Elizabeth as the rightful queen of England. Francis and Mary, refusing to yield this final point, declined to ratify the treaty. Their refusal made comparatively little difference. The French troops left for home. The Protestant Scottish nobles took over the government, and the Scottish Reformation proceeded rapidly. Papal jurisdiction was renounced, the Mass forbidden, and a reformed church set up, though its organization was left for the future. The Treaty of Edinburgh was a notable triumph for Elizabeth, who had adopted a daring and courageous policy and had carried it through to success. Unaided by Spain she had driven the French from Scotland. Her prestige abroad was vastly enhanced, and foundations were laid for an era of cooperation between England and Scotland based upon a common Protestantism and a common hostility to interference from the Continent.

SCOTLAND AND MARY, QUEEN OF SCOTS

Scotland continued to occupy Elizabeth's attention. Francis II of France died in December 1560, a blow that shattered Mary's high position as queen of France. Her uncles of Guise lost their influence at court, and her wish to marry the new King Charles IX, a boy of about eleven, was thwarted by the malice of her mother-in-law, Catherine de Médicis. There was no course open but a return to Scotland.

Scotland was a lawless, backward, and poverty-stricken country, torn by feuds of rival clans and by constant deeds of violence. The power of the Crown was small in the Highlands and in the Cheviot Hills along the border; it scarcely existed in the primitive Western Isles. And even in the Lowlands, centering in the area around Glasgow, Stirling, St. Andrews, and Edinburgh, royal authority was diminished greatly by the exorbitant power of the nobles. There was not much hope that Mary could rule Scotland with success. Her beauty, her bewitching charms and graces, her love of music and dancing, her high spirits and reckless daring, her fondness for war

Mary, Queen of Scots, by Peter Oudry. (National Gallery of Scotland, Edinburgh)

and manly sports, her ambition, and the intensity of her loves and hates—these things made her a fascinating woman to whom men were strongly attracted. Her diplomacy and plottings were bold and clever, but they were also brittle and unrealistic. She was lacking in judgment, in maturity, in the capacity to control her emotions. In short, she was not really intelligent. She had little interest in government. Indeed, she had little interest in Scotland save as a stepping-stone for her ambitions. She did not love Scotland as Elizabeth loved England.

Mary's first years in Scotland were not unsuccessful. She came with a desire to please and she did not question the authority of the Protestant lords whom she found in control of the government; in her half brother, the earl of Moray, an illegitimate son of James V, and even more in her able secretary, William Maitland of Lethington, she possessed sound advisers. She had poor relations with Knox. He thundered against her because she attended Mass; he denounced her gaiety and dancing—the skipping at court, as he called it, was not very comely for honest women. Mary tried to win him, first by her charms and then by her tears, which the crabbed preacher referred to as so much "owling." Nonetheless, conditions in Scotland were better than might have been expected. Had Mary been able to satisfy her ambitions by a brilliant marriage or by the recognition of her right to succeed Elizabeth, she might have remained content. But Elizabeth, for reasons of sound policy, blocked Mary's moves toward marriage and refused recognition of her title to the English succession.

As the two queens drifted into hostility Mary began to chafe. She grew weary of Maitland's tutelage, of Knox's rantings, and of Elizabeth's condescension. When a match with Don Carlos of Spain grew cold, Mary cast her eye upon a young noble at the English court, Henry Stewart, Lord Darnley, a descendant of Margaret Tudor by her second husband, Archibald Douglas, Earl of Angus. Darnley was close to the Scottish throne and was also a possible heir to that of England. Having tricked Elizabeth into allowing Darnley to come to Scotland, Mary proceeded to fall in love with him. He was a pretty boy of nineteen, tall and slender, with a pleasant face and yellow hair, and with the outward graces of the courtier. When Mary married him in July 1565 she did so in defiance of her Protestant councilors, of Knox, and of Elizabeth. Darnley's background was Catholic. The marriage placed Mary at the head of the Catholic party in both kingdoms. At first she was successful. The Protestant lords revolted, but she drove them into England in an exciting campaign in which she rode in armor with her troops and forded a river on horseback during a violent storm.

The marriage with Darnley was ultimately Mary's undoing. He proved to be an impossibly crude youth, not only stupid but vain, insolent, treacherous, and debauched. The court was full of quarrels, and Mary soon regarded her husband with a kind of nausea. She turned for consolation and counsel to a young Italian at her court, David Rizzio, who became her favorite. The folly of her affection for him can hardly be exaggerated. The Scots were grieved "to see their sovereign guided by such a fellow." Darnley, growing jealous, plotted with the exiled Protestant lords; together on March 9, 1566, they entered Mary's chamber during her dinner, seized Rizzio, and murdered him almost in her presence. Mary was a captive. Yet with great presence of mind she persuaded Darnley to desert his fellow conspirators and to escape with her to Dunbar. Her friends rallied round her and once more she was able to drive the Protestant lords into England and recover her position in Scotland. Three months later she enjoyed another triumph, the birth of a son, James, who was to become king of both Scotland and England.

But Mary hated her husband. She was now infatuated with a Scottish noble, James Hepburn, Earl of Bothwell, a reckless and proud young man of about thirty. She could scarcely have chosen a more dangerous love. In February 1567 Darnley was murdered at Kirk o' Field just beyond the walls of Edinburgh. That Bothwell was in touch with the murderers is clear; that Mary approved the deed seems certain. She made no effort to bring him to justice. In April, doubtless by prearrangement, he seized her person and carried her to his castle at Dunbar. A month later they were married. These events were too much for the godly Scots, who now rebelled. Mary's forces and those of her enemies met at Carberry Hill in June. There was no battle, but Bothwell fled from Scotland and Mary was imprisoned in Lochleven Castle. She was forced to abdicate in favor of her infant son. In May of the following year, 1568, she escaped from her prison, raised an army, was defeated at Langside near Glasgow, and fled to England.

Mary went to England of her own will, not at the invitation of Elizabeth. Elizabeth had been foolishly berating the Scottish lords for treating their sovereign so roughly, and Mary hoped that Elizabeth would restore her to the Scottish throne by force.

This was a vain hope: Elizabeth might believe that queens should stand together, but to make war on the Protestant Scots in Mary's behalf would have been a complete reversal of England's Scottish policy. Elizabeth could not hand Mary back to her subjects, for they would most certainly have killed her. Nor could Elizabeth allow Mary her freedom. With her winning ways, her Catholicism, and her claim to the English throne Mary was too dangerous a magnet for those who were discontented with Elizabeth's rule. Hence Mary was kept in honorable confinement, lodged as a guest in various country houses, allowed to hunt and, at first, to correspond with her friends. But her intrigues and plottings were endless; as a result she was guarded more strictly. Her confinement became a lifelong imprisonment that ended on the executioner's block in Fotheringay on February 8, 1587.

ECONOMIC REFORM

When Elizabeth came to the throne the economic prospect was clouded. The finances of the government were in disorder, the currency still was debased, the wool trade was depressed, the marketing of food was disorganized, and there was a dangerous degree of unemployment, poverty, and vagabondage. Improvement in government finance was essential for any economic progress. Most fortunately Elizabeth resembled her grandfather, Henry VII, in her thrift, and in her sense of the value of money. She has been accused of meanness; but in truth her parsimony was one of the secrets of her success, for she kept England solvent while other nations were going bankrupt. From her sister Mary she inherited a debt of £250,000; her annual revenue in the first years of her reign was not above £200,000. Yet from this small sum she paid the ordinary peacetime expenses of government and began to reduce the debt.

To finance her wars she had to find additional income. Knowing that heavy taxation would impair her popularity, she did not ask Parliament for large sums. Income from parliamentary taxation averaged only some £50,000 a year throughout her reign. To pay for war she was driven to diminish her capital by selling Crown lands in times of emergency. There were three periods in which Crown lands were sold in large quantities. The first came in 1559–1560, when she was assisting the Scottish Protestants; the second at the time of the Spanish Armada; and the third in the 1590s, when she had to quell a revolt in Ireland. Her sale of lands averaged some £20,000 a year. This was a diminution of capital, but it was wiser politically than high taxation. And her credit was so good that she could borrow in the Netherlands at a lower rate of interest than could Philip of Spain, with all the wealth of the Indies behind him.

In 1560–1561 the English government completed the reform of the coinage begun by Northumberland about a decade earlier. To restore confidence in the coinage debased and mutilated coins were recalled and new ones issued in which the silver content equaled the face value. The Parliament of 1563 passed a number of laws to stabilize the economy: old statutes against enclosures were re-enacted; the poor law was revised and a new principle was added. Contributions from the richer persons in the parish for the support of the poor—formerly on a voluntary basis—were made compulsory; the people were required to eat fish on Wednesdays and Fridays, not as a matter of religion but as an encouragement to the fishing industry from which the navy drew its seamen. The importation of luxuries, such as jewelry and fine cloth, was restricted, and middlemen were licensed in the grain and cattle trades in order to stabilize the food market.

Parliament also passed the Statute of Artificers (Apprentice), which was a great industrial code. The statute encouraged agriculture and to a lesser degree the cloth trade by making entrance into other occupations more difficult. Anyone wishing to learn some other trade must serve an apprenticeship of seven years. The statute also attempted to stabilize employment and to prevent the lower classes from wandering about. In hiring workmen an employer had to agree to retain them in his service for a certain time, usually a year; and workmen seeking employment had to present a certificate showing that they were entitled to offer their services. At the same time the justices of the peace were empowered to establish the wages that should be paid in various occupations; wages thus determined were to remain in force for a year. The government also encouraged merchants to seek new trades and overseas markets in order to diminish the excessive dependence of English foreign trade upon the city of Antwerp. These measures stabilized the economy and helped to lift the country from the depression of the middle of the century.

THE CATHOLICS

In her religious settlement Elizabeth had aimed at establishing a church which would be accepted by the bulk of the people. In a broad way she was successful, but she was never able to satisfy the ardent Catholics on the one hand nor the radical Protestants on the other.

For some time after 1559 the English Catholics were apathetic and leaderless. In the 1570s their strength and spirit were revived by a movement known as the Counter Reformation, a prolonged, intense, and often successful effort by the Catholic Church on the Continent to set its own house in order, to halt the spread of Protestantism, and to recover the ground that had been lost. The Counter Reformation had many aspects. One was a series of zealous popes dedicated to the task of combating Protestantism. Another was the Jesuit order, or the Society of Jesus founded in 1540 by a Spaniard, Ignatius Loyola. The Jesuits were priests, selected and educated with great care, who formed the church's spearhead against Protestantism. Famous as teachers and missionaries, they accepted the dangerous assignment of propagating the faith among Protestant peoples. Obedience, selflessness, and complete devotion to the interests of the church were fundamental principles of the Jesuits, who worked more often among the upper classes than among the poor, and who were selected in part for their ability to deal with aristocrats and chiefs of state.

Another part of the Counter Reformation was a church council, the Council of Trent, which met intermittently between 1545 and 1563. It defined and sharpened Catholic doctrine, denounced Protestantism, inaugurated reforms, and inspired Catholics with a new intensity—even ferocity—in fighting the battle of the church. The Inquisition, an ecclesiastical court for the suppression of heresy, was active in Spain and Italy but not in northern Europe. The strongest of Catholic rulers, Philip of Spain, became the temporal head of the Counter Reformation and had a deep sense of mission in promoting its success.

The first overt attack of the Catholic Church upon Elizabeth was the papal bull *Regnans in Excelsis,* published against her in 1570 by Pope Pius V. The bull excommunicated Elizabeth, declared her deposed, absolved her subjects from their allegiance (thereby encouraging them to revolt), and called on Catholic princes to enforce its decrees. In many ways it was an ill-timed and inept document: it came too late to assist a Catholic revolt in 1569; it wrongfully accused Elizabeth; and it offended Philip, the only ruler who could enforce it, because he had not been consulted in advance. The English nation as a whole turned fiercely against Rome as an enemy ready to sow seeds of subtle treason among English subjects.

The bull placed English Catholics in a cruel dilemma, for it ended the dual allegiance by which they had hoped to remain loyal to Elizabeth and at the same time true to their church. They must now make a choice: adherence to the queen meant denial of papal authority; obedience to the pope meant treason to England. Many Catholics followed the urge of patriotism and became members of the Church of England; others clung to Rome with a new devotion and politically became more dangerous. Elizabeth and her councilors naturally considered the bull an ultimatum. Henceforth they regarded Catholics as suspected persons ready to plot against the state. Parliament made it treason to bring papal bulls into England, or to deny that Elizabeth was the lawful queen, or to call her a heretic or a schismatic; the property of Englishmen who had fled abroad was to be confiscated unless they returned within a year.

The government became more suspicious because, beginning in 1575, a stream of priests and later of Jesuits came to England from the Continent to work among English Catholics. For some time there had been groups of self-exiled English Catholics on the Continent; in 1568 William Allen, one of the refugees, founded a college at Douai in Flanders to form a center for these groups and to educate the youth among them. Many were trained as priests who then returned to England to work among the English Catholics. Allen, a gifted teacher, inspired his students with a zealous devotion and with a willingness—even a longing—to suffer martyrdom for the ancient faith. Other colleges or seminaries were founded at Rome, Valladolid, and Seville; by 1580 there were one hundred priests secretly at work in England.

Their mission was a spiritual one; they had been commanded to let politics alone. But it was impossible for the English government to regard their activities as purely religious, for religion and politics could not be separated: the patrons of the seminaries were the pope and the king of Spain; the papal bull of 1570 invited English Catholics to be traitors. The English government believed that under the guise of saving souls the priests had come to carry out the bull. An act of Parliament declared it treason to convert an English subject to Catholicism. Hence the priests walked into a trap, for they were hunted down and executed with growing ferocity.

This situation—heroic zeal on one side and the stark necessity of suppressing treason on the other—became more deadly with the arrival of a Jesuit mission in 1580. The Jesuits, like the seminary priests, came to propagate their faith, but circumstances increased the government's suspicions. Gregory XIII, who became pope in 1572, was Elizabeth's sworn enemy. He was zealous, optimistic, and resourceful, but also impetuous and strategically inept. He was the principal sponsor of the Jesuit mission; yet in 1578, shortly before the Jesuits arrived in England, he sent an Italian force, led by the English renegade Sir Thomas Stukeley, to stir up trouble in Ireland. He constantly advocated a Catholic invasion of England—the "Enterprise of England" as it was called. Thus the Jesuits arrived at a moment when the struggle between Rome and Protestant England was becoming a fight to the death.

Two famous Jesuits came to England in 1580. One was Edmund Campion, a man of saintliness, heroism, and ability, who represented the noblest qualities of the Counter Reformation and who brought to English Catholics a new fervor and determination. His object was purely religious. The other Jesuit was Robert Parsons, a subtle and complex character, who abstained from political intrigue only with great reluctance. A skillful writer, politician, and organizer of intrigue, the man of action rather than the priest, he had as his object the overthrow of Elizabeth.

The appearance of the Jesuits resulted in a new code of anti-Catholic legislation known as the Recusancy Laws. The fine of 1s. a Sunday for nonattendance at church was increased to £20 a month; presence at Mass was punishable by a fine of 100 marks and a year's imprisonment. If a Catholic did not pay the fines levied upon him the government could seize his property and retain two-thirds of its income. An earlier law had imposed the death penalty for converting an English subject to Rome; a new law inflicted the same penalty on the convert. Thus, while being a Catholic was punishable by fine and imprisonment, the act of becoming a Catholic could be punished by death. All priests and Jesuits were banished on pain of high treason; their very presence in England made them liable to the death sentence. Young Englishmen in foreign seminaries were summoned home on pain of treason. This code was not enforced to the letter; it was used more often as a threat to keep the Catholics quiet. But there was persecution enough. During the next twenty years some 250 Catholics or persons suspected of Catholicism died on the scaffold or in prison. Although the number is small in comparison with those executed on the Continent, such martyrdom indicates the ferocity of the religious conflict.

THE PURITANS

Elizabeth's church was also assailed by the Puritans. Puritanism had many roots in the past, but its immediate origin is found in the English Protestants who fled the country in Mary's reign. Returning to England as soon as Elizabeth ascended the throne, these Puritans became the religious radicals of her reign. As members of her church, they attended its services and conformed for the most part to its regulations, but were deeply dissatisfied with it. They wished to carry the Reformation to its logical conclusion by destroying every trace of Roman Catholicism and by making a fresh start.

The Puritans represented many shades of opinion and should not be regarded as a compact sect unified in theory and practice. Nevertheless, the teachings of John Calvin lay behind all Puritan thought. Calvin stressed the majesty and omnipotence of God rather than His gentleness and mercy. God was an austere and jealous Jehovah, demanding a strict obedience from all believers. A person's function on earth was to glorify God and to carry out his will. God had a program: to wage a stern and constant battle against evil wherever evil was to be found, in the church, in state, or in the world at large. The Calvinist was thus God's agent, God's warrior, in an endless conflict. One discovered God's will by a study of the Scriptures. And having thus learned the will of God, the Calvinist sought to carry it out with great courage and with small regard for the wishes of earthly kings.

Calvin further taught that if God was omnipotent the realization of God's omniscience, that He must know all things, including the course of future events led Calvin to his doctrine of predestination. According to this doctrine God knew, even before a person was born, whether or not that person was to be saved. Those saved were of the elect, that small and chosen company who did God's will on earth. Those who were not belonged to the majority of humans, the reprobate, who travelled the primrose path to the everlasting bonfire. It might be thought that such a doctrine, imposing upon people God's unalterable decree, would have rendered the Calvinist indifferent about personal conduct; such was not the case. Except in rare moments of doubt, the Calvinist was thoroughly convinced of being one of the elect; and from this conviction the believer derived a sense of exaltation and moral rectitude. But such assurance made for rigidity, for it was believed that Calvinists knew the truth whereas others did not. Nor were they content with going their own way; the Calvinists wished to persuade or, if need be, coerce their fellow mortals into leading godly lives. Believing that nothing in daily life was too trivial to examine and condemn, they were quite ready to inform others of their faults. In Scotland the clergyman in the pulpit would select a wretched member of the congregation and denounce his or her transgressions openly before the whole assembly.

The Puritans, accepting Calvin's theology, challenged the assumptions which underlay Elizabeth's religious settlement and were highly critical of her church. They resented the Tudor doctrine that every member of the state was automatically a member of the state church. This made the church a political body. In the minds of the Puritans the church was not political; it was a voluntary association of believers, a holy society of the elect, and quite independent of the state. The state had no right to establish a church; such was the domain of the clergy. The church had no earthly head; spiritual power flowed from God the Father through Christ the mediator directly to his Church, bypassing queen and Parliament.

Elizabeth assumed that the Roman Catholic Church, if reformed and purged of evil as she and her father had reformed and purged it, could be made acceptable. But the

Puritans, hating Rome, saw nothing but error in the medieval church. The Puritans also disliked the element of compromise in Elizabeth's church. It seemed a makeshift: Protestant in dogma but Catholic in ritual, and established merely to solve the political problem of the diversity of religious belief. As they looked at Elizabeth's church the Puritans saw many things to criticize. They did not like its ritual nor its bishops, who were officials appointed by the Crown to serve the interests of the state. Unfortunately, some Elizabethan bishops displayed a spirit of worldliness and greed which justified sharp criticism. The Crown itself set a bad example, for newly appointed bishops were often coerced into bargains by which a portion of the see's endowment passed into royal hands. Pluralities and nonresidence continued; the lower clergy were often ill-trained and ignorant; the church courts contained abuses. Thus the Puritans had grounds for complaint.

Puritan hostility to the church took many forms. Early in the reign a controversy arose concerning the vestments worn by the clergy. The Puritans considered these vestments too much like those of the Roman priesthood, and they thought that ministers should be permitted to wear whatever vestments they chose. This rather trivial matter became important because the Puritans made it a point of conscience, whereas Elizabeth, as governor of the church, made it a point of obedience. The dispute spread to other matters of form and ritual: to the practice of kneeling at Communion, to the sign of the cross in baptism, to the ring in marriage, to organs and choral singing in churches. As a result of these disputes there were many divergent practices in the church. In 1563 Elizabeth ordered Archbishop Parker to enforce "an exact order and uniformity in all external rites and ceremonies." The archbishop was poorly obeyed.

The controversy then moved to more dangerous ground, for the Puritans began to challenge the authority of the bishops to rule the church. Calvinism stressed the equality or the parity of all clergymen; it rejected bishops as symbols of Roman error and of royal tyranny. The doctrine of parity was given great impetus by Thomas Cartwright, a professor of divinity at Cambridge. From his studies of the New Testament Cartwright drew the conclusion that the Scriptures contained no justification for the government of the church by bishops. The early bishops, he believed, had been preachers and teachers. He insisted that bishops be confined to these ancient functions and that the church be governed by presbyteries, that is, by disciplinary courts composed of local clergy such as were arising in Scotland. Congregations, he believed, should select their own ministers. Such doctrines were undiluted Calvinism. Cartwright gave the Puritans a battle cry: "The bishops must be unlorded." He broadened the conflict from a quarrel over minor points to a clash over fundamentals, for to question the authority of bishops was to question the authority of the queen, who appointed bishops and gave them power. In 1570 Cartwright was deprived of his professorship, and four years later he fled to the Continent.

Puritan hostility to the bishops continued. It reached a raucous climax in the Martin Marprelate libels published between 1587 and 1589. These were anonymous tracts attacking the bishops with great violence but with a ribald humor that made the tracts good reading. They "swept away in a tide of unrestrained jocularity all the traditional reverence for the episcopate." The secret press from which the tracts emanated was discovered by the government, a number of people were punished, and at least one was executed.

Puritan attempts to alter the Church of England took other forms. One was a campaign by Puritan members in the House of Commons. In 1556 the Commons sent Elizabeth a petition asking for reform of certain abuses in the church. In 1571 a Puritan, Walter Strickland, introduced a bill to modify the prayer book. Elizabeth acted quickly. Strickland was summoned before the Council and suspended from the House, to the indignation of the Commons. In the following year the queen commanded that no bills concerning religion be introduced in Parliament "unless the same be first considered and liked of by the clergy." This prohibition impelled a Puritan firebrand, Peter Wentworth, to make a bold defense of the right of free speech in the Commons. He pleaded eloquently for the liberties of Parliament, though he would have used those liberties to Puritanize the church through legislation. The campaign in Parliament failed, and the Puritans turned to other methods.

They held meetings known as "prophesyings" or "exercises," public assemblies of the clergymen of a locality who gathered to study the Scriptures, to discuss the improvement of morals, and at times to denounce notorious offenders. The laity were permitted to attend, though they took no part in the discussions. Such meetings might do good, but they had a Presbyterian flavor and their discussions could easily degenerate into criticism of the church. Elizabeth insisted that they be discontinued. There was also the "classis" movement. A classis was a secret meeting of clergymen with Presbyterian tendencies. These meetings were modeled on the Scottish presbyteries; their purpose was to find subtle ways in which the Anglican service could be given a Presbyterian tone without open challenge of the law.

In 1580 a group of extreme Puritans led by Robert Browne and Henry Barrow broke away from the church altogether and began to preach a new form of religious organization. Church and state, they argued, should have no connection with each other. The congregation, the voluntary association of believers, should be the only ecclesiastical unit and should manage its affairs without supervision or control by any higher authority. These separatists or Congregationalists, as they were called later, worshiped in gatherings known as conventicles in which the forms of the church were not used. The separatists made religion emotional; they rejected the necessity of a learned ministry and relied upon inspiration. They were violently anti-Catholic and violently anti-Anglican. Hence they clashed at once with the government, and Barrow later was executed for seditious words.

Elizabeth was highly irritated by the Puritans, for in rejecting her authority to govern the church they were striking at her authority to govern the state. "There is risen both in your realm and mine," she wrote to the king of Scotland, "a sect of perilous consequence, such as would have no kings but a presbytery and would take our place while they enjoy our privilege. Yea, look we well unto them." Elizabeth's first archbishop, Matthew Parker (1559–1575), a wise and moderate man, found the suppression of Puritanism a difficult matter, partly because he was not given sufficient power. His successor, Edmund Grindal (1576–1583), displayed sympathy with the Puritans. Refusing to obey the queen's command to suppress prophesyings, he was suspended from office.

At Grindal's death in 1583 Elizabeth determined to find a sterner archbishop. She selected John Whitgift, a disciplinarian and an enemy of Puritans. He demanded at once that the clergy acknowledge complete acceptance of the principal tenets of the church; some 200 ministers refused and were suspended. Whitgift developed a new weapon, the Court of High Commission, an ecclesiastical court authorized by the Act of Supremacy. This court, which did not follow the practices of the common law, had no jury and it forced suspects to swear that they would answer all questions truthfully. If a man refused, he was punished by the Star Chamber. If he consented, his answers were used against him and he might be fined or imprisoned without appeal. After the Martin Marprelate libels the government struck hard blows. Puritan leaders were imprisoned, and a few were executed. An act of 1593 inflicted the death penalty upon persons who stubbornly refused to attend the services of the church or who repeatedly worshiped in conventicles. Puritanism declined in the last fifteen years of the reign, Puritans in high office had died, and the religious leaders of the movement had been thinned and silenced by persecution.

CHRONOLOGY

Elizabeth Before the Armada

1558–1603	Elizabeth I
1559	Treaty of Cateau-Cambrésis; Acts of Supremacy and of Uniformity; Elizabethan *Book of Common Prayer*
1560	Treaty of Edinburgh; Scottish Reformation; coinage reform begins
1563	Thirty-Nine Articles of Religion; Statute of Artificers (Apprentices)
1568	Mary, Queen of Scots, flees to England; Douai (English Catholic Seminary) founded in Flanders
1570	Elizabeth excommunicated by Pope Pius V
1580	Jesuits Edmund Campion and Robert Parsons in England; Robert Browne and the Separatists
1581	Statute against Recusants
1587	Mary, Queen of Scots, executed
1587–89	Martin Marprelate Tracts

14. Elizabeth I: The Spanish Armada

CHANGES IN THE ALIGNMENT OF POWERS

For more than half a century before Elizabeth came to the throne the international politics of western Europe had been dominated by the wars and rivalries of France and Spain. During this half century France had been strong, nationalistic, and aggressive under her active rulers Francis I (1515–1547) and Henry II (1547–1559), allied with Scotland, hostile to England, and almost constantly at war with Spain. France had been opposed by Spain under Emperor Charles V (1516–1556), whose vast possessions in the Netherlands, Germany, and Italy were of great potential strength but were weakened by geographical separation and national diversities. Since in the past Spain had been allied with England, Elizabeth at first considered Spain an ally (though not perhaps a friend) and France an obvious enemy.

With the abdication of Charles V, the accession of Elizabeth, and the death of Henry II—all falling within the space of a few years—the old system of international politics dissolved. The new one that replaced it was based on the division between Protestants and Catholics. Although religious differences cut across national frontiers, England emerged as the leading Protestant state and Spain as the Catholic leader. Under a series of weak kings, France sank into chaos and civil war. The French religious wars between Catholics and Calvinist Huguenots continued almost until the end of the century, so that France played a surprisingly minor role in the impending struggle between England and Spain. The Franco-Scottish alliance ended with the Scottish Reformation.

Changes also occurred in Spain and England. Charles V left Austria and Bohemia to his brother Ferdinand, but the rest of his possessions went to his son, Philip II, the former husband of Mary Tudor. Philip became the temporal head of the Counter Reformation, the patron of the Jesuits, and the ruler who sent the Armada of 1588 against England. Horrified to discover that Calvinism was making progesss in the Netherlands, he determined to crush it even at the cost of ruining his richest province. There was thus religious division in Spanish lands as well as in France.

England was the strongest Protestant state in Europe. Although the queen had none of Philip's religious zeal she could not ignore the Spanish menace. And quite naturally she allied, though at first in a clandestine way, with the Calvinists in the Netherlands and with the Huguenots in France. But England also had her religious divisions. What might be called a constant conspiracy was formed between Philip and certain Catholic elements in England and Scotland; the Irish, among whom the Jesuits achieved one of their greatest triumphs, gladly allied with Spain against their English oppressors.

THE BEGINNING OF CONFLICT

The Break with Spain

The first break between England and Spain occurred about 1568. It is worthwhile to examine the causes, though some points will be repeated later. Ten years before, when Elizabeth ascended the throne, Philip had offered her a condescending friendship. But when she established a Protestant church (which he refused to regard as permanent), when she aided Protestants in Scotland and in France, when she made Mary, queen of Scots, her prisoner, and when France grew weak and divided, Philip altered his policy.

Meanwhile another development underscored the clash of religions. The initial phase of Calvinist revolt in the Netherlands took place in 1566 with riots and the destruction of Catholic churches. Elizabeth, who encouraged these actions by propaganda and secret assistance, had no thought of overthrowing Philip's government. She merely wished to return the trouble he was causing her, and to prevent him from making the Netherlands a springboard for an attack on England.

Economic friction also appeared between England and Spain. In the 1560s a famous English merchant and seaman, John Hawkins, made a number of voyages to Spanish America. Though his purpose was peaceful trade, the Spanish were furious at his intrusion; his third voyage ended in disaster when he was treacherously attacked by a Spanish fleet. Anglo-Spanish quarrels, moreover, were disturbing English trade to Antwerp: rather aggressively the English had placed restrictions on Flemish merchants trading in London; and Spanish countermeasures at Antwerp had disturbed the delicate balance of trade. As a result some English merchants had moved their staple to the German port of Emden.

In December 1568, after Hawkins' third voyage, there came a greater shock. A Spanish fleet sailing up the Channel with 800,000 ducats (£85,000) for the Spanish army in the Netherlands was driven into English ports by Huguenot pirates. Elizabeth discovered that since the money was loaned to Philip by Genoese bankers, by contract it remained the property of the bankers until it was delivered in Flanders.

She thereupon seized it as a loan to herself. The Spanish at once laid an embargo on English property in the Netherlands, the English seized Spanish property in England, and trade with the Netherlands ceased. So vital was this trade to both England and Antwerp, however, that it was reopened in 1573. Thus a number of factors were driving Spain and England apart.

Plots in England

Anglo-Spanish tension was increased greatly by a series of plots in England. They began, significantly, with the arrival of Mary, Queen of Scots. The first of them had its origin in aristocratic discontent which drifted into treason. A group of conservative English peers, resentful of the influence of Cecil and other nonnoble councilors and led in the south by the duke of Norfolk and in the north by the earls of Northumberland and Westmorland, were critical of Elizabeth's policy. They were sympathetic to Mary, believing she should be recognized as Elizabeth's successor and restored to the Scottish throne. Moreover, they disliked the growing tension with Spain. Some, though not all, were Catholics and desired to restore the ancient faith. Such sentiments could easily degenerate into treason. The duke of Norfolk began to plot with Mary and with De Spes, the Spanish ambassador, who hoped for a Catholic rising aided by Spanish troops. But Norfolk was not a brave or resolute man. And when in October 1569 Elizabeth summoned him peremptorily to court, he hesitated, obeyed, then tamely allowed himself to be imprisoned in the Tower. Plotting among the southern lords collapsed.

But the north, more valiant and more combustible, differed greatly from the south; it obeyed its own great lords—Percy, Neville, and Dacre; its society was feudal, its religion Catholic. When the earls of Northumberland (Percy) and Westmorland (Neville) also were summoned to court they broke into rebellion. Their followers entered Durham Cathedral, destroyed Protestant bibles, and set up the Mass. For a short time the rebels controlled the north. They made a southern lunge toward Tutbury, where Mary was confined, but she was spirited away and the rebels retreated. The troops of the government closed in upon them, their army broke up, Northumberland and Westmorland fled to Scotland, Leonard Dacre was defeated near Carlisle, and the rebellion was at an end. It had been a dangerous affair.

The rebellion was scarcely over when a new plot, the Ridolfi or second Norfolk plot, developed in 1570–1571. Roberto di Ridolfi was an Italian banker resident in England, an exuberant and overconfident schemer who believed, like De Spes, that many English Catholics were ready to rise against Elizabeth. He plotted with De Spes, with Mary, and with Norfolk, who weakly allowed himself to be drawn into new treasons. The plot called for a Catholic insurrection, a Spanish invasion from the Netherlands, a marriage between Mary and Norfolk, who were to be placed on the English throne, the disappearance of Elizabeth, and the restoration of Catholicism. But Alva, governor of the Spanish Netherlands, regarded the plot as fantastic, Norfolk as a coward, and Ridolfi as a windbag. He refused to act until a revolt in England was well under way and until Elizabeth was assassinated. Meanwhile Cecil discovered the essentials of the plot. De Spes was dismissed in disgrace. Norfolk was convicted of treason and executed in 1572. Parliament clamored for the execution of Mary, that "bosom serpent," as an English statesman called her, but Elizabeth would not consent. These plots made a profound impression upon the English people. Their anger against Mary, their suspicion of Spain, their hatred of Catholicism, their devotion to Elizabeth, who appeared to be their sole protection, were all assuming a deep and passionate character.

France

These events, underscoring the hostility of Spain, caused Elizabeth to review her relations with France. These had been hostile; in 1562 she had committed the blunder of an open alliance with the Huguenots against the French king, hoping to aid them as she had aided the Protestants in Scotland, perhaps even regaining Calais in the process. The Huguenots premitted her to occupy the port of Le Havre, but the venture ended in failure: the Huguenots and the French Crown made peace and joined forces against England; the plague broke out among the English troops in Le Havre; and in July 1563 the place had to be abandoned. Elizabeth withdrew from her luckless enterprise with what grace she could.

Her failure showed her that France, more politically complex than Scotland, was not divided in a simple way between Catholics and Protestants. There was also a middle party, the *politiques,* who regarded peace and political reform as more urgent than deciding the religious quarrel by force of arms. They were Catholic but moderate in religious zeal, nationalist and royalist in character, eager to promote the interests of France, and very hostile to Spain. They resisted the domination of the Huguenots as well as the ultra-Catholic party of the duke of Guise. Catherine de Médicis, who controlled her weak sons Charles IX (1560–1574) and Henry III (1574–1589), supported the *politiques.* Her policy was one Elizabeth could understand, for it was similar to her own policy in England. In England, however, the middle party was moderately Protestant whereas in France it was moderately Catholic.

With great need of support on the Continent, Elizabeth in 1570 began negotiations for a marriage alliance between England and France. Charles IX was married, but he had two younger brothers, Henry, Duke of Anjou (later Henry III), a young man not quite nineteen, and Francis, Duke of Alençon, three years younger. Elizabeth was thirty-seven. Negotiations for her marriage with Anjou were wrecked by his refusal to abandon Catholicism; those with Alençon dragged on for a time and then ended, though they were to be renewed at a later date. But Elizabeth achieved her purpose: the improvement of relations with France. In 1572 the two countries concluded the Treaty of Blois by which each promised to assist the other in case of attack.

Increased cordiality with France was endangered by the Massacre of St. Bartholomew in 1572. Catherine de Médicis had feared that the Huguenot leader, Admiral Coligny, would induce Charles IX to aid the rebels in the Netherlands, thus causing war between France and Spain. Catherine and the party of Guise plotted to assassinate Coligny. Their opportunity came when the Protestant nobles assembled in Paris in August 1572 to celebrate the marriage of the young Huguenot prince, Henry of Navarre, with the king's sister, Marguerite of Valois. Coligny was shot in the streets of Paris but was only wounded. The Protestant nobles there were in a dangerous mood, and Catherine persuaded Charles to sanction their slaughter while they were in his power. The result was a general massacre of Protestants by Catholics which spread from Paris to other cities and with victims numbering seven or eight thousand.

This massacre stirred Protestants throughout Europe to bitter anger. In England there was an outcry for stricter laws against Catholics, for the execution of Mary, and for new measures to ensure Elizabeth's safety. Although Elizabeth could not aid the Huguenots openly without breaking the recent treaty with France, she considered it imperative that the French be kept busy within their own borders and so she connived at assistance to La Rochelle from Protestants in England. At the same time she did not break with the legitimate French government, and normal relations between the two courts gradually were resumed. France was neither England's ally nor her enemy. Thus the wars of religion prevented France from taking an active part in international affairs.

The Revolt of the Netherlands

An important cause of the war between England and Spain was the assistance Elizabeth gave to the Netherlands in their revolt against Spanish rule. The seventeen rich and populous provinces of the Netherlands, comprising both modern Holland and modern Belgium, had fallen under control of the dukes of Burgundy during the later Middle Ages and had eventually become possessions of Spain. The Netherlands had been ruled by Charles V with sympathy and understanding, but Philip's arbitrary and dictatorial government ignored their ancient rights and liberties. Their very prosperity irritated Philip. Far too much of the treasure from America, he thought, found its way into the pockets of Dutch and Flemish merchants. His remedy was the imposition of heavy taxation upon his richest province. Moreover, his rigid orthodoxy was outraged by the growth of Protestantism; he would bring the Netherlands back to the church.

Resentment against his policy broke into revolt in 1566. In the following year he sent the duke of Alva to restore order. Alva, though a good soldier and a hardheaded statesman, was harsh and cruel. He began a reign of terror with bloodshed and confiscation of property which cowed the people and inspired a deep hatred of Spain. On land Alva crushed the revolt.

At sea the rebels were more successful. In 1569 the Prince of Orange, following the tactics of the Huguenots, issued commissions to Dutch privateers to prey upon Catholic commerce. These Dutch Sea Beggars, as they were called, levied a heavy toll on the shipping of Spain as well as that of their own Catholic countrymen. For some time Elizabeth allowed them to dispose of their booty in England and English merchants picked up fine cargoes at bargain rates. But the Sea Beggars, a rough lot, caused disturbances in English ports; in 1572 their visits were prohibited. The result was unexpected: the Dutch privateers turned to the port of Brille in Holland as a new base of operations. This was the signal for a more determined revolt against Spain, and other coastal towns joined forces with the men at Brille. As the war at sea expanded, the defiant spirit of the seaports spread to the interior and created a new revolutionary zeal there. The revolt of the Netherlands had begun in earnest.

In the early years of the war Elizabeth aided the rebels in secret and underhanded ways, but she would not be pushed into an open break with Spain, nor into a Protestant crusade. Her object was not so much to aid the Dutch, though she wanted to keep them fighting, as to guard the welfare and safety of England. She did not wish to drive Philip from the Netherlands but to keep him busy there; moreover, she dreaded intervention by France, for she believed that French domination of the Netherlands would be as dangerous to England as domination by Spain. After 1578, however, the position of the rebels degenerated. In the preceding year Philip had sent a new governor, Alexander Farnese, Duke of Parma, a very able man and the first soldier of the age to combine the qualities of a great general with those of a diplomat. By causing dissension between the Dutch in the north and the Flemings in the south, and by constant military pressure, he gradually broke the resistance of the ten southern provinces and brought them once more under Spanish control. The seven northern provinces, forming the Union of Utrecht in 1579, fought on, though they were hard pressed.

They had hopes of a new champion in Francis, Duke of Alençon, the younger brother of the French king, who campaigned off and on for a number of years in their behalf. The reappearance of French intervention at first alarmed Elizabeth but in 1578 she altered her policy and revived marriage negotiations with Alençon. If he was to drive Spain from the Netherlands he should do so as England's friend. He responded gallantly to Elizabeth's overtures. Paying two visits to England, he was duly smitten by her charms (she was now in her middle forties), and courted her with great fervor and diligence. It was all a bit ridiculous. He was a little man, with a face badly marked by smallpox and with a nose somewhat bulbous in contour. Elizabeth called him her frog. He had an agent in England, one Jean de Simier, whom the queen, with her love for nicknames, referred to as her monkey. "Be assured on the faith of a monkey," Simier once wrote her, "that your frog lives in hope." But Alençon failed on the field of battle and died in 1584, leaving the Dutch in worse plight than before. In the same year William of Orange was assassinated. And the duke of Guise made a treaty with Philip to stamp out Protestantism in France. French aid to the Dutch thus became impossible.

Elizabeth was faced with the fact that if she did not give greater assistance to the Dutch they would surely be conquered. As usual she hesitated. By 1585, however, relations with Spain had reached the breaking point; there was every indication that a Spanish victory over Holland would be followed by a Spanish invasion of England. The Dutch formed Elizabeth's one line of defense abroad: their ruin might well be followed by her own. In 1585 she made a treaty with the Dutch by which she promised to send an army to their assistance at her own charge. She had already loaned them large sums of money, and as a guarantee for repayment the treaty allowed her to occupy the Dutch towns of Brille, Flushing, and Rammekens. In

December 1585 the earl of Leicester sailed to Holland with a powerful force of 7600 men. But Leiscester showed himself to be a poor general and a poorer statesman. He exceeded and disobeyed his instructions, he quarreled with the Dutch and with his own subordinates, he spent money freely, and he complained groundlessly of parsimony at home, for Elizabeth had not spared in equipping the army. His forces deteriorated without substantial achievement, and he returned to England in 1586 with great loss of credit. Sent back to his post in the year following, he was more incompetent than ever. The English campaigns on land during these years brought little but failure and dishonor. Happily the war at sea had more fortunate consequences.

ENGLISH MARITIME ENTERPRISE

It was in Elizabeth's reign that England first became a great sea power with a navy capable of striking heavy blows in waters far from Britain. The background of the Elizabethan navy is to be found, in the first place, in a gradual revolution in naval warfare, the construction and use of warships, and the development of naval gunnery. These changes began in the reign of Henry VIII and were expanded greatly under Elizabeth.

The way in which Englishmen thought of the ocean is also important. An extensive literature arose in the Tudor period dealing with maritime affairs: with maps, mathematics, and navigation; with descriptions of distant lands and of the bizarre adventures of explorers; with propaganda for discovery, the extension of trade, and the planting of colonies. Educated people added these books to their libraries, and there arose that alliance of merchants, seamen, scholars, and gentry which produced the age of Drake and of the Armada. The English were proud of their seamen. Sailors replaced soldiers as the national heroes. In 1589 Richard Hakluyt published the first edition of his famous work, *The Principal Navigations, Voyages, and Discoveries of the English Nation,* in which he told the epic story of English enterprise at sea. Finally, there was a dawning realization that the Atlantic had superseded the Mediterranean as the chief area of European commerce. This shift gave England a splendid geographical location for leadership in Atlantic enterprise.

Voyages of Commercial Expansion

The first venture of which we hear was a voyage to the Atlantic coast of Morocco in 1551 when a group of London merchants sent out two ships under Captain Thomas Wyndham to trade at Agadir. In 1552 he made a second voyage, trading a "good quantity of linen and woollen cloth, coral, amber, jet, and divers other things well accepted by the Moors" in return for "sugar, dates, almonds, and molasses or sugar syrup." This trade became permanent; a Barbary Company was chartered in 1585. Meanwhile Wyndham embarked upon a much more dangerous venture. Accompanied by a Portuguese renegade, Antonio Pinteado, who served as pilot, Wyndham sailed in 1553 to the Gold Coast in tropical West Africa, where he obtained a good quantity of gold. He then went on to the Niger River in search of pepper. The cargo of gold, ivory, and pepper made the voyage a financial success. In the next year Captain John Lok brought home from the Gold Coast four hundred pounds of gold, a substantial fortune.

The Portuguese lodged a formal complaint with the English government. The entire coast of West Africa, they said, was theirs, and no other Europeans should trespass upon it. The English merchants, called before the Privy Council, answered by asserting a principle to which England adhered for generations: only effective occupation of an overseas territory by a European power could confer exclusive rights upon that power. They denied that mere discovery gave perpetual monopoly over vast unoccupied areas. Philip, at that time king of England, prohibited the voyages, but they continued nonetheless. When Elizabeth came to the throne the Portuguese protested again, but received the same answer.

Another venture, born of the depression, began as an attempt to find a northeast passage to the Orient in the waters north of Scandinavia, Russia, and Siberia. In 1553 a group of merchants and courtiers sent out three vessels upon this hopeless quest. Sir Hugh Willoughby, who commanded the expedition, rounded the North Cape of Norway, sailed eastward to the island of Novaya Zemlya, attempted to winter on the Siberian coast, and, with his men, was frozen to death. But one of his ships commanded by Richard Chancellor entered the White Sea and thus came in contact with the Russians. Landing at Archangel, Chancellor made his way to Moscow. He was well received by Czar Ivan the Terrible, who readily granted English merchants the right to trade in Russia; at Chancellor's return to England in 1554 the merchants who had sent him out transformed themselves into the Muscovy Company and began a precarious trade with that country. The company took out cloth and hardware and brought back wax, amber, train oil, tallow, furs, cordage, and timber for masts and spars.

Attempts were also made to find a northwest passage. Early in Elizabeth's reign a friendly controversy arose between Anthony Jenkinson, who favored search for a passage in the northeast, and Sir Humphrey Gilbert, soldier and courtier, who favored the northwest. In 1566 Gilbert set forth his views in *A Discourse for a Discovery for a new Passage to Cataia,* a work which circulated in manuscript for a decade before it was published. Although Gilbert's arguments to prove the existence of a passage were superficial and even childish, he aroused great interest and was widely read. Another propagandist for a northern passage was Dr. John Dee, a mathematician and geographer who invented instruments and devised map projections for determining a ship's location in high latitudes. He also collected much information about the northern seas.

The search for a northwest passage was pursued by Captain John Davis, a scientific explorer, who made three voyages (1585–1587) into the waters between Greenland and Baffin Land. Sailing much farther north than Frobisher had earlier and carefully charting the coasts he visited, he added greatly to geographical knowledge. He was a competent seaman and an intelligent explorer who was not deceived into thinking that every inlet was a northwest passage.

The usual organization of merchants and adventurers for enterprise overseas in the Tudor period was the chartered company—the Barbary Company, the Muscovy Company, the Company of Cathay, and many more. The charters, obtained from the Crown, conferred exclusive rights of exploration, trade, or settlement in a given area. Monopoly was justified by the high degree of risk involved in these ventures and by the large amount of capital required. No individual merchant could afford such danger of loss or provide such sums of ready cash. These companies were of a new type known as joint-stock companies. The investor did not trade in person, as in the regulated companies, but bought shares, as in a modern corporation, letting the company conduct the enterprise and divide the profit or loss among the shareholders. The chartered companies illustrate the free enterprise of the people functioning with the approval of the state; they contrast sharply with the close control of all mercantile ventures exercised by the Crown in Spain and Portugal.

An Eastland Company for trade in the Baltic Sea was chartered in 1579. English merchants had traded in this area in the fifteenth century, but they had been driven back by the Hanseatic League; in the early Tudor period there was only a trickle of English commerce to the Baltic. Now, as the Hansa sank in power, the time was ripe for a new venture. The Eastland Company brought home pitch, canvas, cable, and cordage, and timber for masts and spars. Its establishment was an excellent preparation for the naval struggle with Spain.

Another company was chartered in 1581 to trade in the Mediterranean. English commerce in the Mediterranean, begun under Henry VII, had come to an end in the middle of the century. It had ended partly because the Turks, established in Constantinople and the Levant, were difficult to deal with. They were warriors who regarded merchants as inferior beings sent by Allah to be fleeced. Spain also was hostile to English penetration in the Mediterranean. English merchantmen literally fought their way through the Straits of Gibralter. A Turkey Company was chartered in 1581 and a Venice Company in 1583. In 1592 the two companies merged as the Levant Company which, with many ups and downs in fortune, continued for more than two centuries. Young Englishmen went out to the Levant, learned the native tongues, and traded English broadcloth, kerseys, rabbit skins, tin, and mercury for spices, drugs, indigo, silk, cottoncloth, and linens. This was the modest beginning of England's role as a Mediterranean power. The English East India Company, the greatest of all such dealers, will be discussed later.

Attempts at Colonization

The Elizabethans never established a permanent colony in the New World. Yet despite their failure, they were the founders of the movement which was to people the Atlantic coast of North America with settlers of English blood. The Elizabethans thought and wrote concerning the advantages of planting colonies in America; in 1584 Richard Hakluyt tried to interest the queen by presenting her with his pamphlet, *Discourse of Western Planting.* Attempts at colonization in Elizabeth's reign were connected with three famous men—Sir Humphrey Gilbert, Sir Walter Ralegh, and

Sir Walter Ralegh, artist unknown. (National Portrait Gallery, London)

Sir Richard Grenville. They were not of sailor or merchant stock but were members of the gentry. In 1578 Gilbert obtained a patent permitting him in very general terms to colonize barbarous lands unoccupied by any friendly power. He collected a fleet at once and set sail. What happened on the voyage remains a mystery, but he was soon back in port in a somewhat battered condition. The Spanish accused him of piracy. Raising funds with difficulty, he tried again in 1583. He crossed the Atlantic and landed on Newfoundland of which he took formal possession in the name of Queen Elizabeth. He then sailed to the mainland to select a site for his colony. By now, however, the expedition was failing. His largest ship had deserted shortly after he left England. He lost his supplies and most of his colonists when another of his vessels was wrecked on the coast of modern Nova Scotia. He had no recourse but to turn homeward. Gilbert was drowned on the voyage to England when his ten-ton ship, the *Squirrel,* foundered in a gale off the Azores.

The task of planting a colony in America was carried on by Sir Walter Ralegh, Gilbert's half brother. Obtaining a patent in 1584, Ralegh wisely sent an expedition to find a good location. His captains followed the coast northward from the West Indies to Roanoke Island off the shore of the present state of North Carolina. Roanoke appeared an ideal location. In 1585 Ralegh sent out 100 colonists. Sir Richard Grenville, who commanded the fleet, landed the colonists at Roanoke, placed Ralph Lane, a soldier, in charge, and departed, promising to return in a year's time. By the following summer the colonists, having neglected to plant crops and now quarreling with the Indians, were in desperate straits. In June a large fleet appeared. It was commanded by Francis Drake, who offered the colonists a passage to England. The temptation was too strong to be resisted; the settlers abandoned the colony and came home bag and baggage. Two weeks later a fleet under Sir Richard Grenville arrived at Roanoke with fresh supplies. Though Ralegh's first colony failed partly through bad luck, he was courageous enough to try again. In 1587 he sent out some 150 colonists, with John White as governor, who reoccupied the former settlement on Roanoke Island. Bad luck again dogged Ralegh's enterprise. In 1590 a relief force found the settlement deserted. The fate of the colonists is still unknown.

The English Attack on Spanish America

English colonization in North America was resented by Spain, but the appearance of English seamen in the closely guarded area of the Caribbean was resented much more. The English intrusion into Spanish America may be divided into two parts: first, an attempt at peaceful trade; secondly, a series of plundering expeditions which amounted to undeclared war. The earlier period is connected with the name of Sir John Hawkins, one of the great adventurers of the age. In 1562 he sailed from Plymouth with four ships, secured a pilot in the Canaries, obtained four hundred slaves on the coast of West Africa, and crossed the Atlantic to the island of Santo Domingo. The colonists were eager to buy the slaves, and the authorities seemed willing to wink at the traffic. Hawkins brought home a valuable cargo of hides, sugar, pearls, and some gold. Two years later he sailed again. This voyage was on a larger scale than the first. Elizabeth invested in it, not with money, but by lending a ship from the navy, the *Jesus of Lübeck,* a large but cranky vessel that almost foundered on more than one occasion. Having obtained his slaves—partly by taking them from Portuguese ships—Hawkins sailed to the Spanish Main, that is, to the northern coast of South America between Panama and the mouth of the Orinoco river. The colonists there had been commanded not to trade with him but were eager to do so. Hence a little comedy was enacted: upon the colonists' refusal to trade, Hawkins fired a cannon ball or two at the shore; whereupon the colonists capitulated (having a story for the authorities) and permitted trade to begin. Again Hawkins came home with a valuable cargo.

Unfortunately, his third voyage ended in disaster. Determined to maintain their monopoly, the Spanish punished the colonial governors who had not molested Hawkins, and armed their American fleet more heavily. Hawkins sailed in 1567 with six vessels. With great difficulty he obtained a small number of slaves. After trading along the Spanish Main, he was about to sail homeward when his fleet was struck by a gale which badly damaged the *Jesus.* In order to make repairs Hawkins entered the harbor of San Juan de Ulúa, the port for the Mexican city of Vera Cruz. Hardly had he

Sir Francis Drake. Contemporary engraving. (British Museum)

secured the harbor when a large Spanish fleet appeared. He could have excluded it, but that would have been an act of war, so he permitted the two fleets to anchor side by side. Suddenly the Spanish attacked him, all but destroying his little flotilla. Only two of his ships escaped to make their way home with great suffering. Thus ended the hope of peaceful English trade in the Indies.

Hawkins' disaster at San Juan de Ulúa, which caused great bitterness in England, was followed by English raids that made no pretense at commerce but aimed solely at plunder. By far the most famous of the raiders was Francis Drake, who had served under Hawkins when the Spanish attacked at San Juan de Ulúa. He devoted himself to a one-man war against Spain, completely assured that he represented the forces of light against the forces of darkness. In an expedition in 1571 he lurked in a secret harbor on the Isthmus of Panama while he studied the route by which the Spaniards shipped their treasure. It came largely from Peru, was brought up the west coast by sea to Panama, was carried by mule train across the isthmus to the town of Nombre de Dios on the Atlantic side, where it was stored until a fleet arrived from Spain. Drake saw that Nombre de Dios was the crucial point. In 1572 he entered the town in a surprise attack before dawn and broke into the treasure house, where he saw great quantities of silver. Unfortunately he was wounded and collapsed, and his men carried him to the boats, leaving the treasure behind. But before he sailed for England he captured a mule train within sight of Nombre de Dios, and brought home so much plunder that Elizabeth, fearing a break with Spain, dared not receive him openly but sent him to Ireland for a year or two.

In 1577 Drake sailed on his most famous exploit. Attacks on the Isthmus of Panama had now been rather overdone, and Drake devised a new plan. This was to pass through the Strait of Magellan into the Pacific and to raid the west coast of South America, where the Spaniards considered themselves quite safe. The passage through the strait was fortunately swift, but in the Pacific the fleet encountered foul weather which lasted an entire month. One ship went down with all hands; another was blown back into the strait and then taken to England by the crew, much against the will of John Winter, the commander. Two other ships, mere victualers, had been broken up before entering the strait. Thus Drake was alone in his famous vessel, the *Golden Hind.* He sailed up the west coast of South America, plundering as he went but apparently not taking the life of a single Spaniard. He then went north to California and then across the Pacific, through the Malay Archipelago, around Africa, and so home, with treasure valued by contemporaries at one and a half million pounds. As the second captain to circumnavigate the earth, Drake brought the war with Spain much closer.

The English Navy

The voyages we have been describing taught English sailors many things about their ships. Long voyages to America or north to the Arctic or south to West Africa meant that ships must be able to remain at sea in all weather for extended periods of time. A merchantman trading to the Levant must be large and heavily armed whereas a sea rover in Spanish America must be fast and nimble. Conditions at sea in the sixteenth century almost always approximated conditions of war; and the lessons learned in peaceful trade could be applied directly to battle. A large merchant vessel was a formidable fighting unit that could take its place in combat by the side of the Royal Navy; its sailors felt quite at home in ships built only for war. Finally, from these voyages of maritime enterprise there emerged a generation of famous captains eager to transfer their pursuits from peaceful trade to open war with Spain.

Henry VIII, having been keenly interested in the navy, left a fleet of some fifty vessels great and small, and introduced changes which were to revolutionize naval warfare—although he was only half aware of their implications. Mindful of the possibility of invasion by Catholic powers, he had created a fighting navy, built with the purpose of stopping invasion in mid-Channel and of destroying the army of the enemy at sea. He had given the navy a new role, the defense of the kingdom.

But Henry's ships were not very formidable. They were large ships of a type known as carracks, wide in proportion to their length, built high above the water with towering castles fore and aft from which soldiers could shoot down upon the decks of the enemy. These ships, designed for grappling, carried soldiers who boarded the enemy after the opposing ships had been lashed together and who fought hand to hand with the foe. Although Henry's ships were awe-inspiring, they were poor sailers. Top-heavy and cranky at sea, they rolled and tossed until they developed leaks. Nor could they remain at sea for any length of time without restocking with provisions.

But before the end of the reign, Henry made important innovations. Becoming interested in cannon of unusual size and power, he conceived the idea of placing them in his ships. Because the cannon were too heavy for the flimsy superstructure they were arranged along the sides of the ships on the cargo deck, ports having been cut in the hull through which they could fire broadsides. Here was the beginning of modern naval warfare, for the broadside, when properly developed, could batter and sink the enemy without boarding. Henry also strengthened the navy by building dockyards up the Thames, where ships were safe from enemy action, and by establishing a government board for naval administration.

After Henry's death the fleet so degenerated that Elizabeth inherited only a shadow of her father's naval strength. Her navy remained weak for many years because she had little money to spend on it, and that little was wasted by the dishonesty of the navy board. It was John Hawkins who rebuilt the navy along more modern lines. Having convinced Burghley that the navy board was corrupt, and having become a member of the board in 1578, he began to improve administration, remodel old ships, and build new ones. The normal warship of northern Europe in Elizabeth's reign was the galleon, a heavy fighting ship, more slender, longer, and lower in the water than the carrack, without so much superstructure and with her guns arranged to fire broadsides.

Hawkins entertained advanced ideas concerning naval gunnery and architecture. He increased the length of the ships still further so that they could mount more artillery; he built a gun deck, reserved solely for guns, over the cargo deck; he cut down drastically the old-fashioned castles fore and aft, making the ships faster, steadier, more nimble at sea, and able to sail closer to the wind. The guns were improved in size and quality. Hawkins' ships did not require soldiers but naval gunners and captains who could sail their ships with dexterity. Smaller crews diminished the danger of epidemics and increased the time a ship could remain at sea without revictualing. By 1587, when Hawkins retired from office, he had provided the queen with eighteen large galleons and seven smaller ones, most of them of the latest design and all in readiness for battle. A recent historian has observed that when the Spanish Armada sailed in 1588 "Elizabeth I was the mistress of the most powerful navy Europe had ever seen."

THE SPANISH ARMADA

The enterprise of invading England is first heard of early in Elizabeth's reign among the English Catholic exiles, who wandered about like ghosts on the Continent. Then for a time the project was sponsored by the duke of Guise, who hoped to rescue Mary Stuart. After 1580 it became more and more a Spanish affair. Philip's preparations at first were very slow. They increased in tempo when Elizabeth sent open aid to the Dutch and when Drake made a devastating raid on Spanish America in 1585–1586. Sailing first to Vigo Bay in Spain, then to the Canaries and to the Cape Verde Islands, Drake crossed the Atlantic in eighteen days, captured Santo Domingo, the capital of the West Indies, and Cartagena, the capital of the Spanish Main, leaving a path of destruction behind him. In 1587 he struck again, descending upon the coasts of Spain and Portugal, burning ships in Cadiz Harbor and throwing Spanish plans into chaos.

In reply Philip pushed his preparations with increased ardor. He had become the religious crusader, determined to send forth his fleet at all costs, refusing to weigh dispassionately the enormous difficulties of the enterprise, relying upon God, as it seemed, to perform a miracle in giving victory to Spanish arms. The leading admiral of Spain was the Marquis of Santa Cruz, a veteran of many battles. The Marquis was by then an old man and Philip pushed him hard. In a kind of senile frenzy Santa Cruz gathered ships at Lisbon and frantically loaded them with guns and provisions. In the midst of this senseless rush he died. Philip then appointed the duke of Medina-Sidonia, an aristocratic administrator and a brave and conscientious leader but not an experienced seaman. Medina-Sidonia brought order into the chaos at Lisbon and strengthened the fleet in many ways.

When it sailed against England in the summer of 1588, the Spanish fleet was a powerful fighting force, although events were to reveal its many defects. For one thing, it was less homogeneous than the English fleet. The backbone of its fighting strength consisted, as in England, of some twenty galleons. About half were ships of Castile, whose normal duty was to convoy the treasure fleets from America. About half were Portuguese, a fleet with a great fighting tradition though now in some decay. One galleon belonged to the grand duke of Tuscany, whose beautiful ship had been commandeered by the Spaniards despite his agonized protests. The Armada also contained four galleasses from Naples, light, maneuverable ships which could be heavily armed and which cruised under sail but in combat were propelled by oars. These ships, supplemented by four large merchantmen, made up the first battle line of the Armada. A second line comprised some forty merchant vessels, some very large though without many guns. In addition to these were light, fast ships for scouting, and a large number of victualers and other hulks, slow, cumbersome, and quite helpless in battle. The total was some 130 ships. But the Spaniards had fewer large guns that the English, fewer naval gunners, and insufficient amounts of ammunition. Provisions proved defective. The sailing qualities of the Spanish ships were far below those of England. Of these deficiencies the Spaniards were painfully aware.

There was, moreover, a fatal defect in the planning of the Spanish campaign. The primary purpose of the Armada, in Philip's mind, was to escort Parma's army from the Netherlands to England. Where was the all-important rendezvous between the fleet and the army to take place? The Flemish coast was so shallow that the large Spanish ships could not approach the shore. It would be necessary for Parma to set sail without the Armada's assistance and to rendezvous with the Spanish fleet at sea. This was obviously Philip's plan, for he commanded Medina-Sidonia to meet Parma

Ark Royal, *Lord Admiral Howard's flagship in the battle against the Spanish Armada. Woodcut. (British Museum)*

"off the cape of Margate." Such a meeting at sea, in the face of the English fleet, was the most dangerous operation imaginable. It entirely overlooked the Dutch flyboats, which could sail in shallow water and intercept Parma before he reached the Armada. Parma's naval position was extremely weak. Aside from a few light warships that could not repulse the Dutch, he had nothing but crude canal barges in which he must herd his precious soldiers like cattle. In a word, he could not meet the Armada at sea, and the Armada could not come close to the shore. Parma had explained this situation to Philip but not, apparently, to Medina-Sidonia, who greatly exaggerated Parma's naval strength. The blame for these fatal errors must be laid at Philip's door. He was indeed sending forth his fleet on a mission which only a miracle could render successful.

The Armada sailed from the port of Lisbon on 20 May 1588. As it worked its slow way northward it was buffeted by foul weather, and there was alarming spoilage in the provisions as well as sickness among the men. The duke put in at Corunna in northern Spain to refit. From Corunna he wrote a surprising letter to Philip, suggesting that the entire enterprise be abandoned. But Philip was adamant, and the Armada set sail again on 12 July. Carried by a fair wind, it entered the English Channel. The Spanish ships sailed line abreast in a tight formation which gave the impression of a vast crescent whose wings inclined backward. The victualers sailed safely within the protecting arc of warships. The bulk of the English fleet, commanded by Lord Admiral Howard, with such famous captains as Hawkins, Drake, and Frobisher, was stationed at Plymouth. The English quickly obtained the weather guage of the Spanish, that is, they fell behind the Armada with the wind at their back,

THE SPANISH ARMADA

The Armada 1588.

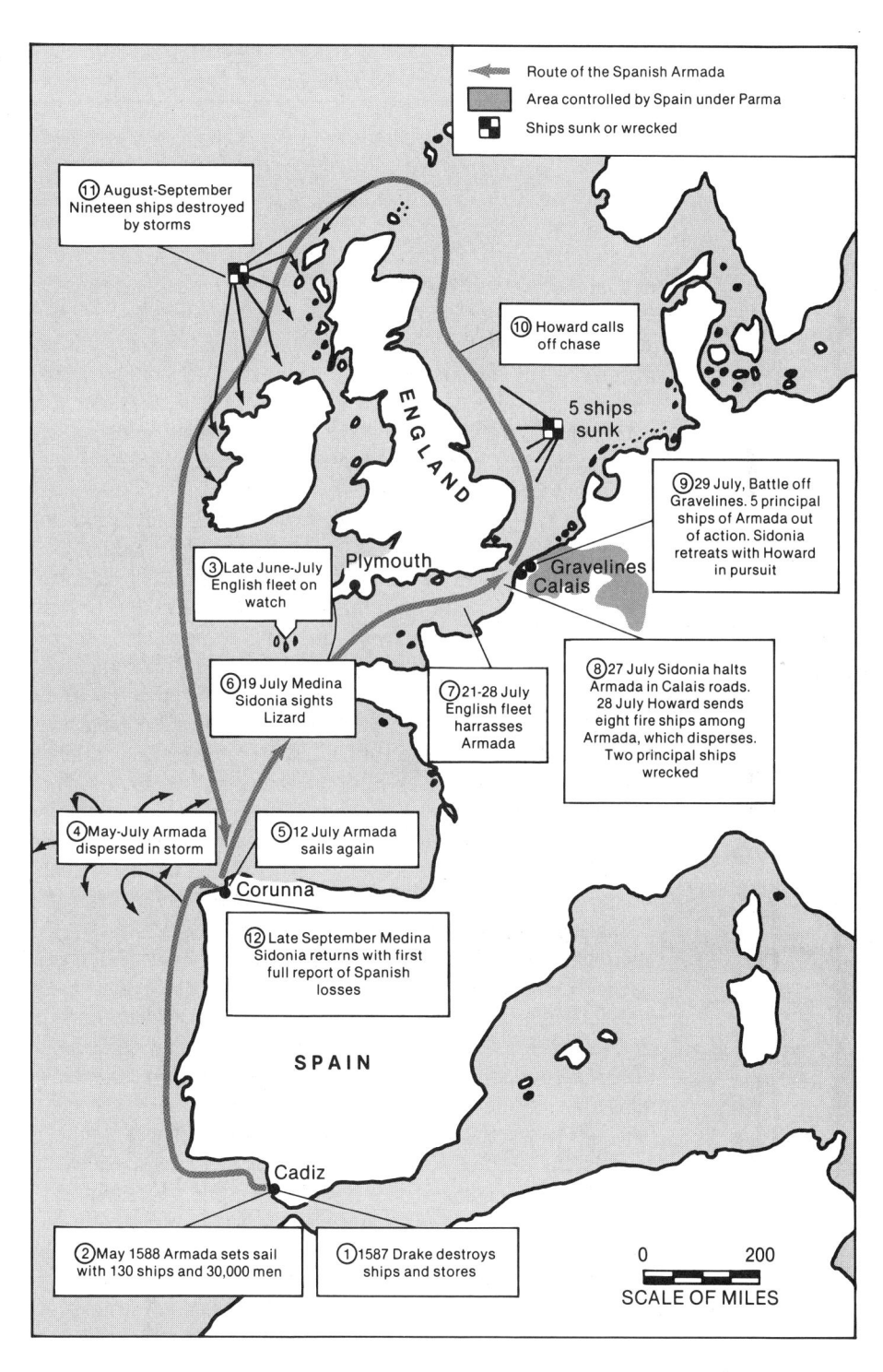

so that they could engage or not at will. Day after day they harried the wings of the Armada in heavy fighting. Their ships sailed line ahead and poured in broadsides, but avoided grappling or fighting in the melee the Spanish had desired.

Undoubtedly the English inflicted more damage than they received. Yet these battles in the Channel were frustrating to both sides. The Spanish crescent was a defensive formation which could do no great harm to the English ships. The English, on their side, found that their gunnery, though better than the Spanish, was less effective than they had hoped. They could not break up the Spanish formation. As Medina-Sidonia approached the strait between Calais and Dover his worries increased. He had no harbor in which to take refuge and no firm word from Parma, he could not drive off the English fleet, and he was running out of cannon balls. On the night of 27 July he anchored off the coast at Calais and sent desperate messages to Parma to send him ammunition and naval assistance. The next night the English sent in fire ships. As these blazing hulks descended upon the Armada, the Spanish captains cut their cables and drifted about in helpless fashion. The formation of the crescent was broken at last.

The English, reinforced by ships which had been blockading the Flemish coast, attacked the next morning in what is known as the Battle of Gravelines. The Spanish fought with great bravery and gradually resumed their old formation, or at least part of it, but now for the first time they were severely beaten. The English could outflank and worry them at will, the English broadsides fired at closer range were more deadly than before, and the Spanish, fleeing for home, sailed into the North Sea a battered and broken fleet. The English followed as far as the Firth of Forth and then turned back. As the Spanish sailed north of Scotland, west of Ireland, and so south to Spain, they were tormented by bad weather, leaking and shattered ships, rotten provisions and lack of drinking water, and fevers among the crews. Some ships made for the coast of Ireland. Without maps or pilots, most of these ships were wrecked, and most of the men were slaughtered, not by the Irish, as is often stated, but by the English, determined to show no mercy. Yet thanks to the fortitude and courage of Medina-Sidonia, almost two-thirds of the Armada reached Spain.

England's victory did not end the war, which dragged on for the rest of Elizabeth's reign. Nor did it produce the sudden eclipse of Spain as a great power, or even give England control of the sea, for Spain at once began to build a new and better navy. In the sixteenth century the forces of destruction which one nation could hurl upon another were still puny. Yet a victory such as that of England was certain to have wide repercussions. It added vastly to England's prestige and lowered that of Spain. All Europe had been watching intently. Protestants in Holland, France, and Germany took new heart; the Dutch became independent in fact if not in international law. The greatest result of the defeat of the Armada was a check to the advance of the Counter Reformation. It was now obvious that Protestantism was not to be swept away. The great Catholic champion had suffered a body blow. "From that time forward, though Spain's preponderance was to last for more than another generation, the peak of her prestige had passed."

England's victory gave her people self-confidence and aggressiveness. The fear of invasion abated, the sense of a great future on the ocean increased. "England in the nineties was a different place from what it had been in the eighties. Elizabeth herself was different. She turned quickly from a defensive to an aggressive policy and with her, as with her councillors, the old fears gave place to a new confidence in England's strength and in England's destiny."

CHRONOLOGY

The Armada

1566	Dutch Revolt begins
1567	Sir John Hawkins driven from Vera Cruz
1569	Northern Rebellion
1570–71	Ridolfi Plot
1572	Massacre of St Bartholomew's Day; Drake captures Spanish gold at Nombre de Dios
1577	Drake circumnavigates the earth
1578	Elizabeth considers marriage with duke of Alençon
1584	Death of William of Orange; French Catholics ally with Spain
1585	Drake captures Santo Domingo and Cartagena; attacks coasts of Spain and Portugal; Roanoke colony founded by Sir Walter Ralegh
1587	Execution of Mary, Queen of Scots
1588	Defeat of Spanish Aramada; death of Robert Dudley, Earl of Leicester
1589	Hakluyt's *Voyages* published

15 Elizabethan England

THE SPANISH WAR, 1588–1603

The War at Sea

After its early climax in the defeat of the Armada, the war with Spain dragged on through the rest of Elizabeth's reign. When neither side could solidly defeat the other the war became one of attrition, fought on several fronts, of which the most important was the sea. Early in 1589 the English dispatched a large fleet of about one hundred vessels commanded by Drake, with twenty thousand troops under Sir John Norris, a famous soldier. This voyage, known as the Portugal expedition, was a failure, partly because of divided counsels. Elizabeth had urged an attack on the ships of the Armada, which still lay scattered and helpless in the ports of northern Spain, but Drake had conceived the notion of starting a revolt in Portugal, then under Spanish control. After stopping briefly at Corunna, where only one Spanish galleon was found, the fleet sailed for Lisbon. The attack was repulsed, and the fleet straggled home with a loss of eight thousand men at a cost of £60,000. It was the failure of the Armada in reverse.

During the next few years an attempt was made to blockade the Spanish coast with the hope of intercepting the treasure fleets from America. But the blockade was intermittent and failed in its purpose. Philip slowly rebuilt and improved his navy. In 1591, hearing that an English squadron was in the Azores, he sent out his new ships in overwhelming force. Most of the English fleet escaped.

In 1595 Drake and Hawkins commanded an attempt to capture the city of Panama and thus cut off the flow of American treasure. The Spanish defense was far stronger than in the past, Drake and Hawkins quarreled, and both died on the voyage, which proved a failure. An expedition in 1596, which succeeded in destroying a

Spanish fleet at Cadiz, was commanded by new men, Lord Thomas Howard, Sir Walter Ralegh, and the young earl of Essex. A third large expedition in 1597 aimed at the Azores produced little except quarrels between the commanders, Ralegh and Essex. The war at sea then declined, and English energies were devoted to warfare in Ireland.

Ireland

When Elizabeth ascended the throne English power in Ireland had sunk to a very low ebb. A lord deputy in Dublin ruled the Pale, and English influence existed in some of the coastal towns. The rest of the country, under its tribal chieftains, was still a Celtic world of feuds, raids, and murders, and of primitive social and economic structure. For a moment around 1540 Henry VIII had taken an interest in Ireland. He had assumed the title of King of Ireland and had followed a policy of persuading the chiefs to surrender their lands to the English Crown and to receive them back again as grants from the king. Under Mary Tudor the Pale was enlarged, though the new territories were not securely held. Elizabeth, having broken with Spain and with the papacy, could not allow Ireland to remain in this unsettled condition. It offered too tempting a base for enemy action against her. Her policy of establishing English control could be accomplished only by conquering the Irish chiefs. The conquest of Ireland occupied her entire reign; at her death it was complete. During these wars the Irish became for the first time ardently Roman Catholic. Catholicism was strengthened because it was a symbol of resistance, because Spain and the papacy were potential allies, and because there was a highly successful mission of the Jesuits. "At the beginning of the reign Ireland was virtually ungoverned and heathen; by the end it was firmly under Engligh control and Roman Catholic."

For many years Elizabeth attempted to conquer Ireland without spending much money, but in the 1590s she was faced with a serious war in Ulster. Ulster lay to the north, the most undeveloped part of Ireland, and had many connections with the Western Isles of Scotland. Its most potent chieftain was Hugh O'Neil, Earl of Tyrone. He had been educated at the English court, but when he returned to Ulster in 1585 he was determined to make himself an independent prince. He was a man of ability, a subtle diplomat who constantly outwitted the English, a soldier who for the first time converted the Irish warriors into half-disciplined troops. Tyrone was also patient, ready to bide his time, but apt to hesitate in a crisis. He and Hugh Roe O'Donnell, Lord of Tyrconnel, led a revolt in Ulster in 1595. Three years later, in a battle on the Blackwater River, Tyrone inflicted a disastrous defeat on the English. He might have marched to Dublin, but instead waited for help from Spain. On two occasions, in 1596 and 1597, Philip had dispatched fleets to Ireland, but both expeditions were ruined by foul weather.

In 1599 Elizabeth sent over her favorite, Robert Devereux, Earl of Essex, with a large and well-equipped army. But Essex wasted his opportunities, concluded a shameful truce with Tyrone, and suddenly, conscious of his failure, abandoned his command and rushed back to England. This ended his career. He was succeeded by

Charles Blount, Lord Mountjoy, an excellent general who gradually broke the power of Tyrone. When the war was all but over, the Spanish finally arrived. A Spanish force of four thousand men landed at Kinsale on the southern coast in 1601. Tyrone came down from Ulster. But by great skill and dash and against greatly superior numbers Mountjoy defeated both Irish and Spanish forces. Tyrone fled north with his shattered army, Tyrconnel was exiled to Spain, the Spanish in Ireland surrendered, and the country lay defeated and prostrate.

Another notable feature of Elizabeth's reign was the planting of English colonies in Ireland. Confiscated lands were granted to English gentlemen, who took out English

Ireland in the 16th century.

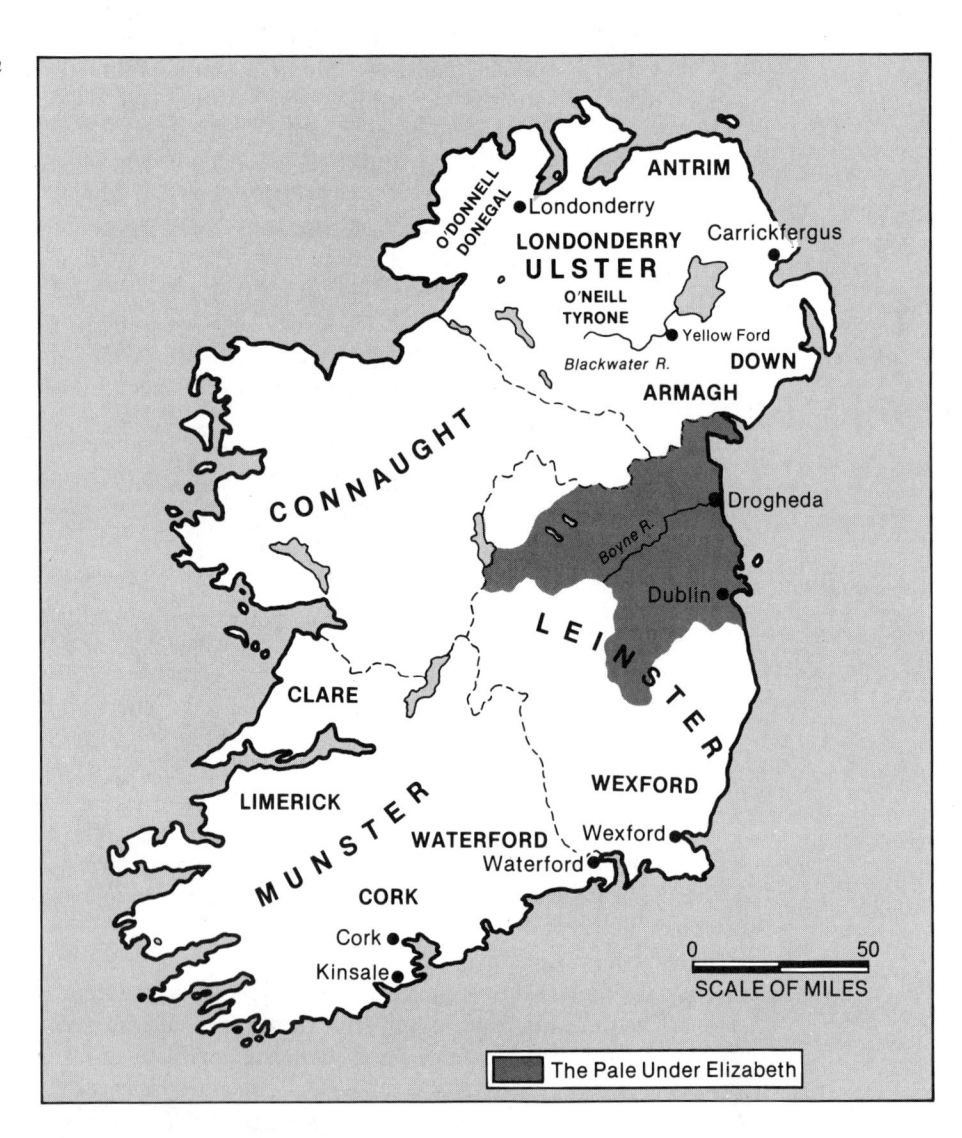

farmers and artisans in much the same way as they later took them to Virginia. Most of these settlements, however, disappeared in the Irish wars.

In addition to the war in Ireland and the war at sea, England also was fighting in the Netherlands and in France. English volunteers served in the Dutch armies, and Elizabeth maintained a separate force in the Netherlands, never less than about six thousand men.

The Cost of War

Operations on such a vast scale were extremely expensive, imposing an almost intolerable strain upon the nation. Between 1588 and 1603 the government spent the unprecedented sum of more than £4 million on the war. About half this amount was provided by parliamentary taxation, the remainder coming from increased customs duties (at a time when trade was declining), from the spoils of war, and from the extensive sale of Crown lands.

The nation was not in a position to carry this heavy burden easily. About one in twenty men were in the armed services, the plague broke out in London and other cities, there was a run of bad harvests, and trade and industry were depressed by the loss and confusion of war. Markets in lands controlled by Spain or in areas whose approach was dominated by Spain were closed to English goods. Moreover, though the exploits of Drake and other raiders stirred the imagination, they were injurious to legitimate commerce, diverting large sums from normal business ventures, undermining international credit, and encouraging a tendency toward monopoly in business ventures. English trading companies, seeing that the volume of commerce was declining, sought to control and monopolize what remained. The Merchant Adventurers, for example, were forced to abandon Antwerp as their staple, were later excluded from the German Empire, and finally settled at Middelburg in Zeeland.

THE EAST INDIA COMPANY

If most trading companies became more interested in the control than in the expansion of commerce, the East India Company was a brilliant exception. All through the sixteenth century the English had longed to sail around Africa to the Spice Islands of the Malay Archipelago, but they had hesitated; they lacked the necessary knowledge of geography, they considered their ships too small for such a lengthy passage, and the Portuguese were already in possession there. These obstacles gradually were removed.

In 1591 a group of London merchants sent out an expedition commanded by George Raymond and James Lancaster. The voyage was an armed reconnaissance, not for trade but for the discovery of trading possibilities; it was to pay its way by the plunder of Portuguese shipping. After rounding Africa the little fleet was struck by a storm which sent Raymond's ship down with all hands. Lancaster continued alone, reached Sumatra and the western coast of the Malay Peninsula, and took some Portuguese prizes. He lost so many of his men through disease, however, that he could scarcely work his way homeward. Another voyage sent out in 1596 under the command of Benjamin Wood was even more disastrous, for only one survivor ever returned.

The loss and sufferings of these voyages might well have discouraged further effort, but the English were now urged forward by the appearance of the Dutch as competitors for the trade of the East, for Holland had grown into a maritime power. In 1595 a Dutch company sent out a fleet which reached the pepper depot of Bantam in Java. The Dutch threw themselves into the Eastern trade with the greatest energy and determination. By 1602 there were so many competing Dutch companies that the Dutch government forced a consolidation by creating a Dutch East India Company. This company, which was little less than a department of state, was backed by abundant capital and by the nation as a whole.

It would be ironic if English voyages had merely paved the way for Dutch success. Therefore, after many delays, an English East India Company was chartered in 1600, consisting of 218 merchants and other adventurers who elected a governor and a directing committee of 24. Happily the first voyage was a brilliant success. Five ships under the command of James Lancaster left England in 1601. Lancaster reached the city of Achin in northern Sumatra, where he obtained permission to buy pepper. He then sailed through the Sunda Strait to Bantam, again obtaining the right to buy pepper and also to establish a factory. These factories, or trading posts, were essential because the sudden arrival of a ship from Europe inflated the price of local products and depressed the price of European goods. Hence it was necessary to leave a group of merchants in a factory to buy and sell over an extended period. For many years Bantam remained the principal station of the English in the Malay Archipelago. Lancaster returned to England with a million pounds of pepper, together with small quantities of cloves, cinnamon, and nutmeg. Before he reached England Elizabeth had died.

GRATUITIES AND FACTION

Decline in Political Morality

The long war with Spain brought unfortunate economic results, as most wars do. It also produced a decline in public morals. For thirty years before the Armada the English had been living under the triple threat of invasion, civil war, and an uncertain succession to the throne. This sense of mounting fear and common danger had produced a high level of national unity, patriotic zeal, and self-sacrifice in the service of the state. Then suddenly the tension eased. The fear of invasion receded. Although the execution of Mary, Queen of Scots, in 1587 may have spurred Philip to greater effort, it removed the danger of a Catholic heir, for Mary's son, King James VI of Scotland, was a Protestant. Safety no longer depended on the single thread of

Elizabeth's life. Puritanism, as a political irritant, subsided. It is small wonder that the morale of the public declined, that the new generation of politicians, though aggressive and confident, were less stable, less restrained, and less careful in distinguishing between integrity and corruption.

The salaries of high officials were meager, often no greater than in the Middle Ages. Elizabeth could not pay salaries in any sense commensurate with the value of the services she received. Officials were expected to live by obtaining payments from everyone—suitors, tradesmen, office seekers—with whom they dealt in the ordinary work of government. There were fees for various services, and these fees had hardened into a tariff. But there were other payments—gifts, gratuities, sometimes bribes—that were given in secret.

The Crown was the fountain of patronage. Hundreds of offices and places were at the queen's disposal; she could give lands and leases on easy terms and many kinds of economic privilege; a word from her could influence patronage in places where she had no direct control. The suitors who thronged the court could not hope for private interviews with her. Hence they turned to officials, to courtiers, to great ladies, to anyone who could enter the queen's privy chamber and bring suits to her attention. Offices were bought and sold, not directly by the Crown, but by bargains between the man who relinquished an office and the man who obtained it. The household of a high official or courtier, such as that of Burghley or of Essex, was a little court in itself. It was filled with followers and clients for whom the great official was expected to obtain favors. If he was successful he attracted new followers, he was offered gratuities, and he added to his influence by surrounding the queen with his adherents.

This was at best a dangerous system and was tolerable only because Elizabeth distributed patronage widely. Quite aware of what was going on, she did not make appointments without private information about those to whom she gave office. But in the last fifteen years of her reign the atmosphere at court degenerated. Burghley's son, Robert Cecil, though a man of ability and character, was not as scrupulous as his father. The new generation was out of touch with the old queen and her ways and she sensed the difference.

The Earl of Essex

The last years of Elizabeth's reign were marked by faction at court as well as by declining honesty. Rivalry arose between the Cecils—Lord Burghley and his son Robert—and Robert Devereux, Earl of Essex. Essex was a cousin of Elizabeth through the Boleyn family; his stepfather was the earl of Leicester, who first introduced him at court in 1584 when he was a youth of seventeen. A handsome young man with a dignified bearing and with great dash and spirit, he at once attracted the queen's attention. His domineering egotism, his impulsive, ill-disciplined, and jealous nature, and his unreasonable ambitions were as yet concealed. He soon won a reputation as a soldier. In the early 1590s a brilliant prospect opened before him. Leicester, the queen's favorite, was now dead, and Burghley, her principal adviser, was growing old. Why should he not fill the place of both and dominate the court?

But he found himself opposed by the Cecils. Burghley's ambition in his old age was to obtain high office for his son Robert. He groomed him for the secretaryship, which fell vacant in 1590; a contest over this office was the first trial of strength between the Cecils and Essex. Elizabeth compromised by leaving the place vacant, though she gave it to Robert Cecil in 1596. Meanwhile the rivalry of the two factions became general. For every vacant office Essex had a candidate whom he urged upon the queen with pressing importunity. There were stormy scenes between them; once Elizabeth boxed his ears. In 1599, on his own urging, he was sent as lord deputy to Ireland. Failing against Tyrone, he conceived the treasonable idea of using the young gallants in his train to force Elizabeth to ruin the Cecils and to give him predominance at court. He returned against orders, only to be arrested and later condemned to the loss of all his offices.

Brooding over his wrongs, insanely jealous of the Cecils, and using violent language against the queen, he allowed his house in London to become the resort of "swordsmen, bold confident fellows, discontented persons, and such as saucily used their tongues in railing against all men." In February 1601 he tried the desperate venture of seizing the court. But the government was forewarned, the city of London did not rise at Essex's urging, and he was quickly confined to his house and forced to surrender. Within ten days he was condemned for treason and within another week he was beheaded. There was great sympathy for him, but the people knew he deserved his fate. The Cecils were left supreme.

THE SPIRIT OF THE AGE

It would be a mistake to strongly emphasize the dislocations caused by the long war with Spain. A broad and general view of society in the age of Queen Elizabeth reveals a brighter and more hopeful picture. What we see is a young and vigorous people emerging from the Middle Ages into the warmer and more intense life of the Renaissance. The Elizabethans were very much alive, alert to the world around them, not merely to grasp the main chance in a material way and to rise in the social scale, but to respond to intellectual and artistic impulses. It was an age of superb writing in prose and verse, of fine achievements in music and architecture. The upper classes were better educated than they had ever been before. Oxford and Cambridge were well attended in the Tudor period, especially by the gentry. The printing press, first introduced in the late fifteenth century by William Caxton, had vastly increased the reading material available to the public.

Along with such alertness went enthusiasm. The Elizabethans were not afraid to throw themselves with vigor into their many undertakings. They were natural and uninhibited, sometimes naîve, sometimes bizarre, but satisfied to be themselves. Self-centered, proud, and self-confident they had a sense of success and achievement arising from good government, increasing wealth, and patriotic pride in the defeat of Spain. They were sure they could succeed at whatever they attempted. Some men of the time were astonishingly versatile. Sir Walter Ralegh, for example, was a courtier and royal favorite, soldier, sailor, discoverer, colonizer, poet, and writer of prose. When in the reign of James I he fell from favor, was cast into prison and decided to write a book; he selected for his topic a history of the world! Interested in chemistry and medicine, he compounded a famous pill which he sent his friends upon request and which doubtless made them much more ill than they had been before.

The Elizabethan Age was a secular age. Despite the Puritans, the Elizabethans were more interested in this world than in the next, in new forms of wealth, in industry, and in overseas expansion. It was not an honest age: people got what they could, marriage was a business arrangement, and great officers of state did not hesitate to accept gratuities. London was full of opportunists out to fleece the unwary. The underworld had a vocabulary of its own. The "conycatcher" "cozened" the "gull," which meant that the trickster cheated the gullible out of his money. The same spirit is found in the monopolies the government permitted. A monopoly might be a legitimate protection for a new invention (as is a patent today) but more normally it was some economic privilege obtained from the queen and shrewdly exploited at the expense of the public. In some ways this was a childish age. There was a love of finery and trinkets, of bright colors, and bizarre costumes, of shows, and parades, and of the wonders and monstrosities of nature. In Fleet Street in London one could see trained bears and monkeys, Indians, dwarfs, large fish, and other marvels. There were pleasures of a simple kind such as singing and dancing around maypoles, though maypoles were not as innocent as they appeared and some sports involved great cruelty to animals.

How can this vitality and exuberance be explained? One can hazard a few guesses. It was in Elizabeth's reign that England felt the full impact of the Italian Renaissance, which came streaming in from many parts of the Continent. During the first half of the century the new learning had been largely devoted to theological debate, but now it broadened into a humanism that was wider, fuller, and more urbane. Although the break with Rome had unpleasant aspects, it was bold and adventurous and freed religious discussion from the trammels of authority. It gave a boost to the national economy. There were also advances in scientific thought, as in the revolutionary concept of Copernicus that the earth revolved about the sun and not the sun about the earth. Equally important were geographical discoveries which opened men's minds to a knowledge of the world as it really was. One must add to these things an outburst of intellectual and aesthetic experience. The Elizabethan scene, moreover, was filled with vivid personalities and bold adventures that stirred the imagination and prompted its people to action.

LITERATURE

Elizabethan writers caught up the exuberance of the age and translated it into a great literature. Writing was stimulated in many ways. The Englishman's pride in his family, in the history of his country, in its language, geography, and antiquities, in its

Illustrations from a songbook. "The Month of May," from Thomas Fella, A Book of Divers Devices, *London, 1622. (Folger Shakespeare Library)*

great deeds on sea and land, provided new and abundant themes on which to write. The improved education of the upper classes created the ideal of the cultured gentleman, who combined patriotism with courtesy, learning, and a love of poetry. A flood of translations from the classics and from contemporary works in French, Spanish, and Italian offered literary forms and subject matter from which Englishmen could borrow. The Elizabethans were ready to experiment; hence the English language as an instrument of literary expression developed wonderfully from the stiffness of the early sixteenth century to the lively flexibility of the later Elizabethans. This period of literary flowering, beginning about 1580, continued into the seventeenth century at least until the death of Shakespeare in 1616.

Much Elizabethan prose, of course, was good without rising to the level of literature. This was true of the many books concerning local geography and antiquities, such as the *Perambulation of Kent* by William Lambarde and the *Britannia* by William Camden, who traveled laboriously from county to county examining local records and antiquarian lore. Historical writing included collections of medieval tales and chronicles by Richard Grafton, John Stow, and Raphael Holinshed; Samuel

Daniel's *History of England;* Francis Bacon's *History of Henry VII;* and John Foxe's *Book of Martyrs,* which dealt with the persecutions of Mary's reign. In his *Annales . . . Regnante Elizabetha* William Camden traced the history of his own time. A work of similar dedication was William Hakluyt's prose epic of English expansion overseas, *The Principal Navigations . . . of the English Nation, made by Sea or over Land.*

When John Lyly published his *Euphues* (1579) and his *Euphues His England* (1580), he did a distinct disservice to English prose. Describing the tiresome adventures of a young Athenian named Euphues, Lyly attempted to give his prose the poetic tone and ornaments of verse. The result, however, was artificial and pedantic, for he introduced such contrivances as farfetched similes, alliteration, and strained antithesis. His sentence structure was dull and monotonous. Yet euphuism became a literary cult; its baneful affectations were copied widely. Only slowly did the realization dawn that prose should not attempt to imitate verse but should describe real things with accuracy and precision. A more spontaneous and realistic style appeared in the tracts of Robert Greene and Thomas Dekker depicting the life of the London underworld. The pamphleteer and satirist Thomas Nash, who attacked the absurdities of euphuism, also carried forward the movement toward realistic and natural writing. Translators of books in foreign languages were forced to be accurate rather than ornate. Moreover, controversy, which aimed to convince the reader, produced straightforward and unadorned prose. The best writing on religion was the treatise, *Of the Laws of Ecclesiastical Politie,* by Richard Hooker, a defense of the Church of England. This work in its melodious flow of well-phrased argumentation, often rose to the plane of great literature. Perhaps the ultimate in compact phrasing and tightly woven form was to be found in the Latinized style of Bacon's *Essays.*

It was in poetry, however, that the Elizabethans excelled. The ode, the madrigal, the song, the eclogue, the ballad, the sonnet—indeed all kinds of lyrics expressing the feelings of the poet—were brought to a high level of excellence. Blank verse became the characteristic form of the drama.

A name famous in poetry was that of Sir Philip Sidney. His high social position, noble spirit, and reputation as the perfect gentleman, together with his early death in the war against Spain, tempted contemporaries to be overlavish in their praise. But Sidney, endowed with high poetic gifts, caught the imagination of his countrymen.

His first work of any length was his *Arcadia,* a prose romance of love and chivalry in which battles and tournaments, plots and counterplots alternated with eclogues or pastoral poems contrasting rural life with the life of a court. The *Arcadia* reflected Sidney's wide reading in the literature of Spain and Italy, but the style betrayed the influence of euphuism. His *Astrophel and Stella* was a collection of 108 love sonnets and 11 songs addressed to Lady Penelope Devereux, the vivacious sister of Elizabeth's favorite, the earl of Essex. Although the first sonnets were rather cold, later ones portrayed a passionate attachment. Their fine phrasing and energetic sentiment place them among the best of their kind. Sidney's *Apologie for Poetrie,* an early attempt at literary criticism, was a prose essay containing advice which poets have fortunately ignored.

Aside from Shakespeare, the finest poet of the age was Edmund Spenser.

A learned poet, he was well acquainted with Greek and Latin literature as well as with French and Italian. In 1580 he accepted a post as secretary to the lord deputy of Ireland and lived in that country until his death in 1599, holding various offices in the English administration. He found Ireland a most uncongenial and depressing place. His lack of sympathy with his surroundings and his sense of exile engendered in him a somber melancholy and despair of the world as he saw it. He retired into a fairyland of his own imagination where virtue triumphed over vice and where a man's duty and desires pointed in the same direction. Of his writings the most important were *The Shepheards Calender,* a series of twelve eclogues; three satires on English society and life at court; a number of splendid lyrics; *The Faerie Queene;* and a prose pamphlet on the state of Ireland.

The Faerie Queene is a long narrative poem placed in a setting of medieval romance in which knights representing virtues such as holiness, temperance, chastity, and justice do battle against opposing vices and appetites. The greatness of the poem is derived from Spenser's high poetic spirit, vivid imagination, and superb mastery of words. He bestows upon his narrative a lush pictorial imagery, a play of fancy, and a flowing melody which waft the reader gently into a fairy world of languorous music and exotic romance.

The drama, of prime importance in Elizabethan literature, was exactly suited to the temper of the age. It satisfied the Elizabethan love of action, of pageantry, and of amusement, as well as the love of songs and poetry. At the beginning of the reign the drama was still in a primitive state. Private theatricals were performed on special occasions at court and at the universities, but there were no public theaters; actors were regarded by the authorities as so many rogues and vagabonds. However, the drama developed with amazing rapidity. Plays became increasingly popular at court. The first company of actors was formed under the patronage of the earl of Leicester in 1574; theaters were soon constructed, not in London itself but across the river in Southwark.

The tremendous possibilities of the drama for public amusement first were demonstrated by the plays of Thomas Kyd and Christopher Marlowe. Kyd's *Spanish Tragedy* (1586), a roaring drama of blood and thunder, possessed plot and stagecraft but was devoid of poetry. The plays of Marlowe were much more important. His fine blank verse brought excellent poetry to the stage for the first time. If his plays were somewhat lacking in plot and characterization, they had a concentration of purpose as their heroes struggled for power in one form or another. Although Marlowe was killed in a tavern brawl in 1592 at the age of twenty-nine, he had already written four great plays: *Tamburlaine, Doctor Faustus, The Jew of Malta,* and *Edward II.*

Dramatists were normally men of education; they thought of themselves as superior to a young playwright, William Shakespeare, who had attended no university but sprang from the despised community of actors. Yet Shakespeare, of course, far surpassed them all. He was especially skillful where most of them failed, in characterization; his plays were filled with characters that have since become immortal. When he turned to drama dealing with the history of England, some of his figures, such as Richard III, were so vivid that they have remained what he made them in defiance of modern research. His unique genius enabled him to write all kinds of plays—fairy plays, romantic and serious comedies, lyrical dramas, histories, profound tragedies, fanciful plays—all with greatness and success. It was his universal appeal and understanding of all mankind and his excellence in all forms of poetry that made him one of the greatest of writers. His work may be divided into three periods. The first, from about 1592 to about 1600, a time in which by a curious chance his rivals disappeared and he had the stage to himself, was the period of most of the histories, of *A Midsummer Night's Dream, Romeo and Juliet,* and the romantic comedies. Then came a more somber era (1601–1608) in which he wrote his great tragedies, *Hamlet, Othello, King Lear,* and *Macbeth,* his Roman plays, and a few rather gloomy comedies. In a final period, from 1608 until his death in 1616, his mood became tranquil and gently disillusioned. The plays of this time were *Pericles, Cymbeline, The Winter's Tale,* and *The Tempest.* A great dramatist, he was one of the greatest of poets, whose marvelous imagery and inventiveness, enormous vocabulary, and superb felicity of diction have molded English literature and language from his day to this.

THE SOCIAL STRUCTURE

The Nobility

The nobility of Elizabeth's reign was a subdued and diluted version of the medieval aristocracy. In the fifteenth century, as we know, the nobles had been powerful, troublesome, and numerous. Seventy-three temporal peers had attended the Parliament of 1453–1454. However, those nobles who survived the Wars of the Roses were disciplined by the early Tudor kings. At the same time, Henry VII and his son were under pressure to ennoble their supporters. Henry VII created eleven peers; Henry VIII, thirty-eight; Edward, seven; and Mary, nine. The new nobility was loyal to the dynasty that had brought it into being, and the Tudor peerage, on the whole, was submissive and obedient. The bloody baron had become the sophisticated courtier. But noble families have a way of dying out. In 1547 there were only fifty-four temporal peers. Elizabeth, very conservative in her creations, ennobled only fourteen new peers during the course of her long reign. At her death there were fifty-nine lay nobles.

The conception of a noble in the reign of Elizabeth was that of an exalted, eminent, and wealthy person who sprang from an ancient lineage or who had performed great public service, or, better yet, who combined the two. He should be a man of action, not of contemplation. He could be called upon to perform high public functions without remuneration. He might be asked to lead an embassy abroad, a most costly duty. Nobles were placed in command of military expeditions. They were made lords lieutenants, lord deputies of Ireland, or presidents of the Council of the north. The greatest of them owned town houses in London and were expected to add to the splendor of the court. Thus, though they had lost their medieval power and importance, they performed a number of useful functions.

Nobles lived in the grand manner with elaborate households, rural palaces, fine furniture, and costly clothes. They offered liberal hospitality and spent money freely as they moved about the country. At death, after elaborate funerals they were laid in expensive tombs. Some of them lived so extravagantly that they ended in financial ruin. Land was more stable than other forms of wealth. In an age of inflation, increasing land values, and higher rents, a noble might prosper through the careful management of his estates. It is interesting that the Crown, which suppressed the nobles in the early part of the century, later became solicitous for their welfare, regarding them as a class to be preserved and protected.

The Gentry

Country gentlemen as a class were becoming the most wealthy and powerful in the kingdom. Having acquired much of the land of the monasteries, they continued to increase their possessions at the expense both of the nobility and of the Crown, and, engaging in a hundred local activities, controlled the administration of rural England as justices of the peace. They were the great men of the countryside, accustomed to power, authority, and respect. Country gentlemen had many connections with well-to-do lawyers and merchants in the towns. They crowded into the House of Commons and filled many offices in the central as well as in the local government. They set the patterns of social behavior and of humane manners.

Although some gentry families had held their lands since the Middle Ages, there was great fluidity in the class of country gentlemen in the Tudor period. Some yeomen were wealthy enough to push into the lower ranks of the gentry. Rich merchants and businessmen in London, successful lawyers like Sir Edward Coke, officials who had climbed to the top, such as Sir Nicholas Bacon and Sir William Petre, bought estates in the country and established country families. Perhaps the most spectacular ascent was that of the Cecils. The first Cecil of whom we hear in England was a man-at-arms under Henry VII. In the second generation a Cecil was a knight; in the third, a baron; in the fourth there were two branches of the family, each headed by an earl. Younger sons of the nobility also belonged to the gentry class, sometimes holding lands from their fathers or brothers. There were, of course, gentry who fell upon evil days and sold their property, but the trend was upward. The country gentleman was not what we call a dirt farmer. He was a landlord who lived upon rents, but he often retained a home farm which he managed himself, and he knew something about agriculture, and about soils, crops, and orchards.

There were various types of country gentlemen. A few were very rich and were closely associated with the nobility. Such men lived as lavishly as the nobles, though they could ruin themselves in the process. On the other end of the scale was the rustic type, the homespun squire who probably lived far from London and was glad to be home after his brief visits to the capital. He was on intimate terms with his tenant farmers, whom he met at the village alehouse and with whom he talked about crops and cattle. He was fond of hunting and decorated his hall with the skins of foxes and polecats and other trophies of the chase. But there was also the more intellectual type of country gentleman who had a library of the classics as well as books on

Hardwick Hall, Derbyshire. Note the large glass windows. (Copyright Country Life*)*

history and government. He was interested in the law because he was a justice of the peace and because he was apt to be involved in lawsuits with his neighbors. He was a university man; perhaps he had taken a grand tour which brought him in touch with French or Italian art and letters. He had an interest in architecture and music. The commonest type of country gentleman, however, was not extremely rich, or boorish, or intellectual. He was a business type who wished to make a profit from his estates, to stand well with his neighbors, and to perform his duties in local government.

Technically a man was a member of the gentry if the Heralds' College had granted him a coat of arms and the right to gentility. This college consisted of the earl marshal, who kept order at the royal court, and kings, heralds, and pursuivants with goodly titles, such as Garter King-of-Arms, Clarenceux King-of-Arms, York Herald, Rouge Dragon, Rouge Croix, Blue Mantle, and Portcullis. The duties of the college were to construct coats of arms, to record pedigrees of gentle families, and to supervise funerals.

A country gentleman took great pride in his estate. With a deep sense of continuity, he regarded himself as the trustee of his property in which he held only a life interest and which he must pass on to his heir, enlarged if possible but certainly not diminished. The Tudor gentry were great builders. Tudor houses combined English medieval tradition with the new influence of the Renaissance.

The Renaissance brought attention to balance and symmetry and to decorative columns and porticoes. Great houses continued to be built around courts, sometimes

"Dancing Scene," from Roxburghe Ballads, *Vol. 2, late 16th to early 17th century. (British Library)*

in the shape of the capital letter H. Such a house would have two open courts with an entrance at each end, with the great hall as the crosspiece, and with the private apartments of the owner forming one side of the H and those of the kitchen and servants forming the other. A house might also be built in the shape of the letter E. Here the great hall was placed in the middle of the long side of the E, thus separating private rooms from the servants' quarters.[1] There were many fireplaces, chimneys, and bay windows. Furniture, though ponderous, was becoming more comfortable and better looking. Even the poor had pewter bowls and spoons. Guests brought their own knives, which were carried in sheaths. Forks were not in common use, and people still ate with their fingers, washing them in bowls after meals. A Tudor house had a flower garden and perhaps a deer park, but there was little or no landscaping.

[1]An added attraction of an E-shaped house was that it resembled the first letter of Elizabeth's name.

The Common People

The largest number of people were those we can call the "common" people or the peasantry.[2] As with the upper classes, there was a highly stratified hierarchy. The people in this class had no real social status, but there was a highly developed system of economic status. At the top were the yeomen, who managed and worked on their own substantial farms. Some had freehold (land owning) status. Many more had leases and paid rents. The leases held by yeomen were usually long term and could be inherited. Rents were usually based upon earlier, medieval land values and were low by inflationary standards. It was in the interest of the landlords to negotiate these leases whenever possible. Some yeomen were close to the lower levels of the gentry in economic terms. However, the yeoman worked in the fields and did not lead a "gentle" life.

Below the yeomen were the general run of tenant farmers. Some had written leases (copyholders), others did not. In general, however, they had smaller holdings than the yeomen and shorter-term leases which were more easily adjusted by the landlords. This class suffered more from inflation, as a result.

At the bottom was a large class of cotters or landless agricultural laborers. Written evidence by or about them is scarce and we know little about their lives in any detail. The enclosure movement had led to regional patches of unemployment. Some laborers had been reduced to the level of seasonal and/or part-time workers. The maintenance of a family and a home was nearly impossible for these people. The children of many of the laborers left the land for the towns and cities, or became vagabonds or beggars.

Women in the class of yeomen and tenant farmers were responsible for the home and all meals. They also tended the vegetable and herb gardens. Where farm work was seasonal for the men, it was year-round for their wives. "From my sad cradle to my sable chest, Poor pilgrim, I did find few months of rest."

Local Government

The Tudors achieved a revolution in local government. Broken and debased in the fifteenth century, the government of rural England was reconstructed and developed in a remarkable way. There was a great extension of the administrative activities of local officers and an increased control and supervision from the central government. Country gentlemen served willingly, without pay, out of devotion to their counties and for enhanced prestige among their neighbors. The most important officers of local government were lords lieutenants, the sheriffs, and the justices of the peace.

The lord lieutenant was almost always a noble, often a member of the Privy Council and an important figure at court. He was placed at the apex of the system of local government. A Tudor creation, he was first appointed by Henry VIII to organize local military precautions in times of emergency and to act as a connecting link between the Crown and the provinces. He received instructions from above and

---

[2]In England the class of farmers can be called "the peasantry." No one individual person is called a "peasant," however.

exercised authority on the spot. But since he was often away from his county, country gentlemen were appointed as deputy lieutenants. They were the cream of the local gentry, numbering nearly 200 by the end of Elizabeth's reign. The principal duty of the lord lieutenant was the training of the militia in gatherings known as musters. Here the best men were selected for the trained bands, their armor and weapons were inspected, and they were drilled by professional soldiers called mustermasters. The gentry provided a quota of light horsemen. The system was rather amateurish, for the periods of training were too brief. The militia was not expected to function outside its own county and was not used for expeditions overseas.

Additionally the lord lieutenant had other functions. When the government issued privy seals, that is, letters requesting loans, the requests were distributed by the deputy lieutenants and justices of the peace—a most unpleasant duty. A lord lieutenant might be asked to enforce the laws about religion, to administer relief in times of famine, to regulate markets, and to prevent the export of wheat. The lord lieutenant often held the office of *Custos Rotulorum,* the keeper of the shire records, though the actual work was done by a clerk of the peace.

Though he had lost most of his medieval power the sheriff was still important. Sheriffs were nominated by the privy councilors and judges, who met once a year and prepared lists of three names for each shire. Of these the queen selected one. This was an office that men so wished to avoid that they offered bribes to escape it. The sheriff was now the executive officer of the county court. He made arrests, kept suspects in jail, brought prisoners into court, impaneled juries, and carried out the sentences imposed. He did not make decisions but performed the unpleasant function of local justice.

He had many miscellaneous duties, some of which involved great expense, and although he served for one year only, he was usually much the poorer when his term of office ended. He must collect debts owing to the Crown and might be held responsible for the payment of any money he could not extract from others. The dignity of his office must be maintained. He traveled about with thirty or forty men in his train, he entertained judges and ambassadors, he met the queen with a large escort when she came into his county. Having charge of the Crown lands in his shire, the sheriff also summoned the county court for the election of the knights of the shire. He had a bad name for trickery in parliamentary elections. He must also help keep the peace, must suppress riots, must bring to London persons wanted by the Council, and in general must assist in the work of local justice. In all this he was aided by undersheriffs and bailiffs.

The Justices of the Peace

The persons on whom local government depended most were the justices of the peace, who formed a group unique to England, for they were unpaid local magistrates drawn from the upper strata of the gentry. They worked hard at their judicial and administrative tasks, which constantly grew heavier during the Tudor period.

Justices of the peace were either ordinary justices or justices of the "quorum." Those of the "quorum" had legal training and experience and one of them had to be present when certain judicial work was being done. But all the justices of the peace knew something about the law. Of numerous guidebooks to tell them of their duties, the best known was William Lambarde's *Eirenarcha: Or the Office of the Justices of Peace*. The justices were selected by the Lord Chancellor with the help of privy councilors and judges. In a large county such as Devon there might be fifty or sixty justices; in other counties, less than half that number. To be a justice brought local honor and distinction; to be excluded was an affront that was deeply resented. The plays of the time made fun of the justices, and Shakespeare left a famous caricature in his picture of Justice Shallow. But the standard was normally high.

We first hear of justices of the peace in the fourteenth century, when they were appointed to assist the itinerant justices and to help keep the peace. A statute of 1361 permitted them to try cases themselves. In the Tudor period one justice acting alone could punish petty offenses brought to his attention by an accuser or by the petty constable, the policeman of the village. He could punish drunkenness, or card playing on the Sabbath, or the refusal to work at harvest time. He could order that a vagabond be whipped. He could force suspected persons to give bond to keep the peace or to appear in court. Or he could hold them in jail until they were tried. It was his duty to stop a riot before it became dangerous, though he himself could not punish the rioters. Two justices acting together in what were known as petty sessions could ask the sheriff to impanel a jury to determine minor cases. Four times a year the justices of the county met at the Quarter Sessions. All the legal officials of the county were present: justices, sheriff, high constables (there were usually two for each hundred), petty constables, jailors, jurors, and the clerk of the peace. For three days the justices of the peace tried cases. An account of each case was then sent up to London. The trial of serious crimes, such as felonies, was left to the itinerant justices, who visited each locality once a year.

Aside from judicial work, the justices of the peace engaged in an enormous amount of administrative activity. They helped conduct the musters, they apprenticed pauper children to a trade, they levied small rates for the support of maimed soldiers, they met yearly to fix wages and prices for their locality, they licensed inns and alehouses and closed places that became disorderly, and they looked to footpaths, roads, ferries, and bridges. They spent an enormous amount of time administering the poor law. The care of the poor was a heavy burden, for the country swarmed with vagrants of all kinds—some poor impotent wretches broken by age or disease, some sturdy beggars apt to be in all kinds of mischief. At the beginning of the Tudor period the government had no solution but harsh repression. Gradually it was recognized that poverty was not always the result of idleness or vice. Various statutes concerning the poor were made into a code in the Parliaments of 1597 and 1601. The law provided that each parish was responsible for its own poor, that is, for persons who had been born in the parish. Vagabonds were whipped and told to return to the parish of their birth. There they were supported in a workhouse, a place where work was provided but where the impotent poor also were lodged. The workhouse was financed by a parish rate. Officials known as overseers of the poor

Old London Bridge. Detail of an engraving by Claes Jansz Visscher, imprinted 1885. (Folger Shakespeare Library)

acted under the direction of the justices of the peace. Thus although an effort was made to cope with this serious problem, harshness and injustice remained. Each parish tried to shift as much of the burden as possible upon neighboring parishes, and justices of the peace constantly had vagrants thrust upon them for whom they did not know how to provide.

LONDON

Not knowing where else to go, many of the poor drifted to the towns, especially to London, which grew so rapidly that by the end of the reign it may have numbered 250,000 persons. The government disliked this growth, for it added to the danger of the plague and to the possibility that some fanatic might attempt the life of the queen.

There were proclamations against the erection of new houses and the crowding of poor people into tenements and slums. The worst slums were just outside the city walls, which formed a rough half circle on the north bank of the Thames. Within the walls the houses were tall, narrow, half-timbered buildings inhabited for the most part by respectable merchants, manufacturers, and tradesmen. The city was expanding in various directions: eastward down the Thames, along the main roads leading from the city, and into the area toward Westminster, that is, into Holborn and the district north of the Strand. There were many buildings in Southwark across London Bridge. Here were the Tabbard and the White Hart, inns from which travelers rode to Canterbury and Dover; theaters, the Globe and the Swan; Paris Garden, where there were bull- and bear-baitings; and for the rest a rather disreputable area.

The Thames was the heart of the city. The queen, the lord mayor, and some of the livery companies had barges that were used on state occasions; there were innumerable small boats; and thousands of watermen rowed passengers up and down the river. The river was used for pageants and processions for which there might be fireworks and music. It made London and Westminster one town. The finest houses lined its northern bank. At the eastern corner was the Tower of London, used not only as a state prison but as a mint, an arsenal, a repository for government documents, and a zoo. Along the city front were docks and markets, the Steelyard of the Hanseatic League, the Customs House, and several towers and old priories converted into fashionable apartments, the gardens of the Inns of Court. West of the city the houses of the aristocracy followed the river, their gardens running down to the water's edge. At Westminster one found the royal Palace of Whitehall, government buildings, the Parliament house, and Westminster Abbey. In the center of the city was St. Paul's, an ancient Gothic cathedral later destroyed in the great fire in 1666. Famous streets in London were Fleet, Cheapside, Cornhill, Lombard, and Leadenhall, where prosperous merchants operated their shops. The streets of London were narrow, dirty, and noisy with carts, coaches, and the cries of hucksters shouting their wares. There were famous inns: the Mitre, the Mermaid, the Dagger, the Boar's Head, and the Devil at Temple Bar, with a sign showing St. Dunstan pulling the Devil by the nose.

THE COURT

At Whitehall Palace we enter the world of the court. Elizabeth shared to the full her people's fondness for fine clothes, jewels, and costly trinkets, for music and dancing, and for riding and the chase. Even in the early years of the reign, when frugality was a necessity, foreigners were impressed with the gaiety of the court, its banquets, plays, and masques, and its water parties on the Thames. Elizabeth's suitors added to the glitter with their expensive costumes, elaborate retinues, and quaint devices, such as the bleeding hearts one admirer embroidered on the coats of all his train. Tournaments were reduced to spectacular foolery.

For the government of the court three principal officers were responsible. One was the lord chamberlain, a dignified major domo who was responsible for the section of the palace in which the queen lived. Under his supervision were special departments, such as the beds, the wardrobe, the jewel house, the sergeants at arms, the chapel, the revels, the queen's barge, and many others. He was in charge of entertainments and of ceremonial occasions. A second official was the lord steward, who supervised the purchase of provisions and the preparation of food. It is probable that two of his subordinates, the treasurer and the comptroller of the household, together with the cofferer (who was responsible for purveyance), did most of the work. They formed a little court called the Court of the Green Cloth, which settled disputes with tradesmen. Below these officials were the kitchen, the bakehouse, the pastry, the cellar, the buttery, the spicery, the chandlery, the confectionery, the laundry, the boiling house, the scullery, and many more. A third important official, the master of the horse, who was always a favorite of the queen and in constant attendance upon her, was in charge of the stables, hunting, picnics, and other outdoor activities.

The life of the court revolved around the presence chamber, the privy chamber, and the queen's withdrawing rooms. The presence chamber was open to anyone in proper attire who was entitled to appear at court. It contained a throne. Here Elizabeth received ambassadors and distinguished guests in formal interviews, and here young courtiers and country gentlemen might be presented to her. Admission to the privy chamber, on the other hand, was very difficult. Gentlemen ushers stood guard at the door. Elizabeth sat in the privy chamber with her ladies and intimate friends. Nobles and their wives normally were admitted, and great councilors came to consult with the queen. Behind the privy chamber were the queen's withdrawing rooms, where she ate and slept, surrounded by the ladies of her bedchamber and her famous maids of honor, a group of girls of good family who attended her, read to her, and entertained her with music and dancing in which she herself took part even in her later years.

The queen always desired to be seen and loved by the people. Every year she made a progress through some part of the kingdom and was received with elaborate ceremonies by towns and by members of the nobility and gentry with whom she visited. A progress was a complicated affair which required long preparation. Hundreds of carts carried the royal wardrobe and household furnishings, for the queen brought her own things with her, so that a gentleman whom she visited often need do no more than offer her his house. But doing so was thought to be cheap, and usually the queen was received in sumptuous style. There were pageants, plays, and all kinds of curious devices such as ships, goddesses, nymphs, and fairies who welcomed her with songs and dances. It was all highly artificial yet pleasing and glamorous.

THE PRIVY COUNCIL

Alongside the frivolity of the court was the serious business of government. Although the queen made decisions with the advice of a few great councilors, the Privy Council as a body did an enormous amount of administrative and judicial work.

It was composed of some twelve to twenty high officials, normally including the archbishop of Canterbury, the lord chancellor, the secretary (there were sometimes two), the lord treasurer, the chancellor of the Exchequer, the lord privy seal, the lord admiral, the lord chamberlain, the master of the horse, the chancellor of the duchy of Lancaster, the lord warden of the Cinque Ports, and perhaps a few nobles whose judgment the queen respected. The councilors, of course, held office at the pleasure of the queen. They debated questions of high policy only when she asked them to do so, and most of their work was concerned with detail. As in the latter years of the reign of Henry VIII,[3] the Council watched the operation of local government, corresponded at length with lords lieutenants, sheriffs, justices of the peace, and local councils, instructed English ambassadors abroad, and supervised the royal household. Increasingly it dealt with economic questions, with the enforcement of religious laws, with military and naval operations, with London, with Ireland, and with the poor law—no matter was too small for the Council's attention. It also heard petitions and acted as a court. All councilors, moreover, now sat as judges in the Star Chamber. The Council did not keep a record of its debates but merely of its decisions and of the enormous number of letters which it wrote in the course of business. The Council was the Crown in action, the administrative machine that controlled the work of government.

PARLIAMENT

The House of Commons in Queen Elizabeth's time grew steadily in strength and influence. The reign of Henry VIII, as he have seen, had been for the Commons a time of training in the art of legislation and a period of growing self-confidence. In the reign of Elizabeth they became far more aggressive and independent. They assumed that they had a recognized place in the counsels of the nation, they were developing parliamentary procedures and making their privileges realities, and they were much more in the public eye. Resenting manipulation by the Crown, they criticized royal policy with surprising freedom.

The Tudor conception of the role of the Commons was very conservative. Henry had believed that the Commons should do three things: vote taxes as the need arose; pass or reject the legislation proposed by the Crown; and give advice to the sovereign, though only when requested. Elizabeth held similar views. Members were told in 1593 that they might "say yes or no to bills; but they were not to speak of all causes as they listed or to frame a form of religion or a state of government as to their idle brains seemed meetest. No king fit for his state would suffer such absurdities."[4] The Commons were thus to play a negative and advis-

---

[3]See page 247.
[4]This is a slight modification of a document quoted in J. E. Neale, *Elizabeth I and Her Parliaments 1584–1601* (London: J. Cape, 1957), p. 249.

ory role; they were not to initiate policy; and there were high matters of state—religion, the queen's marriage, the succession—with which they should not meddle.

Henry had manipulated Parliament, and so did Elizabeth, though she acted with more finesse than her father had shown. Much of this manipulation was justified. The Commons met only occasionally[5] and possessed little organization. Because members were apt to wrangle and to criticize the government in an irresponsible way some leadership was necessary. It was supplied by the privy councilors who were members of the Commons. Clustered in a group close to the speaker, these men formed a kind of ministerial bench and were, in fact, the leaders of the Commons. They introduced the most important laws, they guided the course of debate, they made clear the need for subsidies, they answered criticism of the government, they were members of almost all committees, and they formed a breakwater against the demands of the Commons for more liberty in the house and for less autocratic rule in church and state. The councilors were supported by a group of lesser officials who held some place in the government or in the royal household.

The speaker was important. Elected in theory by the Commons, he was in reality a nominee of the queen from whom he received his fees and other rewards. He was not the impartial moderator of modern times but a servant of the Crown, eager to promote the business desired by the ruler. The primitive state of parliamentary procedure gave him great power: he could determine the order of business; he worded the questions on which the Commons voted; and since most votes were decided by a shout of "Aye" or "No," it was the speaker who declared whether a question had been carried. He and the privy councilors could hold whispered consultations, take part in naming the members of committees, give the floor, stop a debate, and even adjourn the house for the day. Elizabeth preferred to remain in the background, leaving the details of parliamentary management to her ministers, but when she did intervene she did so with skill and vigor in speeches that were models of persuasion and eloquence. Her regal bearing and tactful management, her alternation of gracious affability and tart reproof created in her subjects a loyalty tinged with awe. Her success in dealing with the Commons was due in no small part to her unique and masterful personality.

Elizabeth was not unopposed in her manipulation of the Commons. A principal source of opposition was the growing strength of the country gentlemen who, as a class, were becoming the most influential in the kingdom. They found a seat in Parliament most attractive as a symbol of local as well as national importance. As they crowded into the House of Commons they added greatly to its wealth, its talent, and its social standing. An astonishing number of the important people of Elizabethan England sat in the House of Commons. Such a body—so self-assured, aggressive, talkative, sophisticated, and elite—could not be excluded from a larger part in shaping the national destiny.

As in the Middle Ages, the Commons were divided into knights of the shire

---

[5]There were ten Parliaments in Elizabeth's reign, meeting in thirteen sessions.

and burgesses of the towns. The number of knights remained constant at 90 during the reign of Elizabeth. But the number of burgesses steadily grew larger throughout the Tudor period. There were 224 borough members in the first Parliament of Henry VIII; 308 in the first Parliament of Elizabeth; 372 in her last (when knights and burgesses together totaled 462). It was the prerogative of the Crown to grant a city or a borough the right to return members, and the Tudors were lavish with such grants. If the boroughs, new and old, had always returned their own citizens, there would have been about four burgesses in the Commons to every country gentleman representing a shire. Actually, the proportion was reversed; there were about four members of the gentry to every burgess. Members did not have to reside in the constituencies they represented. As a result the gentry pushed into the seats of towns and cities. It has been estimated that in the Parliament of 1584, for example, there were about 240 country gentlemen, about 75 officials, about 53 practicing lawyers, and about the same number of townsmen.

Another source of opposition to Elizabeth in the Commons was the rise of Puritanism. The Puritans, as we have seen, attempted to modify the Church of England through legislative action. Their campaign deeply annoyed Elizabeth, who did not hesitate to strike back. Her methods of vengeance raised questions of parliamentary privilege.

Despite these differences and tensions there was an essential harmony between Elizabeth and the House of Commons. Scholars across the generations have disagreed as to whether Elizabeth or her ministers were responsible for the final decisions. Most agree, however, that the reign of Elizabeth was largely a successful one. Her parliament shared with her a common purpose of promoting England's safety and welfare. The Commons' veneration for their heroic sovereign grew with the years. They loved her for the dangers she had passed. That she also loved them was clear throughout her reign and showed brightly in the words with which she bade them a last farewell in 1601: "Though God hath raised me high, yet this I count the glory of my crown, that I have reigned with your loves . . . It is not my desire to live or reign longer than my life and reign shall be for your good. And though you have had, and may have, many mightier and wiser princes sitting in this seat, yet you never had, nor shall have, any that will love you better."

Elizabethan England, or perhaps one should say Tudor England, has been regarded as one of those remarkable ages which occur seemingly at random, in one place or another, in one century or another. The Golden Age of Greece, the Rome of Caesar and the *Pax Romana,* the Florentine Renaissance, all were among the company Elizabethan England kept. Despite the great intellectual and artistic appeal of these great ages for us today, we must remember that life for most people consisted of exhausting labor and few intermittent pleasures. The Church, or at least the great cathedrals, provided the only places and occasions where the great cultural attainments of the elite were shared with all classes and conditions of people. The role played by the Church did not pass through the next century unchallenged.

CHRONOLOGY

Elizabethan England

1563	Foxe's *Book of Martyrs*
1574	Actors company formed; theaters built
1578–80	John Lyly publishes *Euphues*
1588–97	War with Spain
1589–96	Edmund Spenser and the *Faerie Queene*
1590	*Arcadia* by Sir Philip Sidney
1590s	Rivalry of Robert Cecil and earl of Essex
1592	Christopher Marlowe, author of *Doctor Faustus*, is killed.
1592–1600	William Shakespeare writes histories, *Romeo and Juliet*, and *A Midsummer Night's Dream*
1595–1601	Ulster Rebellion; Ireland conquered
1600	East India Company chartered
1601	Death of Essex; triumph of Cecil; Elizabethan Poor Law
1601–1608	Shakespeare's *Hamlet, Othello, King Lear, Macbeth*
1608–1616	*The Tempest, The Winter's Tale;* death of Shakespeare

16 James I: The Prerogative Challenged

For over a century the Tudors had taught their subjects that loyalty to the Crown was the greatest of virtues and disloyalty the blackest of crimes. Yet forty years after Elizabeth's death a large proportion of the people took up arms against the king in the English Civil War. What were the causes of this astounding turn of events? The search for these causes has dominated, if not bedeviled, the work of historians in recent decades, with little more than exhaustion to show for their efforts. Historians have often assumed in an uncritical way that the fault lay entirely with the luckless Stuart sovereigns, James I (1603–1625) and his son, Charles I (1625–1649). The Stuarts, it must be admitted, were inept rulers. But it should be remembered that Elizabeth, despite the glories of her reign, left problems of the most serious kind to her successors. Her religious settlement, wise as it was, satisfied neither Roman Catholics nor Puritans. Parliament, grown more aggressive, more loquacious, and more difficult to manage, was reaching for control of policy. If that control were obtained, the Commons and not the king would be supreme. Elizabeth left public finance in an unstable condition. With all her parsimony she had done no more than make ends meet; the growing cost of government in a time of inflation was certain to be a thorny question. Public virtue had declined, while corruption in the government was on the increase. Even relations with foreign states were not as satisfactory as they appeared. It is true that Spain was a defeated power in 1603, but Catholicism was regaining strength throughout Europe. If Spain improved her international position, the outlook for England might darken. And meanwhile, as the war with Spain had dragged on, Elizabeth's relations with the Dutch and with Henry IV of France had grown cooler. It is not surprising that James I was unable to deal with these problems successfully. That he may be held responsible for civil war in 1642 is another question.

THE BRITISH SOLOMON

James's character contained so many contradictions that it is not easy to describe him in a few words. His councilors admired the ease and rapidity with which he comprehended business and made his decisions. He had a good memory and more than a touch of native shrewdness. James was a learned man, fond of study, especially in the area of theology. Hating war and violence, James hoped to keep England at peace; indeed, to bring peace to all of Europe. His desire was to rule well and to be good to the Church of England. An affectionate man, he wanted to be on terms of friendly intimacy with those about him. He could be jovial, witty, kindly, and good-natured.

After his death certain scandalous writers, hoping to please the Puritans, described him as a ridiculous person, a buffoon in purple, an impossible pedant without dignity or judgment. While such an interpretation was superficial it is true that his good qualities were rendered all but useless by grave defects in his character. He was astonishingly vain. No flattery was too gross, no praise too extreme for his taste. He held a lofty opinion of his own wisdom, delighting in being compared with Solomon. In his more exalted moments he felt a celestial proximity to Heaven, as though he and the Deity had much in common. He was lazy and self-indulgent, lacking in control of his emotions and given to bursts of temper. Although he was determined to dictate policy, the drudgery of daily attention to the details of government was repugnant to him, and he left it to his councilors.

Disliking London, he much preferred a country life, partly to escape the press of business, partly to indulge his love of hunting, partly to retire with his boon companions to some distant palace or country house where he could be jovial, intimate, careless, idle, and debauched. He lingered in the country for weeks at a time, at his "paradise of pleasure," when his presence was urgently needed in London. This bold hunter was normally quite timid, apprehensive, and constantly fearful of danger and of assassination. He wore heavy padded clothes which would resist the sudden thrust of a dagger. James was also very extravagant, and lacked Elizabeth's ability to scrutinize the whole fabric of public finance. Any money that came into his hands was regarded as a windfall to be squandered at once. He also lacked her power to command. "When he wishes to speak like a king," wrote Tillières, the French Ambassador, "he rails like a tyrant and when he wishes to yield he does so with indecency."

James's Scottish Background

James's training and experience as a Scottish king did not fit him to solve the difficulties left by Elizabeth. Placed on the Scottish throne as an infant, he was for many years a helpless pawn in the hands of the Scottish nobility. He lived in constant danger of capture by rival bands of nobles who wished to control the government, and especially by the wild young earl of Bothwell. Bothwell's constant misbehavior

James VI and I, artist unknown. (National Galleries of Scotland, Edinburgh)

had gradually reduced him to the life of an outlaw, but he had the notion that he could recoup his fortunes if only he could obtain possession of the king. At the same time a group of northern earls, Catholic in religion and pro-Spanish in politics, plotted and rebelled against him. The Scottish nobles did not regard the king as a sovereign lord but rather as a feudal suzerain against whom revolt was no great crime. They were themselves little kings in their own districts, combining the authority of feudal chieftains, landlords, magistrates, and heads of clans. They could raise the whole countryside against the government. In trying to suppress them James had little assistance from the weak middle class. He had to build his own power, as Henry VII had done in England. Scotland could only be ruled by tyranny—but tyranny was an evil heritage for a future king of England.

James also had to contend with the strident claims of the Scottish Kirk. John Knox, the leader of the Scottish Reformation, proclaimed that the laws of God should rule the state. Kings who fought against God, that is, kings who opposed the Kirk, should be brushed aside. Andrew Melville, who led the Kirk in James's reign, molded the theocracy of Knox into the famous doctrine of the two kingdoms. Melville made a distinction between the civil power of the king, to be exercised in temporal affairs, and the spiritual power of the Kirk, to have jurisdiction in matters of religion. The spiritual power, Melville contended, flowed directly from God to his Kirk; thus the ministers ruled the Kirk by divine right of the most immediate kind. The king was to have no share in ecclesiastical affairs. But although the independence of the Kirk was inviolable, the independence of the state was not. God spoke through his clergy, and to God's word the king should render obedience. As a matter of fact, the ministers interfered constantly in the temporal affairs of the state. Had they had their way, they would have dictated to James on all occasions. They denounced and bullied him brutally; in return he hated and loathed them. This was poor training for a king who would have to deal with the English Puritans.

In combating the pretensions of the ministers and the lawlessness of the nobility, James adopted a theory of government known as the divine right of kings. He did not originate it, but he became its ardent advocate, dwelling upon it constantly in his speeches and writing a concise and lucid description of it in 1598, *The Trew Law of Free Monarchies*. According to this theory, kings were placed on their thrones by God. Many passages in the Scriptures could be cited in support of this belief, especially those in the Old Testament in which the Israelites begged God to send them a king. God made kings, and only God could unmake them. It was God's decree that subjects obey their king, offer no resistance, and refrain from criticism, even in secret thought. Evil kings as well as good ones came from God; the only recourse of the people lay in prayers and sobs to Heaven.

James also employed history to reinforce his argument. King Fergus I, coming out of Ireland, had conquered Scotland (according to the version of Scottish history held in James's reign), and William I had conquered England. These rulers, James argued, had acquired rights in their kingdoms which amounted to absolute ownership. Absolute ownership brought absolute power. As the king was overlord of the whole land, "so was he master over every person that inhabiteth the same, having power over the life and death of every one of them." James drew an analogy from feudalism, giving the king as lord of the kingdom all the rights a feudal baron held over his fief. In a word, the king was above the law, above the church, above the Parliament. Such views were not likely to commend themselves to the English House of Commons.

During James's last years in Scotland he made surprising progress in translating his theory into fact. He dealt the nobility shrewd blows. He drove Bothwell into exile and forced the northern earls to take temporary refuge on the Continent. He imposed bishops upon the Kirk. With the aid of his able adviser, John Maitland of Thirlestane, he created a strong and loyal bureaucracy which could be trusted to govern the country in his interest. The Scottish Parliament was subject to his will. His methods, however, were those of a despot.

There were other ways in which his rule in Scotland was an unfortunate preparation for his rule in England. Early in life, under the guidance of bad advisers, he learned to intrigue with every foreign power from which he thought he might derive some benefit. He gave Elizabeth protestations of friendship but at the same time courted the good will of her enemies. In his desire to obtain the English succession he sent secret envoys to Catholic rulers, hoping to win their approval or at least to blunt their hostility. He gave them the impression that he was not unfriendly to Catholicism and, indeed, that his conversion was not to be despaired of. He conveyed the same impression to the pope. Thus he offered a secret hand of friendship to the Catholic world and was in touch with Elizabeth's foes. At the same time he secretly courted the English Puritans; yet he posed in public as the champion of the Church of England. Such scattered insinuations and contradictory half promises were certain to cause future trouble. Finally, his training in finance was very bad. A starveling prince, his poverty in Scotland was excruciating. He learned to try any dodge, however low, which offered hope of a little cash. He borrowed from his councilors and asked them to employ their private credit in his behalf. He was careless about money, in part because he never had any to be careful of.

THE RELIGIOUS SETTLEMENT

The Puritans

In Scotland James had been content with the simple ritual of the Presbyterian Kirk, but in England he became an ardent supporter of Elizabeth's church. He liked its ceremonies, partly no doubt for themselves, partly because they stressed the divinity of kings. He liked the upper clergy, many of whom were his personal friends. Above all, he liked a church which was under the firm control of bishops and of which he was the acknowledged head.

He sympathized with a movement which may be referred to as Anglican, though described in his day as anti-Calvinist, anti-predestination, or Arminian.[1] Refusing to consider the church as a political compromise, a convenient halfway house between Rome and Geneva, the Anglicans sought a more convincing foundation. Turning to the primitive church during the first five centuries of the Christian era before the rise of the medieval papacy, they studied early creeds and councils and the writings of the early fathers and reached the conclusion that the Church of England, as reformed in the sixteenth century, was the true descendant of primitive Christianity. They regarded the church of Rome as one which had fallen into error but which nonetheless had preserved in medieval times the primitive truths and godly ceremonies of the early church. Anglicanism was a conservative reaction against the rigidity of the Puritans. Its outlook was broader, more moderate, and more humane. Unfortunately its theoretical advantage was lessened by its practice. Closely allied with the king, it did not criticize the vice and corruption of the court. It was ready to strike at humble folk who were Puritans but was strangely complacent about the errors and wickedness of the great.

While James was on his journey from Scotland, he was presented with the

---

[1] Arminius was a Dutch professor of theology who rejected the doctrine of predestination.

James I attending a sermon at St. Paul's Cross. 17th century panel painting. (Society of Antiquaries)

Millenary Petition, signed, it was said, by one thousand Puritan clergymen. The petitioners asked for discontinuance of the use of the sign of the cross in baptism, of the ring in marriage, of the terms "priest" and "absolution." They wished the rite of confirmation abolished, the wearing of the surplice made optional, and the length of the service and the amount of choral singing curtailed. They asked also for a more learned ministry, for an end to pluralities and nonresidence, for reform of the ecclesiastical courts, and for stricter observance of the Sabbath. The king reserved judgment, but he agreed to hold a conference between Puritans and Anglicans. In January 1604 this conference took place at Hampton Court. Surrounded by his bishops and councilors, James admitted a delegation of four leading Puritans and asked them what alterations they desired in the church. In addition to the points of the Millenary Petition, they asked that the doctrine of predestination be more fully recognized, that the clergy be permitted to administer Communion without subscribing to the full doctrine of the church concerning it, that there be a new translation of the Bible,[2] and that the Apocryphal books should not be read in church. As these

---

[2]The new translation, the King James Bible, was published in 1611.

points were made they were interrupted and scoffed at by the bishops, and James grew irritable.

It was then that Dr. Rainolds, the principal Puritan spokesman, used the unfortunate word "presbytery," which made the king believe that the Puritans were Presbyterians. He turned upon them in fury. A Scottish presbytery, he cried, "as well agreeth with a monarchy as God and the Devil. . . . Stay, I pray you, for one seven years before you demand that of me; and if you find me pursy and fat and my windpipes stuffed I will perhaps hearken unto you. For let that government be one up . . . we shall all have work enough, both our hands full. But, Dr. Rainolds, till you find I grow lazy, let that alone. . . . No bishop, no king. When I mean to live under a presbytery I will go into Scotland again, but while I am in England I will have bishops to govern the Church." As for the Puritans, "I will make them conform themselves or I will harry them out of this land." And so the abashed Puritans in their black gowns hastened from the court of Solomon.

James was much pleased with his part in the conference. In truth, he had done great harm. He had first encouraged the Puritans, called them to argue a case that was already decided against them, and then treated them with scorn and contempt. Clergymen who would not conform to the regulations of the church now were deprived of their livings or suspended from them. The Puritans claimed that some three hundred ministers were thus removed, but the church placed those deprived at fifty. Recent research has raised that number to about ninety. There was no further attack on the Puritans during the reign, though James's Declaration of Sports in 1618, permitting games and dancing after church on Sundays, was highly offensive to them. Drawing together into a hard core of opposition, they found much to criticize in James's government, and they were strongly supported by the House of Commons. A few refused to conform at all. A little congregation in the town of Scrooby in Nottinghamshire fled with their ejected ministers to Holland; from there in 1620 they sailed in the *Mayflower* to America. It was thus that the Pilgrims came to New England.

The Catholics

James was more enlightened and more tolerant in dealing with the English Roman Catholics than with the Puritans. He feared and distrusted Roman priests, especially Jesuits, but he distinguished between them and the laity for whom he had much sympathy and to whom he hoped to give a restricted toleration. He was, he said, opposed to persecution; on the other hand, he could not permit the number of Catholics to increase. He therefore asked two things of them: first, that they be loyal subjects, and second, that as a token of outward conformity and obedience they attend the services of the Church of England. In return he would allow the savage penal code of Elizabeth, with its heavy fines, to remain in abeyance. For about a year and a half the fines were not levied, and the king was on his way to toleration.

James found his policy of toleration difficult to maintain. It was strongly opposed by the Anglican bishops, his councilors, and his judges. Queen Anne, who was a

Catholic, favored her coreligionists in an irritating way. Pope Clement VII, deceived by James's hints before 1603, believed James was about to become a Catholic. There was a suspicion that Sir Walter Ralegh and his follower Lord Cobham were plotting with the ambassador from the Spanish Netherlands to place James's cousin Arabella Stuart on the throne. As a result of these irritations, James turned back to the Elizabethan code in February 1605.

The Gunpowder Plot of November 1605 was the result of James's broken promises to the Catholic world. It seems to have originated in the mind of Robert Catesby as early as 1603. Catesby was a Roman Catholic gentleman who had been active in many Catholic enterprises. By May 1604 he had confided his plan to four men, including his friend Thomas Percy, a relative of the earl of Northumberland, and Guy Fawkes, a soldier of great toughness of character brought over from the Spanish Netherlands. The plot involved placing barrels of gunpowder under the Parliament house and, at the opening of the next session of Parliament, to blow up the king, the queen, and Prince Henry, bishops, nobles, councilors, judges, knights, and burgesses—all in one thunderclap. The conspirators rented a house which had a cellar running under the Parliament building. Into this cellar Guy Fawkes carried some twenty barrels of gunpowder, placed iron bars upon them to increase the impact of the explosion, and laid over all a covering of faggots. The conspirators, however, ran out of funds and were forced to confide their secret to a number of people. One of these was Francis Tresham, who betrayed the plot. He wrote his brother-in-law, Lord Monteagle, to stay away from Parliament on the appointed day, and Monteagle took the letter to the government. It was not until late at night, on the eve of the meeting of Parliament, that Guy Fawkes was discovered keeping watch over the gunpowder.

The Gunpowder Plot made a tremendous impression on the men of the time. Parliament passed stricter laws against Catholics. Although James was thoroughly terrified he tried to salvage something of his program of toleration. He devised a new oath, the Oath of Allegiance, which could be offered to Catholics. It was thought that loyal ones would take this oath, whereas those who were disloyal would not. The oath, in fact, made this distinction rather neatly. James soon returned to a policy of remitting the penal fines for Catholics who were willing to take the oath. After 1614, as we shall see, his diplomacy drew him closer to Spain, and Spain demanded that the English Catholics be treated well. Hence in the later years of the reign they were better off than might have been expected.

THE PARLIAMENT OF 1604–1610

The great constitutional issue of the Stuart period was the clash of king and Parliament; in fact, the entire history of the seventeenth century was to revolve about this theme.[3] The quarrel began with surprising suddenness after James's accession. A ruler who paraded the divine right of kings and a Parliament intent upon

---

[3] The seventeenth century has been called "the Century of Revolution" by historian Christopher Hill.

increasing its control of policy were certain to come to blows. James's government brought evils the Commons were not slow to point out. Redress of grievances became their constant cry, but grievances meant more than new abuses. Under a ruler for whom the Commons felt no affection, as they had felt affection for Elizabeth, many aspects of government that had been tolerated before 1603 now seemed outmoded and insufferable. For some the time had come for reform. But reforms often involved a lessening of royal authority or royal revenues. As James saw it, the Commons were demanding a fundamental change that would shift power from the king to themselves: they were grasping at control of the executive. Naturally the king fought back, and thus the question of sovereignty became a major issue. Where did ultimate authority lie? And where should disputes be settled if neither the king nor Parliament would yield? The constitutional prinicple of the sovereignty of "king-in-parliament" worked only when the two would or could work in cooperation. If one or the other stubbornly refused, the path to follow was less clear.

James knew little about the English Parliament. He knew only the Paliament of Scotland which, for all its age, was a weak and primitive body that could easily be manipulated. In dealing with the English House of Commons James committed many blunders. He made too many speeches, sent too many messages, often couched in a scolding and didactic tone, and was much too quick to interfere in parliamentary business. This interference not only irritated the Commons but disturbed those avenues of influence still open to the Crown. James's principal minister, Robert Cecil, soon to be earl of Salisbury, had managed the parliamentary business of the Crown during Elizabeth's last years. He continued to do so in the new reign, though he worked under disadvantages. Now a member of the House of Lords, he could speak to the Commons only when committees from both houses met in conference. He could make use of the speaker as well as a group of officials and courtiers in the Commons, of whom the most able was Sir Francis Bacon. But Bacon was not a councilor; in fact, the number of councilors in the Commons was very small, and hence the Crown was not as well represented in the lower house as it had been under Elizabeth. Rather strangely, Salisbury had not attempted to influence elections in 1604; he could compensate for his error only by managing by-elections as the Parliament progressed. Above all, he was frustrated by the constant meddling of the king, who followed events in Parliament closely, day by day and even hour by hour, in order to send his principal minister detailed—and misguided and disturbing—instructions.

A quarrel arose as soon as Parliament met in 1604. Two men, Sir Francis Goodwin and Sir John Fortescue, claimed to have been elected to the same seat in the Commons. Where was this question to be settled? James announced that since the writs summoning Parliament had been issued by the Chancery, the Chancery had the right, if it suspected irregularity, to issue a writ for a new election. This had been the Tudor practice. But the Commons demanded the right to settle election disputes, and they promptly declared that Goodwin had won the seat in question. James asked them to confer with the Lords. The Commons refused, claiming the Lords had nothing to do with the question. Somewhat taken aback, the king told the Commons to confer with the judges and then report their findings to the Privy Council. Again the Commons refused.

James then sent them a peremptory message, commanding "as an absolute king that there might be a conference between the House and the judges," he and his councilors to be present. The Commons were astonished but decided to give way. "The prince's command is like a thunderbolt," said a member, "his command upon our allegiance like the roaring of a lion. To his command there is no contradiction." Fortunately the conference went well. James suggested a compromise: that the election of both Goodwin and Fortescue be voided, that neither stand again for the seat in question, and that a new election be held. The Commons agreed. James was delighted with his own graciousness and wisdom. But the Commons had won, for thereafter they settled election disputes without challenge. James had lost much and gained nothing.

The Commons then turned to grievances. They debated purveyance, the right of the monarch to live off the country as he traveled about. The difficulty was that James traveled a great deal and allowed his purveyors to exceed their rights. The Commons also objected to the court of wards, a court set up by Henry VIII that administered the estates of minors who were wards of the king. Wardship was undoubtedly the source of great abuse. The Commons further showed much sympathy for the Puritans, especially for the "silenced brethren" who had been ejected from their churches. When James wished to assume the style of king of Great Britain, the Commons refused their consent. They also declined to vote new taxes, since payments still were due from taxes voted to Elizabeth. At the end of the session the Commons drew up a famous document, the Apology of 1604. It was a bold declaration of right, a lecture to a foreign king upon the constitution of his new kingdom. An important point concerned the origin of parliamentary privilege. In the case of *Goodwin v. Fortescue* James had declared that the Commons "derived all matters of privilege from him and by his grant," but the Apology asserted that parliamentary privileges were the right and inheritance of the Commons—no less than their lands and goods—and did not spring from royal grace. Surveying the events of the session, the Commons justified their actions at every turn, and added a statement that the king could not alter laws on religion without their consent. James replied with a scolding speech, and so the session ended.

The parliamentary session of 1606–1607 was devoted largely to the question of closer union between England and Scotland. The two kingdoms, of course, now had the same ruler but otherwise were distinct and independent. It was James's noble ambition to draw them together into a perfect union. He would have one kingdom with one king, one faith, one language, one people alike in manners and allegiance. The names of England and Scotland should disappear in the name of Britain, the border should be erased and become the middle shires, the Englishman and the Scot should love one another as brothers. But James was in too much of a hurry. He forgot the long and mutual hostility of the two nations. Unfortunately he had brought with him to England a large number of Scots to whom he had been excessively generous, thus arousing the jealousy of the English courtiers. It is not surprising that his proposals were coldly received by the English House of Commons.

In 1606 James proposed four preliminary steps to union: the repeal of hostile laws, that is, laws of each country aimed at the other; mutual naturalization; a commercial treaty looking toward free trade; and improvement of justice along the border. The hostile laws were repealed without question, but the rest of the program met with intense opposition. A commercial treaty was completely refused, and the measures for border justice were reduced significantly. Debates on naturalization were long and interesting, but the Commons declined to naturalize the Scots unless English law was imposed on Scotland. The king grew angry, and the session ended with little accomplished. In the next year, 1608, James obtained from the English judges a decision that Scots born after the union of the Crowns were citizens of both kingdoms. The judges were unanimous in determining the status of the *post-nati* in Calvin's case. Even Sir Edward Coke supported this victory for the royal prerogative.

A major crisis developed in the parliamentary sessions of 1610. Debate revolved about the fundamental questions of the royal prerogative and the royal finance. The prerogative—that sovereign power inherent in the king to act on his own authority—had been brought to the fore by a number of issues. There had been a feud between the courts of the church, especially the Court of High Commission, supported by the combative archbishop of Canterbury, Richard Bancroft, and the courts of common law, supported by the famous judge, Sir Edward Coke, who loved the common law and became its champion against the church courts and against the royal theory of divine right. In defense of the common law Coke could be the most obstinate and difficult of men. On more than one occasion, when the king stormed at him, he fell upon his knees; yet even in that position he clung to his opinions.

A dispute arose about an ancient writ, the writ of prohibition, through which the common-law judges exercised considerable control over the courts of the church. This writ halted proceedings in any ecclesiastical court until the judges were satisfied that the matter in dispute fell properly within the jurisdiction of that court. In 1605 Archbishop Bancroft appealed to the king against the writ of prohibition. All judicial authority, he argued, began in the Crown and flowed in two streams, the temporal jurisdiction to the courts of common law, and the spiritual to the courts of the church. The two systems were on an equality, the writ of prohibition should be ended, and the king should decide disputes between the two jurisdictions. But Coke answered sharply that the writ of prohibition was a part of the law, and the law could be altered only by Parliament. Two years later Bancroft asserted that the king, as supreme judge, should hear and decide doubtful cases. "To which it was answered by me," wrote Coke, "that the king in his own person cannot adjudge any case, but this ought to be determined and adjudged in some court of justice. . . . "

The prerogative was connected closely with the question of finance. James had been living far beyond his means and had run deeply into debt. In 1608 he appointed Salisbury lord treasurer. Salisbury found that he could not lessen expenditure; he could inly increase the revenue, as he did substantially. Among other expedients he levied impositions, that is, customs duties over and above the normal schedule of tonnage and poundage authorized by Parliament. It was a dangerous experiment, for the Commons were certain to object. But Salisbury had a legal decision in his favor. In 1606 a merchant named Bate, who imported currants from the Levant, had refused to pay impositions and had been tried in the Court of Exchequer. The decision was that, since the prerogative included the regulation of commerce and

Robert Cecil, Earl of Salisbury, attributed to J. de Critz, 1602. (National Portrait Gallery, London)

since impositions formed part of that regulation, the duties were legal though they had not been voted by Parliament.

The sessions of 1610 were stormy ones. The Commons insisted on discussing grievances. In a long and important debate on impositions the Commons asserted firmly that these levies were illegal unless they were granted by Parliament. Other aspects of the prerogative came under attack: the Court of High Commission, the use of proclamations to modify law, and the jurisdiction of the council of Wales over certain English shires. In July a petition of grievances was presented to the king. It was so long, said James, that he thought he might use it for a tapestry.

Meanwhile Salisbury, who was striving to extract money from the Commons, proposed that in addition to a grant of the customary kind, though of unusual size, the Commons should vote the king a permanent revenue. In return Salisbury offered that the king would abandon purveyance and most of his feudal rights, including wardship. This bargain known as the Great Contract was tentatively approved in July of 1610, but by autumn both sides wished to end it, to Salisbury's infinite sorrow. James dissolved his first Parliament in anger early in 1611.

THE PARLIAMENT OF 1614

James's first Parliament had lasted for seven years; his second, for two months. Impelled by his abject poverty, he very reluctantly summoned Parliament again in 1614. The debt was high, bills were unpaid, and future revenues were anticipated. The decay in public finance had turned to dead rot. When James faced the Commons he tried to be conciliatory and he offered a number of small concessions. Brushing aside these concessions rather impolitely, the Commons turned to more fundamental grievances. They began by a searching inquiry into the recent elections, for they had heard that a group of courtiers had plotted to influence elections on a large scale in return for promises of office. This rumor was false, and the Commons found little to complain of. Nonetheless, they expelled a privy councilor, Sir Thomas Parry, for corrupt electioneering practices, and questioned the right of the Attorney General, Bacon, to sit in the Commons.

It was clear that the Commons would debate grievances thoroughly before they turned to supply. When they took up the delicate matter of impositions, the debate grew heated. They asked the House of Lords for a conference on impositions, but the Lords refused. One bishop in the Lords made such a violent attack on the lower house that the Commons resolved to conduct no business until they received satisfaction. This sullen resolve annoyed the king, who warned them he would dissolve the Parliament if they did not vote supply. The Commons stood their ground; so did James. The Parliament was dissolved after a session of two months without passing a single bill. The king was furious: the Commons had rejected his proffered love, had assailed his prerogative, and had spoken irreverently of kings. Perhaps they sought his life. One member foolishly spoke as though there might be a massacre of the Scots in London. Thereafter, James was through with Parliaments. If he had had his way, there would have been no more Parliaments in England.

DEGENERATION IN GOVERNMENT

For the next seven years, from 1614 to 1621, James ruled without a Parliament. Unfortunately these were years of failure, of scandal, and of increasing difficulties both at home and abroad. The efficiency and the standards of government degenerated. During the first decade of the reign the king's chief minister had been Robert Cecil, Earl of Salisbury, who, as principal secretary, master of the court of wards, and lord treasurer, had been the pivot about which the entire administration revolved. If he was not a great man, he at least came close to greatness. His solid judgment and steady nerve, his prudence, sagacity, and self-control, and his tremendous industry kept affairs on an even keel and continued Tudor ideals of government in the first years of the Stuart period. Amid endless routine he did not lose sight of larger objectives. He was a man of wit and liveliness, a spirited writer and speaker, a cultured gentleman who could be warm and generous in friendship. But after his death in 1612, government fell into weaker hands.

The Howards

Several members of the Howard family became important. Henry Howard, Earl of Northampton, a man greatly trusted by James, was a worthless, self-seeking, and crafty courtier. His intense jealousy led him to dislike his colleagues. His Catholicism was only half-concealed, and he stood constantly for leniency to Catholics, severity to Puritans, alliance with Spain, and an end to Parliaments. He died in 1614. His nephew Thomas Howard, Earl of Suffolk, later lord treasurer, was a brave sailor and a loyal subject, but he was lax and easygoing, and had small strength of character. A distant cousin, Charles Howard, Earl of Nottingham, had commanded the English fleet against the Armada. He continued to be lord admiral in James's reign, but as he grew old he permitted the navy to fall into decay. Against the Howards there arose a party of opposition: Lord Chancellor Ellesmere, very Protestant and anti-Spanish; Archbishop Abbot; and William Herbert, Earl of Pembroke, the richest peer in England. The rivalries of these two factions dominated politics for many years.

George Villiers, Later Duke of Buckingham

A new favorite arose at court. This was George Villiers, a handsome young man who caught the fancy of the king in 1614. Villiers was to have a remarkable career. By 1617, when he was only twenty-five, he had become the master of the horse, a knight of the garter, earl of Buckingham, and a member of the Privy Council. He was private secretary and boon companion of the king, the channel through which suits and requests for patronage came to the ruler. He did not at first aspire to dominate policy. Rather, he gloried in his control of patronage, for this was the highest ambition of the courtier. Great men and small paid homage to him, the king foremost among his worshipers. It is small wonder that his head was turned, that he became vain, willful and arrogant, easily offended by opposition, and determined to have his way.

His rise to power brought many evils. He and his extortionate mother, Lady Compton, developed a system of spoliation and blackmail; they used Buckingham's influence with the king to extract money from all aspirants to office. But in his pride and egotism, Buckingham went further. Those who attained a place in the government must do more than pay for it: they must acknowledge their subservience to him. The ministers of state must be his creatures, swelling the crowd of his hangers-on and making the world aware of their dependence. Deviation from his wishes meant loss of office, and his path became strewn with men whom he first advanced and later ruined. His ascendancy increased the debauchery at court, where the king often was intoxicated at his jovial suppers.

In 1618 Buckingham was able to drive from office the Howards, who had always

Inigo Jones, the architect. Portrait sketch by Anthony Van Dycke. (Trustee of the Chatsworth Settlement)

been hostile to him as an upstart. The year 1618 was one of great financial difficulty. The fiscal picture became so dark and the means of raising money so shameful—such as the sale of peerages—that even James knew something must be done. A movement for reform began. Joining this movement, Buckingham found in Lionel Cranfield a man willing to do the required work. Cranfield, a successful merchant and capitalist, had become a financial adviser of the government and was later to attain high office. In 1618, with Buckingham's backing, he investigated many departments—including the Treasury over which Suffolk presided—and showed many ways in which the king could save money. His investigations produced a struggle between Buckingham and the Howards. It was easy to show that Suffolk had mismanaged money and was probably corrupt. He was tried for embezzlement of funds, found guilty, and dismissed from office. Nottingham, the ancient lord admiral, was induced to resign without a trial, and his office was given to Buckingham. As other Howards fell in rapid succession Buckingham was left supreme. Although a few great personages at court owed him nothing, the majority of officials now received their places from him and were dependent on his good will. His appointments were not all bad. He tended to give office to devoted and efficient bureaucrats who would do as they were told; and he developed skill in obtaining work from these officials. But he and the king made all the important decisions.

The King and the Judges

Early in the reign, as we have seen, the king had clashed with the great lawyer, Sir Edward Coke. The points at issue had been fundamental: the rivalry of the courts of common law with the extralegal or prerogative courts; and the relation of the Crown to the common law. Several important cases between 1610 and 1616 underscored these issues and pointed to new ones: in 1610, in one such case, Coke delivered a clear and important opinion concerning royal proclamations, which had been increasing during James's reign. The king, said Coke, could not add to existing law or create new offenses by proclamation. He could issue proclamations only to admonish his subjects that certain laws existed and must be obeyed. In another, the Bonham Case, Coke made an unsuccessful effort to introduce the principle of judicial review. He held that "when an act of Parliament is against common right and reason or repugnant or impossible to be performed, the common law will control it and adjudge such act to be void." He would thus have allowed the judges to decide whether an act of Parliament was or was not to be enforced. This principle, so important in American history, was never established in England.

In *Courtney v. Glanvil* (1615) Coke made a crude attack upon the court of chancery, arguing that once a case had been decided in the common-law courts that case could not be reopened in the chancery. James, who regarded it as a court under his special protection, was highly irritated, and his anger was increased by two other cases which involved another principle—the independence to the bench. The Peacham Case (1615) concerned a soured and broken clergyman, Edmund Peacham, who secretly wrote notes for a sermon predicting the death of the king. James, intent on severity, decided to consult the judges before the trial, not an unusual procedure. The novelty was that James, fearing that Coke might prove difficult, hit on the plan of consulting the judges one by one and not as a group. Coke objected, declaring that "this auricular taking of opinions, single and apart, was new and dangerous." Finally, in the case of Commendams (1616), James asked the judges to postpone their decision until he had consulted with them. Coke persuaded them to reply that they could not delay justice at the king's command. In a great rage James called the judges before him; they fell upon their knees. The king then asked them whether in the future they would be willing to delay a case involving the interests of the Crown until they had spoken to him. All agreed, save Coke, who merely said that he would do what it was fitting for a judge to do. Later that year he was dismissed from the bench. By this drastic action James freed himself from the opposition of the judges, but he struck a heavy blow at the moral weight of their decisions. Coke's shortcomings were forgotten; he became a martyr of the commonwealth, a symbol of the widely held conviction that the liberties provided by the common law should be left as they were.

Foreign Affairs

England's international position, as well as her government, declined alarmingly during the interparliamentary period between 1614 and 1621. To understand this decline we must briefly review the first part of the reign. When James ascended the English throne in 1603 he was in a strong position relative to foreign powers. He was king of the most powerful Protestant state, strengthened by union with Scotland. His prestige was high in Scandinavia, northern Germany, and Holland. He was on good terms with certain Catholic states opposed to Spain: France, Venice, and Tuscany. To English friendship with France he could add the ancient tradition of Franco-Scottish alliance. Thus when he stepped into Elizabeth's place as a leader of Protestant and anti-Spanish Europe, he inherited her strength but added some of his own.

James's great departure from Elizabeth's policy was his belief that he could lead Protestant Europe and at the same time be a friend of Spain. In the past he had feared Spain greatly, but he now considered himself sufficiently powerful and well established to offer Spain his friendship and thus to make complete the circle of his amity. He was, as we know, a man who loved peace, whose ambition was not merely to keep England out of war, but to make peace universal throughout Europe. Friendly with all nations, allied with Protestant states, and on peaceful terms with Spanish lands: this was his noble vision of bringing peace and concord to Europe as a whole.

This vision, of course, was an empty one, and his failure in foreign policy was to prove the most shameful of his reign. The reasons are clear. His cardinal error was to believe that he could be a Protestant champion and at the same time a friend of Spain. This basic contradiction involved him in countless difficulties. His policy, moreover, was a personal policy he never explained to his people, who regarded him as more pro-Spanish than he was. They allowed him to be without funds, and Parliament was tempted to make for the first time a serious demand for a voice in shaping foreign policy. James was not merely averse to war; he regarded it with terror. He could not bear the sight of a naked sword or of men drilling for combat. The story was told that once when a soldier attempted to kiss his hand, the king suddenly drew it back, afraid it would be bitten. His fear of assassination played an important part in his diplomacy. Believing the king desired peace at any price, his enemies came to count on his inaction. Since he had no money he could neither fulfill his commitments nor make good his threats. Thus he became a defender who could defend no one, a champion who could do nothing but talk.

For the first decade of his reign he was much closer to Protestant Europe than to Spain. Although he made peace with Spain in 1604, thus ending the long war, the peace was no surrender. James promised not to assist the Dutch, but he allowed them to raise money and volunteers in England, whereas a similar concession to Spain meant nothing. He did not accept the Spanish claim of monopoly in the New World; in the end the treaty said nothing about Englishmen in the Spanish Indies (where they continued to go at their own risk). England and Scotland benefited by the peace. They could trade in Spain and in the Netherlands; Ireland could be pacified without fear of Spanish intervention; and Spain was left fighting the Dutch and in constant danger of war with France.

Nevertheless, the peace was an uneasy one. James quarreled with Spain over one issue after another, and as a consequence drew closer to Protestant and anti-Spanish Europe. When he looked for a bride for Prince Henry, he turned to anti-Spanish lands—France, Savoy, and Tuscany. In 1613 his daughter Elizabeth was married to Frederick V of the Palatinate, the leading Calvinist ruler in Germany. This marriage brought James into close contact with the Protestant princes of southern Germany, who in 1608 had formed a defensive alliance know as the Protestant Union. James in effect became a member. His position as Protestant champion was enchanced, and his relations with Spain became so strained that many Englishmen thought, and hoped, that the Elizabethan war with Spain would be renewed.

Then, about 1614, a shift occurred. James's international position weakened while that of Spain improved. The deaths of Henry IV of France in 1610, of Salisbury and Prince Henry in 1612, were each a grievous blow to England. Unfortunate quarrels separated James from the Dutch, from Savoy, and from France. The efficiency of English government declined and the breach with Parliament widened. Meanwhile Spain had grown stronger, at least in her relations with other powers. She had concluded a truce in 1609 with the Dutch; her relations with France had greatly improved; and she had in England a most astute ambassador, Sarmiento, later Count Gondomar.

As a result, James became more conciliatory; treating with Spain as with an equal or even a superior power, he drifted into a policy of appeasement. Left without funds by Parliament in 1614, he began negotiations to arrange a marriage between his second son, Prince Charles, and a Spanish infanta (princess) who would, he assumed, bring him a large dowry. Sarmiento eagerly advocated the marriage, but the Spanish government did not. Nonetheless, in 1615 the Spanish drew up articles to serve as a basis for negotiations. They stipulated that English Catholics be permitted the exercise of their religion through nonenforcement of the penal laws. The infanta must control the education of her children, who must be baptized according to the Roman Catholic use. They must be free to choose their own religion and, if they selected Catholicism, they must not be debarred thereby from the English succession. The infanta's household must be Catholic, her chapel must be large and open to the public, her priests must wear their normal habits. James's first reaction to these articles amounted to a refusal, but in the end he accepted them as a basis for negotiation. In 1617 the Spanish raised their terms. The English penal laws must be repealed altogether; until this was done the infanta was to remain in Spain and not a penny of the dowry was to be paid. The prince must come to Madrid for his bride, the implication being that his visit would result in his conversion. James knew that he could not repeal the penal laws; only Parliament could repeal them and such action by the Puritan Commons was unthinkable. Hence the negotiations were deadlocked. Yet James still hoped for a Spanish dowry, and the Spanish continued to negotiate with him, if only to separate him from old friends.

It was at this unfortunate moment in 1618 that Sir Walter Ralegh returned from his last voyage to the Spanish Indies. A prisoner in the Tower since 1603, he had been released in 1616 in order to seek a gold mine which he believed to exist on the Orinoco River in modern Venezuela. Delighted at the thought of gold, James seems to have convinced himself that Ralegh's voyage would make the Spanish more eager for the marriage treaty. Although Ralegh had solemnly pledged not to molest the Spaniards, he returned to England not only without gold but guilty of an attack upon a Spanish settlement. Under sharp pressure from Spain, James weakly sent Ralegh to the block, to the bitter indignation of the people.

The Thirty Years' War

In 1618 a great war broke out between Protestants and Catholics in Germany. It began as a revolt in the kingdom of Bohemia. The aged and childless Emperor Matthias, seeking to establish his cousin, Ferdinand of Styria, as successor to his dominions, had demanded in 1617 that the Bohemians accept Ferdinand as their future king. The Bohemian nobles, who were largely Protestant, refused. They rose in rebellion, broke into the palace at Prague, seized the emperor's agents, and flung them out of the window. The rebels, soon in possession of Bohemia, appealed to James for assistance, while the emperor appealed to Spain. But James's mind was taking a turn of its own. A suggestion had come to him from Spain that he, as a virtuous prince, should mediate between the emperor and the Bohemians. He eagerly accepted this proposal, not realizing it was a trick; for while he vainly attempted to mediate, Spain was left free to aid the emperor. Meanwhile, Matthias died and Ferdinand was elected emperor. Thereupon the Bohemians deposed him as their king and elected in his stead James's son-in-law, Frederick of the Palatinate. Frederick hesitated as well he might, then accepted, and traveled to Prague in October 1618.

These events caused a surge of anti-Catholic and anti-Spanish sentiment in England. James, under heavy pressure to drop his friendship with Spain and to assist his son-in-law, was in great confusion. He sharply criticized Frederick's rashness in accepting the Bohemian crown. James hated all war; but from a war to support revolt and usurpation he shrank as from the plague. He loathed the vexation of action. He had no army, and he could obtain one only by summoning Parliament. To send assistance to Frederick would ruin his reputation as the peacemaker of Europe and would end all hope of the Spanish match. The Spaniards would foster plots among the English Catholics, and his life would be in danger. Yet Frederick was his son-in-law, and Frederick's wife was his daughter. Should he desert his own flesh and blood? Torn and perplexed, the king sank into irresolution. To the exasperation of his people, month after month slipped by without taking action.

Meanwhile the Catholic powers made their plans. A secret agreement between Ferdinand and Philip III of Spain provided that Ferdinand should move against Prague while Philip created a diversion by attacking the Palatinate from the Spanish Netherlands. There is no doubt that Philip was most reluctant; his decision might have been different if James had shown clearly that he would defend the Palatinate. For although the Bohemian adventure was an act of aggression, a Spanish attack on the Palatinate would be equally aggressive. The Palatinate was Frederick's rightful possession.

A Catholic conquest of it would dissolve the Protestant Union and threaten every Protestant interest in southern Germany.

In August 1620 the blow fell when a Spanish army attacked the Palatinate. The emperor moved into Bohemia, defeated Frederick, and sent him fleeing northward for his very life. The Bohemian venture was over, and the Palatinate was in grave danger. It was under these circumstances that James summoned the next Parliament.

THE PARLIAMENT OF 1621

The Parliament of 1621 was the most important of James's reign. If the king obtained supplies, he could defend the Palatinate and perhaps could stem the tide of Catholic victory. Without money he was helpless. In view of these sobering considerations both the king and Commons acted for some months with marked restraint. Yet the Commons were in a grim mood. A mistaken foreign policy, they believed, was exposing their country and their religion to untold dangers. For one thing, they regarded the Spanish match with deep alarm. For another they were keenly aware that at home grave abuses had crept into the government. A perplexing economic depression rendered them even more irritable. They were determined, not only to improve foreign policy where they could, but also to launch a broad and searching investigation of domestic conditions.

Warned away from criticism of the king's foreign policy, the Commons turned to grievances at home. They made a thorough inquiry into patents and monopolies. These patents brought little money to the Crown but were highly profitable to certain courtiers, including a number of Buckingham's relatives. So alarmed was Buckingham that he posed as a reformer and allowed his relatives to be punished. The Commons also wished to investigate the so-called referees, that is, the councilors to whom patents had been referred for appraisal before they had been granted. Had the Commons brought formal charges against the referees, they would in effect have revived the medieval practice of impeachment. James managed to stop this attack upon his ministers, but hostility to the referees continued. When sudden dramatic charges of bribery were brought against Bacon, now lord chancellor, the Commons pushed the accusations and forced Bacon out of office. Meanwhile the foreign situation deteriorated and Frederick's cause was near collapse.

In the autumn session of the Parliament the Commons could be restrained no longer. They entered upon a long debate on foreign policy in which member after member pointed to Spain as the great enemy. Let the war be against Spain, not by pottering in the Palatinate, but by attacking Spain and the Spanish Indies on land and sea in true Elizabethan fashion. Let measures be taken against the Roman Catholics at home. The debate reached its crescendo in a violent speech by Sir Edward Coke, who poured forth vituperation upon Spain and Catholicism. The Commons voted one subsidy to aid the Palatinate over the winter. Then they prepared a petition asking for the enforcement of the anti-Catholic laws, for a war with Spain, and for a Protestant marriage for the prince.

Upon hearing of the petition James dashed off an angry letter to the Commons. They were, he said, debating matters far above their reach and capacity. He commanded them not to meddle with his government nor "deal with our dearest son's match with the daughter of Spain, nor touch the honor of that king." He added "that we think ourselves very free and able to punish any man's misdemeanors in Parliament as well during their sitting as after; which we mean not to spare henceforth." In reply the Commons drew up a protestation. It declared that their privileges were their undoubted birthright and inheritance, that weighty affairs of the kingdom should be debated in Parliament, and that every member had freedom of speech and freedom from arrest. James then dissolved the Parliament in bitter anger. Coming to the Council chamber, he called for the Journal of the Commons and with his own hands tore out the page citing the protestation.

JAMES'S LAST YEARS

The dissolution of Parliament marked the eclipse of James as a potent and respected ruler. A feeble old man sinking into his dotage and cut off from the sympathy of his people, he found his position hopeless in both domestic and foreign affairs. At home his finances fell once more into disorder. Prince Charles and Buckingham, impatient with his fumbling timidity, were eager to take control of policy. He lacked the power to intervene in continental affairs. He could not send assistance to Frederick in the Palatinate. He could only ask Spain to be kind. But he had to ask for a great deal: that the Spaniards withdraw their victorious forces from the Palatinate, that they persuade the emperor to do the same, and that, if the emperor refused, they make war upon their Catholic kinsman to please the Protestant king of England.

Though such cooperation seemed impossible, James thought it might be accomplished through the Spanish match; negotiations to this end continued through 1622. They reached their climax in 1623, when Charles and Buckingham, with romantic folly, determined to go to Spain in person, to conclude a marriage treaty quickly, and to "bring back that angel," the infanta, with whom Charles imagined himself to be in love. Luckily the two young men reached Spain in safety. But the Spanish, with the prince in their possession, naturally raised their terms. James must now proclaim that the penal laws were suspended, must swear that they would never be reimposed, and must obtain the consent of Parliament for his action. Until these things were done, the infanta was to remain in Spain even after her marriage. Charles foolishly agreed to these impossible terms; and James, terrified lest his dear son was a hostage, sadly swore the required oaths.

The Spanish marriage never took place, for Charles was at last awakened from his romantic dream. Anger and resentment against Spain extinguished his infatuation for the infanta, and when he and Buckingham returned to England, they demanded a complete reversal of policy. They wished to make war on Spain, to build a great European alliance against her, and to restore Frederick to the Palatinate by force. The old king was horrified. But his son and his favorite, treating him with some brutality, hurried him into policies he detested. A Parliament in 1624 was easily persuaded to demand an end to the Spanish treaties and the beginning of a war. The Commons voted a small supply, promising to give more when war was declared. English diplomats were dispatched in all directions to form an anti-Spanish front.

In this search for allies Charles and Buckingham turned to France, proposing a marriage between the prince and Henrietta Maria, sister of the French king. Unfortunately, and largely out of pride, the French demanded that the English Catholics be given terms as favorable as those in the abortive treaties with Spain. This condition was accepted. James died in March 1625, leaving his son a discontented kingdom, an empty treasury, a war with Spain, and a marriage treaty with France that could not possibly be fulfilled.

CHRONOLOGY

The First Stuart

1603–25	James I (and VI of Scotland)
1603	Millenary Petition
1604	Hampton Court Conference; the "Apology"
1605	Gunpowder Plot—Guy Fawkes; dispute over Writ of Prohibitions
1606	Bate Case; impositions approved
1607	Jamestown settled
1608	Scots born after accession of James to be citizens of England and Scotland—Calvin's case
1610	Salisbury's Great Contract proposed and rejected; Sir Edward Coke and Royal Proclamations
1611	Authorized Version of Bible—King James Bible
1612	Death of Salisbury
1616	Sir Edward Coke dismissed
1618	George Villiers in power; Declaration of Sports; Thirty Years' War; Lionel Cranfield, Earl of Middlesex, and financial reform
1620	Pilgrims sail on *Mayflower*

17

The Reign of Charles I to 1642

THE NEW KING, 1625–1649

King Charles I, born in Scotland in 1600 and brought to England in 1604, was very delicate as a child. As a young man at court he was healthy, though not robust, fond of theatricals and sports, an excellent horseman who delighted in hunting and in running at the ring. His early contacts with his father and Buckingham were not happy. He resented the glamorous favorite whom all must worship. James made matters worse by showing that he was fonder of Buckingham than of his son. Quarrels between the two young men became so numerous that the king called them before him in 1618 and commanded them on their allegiance to become more friendly. Thereafter their relations improved.

Although Charles was frequently embarrassed by his father's lack of dignity, he was at the same time overawed and silenced by James's rapid conversation, quick intelligence, and choleric temper. Charles was slow and halting in thought and speech and so it is probable that he felt himself inferior. If we assume these were his feelings and that he struggled to overcome them, his character becomes clearer. He schooled himself to be a brave and courageous person. With a natural love of propriety, he perhaps took refuge in laying emphasis upon what was decorous and orderly. His first act as king was to cleanse the court of the bawds and drunkards whom his father had tolerated. His family life was always dignified and correct. Perhaps to counteract any feeling of inferiority he developed a lofty and majestic deportment toward all with whom he dealt. He accepted fully the theory of the divine right of kings. James had stressed the divine origin of kingship; Charles dwelt upon the duty and obedience owed to a ruler by his subjects. He believed that opposition to the royal will was sin; and this became the constant theme of sermons by the Anglican clergy. It followed that if the people were wicked enough to force concessions from the king, the king need not keep his word to them but could revoke his promises when opportunity served. Charles thus acquired an unpleasant reputation for deceit and unreliability. There was a cold, unsympathetic rigidity about this man; he lived in his own world, alien to the feelings and ambitions of others. Nor could he understand the moral force of Puritanism or the aspirations of the Commons. In his mind the Church of England was the only possible church, and monarchy by divine right the only possible government. Such a king was certain to turn to dictatorial and arbitrary rule.

Charles, however, did not possess the vigorous personality necessary for an absolute sovereign. Left to himself he could not make incisive decisions or take strong action, and so he leaned on others more resolute than he. He relied at first on Buckingham, whose complete self-confidence and lavish extravagance symbolized the magnificence and glory of kingship. Later he was influenced by his wife who, reflecting the absolutism of France, urged her husband to play a kingly and decisive role. Later in the reign Charles relied on Archbishop Laud and on Thomas Wentworth, earl of Strafford, both advocates of authority, discipline, and coercion. When these props were gone, Charles was left with courage and tenacity, but little more.

THE CLASH WITH THE COMMONS

Diplomacy, War, and Parliament

When Charles ascended the throne in 1625 he did not understand that he was already in an awkward position. He was the unhappy heir of all the grievances and discontents that had arisen in the reign of his father. There were additional difficulties of his own making. Since he could not fulfill the terms of the marriage treaty with France, he was very likely to have difficulties with that country. He was committed to war with Spain; he and Buckingham, hoping to build a great anti-Spanish front, had promised large sums to King Christian of Denmark, the Dutch, and Count Mansfeld, Frederick's freebooting general. Money must also be spent on the English fleet. Unless Parliament came to Charles' assistance, he could not hope to honor these huge commitments. His one military venture had been Mansfeld's expedition in 1624, which had proved a shameful fiasco. The plan had called for Mansfeld to lead an English army directly across France to the relief of the Palatinate. To this the French objected; and after great uncertainty and change of plan, the English soldiers landed at Flushing in Holland. Unpaid, starving, stricken with fever, they had dwindled in a few months from an army of 12,000 men to some 3000 useless wretches.

Charles was also in difficulty at home. The terms of the French treaty were unknown, but it was suspected that they favored the Roman Catholics. Henrietta Maria, the pretty little French princess who was to be Charles's wife, was regarded as a missionary of her Catholic faith. Moreover, it soon became evident that Charles favored the High Anglican or Laudian school of churchmen. Laud's views were Arminian, not popish. But the reliance of the Arminians on the primitive church rather than on the Scriptures alone, their insistence on the continuity of the Church of England with the Roman Catholic Church before the Reformation, and their revival of medieval ritual appeared to presage a return to Roman Catholicism. The lofty position of the Anglican bishops in Charles's reign gave great offense. Their claim that episcopacy was divine in origin, their persecution of the Puritans in the Court of High Commission, their increasing pomp and dignity, and their employment by the king in high offices of state aroused the strong antagonism of many people. The courteirs were jealous of Buckingham's monopoly of power and of royal favor. And, finally, the economic depression of the 1620s had not yet lifted. It deepened momentarily in 1625 because of the plague which settled upon London and disturbed every phase of social and economic life.

Amid these difficulties Charles and Buckingham should have approached their first Parliament with care. But they acted with blind self-confidence, assuming that their success in 1624 would repeat itself. The Commons, summoned for May 17, 1625, were kept waiting in plague-stricken London for a month before Parliament began. The departure of Henrietta Maria from France had been delayed, and Charles did not wish to meet Parliament until she arrived. His opening speech was vague. He had been advised by Parliament to break with Spain, he said, and he now needed money to conduct the war, but he did not say how much was required or where the war was to be fought. This last point was important, for the Commons wanted a war at sea in the Elizabethan tradition, not a costly war in Germany. Charles's councilors in the House of Commons, having no instructions, were equally noncommittal. Taking advantage of this uncertainty, the opposition moved and carried a vote for a small supply of two subsidies. This action contained an element of trickery, which was unfortunate, but the government had invited some such move by its laxness in stating its case. About a week later Charles attempted a similar device. His councilors gave the Commons for the first time an account of the situation abroad and asked for a large amount of money. But members had been slipping away from London and the plague. Attendance was thin and those who remained refused to commit their fellow members to heavy taxation.

Charles then adjourned Parliament to Oxford, where the Commons reassembled in a rather sullen mood. At Oxford Charles and Buckingham committed new tactical blunders. Buckingham offended the Commons by summoning them before him and speaking to them as though he himself were king. The Commons criticized him sharply, attacked an Arminian divine, Richard Montague, and refused to increase their former grant. The Parliament then was dissolved. It had set a pattern of mismanagement by the Crown, of distrust between king and Parliament, and of refusal by the Commons to grant adequate supply.

Meanwhile the king and Buckingham had been gathering a great fleet at Plymouth for an attack on Spain. They hoped to assault Cadiz as Drake had done in 1587. But everything went wrong. The expedition contained only nine ships of the Royal Navy; the rest were merchant vessels pressed into unwilling service. Ten thousand soldiers and five thousand sailors were also pressed, but the former were largely vagabonds who could not be turned into an effective army. The expedition did not sail until October 1625, when the fair weather of the summer months had ended. After a long march without food in the heat of the Spanish sun, the soldiers discovered a quantity of wine and promptly became intoxicated. They could have been slaughtered by a determined attack. There was no alternative but to send them back to the ships and abandon the assault upon Cadiz, which had been strongly reinforced. Buckingham's great enterprise had ended in disaster.

The Parliament of 1626

It was under the shadow of this failure that Charles's second Parliament met early in 1626. The king had no choice but to summon it because of his many commitments and his lack of money. Knowing that Parliament would be difficult, he made what preparations he could. He ordered a strict enforcement of the penal laws against the Roman Catholics, thus breaking the pledges of the marriage treaty with France. He excluded certain leaders of opposition in the Commons by appointing them sheriffs.

In the Commons a new leader appeared, Sir John Eliot, a man of high ideals and patriotism, but of less ability and prudence than were possessed by the men whom Charles had excluded. Eliot's fiery oratory was apt to lead the Commons into rash and violent action.

The Commons, determined to have a strict accounting for what had happened, began to investigate the responsibility for Mansfeld's disaster and soon launched into a broad attack on Buckingham. They tried to impeach him, but they did so with more violence than skill. Eliot and Sir Dudley Digges, laying the charges of the Commons before the Lords, used language for which Charles sent them to the Tower. The impeachment failed, largely because the king withheld evidence and thus prevented the Commons from proving their case. In a tantalizing way the Commons had passed a resolution to give the king three subsidies but had not put the resolution in the form of a bill. After the attack on Buckingham failed, the resolution was allowed to lapse, and Charles received no money from this Parliament, which was shortly dissolved.

Charles's allies on the Continent were ruined because he could not send them the money he had promised. Mansfeld, ordered to assist the Dutch, was defeated; Christian of Denmark was badly beaten, largely because his troops would not fight without pay. Charles made matters worse by drifting into a war with France.

Louis was angered when Charles enforced the penal laws despite the marriage treaty. A coolness arose between Charles and Henrietta Maria, whose French attendants were disliked in London. Eventually Charles sent them back to France, thus breaking the treaty once more. Moreover, James and Buckingham had promised to lend the French eight English ships to be sent against the Huguenots at La Rochelle who were defying the French government. But the use of English ships to repress Protestants caused such a furor in England that Buckingham tried to prevent the delivery of the ships to France. Charles now posed as the protector of the Huguenots against Louis, each nation seized the merchant vessels of the other, and war soon followed. In June 1627, a large English expedition sent to the relief of La Rochelle made a landing nearby on the Île de Ré. But a French fort on the island could not be caputred, an English army was cut to pieces, and the expedition, another dismal failure, returned to England.

The Forced Loan of 1627

Meanwhile Charles, in trying to raise money, determined in 1627 to levy a forced loan. The money was to be collected as though it had been voted by Parliament and was to amount to five subsidies. But the widespread opposition was increased rather than lessened by the sermons of Arminian clergymen, who preached the religious duty of obedience. Sir Randolph Crew, chief justice of the King's Bench, was dismissed for refusing to declare that the loan was legal. So many men declined payment that pressures of various kinds were applied; a number of the gentry were imprisoned. Five of them brought matters to a head by applying for writs of habeas corpus, which enabled them to ask why they had been put in prison; their purpose was to force the courts to declare whether or not a refusal to contribute to the recent loan was a legal cause for imprisonment. The judges were placed in a difficult position, for it was obvious that a man could not be imprisoned merely because he would not lend his money. The judges therefore returned the knights to jail without giving any reason. But the nation believed that the judges endorsed the view that imprisonment for refusal to lend money was legal and that the king could keep men in jail indefinitely without showing cause. The episode was regarded as a dangerous attack upon personal liberty and on the rights of property.

Discontent was increased by two other grievances. Without means to feed or house his troops, Charles began to billet them in private homes. A householder was informed that he must give board and lodging to two or three soldiers, who might well be lawless rogues, and it was suspected that persons who had refused to lend their money were the first to have soldiers billeted on them. In order to deal with the many quarrels between the soldiers and their reluctant hosts and to maintain discipline in the rabble that Charles called his army, martial law was proclaimed in certain areas. These four points—forced loans, imprisonment without cause shown, billeting, and martial law—formed the basis for debate and action in Charles's third Parliament, which met in 1628.

The Petition of Right

The Parliament of 1628 differed from its predecessors. The Crown was desperate, for government simply could not be carried further without funds. The Commons, on their side, were in deadly earnest. Goaded by the nation's military defeat and by the Crown's attacks on personal liberty, they displayed a new hardness and determination.

Before the Parliament met, Buckingham had talked of a standing army, obviously to beat down opposition, and the government had considered highly dubious expediants for raising money. These wild plans were dropped and the Crown concentrated instead on winning support in the coming session. Key opponents were offered office and other rewards if they would side with the king, royal officials in the Commons were given better instructions, and an attempt was made to influence elections. All such interference failed completely. Men who had been imprisoned because they had refused to lend money were overwhelmingly elected.

The members of this House of Commons were men of position and wealth, able, it was said, to buy out the House of Lords thrice over. The opposition leaders were in complete control and had by now developed procedures—such as the committee of the whole house—by which they could obtain quick action in the Commons. They decided to drop the impeachment of Buckingham and to concentrate on the defense of personal liberties. They began by passing resolutions against unparliamentary taxation and against imprisonment without cause shown. When these resolutions were modified by the Lords, the Commons attempted to frame a bill that would guarantee the liberties of the subject. But it proved difficult to turn the wording of their resolutions into the wording of a bill. If a bill required the king to confirm old statutes and ancient liberties, the implication was that those liberties no longer existed. A member remarked that if "we tell our constituents we have confirmed old statutes, they will ask us when those statutes had been repealed." Hence the Commons adopted the happy idea of Sir Edward Coke that they employ the device of a Petition of Right to redress specific infractions by the king. Such petitions were used in the law courts in cases in which petitioners, claiming that the king had overridden the law, asked merely that they be given the law's protection. The form of a petition enabled the Commons to assert that the laws had been broken and to demand that the king not break them again. Charles endeavored to answer in vague terms, but in the end, in return for a substantial grant, he gave a firm assent.

The Petition of Right contained four points: no man thereafter should be compelled to make any gift, loan, benevolence, tax, or such like charge without common consent by act of Parliament; no man should be imprisoned or detained without cause shown; soldiers and sailors should not be billeted on private individuals against the will of these individuals; and commissions for martial law should not be issued in the future. The Petition of Right, regarded as one of the great documents of English liberty, had its weaknesses: it was not a statute, it contained loopholes, it had to be modified by later generations because it deprived the king of powers a government trusted by the people could be allowed to possess. Nonetheless, it set a limit to the arbitrary power of the Crown and was the first great check upon Stuart absolutism.

Those who hoped it would bring peace between king and Commons were shortly disappointed. Largely because of Eliot's impetuous and unreasonable tactics, the Commons drew up a remonstrance which complained of other grievances and attacked both Laud and Buckingham. A second remonstrance declared that the collection of tonnage and poundage without consent of Parliament was a breach of liberty. The duties of tonnage and poundage formed the normal schedule of the custom. For generations they had been granted to every king for life upon his accession. In 1625, however, they had been given for one year only, but the Commons' bill to this effect had never become law. Without the customs the king was all but penniless. Eliot's audacious move was beyond the wishes of moderate men. In reply the king prorogued Parliament, which did not meet again until early in 1629.

Charles and Buckingham learned little from their failures. Laud and other Arminian churchmen now were advanced to important posts. A new expedition was prepared for the relief of La Rochelle. Ships, ordnance, and provisions of all kinds were assembled at Portsmouth in the summer of 1628. Soldiers and sailors were rounded up in the usual way. But, as before, all plans went awry. The sailors were so mutinous for lack of pay that Charles himself went down to Portsmouth to pacify them. The movement of soldiers through the country revived the problem of billeting. Localities were assured in solemn terms that the king would pay for the support of his troops. But the presence of the soldiers was deeply resented, people would do nothing for them, and some Irish troopers were found to be pawning their arms in order to obtain money for food. Meanwhile merchants were refusing to pay customs duties not authorized by Parliament.

Everywhere murmurs arose against the hated duke of Buckingham. One John Felton, an unpaid and unpromoted lieutenant in the navy, bought a butcher's knife, made his way on foot to Portsmouth, and stabbed Buckingham to death as he stood amid his followers. The people rejoiced, and Felton was a popular hero. But Buckingham's blood separated Charles from his subjects in a new and bitter way. The fleet set sail for La Rochelle in September despite the lord admiral's death. But La Rochelle, where the hard-pressed garrison had been subsisting on a diet of boiled leather, surrendered to the French king in October, and the English fleet returned without glory.

Parliament met in a short and stormy session in 1629. The Commons turned at once to the collection of tonnage and poundage without their consent. They attacked the Arminian clergy, who were represented as undermining sound religion. Charles determined to end the debate. He sent a message to the Speaker to adjdourn the house. There followed a famous scene on 2 March 1629, when the Speaker sought to leave the chair but was held down by force while the Commons passed three resolutions: that whoever should introduce innovations in religion by bringing in popery or Arminianism should be accounted a capital enemy of the king and kingdom; that whoever should advise the levying of tonnage and poundage without consent of Parliament should be accounted the same; and that whoever should pay tonnage and poundage levied without the consent of Parliament should be held a betrayer of the liberty of the subject and a capital enemy of the king and kingdom. Meanwhile the king's messengers were hammering at the locked doors of the lower house. Once the resolutions were passed, the doors were opened and a royal message announced the adjournment of the Commons. A week later Charles dissolved Parliament and imprisoned a number of the opposition leaders. Some were soon liberated but others stayed in prison for years. Charles was through with Parliaments for eleven years.

CHARLES'S PERSONAL RULE

Charles was now able to rule England according to his own conception of government. He was not without idealism. He wished to be a conscientious and patriarchal king who, with the aid of his councilors, would protect his subjects in all walks of life from suffering wrong. He thought of himself as the guardian, not only of the people, but of the church and the ancient constitution against irreligious and seditious persons. The difficulty was that Charles reserved to himself, as king, all power to decide what the church should be, what rights should be protected, and what laws should be obeyed. The people were not to share in determining these matters: their duty was to obey. Charles thought in terms of the complete unity of church and state. To attack the one was to attack the other. Men who criticized the church could not be loyal subjects. Charles was prone, moreover, to determine in his own mind what the laws should mean and then to dismiss any judge who disagreed with him.

A number of reasons can be suggested to explain why Charles was able to rule for eleven years without summoning a Parliament. It is probable that the views of members of the House of Commons were more radical than those of the nation as a whole, for the English were a conservative people. Charles did not look like a tyrant. His decorous court, his habit of doing things in the traditional way, and his mediocre councilors—all made his government appear normal and innocuous. England was accustomed, when Parliament was not in session, to be ruled by the king, the Council, the law courts, and the justices of the peace. All these organs of government continued to function. Moreover, the period of personal rule was a time of economic prosperity. England was at peace, and the economy had recovered from the depression of the 1620s. Charles did not demand large sums of money. Had they been willing, the English could easily have paid what he asked.

Charles was able to withdraw rather easily from the wars in which he had become involved. In April 1629 he made peace with France without difficulty. The fall of La Rochelle showed that he could not defend the Huguenots; the terms offered them by Louis made it clear that Charles need not make the attempt. About the same time Christian IV of Denmark withdrew from the war in Germany. He had been defeated, but his enemies, afraid of Sweden, gave him favorable terms. His withdrawal relieved Charles of an embarrassing ally and enabled him to make peace with Spain more easily in 1630. Nonetheless, the treaty with Spain was a rather shameful conclusion to the long years of English intervention on the Continent since the beginning of the Thirty Years' War. The net result of English efforts was the loss of the Palatinate, the desertion of the Dutch, the fall of La Rochelle, and the defeat of Christian IV—a dismal record.

The great war in Germany was entering a new phase. Sweden, under her famous King Gustavus Adolphus, invaded northern Germany on the Protestant side. Allied with France, she faced the Hapsburgs of Spain and Austria. The two alliances were fairly evenly matched. Hence Charles could evade the burden of defending Protestantism on the Continent and could decide with which camp he wished to ally. He hoped to employ this advantage to regain the Palatinate by diplomacy. But his weak and vacillating policy, his bargaining with one side and then with the other as the fortunes of war swayed back and forth, rendered him despicable. No one wanted as an ally a king who had no military power and who might desert his friends at a moment's notice.

Charles I (1625–1649) dining in public, by Gerrit Houckgeest. (Her Majesty, Queen Elizabeth II)

Finance

Blessed with peace abroad and with tranquility at home, Charles seemed secure. In love with his queen, happy with his collection of art treasures, he believed himself to be the most fortunate king in Christendom. But by a long series of highhanded actions he gradually alienated his people and prepared the way for the sea of troubles which overwhelmed him in the 1640s. Charles's revenues from extraparliamentary sources during his years of personal rule were large but not large enough for his needs. To make ends meet he was forced to ignore the debt, to curtail expenses, and to find new sources of income. In 1629 the debt from the war years stood at nearly £1 million. Most of it never was repaid, the loudest creditors being soothed by favors and privileges of various kinds. Expenditure at court and in the administration was decreased. Ship money was a means by which Charles hoped to be relieved of the cost of the navy.

New income was raised by several devices, among them the distraint of knighthood. In the late thirteenth century Henry III and Edward I, finding that landowners attempted to evade the duties of knighthood, decreed that every man who held land worth £20 a year should become a knight. Raising the sum to £40 a year, Charles enforced this ancient rule and collected fines and compositions from persons who had neglected to be knighted. More than £100,000 were raised by this means within two years. The payments, however, were extracted from the landed classes, which were Charles's natural supporters. The value of the fines was not worth the irritation they aroused. Charles also revived the ancient laws and boundaries of the medieval forests. These forests, it will be remembered, had been extensive areas set aside for the royal sport of hunting. Redefining the forest boundaries, Charles imposed fines for the disregard of obsolete rules everyone had forgotten. For example, almost the entire county of Essex was found to be a forest, and forest law was enforced upon land which had been in private hands for centuries. As a matter of fact, very little money came to the Treasury by this means; although the fines could not be collected they aroused strong animosity among the upper classes. Wealthy families also were incensed by the increased revenues Charles obtained from the vexatious court of wards.

Moreover, Charles offended industrialists and merchants. He imposed a fine of £70,000 on certain London companies because they had not fulfilled their promises in the colonization of Ulster. Of this huge fine, he obtained only £12,000 after a long dispute. He irritated the people at large by granting monopolies to certain retailers of soap, bricks, coal, and salt. Monopolies had been declared illegal by the Parliament of 1624, but Charles evaded the letter of the law by giving monopolies to corporations rather than to individuals.

His most famous expedient was ship money. The Crown possessed an unchallenged right to impress ships from the port towns in times of emergency. Hence the first levy of ship money in 1634 for an expedition against pirates did not arouse resistance. In the following year, however, ship money was demanded once more, this time from the inland counties as well as from the ports. Opposition increased, but the money was collected. But a third levy, in 1636, met widespread hostility, for it was evident that ship money was becoming a permanent form of extraparliamentary taxation. John Hampden, a wealthy gentleman of Buckinghamshire, refused to pay. His case, watched intently by all England, came before the Exchequer Chamber in 1637, when the judges decided, though only by a vote of 7 to 5, that ship money was legal in time of danger and that only the king could decide when danger existed. Ship money continued to be levied, though its collection grew more difficult. But the Hampden Case dramatized the arbitrary nature of Charles's government. Disaffection was widespread against a system of rule and taxation in which Parliament had no share.

Persecution of Puritanism

An even deeper hostility was aroused by Charles's ecclesiastical policy. Favoring the Arminian or High Anglican churchmen, he promoted them to places of trust both in the church and in the state and defended them vigorously against the attacks of the

House of Commons. To the Puritans and to many moderate Anglicans, the Arminians seemed to be heading toward Rome. This impression was confirmed by the pro-Spanish policy of James and at times that of Charles, by the presence of Henrietta Maria and many Roman Catholics at Charles's court, by his failure to strike a blow on behalf of continental Protestantism, and by the fact that the anti-Catholic laws were unenforced whereas the full force of the law was used to persecute Puritans. It was this seeming partiality that caused dislike.

We can understand the situation better if we look at Archbishop Laud, who was hated with a violence difficult to grasp. He was a scholar, a patron of his Oxford college, a brave and resolute man, and a skillful administrator who improved the organization of the church. But although tolerant in theory, he was utterly intolerant in practice; he was a disciplinarian, an advocate of authority and of obedience. Harsh and uncompromising, he took an almost savage pleasure in punishing his opponents. Moreover, he was a meddlesome person, as zealous in matters of petty detail as in the enforcement of broad policy. And he was unfair. The Arminian clergy were to enjoy every facility for expressing their opinions, but the Puritans were to be silenced; Arminians were encouraged to defend their church, but the slightest criticism of it was to be suppressed. Laud's partiality was driven home because he was important in the state as well as in the church. A member of the Privy council, of the court of High Commission, and of the Star Chamber, he was also on commissions for the Treasury and for foreign affairs. He freely employed the power of the state to enforce his ecclesiastical policy. Sitting on the bench in cases involving Puritans, he was both a judge and a party to the suit. His lack of a sense of fair play, his great power, and his ostentatious manner of life aroused resentment, a resentment which spread to the bishops as a whole.

Laud's aim was to suppress all religious services except those of the Arminians, to hold the clergy to strict obedience and conformity, and to stifle criticism of his church. Laud's ceremonial was forced on congregations who were not permitted to worship elsewhere. Criticism of the church was brutally suppressed. No book or pamphlet could legally be printed or sold without a license, and Puritans who wrote secret pamphlets attacking the church were punished harshly. In 1630 Alexander Leighton was whipped, pilloried, and mutilated for printing abroad *An Appeal to Parliament; or Sion's Plea against Prelacy,* in which he challenged the doctrine that episcopacy was divine in origin. Four years later William Prynne, a rather obnoxious Puritan lawyer, was sentenced to life imprisonment, to a fine of £5,000, to disbarment, to mutilation, and to the pillory because of his *Histrio-Mastix: A Scourge of Stage Players,* an attack on the drama which was interpreted as a reflection on the queen. In 1637 Prynne was tried again for further pamphlet writing; Henry Burton, a clergyman, for his sermons; and John Bastwick, a doctor, for writings against the bishops. All three were sentenced to the pillory and to mutilation: and Prynne, having lost his ears in 1634, had the stubs scraped and was branded on the cheek with the letters "S.L." (Seditious Libeler). It is small wonder that by 1640 the Puritans were wholly estranged from the church.

The Explosion in Scotland

The year 1637 may be considered the first year of open opposition. It was the year of the Hampden Case, resisting ship money, and of the trial of Prynne, Burton, and Bastwick. It was also in 1637 that serious trouble arose in Scotland.

Charles handled his Scottish subjects in so highhanded a manner that he slowly drove them into rebellion. He began with an Act of Revocation in 1625 by which he recalled all grants of land (including church lands and tithes) made by the Crown since 1540. Such acts of revocation were not uncommon in Scotland, but Charles's act was so sweeping and covered so long a period of time that it affected almost every substantial landowner in the country. In 1627 he permitted the Scots to redeem their estates by money payments, but he had thoroughly alienated the upper classes. He forgot that James, as a matter of policy, had increased the loyalty of the Scottish nobility and gentry by grants from the possessions of the ancient church.

When Charles visited Scotland in 1633 he added new irritations. He introduced English innovations into the Scottish coronation service and permitted Laud to flaunt Arminian ritual before the eyes of the horrified Scots. When he attended the Scottish Parliament he noted the names of those who opposed his wishes. Upon his return to England he decided that changes should be made in the government and in the Kirk of Scotland. Very unwisely he excluded the lords of session, that is, the judges of Scotland's high court for civil cases, from membership in the Privy Council. The power of the Scottish bishops on the Council was thus increased, and in 1635 Charles named Archbishop Spottiswoode as chancellor of Scotland.

More dangerously he decided that the liturgy of the Kirk should be based on the English *Book of Common Prayer.* The prayer book prepared for Scotland used to be called "Laud's Liturgy," but a recent study has shown that it was largely the work of the Scottish bishops. Their modifications of the English prayer book, to make it more palatable for the Scots, were carefully supervised by the king. When it was used for the first (and last) time in St. Giles's Cathedral in Edinburgh in 1637 it provoked a famous riot. All Scotland was in an uproar. The Scots appointed a body of commissioners, often called the Tables, who formed a sort of opposition government. To consolidate public opinion, they issued a famous document known as the National Covenant. It contained a pledge to resist the recent innovations in religion and to support the authority of the Crown. These two points were obviously inconsistent, but they united Scotland for the moment, and thousands of persons eagerly subscribed to the Covenant. Scotland was in revolt. If Charles were to enforce his prayer book he would have to do so by military might.

THE BISHOPS' WARS AND THE SHORT PARLIAMENT

For a moment Charles bowed before the storm in Scotland. He promised that a General Assembly would meet in 1638 and a Scottish Parliament in 1639. As soon as the Assembly convened it summoned the Scottish bishops to appear before it; on their refusal, the Assembly abolished episcopacy. It proceeded to do away with the prayer book of 1637, with the canons by which the book was to have been enforced, and with the Five Articles of Perth which called for the use of High Anglican liturgical practices. It then re-established the presbyterian form of church government and decreed that nonpresbyterian clergymen should be expelled from their pulpits.

When Charles refused to recognize the actions of this Assembly both sides prepared for war. Without funds, Charles summoned the English nobility to serve at their own charge and called out the militia of the northern counties. But the men were untrained, their equipment was defective, and they were unpaid. A troop of the king's horse pushed into Scotland, saw the Scots army, turned without fighting, and fled south across the border. An invasion of Scotland became an impossibility. Charles concluded the Pacification of Berwick with the Scots in June 1639, by which both sides agreed to disband their forces. A new General Assembly and a Scottish Parliament were to determine the future government of Scotland.

This pacification was short-lived. The General Assembly confirmed all that its predecessor had done, the Parliament repealed laws in favor of episcopacy and increased its own powers, the Scottish army remained in existence. A second Bishops' war was inevitable. But Charles's resources were so limited that the momentous decision was taken to summon a Parliament in England. Charles's councilors argued that a Parliament would show the people that the king wished to obtain funds in the old accustomed way. If Parliament did not vote him supplies in his great emergency he would be free to use any means at his disposal to raise money for war. Councilors hoped that anti-Scottish feeling in England would bring support for the king; Wentworth, now summoned back from Ireland, thought that the Commons could be managed.

The result was the Short Parliament, which met from 13 April to 5 May 1640. Many of the popular leaders were returned. The Commons were told in an arrogant way that they should vote money at once and that the king would then listen to any grievances they might have. The answer of the Commons is to be found in a speech by John Pym, who presented in a moderate but devastating way the long list of grievances which had accumulated since 1629. Beginning with Charles's attacks on parliamentary privilege, Pym traced the innovations in religion and the assaults on the rights of property. He called for reform and when he sat down there were cries of "A good oration!" Under his leadership, the Commons began a systematic collection and examination of popular complaints. Grievances were to precede supply. The king, angry at a rumor that the leaders of the Commons were in secret communication with the Scots, dissolved the Parliament.

Charles was left with the old problem of fighting a war without money. His principal adviser at this crisis was Thomas Wentworth, now earl of Strafford, known to the people as "Black Tom the Tyrant." Strafford, one of the popular leaders in the 1620s, had been imprisoned in 1627 for refusing to lend money to the king. But after the Petition of Right he had come over to the side of the Crown and for this had been accused of apostasy. He was a masterful man whose temper was autocratic. He had no interest in free institutions and no sympathy with Puritanism. Skillful and resolute as an administrator, he believed in authority, demanded unquestioning obedience, and was prone to drive at what he desired without too nice an attention to legality. It was natural for such a man to take his place with the king. From 1628 to 1632 he was president of the Council in the North; from 1632 to 1640, lord deputy in Ireland. It was only toward the end of Charles's personal rule that this hard, bold, and determined man was summoned from Ireland to become one of the king's principal counselors. After the dissolution of the Short Parliament he advised Charles to prosecute the war against the Scots with vigor, to consider himself free from all normal rules of government, and to do anything "that power might admit." "You have an army in Ireland you may employ here to reduce this kingdom." Was "this kingdom" Scotland, or was it England?

It was easier to speak boldly than to raise an army. Loans could not be obtained either from London or from sources overseas. Charles called out the militia from the southern part of the country, but the men were not only half trained but half mutinous. Many of them deserted; others broke into disorders which often were demonstrations against the Laudian church. England's heart was not in the war, and the arbitrary methods of the government only increased the general discontent. The Scots, therefore, took the initiative. Crossing the Tweed unopposed on 20 August 1640, they occupied the two northern counties of Northumberland and Durham, upon which they levied £850 a day for their support. The Scots, however, had no intention of pushing farther south. With two counties and with the coal fields around Newcastle in their possession, they held hostages enough. On all sides in England the demand arose for a meeting of Parliament. Charles, not yet convinced, summoned instead a Great Council consisting only of peers, such as had not met in England for at least two centuries. The peers arranged a treaty with the Scots that left things as they were until a more lasting settlement could be made. Thus a meeting of Parliament became absolutely necessary. Charles summoned one for 3 November 1640. The years of "personal rule" and the policies of "Thorough" (or the strict and stern enforcement of the laws) attributed to Strafford and Laud were at an end.

THE FIRST YEARS OF THE LONG PARLIAMENT

The members of the House of Commons who assembled in November 1640 were in a determined mood. Estranged from the Crown by years of arbitrary government, they believed that the time had come for the removal of abuses and for curtailment of the royal prerogative. The king, defeated and bankrupt, was in their power. And yet it is probable that most members thought in the traditional fashion of redressing wrongs and driving out "evil counselors." They had no thought of revolution or of removing the king from office. But a group of leaders—men such as John Pym and John Hampden in the Commons and a handful or Puritan peers—wanted something more than did ordinary members. Not that these leaders thought in terms of physical revolt. What they wanted was a transference of power from the king to the House of Commons. It seemed intolerable to them that a wrong-headed king whose government was in shambles should formulate policy which he could not carry out—while members of the gentry, upon whom the execution of government rested, had no share in decision making. These leaders believed that sovereignty should pass from the king to Parliament. During the next few years a majority of members came to agree with them.

The Commons began by striking at the ministers of the king. It was resolved at once to impeach the earl of Strafford. In this the Commons were prompted as much by fear as by determination to punish evil deeds; they secured Strafford's imprisonment even before the charges against him were formulated. Laud also was imprisoned, but he was not thought dangerous; his trial and execution did not take place until 1644–1645.

Strafford's trial before the House of Lords began in March 1641 and ended three weeks later without a verdict. He was accused of treason for attempting to subvert the fundamental laws of the realm and for advising the king to substitute an arbitrary and tyrannical government, but it soon became evident that the Commons' case was weak. The basic definition of treason was an offense against the king, of which Strafford was not guilty. He was accused, in fact, of treason against the nation, a new concept in law. His words to the king, "You have an army in Ireland you may employ here to reduce this kingdom," might well have referred to Scotland, as he claimed they did; in any case they rested on the oath of only one witness. The impeachment seemed likely to fail.

When the Commons discovered that certain courtiers were plotting to bring down the army from the north in order to dissolve the Parliament, they dropped the impeachment in a panic and substituted a bill of attainder, which required no proof, but which must pass the Lords and be signed by the king. There was now a great deal of tumult. Mobs from the city, sometimes composed of well-dressed persons and sometimes of mere rabble, milled around Westminster. Danger arose that the mob might attack the palace; cries were heard demanding the life of the queen. Threatened with violence, the lords passed the bill in a very thin house, and the king, after days of agony, signed it, to his great loss both in strength and in honor. Strafford was executed next morning.

To secure their position the Commons passed the Triennial Act, which provided that no more than three years should elapse between the dissolution of one Parliament and the meeting of the next; and an act declaring that the Parliament now assembled should not be dissolved without its own consent. When Charles signed the second of these bills, he lost his last shred of power over the Commons. The most basic control of Parliament by the Crown had been its right to summon and dissolve at will; with the curtailment of this power the Crown was indeed laid low. Charles had decreed a perpetual Parliament.

A series of important acts followed. Ship money, forest laws, and distraint of knighthood were swept away. Tonnage and poundage, though granted for a short time, was declared illegal without the consent of Parliament. Another measure abolished the Star Chamber, the High Commission, the Council in the North, the power of the Privy Council to deal with the property rights of the people, and the jurisdiction of the Council of Wales in so far as it resembled that of the Star Chamber.

The courts of common law remained supreme, victorious in their long contest with the prerogative courts.

The early work of the Long Parliament, which we have been describing, was done with surprising unanimity, but when the Commons turned to religious issues their unanimity disappeared. They could agree that the penal laws against Catholics should be enforced, that the church should not be Laudian, that Parliament should exercise some control over it, but here agreement ended. As differences multiplied, a royalist party began to take shape in the Commons. It was composed of moderate Anglicans, people loyal to the Church of England and to its prayer book who desired to retain episcopacy with the excessive power of the bishops curtailed. But a majority of the Commons wished to overthrow the church, to end it root and branch, and to set up some form of Puritanism in its place. What form was that to be? Presbyterianism, although strong in London and in other parts of the country, did not as yet command much support in the Commons. The same was true of Independency, or Congregationalism, though the few members who supported it wielded considerable influence. Pym, followed by a majority of the Commons, thought in terms of a Puritan state church controlled by lay commissioners who in turn would be controlled by Parliament. This solution in effect would transfer to Parliament the ecclesiastical supremacy the Crown had exercised since the Reformation. As these Puritan groups emerged, the Anglicans drew together, not only in defense of the prayer book and a reformed episcopacy, but in defense of the king, whose powers, it was thought, should not be reduced any further.

Division between Puritans and Anglicans was increased greatly in the autumn of 1641, when news arrived of a rebellion in Ireland. With Strafford, who had ruled Ireland with a heavy hand, now gone, the Irish Catholics saw an opportunity to turn on their oppressors. They had hoped for a general insurrection, though what took place was a rising in Ulster, where there were many English and Scottish landowners. The stories that reached England were greatly exaggerated, but it is certain that some thousands of Protestants were murdered and that thousands more died of exposure and privation. The Commons, vowing to revenge such brutality, voted money at once for an efficient army. This raised a fundamental issue, for the Commons dared not entrust the new army to the king, and the king could not entrust it to the Parliament. In this crisis Pym and other Puritan leaders drew up the Grand Remonstrance, a long document of 204 clauses which reviewed past grievances over many years, set forth the remedies advocated by Parliament, and demanded that the king employ officers and ministers of state whom the Commons could trust. The Grand Remonstrance was opposed by the royalists, who now formed a compact party. The debates on the Grand Remonstrance became so heated that there was danger of a scuffle on the floor of the Commons. In the end the Remonstrance passed by the slim majority of 159 to 148.

Events now moved rapidly to the outbreak of war. Tumults and mobs at Westminster became common. The bishops, fearing attack, ceased to attend the House of Lords. Men drew their swords in the streets; the names of Cavalier and Roundhead came into use. Charles had a party in each house, but in a wild and foolish move he ordered his attorney general to prepare impeachment proceedings against five of the leading Puritans in the Commons. When that house would not surrender them, Charles took the fatal step of coming in person to the Commons in an attempt to arrest the five members. This was regarded as a monstrous breach of privilege—as it was—though no worse a violation of constitutional principles than the Commons' use of the mob to terrorize Westminster. The five members had slipped away to London. Four thousand men came up from Buckinghamshire to defend their hero Hampden. The Commons sent one of their number, Sir John Hotham, to secure the arsenal at Hull and passed an ordinance which placed their nominees in control of the militia. Charles withdrew to Hampton Court and sent the queen to France. In March 1642 he went to York, in April he was refused admission to Hull, and in August he raised his standard at Nottingham. The Civil War had begun.

THE CAUSES OF THE CIVIL WAR

The years between 1640 and 1660 have traditionally been treated as a single period—the Puritan Revolution, or more recently, the English Revolution. One result of this was to confuse the causes of the Civil War of 1642–1646 with those factors that caused the revolution of 1649–1660. More recently historians have come to make a distinction between the causes of the Civil War and the causes of the revolution which grew out of the Civil War. Whatever were the forces at work in society in general that surfaced in the late 1640s and the 1650s, they might not have surfaced when and how they did if there had been no Civil War to impel them.

The search for explanations, if not causes, of the events of the 1640s and 1650s began with the participants themselves. James Harrington, Thomas Hobbes, and Sir Edward Hyde, later earl of Clarendon, all contributed to the ongoing debate. Harrington's *Oceana* (1656) credited the rise of the gentry with being the force behind the rebellion. Hobbes's *Behemoth, or the Long Parliament* (1600) saw the emergence of a bourgeois ideology, and Clarendon's *History of the Rebellion and Civil Wars in England* (1702–4) was a pro-Royalist narrative history which concentrated on the events and people of the reign of Charles I.

In the nineteenth century scholars such as S. R. Gardiner, in his monumental *History of England,* saw a "Puritan Revolution" in which there was a struggle for political and religious liberty. Karl Marx and his followers saw a distinct phase in the history of class struggle—the overthrow of the feudal aristocracy by the bourgeoisie. The twentieth century has seen many historians, beginning with R. H. Tawney, seek to explain the period by combining the ideas of Harrington, Hobbes, and Marx. The rise of the gentry has been seen as the result of modern managerial techniques (Tawney). This rise has also been attributed to the gentry's connections with the royal court (Trevor-Roper). Lawrence Stone *(Crisis of the Aristocracy)* thought the temporary crisis faced by the titled nobility gave the illusion of such a rise. Christopher Hill's many books have depicted a form of bourgeois revolution. Perez Zagorin saw a struggle between "court" and "country." Margaret Judson *(Crisis of the Constitution)* saw a struggle for constitutional sovereignty between the Crown and

Parliament. This view was in the tradition of Wallace Notestein, who had earlier seen the House of Commons attempting to take the initiative in formulating legislation and making policy. Each of these scholars sought answers by looking beyond the reign of Charles I to that of James I, Elizabeth I, and even Henry VIII.

Many contemporary scholars cite more immediate causes for war and revolution. Some see a dissolution of what had been a well-run state (Conrad Russell), or else immediate conflicts over the rigid enforcement of Anglicanism by Charles and Laud (Tyacke), or the struggle between national and local governments and their respective leaders (Alan Everitt, Clive Holmes, and J. S. Morrill). Such debates have raged for three hundred years and are likely to continue.

Economic issues also played a part in bringing about the Civil War. During the early Stuart period the aggressive country gentleman, as well as the opportunistic merchant and industrialist, saw many ways in which economic profit could be made. What these men wanted was greater freedom, especially in dealing with labor, and a relaxation of Tudor control of economic life. The early Stuarts, however, believed that the regulation of the economy was a royal prerogative to be employed for the protection of the Crown and for the advancement of the general good. Desiring stability rather than progress, James and Charles were suspicious of private enterprise; they resisted economic change which, they feared, might cause unemployment and social unrest. They stood for the *status quo*. Moreover, they regarded themselves as patriarchal rulers who protected the poor against the wealthy. But their efforts in this direction were so feeble, their economic policies so inconsistent, contradictory, and full of exceptions imposed by poverty, that they irritated the landed and business classes without bringing noticeable relief to the poor.

Inflation kept up the price of agricultural products. The country gentleman who could engage in the national industry of feeding London or who owned property rich in minerals or timber could make a good thing of his estates. The agricultural frontier was moving westward into Wales and northward toward the border. Wishing to bring more land under cultivation, landowners enclosed their estates, drained marshes, and encroached upon the wasteland between villages. The government resisted these moves, partly because they injured the poor, partly because they offered opportunity to levy fines upon the rich. Nevertheless, wealthy men who loaned money to the king were allowed to act as they pleased.

The same tendencies may be seen in commerce and industry. In James's first Parliament a demand arose for freer trading conditions, that is, for a curtailment of the monopolies enjoyed by the London trading companies. But the Crown defended the rights of the London companies. Moreover, many merchants resented the government's weakness in opposing the Dutch and in allowing the navy to decay, so that it gave little protection to English seaborne trade. Industry had expanded steadily in the century before the Civil War. To a considerable extent this expansion was based upon a greater use of coal in heating houses and in new industrial techniques. A remarkable growth had taken place in the amount of capital invested in business enterprises. London grew steadily as an economic center; the population slowly increased. Yet capitalists found that they were commanded to do uneconomical things such as keeping their workpeople employed when trade was slack, that the

Star Chamber was used when the common law courts would not support the Crown, that the middleman was disliked, that economic regulation became complex and rigid, that the government broke its own rules, that monopolies increased, and that interference by the Crown in economic life did more harm than good.

As for the poor, they obtained little benefit either from the expansion of the economy or from the policy of the state. The population, though not large, was greater than the economy of the time could absorb. Underemployment and extremely low wages were common, with no protection against disaster, and little done to relieve the poor. The poor, it may be noted, did not support the king during the Civil War. The business classes, with some exceptions, were alienated; the landed aristocracy was divided at least in sympathy.

CHRONOLOGY

The Personal Rule

1625–1649	Charles I
1627	Relief of La Rochelle a failure; forced loan; Five Knights' Case
1628	Petition of Right
1629	"Personal Rule" begins
1630	Peace with France and Spain; Puritans settle Boston Bay
1637	Ship Money Case (John Hampden); trials of Prynne, Burton, and Bastwick; Scottish National Covenant
1639	First Bishops' War
1640	Second Bishops' War; Short Parliament; Long Parliament begins; Strafford impeached; Laud imprisoned
1641	Strafford convicted and executed; Triennial Act; rebellion in Ireland; Grand Remonstrance
1642	Militia Bill and Civil War

18 The Civil Wars and the Rule of the Saints

The Civil Wars were fought between the king and Parliament. A look at how the wars started and how different groups and individuals chose sides may give us a better understanding as to their causes.

The Civil Wars were fought with spirit and resolution. The fighting began in a rather amateurish way, but both sides soon acquired professional technique from veterans returning from the wars on the Continent. Friends and relatives found themselves on opposite sides. Both sides, seeking the support of noncombatants, treated them with respect. A fiercer spirit prevailed when Englishmen fought Scots or Irishmen; yet the war in England generally was conducted with honor and humanity.

HOW THE COUNTRY WAS DIVIDED

Some eighty of the nobility sided with the king, some thirty against him. The nobles felt instinctively that their greatness was bound up with that of the Crown; they feared the mob and the chaos of revolution. Some had a sense of personal gratitude to Charles. "Had I a million crowns or scores of sons," wrote Lord Goring, "the king and his cause should have them all. . . . I had all from the king, and he hath all again." Of the nobles supporting Parliament, a few were Puritan, a few hoped to be on the winning side. The gentry were divided, the majority for the king, a large minority for Parliament. They were influenced by the same considerations as were the nobles, though Puritanism was stronger among them than among the peers. Accustomed to riding, they had the makings of excellent cavalry officers, and they often brought a body of horsemen with them for the king's service. "The honest country gentleman," wrote a Royalist, "raises the troop at his own charge, then gets

374

a Low Country lieutenant to fight his troop for him, and sends for his son from school to be cornet." The yeomen tended to side with the gentry of their areas; the peasants were indifferent. Although a few London merchants were Royalists, the business classes of the towns sided with Parliament; London, which was strongly Presbyterian, supplied the Commons with an inexhaustible source of men and money.

To some extent every locality was divided; the war began with a great number of small clashes as each side attempted to capture military stores and to control the militia. There was, however, a rough geographical division. The north and the west of the kingdom sided with the king, the south and the east with Parliament, while much of the Midlands formed a no-man's land. The king's territory was excellent recruiting ground, though his soldiers were difficult to discipline, prone to plunder, and apt to disappear if they did not receive their pay. The shires under Parliament's control were more amenable to discipline and to taxation, the London-trained bands were the best infantry in the kingdom at the beginning of the war, and Parliament secured the three principal arsenals of London, Hull, and Portsmouth.

Parliament held two great advantages; the first was sea power. The adherence of the navy permitted Parliament to control and to continue foreign trade, to collect customs, to hinder the king in importing munitions, and to maintain coastal towns behind his lines. Parliament's second advantage lay in money. By controlling the richer and more populous portions of the country, it could levy assessments on prosperous farming counties, sequester Royalists' estates, and raise loans in London. Although the pay of its soldiers was often in arrears, Parliament could always find new recruits. The king, on the other hand, depended almost entirely on the generosity of his followers; great nobles, such as the earls of Worcester and Newcastle, gave him huge sums. But the most lavish private gifts run out at last and are a poor substitute for taxation. As the king's finances became more and more desperate, recruiting fell off, and munitions were difficult to come by. The fact that royal troops lived off the countryside made the peasants hostile.

The first Civil War thus saw the king, the titled aristocracy, the Church of England, the North and the West, and a narrow majority of the gentry fighting against the House of Commons, London, other commercial centers with the merchant class, the South and the East, Puritans, and a large minority of the gentry. In many cases the choice of sides was a very personal one. Behind it all, it must be remembered, the House of Commons and the king could no longer trust each other. If there had been no Parliament in session, there would probably have been no Civil War.

THE CIVIL WAR OF 1642–1646

The king held an initial advantage, partly because the parliamentary general, the earl of Essex, was so dilatory that he allowed the king to grow strong. Charles moved west from Nottingham to Shrewsbury, seeking recruits and weapons. By

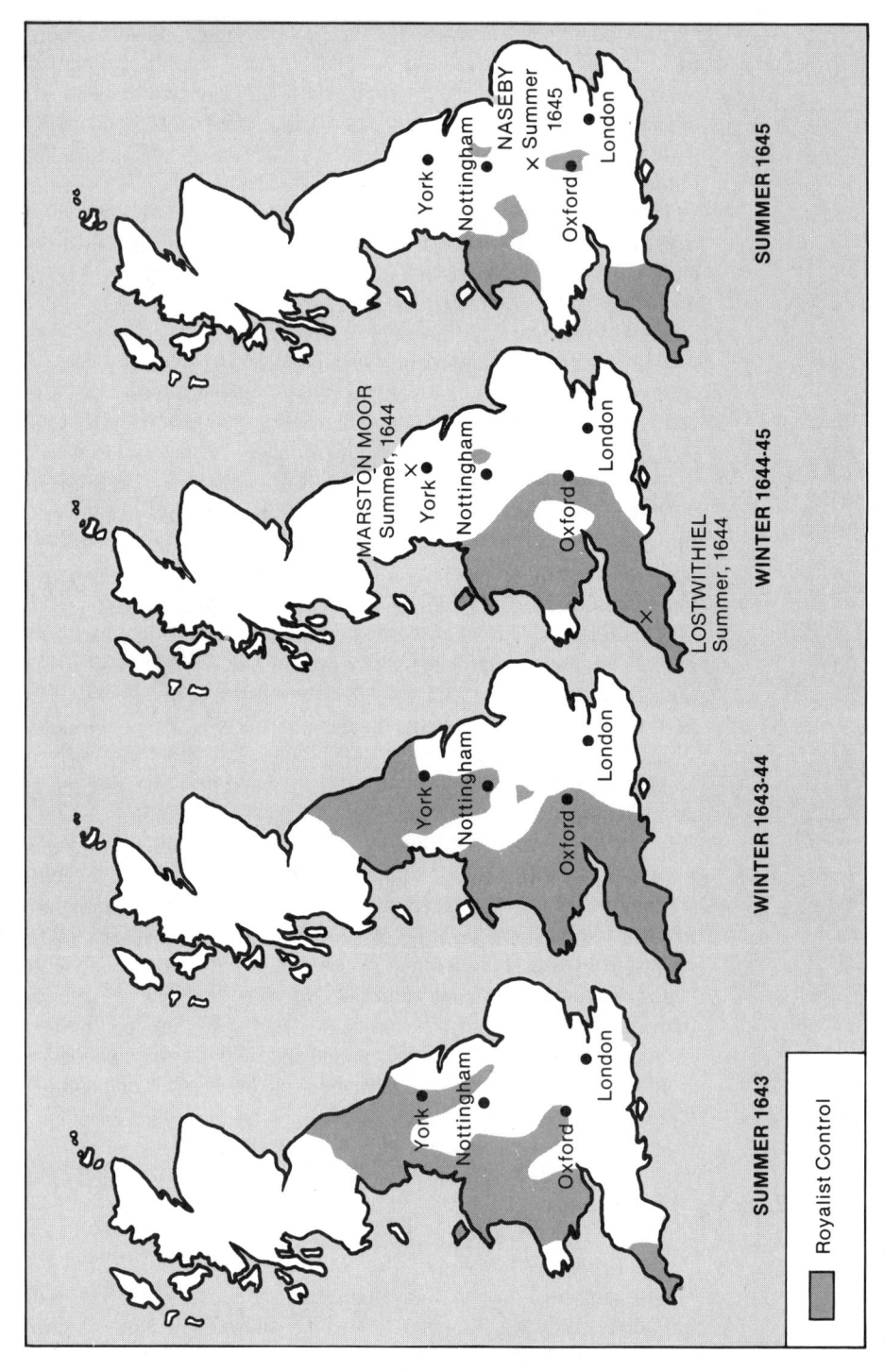

Areas under royal control.

October 1642 he was able to march toward London, hoping to end the war at a blow. Essex met him at Edgehill in Warwickshire in the first battle of the war. Charles's cavalry, commanded by his impetuous nephew, Prince Rupert of the Palatinate, drove Essex's horsemen from the field, but most of the parliamentary foot stood firm and the king's infantry was badly mauled. The fruits of victory fell to Charles, who entered Oxford and continued his march toward London. Although Rupert stormed Brentford a dozen miles from the city, the London-trained bands supported Essex. Charles withdrew to Oxford, which became his headquarters for the remainder of the war. He had shown more skill and daring than Essex, but he had failed to win the war in a single decisive campaign.

There was one parliamentary officer who studied these events to advantage. Oliver Cromwell, watching the battle at Edgehill, saw clearly that the parliamentary forces could never be victorious until their cavalry was equal to that of the king. He said to his cousin, John Hampden, "Your troops are most of them old decayed serving-men, tapsters, and such kind of fellows; do you think that the spirits of such base, mean fellows will ever be able to encounter gentlemen that have honor, and courage, and resolution in them? You must get men of a spirit that is likely to go as far as gentlemen will go, or you will be beaten still." Cromwell was a member of the gentry, owning estates around Huntingdon, and he obtained leave to go home to raise a troop of cavalry.

This famous troop, expanding gradually from 80 to 1100 men, was to give its spirit to the whole parliamentary army. Most of its soldiers were farmers, many owning their land and their horses. They were very religious, "having the fear of God before them and making some conscience of what they did." Cromwell was proud of his troop. "I have," he wrote, "a lovely company." Enforcing rigid discipline, he trained his men carefully. He taught them to look after and groom their horses and to keep their weapons bright and ready for use. Each trooper was armed with a pair of pistols and a sword and was protected by a light helmet called a pot and by two pieces of armor, known as back and breast, which fitted over the upper part of the body and were laced together at the sides. Cromwell trained his men to charge "at a good round trot," firing their pistols as they met the enemy and then relying upon the sharpness of their swords.

Cromwell had a natural aptitude for war. An introvert in his religious life, forever seeking flaws in his soul, he was an extrovert in battle, with a capacity for instant decision and a wonderful alertness and vitality. He was "naturally of such a vivacity, hilarity, and alacrity as another man hath when he hath drunken a cup too much." He created his own troop and selected his own officers; he saw that his men received their pay and their supplies. At first he was merely a dashing cavalry officer, but he grew with astonishing rapidity, developing into a superb general by whom all the arts and techniques of war—military, logistic, psychological—were employed with masterly success.

Following the Battle of Edgehill Parliament increased the efficiency of the war effort by dividing its territory into groups of counties known as associations. Of these the Eastern Association, consisting of East Anglia and the counties from Lincolnshire down to Hertford, was the most important. An army raised in this area was

Sir Thomas Fairfax, from Joshua Sprigg, Anglia Rediviva; England's Recovery, *London, 1647. (Department of Special Collections, Wilson Library, University of Minnesota)*

commanded by the Presbyterian earl of Manchester. Cromwell's regiment formed part of this army.

The fortunes of the king in the Civil War reached their height in 1643. In addition to the army at Oxford, there was a royal army in the north under the earl of Newcastle, who in the previous year had moved from Durham into Yorkshire, pushing back the parliamentary forces under Lord Fairfax and his son Sir Thomas. In 1643 Newcastle entered Lincolnshire and soon occupied the entire county. In the southwest a third army overran Cornwall and Devon except for the walled towns. With the capture of Bristol in July the king's hold on the west seemed secure. Thus, he occupied a central position at Oxford, with supporting forces on each flank, and there was scope for a broader strategy. Essex opened the campaign with a lunge toward Oxford, but he was checked and withdrew, allowing the queen, who had landed in the north, to enter Oxford with a large convoy of reinforcements and supplies. Encouraged by these successes, Charles planned a three-pronged assault on London by a converging movement of all his armies. But Newcastle hesitated to push south while Hull remained uncaptured in his rear; a similar dread haunted the

Royalists in the west, for they had not taken Plymouth. Charles therefore turned west to besiege the fortified city of Gloucester. Parliament was in difficulty, but it rose to the occasion, imposed new taxes, and sent Essex to Gloucester's relief. Charles abandoned the siege and met Essex at the Battle of Newbury, which was called a draw, though the king's losses were greater than those of Essex.

A crisis in the war was approaching, and both sides sought allies. The king turned to Ireland, where his Lord Deputy, Ormonde, held Dublin with a small Royalist force. Arranging a truce with the Irish Catholics, Ormonde sent troops to England, though they were not numerous enough to make any great difference. Charles was soon hoping for aid from the Irish Catholic rebels; a secret treaty was arranged which made them large concessions in return for assistance. Unfortunately a copy of the treaty was captured by Parliament, and great discredit was brought upon the king, for the use of Irish troops in England was abhorent to all parties.

Meanwhile Parliament approached the Scots, asking for a political alliance for the resolute prosecution of the war. But the Scots wanted a religious covenant. They knew that the Presbyterian party held a strong position in the House of Commons and that Parliament was in great need of assistance. They demanded and secured the Solemn League and Covenant, a treaty containing an implied promise that Parliament would establish Presbyterianism as the state religion in both England and Ireland. This treaty had far-reaching results. It divided the Commons between the Presbyterians and another party, the Independents, to whom we will turn presently. Eventually, when the Independents came to power, the treaty brought war between England and Scotland but meanwhile it helped enormously in defeating the king.

In January 1644 a well-equipped Scottish army of twenty-one thousand men crossed the border into England. The military picture suddenly was altered. Newcastle, the king's general, turned to face the Scots and was thrown on the defensive. He was driven into York, where he was besieged by the Scots, by the Fairfaxes, and by Manchester's forces. Prince Rupert, coming to the rescue from the west, broke up the siege but made the mistake of following the parliamentary armies as they retreated and of forcing a battle at Marston Moor in July 1644. The result was a Royalist disaster. Rupert retreated with his cavalry, having lost his infantry, his guns, and his baggage. The king's hold on the north of England was crushed.

Elsewhere Charles did not fare badly. Essex was defeated in Cornwall, and a second Battle of Newbury ended in a draw, though the king should have been routed. Meanwhile the great adventurer, James Graham, marquis of Montrose, was raising the Scottish Highlands for the king, to the consternation of the Lowland Scots. Nevertheless, Charles was in a precarious position. He was almost without money or even a resolute plan.

Meanwhile Parliament reconstructed and improved its army. There had been a quarrel between Cromwell and the earl of Manchester in which, with his usual force and bluntness, Cromwell had accused the earl of inefficiency and of wishing to make peace with the king. As a result Parliament passed the Self-denying Ordinance, which forced the resignation of persons holding commands, civil or military, who were members of that Parliament. Essex, Manchester, and Waller were eliminated; Fairfax became general, Skippon, major general; the office of lieutenant general, left open for a time, was given to Cromwell. By the Self-denying Ordinance he should have been passed over, but he had a great following in the army and his services were too valuable to lose. His appointment was an indication that in a crisis the army could force its will upon the Commons. The New Model Army, as it was called, was better led and better organized; the soldiers were paid regularly by a monthly assessment levied on all the counties under Parliament's control. It was this army that speedily brought the war to a close. Charles, with no firm plan, foolishly marched into enemy territory and was crushed at Naseby in June 1645, another battle in which Cromwell played a distinguished part. Thereafter the king was a fugitive and the war subsided into sieges and small operations. In May 1646 Charles surrendered himself to the Scots.

PRESBYTERIANS AND INDEPENDENTS

To defeat the king was far easier than to construct a new government. The king could not be restored as if nothing had happened; nor could the House of Commons, which had fought a war and governed the country for five years, be set once more in its old position. King and Parliament would have to cooperate in a new government, and many wounds would have to be healed. These problems proved too difficult for solution. There were bitter quarrels—between Presbyterians and Independents, between Parliament and the army, and between England and the Scots—until chaos threatened and the Second Civil War was fought. Then the army, bitter against the king, seized control of Parliament and brought Charles to his tragic death.

When Royalist members left Parliament at the beginning of the Civil Wars, the party that remained was the Root and Branch party, determined to destroy the Anglican Church. In 1642 it summoned a meeting of clergymen, known as the Westminster Assembly, to suggest reforms. The Solemn League and Covenant gave power to the Presbyterians in the Commons, and the church gradually assumed a Presbyterian tone. A Directory took the place of the Prayer Book, the hierarchy of the Church of England was abolished, there was a new Confession of Faith as well as a new Catechism. The new church, when fully constructed, would be a Presbyterian Church, though it would be subject to Parliament and not free and sovereign as in Scotland.

A new form of ecclesiastical government—that of the Independents—was emerging in England. The Independents had begun in the reign of Elizabeth when a group of religious radicals, the Brownists or Separatists, broke from the church and set up their own congregations. The churches in New England and some English churches in Holland were of this type. They rejected any kind of ecclesiastical hierarchy, whether Anglican or Presbyterian. Each congregation, they believed, should be complete, autonomous, and sovereign in itself. Uncontrolled from above, it should select its own minister and should determine its own beliefs and ritual. The Independents laid great stress on individual interpretation of the Scriptures and believed that man could discover God's will as well as find a guide to conduct in the

Bible. "If thou wilt seek to know the mind of God in all that chain of Providence," wrote Cromwell, "seek of the Lord to teach thee what that is; and He will do it." Hence the Independents believed in new revelations, new directives, to be found in God's written word. The result was great diversity of doctrine and a great variety of sects—Congregationalists, Anabaptists, Antinomians, Fifth Monarchy Men, Seekers, Quakers,[1] and, to the far left, the Diggers, who rejected church buildings and all ritual and made religion a silent communion of the spirit between God and man. The Independents were weak in the House of Commons. They could number only fifty or sixty votes. But their leaders, such as Sir Henry Vane the Younger and Oliver St. John, were so able that they exerted an influence out of proportion to their numbers.

Presbyterians and Independents represented not only two churches but two philosophies of government. The Presbyterians proclaimed the sovereignty of Parliament. Like the members of the General Assembly in Scotland, they believed that God had given them the right to rule the state. The Independents, on the other hand, found sovereignty in the people. Democracy in the Independent churches led to democracy in politics. Just as a congregation selected its pastor, so the people should select their governors; Parliament should be kept close to the sovereign people by frequent elections. Just as the church was a voluntary association of believers held together by a covenant, so the state was an association of freemen held together by a contract. The government should not interfere in matters of the spirit. There should be liberty of conscience for every individual to believe and worship as he wished. Thus the ideas of modern political democracy were foreshadowed by the Independents.

If weak in the House of Commons, the Independents were strong in the army. All sorts of sects were to be found among the soldiers. Trusting in new revelations, they believed that God, by the victories He had given them, had marked them as the protectors of religion with a mission to control the state. The soldiers were hostile to the king. He had been their enemy, and they could not trust themselves under his power in any form of restored monarchy.

The army looked to Cromwell as its leader in politics as well as in war. He was popular with the soldiers, jovial and familiar with them, and did not stand on his dignity; and if a fiery temper underlay his joviality, this did not make him less popular. He represented their views much better in religion than he did in politics. He has been called the great Independent. Though he did not associate himself with any one sect, he sympathized with the spirit of all of them and embodied their religious ideals. As a young man of about twenty-eight he had experienced a conversion through which, after great mental and spiritual agony, he became convinced that he was one of God's elect, chosen by the Almighty to fulfill His plans on earth. It was Cromwell's primary aim to discover the will of God, and for this purpose he devoted long periods to prayer and meditation. He was a strong advocate of liberty of conscience, and he defended the sectaries in the army against the intolerance of the Presbyterians. After the Battle of Naseby he wrote to the speaker of the House of Commons:

---

[1] Antinomians believed Christ relieved Christians from obedience to the moral law; Anabaptists required rebaptism for true believers; Fifth Monarchy Men looked to an imminent second coming of Christ; Seekers rejected organized religion and sought truth elsewhere; Quakers also sought piety and tranquility outside a formal church structure.

Honest men served you faithfully in this action. They are trusty; I beseech you in the name of god not to discourage them. He that ventures his life for the liberty of his country, I wish he trust God for the liberty of his conscience, and you for the liberty he fights for.

In politics Cromwell did not represent the soldiers so well: his political views were those of the landowning classes. Because of his strong sense of property and his dread of chaos he labored to make the soldiers obedient to Parliament and to restrain them from using force in politics. He thus exposed himself to the suspicion of the radicals and to the charge of hypocrisy.

Parliament and the Army

Shortly after the war came to an end, the relations between Parliament and the army became extremely tense. There was no hope that Parliament, with its intolerant Presbyterian majority, would accept the Independent and democratic ideas of the soldiers. The soldiers may well have been motivated by military as much as by political considerations. The Presbyterian leaders foolishly planned to disband the army, not only without indemnity for acts committed in war but also without arrears of pay. They hoped to persuade the disbanded soldiers to enlist for service in Ireland. The degree of discontent in the army became alarming. The soldiers organized themselves politically by electing representatives called Agitators or Agents to present their views to Parliament. When the army refused to disband in the spring of 1647, the Presbyterian leaders determined to disperse it by force. The plan was to

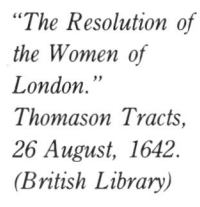

"The Resolution of the Women of London." Thomason Tracts, 26 August, 1642. (British Library)

bring the Scottish army into England and to employ it against the men who had won the war. At this point the army mutinied. It began by arresting the king.

Charles had been a prisoner of the Scots for eight months. He had been negotiating both with them and Parliament, but had refused Presbyterianism; in January 1647 the Scots in disgust handed him over to the English and crossed the border into their own country. In June he was seized by the English army. In August the army occupied London, and the radicals, or Levelers, drew up the Agreement of the People, to be laid before the House of Commons. This famous document demanded that the Parliament then in session be dissolved, that there be an election every two

Charles I, from Bibliotheca Regia . . . containing a collection of such of the pages of His Late Majesty . . . as have escaped the Wreck and Ruins of these times, *London, 1659. (Department of Special Collections, Wilson Library, University of Minnesota)*

years, that electoral districts be made equal, and that there be universal manhood suffrage. The king and the House of Lords were not mentioned and presumably would disappear. An assertion of natural rights followed: all Englishmen should enjoy freedom of conscience, freedom from impressment, and equality before the law. Cromwell and many officers would have been satisfied with a limited monarchy, but in the Agreement of the People the soldiers were demanding a democratic republic based on a written constitution, both novel ideas in English history. At Cromwell's urging, the Agreement was modified and presented to Parliament in the form of proposals.[2]

Events suddenly took a dramatic turn, for on the night of 11 November 1647, the king escaped from Hampton Court and made his way to the Isle of Wight off the southern coast. He had concluded a secret agreement with the Scots that he would establish Presbyterianism throughout his dominions for three years if they would restore him to his throne. There followed the Second Civil War in 1648. It consisted of scattered risings by Cavaliers, the desertion of part of the fleet, and an invasion from Scotland, but these sporadic moves were not directed by any master mind. The people as a whole were apathetic. Local risings were quelled without great difficulty, and in a lightning campaign Cromwell overwhelmed the Scots at Preston, Wigan, and Warrington in the northwest of England.

The Death of the King

After these victories the English army assumed control. Its mood was one of harsh severity against the king, whose intrigues with all parties, and especially his last treaty with the Scots, which resulted in the Second Civil War, hardened the hearts of the soldiers against him. "We came to a very clear resolution," wrote one of them, "that it was our duty, if ever the Lord brought us back again in peace, to call Charles Stuart, that man of blood, to account for the blood he had shed, and mischief he had done to the utmost against the Lord's cause and people in these poor nations." London was occupied once more in December 1648. Parliament was dealt with in a simple way. Colonel Pride, placing his musketeers at the door of the House of Commons, excluded about 140 Presbyterian members (arresting 45 of them) and admitted only the Independents, some 50 or 60 strong. This was known as the Rump (sitting) Parliament.

A court was then set up to try the king. Charles refused to recognize its jurisdiction, but it condemned him to death for treason against the nation. Charles met his fate with fortitude and courage on January 30, 1649. Steadfast in his opinions, he said on the scaffold,

> For the people I desire their liberty and freedom as much as anybody whomsoever; but I must tell you that their liberty and freedom consists in having government, in those laws by which their life and goods may be most their own. It is not their having a share in government; that is nothing pertaining to them.

---

[2]This document in modified form appeared again in 1649. See Charles Firth, *Oliver Cromwell and the Rule of the Puritans in England* (London: Putnam, 1901), pp. 177, 183, 236–237.

The Trial of King Charles I, 1648. (British Museum)

He then prayed for a moment, laid his comely head on the block, and signaled the executioner to strike. At one blow his head was severed from his body. A groan broke from the people—"such a groan," wrote a spectator, "as I never heard before, and desire I may never hear again."

THE COMMONWEALTH, 1649–1653

Shortly after the king's execution Parliament abolished the office of king as dangerous and unneccessary. It also abolished the House of Lords. "England," it declared, "shall henceforth be governed as a Commonwealth, or a Free State, by the supreme authority of this nation, the representatives of the people in Parliament." On another occasion the Commons affirmed that the people were, under God, the origin of all just power. But despite these democratic sentiments, the members of the House of Commons, now about ninety Independents, clung to power with the utmost tenacity. The army strongly desired an election, but no election was held. The Commonwealth was in reality a continuation of the rule of the Long Parliament under a new name. Parliament was more powerful than ever, for there was neither a king nor a House of Lords to impose restraint.

The Commons appointed a Council of State to which administrative power was entrusted; the Council, however, was to be elected annually by the Commons, and thirty-one of its forty-one members were also members of Parliament. It was no more than the Commons in administrative session. Nor could Parliament claim to represent the nation. Large areas of the country had no members in the Commons. Parliament represented only the Independents, who were a handful of sectaries, a fraction of the whole people. Parliament, moreover, did not meet occasionally as in the past. It remained in session the year round: there seemed no hope of ending it, for it could not legally be dissolved without its own consent. The Commons contained energetic and dedicated men, some of them very able, but it is not surprising that their government was highly unpopular. The army, taking its stand on the principles of the Agreement of the People, was deeply dissatisfied; it tolerated the new government only because there were enemies on every side.

At home the Commonwealth faced the hatred of Royalists and Presbyterians. These groups, and many persons outside them, could never forgive the Puritans for killing the king. The Independents had thought of Charles's death as just retribution, but it proved to be their most egregious blunder. To lay violent hands upon the king, to touch the Lord's anointed, to shed his blood as though he were a common criminal was to shock and horrify a large proportion of the people. Charles haunted the Independents from his grave. The reaction in his favor that had begun before his death was greatly intensified by the appearance of *Eikon Basilike,* a touching book about his last days of suffering. It was written by a clergyman, Dr. Gauden, who drew largely on his own imagination, but Royalists were certain that it had been written by Charles himself and that its noble thoughts were those of the king. This book kept green among Cavaliers the memory of their martyred ruler.

The popular image of the king now altered. Charles, the friend of Laud, the imposer of ship money, the shady trickster, and the man of blood disappeared; Charles the Martyr took his place. John Milton hoped to shatter this image in a learned pamphlet, *Eikonoklastes,* but no one read it. The death of the king was remembered, his weakness forgotten. For the moment the Commonwealth had little to fear from Royalists or Presbyterians. The Royalists were battered and impoverished, their estates sequestered and redeemable only by the payment of large fines. The Presbyterians, though strong among the business classes in the towns, went no further than a sullen passive resistance.

The Commonwealth was also under attack from the political radicals, known as the Levelers. Their leader, John Lilburne, a restless and unreasonable man, was an energetic pamphleteer. He denounced the Commons for refusing to grant annual elections, manhood suffrage, and complete religous liberty. He said bitter things about Cromwell, whom he regarded as a traitor to democratic principles. Cromwell believed that Lilburne was politically dangerous and ought to be suppressed. "I tell you," he said in the Council, "you have no other way to deal with these men but to break them, or they will break you." Lilburne was sent to the Tower.

Cromwell was wise enough to ignore a small and harmless group who called themselves True Levelers and were known as Diggers. Their leader, Gerrard Winstanley, was a religious mystic who applied the principle of equality not only to politics but to social and economic life. He envisaged a kind of communist utopia. Believing that the poor had been excluded from their birthright, the land of England, he wished the people to take over the land and to hold it in common. His desire was to eliminate landlords, clergymen, and lawyers. But Winstanley, a gentle rebel, began his revolution by leading a group of poor men to a village near London, where they squatted on the common, dug up the ground, and planted beans. They were shortly dispersed by the landowners of the village.

Charles's death produced a violent reaction abroad. In Russia the Czar imprisoned English merchants. In Holland the Stadtholder, William II, who had married Charles's daughter Mary, allowed Royalist privateers to refit in Dutch ports. An English ambassador at The Hague and another in Madrid were murdered by Royalists almost with impunity. France was openly hostile; Spain was a little more friendly only because she was at war with France. The Puritans were regarded on the Continent as barbarians, revolutionists, and blood-stained villains.

Surrounded by enemies, the Commonwealth perforce became a military state. It maintained an army of forty-four thousand men, of whom twelve thousand were to be sent to Ireland. This army, the finest in Europe, was commanded by officers who made it their career. The men were well paid. The famous redcoat of the British soldier was now introduced and made universal. The navy was reorganized, and some forty warships were built within three years. There was much for these forces to do. The navy hunted down royalist privateers, for some of Charles's followers, desperate in poverty, had taken to the sea and preyed upon English commerce. Small nests of Royalists were cleared from the Channel Islands, from the Scilly Isles off the coast of Cornwall, and from the Isle of Man. The North American and West Indian colonies were forced to submit to the Commonwealth. From 1652 to 1654 there was an important and fiercely fought naval war with the Dutch. Meanwhile the army had rough work to do in Ireland and Scotland.

Ireland and Scotland

Ireland was very dangerous for the Commonwealth in 1649. For some years she had been left to her own devices, but the Second Civil War and the execution of the king produced an alliance of Protestant Royalists and Irish Roman Catholics. Ireland, if left alone, would not only be independent; she would become a base for an invasion of England. Parliament therefore turned to its best general and in the summer of 1649 Cromwell landed in Dublin with a well-equipped army of some twelve thousand men. There was no Irish army that could meet him in the field; instead, the Irish relied on fortresses and walled towns to delay his progress. Cromwell at once struck north at Drogheda. When the town refused to surrender, Cromwell took it by storm and put the entire garrison of twenty-eight hundred men to the sword. Though this massacre was justified by the rules of war, it would not have happened in England and was done in a spirit of revenge. Cromwell believed that he had come to Ireland not only as a conqueror but as a judge. He termed the slaughter at Drogheda a "righteous judgment of God upon these barbarous wretches." Another massacre took place at Wexford, though, Cromwell did not order it. The terror inspired by these incidents induced other towns to capitulate; by the end of 1649 all the southern and eastern coast, with the exception of Waterford, was in English hands. Early in 1650 Cromwell struck inland into Munster and captured Kilkenny, the seat of the Roman Catholic alliance.

Cromwell left Ireland in the summer of 1650. The conquest, completed by his lieutenants, was over by 1652, when the country was utterly devastated, a third of the population had perished, and a traveler could journey for miles in some areas without seeing a living creature. The settlement of Ireland after the war was harsh. The lands of all Roman Catholics who had taken part in the rebellion were confiscated and allotted either to Englishmen who had advanced money for the campaign or to Cromwell's soldiers as arrears of pay. Some Catholics received inferior land in Connaught as compensation, but many received nothing. It is said that two-thirds of the land in Ireland changed hands, and a large part of the Irish upper classes were ordered to move into Connaught or county Clare. Ireland became a country in which the great landowners were Protestant. Cromwell's soldiers, however, who were small farmers, often married Irish women, though they were forbidden to do so. In a few generations their descendants were Catholic in religion and Irish in sympathy. The Irish peasants remained as landless laborers on the estates of the new owners. Cromwell's settlement in Ireland included a number of other points. Anti-Catholic laws were enforced, and an attempt was made to strengthen Protestant congregations. There was impartial justice in the courts, Ireland obtained thirty members in the English Parliament, and free trade was established between the two countries. But these measures benefited the English in Ireland rather than the Irish themselves. Irish hatred of England grew to white heat.

In Scotland the Presbyterians, deeply offended by the triumph of the Independents in England and by Charles's execution, at once proclaimed Charles II as their king. They sent envoys to England who demanded that he also be recognized there and that the terms of the Solemn League and Covenant be honored. In reply the English expelled the envoys and prepared for another war. This was a national war, for Scotland, like Ireland, was attempting to dictate to England how she should be governed; the struggle became one for supremacy in Britain. The Scots turned to Charles II, an exile in the Netherlands, then about twenty years old. He was told that they would place him upon the English throne on condition that he accept the Covenant and establish Presbyterianism in both England and Ireland. He resisted these terms until Cromwell's victories in Ireland ended all hope of aid from that country. Then Charles came reluctantly to Scotland. The Scots knew his acceptance of the Covenant was hypocritical, yet they insisted upon it. Charles found himself a semiprisoner of the Kirk. He was forced to deplore in public the episcopacy of his father and the Catholicism of his mother; many years later he remarked that he would rather be hanged than return to the accursed land of Scotland.

Cromwell crossed the border in July 1650. At Dunbar on September 3 he caught the Scots in an awkward position and inflicted a crushing defeat on them. Three thousand Scots fell in the battle and ten thousand were taken prisoner. The effect in Scotland was overwhelming, for the ministers had been confident of victory. Charles was able to gain some control of policy. In the next year he led an army into England, hoping for an uprising in his favor, but his army was annihilated at the Battle of Worcester. In this battle Cromwell did not merely defeat the enemy; he wiped it out. Scarcely a Scot reached home after that ordeal. Charles wandered as a fugitive for some six weeks before he found a boat to take him to France. The English conquest of Scotland followed shortly. Annexed to England, she lost her Parliament and General Assembly, though local churches were let alone. English rule in Scotland was impartial, efficient, and deeply resented.

The End of the Commonwealth

Despite these victories, there was strong sentiment in the army that the Commonwealth was a provisional government which should be superseded by something more stable and lasting. Cromwell urged the Commons to fix a date for their dissolution, but the date they determined upon was 1654, three years in the future. Meanwhile the management of constant war occupied their energies, and they had no time for much-needed reforms. A law was finally passed granting amnesty to the defeated Royalists, but it was weakened by many exceptions. There was also need for legal and social reform, for the normal relations of debtor and creditor and of landlord and tenant had been disturbed. The prisons were full of debtors; the country swarmed with beggars. Parliament appointed a commission to review the law, but few of its suggestions were adopted. A reorganization of the church was also necessary. Presbyterianism had been established in London and in a few other places, but in large portions of the country each congregation went its own way. A group of clergymen headed by John Owen, who had been Cromwell's chaplain in Ireland, presented Parliament with a comprehensive scheme for the settlement of the church. But the result was nil.

The irritation of the army with Parliament increased. When a bill was finally introduced for a new election, the commons changed it into a plan for their continuance in power, suggesting that they should remain members of all future Parliaments, and that elections should merely add to their number. Cromwell and the army officers objected and believed that the bill would be defeated. Then suddenly in April 1653, Cromwell learned that the bill was about to be passed. He came down to the Commons, berated the members soundly, and called in his musketeers. The members then filed out of the chamber and the door was locked behind them.

Like the execution of the king, the dissolution of Parliament by force proved to be a political blunder. The House of Commons had been the one last shred of legality covering the actions of government, and the only link with the old constitution. Military might was revealed as the sole source of power. Cromwell spent the rest of his life trying to give the rule of the sword some sort of constitutional form.

THE BAREBONES PARLIAMENT AND THE INSTRUMENT OF GOVERNMENT

At the dissolution of the Long Parliament, some people wished Cromwell to be king. His picture was hung up in London with the inscription:

Ascend three thrones, great captain and divine,
I' th' will of God, old Lion, they are thine.

Cromwell dismissing the Rump Parliament, 1653. Contemparary Dutch engraving. (British Museum)

But Cromwell had no wish to become either a king or a military dictator. As commander in chief he considered himself temporarily in authority but he desired to lay that authority down and divest the army of governmental power. He and the army officers determined to summon a new assembly and to place power in its hands. This assembly, however, was not elected by the old franchise. Independent churches were asked to make nominations, and from this list Cromwell and the officers selected 140 persons. They were all Puritan notables—preachers, idealists, reformers—but had no experience in government. They were strongly influenced by the Fifth Monarchy Men, who believed that Christ would soon come to rule the world and that, until his coming, "His saints should take the kingdom and possess it." This assembly was nicknamed the Little or Barebones Parliament, since one of its members was an Anabaptist preacher named Praise-God Barbon or Barebones, who seems to have contributed nothing but his name. The Parliament entered upon a reckless course of hasty and unwise reform. It abolished the court of chancery after

Oliver Cromwell, from Gregorio Leti, Historia, e memorie recondite sopra alla vita di Oliverio Cromvele, Amsterdam, 1692. (Department of Special Collections, Wilson Library, University of Minnesota)

one day's debate. It appointed a committee to codify the law, which was to be so reduced that a man could carry it in a little book in his pocket. Some members wished to abolish the law entirely and to substitute the laws of Moses. Tithes were to be abolished before any other way was found for the support of the church. Cromwell and the army officers were disgusted and alarmed, and so were the more moderate members of the Parliament. these moderates met early one morning, marched from the Parliament building to Whitehall, and returned to Cromwell the powers he had given them. The rule of the Barebone saints was over. It had lasted from July to December 1653.

Cromwell then accepted a plan advanced by certain army officers that the government should consist of a lord protector, a Council of State, and a Parliament. The plan was in the form of a written constitution, the only written constitution ever to be in effect in England. This Instrument of Government, as it was called, was written because its authors wanted something permanent, fundamental, and unchangeable. In religion they thought of a covenant between God and man, and so in politics they were led to think of a contract between man and his governors. The army officers were more conservative than they had been in 1649; the franchise was limited to property holders; Parliament was to meet only once in three years and then for only five months; it could not vote away the constitution; and there was a portion of the revenue it could not control. On the other hand, the protector had no veto; he must consult the council or Parliament or both. The councilors held office for life and could name the protector's successor. Thus the army officers built checks and balances into their constitution. The document is also interesting because in it one can see the old constitution creeping back. Finally, it guaranteed religious liberty to all Christians except to Catholics and to members of the Church of England.

THE PROTECTORATE, 1653–1659

It is ironic that Cromwell, having defeated the king in the name of Parliament, discovered as protector that he could not manage the House of Commons any more than could Charles I. Cromwell wished to rule with Parliament's consent and cooperation and not by military force; he also feared an all-powerful Parliament such as the Long Parliament, and he was determined to maintain religious toleration. He therefore took his stand on the Instrument of Government.

His Parliaments, on the other hand, were hostile to military rule and to the Instrument of Government as the work of the army. They assumed the lofty tone of the Long Parliament in claiming to be the supreme power in the state. Cromwell's first Parliament (1654–1655) began at once to amend the constitution, making elective the office of protector, bringing the council more under Parliament's control, seeking to limit religious toleration, and trying to reduce the size of the army as well as to subject it to parliamentary authority. Cromwell protested and offered compromises. He dismissed the Parliament at the earliest possible moment.

In 1655 he made a serious blunder. Amid rumors of Cavalier plots Cromwell divided the country into twelve districts and placed a major general in charge of each. This was effective as a police measure, but it brought the power of the army to every person's doorstep and intensified the hatred of military rule. The elections to Cromwell's second Parliament in 1656 went against the government. Although about a hundred members were excluded as dangerous, the Commons showed little interest in toleration and great hostility to the major generals. But they had a strong desire to return to the old constitution.

This desire took the startling form of asking Cromwell to assume the title of king. One of his Secretaries wrote:

Parliament will not be persuaded that there can be a settlement any other way. The title is not the question, but it's the office, which is known to the laws and to the people. They know their duty to a king and his to them. Whatever else there is will be wholly new, and upon the next occasion will be changed again. Besides they say the name Protector came in with the sword. . . . nor will there be a free Parliament so long as that continues, and as it savors of the sword now, so it will at last bring all things to be military.

The proposal, known as the Humble Petition and Advice, was made to Cromwell by Parliament in March 1657. He rejected it. While he saw the advantage of a settlement that would bring a sense of permanence, he knew that most of his old fellow soldiers would be deeply offended. In May the Humble Petition and Advice was presented to him again, with the word "protector" substituted for "king." This time Cromwell accepted, and he became hereditary protector, a king in all but name. There was also to be a second chamber of Parliament to which he could appoint members for life. He was also given a more ample revenue. Parliament asked for and obtained the right to control its own election disputes; the power of the Protector to exclude members was dropped. But in a second session of this Parliament a quarrel arose between the two houses. Moreover, the hard core of republicans in the Commons was violently opposed to the new arrangements. Before another Parliament met, Cromwell was dead (3 September 1658).

Cromwell's contemporaries judged him with the utmost severity. To Clarendon, the Royalist historian of the Great Rebellion, he was "a brave bad man," possessing "all the wickedness against which damnation is pronounced and for which hell fire is prepared." Clarendon, though he condemned, could not refrain from admiration, but most Royalists saw nothing to palliate the blackness of Cromwell's character. He also was assailed from the left by radicals who believed that he had betrayed the cause for which he had fought and had been led by ambition to grasp the sovereign power in the state. "In all his changes," wrote the republican Ludlow, "he designed nothing but to advance himself." These views reflect the fact that he was the leader of a party and not of the nation.

A more sympathetic estimate by his steward, John Maidston, described Cromwell the man—his fiery temper, his marvelous courage, his unselfishness and devotion to a cause, his promptness and vigor in action, his deeply religious nature, his strength and depth of character, his compassion for persons in distress. "A larger soul," wrote Maidston, "hath seldom dwelt in house of clay." Much of his work was destroyed by the Restoration; yet his great achievements stand out clearly. His superb ability as a soldier broke the absolutism of the Stuarts and changed the course of English history. He held the British Isles together and saved England from anarchy, taking hold as a strong executive in the face of chaos. Cromwell advanced the cause of religious toleration. He raised England's prestige and added to her possessions overseas, and gave her for the first time a colonial and imperial policy.[3] To this last point we must now turn our attention.

---

[3] See the estimate of Cromwell in the last chapter of Charles Firth, *Oliver Cromwell and the Rule of the Puritans in England.*

OVERSEAS EXPANSION

The Rise of the Dutch

English expansion overseas in the Stuart period developed naturally from the achievements of the Elizabethans. Brilliant as those achievements had been, they were for the most part experimental; when Elizabeth died in 1603 England did not possess a single colony. It was in the seventeenth century that they intensified their efforts and learned the difficult lesson that colonies must be built slowly through toil and patience and not merely through bold adventure.

Conditions of international rivalry had altered. The Elizabethans had thought of Spain as their great opponent, a belief which persisted in the reign of James I, though Spain was falling rapidly into decay. For the first three quarters of the seventeenth century it was the Dutch and not the Spanish who were England's commercial rivals. While fighting their fierce wars of independence against Spain, the Dutch had become a great maritime power. Their East India Company was far stronger and more wealthy than its English rival. During the early seventeenth century Dutch fleets swept through the Caribbean, driving the Spanish from the sea; and in 1628 Piet Hein—a Dutch Sir Francis Drake—captured the whole of the Spanish treasure fleet. By 1626 Holland had planted a settlement on the island of Manhattan; in the 1620s a Dutch West India Company established itself in northern Brazil. All over the world—in the East, the West, the Levant, Russia, the Baltic, the herring fisheries of the North Sea, and in the whaling areas of the arctic—wherever the English went to trade, to fish, or to colonize, there were the hardheaded Dutch eager to drive them out. Holland possessed a great merchant marine and hoped to monopolize the carrying trade of the world.

The English were slow to recognize the challenge of the Dutch, though there were warning voices. Sir Walter Ralegh wrote a pamphlet declaring that Holland "possessed already as many ships as eleven kingdoms, England being one of them." In 1614 Tobias Gentleman warned that the English neglected fishing: "Look but on these fellows that we call the plump Hollanders, behold their diligence in fishing and our own careless negligence." Another author contrasted the smallness of England's foreign trade with that of "our neighbors the new Sea-Herrs." These warnings fell upon deaf ears. King James, intent on the Spanish match, would do nothing; and King Charles, without resources, could do nothing if he would. It was left for the Puritans to beat back the Dutch.

English Colonies in America

Between the old war with Spain and the new ones with Holland there was an interval in which the English sought to expand overseas through the arts of peace. During the first half of the seventeenth century Englishmen swarmed to North

America and even more to the West Indies. A mass migration such as England had never seen before, it consisted of two waves. One planted Virginia, Maryland, and the English West Indies. In 1606 two companies were founded, the Plymouth and the London, to establish colonies in North America under the supervision of a royal council. The Plymouth Company accomplished nothing permanent, but the London Company in 1607 planted a colony at Jamestown in Virginia. After a period of intense suffering, the colonists found a staple crop in tobacco, much to King James's disgust, for he had conceived a strong aversion to that expensive luxury, that "precious stink." The affairs of the company became involved in English politics, and in 1624 the king dissolved the company and took Virginia under his control, making it the first Crown colony. In 1632 George Calvert, Lord Baltimore, a Roman Catholic who had been one of James's secretaries, obtained permission to establish a colony in the northern part of Chesapeake Bay. This project, carried out by his son, resulted in the founding of Maryland in 1634.

Tiny English settlements were also attempted in Guiana—an unoccupied area between the Spanish in modern Venezuela and the Portuguese in Brazil—and on the Amazon and Orinoco rivers. These settlements were failures, but they led to colonies in the West Indies. The Spanish had ignored the smaller islands, for they contained no gold, were densely wooded, and were inhabited by savage Carib tribes who had the unpleasant habit of eating Europeans.

A number of motives lay behind this wave of colonization. The first was economic, the desire for products unobtainable at home—the precious metals, naval stores, cotton, tobacco, sugar, and rare woods. There was also a social motive. England teemed with beggars, and it was thought that the country was overcrowded; hence the idea that colonies might drain off surplus population. Moreover, an English base in the New World was regarded as a great advantage in any future war with Spain. Propaganda in favor of colonization often spoke of the mission of converting the Indians, although, as a matter of fact, little was done in this direction; England did not become a missionary nation until the nineteenth century. And finally, colonial trade would help to build the merchant marine.

Another wave of expansion sprang from religious motives and produced the colonies in New England. Groups of Separatists emigrated to Holland in the early seventeenth century; in 1620 the Pilgrim Fathers crossed the Atlantic in the *Mayflower* and founded a colony at Plymouth. About ten years later a larger group of Puritan malcontents, led by men of more wealth and social standing than the Pilgrims, formed the Massachusetts Bay Company. They settled in the area of Boston and were soon the largest colony in North America, for Laud's persecution drove thousands across the Atlantic. Colonization in New England was not a normal phenomenon of overseas expansion. Rather, it was a secession of a part of the English race from the religion and government of the homeland. The Pilgrims felt a hostility toward England which for a number of years was a part of the American tradition.

The Navigation Acts of 1650 and 1651

After the Commonwealth was established in 1649 its attention was focused on the West Indies, where strange events had been taking place. About 1640, at the suggestion of Dutch traders, the English began to cultivate sugar with astonishing results. By concentrating on sugar processing, the West Indies sprang suddenly into wealth and importance. Small holdings were thrown together into large plantations, the landless were left to shift for themselves as best they could, and black slaves were imported to work the fields of sugar cane. From these changes the Dutch profited greatly. They extended credit to the planters, sold them slaves, and bought their sugar, taking it to Holland. The West Indies might be English colonies, but all the advantages were going to the Dutch. Moreover, at the end of the Civil Wars, many Royalists went to the islands. Barbados and Antigua, as well as Virginia and Maryland, recognized Charles II as king after the death of his father.

In 1650 Parliament passed an ordinance forbidding all trade with the colonies as long as they remained in rebellion. This was by way of punishment. The ordinance also contained a clause prohibiting trade by foreign vessels with any English colonies at any time, a provision thereafter enforced. A naval expedition in 1651 reduced the colonies to submission, though some clandestine trade with the Dutch continued. There followed the famous Navigation Act of 1651, which was the basis of English trade for nearly two hundred years. It declared that products from Asia, Africa, and America could be brought to England or to her colonies only in English or colonial ships of which the master and a majority of the crew were English. Products from Europe, the ordinance continued, might come to England only in English ships or in the ships of the country producing the goods. Thus foreign traders were excluded from English colonies, colonial goods must come to England in English ships, and European goods must come either in English ships or in ships of the nation in which the goods were produced. The colonists might take their products to foreign ports if they could gain access, but the bulk of their trade would be with England; the carrying trade of the Dutch was thus dealt a heavy blow. The English Parliament was legislating for the empire as a whole and was drawing the mother country and the colonies closer together.

The First Dutch War, 1652–1654

The Navigation Act of 1651, the culmination of a long period of friction, brought war between England and Holland. "The English are about to attack a mountain of gold," groaned a Dutchman; "we a mountain of iron." The mountain of gold was the vast merchant marine of Holland. During the war it sailed in convoys protected by warships, for the Dutch had to continue their trade in order to live. The mountain of iron was the English battle fleet built by the Commonwealth. Its warships were large, solid, and heavily armed; its administration was excellent; its movements were directed by the state. Three of Cromwell's soldiers—Blake, Monck, and Deane—took to the sea and gave to the navy the martial spirit of the New Model Army. The fighting was hard, close, and deadly. Both fleets sailed in line ahead formation, but the lines were often broken, and battles developed into furious melees in which new techniques developed rapidly. At first the Dutch won some advantage, but a battle in June 1653 damaged their fleet and permitted the English to blockade their coast, halting commerce and ruining hundreds of Dutch merchants. After nine pitched battles in two years, both sides were glad to make peace in 1654. The Dutch accepted the Navigation Act of 1651, agreed to salute English ships in the Channel, and paid damages for injuries inflicted upon the English East India Company. The peace, however, was a truce, and Anglo-Dutch rivalry continued.

Cromwell's Western Design

Cromwell, the first English ruler systematically to employ his power to win new colonial possessions, conceived the idea of uniting English colonies in North America with those in the West Indies, at the same time extending English possessions in both areas to form a great dominion in the West. During the Dutch war he encouraged the colonists in New England to attack the Dutch "in the Manhattoes," and, when this project was ended by peace in Europe, to attack the French in Canada. The whole area from the Penobscot River in modern Maine to the mouth of the St. Lawrence fell into English hands, though it was restored to France in 1668. When the Dutch war was over, Cromwell turned to the Spanish West Indies. He was encouraged by some of his advisers to underestimate the difficulties of the enterprise.

In 1655 Cromwell sent an expedition against the Spanish Islands, but it was not prepared with his usual care. The sailors were of good quality, but the troops consisted of men rejected by the army in England or pressed from the London slums; three thousand recruits picked up in Barbados were derelicts, "the most profane debauched persons that we ever saw." It is small wonder that an assault on Santo Domingo was a total failure. The commanders of the expedition, Admiral Penn (whose son was the founder of Pennsylvania) and General Venables, fearing the wrath of Cromwell, determined to attack Jamaica, which was weakly held by a few hundred Spanish planters. The English army, some ten thousand strong, gallantly captured this island. Cromwell was deeply chagrined, the more so because he found himself at war with Spain in Europe, but he determined to retain Jamaica, which became in time an important sugar island. His grandiose dream of a western dominion faded away, but it was the beginning of England's age-long effort to build an empire overseas.

The English East India Company

The English East India Company, as we have seen, had made an excellent beginning. Even before the friction with the Dutch had become so acute, the English had begun to turn to India. Here the Portuguese were established along the western coast, though their hold was weak. In 1612 Captain Best, after driving away a

India and the East Indies in the 17th century.

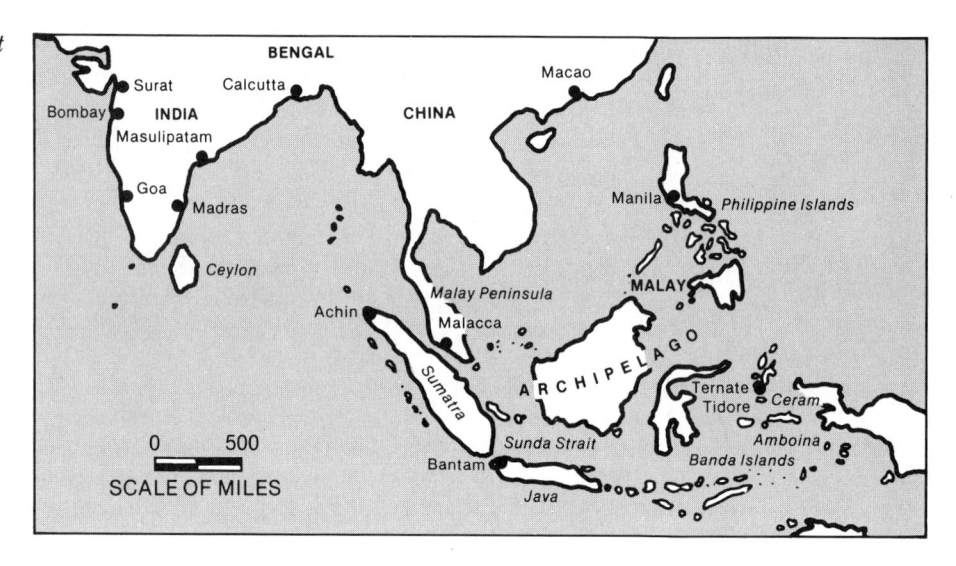

Portuguese fleet, secured from the local Mogul Governor the right to establish a factory at Surat. In 1622 the English drove the Portuguese from Ormuz at the mouth of the Persian Gulf and obtained a factory there. In 1635 a treaty was made with the Portuguese by which the English were permitted to trade in Portuguese ports. Surat remained the principal English trading area until Bombay was secured in the reign of Charles II. On the eastern coast of India the English established themselves first at Masulipatam in 1611 and later at Madras in 1639. It was not until later in the century that a firm foothold was secured in the area of Bengal. The English brought home muslins and other cotton fabrics, saltpeter, and indigo (a blue dye).

In the East the company was making headway, but difficulties arose at home. The company's system of bookkeeping was cumbersome, for each voyage was handled as a separate venture. It was accused of taking coin out of England and bringing back luxuries. Parliament was hostile because the company was a monopoly. Worst of all, it could not rely on the king, from whom it held its charter. Both James and Charles permitted interlopers to go to India, where they acted more like pirates than merchants, causing the company great harm. The company also suffered from the dislocations of the Civil Wars; for a time it ceased to trade as a corporation, though it licensed private merchants to trade as individuals. Cromwell restored the fortunes of the company and set it trading once more with a new charter in 1657.

ECONOMIC CHANGE

Historians now regard the two decades between 1640 and 1660 as highly important in the economic history of England. It was during this time that the capitalist classes—agricultural, industrial, and commercial alike—freed themselves from the

ECONOMIC CHANGE 399

The Atlantic Ocean 1660.

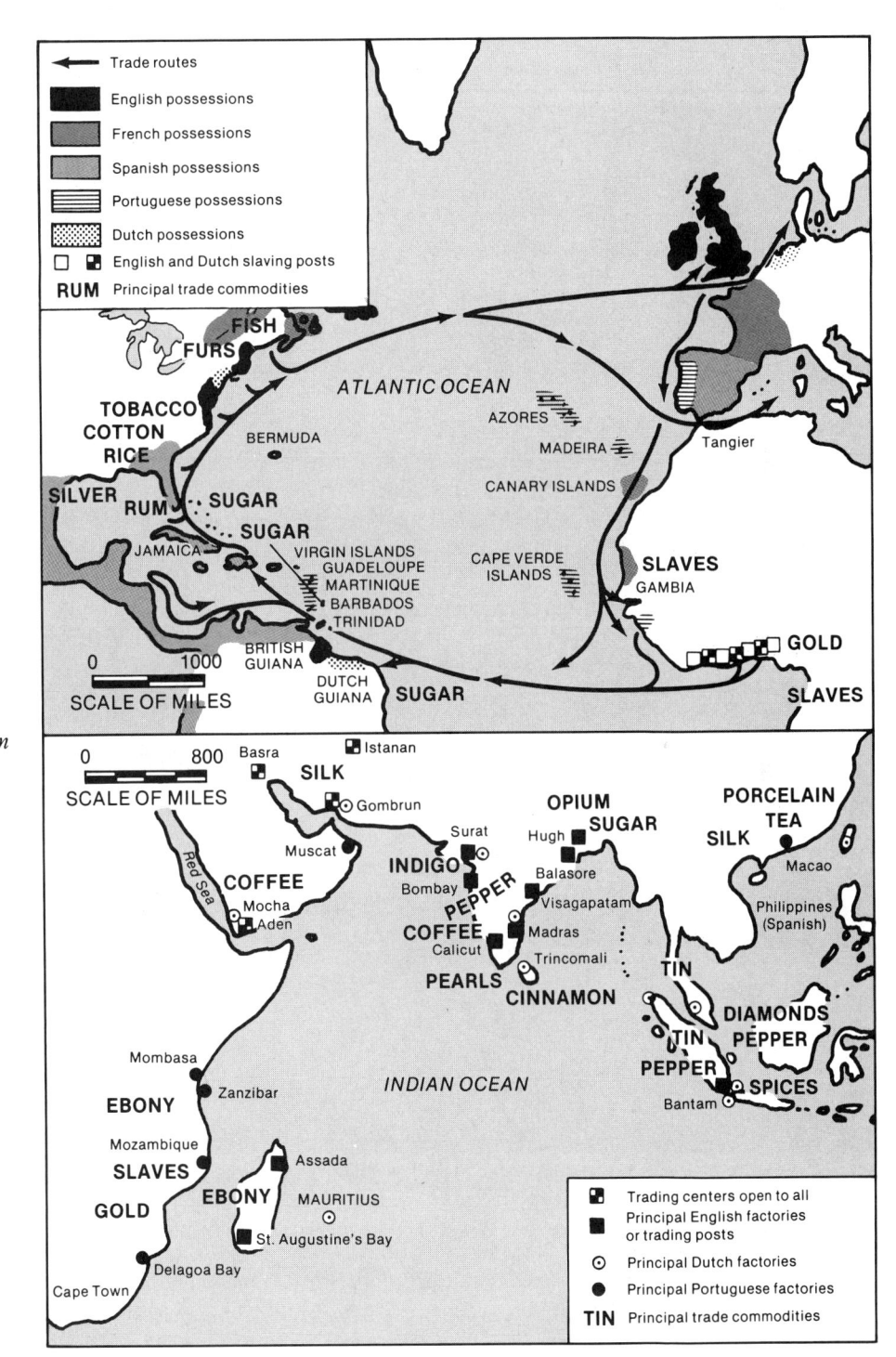

The Indian Ocean 1660.

control over economic life formerly exercised by the Crown. "The fall of the absolute monarchy was the turning point in the evolution of capitalism." Thereafter wealthy people were at liberty to do as they pleased with their property and to manage their affairs for their own economic advantage.

A tremendous amount of land was bought and sold during this period. The government sold quantities of Crown lands—so that there was little left by 1660—and also much property belonging to the Church of England. Estates of well-to-do Royalists were sequestered and could be recovered only by the payment of heavy fines, while other estates were confiscated and sold. Moreover, many Royalists, under pressures of all kinds, sold their lands privately. These people, after the Restoration of 1660, could usually recover confiscated estates through legal action; but for lands sold privately there was no redress. Yet the majority of Royalists survived. Much land was purchased during this period by those who had made money in trade or who were connected in some way with the government. Thus the landowners after 1660 were both Cavaliers and Roundheads.

The emancipation of the landed classes may be said to have taken place in three distinct phases. In the first place, there was obvious freedom from the restrictions and burdens imposed by the government of Charles I. Indeed, the government now did everything it could to encourage agricultural productivity. Opposition to enclosing disappeared; acts were passed for the draining of the fens; improved farming methods, such as the use of clover in a better rotation of crops, were supported by the government, which also felt a new responsibility for transportation and for a postal service. In the second place, the landowning classes profited enormously from the abolition of feudal or military tenure and an end to the court of wards. Feudal tenure was now converted into freehold or common socage. So great was the desire of landowners for this relief that feudal tenure was abolished thrice over, in 1646, in 1656, and in 1660. The change has been called "possibly the most important single event in the history of English landholding." It deprived the Crown of a vital means of controlling the upper classes and it gave landowners the absolute right to do as they pleased with their estates. Knowing that their titles were secure, they were much more inclined to invest money in long-term improvements. Finally, the landed classes were able to defeat efforts by the Levelers and by other radical groups to obtain permanent rights in the land for copyholders and small tenants. Indeed, the man who bought land as an investment and the Royalist who recovered his estates after a costly struggle were apt to regard the poor with little sympathy. The temporary assertiveness of the lower classes was something to be suppressed. Hence the new developments in agriculture, although they caused productivity to leap forward, brought small benefit to the poor. There was a grave problem of rural poverty at the end of the century.

A similar story may be told of industry. The government no longer attempted to regulate prices or wages or hours and conditions of labor, or to supervise the quality of workmanship. Industrial monopolies came to an end; economic favors were no longer available to parasitic courtiers. Employers were free to conduct business enterprises along economic lines. Moreover, the common law courts, which protected the rights of the individual, were now supreme. As for the merchants, the state was willing to use diplomacy and even armed force to advance their interests in overseas expansion.

THE END OF THE PROTECTORATE

After Cromwell's death the Protectorate crumbled, and events moved quickly to the restoration of the Stuarts. Richard, Oliver's son, lacked the character and experience to remain in power. His first move was correct, for he refused a demand of the army to be allowed to select its own commander in chief. In January 1659 he summoned a Parliament which on the whole was ready to support him; but under pressure from the army he dissolved it in April. This action ended his short rule as protector. The army, left in control, recalled the Long Parliament, quarreled with it, and dismissed it. But army opinion was divided; at this point General Monck, the commander in Scotland, determined that the nation, not the army, should decide what it wished to do. Monck marched down from Scotland, outwitted the army leaders in London, recalled the Long Parliament once again, obtained a majority by adding the Presbyterian members expelled in 1648, and forced it to dissolve itself and to issue writs for a free Parliament elected under the old historic franchise. This Parliament met in April 1660 and invited Charles II to return to England. He required little urging.

CHRONOLOGY

Civil Wars, Commonwealth, and Protectorate

1607	Jamestown, Virginia settled
1620	Pilgrims land at Plymouth
1630	Boston Bay colony
1643	Solemn League and Covenant
1644	Battle of Marston Moor; Royalist disaster
1645	Self-Denying Ordinance; New Model Army; Battle of Naseby

(continued on next page)

Chronology, continued

1646	Charles I a prisoner
1647	Agreement of the People; Charles escapes
1648	Second Civil War; Charles recaptured; Prides's Purge
1649	Trial, conviction, and execution of Charles I; monarchy and House of Lords abolished
1649–53	Commonwealth of England, Scotland, and Ireland; Levellers in opposition; Ireland and Scotland conquered
1651	Navigation Act
1652–54	First Dutch War
1653	Long Parliament dissolved; Barebones Parliament; Instrument of Government; Cromwell lord protector
1655	Rule of major generals; conquest of Jamaica
1657	Humble Petition and Advice; East India Company rechartered
1658	Cromwell dead; Richard Cromwell lord protector
1660	Restoration of Charles II; feudal tenures abolished

19

Restoration and Revolution

THE RESTORATION

The Restoration of 1660 was a rejection of the constitutional experiments of the Puritans and a return to the ancient form of government by King, Lords, and Commons. But neither kingship nor Parliament had remained unchanged. The Crown had lost many powers. Charles II and his minister, Edward Hyde, Earl of Clarendon, wisely retained the early legislation of the Long Parliament which had been accepted by Charles I. This meant that many of the old devices for raising money and for exalting the prerogative were now gone. The king was left entirely dependent upon Parliament for money; the prerogative courts disappeared. The Crown did, however, retain control of the executive branch of government. As such, Charles II appointed his ministers, bishops, and judges, directed foreign affairs, controlled the army and navy, and supervised the daily administration and the expenditure of funds. He also summoned and dissolved Parliament. A new Triennial Act in 1664 called for a session of Parliament every three years but provided no machinery to make these sessions obligatory. Charles retained the veto and an undefined prerogative of suspending and dispensing with statutes in times of emergency.

Parliament in 1660, however, held a far stronger position than before the Civil Wars. Neither Parliament nor the king could forget that for twenty years the Commons had controlled administration, had raised armies, built a navy, fought wars, eliminated monarchy and the House of Lords, declared itself the supreme power in the state, and, above all, had brought a king to the block. Parliament after 1660 possessed an indisputable sovereignty in taxation and legislation; moreover, its competence had become all-embracing. There was no sphere in which it could not act. It assumed at once the right to arrange a settlement of the church. Parliamentary privilege was now sacred; older methods of royal influence, such as the control of the Speaker, became impossible. Charles met a storm of protest when he attempted to create a new parliamentary borough. The Commons audited his accounts and impeached his ministers. Thus Parliament entered upon the heritage of the Puritan Revolution. The great challenge of the future was to devise a means by which the Commons could control the executive without continuous crises.

Charles II

When Charles II landed at Dover in May 1660 and made his way through shouting throngs to London, the kingdom was wild with joy. Maidens strewed flowers in his path, loyal healths were drunk in endless numbers, maypoles were set up again, and Cromwell's corpse was exhumed from Westminster Abbey and hanged at Tyburn. England was England once more. The people had a king. They knew what they wanted—but they did not know what they were getting.

Charles II, born in May 1630, was a dark and ugly baby who became a dark and ugly man. He was tall and athletic and always enjoyed excellent health. His education

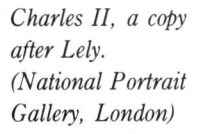

Charles II, a copy after Lely. (National Portrait Gallery, London)

was interrupted by the Civil War. As a youth he roamed about the Continent, in poverty, idleness, hopelessness, and debauchery. He grew up to be lazy and irresolute, prone to follow the course of least resistance, untrustworthy, ungrateful, and irreligious. Having few principles of any kind, he saw virtue only in dissimulation and compromise; he believed that every man and woman could be bought at a price. Because his funds were curtailed by Parliament, he used his control of foreign affairs to obtain subsidies from the king of France for which he was ready to betray the religion of his country. His sympathies were French and Roman Catholic. Confident that God would not damn a man for a little pleasure, he drank heavily, kept a harem of mistresses, and made Whitehall a licentious and wicked place. However, Charles's good qualities should not be forgotten. He made no pretense at being anything but what he was. Witty, charming, and amusing, he possessed a keen intelligence and discernment of character. He was loyal to his family and affable with his subordinates without a loss of dignity. The king had an interest in commerce, he loved the sea and the navy, he dabbled in chemistry, and was a patron of science. Though he desired a policy of religious toleration, his dark dealings with France and his sympathy with a religion hated by his people portended an explosive violence which poisoned the atmosphere at Westminster.

The Convention Parliament

While Charles was still on the Continent he had issued the Declaration of Breda, in which he promised to abide by Parliament's decision on the principal issues requiring immediate settlement. The Convention Parliament, which sat until December 1660, took action on three of these issues. An act of indemnity pardoned all those who had fought against Charles I or had taken part in the governments of the interregnum, except for some fifty persons whom the act listed by name. Of these, thirteen were executed, twelve being regicides; the thirteenth, Sir Henry Vane, was considered too dangerous to live. In an age as cruel as the seventeenth century, these thirteen lives were but a mild revenge for a Civil War and the death of a king.

Closely connected with indemnity was the question of a land settlement. Any solution was certain to cause injustice and bitterness. It was decided that Royalists whose estates had been confiscated by the Puritans should be allowed to recover their lands through the courts, but that those who had sold their estates should receive no compensation. This decision was important for the pattern of landownership in the following century. It meant that many Puritans who had purchased estates during the interregnum were able to retain them after 1660. The future landowners of the kingdom were to be the descendants of Roundheads as well as of Cavaliers. The great families who had sided with Charles I were more successful in recovering their former property than were the smaller Royalists; and these great families often added to their holdings after 1660 by purchases from Royalists who were in need. There was thus a tendency for more and more land to accumulate in a few hands. The large landowners turned against James II in 1688 and often profited from the revolution in that year. Hence there emerged two classes that will become familiar in the eighteenth century: the great Whig magnate owning vast estates, and the small Tory squire, sullen, resentful, and dissatisfied.

The Convention Parliament had also to provide the king with money. The system of taxation and of government finance was antiquated, but there was no time for reform. Since money was required at once to pay off the army, Parliament quickly raised the necessary funds by levying direct assessments upon local areas. To meet ordinary expenses of government, it granted to Charles II the customs duties and an excise on beer, ale, tea, and coffee. This revenue was expected to amount to £1,200,000 a year, but unfortunately it never reached that amount. In return for this grant Charles surrendered the right to wardship and to other survivals of the age of feudalism. Feudal tenures were abolished; the great landowners now held their estates in common socage. They benefited greatly from the change, for they were relieved of heavy payments and became more independent of the Crown.

The Clarendon Code

There remained the question of a religious settlement—a most difficult question, for the country was thoroughly divided. Of England's nine thousand parish churches, some two thousand were held by Presbyterian clergymen and perhaps four hundred by Independents. There was also a large number of sectaries, comprising perhaps a tenth of the population, who went their own way, as did the Quakers, in various forms of unregulated religious life. But the Anglican clergymen, who now returned from exile or emerged from hiding, naturally expected to be restored to their former livings. So long as the Convention Parliament remained in session there was a possibility of compromise. This Parliament contained many Presbyterians who hoped that their opinions would carry weight and who were willing to accept bishops associated in some way with synods. The king was ready for toleration, and Clarendon was disposed to be moderate. A few Presbyterians were offered preferment in the church, but the moment of possible compromise quickly passed. A conference between Anglican and Presbyterian leaders broke down completely and Anglican bigotry hardened against all nonconformists. The Cavalier Parliament, elected early in 1661, contained a majority of Royalist Anglicans determined to restore the church as it had been before the Civil Wars, to drive out the Puritans, and to exclude them from political life.

Hating and fearing all forms of nonconformity, the Cavaliers passed a number of acts known collectively as the Clarendon Code, though Clarendon was only partially responsible for them. The Corporation Act of 1661 excluded from the governing bodies of the towns all persons who refused to swear to the unlawfulness of resistance to the king and who declined to receive the Communion according to the rites of the Church of England. The Act of Uniformity in 1662 issued a new Prayer Book and provided that clergymen must either accept it or resign their livings. Some twelve hundred clergymen refused, vacating their churches. Their number is an indication of the strength of nonconformity. The Conventicle Act of 1664 imposed

Edward, Earl of Clarendon, from Edward, Earl of Clarendon, The History of the Rebellion and Civil War in England, *Oxford, 1702. (Department of Special Collections, Wilson Library, University of Minnesota)*

harsh penalties on those who attended religious services in which the forms of the Anglican church were not used. The government was afraid that conspiracies might be plotted in nonconformist gatherings; the king attempted and failed to modify the Act of Uniformity by dispensing with it in individual cases. An even harsher Conventicle Act became law in 1670. In 1665 the Five Mile Act prohibited clergymen from coming within five miles of a parish from which they had been ejected. A licensing act permitted the archbishop of Canterbury and the bishop of London to control the press and the printing of books.

The Clarendon Code brought about great social changes. It divided religious life in England into two parts: the Church and nonconformity. The Church, purged of

Puritans and fanatics, was to hold the position of power: it regained its church buildings and other property, it could levy tithes, and it controlled education on all levels. Nonconformists were excluded from the universities, from many professions, from municipal government, from all offices under the Crown (by the Test Act of 1673), and from membership in the House of Commons. A social stigma became attached to nonconformity. Persons outside the Church were considered fanatic, ignorant, and "low class." Indeed, in the eighteenth century the Church was sometimes regarded as synonymous with Christianity.

These disabilities undoubtedly weakened the nonconformists greatly. People of power and ambition eventually yielded to public pressure and moved into the church; in the eighteenth century there were few persons of importance who were not Anglicans. Nonconformity, on the other hand, was now lawful. The Tudor doctrine that everyone must belong to the state church had been abandoned. Nonconformity was strong enough to remain a permanent element in English life. It had struck deep roots among the lower middle class, among shopkeepers, artisans, and small farmers. Deprived of many of the opportunities of their fellow citizens, nonconformists entered trade and business. Their industry, thrift, and sobriety brought them material success, and they eventually became merchants, bankers, and manufacturers. They were further strengthened by the rise of Methodism in the eighteenth century. As they gradually emerged from their disabilities, they formed a group apart, with a culture and a morality of their own.

THE FALL OF CLARENDON

For seven years the earl of Clarendon remained Charles's principal minister and lord chancellor. His position seemed secure, not only because of his great services during the interregnum but because his daughter Anne Hyde had become first the mistress and then the wife of James, Duke of York, the heir presumptive to the throne. But although Clarendon possessed ability and noble character, he was proud, austere, and rigid. He returned to England in 1660 to find himself old-fashioned and out of touch with the times. He was hated by the buffoons and loose women around the king, whom he irritated by lectures on morality. He was suspicious of Parliament, to which he assigned a subordinate role it resented. With many enemies, he was apt to be blamed when anything went wrong. He fell from power in 1667, largely because of mischances in foreign affairs for which he was only partially responsible.

The first was the choice of a Portuguese princess, Catherine of Braganza, as Charles's wife. Portugal offered England generous terms for a marriage alliance. The dowry was to be £800,000 in cash, along with the town of Bombay in India and the fortress of Tangier in North Africa near Gibraltar. The English were to be permitted to trade throughout her empire. The marriage was pleasing to France, for Louis XIV welcomed an alliance that weakened Spain. The Dutch, however, were furious: they wanted the Portuguese empire for themselves. The marriage alliance was accepted in London, but the results proved disappointing. The short and dumpy figure of the bride, her prominent teeth and her stolid manner contrasted sadly with the allurements of Lady Castlemaine, that voluptuous goddess who presided at Charles's court. Moreover, Catherine was childless. Bombay was a fever-ridden and profitless possession in 1661, though it became valuable later. Tangier's value as a Mediterranian base was not appreciated, and because it proved very costly Tangier was abandoned in 1683. Portugal appeared to have had the better of the bargain, for she gained a strong ally.

In 1662 Charles sold Dunkirk to the French. The cost of its garrison was heavy and it was difficult to defend from an attack by land. Dunkirk, conquered from Spain by Cromwell's redcoats, was highly prized in England; hence its sale was most unpopular. To England's great cost it was to be used later by Louis XIV as a base for privateering.

Then came a second naval war with Holland (1665–1667), which has been called the clearest case in English history of a purely commercial war. Rivalry between the two countries was again at fever pitch; even before war was declared, there had been fighting over slaving stations in West Africa, and an English squadron had seized the New Netherlands in America. This war, like the first, was a war of fierce naval engagements between large and powerful fleets. It was fought for the most part in the seas between Britain and the Continent. By 1666 both sides were feeling the strain. The Dutch, having raised enormous loans, were at the end of their financial resources; England suffered two calamities which for the moment quelled her fighting spirit.

In the spring of 1665 the plague appeared in London, killing some sixty-eight thousand persons before it subsided late in 1666. Everyone fled London who could, leaving a desert of closed houses, of houses with a red cross painted on the door which meant that the plague was within, of panic and misery which paralyzed economic life. This was the final visitation of the bubonic plague, endemic in England since the fourteenth century and carried by the fleas on black rats; one explanation for its failure to return is that black rats were then driven out by brown.

To worsen matters, the Great Fire of London blazed forth in September 1666. Starting accidentally near London Bridge and driven by a high wind over parched land, the fire destroyed the greater part of the old city. The people, more intent on flight and on saving their household goods than on putting out the flames, fled through the suburbs to the countryside beyond. The fire lasted four days, destroying some thirteen thousand houses, eighty-four churches including St. Paul's, and many public buildings, none of them covered by insurance. The people stumbled back over hot ashes to begin building London anew. The new houses were usually made of brick instead of wood and plaster.

Bankrupt and without allies, England now sought peace and began negotiations. Peace was made at Breda in July 1667. The English retained New York and New Jersey; the Dutch, most of the places in dispute along the African Coast and in the East Indies. The Navigation Act was modified slightly in Holland's favor, and the English flag need be saluted only in the Channel. The war had been far from glorious.

Clarendon, as so often, received the blame. Yielding to his minister's enemies, Charles dismissed him from office. Clarendon then was impeached by the Commons, fled abroad, and spent his exile writing his famous *History of the Great Rebellion*.

THE CABAL AND THE SECRET TREATY OF DOVER

For some time after the fall of Clarendon there was no chief minister. Charles attempted a more personal rule and personal direction of foreign policy. Five of his ministers, whose initials formed the acronym "CABAL," were of more importance than the rest. One was Sir Thomas Clifford, later lord treasurer. His patron, Lord Arlington, principal secretary of state, was an experienced and industrious diplomat whose policy in general was anti-French. Both men died Roman Catholics. A third member of the CABAL, George Villiers, second duke of Buckingham, the son of the favorite of James I, was a despicable person, said to be "without principles either of religion, virtue, or friendship." He later drifted into opposition. Lord Ashley, afterward earl of Shaftesbury, was more important. A man of great courage and resourcefulness, though given to violent action, he was a strong Protestant and an opponent of arbitrary government. Like Buckingham, he was to turn against the Crown. The last of the five, Lauderdale, advised the king on Scottish affairs.

European politics in the second half of the seventeenth century centered upon two great facts: the decay of Spain and the aggressiveness of Louis XIV. Spain's sun had set in 1659 at the conclusion of a long war with France. With the death of the Spanish king Philip IV in 1665 and the accession of his sickly and half-witted son, Charles II, the Spanish empire seemed ready for dismemberment. It was still a splendid empire, including large portions of Italy and scattered footholds throughout the Mediterranean, the Spanish Netherlands, Mexico, Central and South America except Brazil, most of the larger West Indian islands, the Philippines, Morocco, and the Canary Islands. Louis XIV cast a covetous eye on these valuable territories. He had married a Spanish princess, Maria Theresa, a daughter of Philip IV; and in 1667 he put forward a claim to the Spanish Netherlands based in part on the nonpayment of his wife's dowry and in part on the law of "devolution" which governed the inheritance of property in the Netherlands. Louis attacked this area and was soon in possession of a number of fortresses within Spanish territory.

Charles's diplomacy during these years was unsettled, with many shifts and little purpose. His basic principle was friendship with France. Louis was the grand monarch of Europe, wealthy, powerful, magnificent, the symbol of absolutism and Catholicism, the model of etiquette and manners, the observed of all observers, with rich merchants, splendid diplomats, and superb armies. Charles regarded him with envy, with admiration, and with the hope of obtaining money, but his first move was to form a Triple Alliance with Holland and Sweden in 1668 to prevent Louis from absorbing the whole of the Spanish Netherlands and also, perhaps, to raise the price of English friendship. Meanwhile Louis made a secret treaty with Emperor Leopold of Austria for the division of the Spanish empire if the Spanish king died while still young, as everybody assumed he would. Hoping for greater things to come, Louis called off the war in the Netherlands in 1668; the Triple Alliance had little to do with his decision.

Louis was angry with the Dutch. They had dared to oppose his ambitions, they were France's commercial rivals, and he wanted to ensure their noninterference when the Spanish empire was divided. To isolate the Dutch, Louis sought an agreement with England. The result was the Treaty of Dover in 1670. Charles's motives in making this treaty are still debatable. Perhaps he was misled by his need for money or by his love for his sister Henrietta, who had married the brother of the French king. At any rate, the treaty was a shameful one. In it Charles declared that he was convinced of the truth of the Catholic religion and that he would announce his conversion when his affairs permitted. He had every reason to believe, the treaty stated, that his people would accept his decision, but if not, Louis agreed to provide 6000 French troops to assist in its enforcement. Meanwhile, as a token of friendship, Louis was to send Charles £166,000. (By later agreements during the next eight years Charles obtained additional subsidies. He received in all some £742,000.) The treaty also provided that England and France join in a war against the Dutch and that the English might annex certain parts of Holland, which, however, they must conquer for themselves. A public treaty contained the clauses concerning the Dutch war; the other clauses remained secret. Just before the war began in 1672, Charles issued a sweeping Declaration of Indulgence by which he suspended the penal laws against both Catholics and nonconformists.

Parliament met in an unpleasant mood in January 1673, deeply suspicious of the king. The Commons did not know the secret terms of the Treaty of Dover, but they made some shrewd guesses. "The public articles are ill enough," said a member. "What are then the private articles?" The war with Holland began abruptly with no immediate cause. The Commons were anti-Catholic and anti-French. Commercial rivalry with Holland was beginning to abate, and there was a dawning realization that France, not Holland, was the great enemy.

The Declaration of Indulgence was a bold use of the suspending power. A new apprehension was appearing—the dread of arbitrary government at home. Popery, France, and despotic power were emerging as the things to be feared. The Commons voted money for the Dutch war, but not until Charles withdrew the Declaration of Indulgence. Parliament then passed the Test Act, which prohibited anyone from holding office under the Crown, either civil or military, until he had taken the Anglican Sacrament and made a declaration against transubstantiation which no Roman Catholic would accept. All Catholic officials, including the duke of York, were driven from office.

The war did not go well. It differed from the first two wars because the Dutch, regarding France as their principal enemy, stood on the defensive at sea. One large naval battle, off the Texel in 1673, demonstrated that the English could not hope to invade Holland and that they must lift their blockade of the Dutch coast. Parliament was so insistent that Charles withdraw from the war that he did so in 1674. He had gained nothing from his crafty dealings: his Declaration of Indulgence had failed, and the Dutch war had sacrificed men and money to little purpose. Ashley and Buckingham were soon to join the opposition. Thus the year 1674 may be taken as a dividing date in the reign. Charles's attempt at personal government had broken down, leaving a legacy of fear and confusion.

DANBY, POLITICAL PARTIES, AND LOUIS XIV

The Cabal broke up after the third Dutch war. Charles's principal minister from 1674 to 1678 was the lord treasurer, Thomas Osborne, soon to be earl of Danby, a robust and vigorous man with a policy of his own. Pro-Dutch, anti-French, and anti-Catholic, he hoped, on the one hand, to draw Charles away from his unpopular policies and, on the other, to rekindle in the Commons their former loyalty to the Crown. He offered Parliament strong support of the Church of England and sound administration of public finance.

Danby paid attention to the management of the Commons. The Commons were divided, as they had been in the first part of the century, into a Court party, which normally supported the king, and a Country party, which normally opposed him. These groups now were organized into political parties, though they lacked the discipline and clear-cut division of parties today. Danby cultivated the members of the Court party, not only by offering them policies which he hoped they would like, but by judicious distribution of offices, pensions, and even payment in cash. His efforts called forth a corresponding organization of the opposition. This was the work of Shaftesbury, who drew the Country party together, established a party headquarters in London known as the Green Ribbon Club, and gradually developed an organization throughout the kingdom. He was in close contact with the political thinker John Locke, whose theories of limited monarchy were to exert great influence. Later in the reign the terms "Whig" and "Tory" came into use. The Tories, led by Danby, supported the church and the prerogatives of the Crown. The Whigs, following Shaftesbury, stood for limitation of royal power and for increased toleration for Protestants though not for Catholics.

Thus Danby organized the Court party but failed to conciliate Parliament as a whole. The Commons were tense and nervous. Their nervousness was increased by the policy of Charles and Louis as well as by a panic that resulted from a supposed Popish Plot.

After 1674 England was officially neutral in the war between Holland and France, which continued until 1678. Louis had found the war unexpectedly difficult, for the Dutch had discovered a leader in their young Stadtholder, William III, who succeeded in building a coalition of powers against France. The Commons became more and more anti-French. In 1677–1678 Charles was induced to take a step away from France by consenting to a marriage between Mary, the elder daughter of James, Duke of York, and William III. By the Treaty of Nimwegen in 1678 Louis made peace with the Dutch, who lost no territory in Europe, but, battered and broken, ceased to be a great power.

THE POPISH PLOT

The English, who by now had been living for years in an atmosphere of tension, were thrown into panic in 1678 by the false disclosures of two informers, Titus Oates and Israel Tonge. Oates was a rascal whose vices had caused him to be ejected from school, from an Anglican living, and from a Jesuit seminary. Coming forward with astonishing effrontery, he declared that he knew of a Jesuit plot to assassinate the king and to place James, his Catholic brother, on the throne. This central lie was surrounded by many lesser ones and by accusations against innocent persons. Oates had stumbled on a few facts which gave a superficial appearance of truth to his stories. It was discovered that a group of Jesuits had held a secret meeting in London and that Edward Coleman, a secretary of James's second wife, Mary of Modena, had been in dangerous correspondence with Catholics in France. Israel Tonge, the other informer, was a half-crazed clergyman, a D.D. from Oxford, who probably believed he was telling the truth.

He and Oates had first made their revelations before a London justice of the peace, Sir Edmund Berry Godfrey, who, disappearing suddenly, was found dead with a sword thrust through his back. His mysterious death was followed by a furious wave of false accusations against Catholics. Many were put to death, even though persons in authority, including the king were convinced of their innocence. For almost two years the panic continued, Oates living like a king, with no one daring to contradict his lies. The Commons listened gravely to evidence brought before them by ratcatchers, they impeached Catholic peers, and they passed a bill strengthening the terms of the Test Act. They turned on Danby, who, at Charles's command, had written one of the king's letters to Louis. Shaftesbury wildly accused the queen of treason. To save his minister from impeachment, to save his queen, and perhaps even to save the powers of the Crown, Charles dissolved the Cavalier Parliament in January 1679.

THE EXCLUSION STRUGGLE

The Catholic episode gave a new turn to English politics. Led by Shaftesbury, the Whigs embarked on a campaign to exclude the Catholic duke of York from the succession to the throne. This policy first appeared in Charles's second Parliament, elected in February of 1679, a violent Parliament in which the opposition was in full control of the Commons. It imprisoned Danby, brushed aside a compromise advanced by Charles to limit his brother's powers as king, and introduced a bill excluding James from the throne. Charles's answer was to send his brother into temporary exile and to prorogue Parliament, which he dissolved in the summer.

The question of exclusion continued to be the storm center of politics, but

Shaftesbury and other Whigs encountered difficulty in selecting a candidate to take James's place. The most obvious choice was Mary, James's elder daughter, a Protestant who had married William III. But the time had not yet come when England would accept a Dutchman as king, and Shaftesbury was anti-Dutch. He made the error of championing Charles's illegitimate son, James Scott, duke of Monmouth. Monmouth was a soldier, quite romantic in his way, but brainless, vain, and irresponsible. The Whigs were divided; some favored the succession of James with limited powers, some favored Monmouth, some Mary, and some a republic. Charles called two more Parliaments, in 1680 and 1681. The first introduced another exclusion bill which was stopped in the Lords. The second, which met in Oxford, was a wild affair to which the Whigs came armed as though to begin an insurrection. The members from London had the motto "No Popery, No Slavery" woven into their hats. This Parliament lasted for only one week and was the last to be summoned by Charles II.

Royalist Reaction

The violence of the Whigs, which appeared to be leading the nation into another civil war, caused a reaction in favor of both the king and the duke of York. Charles regained much of his early popularity. Emboldened by the support of the Tories, he ventured to arrest Shaftesbury for treason, though Shaftesbury was acquitted by a London jury. Thereupon Charles secured the appointment of Tory sheriffs who could be trusted to pack the juries of the capital. He also challenged the London charter. The charters of many other towns were examined and remodeled so as to exclude Whigs from the municipal corporations.

At first the Whigs turned from opposition to conspiracy. Some of the Whig leaders—Shaftesbury, Lord Russell, the earl of Essex, and Algernon Sidney—held secret meetings in which they talked of revolt, although their plans never reached a very advanced state. Meanwhile Monmouth was plotting in an irresponsible way with more questionable characters, and a scheme known as the Rye House Plot was devised to assassinate the king and his brother. When this was betrayed to the government, the Whig leaders, whether they were connected with it or not, knew that their cause was lost. Shaftesbury fled to the Continent, followed by Monmouth. Essex committed suicide. Russell and Sidney were convicted, not for a part in the Rye House Plot, but for their opinion that resistance to the king was lawful. Both were executed, though they were men of character and principle. Meanwhile the Tories rallied about James, displaying an extraordinary loyalty to him and proclaiming the doctrines of divine right and of nonresistance. It was their practice to fall upon their knees and drink his health as they shouted a loud "Huzzah!" They assumed that he would be a Tory king who would keep the Whigs under control, would uphold the Church of England, and would regard his Catholicism as a private affair.

In February 1685 King Charles suffered a sudden stroke and died within a few days. As the king was dying, a Catholic priest who had helped him to escape from Cromwell's forces after the Battle of Worcester was admitted to his bedchamber and received him into the Roman Church.

JAMES II, 1685-1688

King James II was fifty-one when he ascended the throne. As a young man he had served in the armies of France and Spain and was accounted a good officer. In Charles's reign he had become lord admiral, had been a successful naval administrator, and had seen action as the commander of an English fleet against the Dutch. But as king he was impossible—dull, obstinate, rigid, brusque, suspicious, blind to public opinion, and determined to have his way whatever the consequences. It is possible that he suffered a mental decline about the time he secured the throne. His soldiering left him with an inflated confidence in military power and with a callousness toward human suffering. He practiced his Catholicism openly. In less than four years he drove his people to revolution and lost his throne.

He began his reign in a strong position. The Whigs were crushed, the Tories blindly loyal. Tory town corporations could be trusted to return Tory members to the House of Commons. Thus fortified, James summoned Parliament in May 1685. It was a packed assembly, strongly Tory. The king promised "to preserve the government in Church and State as it is now by law established," and then demanded money. The Commons obligingly granted him the customs for life, so that he had an ample revenue. The Revolution, when it came, was not caused by quarrels over finance.

Meanwhile an event took place which appeared to add to his power. This was a rebellion in the southwest of England led by the duke of Monmouth. Fleeing from England in the last years of Charles's reign, Monmouth traveled to Holland where William III advised him politely to go and fight the Turks. Instead, he obtained a ship and some ammunition in Amsterdam and landed at Lyme Regis in Dorset in June 1685. Here he proclaimed himself the rightful king. The gentry did not join him, but some 6000 of the peasants, armed chiefly with scythes and other farming implements, flocked to his standard. The area was a clothmaking district in which much poverty and unemployment existed. There was not the slightest hope of success. The local militia retreated at first but soon was stiffened by regular troops, and at the night Battle of Sedgemoor Monmouth's men blundered into an impassable ditch, where they were slaughtered without mercy. This pathetic rising, the last peasants' revolt in England, was savagely punished. Some three hundred peasants were executed and some eight hundred more were sold as slaves in the West Indies. The country was shocked by the butchery of these poor simple folk. Moreover, James used the rebellion as an excuse to increase the size of the army.

In November James summoned Parliament into its second and final session. He demanded a large sum of money for the support of the army, which contained many Roman Catholic officers who had not complied with the requirements of the Test Act. The Commons, pointing to these officers, offered a considerable grant if the Test Act were enforced. But the king declined, and Parliament was prorogued after a session of about ten days. It never met again in James's reign. The king in effect had asked the Commons to repeal or modify the Test Act, and the Commons had refused to do so.

These developments startled the Tories, who had made themselves champions of hereditary succession and nonresistance. But they were also champions of the Church of England and of a constitution which might allow the king high prerogatives but debarred him from despotic power. They regarded the Test Act as the bulwark of Anglican supremacy; moreover, they loathed the thought of rule by the sword, for they had suffered more from Cromwell's army than had any other section of the people. If their loyalty had blinded them to reality, it had also blinded the king. James seems to have imagined that the Anglicans were so close to Rome, and the Tories so committed to nonresistance, that he could obtain the repeal of the Test Act and could then place Roman Catholics in positions of authority. He should have been warned by the parliamentary session of November 1685 that he was in error.

Nevertheless, he pressed forward. About half the army was encamped on Hounslow Heath outside London with the obvious intention of overawing the city. Roman Catholic recruits were brought over from Ireland. A famous case in the courts established a means of retaining Catholic officers. A collusive suit was brought against Sir Edward Hales, who was a Roman Catholic officer in the army, but Hales pleaded that he held a dispensation from the king to retain his place despite the Test Act, and the judges agreed that the dispensation was legal. A Catholic commanded the army in Ireland, another the fleet in England. The earl of Sunderland, a vigorous but reckless man, Judge Jeffreys, the cruel judge who had dealt so harshly with the Monmouth rebels, and a Jesuit, Father Edward Petre, zealous but unwise, became the king's closest advisers.

In 1686 James attempted to bend the Church of England to his will by creating a court of Ecclesiastical Commission with large powers over the clergy. This court was illegal, for the old High Commission had been abolished in 1641 and the creation of similar courts had been forbidden. The Ecclesiastical Commission began by suspending Henry Compton, bishop of London, from office. It then turned upon the University of Oxford, where three colleges—Christ Church, University, and Magdalen—were placed under Roman Catholic rule; the fellows or faculty of Magdalen College were expelled because they would not elect the king's candidate as their president. Oxford was an Anglican and Tory stronghold; hence the king was attacking his own supporters. Moreover, the fellows of an Oxford college, like parish priests, held their livings as freehold property, from which they could be ejected only through due process of law. The tyranny of the king placed the living of every clergyman in jeopardy.

Having thus alienated the church, James sought the support of the nonconformists. In April 1687 he boldly issued a Declaration of Indulgence which suspended all the penal laws, leaving both Catholics and nonconformists free to worship in public and to hold office. From dispensing with the law in a specific instance, as in the case of Sir Edward Hales, the king now moved to the suspension by prerogative of a long list of statutes. Had it succeeded, the king would have been free from all legal restraints.

Knowing that he could not maintain his position without the approval of Parliament, James began a campaign to pack the Commons. The town charters again were remodeled, Tories were expelled from town corporations, and Roman Catholics were introduced in their places. Naming Catholics as lords lieutenants of counties, he instructed them to ask the justices of the peace whether, if they were returned to

Parliament, they would vote for the repeal of the Test Act. The answer was so universally negative that James did not summon Parliament again.

Meanwhile, the great question remained: would the nonconformists accept the toleration offered to them by the king and ally with him against the Church of England? A few of them did, although they knew that in the long run they could expect but short shrift from a Catholic government. The Church of England promised that if ever it came to power it would grant them toleration. William III also issued a declaration supporting religious toleration for nonconformists, though not their admission to office. More and more through 1687 the dissenting bodies supported the church against the Crown. Opponents were uniting against James.

Two events in 1688 produced the Revolution. One was the trial of seven bishops. In May James had reissued the Declaration of Indulgence with the command that it be read on two successive Sundays in every parish church. Sancroft, the archbishop, and six other bishops petitioned the king to withdraw this command. They printed and distributed their petition, which was a technical breach of the law; the king prosecuted them for publishing a seditious libel against his government. The nation waited breathlessly as the seven bishops, men of high character and unquestioned loyalty, were tried by a London jury. The verdict "Not guilty" set the whole people rejoicing; the soldiers cheered on Hounslow Heath.

The second event which precipitated the Revolution was the birth of a son to James and his queen, Mary of Modena, on June 10, 1688. They had been married for fifteen years, their other children had died, and it had been assumed that they would have no more. As long as James was childless by his second wife, the throne at his death would go to one of his grown Protestant daughters, Mary or Anne. But the birth of a son altered this picture. The little prince, known in history as the Old Pretender, would take precedence over his older sisters. The fact that he would certainly be brought up in the Catholic faith opened the prospect of an endless line of Roman Catholic kings. So surprising was his birth that Catholics pronounced the event a miracle, but Protestants spread the story that the child was not of royal parentage but had been brought into the palace in a warming pan. His birth changed the course of history. A group of Whig and Tory leaders, acting together, extended an invitation to William III to invade England with a military force around which the country could rally in revolt against its present king.

THE GLORIOUS REVOLUTION

William viewed the possibility of intervention in England from the standpoint of a continental statesman. The great object of his life was opposition to Louis XIV; if he came to England he would come in order to strengthen his position against France. But developments on the Continent and in England seemed to be converging. A new war against Louis was about to begin. James, as Louis' ally, might perhaps bring England in on the French side. Resentment against James in England seemed to be about as strong as it was likely to become. By the beginning of 1688, William, who was in touch with Whig and Tory leaders, appears to have made up his mind to intervene if he could, but he acted cautiously. He refused to come, as Monmouth had done, without an invitation, and he refused to come without an army, although the presence of Dutch troops in England would certainly cause irritation.

Events played into William's hands. The Dutch naturally feared that Louis would attack them while their army was away, but the grand monarch, less interested in England than in the Rhine, sent his armies eastward against the Palatinate, opening the way for William's enterprise. Louis offered James the aid of the French fleet, but James declined this assistance; as a matter of fact, Louis had few ships to send, for his fleet was largely in the Mediterranean. Not without reason Louis believed that William's invasion would lead to a civil war which would neutralize both England and Holland while the French freely conquered parts of Germany. Hence William sailed unopposed. A fresh "Protestant" wind from the east carried him through the Channel. On 5 November, the anniversary of the Gunpowder Plot, William and his army landed safely at Torbay in Devon.

James in a panic made many concessions, but it was too late. He advanced with his army to Salisbury, returned to London, then did the one thing that was certain to overthrow his government: he ran away. Leaving London late at night, he took ship near Chatham, but was captured by some English fishermen and brought back to England. William wanted no royal martyr. The king was left unguarded and obligingly escaped once more, this time making his way to France. The English were left with little choice but to accept William as their king.

William assumed temporary control of the government and summoned a free Parliament, which met in February 1689. Whigs and Tories, sobered by a sense of crisis, met in a conciliatory spirit, though party differences soon appeared. The Whigs wanted a declaration that the throne was vacant: such a statement would break hereditary succession and give the next king a parliamentary title. The Tories, half ashamed of their opposition to James II, wished to soften the Revolution by asserting that the king had abdicated, thus absolving themselves from the sin of having deposed him. Some Tories hoped that he might be brought back with limited powers, or that William might be regent, or that Mary might be queen with William as prince consort. These suggestions were swept away by the course of events. James had no intention of returning without a French army to re-establish his former powers; William refused to be anything but king; and Mary declined to be queen unless her husband shared the royal title with her. The Commons therefore drew up a statement declaring that James, having broken the fundamental laws and having withdrawn himself out of the kingdom, had abdicated the government and that the throne was thereby vacant. William and Mary were then made joint sovereigns, with the administration vested in William.

The Revolutionary Settlement

Within the next few years Parliament passed a number of acts which, taken together, formed the revolutionary settlement. Although they sprang largely from the deposition of James II, they were remarkable for their broad conception of liberty, a theme inherent in the Puritan revolt against Charles I but made acceptable to the upper classes after 1660 by a group of political thinkers—Algernon Sidney; Henry Neville; George Savile, Marquis of Halifax; and above all, John Locke. These men rejected the egalitarian democracy of the Independents and placed political power in the hands of the property-owning classes, but insisted that all men possessed inalienable rights to personal liberty and to religious equality (though there was to be no religious toleration for Catholics).

Of these thinkers the most important was John Locke, who believed that philosophical principles must be founded on human experience. In its simplest terms, his political theory was that of a social contract between governors and governed. Rejecting all notions of divine right, hereditary succession, nonresistance, and the all-powerful state, he held that governments could be justly overthrown when they ceased to fulfill the functions for which they had been established. Locke argued further that man had certain inalienable rights, such as religious liberty and equality before the law, with which the state could not interfere. Before governments had come into existence, he argued, men were free and equal and bound only by moral law. The great end for which they had placed themselves under governments was the protection of their property. The preservation of life, liberty, and property was the solemn trust placed in the hands of the state. Governments must be limited in power to prevent them from degenerating into tyranny; this should be done by introducing checks and balances, of which the most important was the division into executive, legislative, and judicial branches which imposed restraints upon each other. Locke's reasonable, utilitarian, and liberal approach made a strong appeal to the people of his time, deeply affected government throughout the eighteenth century, and appeared in the American Constitution.

As the greatest constitutional document since Magna Carta, the Bill of Rights (1689) began by asserting that James II, abetted by evil advisers, had sought the destruction of the Protestant religion and the laws and liberties of the country. Certain actions therefore were declared illegal: the use of the suspending power without parliamentary consent; the dispensing power, first "as it hath been exercised of late," and secondly altogether; the court of Ecclesiastical Commission; the levying of money in any way other than that in which it had been granted; a standing army in time of peace without the consent of Parliament. It was further declared that elections to Parliament should be free; that free speech in Parliament should not be questioned except by Parliament itself; that Parliaments should be summoned frequently; that subjects might petition the king; that excessive bail and cruel and unusual punishments were prohibited; that jurors in treason trials should be freeholders; and finally that no Roman Catholic, nor anyone marrying a Roman Catholic, should succeed to the throne and that all future kings should subscribe to the Test Act as revised in 1678.

The Bill of Rights has been criticized because it did not deprive the king of power more completely. He remained the hereditary head of the administrative part of the government. But while this practical document sought to end abuses, it did not attempt to provide for all contingencies. Rather it asserted a number of principles which established England as a limited monarchy. It affirmed the ancient doctrine that the king was under the law, it implied the existence of a contract between the king and the nation, it asserted the sovereignty of Parliament, and it set forth the elementary legal rights of the subject. The Bill of Rights was typical of English constitutional documents in that its wording was largely limited to the specific needs of the moment. Any larger significance is always implied, not stated. In such implications the Bill of Rights has had incalculable influence at home and abroad.

The Coronation Oath (1689), prepared for the new sovereigns, was an adjunct to the Bill of Rights. This oath pledged William and Mary to rule according to "the statutes in Parliament agreed upon, and the laws and customs of the same." Former oaths had merely referred to the laws and customs of earlier kings; but now the words "the statutes in Parliament" were introduced for the first time. The new rulers also swore to uphold "the Protestant Reformed Religion established by law," as well as the Church of England and Ireland "as by law established." Although the words appear redundant, many people believed that the Church of England was too close to Roman Catholicism; Parliament included the words "Protestant" and "Reformed," words which referred to the changes brought about in the Church of England under Henry VIII and Elizabeth.

The Toleration Act (1689)[1] granted the right of public worship to Protestant nonconformists but debarred them from office in the central or local government. The Test Act and the Corporation Act remained in operation; the rest of the Clarendon Code was not enforced. The Toleration Act did not extend liberty of worship to Catholics or to Unitarians, but thereafter they were normally let alone.

A Mutiny Act of 1689, which had to be renewed annually and thus necessitated a meeting of Parliament every year, authorized the maintenance of military discipline in the army by courts-martial. Although annual sessions of Parliament had now begun, a Triennial Act in 1694 provided that Parliament should meet at least once every three years and should not be longer than three years in duration. A Trials for Treason Act (1696) stated that a person on trial for treason should be shown the accusations against him, should have advice of counsel, and should not be convicted except upon the testimony of two independent witnesses. Censorship of the press was allowed to lapse in the same year, though laws against libel remained very strict.

The House of Commons consolidated its control over finance. It assumed full responsibility for military and naval expenditures which were met—after a consideration of the estimates—by appropriations and not by grants to the king. The use of appropriations greatly assisted the government in negotiating loans, which were facilitated further by the establishment of the Bank of England in 1694. The Commons, moreover, appointed certain members as commissioners for public accounts, though the commission did not at first work closely with the Treasury. A grant known as the civil list was voted to the king to cover the expenses of civil government. It became the custom to vote this money for the reign of the sovereign.

The Act of Settlement in 1701 provided that if William or Mary's sister, Anne should die without children (Queen Mary had died in 1694), the throne should

---

[1] The exact title was "An Act for exempting their Majesties' Protestant Subjects, differing from the Church of England, from the Penalties of certain Laws."

descend, not to the exiled Stuarts, but to Sophia, electress dowager of Hanover, a granddaughter of King James I, or to her heirs.[2] The opportunity was taken to impose new restrictions upon the king: he must in future be a member of the Church of England; should he be a foreigner, he must not involve England in war in defense of his foreign possessions; he must not leave the British Isles without the consent of Parliament; a royal pardon could not be pleaded in bar of impeachment; judges should hold office during good behavior and could be dismissed only upon a joint address of both houses of Parliament. The final point was perhaps the most important. The judges were now independent of the Crown and were becoming the cold and impartial deities of modern times.[3]

Thus England declared herself to be a limited monarchy and a Protestant state. The ancient belief that kings governed by some divine dispensation and were supported by sacred prerogatives was dead; for all practical purposes, sovereignty resided in the nation.

SCIENCE AND THE ARTS

The age of the later Stuarts contained more than plots, intrigues, and revolutions. It was an age of great activity in overseas expansion, as will be explained briefly in the next chapter. It was also an age of intellectual and literary endeavor. Its achievements in science were remarkable. A growing interest in science earlier in the century, inspired by Francis Bacon and by the French philosopher Descartes, flowered in the reign of Charles II. The king himself, his cousin Rupert, and his favorite, the duke of Buckingham, had their private laboratories. These dilettante experiments by prominent persons constituted a danger to the spirit of pure scientific inquiry, which nevertheless made great progress. The Royal Society was founded in 1662 to promote experiments in physics and mathematics. For some time the society included talented men from various walks of life: John Aubrey, who wrote brief lives of his contemporaries; Sir Christopher Wren, the architect; John Evelyn, the botanist and numismatist; Samuel Pepys, the naval administrator and diarist; John Locke, the philosopher; and Sir William Petty, the statistician. There were also scientists: Robert Boyle, physicist and chemist, who formulated the law concerning the elasticity of gases; Isaac Barrow, a mathematician; Robert Hooke, mathematician and physicist; and Jonathan Goddard, who made telescopes. After 1684, influenced by the discoveries of Isaac Newton, the society became more purely scientific. Professor of Mathematics at Cambridge at twenty-seven, Newton was one of the great mathematicians of all time. His many discoveries concerning gravitation, calculus, optics, dynamics, and the theory of equations revealed his genius. He was president

---

[2]See genealogical table on page 423.
[3]Two other provisions of the act—that business normally transacted in the Privy Council should not be transacted elsewhere and that officeholders under the Crown should not be eligible for membership in the House of Commons—never became operative.

St. Paul's Cathedral (Britain on View Photographic Library, BTA/ETB)

of the society for twenty-four years. His *Principia Mathematica* (1687) became the foundation of modern science.

There was as yet no thought of a clash between science and religion. Boyle and Newton were both religious men; the first historian of the Royal Society, a clergyman, praised its endeavors "to increase the powers of all mankind and to free them from the bondage of errors." Yet these scientists were finding paths to truth which were entirely outside theology. They were creating a mode of thought which regarded the age of miracles as past, rejected the new revelations of the Puritans, and believed that the universe was governed by natural law. One result was the decline of superstition. There was, for instance, less belief in witchcraft.

The great name in music in this age was that of Henry Purcell, a man of genius, who "wrote masterpieces in every department of music practiced in his time." Before the Civil Wars English music for the most part had been either church music or madrigals. It now broadened into many other forms. Purcell wrote operas,

HOUSE OF STUART

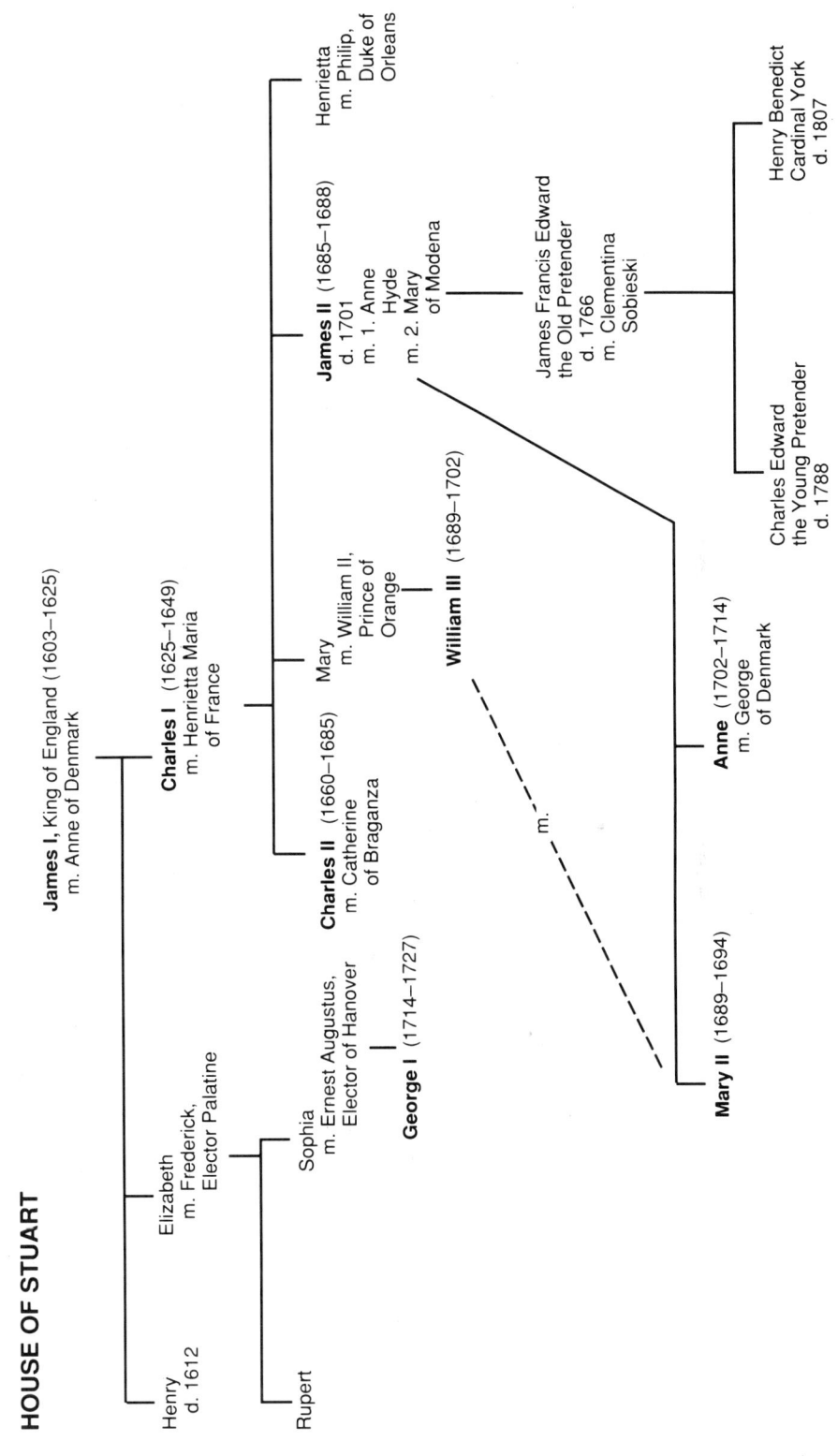

- Henry d. 1612
- Elizabeth m. Frederick, Elector Palatine
  - Rupert
  - Sophia m. Ernest Augustus, Elector of Hanover
    - **George I** (1714–1727)
- **James I**, King of England (1603–1625) m. Anne of Denmark
- **Charles I** (1625–1649) m. Henrietta Maria of France
  - **Charles II** (1660–1685) m. Catherine of Braganza
  - Mary m. William II, Prince of Orange
    - **William III** (1689–1702) m. Mary II (1689–1694)
  - **James II** d. 1701, m. 1. Anne Hyde, m. 2. Mary of Modena (1685–1688)
    - Mary m. William II, Prince of Orange
    - **Anne** (1702–1714) m. George of Denmark
    - James Francis Edward the Old Pretender d. 1766 m. Clementina Sobieski
      - Charles Edward the Young Pretender d. 1788
      - Henry Benedict Cardinal York d. 1807
  - Henrietta m. Philip, Duke of Orleans

incidental music for plays, and sonatas for strings and harpsichord. The violin was introduced into England in the reign of Charles II, when the first public concerts were given. In architecture the outstanding figure was Sir Christopher Wren, who built the modern St. Paul's Cathedral after the Great Fire. The great dome of the new cathedral, which is of the Renaissance style of architecture, still dominates the financial center of the city.

English drama had ceased for a time when the Puritans closed the London theaters, and there were only two theaters open in the early years of Charles II. The theaters of the Restoration, depending largely upon the patronage of the royal court, reflected the degenerate taste of Charles's courtiers. Plays were either heroic tragedies, melodramas of knightly love, or comedies of manners, witty but coarse and cynical. The technique of play acting was improved. Scenery now was used, and female parts were performed by actresses and not by boys, as in Shakespeare's time.

CHRONOLOGY

Restoration and Revolution

1660–1685	Charles II
1661–1665	Clarendon Code
1662	Act of Uniformity; Royal Society founded
1665	London struck by plague; second Dutch War begins
1666	Great Fire of London
1667	England acquires New York and New Jersey; fall of Clarendon; the CABAL
1670	Treaty of Dover
1672	Third Dutch War begins
1673	Test Act; Catholics removed from office
1674	End of CABAL; Danby in power; Shaftesbury in opposition
1678	Popish Plot and Titus Oates
1679–81	Exclusion Struggle; Whig v. Tory

(continued on next page)

Chronology, continued

1683	Rye House Plot
1685–88	James II
1685	Monmouth's Rebellion crushed
1686	James creates Court of Ecclesiastical Commission
1687	Sir Isaac Newton's *Principia Mathematica*
1688	Declaration of Indulgence; birth of son to James; trial of seven bishops; invitation to William of Orange; William lands; James flees
1689	William and Mary placed on throne; Bill of Rights and Coronation Oath; Toleration Act; Mutiny Act
1690	John Locke's *Treatises on Government*
1694	Triennial Act; Bank of England founded; death of Mary II
1696	Trial for Treason Act
1697	St. Paul's Cathedral; Sir Christopher Wren
1701	Act of Settlement

20

William III and Anne

WILLIAM III, 1689–1702 AND MARY II, 1689–1694

In the difficult years following the Revolution, England was fortunate in having as great a king as William III. He was not a popular ruler. His thoughts were forever on his beloved Holland, his intimates were mostly Dutchmen, and he never confided in English generals or statesmen. Small, slightly deformed, a sufferer from asthma and from a tubercular lung, he was not impressive physically. Since the smoke of London gave him a cough, he spent his time in the country as much as possible. Hence there was no court to bring him into contact with the people, as there has been under Queen Elizabeth or Charles II. He was a cold man, without social arts or graces, an exacting taskmaster, liked by the army but by few persons outside it.

William's virtues were those of the soldier–bravery in mortal danger, stoic composure in adversity, and the highest sense of duty. His life was dominated by a hatred of Louis XIV. In governing England William was somewhat highhanded, for he was an autocrat who despised the quarrels of Whigs and Tories, but he displayed both patience and magnanimity toward them. He knew that he was surrounded by treachery, that many Tories and some Whigs were in touch with James II. Yet with great forbearance, he ignored this double-dealing and employed false men if he considered them useful. He was happiest when on the battlefield. But his gifts as a soldier were far less than his powers as a diplomat and statesman. Aside from ruling England and Holland, he held together an alliance against France, fought a long war from 1689 to 1697, and prepared for a greater war which came under his successor, Queen Anne.

WAR WITH FRANCE

Ireland

William was forced at once to turn his attention to Ireland. James II had been good to the Irish Catholics, and when he called on them for help they rose in his behalf. In March 1689 James arrived in Dublin with French officers and French money. The island was soon in Catholic hands. Protestants fled to England or went into hiding or crowded into Londonderry, which withstood a siege lasting 105 days. A Catholic Parliament re-established the Roman Catholic Church and began to restore the land to its former Catholic owners. Early in 1690 some seven thousand troops arrived from France, creating a dangerous threat to England. But James's cause did not prosper. The closer he associated himself with Irish Catholicism, the less was his hope of regaining England. Moreover, his counsels were divided: he thought in terms of the English throne, but the Irish aimed at independence, and the French at a long war that would cause William a maximum amount of harm. William landed in Ireland in June 1690 with an army of thirty-six thousand men. On July 1 he fought the Battle of the Boyne, completely defeating James, who immediately fled to France. Within a year the Irish rebellion was crushed.

The Irish received condign punishment. They were hated and feared both as Catholics and as rebels, and England began a policy of ruthless repression and of impregnable Protestant ascendancy. Thereafter Catholics could neither hold office, sit in the Irish Parliament, nor vote for its members. They were barred from all learned professions save medicine, subjected to unjust and discriminatory taxation, made to suffer legal disabilities in dealings against Protestants, and excluded from almost every means of acquiring wealth, knowledge, or influence. Neither could Catholics purchase land or hold long leases. If the family owned land, it was divided at death among the sons, unless the eldest became Protestant, in which case he got it all. Catholic worship was not forbidden, but it was hedged with severe restrictions.

There was also a repressive economic code. The Irish could neither trade with the colonies, nor could colonial products come to Ireland except by way of England. Thus Ireland's shipping was all but destroyed; her many fine harbors brought her little profit. A prosperous trade in exporting cattle and sheep to England was ended, though the Irish exported cattle to other parts of Europe. They developed the manufacture of woolen cloth, but this was restricted, and in 1699 the export of woolen cloth was forbidden. Nor could raw wool be sent to England. The manufacture of linen was encouraged, but the industry was retarded by lack of capital.

The mass of the population thus was compelled to wring a precarious subsistence from the soil. It is small wonder that the Irish peasants learned to hate the law and to regard it as the enemy. But religion gave them depth and earnestness and a love of ancient custom. It taught conjugal fidelity; the Irish became a chaste people with a delicate sense of female honor. The peasant was affectionate toward family, sympathetic toward the sufferings of others, grateful for kindness, polite, tactful, and hospitable to strangers. Their character displayed contradictions. The Celtic temperament was cheerful, but sufferings produced a strain of religious and poetic melancholy. They could be patient and submissive under great provocation, yet brood over ancient wrongs while awaiting the hour of sudden revenge.

Anglo-French Colonial and Commercial Rivalry

The support given by Louis to James's enterprise in Ireland brought war between England and France. Parliament voted supplies at once to meet the French and Irish danger; war was declared against France in May 1689. The English, however, were thinking of the security of their new regime and of the defense of their country from invasion. It is conceivable that once Ireland had been subdued, England would not have joined in the European war against France. Her entry was due in no small measure to colonial and commercial rivalry.

Both Charles II and his brother gave great encouragement to commerce and colonization, courtiers and politicians followed their example, and the amount of capital available for investment increased. The result was a burst of activity in overseas expansion unequaled since the reign of Elizabeth. The older trading companies, which had suffered heavily during the Civil Wars, entered a period of prosperity. The East India Company under a new charter of 1661 did exceptionally well. On the average, the company paid dividends of twenty-five percent; at the height of its prosperity in 1683 the price of its stock had risen fivefold.

Several new companies were established. The Royal Adventurers of England Trading to Africa, chartered by Charles in 1662 with James as governor, brought slaves from West Africa to the New World. It was ruined by the second Dutch war and its stock was taken over in 1672 by a new body, the Royal African Company. James again was governor. The Hudson's Bay Company, the only one of these early companies still in existence, was begun when Prince Rupert, the Royalist general of the Civil War, became interested in the possibilities of the fur trade in the area of Hudson Bay. He obtained a charter in 1670. The company, always very conservative, operated on a modest scale and prospered in spite of French attacks.

Meanwhile the colonies in the New World were expanding. New York and New Jersey were acquired from the Dutch; the Carolinas and Pennsylvania were founded. The population of the English settlements in North America had risen by 1688 to perhaps 200,000 persons. In the British West Indies the large island of Jamaica developed slowly, and the administration of the settlements was tightened and improved.

A famous code of laws, the Acts of Trade, was devised to control colonial commerce. An act of 1660, based on the Navigation Act of 1651, provided that the trade of the English colonies, both export and import, must be conducted in English ships, and that certain enumerated articles, such as sugar, tobacco, cotton, ginger, indigo (the list grew longer in later years), must be shipped only to England or to other English colonies. From the non-English parts of Asia, Africa, and America, goods could be brought to England only in English or colonial ships directly from the place of origin. But since English vessels normally were excluded from the possessions of other powers, the practical effect of this provision was to confine the colonial trade of England to her own colonies. Colonial products other than the enumerated articles could still be taken to foreign ports. Of these products the most important were fish from the Newfoundland Banks, which were shipped to southern Europe and sold for cash, thus helping to create a favorable balance of trade. The Staple Act of 1663 provided that manufactured goods from the Continent could enter the English colonies only if the goods had been brought to England before they were shipped across the Atlantic. Finally, the Plantations Act of 1673 concerned the enumerated articles, which had long been a subject of contention. New England skippers took sugar and tobacco to continental ports in defiance of the act of 1660. To end this illegal traffic, the Plantations Act imposed new duties on exporters of enumerated articles at the port of lading unless the exporters gave security that the goods in question were bound for England.

Although the Acts of Trade have been condemned by modern historians as crude and selfish, they were not so regarded in the seventeenth century. Since the colonies had been founded by English enterprise, it was considered only just that their trade be channeled to England. The mercantile theory of the time embodied the ideal of a self-sufficing empire in which merchandise need not be purchased from foreign countries. Tropical products from the West Indies, it was thought, added directly to the wealth of England since they could not be produced at home and were often re-exported for sale on the Continent. It was argued further that the colonies were defended by the English navy and were heavily protected in the English market. The colonists made little or no objection to the exclusion of foreigners from colonial ports. What they disliked was the necessity of taking the enumerated articles to England. The Acts of Trade were not as oppressive in the seventeenth century as they became in the eighteenth. Devised by men well versed in colonial trade, they prevented the Dutch from exploiting English colonies; the English merchant marine throve under their operation. English tonnage doubled in the first decade after 1660 and continued to increase rapidly. American trade, which in 1670 amounted to one-tenth of all English foreign commerce, rose to one-seventh in 1700.

Important as it was, colonial trade was only a fraction of England's foreign business. The Merchant Adventurers and the Eastland, Muscovy, and Levant companies carried English commodities, especially woolen cloth, throughout central and northern Europe and into the Near East. The tendency at the end of the seventeenth century was to throw open these trades to a larger number of English merchants; the great trading companies became less exclusive than their structure implied. There were also unincorporated merchants who traded with Spain and Portugal. Commerce was becoming the very lifeblood of the nation. The age was one in which the techniques of manufacturing were still primitive, but in which there was no lack of capital or of business skill; the mercantile instincts of the nation turned to commerce rather than to industry. The growing community of merchants and capitalists was acquiring greater influence at Westminster than it had possessed in the past and was becoming one of the most powerful forces in the kingdom. Thus the rise of France as a colonial and commercial rival was a matter of grave concern.

In a general way the history of French expansion overseas parallels that of

England, though the French moved more slowly and founded fewer colonies. The first permanent colony was founded in 1608 at Quebec; about the same time a colony was planted at Port Royal in Acadia (Nova Scotia). The number of French colonists in Canada in 1689 was probably less than 15,000, but they ranged over an enormous area from the St. Lawrence Valley westward through the Great Lakes and down the Mississippi. The French islands in the West Indies were equal or even superior to the English ones. The French held slaving stations around St. Louis on the Senegal River in West Africa. Its early factories in India were located at Surat (1668), at Pondicherry (1674), which grew into its best town; and at Chandarnager (1690) on the Hooghly River in Bengal. These colonies were supported by the French state, by a fine navy, and by a growing mercantile marine. It is not surprising that English merchants regarded this French expansion with apprehension.

England's entry into the war against Louis in 1689 constituted a change of policy. The ancient hostility of the two countries in the later Middle Ages had subsided in the reign of Queen Elizabeth, and for almost a century, except for brief periods of hostility, England and France had been at peace. This amity was now broken. There began a century of conflict, a new Hundred Years' War, which was concluded only when Napoleon was defeated at Waterloo in 1815.

The War of the League of Augsburg, 1689–1697

The aggressions of Louis XIV against his neighbors gradually surrounded France with a ring of hostile states that formed the League of Augsburg in 1686 for their mutual protection. Just as the Revolution was taking place in England, a war broke out in 1688 when Louis attacked the Palatinate. Aligned against him were the members of the so-called Grand Alliance of England, Holland, Austria, Spain, a number of the German states, of which Brandenburg, Saxony, Hanover, and Bavaria were the most important, and later Savoy and the papacy. Sweden had joined the league in 1686 but took no part in the war. Such an alliance might appear invincible. But France had the advantage of inner lines, whereas the allied powers, scattered around the circumference, were divided by jealousies and conflicting ambitions. Decisive action depended upon what England and Holland could accomplish at sea and in the Spanish Netherlands.

The French navy, which was able at first to challenge the fleets of both England and Holland, secured temporary control of the Channel at the time of James's expedition to Ireland. But the French fleet could not control both the Channel and the Mediterranean. It was defeated by the English in 1692 at La Hogue in the Channel near Normandy; when Louis began operations against Spain and Savoy in 1694, an English squadron entered the Mediterranean, blockaded the French in Toulon, and disrupted the assault on Spain.

On the other hand, Louis had the better of the fighting in the Spanish Netherlands. He possessed every advantage of veteran troops, excellent generals, and strategic positions. He captured Mons in 1691 and Namur in 1692 and defeated William in the Battle of Steenkerke in the latter year. William again was defeated in 1693. Although

William retook Namur in 1695, Louis was winning the war on land and was dividing the allies by his diplomacy. Nevertheless, Louis was ready for peace in 1697 and so were his opponents. The Peace of Ryswick in that year provided that France restore all her conquests since 1678 except Strasbourg, allow the Dutch to garrison a line of fortresses in the Spanish Netherlands along the French frontier, and acknowledge William as King of England. The peace merely provided a breathing space before the opening of another war.

WILLIAM AND ENGLISH POLITICS

Meanwhile William was contending with political factions in England. Politics at this time are difficult to understand because although we hear of Whigs and Tories they were not like modern parties. Of the many reasons for this, perhaps the most important was the position of the king. William kept power in his own hands as far as possible. He insisted on having complete control over the army and over foreign affairs, he did not allow Parliament to meet when he was abroad, and he rarely took an English minister with him when he went to the Continent. Acting as his own prime minister, William was at liberty to control policy and to make appointments. He used all the powers of the Crown which had not been taken away and resisted any encroachment on those powers. With so strong and energetic a ruler, modern political parties which today control policy and distribute patronage were impossible.

Modern political parties were also impossible because of the aristocratic nature of society. Country gentlemen with wealth and local influence could obtain election to the House of Commons through their own efforts and were completely independent of any party organization, speaking and voting as they pleased in Parliament. There were also family groups of members. A great noble holding large estates could secure the return of his relatives, employees, and other connections; this group looked to him and not to a party for leadership. Political parties in the modern sense were also out of the question because there was no connection between a change of ministers and an election to the House of Commons. William did not appoint ministers because their party had won a majority. Indeed the reverse was true, for the king's ministers could build a Court party in Parliament. At least a hundred members were placemen who held some office in the gift of the Crown, and this patronage could be used to influence elections and to obtain votes after Parliament assembled. Members might storm at ministers but could not turn them out except by the clumsy method of impeachment.

Both parties were affected by the Revolution. The Tories lost their political philosophy. Some of them were Jacobite, but the majority accepted Locke's utilitarian view of kingship. Yet they could not pay William the respect they had accorded the Stuarts; they thought of him as the enemy of their church. The Tories represented the interests of the landowning gentry who had no inclination to pay high taxes for the support of a war on behalf of commerce. The Whigs had attacked the prerogatives of the Stuart kings but now found themselves with a ruler who used his prerogatives with vigor. Hence they were goaded into seeking further reduction in the powers of the Crown and further increases in the powers of Parliament. They stood for religious toleration, for the commercial interests of merchants and bankers, and for a vigorous prosecution of the war against a commercial rival. Finally, because both parties contained moderates and extremists their condition was confused and fluid.

Under these circumstances both the ministers of the king and the opposition to him in the Commons were apt to be coalitions of both parties; the best descriptive terms are a Country party in the Commons which criticized the government and a Court party which defended it. In the first part of the reign the Whigs had a majority in the Commons. Irritated by the king's appointment of both Whigs and Tories to the ministry, the Whigs set themselves to annoy the government. They voted money for only short periods, they made inquiries into military and naval mishaps, they set up committees to audit the accounts, they forced William to cancel grants made to his favorites, and they dealt with the affairs of the East India Company, which had previously been the province of the Crown. William naturally was irritated, but he discovered that the Tories also opposed him. They lacked enthusiasm for the war, they sought to reduce the size of the army, and some of them were in correspondence with James II.

Since the prosecution of the war was all-important to William, he brought a majority of Whigs into the government. Between 1694 and 1698 the ministry was largely Whig, although a moderate Tory, Sidney Godolphin, an official in the Treasury who was a kind of indispensable civil servant, remained in office. The leading Whigs were known as the Junto. The best work of the Whigs was the founding of the Bank of England in 1694. The subscribers to a government loan of £1,200,000 were incorporated by Parliament as a joint-stock bank with the right to issue notes and discount bills. This was a modest beginning, but the bank helped to finance the war, and since the government was not required to repay the loan so long as it paid interest, the arrangement was the origin of the national debt.

After the Peace of Ryswick in 1697, the country eagerly turned away from war. A new leader appeared in the Commons, Robert Harley, who won much popular approval but greatly angered the king by demanding a reduction in the cost of government, a smaller army than William advised, and an end to royal gifts to favorites. The Whigs were discredited by this attack and by revelations that some of them were in secret correspondence with James II. The king gradually replaced them with Tory ministers, of whom Godolphin and John Churchill, Earl of Marlborough, were the most important. Such was the situation at the end of the reign.

THE PARTITION TREATIES

The problem of the fate of the Spanish empire was growing more pressing in the last years of the century. The Spanish king, Charles II, though taking an unconscionable time in dying, would certainly do so soon. The two strongest claimants to the inheritance of Spain were Louis of France and Emperor Leopold of Austria, both of whom had married sisters of the Spanish king. A third possible heir was Leopold's grandson, Prince Joseph Ferdinand of Bavaria, who was still a child. William's great fear was that the Spanish Netherlands would fall to France, and he devoted his last years to the completion of two partition treaties with Louis by which he hoped to divide the Spanish possessions without a war and without France's obtaining the Netherlands. But neither Spain nor Austria was consulted about these treaties. The Spanish, resentful at the proposed dismemberment of their empire, believed that France could unite their possessions better than could Austria; hence Charles II, now really on his deathbed, was induced to sign a will which left the Spanish empire to Philip, Duke of Anjou, a grandson of Louis XIV, on condition that it not be divided. Louis had before him the prospect of enormous new possessions but also the sobering thought that they would have to be fought for. His decision was to accept the will.

It appeared at first that no general war would follow. Holland recognized Philip as king of Spain, and the English seemed willing to do the same, for the will provided that if Philip accepted the crown of Spain he should forfeit that of France. Louis, however, made a number of miscalculations. Hoping to prevent a war by frightening his opponents, he seized a number of strategic points in the Spanish Netherlands, in Cologne, and in Milan. These moves showed clearly that, though Philip might become the King of Spain, his policy would be dominated by France. Nor did Louis give any indication that Philip, if King of Spain, would renounce his claim to the French crown. Moreover, it became evident that French merchants would be permitted to exploit the Spanish empire: a French company was given the right to supply the Spanish colonies with African slaves. Above all, at the death of James II, Louis recognized James's son, James Edward, the Old Pretender, as king of England, a gratuitous insult which united the English against France. Tories as well as Whigs, determined to preserve the revolutionary settlement, agreed that the country must prepare for war. Preparations were under way when William died in March 1702.

QUEEN ANNE, 1702–1714

The reign of Queen Anne may seem to be dominated by the great war with France. And in a sense it was. But behind the war clouds the reign was studded with brilliant names and could boast notable achievements: Marlborough in war and diplomacy; Newton in science; Wren in architecture; Godolphin, Somers, Halifax, Harley, and Bolingbroke in politics; Pope, Swift, Defoe, Congreve, Addison, and Steele in literature—all added luster to what is often called the Augustan Age. English wealth and commerce increased while Louis' power was beaten down, the empire was enlarged, and a lasting union with Scotland was effected.

These achievements cannot be attributed to Queen Anne, a semi-invalid who suffered from gout and who had borne some sixteen children, only to see them die. A woman of very mediocre abilities, she was slow-witted, obstinate, opinionated—and rather dowdy in appearance. She disliked both the memory of William and the thought that the Hanoverians would succeed her. She was pious and devout, a strong supporter of the Church of England and of the Tory party, fond of female favorites, though devoted to her sponge of a husband, Prince George of Denmark, of whom Charles II had said, "I have tried him drunk and tried him sober, and there is nothing in him." Anne's one hobby, it has been remarked, was eating. Yet she had both courage and a sense of duty. She tried to play her part and to maintain her prerogatives. Disliking political parties, she once burst out, "Why for God's sake must I, who have no thought but for the good of my country, be made so miserable as to be brought into the power of one set of men?" Yet she could not avoid dependence on her ministers. A small inner group of advisers supplied the leadership which William had exercised personally, and thus the practice of limited monarchy was advanced during her reign.

The Marlborough-Godolphin Coalition

Anne began her reign by selecting a coalition ministry consisting of both Whigs and Tories. The most important members were the earl of Marlborough, who was captain general (that is, supreme commander of the army), and Sidney Godolphin, the lord treasurer. Marlborough, one of England's greatest generals, was a man of extraordinary gifts both as a diplomat and as a soldier. He had spent all his life at court or at war, having fought at Tangier, in Flanders, in Alsace, in Ireland, and in Flanders again before he became commander in chief. He was a splendid tactician. Armies were still small enough for a single mind to direct their movements during battle, and one must imagine Marlborough deploying troops, placing artillery, at times leading a charge in person. He taught his cavalry to charge home (as Cromwell had done), and his infantry to fire in a single volley by platoons. The grenade and the bayonet were new weapons that made close fighting more deadly. Marlborough was equally successful in planning grand strategy and in viewing campaigns as a whole. At the same time he was an excellent diplomat. Year after year he traveled from one capital to another, holding together an alliance of nations with diverse and selfish aims. His strong position at home made it possible for him to coordinate war and politics. Yet, there were serious flaws in his character. He was much too fond of money. As a young man he did not scruple to obtain advancement by becoming one of the lovers of Lady Castlemaine, the mistress of Charles II. A servant of James II, he deserted him, though only when his cause was hopeless; a servant of William, he corresponded secretly with James.

His wife Sarah, was an avaricious, violent, and overbearing woman who for many years was a favorite of Queen Anne. To place themselves on a basis of complete equality, Anne and Sarah called each other Mrs. Morley and Mrs. Freeman. This connection aided Marlborough greatly, though his wife was so partisan and vehement a Whig that she made it difficult for him to work with the Tories. Godolphin, as we have seen, was a very able administrator, sound and steady, a moderate Tory with a touch of the Jacobite. At the beginning of the reign Anne wrote to Sarah, "We four must never part till death mows us down with his impartial hand." Other members of the coalition were Somers and Halifax from the Whig Junto, Robert Harley, a moderate Tory, and a number of High Tories.

The High Tories of the coalition proved to be difficult. They raised the cry that the church was in danger, and twice attempted to pass occasional conformity bills which would have prevented nonconformists from qualifying for office by occasionally taking the Anglican sacrament. Their view of England's role in the war differed from that of Godolphin and Marlborough. Marlborough's strategy was to drive the French from the Netherlands, defeat them in a pitched battle, and so open the way for a march on Paris. But the High Tories, less interested in the war, wished England to rely on sea power and to play only an auxiliary part in the war on land. Marlborough and Godolphin broke with the High Tories, several of whom were dismissed in 1703. Robert Harley became secretary of state in 1704. Thereafter the three principal ministers, known as the Triumvirate, were Marlborough, Godolphin, and Harley. At the same time a brilliant young member of the Commons, Henry St. John, later Viscount Bolingbroke, was made Secretary at War. This moderately Tory ministry was displeasing to the extremists of both parties and would not have survived for long had not Marlborough won the victory of Blenheim in 1704.

The War of the Spanish Succession, 1702–1713

The first years of the War of the Spanish Succession did not go well. Allied with Spain, Savoy, Bavaria, and Cologne, Louis was in a strong position. He had placed French troops in a number of strategic places, and his fleet at Toulon dominated the western Mediterranean. Arrayed against him was the Grand Alliance of England, Holland, and Austria as well as Denmark, Prussia, Hanover, and lesser German states. But it was difficult, as before, for the allies to work together. Success depended largely on good relations between England and Holland, which for the most part were maintained, though the Dutch, who undoubtedly were making great sacrifices, were fearful of the pitched battles desired by Marlborough. For two years Marlborough's campaigns in the Netherlands and along the lower Rhine accomplished little, as did English operations at sea.

Successes in these years were diplomatic rather than military. In 1703 both Savoy and Portugal joined the allies. The adherence of Savoy was helpful in northern Italy and on the upper Danube against Bavaria, while the port of Lisbon supplied a naval base close to the Mediterranean. The Portuguese, however, came in only on conditions. They asked that the Emperor's son, the Archduke Charles, be declared king of Spain instead of Philip, Louis' grandson; that Charles come in person to Lisbon; and that the war continue until Spain had been won for Austria. These conditions were accepted, though they forced the allies to fight in Spain under disadvantages which in the long run proved insurmountable. There was also a commercial treaty between England and Portugal, the Methuen Treaty, by which English cloth entered Portugal and Portuguese port wine entered England at low custom rates: hence the English taste for port during the eighteenth century.

In 1704 the fortunes of the allies rose greatly. To assist the Austrians, who were pleading for help, Marlborough conceived the bold design of taking his army up the

The Netherlands 1700.

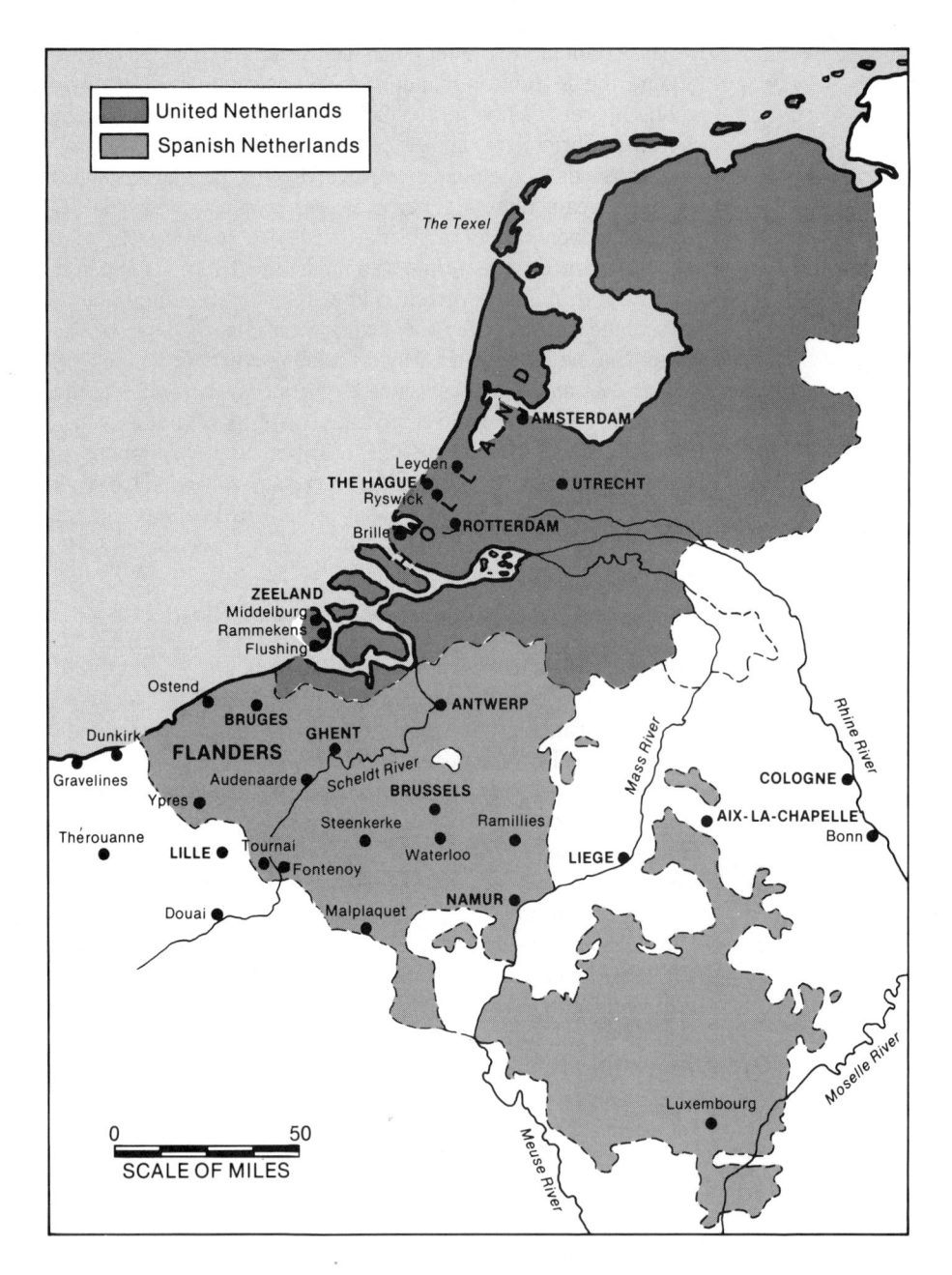

Rhine and into Bavaria to disable the Bavarians before they and the French could attack Vienna. They defeated the Bavarians at the Battle of the Schellenberg, and on August 13, 1704, met and overwhelmed a combined French and Bavarian army at Blenheim. Blenheim was a decisive battle. For the first time in two generations a large French army suffered a crushing defeat. Austria was saved, its future aggrandizement was assured, and Louis lost all hope of extending his territories beyond the Rhine. The Godolphin-Marlborough coalition was strengthened in England and remained in power for four more years. Coincidentally, Admiral Rooke captured Gibraltar and beat off a French fleet at nearby Málaga. Gibraltar remained in English hands despite counterattacks by the French and Spanish.

In the years following Blenheim the war went steadily against Louis except in Spain. Marlborough won the important victory of Ramillies in 1706, with the result that the French were cleared from the Spanish Netherlands; after another victory, Oudenaarde, in 1708, he might have pushed on to Paris but was restrained by the fears of his allies. In 1709 Louis attempted to make peace, but was offered such hard terms that he determined to continue the war. Making a supreme effort, he raised new armies and inspired France to heroic exertion. Marlborough's costly victory in the Battle of Malplaquet, also in the Netherlands, was really a strategic victory for Louis, for it stopped an advance to Paris and retrieved the reputation of French arms. In Spain, on the other hand, the allies were unsuccessful. The Spanish people did not want the Archduke Charles as their king. They wanted Philip of France, and they rallied so effectively to his cause that the allies abandoned Madrid. The Austrian cause in Spain was hopeless.

English Politics, 1705–1710

Two alterations, both gradual, took place in the relative position of parties during these years. The first came as a result of the elections in 1705 and 1708, when the Whigs increased their strength in the House of Commons. The old Whig Junto of William's reign was loud in demanding office, and since the Whigs favored the vigorous prosecution of the war, the government gradually yielded. Thus the ministry of Marlborough and Godolphin gradually was shifted from one that was moderately Tory to one containing many Whigs. The queen was most reluctant to make these changes. She thought of the Whigs as the opponents of her church and of the prerogatives of the Crown, both of which she was determined to defend. It was only with the greatest difficulty that she was persuaded to admit Whigs to office.

Following the election of 1708, however, the Marlborough-Godolphin-Whig coalition began to disintegrate. The basic cause was war-weariness among the people. The war was very costly, and although Marlborough's victories were most satisfying, they did not appear to be bringing the war to a conclusion. It was remembered that Louis had offered to make peace in 1709. The government also was weakened because Anne was at last growing tired of the domineering Sarah and was turning to a new favorite, Mrs. Abigail Masham. Mrs. Masham, a cousin of Robert Harley, was a Tory who favored a purely Tory ministry.

A famous trial in 1710 which further undermined the position of the coalition was that of Dr. Sacheverell, a Tory clergyman who attacked the Whigs in his sermons, declared that the church was in danger, and denounced the principles of the Revolution by defending divine right and passive obedience to kings. Though Sacheverell's true aim was notoriety, he did gain a great following. There was no doubt that his utterances were treasonous. The government successfully impeached him but then, knowing that severity would be unpopular, gave him a ridiculously light sentence. Sensing that the country was turning against the Whigs, Anne began to break up the ministry. She dismissed Sarah after a stormy scene, then dropped Sunderland and Godolphin, along with the Whigs of the Junto. Tories were brought in, of whom the chief was Robert Harley, lord treasurer, later the earl of Oxford, and St. John, secretary of state, later Lord Bolingbroke. Though he had won the war, Marlborough was dismissed in 1711.

The Treaty of Utrecht, 1713

The Tory ministers at once set about making peace with France. Their methods were dishonorable, for they made secret preliminary agreements with Louis safeguarding English interests before they consulted their allies. Yet the settlement was not unjust and brought England many benefits. Louis recognized Anne and the future sovereigns from Hanover as the rightful rulers of England; he banished the Old Pretender from France. The fortifications of Dunkirk, a center for French privateers, were destroyed under the supervision of English troops. England obtained important colonial concessions. The area of Hudson Bay, Acadia (Nova Scotia), and the island of Newfoundland were ceded to her by France, as was also the French portion of St. Kitts in the West Indies. From Spain England secured Gibraltar, the island of Minorca in the Mediterranean, a monopoly of supplying Spanish America with black slaves, and the right to send one ship each year to the fairs at Vera Cruz or at Cartagena.

The settlement on the Continent recognized Philip as king of Spain but provided that he renounce his claims to the French throne and that the crowns of France and Spain never be united.

The Treaty of Utrecht left France in an exhausted and bankrupt condition from which she recovered only slowly. Her colonial and commercial development also received a serious reversal, though they resumed their progress much more rapidly than did France as a whole. The Dutch sank into the position of a second-rate power—secure, wealthy, but unimportant. England emerged from the war with the most lively and busy colonial empire in the world and the largest navy. It is an indication of the prime importance of commerce to England that the Tory ministers who made this treaty were no less intent on colonial and commercial advantage than the Whigs would have been.

The Hanoverian Succession

Having dismissed her Whig ministers and appointed Tory ones in 1710, Anne dissolved Parliament. The result was a Tory victory, for she had gauged the temper of the electorate correctly. The Tories appeared to be firmly entrenched, with a

Tory queen, Tory ministers, and a Tory House of Commons. Yet within four years their party was fragmented and ruined, never to be revived in its early eighteenth-century form. The cause of this debacle was the entanglement of the Tories with Jacobitism. The story has sometimes been written as though they engaged in a deep and sinister plot, but in truth they were drawn into Jacobite dealings by the necessities of their position.

Their task was to make peace after the Whigs had won the war. Though their policy was correct, their methods, as we have seen, were questionable, for they safeguarded English interests by deserting their allies. As this came to light, the allies were deeply incensed—none more so than George, the elector of Hanover. For various reasons he had wished to fight France to a finish, and was furious over the Tory policy. So were the Whigs. Indeed, so vehement was Whig hostility that Anne was forced to create twelve Tory peers to pass the treaties through the House of Lords. Thus George of Hanover and the Whigs were drawn together. The Tories, fearful of the future, believed that if George became king they would be impeached for treason. Like many statesmen of both parties, they had occasionally flirted with Jacobitism in the past. Now they began to go further in their messages to the exiled Stuarts.

James II, of course, was dead. His son, James Edward, the Old Pretender, a young man in his early twenties, was not a promising candidate for the throne. He was a devout Catholic, his health was poor, and though he was always dignified and correct, there was a settled melancholy about him, as though he knew himself to be a man doomed to futility. His principal disadvantages as a possible king of England were his Catholicism and his dependence on France. Early in 1714, after a serious illness of the queen, Oxford, acting through the French Ambassador, inquired of the Pretender whether he was prepared to alter his religion if called to the English throne. When he replied in most definite terms that he was not he ended all chances of a Stuart restoration.

The Tories had made no secret of their approach to the Pretender, and a debate in Parliament, in which the Whigs charged that the Protestant succession was in danger, caused a quarrel between Oxford and Bolingbroke. Oxford, though an able administrator, had grown irresolute and dilatory and was intoxicated frequently. Bolingbroke, a vehement man who hated half measures, was no more Jacobite than Oxford, but he loathed a policy of drift and believed that the Tories should obtain a position of power so that they could bargain with George when the crisis arrived. He asked Anne to dismiss Oxford, which she did in July 1714. Then suddenly the crisis came. Anne was on her deathbed, but Oxford's successor as lord treasurer had not been appointed. The Privy Council, which met without the queen, was dominated by men who did not wish a Roman Catholic sovereign. They determined to suggest the duke of Shrewsbury as treasurer, and Anne accepted the appointment, perhaps without knowing what she was doing, for she died two days later. Shrewsbury, like his fellow councilors, was resolved to promote the Hanoverian succession. Bolingbroke was helpless, and all hope of a Stuart restoration disappeared.

Scene in a coffe-house, c. 1700. (Grouache, British School, British Museum)

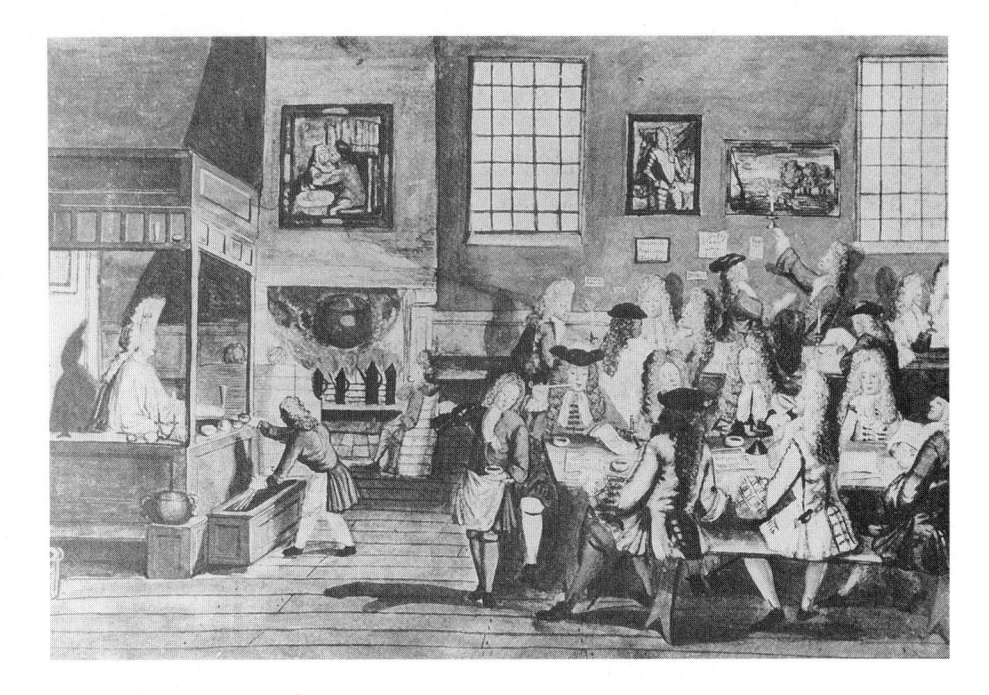

The Scottish Union, 1707

The most important achievement of the Whigs in domestic affairs during the middle years of Anne's reign was the completion of a union between England and Scotland. At the time of the Restoration in 1660 the Cromwellian union had been dissolved. Scotland had reverted to its former position under the early Stuarts, becoming once more a separate country with its own Privy Council and Parliament. But its king remained the king of England. Charles II governed Scotland harshly through a secretary in London and an amenable Privy Council in Edinburgh. Episcopacy was re-established; the Lords of the Articles again dominated the Scottish Parliament.

It is not surprising, therefore, that the Revolution in 1688 appeared to the Scots as an opportunity to strike for greater freedom. They wished not only to be rid of a Catholic sovereign, but also to overthrow a despotic government, to reassert Presbyterianism, and to obtain a free Parliament. Hence a Scottish Convention Parliament summoned by William used stronger language than was used in England, declaring that James II had "forfeited" the Scottish throne, which was thereupon offered to William and Mary. But this offer was accompanied by an urgent request for parliamentary liberty and by a complaint that episcopacy was an intolerable grievance. Before William could respond, a revolt took place in the Highlands. It was soon dispersed.

William decided, however, that he could keep his throne in Scotland only by making concessions. He permitted the re-establishment of Presbyterianism and allowed the Lords of the Articles to be abolished, so that the Scottish Parliament was at liberty to conduct business as it chose. There was danger in this concession: the Parliaments in the two kingdoms could now go separate ways, for there was nothing uniting them except the royal veto.

Despite William's concessions, Scotland never was reconciled to his rule, and bitterness against England was increased greatly by a commercial failure in 1699. The Scots, debarred as aliens from trade with the English plantations (though they engaged in a good deal of smuggling), founded in 1695 a Scottish company to trade with Asia, Africa, and America. It was hoped at first that some capital could be secured from England, but the English Parliament opposed the plan, and in the end capital came only from Scots. Persons of every rank subscribed to the venture. The plan to trade in Asia and Africa was abandoned because of English opposition, and the company decided to plant a colony on the Isthmus of Panama. Ignoring local conditions and strangely discounting the certain hostility of Spain, the company sent out three ships with colonists and with goods (including periwigs) to be sold to the Indians. But the climate in Panama was unhealthy, the Spanish attacked the colony, and William, allied with Spain against France, would send no help. The venture ended in failure, with hundreds of Scots losing their savings in this hapless enterprise.

Smarting under this debacle, for which they blamed the English, the Scots were incensed further by the English Act of Settlement in 1701, which arranged for the Hanoverian succession without prior consultation with Scotland, and by the English declaration of war against France in 1702. In 1703 the Scottish Parliament passed an act which forbade the king to involve Scotland in war without its consent. Parliament also passed the famous Act of Security—a kind of declaration of independence—providing that unless Scotland received broad securities, she would not accept the same ruler as England after the death of Queen Anne. Fearing that Scotland might ally with France, English statesmen resolved on a closer union between the two parts of Britain. Commissioners were appointed to prepare a union with Scotland, and the threat was made that if this union were not completed quickly Scottish trade to England would be sharply curtailed.

The Scots were in a cruel dilemma. An alliance with France while England and France were at war would be disastrous. A restoration of the Catholic Stuarts would spell the ruin of the Kirk. Moreover, the only remedy for Scotland's economic plight lay in trade with England and her colonies. Scotland, in a word, faced disaster unless she accepted union. And therefore, despite its anger, the Scottish Parliament appointed commissioners to meet with those of England. A union of the two countries was accepted in 1707. The Scots gave up their Parliament. Thereafter they were to send forty-five members to the English House of Commons and sixteen representative peers to the English House of Lords.

In return the Scots received freedom of trade with England and with the English colonies. They retained Presbyterianism as their national church; they also retained their law, their local government, and their banking system. Customs duties and taxation in the two countries were amalgamated. Since Scotland would now be

HOUSE OF HANOVER

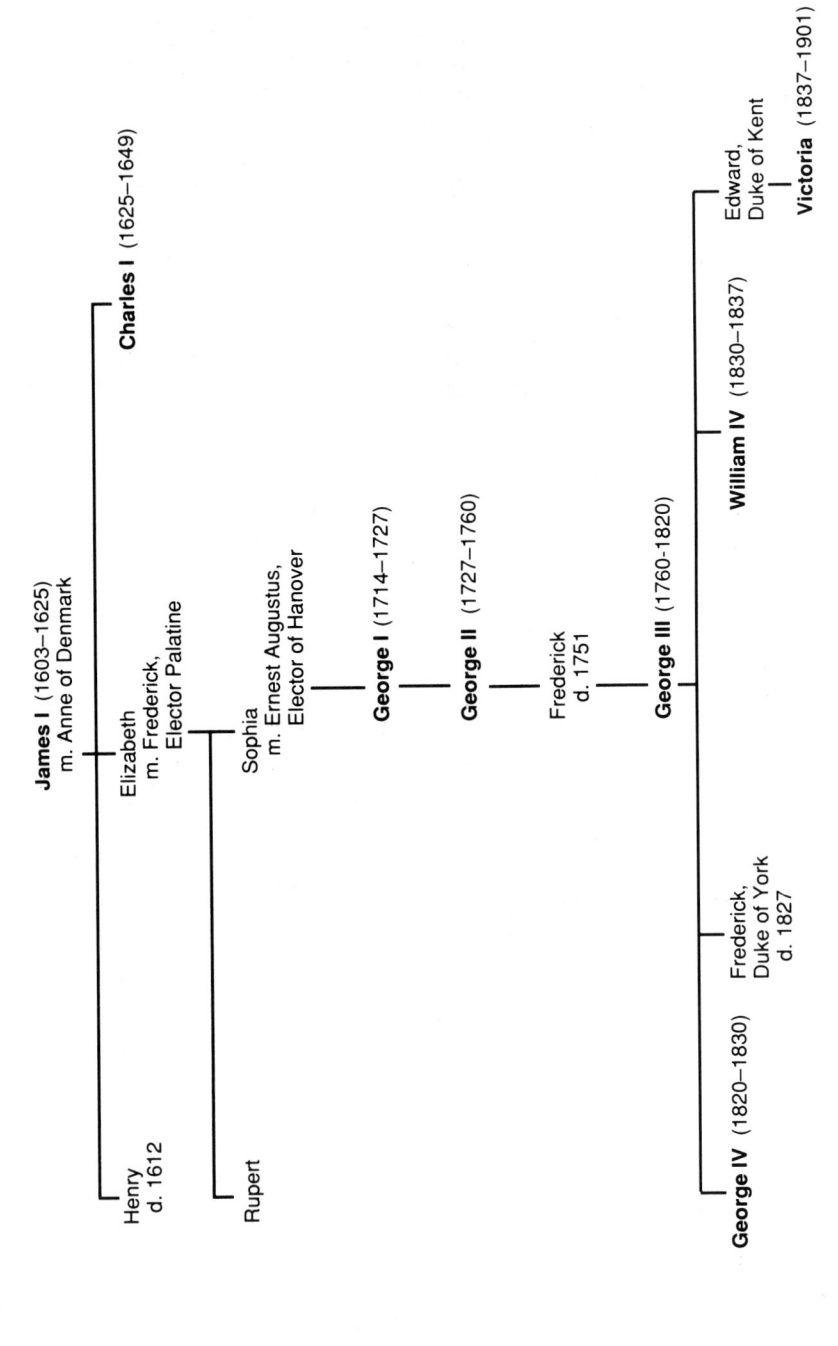

James I (1603–1625)
m. Anne of Denmark
- Henry d. 1612
- **Charles I** (1625–1649)
- Elizabeth m. Frederick, Elector Palatine
  - Rupert
  - Sophia m. Ernest Augustus, Elector of Hanover
    - **George I** (1714–1727)
      - **George II** (1727–1760)
        - Frederick d. 1751
          - **George III** (1760–1820)
            - **George IV** (1820–1830)
            - Frederick, Duke of York d. 1827
            - **William IV** (1830–1837)
            - Edward, Duke of Kent
              - **Victoria** (1837–1901)

partially responsible for the combined national debt, she was given a considerable sum of money, about £398,000, known as the Equivalent. This made the union a little more acceptable; much of the Equivalent was used to compensate investors in the disastrous attempt to plant a colony in Panama.

The union gave economic opportunity to Scotland and relieved England from the danger of a Franco-Scottish alliance. In the long run it brought lasting benefits to both countries, but for at least half a century it was bitterly resented in Scotland.

CHRONOLOGY

Last of the Stuarts

1689–94	William and Mary; William III rules alone until 1702
1689–97	War of the League of Augsburg
1690	Battle of the Boyne; Ireland crushed
1694	Bank of England; beginning of national debt
1702–14	Queen Anne
1702–13	War of the Spanish Succession
1704	Battle of Blenheim; Marlborough and Godolphin in power; Gibraltar captured
1707	Act of Union with Scotland
1710	Trial of Dr. Sacheverell
1711	Marlborough dismissed; Harley (Oxford) and St. John (Bolingbroke) in power; House of Lords "packed"
1713	Treaty of Utrecht

Suggestions for Further Reading

BIBLIOGRAPHIES

Bonser, Wilfred, *An Anglo-Saxon and Celtic Bibliography* (450–1087), 2 vols., 1957.
Brown, L. M. and I. R. Christie, *Bibliography of British History, 1789–1851*, 1977.
Davies, Godfrey, *Bibliography of British History: Stuart Period, 1603–1714*, rev. Mary Keeler, 1970.
Gross, Charles, *The Sources and Literature of English History*, 1915.
Hanham, H. J., *Bibliography of British History, 1815–1914*, 1976.
Pargellis, Stanley and D. J. Medley, *Bibliography of British History: The Eighteenth Century, 1714–1789*, 1951.
Read, Conyers, *Bibliography of British History: Tudor Period, 1485–1603*, 2d ed., 1959.
Smith, Robert A., *Late Georgian and Regency England, 1760–1837*, 1984.

The North American Conference on British Studies has sponsored the following bibliographical handbooks:
Altschul, M., *Anglo-Norman England, 1066–1154*, 1969.
Wilkinson, Bertie, *The High Middle Ages in England, 1154–1377*, 1978
Guth, D. J., *Late-Medieval England, 1377–1485*, 1976.
Levine, Mortimer, *Tudor England, 1485–1603*, 1968.
Sachse, William L., *Restoration England, 1660–1689*, 1971.
Altholz, J. L., *Victorian England, 1837–1901*, 1970.
Havighurst, A. F., *Modern England: 1901–1970*, 1976.

REFERENCE WORKS

Cockayne, George E., *The Complete Peerage of England, Scotland, Ireland, Great Britain, and the United Kingdom,* ed. Vicary Gibbs, et al., 13 vols., 1910–1959.
Drabble, Margaret, ed., *The Oxford Companion to English Literature,* 5th ed., 1985.
Fryde, E. B., D. E. Greenway, S. Porter, and I. Roy, eds., *Handbook of British Chronology,* 3d ed., Royal Historical Society, 1986.
Gilbert, Martin, *British History Atlas,* 1968.
Haigh, Christopher, *The Cambridge Historical Encyclopedia of Great Britain and Ireland,* 1985.
Langer, William L., ed., *An Encyclopedia of World History: Ancient, Medieval, and Modern, Chronologically Arranged,* 5th ed., 1973.
McEvedy, Colin and Richard Jones, *Atlas of World Population History,* 1978.
Rogers, Pat, *The Oxford Illustrated History of English Literature,* 1987.
Stephen, Leslie and Sidney B. Lee, eds., *The Dictionary of National Biography from the Earliest Times to 1900,* 1921–1922.

JOURNALS

Albion
American Historical Review
Bulletin of the Institute of Historical Research
Economic History Review
English Historical Review
Historical Journal
History
History Today
Journal of British Studies
Journal of Modern History
Past and Present
Times Literary Supplement (London)

PREHISTORIC BRITAIN

While interest in Stonehenge never ceases and answers to its riddles are yet to be found, the important current work in this field is seeking to show continuity from one group and period to another, rather than sharp contrasts. The Beaker folk, for example, may be older inhabitants in a new era rather than new arrivals from the

Continent. Darvill has made an important addition to the continuing work of Colin Renfrew, among others.

Atkinson, R. C. J., *Stonehenge*, 1956.
Darvill, Timothy, *Prehistoric Britain*, 1987.
Fox, Sir Cyril Fred, *Pattern and Purpose: Early Celtic Art in Britain*, 1958.
———*The Personality of Britain: Its Influence on Inhabitant and Invader in Prehistoric and Early Historic Times*, 1947.
Powell, T. G. E., *The Celts*, 1958.
Refrew, Colin, *Before Civilization*, 1973.
Stover, Leon E. and Bruce Kraig, *Stonehenge: The Indo-European Heritage*, 1978.

ROMAN BRITAIN

Historians, here too, are looking for continuity rather than sharp lines of difference, especially on the subject of prehistoric and Roman villas. Roman London is continually baring its secrets to the archaeologists and the tunnel diggers. Salway's addition to the Oxford *History of England* series is most welcome.

Birley, Anthony, *The People of Roman Britain*, 1980.
Blair, Peter Hunter, *Roman Britain and Early England 55 B.C.–A.D. 871*, 1963.
Burn, A. R., *Agricola and Roman Britain*, 1953.
Collingwood, R. G. and J. N. L. Myers, *Roman Britain and the English Settlements*, 1937.
Collingwood, R. G. and I. A. Richmond, *The Archaeology of Roman Britain*, rev. ed., 1969.
Richmond, I. A., *Roman Britain*, rev. ed., 1964.
Rivet, A. L. F., *Town and Country in Roman Britain*, 1958.
Salway, Peter H., *Roman Britain*, 1981.
Todd, Malcolm, *Roman Britain, 55 B.C.–A.D. 400*, 1981.

ANGLO-SAXON ENGLAND

Historians of Anglo-Saxon England are now less sure of a total break at the time of the Roman evacuation. They are also increasingly inclined to see presages of feudalism prior to the Norman Conquest in 1066. Scholars also are increasingly interested in showing links between England and the Continent. All in all, however, Anglo-Saxon England is still viewed as a distinct society, linked with, but different from, the Roman, Norman, and Continental.

Alcock, Leslie, *Arthur's Britain: History and Archaeology, A.D. 367–634*, 1973.
Beresford, Maurice, *The Lost Villages of England*, 1954.
Blair, Peter Hunter, *An Introduction to Anglo-Saxon England*, 2d ed., 1977.
Brown, David, *Anglo-Saxon England*, 1978.

Chaney, William A., *The Cult of Kingship in Anglo-Saxon England,* 1970.
Duckett, Eleanor S., *Alfred the Great,* 1956.
———, *Anglo-Saxon Saints and Scholars,* 1948.
Finberg, H. P. R., *The Formation of England: 550–1042,* 1976.
Jolliffe, J. E. A., *Pre-Feudal England: the Jutes,* 1933.
Laing, Lloyd and Jennifer, *Anglo-Saxon England,* 1979.
Lapidge, Michael and H. Gneuss, *Learning and Literature in Anglo-Saxon England,* 1985.
Maitland, F. W., *Domesday Book and Beyond,* reprinted 1966.
Myres, J. N. L., *The English Settlements,* 1985.
Orwin, C. S. and C. S., *The Open Fields,* 3d ed., 1967.
Owen, Gail R., *Rites and Religions of the Anglo-Saxons,* 1981.
Quennel, M. and C. H. B., *Everyday Life in Anglo-Saxon, Viking and Norman Times,* 1959.
Sawyer, R. H., *From Roman Britain to Norman England,* 1978.
Stenton, Sir Frank, *Anglo-Saxon England, c. 550–1087,* 3d ed., 1971.
Whitelocke, Dorothy, *The Beginnings of English Society,* 1952.

1066–1485

Continuity is again a common theme. The year 1066 is still viewed as a bridge rather than a fence. Biographies of kings, prelates, and administrators are important. Administrative history, as well as that of the family estate, is once again becoming of interest on governmental and ecclesiastical levels. The roles of women, the peasantry, and the urban dwellers are also of increasing interest. Studies in the later middle ages increasingly look forward to the Tudor Age. The years 1485 and 1066 share a position on the historical continuum; neither is viewed as a breaking point.

Church and State

Appleby, John, *England Without Richard,* 1965.
———, *John, King of England,* 1958.
———, *The Troubled Reign of King Stephen,* 1970.
Barlow, Frank, *The Feudal Kingdom of England, 1042–1216,* 2d ed., 1955.
Bean, J. M. W., *The Decline of English Feudalism, 1215–1540,* 1968.
Beeler, John, *Warfare in England, 1066–1189,* 1966.
Brooke, Christopher, *From Alfred to Henry III, 871–1272,* 1961.
Chibrall, Marjerie, *Anglo-Norman England: 1066–1166,* 1987.
Chrimes, S. B., *An Introduction to the Administrative History of Medieval England,* 3d ed., 1966.
Dobson, R. B., *The Peasants' Revolt of 1381,* 1970.
Douglas, David, *William the Conqueror,* 1964.
Fryde, E. B. and Edward Miller, eds., *Historical Studies of the English Parliament.* Vol. 1, *Origins to 1399,* 1970.

Fryde, Natalie, *The Tyranny and Fall of Edward II, 1321–1326,* 1979.
Green, Judith A., *The Government of England under Henry I,* 1989.
Griffiths, Ralph A., *The Reign of Henry VI,* 1981.
Gwin-Wilson, Chris, *The Royal Household and the King's Affinity: Service, Politics and Finance in England, 1360–1413,* 1986.
Hollister, C. Warren, *The Impact of the Norman Conquest,* 1969.
———, *Monarchy, Magnates and Institutions in the Anglo-Norman World,* 1986.
Holmes, G. A., *The Later Middle Ages, 1272–1485,* 1962.
Holt, J. C., *Magna Carta,* 1965.
Jacob, E. F., *The Fifteenth Century,* 1961.
Jenkins, Elizabeth, *The Princes in the Tower,* 1978.
Jolliffe, J. E. A., *Angevin Kingship,* 2d ed., 1963.
———, *The Constitutional History of Medieval England from the English Settlement to 1485,* 4th ed., 1961.
Jones, Thomas, *The Becket Controversy,* 1970.
Kelly, Amy, *Eleanor of Aquitaine and the Four Kings,* 1950.
Kendall, Paul M., *Richard the Third,* 1955.
Knowles, David, *The Monastic Order in England, 943–1216,* 1940.
———, *The Religious Orders in England,* 3 vols., 1963.
———, *Saints and Scholars,* 1962.
———, *Thomas Becket,* 1970.
Lander, J. R., *Conflict and Stability in Fifteenth Century England,* 1969.
———, *Crown and Nobility, 1450–1509,* 1976.
———, *Wars of the Roses,* 1966.
Lyon, Bryce, *A Constitutional and Legal History of Medieval England,* 1960.
McFarlane, K. B., *Lancastrian Kings and Lollard Knights,* 1972.
McIlwain, Charles H., *The High Court of Parliament and Its Supremacy,* 1910.
McKechnie, W. S., *Magna Carta: A Commentary on the Great Charter of King John,* 1914.
McKisack, May, *The Fourteenth Century,* 1959.
Oman, Sir Charles, *The History of the Art of War in the Middle Ages,* 1953.
Painter, Sidney, *The Reign of King John,* 1949.
Perroy, Edouard, *The Hundred Years' War,* 1951.
Plucknett, T. F. T., *Edward I and Criminal Law,* 1960.
Pollock, F. and F. W. Maitland, *The History of English Law before the Time of Edward I,* 2 vols., reissued 1968.
Poole, Austin L., *From Domesday Book to Magna Carta, 1087–1216,* 2d ed., 1955.
Powell, J. Enoch and K. Wallis, *The House of Lords in the Middle Ages,* 1968.
Powicke, Sir Maurice, *The Thirteenth Century, 1216–1307,* 2d ed., 1962.
Prestwich, M. C., *War, Politics and Finance Under Edward I,* 1972.
Prestwich, Michael, *The Three Edwards: War and State in England, 1272–1377,* 1980.
———, *Edward I,* 1988.
Richardson, H. G. and G. O. Sayles, *The Governance of Mediaeval England from the Conquest to Magna Carta,* 1963.
Ross, Charles, *Edward IV,* 1974.
———, *Richard III,* 1981.

———, *The Wars of the Roses*, 1976.
Stenton, Doris M., *English Justice Between the Norman Conquest and the Great Charter, 1066–1215*, 1964.
Stenton, Sir Frank, *The First Century of English Feudalism, 1066–1166*, 2d ed., 1961.
Thorpe, Lewis, *The Bayeux Tapestry and the Norman Invasion*, 1973.
Tout, T. F., *Chapters in the Administrative History of Mediaeval England*, 6 vols., 1920–1937.
———, *The Place of the Reign of Edward II in English History*, 2d ed., 1936
Treharne, R. F., *The Baronial Plan of Reform, 1258–1263*, rev. ed., 1971.
Tuck, Anthony, *Richard II and the English Nobility*, 1973.
Van Caenegem, R. C., *The Birth of the English Common Law*, 1973.
Warren, W. L., *Henry II*, 1973.
———, *King John*, 1961.
———, *The Governance of Norman and Angevin England, 1086–1272*, 1987.
Wilkinson, Bertie, *The Creation of Mediaeval Parliaments*, 1972.
———, *The Later Middle Ages in England, 1216–1485*, 1969.
Williamson, Audrey, *The Mystery of the Princes, An Investigation into a Supposed Murder*, 1978.
Wolffe, B. P., *The Royal Demesne in English History: The Crown Estate in the Governance of the Realm from the Conquest to 1509*, 1971.

Economic, Social, and Intellectual

Barnie, John, *War in Medieval English Society: Social Values and the Hundred Years' War*, 1974.
Bennett, H. S., *The Pastons and Their England*, 1922.
Boase, T. S. R., *English Art, 1100–1216*, 1953.
Brewer, D. S., *Chaucer*, 3d ed., 1973.
Brooke, Christopher, with Gilbian Keir, *London, 800–1216: The Shaping of a City*, 1975.
Evans, Joan, *English Art, 1307–1461*, 1949.
Finn, R. Welldon, *An Introduction to Domesday Book*, 1963.
Gairdner, J., ed., *Paston Letters*, 6 vols., 1904.
Galbraith, V. H., *The Making of Domesday Book*, 1961.
Gransden, Antonia, *Historical Writing in England, c. 550–c. 1307*, 1974.
Gwin-Wilson, Chris, *The English Nobility in the Middle Ages: The Fourteenth-Century Political Community*, 1987.
Hanox, Rosemary, *Richard III: A Study of Service*, 1989.
Harawalt, Barbara A., *The Ties that Bound: Peasant Families in Medieval England*, 1986.
Holmes, G. A., *The Estates of the Higher Nobility in Fourteenth-Century England*, 1957.
Kanner, Barbara, ed., *The Women of England from Anglo-Saxon Times to the Present*, 1979.
Kendall, Paul M., *The Yorkist Age*, 1955.
Leff, Gordon A., *Paris and Oxford Universities in the Thirteenth and Fourteenth Centuries: An Institutional and Intellectual History*, 1968.
McFarlane, K. B., *John Wycliffe and the Beginning of English Non-conformity*, 1953.
———, *The Nobility of Later Medieval England*, 1973.

Norton-Smith, John, *Geoffrey Chaucer*, 1974.
Painter, Sidney, *Studies in the History of the English Feudal Barony*, 1943.
Poston, M. M., *The Medieval Economy and Society 1100–1500*, 1972.
Power, Eileen, *Medieval Women*, ed. M. M. Poston, 1975.
Rashdall, H., *The Universities of Europe in the Middle Ages*, 3 vols, 1936.
Robson, J. A., *Wyclif and the Oxford Schools*, 1961.
Roth, Cecil, *A History of the Jews in England*, 2d ed., 1964.
Southern, R. W., *Robert Grosseteste: The Growth of an English Mind in Medieval Europe*, 1988.
———, *Western Society and the Church in the Middle Ages*, 1970.
Stenton, Doris M., *English Society in the Early Middle Ages (1066–1307)*, 2d ed., 1952.
———, *The English Woman in History*, 1957.
Stoll, Robert, *Architecture and Sculpture in Early Britain: Celtic, Saxon, Norman*, 1967.
Swanson, Heather, *Medieval Artisans: An Urban Class in Late Medieval England*, 1989.
Swanson, R. N., *Church and Society in Late Medieval England*, 1989.
Thrupp, Sylvia, *The Merchant Class of Medieval London, 1300–1500*, 1948.
Titow, J. Z., *English Rural Society, 1200–1350*, 1969.
Trevelyan, G. M., *England in the Age of Wycliffe*, 1920.
Ziegler, Philip, *The Black Death*, 1969.

THE TUDORS (1485–1603)

Biography continues to play an important role in Tudor historiography. Scholars are increasingly looking at the role of religion in the life of the people before, during, and after the Reformation. The Reformation is still viewed as being an affair of state. Henry VIII, for good or ill, is still a force to be reckoned with. Elizabeth and Elizabethan England is increasingly being examined more critically. The queen is less secure on her pedestal, Parliament is less likely to be taking "the initiative," and Puritanism is being examined in terms of ordinary people, not just leaders.

Church and State

Anglo, Sydney, *Spectacle, Pageantry, and Early Tudor Policy*, 1969.
Black, J. B., *The Reign of Elizabeth, 1558–1603*, 2d ed., 1959.
Bradshaw, Brendan, *The Irish Constitutional Revolution of the Sixteenth Century*, 1979.
Bush, M. L., *The Government Policy of Prector Somerset*, 1975.
Canny, Nicholas, *The Elizabethan Conquest of Ireland: A Pattern Established, 1565–76*, 1976.
Chrimes, S. B., *Henry VII*, 1972.
Crowson, P. S., *Tudor Foreign Policy*, 1973.
Dickens, A. G., *The English Reformation*, 1964.
———, *Thomas Cromwell and the English Reformation*, 1959.
Dietz, F. C., *English Government Finance*, rev. 1964.

Elton, G. R., *England Under the Tudors*, 1955.
———, *The Parliament of England, 1559–1581*, 1986.
———, *The Policy and Police: The Enforcement of the Reformation in the Age of Cromwell*, 1972.
———, *Reform and Reformation, England, 1509–1558*, 1977.
———, *Reform and Renewal: Thomas Cromwell and the Common Weal*, 1973.
———, *The Tudor Constitution*, 1960.
———, *Tudor Revolution in Government*, 1953.
Fox, Alistain, and John Guy, *Reassessing the Henrician Age: Humanism, Politics and Reform, 1500–1550*, 1986.
Fraser, Lady Antonia, *Mary, Queen of Scots*, 1969.
Guy, John, *Tudor England*, 1988.
Haigh, Christopher, ed., *The English Reformation Revised*, 1988.
Hughes, Philip, *The Reformation in England*, 3 vols., 1954.
Hurstfield, Joel, *Elizabeth I and the Unity England*, 1960.
Ives, E. W., *Anne Boleyn*, 1986.
Jordan, W. K., *Edward VI: The Threshold of Power*, 1970.
———, *Edward VI: The Young King*, 1968.
Knappen, M., *Tudor Puritanism*, 1939.
Lehmberg, Stanford E., *The Reformation of Cathedrals: Cathedrals in English Society, 1485–1603*, 1989.
———, *The Reformation Parliament*, 1969.
Loach, Jennifer, *Parliament and the Crown in the Reign of Mary Tudor*, 1986.
Loades, D. M., *The Reign of Mary Tudor*, 1979.
MacCaffrey, W. T., *The Shaping of the Elizabethan Regime*, 1968.
McConica, J. K., *English Humanists and Reformation Politics Under Henry VIII and Edward VI*, 1965.
McGrath, Alisten E., *Reformation Thought: An Introduction*, 1988.
McGrath, P., *Papists and Puritans under Elizabeth I*, 1967.
Mackie, J. D., *The Earlier Tudors, 1485–1558*, 1957.
Mattingly, Garrett, *The Armada*, 1959.
———, *Catherine of Aragon*, 1941.
Neale, J. E., *Elizabeth I and Her Parliaments*, 2 vols., 1957.
———, *Elizabethan House of Commons*, 1949.
———, *Queen Elizabeth*, 1934.
Notestein, Wallace, *The Winning of the Initiative by the House of Commons*, 1924.
Pollard, A. F., *Henry VIII*, 1902.
———, *Thomas Cranmer and the English Reformation*, 1904.
———, *Wolsey*, 1929.
Powicke, F. M., *The Reformation in England*, 1941.
Prescott, H. F. M., *Mary Tudor*, 1953.
Read, Conyers, *Lord Burghley and Queen Elizabeth*, 1960.
———, *Mr. Secretary Cecil and Queen Elizabeth*, 1955.
Scarisbrick, J. J., *Henry VIII*, 1968.
Smith, Lacey Baldwin, *Henry VIII: The Mask of Royalty*, 1971.

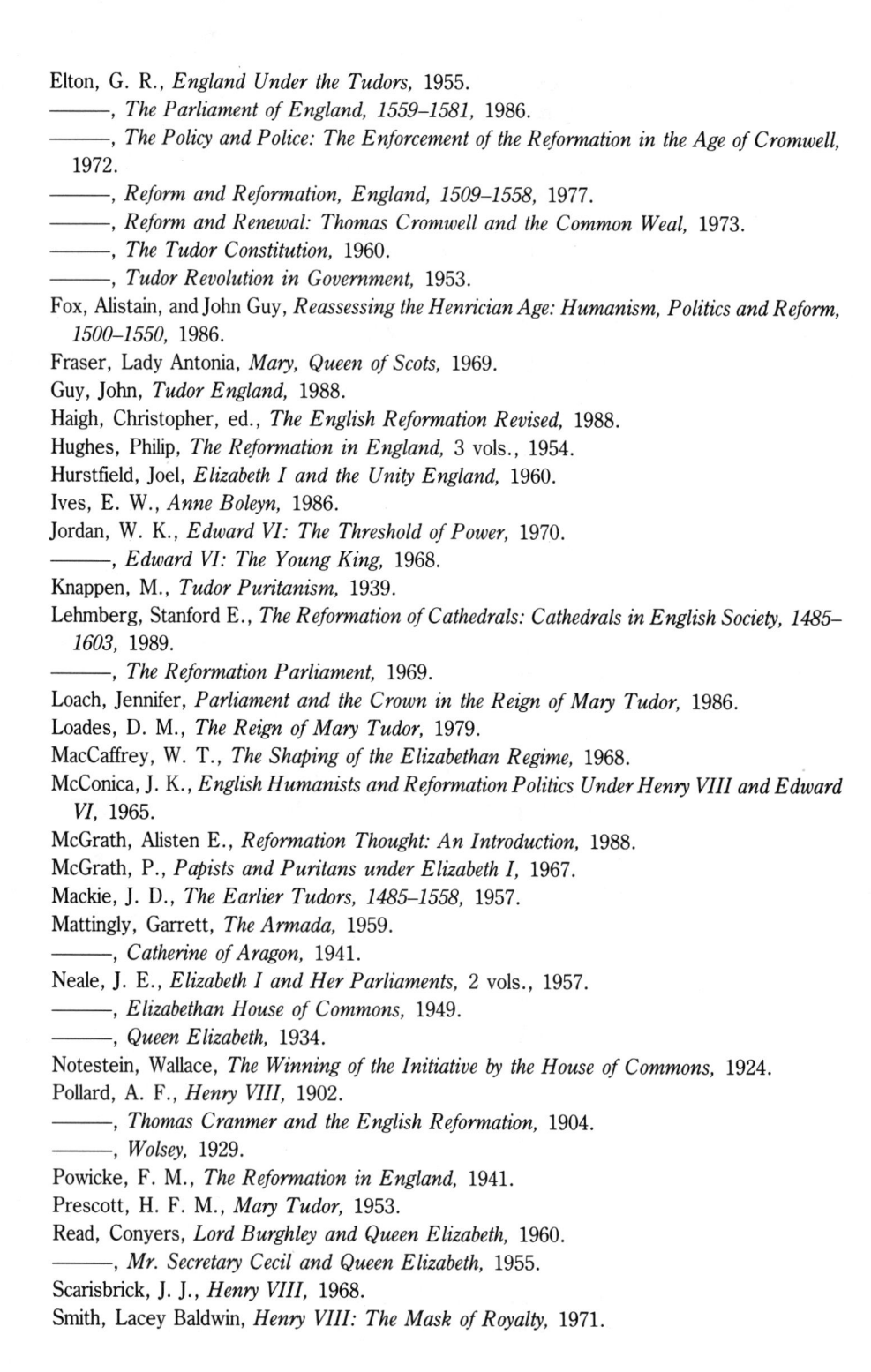

———, *Elizabeth Tudor*, 1975.
———, *Treason in Tudor England*, 1986.
Storey, R. L., *The Reign of Henry VII*, 1968.
Wernham, R. B., *Before the Armada*, 1966.
Williams, Neville, *The Cardinal and the Secretary, Thomas Wolsey and Thomas Cromwell*, 1975.
Zeeveld, W. G., *Foundations of Tudor Policy*, 1948.

Economic, Social, and Intellectual

Caspari, F., *Humanism and the Social Order in Tudor England*, 1954.
Collinson, P., *The Elizabethan Puritan Movement*, 1967.
Cornwall, Julian, *Revolt of the Peasantry, 1549*, 1977.
George, C. H. and K., *The Protestant Mind of the English Reformation, 1570–1640*, 1961.
Hexter, J. H., *More's Utopia: The Biography of an Idea*, 1952.
Howell, Roger, *Sir Philip Sidney: The Shepherd Knight*, 1968.
Jones, W. R. D., *The Tudor Commonwealth, 1529–1559*, 1970.
Jordan, W. K., *Philanthropy in England, 1480–1660*, 1959.
Lovejoy, A. C., *The Great Chain of Being: A Study of the History of an Idea*, 1936.
Miller, Helen, *Henry VIII and the English Nobility*, 1986.
Outhwaite, R. B., *Inflation in Tudor and Early Stuart England*, 1969.
Rappapert, Steve, *Worlds within Worlds: Structures of Life in Sixteenth-Century London*, 1989.
Rowse, A. L., *The England of Elizabeth*, 1951.
———, *The Expansion of England*, 1955.
Stone, Lawrence, *The Crisis of the Aristocracy, 1558–1641*, 1965.
Van Baumer, F. L., *The Early Tudor Theory of Kingship*, 1940.

THE STUARTS (1603–1714)

The causes of the English (Puritan) Revolution continue to be of interest, and regional studies have become very important. How things actually worked is of more concern than are the great clashes of ideologies. Scholars of the Revolution are examining local governmental, economic, and social institutions and their impact upon the national scene. The rise of modern science and its political and broader intellectual influences is a subject of increasing importance. Scholars are also seeking the origins of the modern family and modern gender roles in the Tudor and, especially, the Stuart years.

Church and State

Aylmer, G. E., *The King's Servants*, 1961.
———, *Rebellion or Revolution? England, 1640–1660*, 1986.

Baxter, Stephen, *William III*, 1966.
Bottigheimer, Karl, *English Money and Irish Land*, 1971.
Bowen, Catherine Drinker, *The Lion and the Throne: The Life and Times of Sir Edward Coke*, 1956.
Brailsford, H. N., *The Levellers and the English Revolution*, 1961.
Bridenbaugh, Carl, *Vexed and Troubled Englishmen, 1590–1642*, 1968.
Brunton, D. and D. H. Penninton, *Members of the Long Parliament*, 1954.
Canny, Nicholas, *Kingdom and Colony: Ireland in the Atlantic World, 1560–1800*, 1988.
Churchill, Sir Winston S., *Marlborough, His Life and Times*, 6 vols., 1933–1939.
Clarendon, Earl of, *History of the Great Rebellion*, 1888.
Clark, Sir George, *The Later Stuarts, 1660–1714*, 1934.
Davies, Godfrey, *The Early Stuarts, 1603–1660*, 1959.
———, *The Restoration of Charles II*, 1955.
De Krey, Gary Stuart, *A Fractured Society: The Politics of London in the First Age of Party, 1688–1715*, 1985.
Feiling, Keith, *A History of the Tory Party*, 1924.
Fink, Zera, *The Classical Republicans*, 1962.
Firth, C. H., *The Last Years of the Protectorate*, 1909.
———, *Oliver Cromwell and the Rule of the Puritans in England*, 1900.
Fletcher, Anthony, *The Outbreak of the English Civil War*, 1981.
———, *Reform in the Provinces: The Government of Stuart England*, 1986.
Foster, Elizabeth Read, *The House of Lords, 1603–1649: Structure, Procedure, and the Nature of its Business*, 1983.
Gardiner, S. R., *History of England, 1603–1656*, 18 vols., 1894–1904.
Green, David, *Queen Anne*, 1971.
Gregg, Pauline, *Free Born John: A Biography of John Lilburne*, 1961.
Haley, K. H., *First Earl of Shaftesbury*, 1968.
Haller, William, *Liberty and Reformation in the Puritan Revolution*, 1955.
———, *The Rise of Puritanism, 1570–1643*, 1938.
Havran, Martin J., *Catholics in Caroline England*, 1962.
Hexter, J. H., *The Reign of King Pym*, 1941.
Hill, Christopher, *Puritanism and Revolution*, 1958.
Holmes, Geoffrey, *Britain after the Glorious Revolution*, 1969.
———, *British Politics in the Age of Ann*, 1968.
Horewitz, Henry, *Parliament, Policy and Politics in the Reign of William III*, 1977.
Hulme, Harold, *The Life of Sir John Eliot*, 1957.
Hutton, Ronald, *The Restoration: A Political and Religious Victory of England and Wales, 1658–1667*, 1985.
Jones, Colin, Malwyn Newitt and Stephen Roberts, eds., *Politics and People in Revolutionary England*, 1986.
Jones, J. R., *Charles II: Royal Politician*, 1987.
———, *The First Whigs: The Politics of the Exclusion Crisis, 1673–83*, 1961.
———, *The Revolution of 1688 in England*, 1972.
Judson, Margaret, *The Crisis of the Constitution*, 1949.
Keeler, Mary F., *The Long Parliament, 1640–41*, 1954.

Kenyon, J.P., *Robert Spencer, Earl of Sunderland, 1641–1702*, 1958.
———, *The Stuart Constitution, 1603–1688*, 1966.
Kishlansky, Mark, *The Rise of the New Model Army*, 1979.
Macaulay, T. B., *History of England*, 6 vols., 1849–1861.
MacCormack, J., *Revolutionary Politics in the Long Parliament*, 1974.
Moir, Thomas L., *The Addled Parliament of 1614*, 1958.
Morrill, J. S., *The Revolt of the Provinces*, 1976.
Ogg, David, *England in the Reign of Charles II*, 2 vols., 1956.
———, *England in the Reign of James II and William III*, 1953.
Ogilvie, Charles, *The King's Government and the Common Law, 1471–1641*, 1958.
Pawlisch, Hans P., *Sir John Davies and the Conquest of Ireland: A Study of Legal Imperialism*, 1985.
Pearl, Valerie, *London and the Outbreak of the Puritan Revolution, 1625–1642*, 1961.
Plumb, Sir John H., *The Growth of Political Stability in England, 1675–1725*, 1967.
Prall, S. E., *The Agitation for Law Reform during the Puritan Revolution, 1640–1660*, 1966.
———, *The Bloodless Revolution: England, 1688*, 1972.
———, *The Puritan Revolution: A Documentary History*, 1968.
Richardson, R. C., *The Debate on the English Revolution*, 1989.
Roberts, Clayton, *The Growth of Responsible Government in England*, 1966.
Roots, Ivan, *The Great Rebellion, 1642–1660*, 1966.
Russell, Conrad, *The Origins of the English Civil War*, 1973.
———, *Parliaments and English Politics, 1621–1629*, 1979.
Schwoerer, Lois, *The Declaration of Rights, 1689*, 1981.
———, *"No Standing Armies": The Antiarmy Ideology in Seventeenth-Century England*, 1974.
Snow, Vernon, *Essex the Rebel: The Life of Robert Devereux, the Third Earl of Essex, 1591–1646*, 1970.
Solt, Leo, *Saints in Arms*, 1959.
Speck, W. A., *Reluctant Revolutionaries: Englishmen and the Revolution of 1688*, 1989.
Stone, Lawrence, *The Causes of the English Revolution, 1529–1642*, 1972.
Trevelyan, G. M., *England Under Queen Anne*, 3 vols., 1930–34.
———, *The English Revolution, 1688–1689*, 1938.
Trevor-Roper, H. R., *Archbishop Laud*, 1940.
———, *Catholics, Anglicans and Puritans: Seventeenth-Century Essays*, 1988.
Tyacke, Nicholas, *Anti-Calvinists: The Rise of English Arminianism, c. 1590–1640*, 1987
Underdown, David, *Pride's Purge: Politics in the Puritan Revolution*, 1971.
Van der Zee, H. and B., *William and Mary*, 1973.
Wedgwood, Dame Veronica, *The King's Peace*, 1955.
———, *The King's War*, 1958.
———, *The Trial of Charles I*, 1964.
Western, J. R., *Monarchy and Revolution: The English State in the 1680s*, 1972.
Willson, David Harris, *King James VI and I*, 1956.
———, *The Privy Councillors in the House of Commons, 1604–1629*, 1940.
Worden, Blair, *The Rump Parliament, 1648–1653*, 1974.
Zaller, Robert, *The Parliament of 1621*, 1971.

Economic, Social and Intellectual

Astor, Margaret, *England's Iconoclasts,* Vol. I, *Laws against Images,* 1988.
Brooks, C. W., *Pettyfoggers and Vipers of the Commonwealth: The 'Lower Branch' of the Legal Profession in Early Modern England,* 1986.
Chambers, J. D., *Population, Economy, and Society in Pre-Industrial England,* 1972.
Clarkson, L. A., *The Pre-Industrial Economy in England, 1500–1750,* 1971.
Cliffe, J. T., *Puritans in Conflict,* 1988.
Collinson, Patrick, *Godly People: Essays on English Protestantism and Puritanism,* 1983.
Earle, Peter, *The Making of the English Middle Class: Business, Society and Family Life in London, 1660–1730,* 1988.
Gooch, G. P., *English Democratic Ideas in the Seventeenth Century,* 1959.
Harris, Tim, *London Crowds in the Reign of Charles II: Propaganda and Politics from the Restoration until the Exclusion Crisis,* 1987.
Hill, Christopher, *The Economic Problems of the Church, from Whitgift to the Long Parliament,* 1956.
———, *Society and Puritanism in Pre-Revolutionary England,* 1964.
———, *A Tinker and a Poor Man: John Bunyan and His Church,* 1988.
———, *The World Turned Upside Down,* 1972.
Jacob, James R., *Henry Stubbe, Radical Protestantism and the Early Enlightenment,* 1983.
Jacob, Margaret, *The Newtonians and the English Revolution,* 1974.
Katz, David, *Sabbath and Sectarianism in Seventeenth-Century England,* 1988.
Laslett, Peter, *The World We Have Lost: England Before the Industrial Age,* 1965.
Manning, Brian, *The English People and the English Revolution,* 1976.
Notestein, Wallace, *The English People on the Eve of Colonization,* 1954.
Phillips, John, *The Reformation of Images: Destruction of Art in England, 1535–1600,* 1973.
Pocock, J. A., *The Ancient Constitution and the Feudal Law,* 1957.
Prest, W. R., *The Rise of the Barristers: A Social History of the English Bar, 1590–1640,* 1986.
Sharpe, Kevin, *Criticism and Compliment: The Politics of Literature in the England of Charles I,* 1987.
Stone, Lawrence, *Family, Sex, and Marriage in England, 1500–1800,* 1977.
Supple, B. E., *Commercial Crisis and Change in England 1600–1642,* 1959.
Tawney, R. H., *Business and Politics Under James I,* 1959.
———, "The Rise of the Gentry, 1558–1640," *Economic History Review,* XI (1941), 1–38.
Thomas, Keith, *Religion and the Decline of Magic: Studies in Popular Beliefs in Sixteenth and Seventeenth Century England,* 1971.
Thompson, Roger, *Women in Stuart England and America,* 1974.
Trevor-Roper, H. R., "The Gentry, 1540–1640," *Economic History Review,* Supplement I, 1953.
Turner, F. C., *James II,* 1948.
Underdown, David, *Revel, Riot and Rebellion: Popular Politics and Culture in England, 1603–1660,* 1987.
Walzer, Michael, *The Revolution of the Saints,* 1965.
Westfall, R. S., *Science and Religion in Seventeenth-Century England,* 1958.
Zagorin, Perez, *The Court and the Country: The Beginning of the English Revolution,* 1969.
———, *A History of Political Thought in the English Revolution,* 1954.

Index

Page numbers in italics refer to illustrations. Page numbers followed by "n" refer to footnotes.

Abbot, George, 344
Abelard, 124, 127
Acadia, 430, 438
Acre, 97
Act for the Submission of the Clergy, 241, 242
Act in Absolute Restraint of Annates, 242
Act in Conditional Restraint of Annates, 242
Act of Appeals, 242, 244–245
Act of Revocation, 366
Act of Security, 441
Act of Settlement, 420–421
Act of Succession, 242–243
Act of Supremacy, 242, 276, 288
Act of Uniformity (1548–1549), 254, 255
Act of Uniformity (1559), 276
Act of Uniformity (1662), 406
Acton Burnell, burgesses at, 155
Acts of Trade, 428–429
Addison, Joseph, 433
Adela, mother of Stephen of Blois, 80
Adelard of Bath, 124–125
Adolf of Nassau, King of Germany, 150
Adrian IV, Pope, 123
Advowson, right of, 25
Africa, 222, 223, 296, 299, 311, 409, 428, 430
Agadir, 295
Agincourt, battle of, 162, 191
Agitators, 382
Agreement of the People, 383–384, 386
Agricola, 12
Agriculture: Anglo-Saxon, 22, 39–40, *40*, 47; Celtic, 10; Elizabeth I and, 282;

Agriculture *(cont.)*: in fifteenth century, 201; in fourteenth century, 170–171; geographic features and, 2; in Norman England, 68–69; in seventeenth century, 372, 400–401; in sixteenth century, 262–266; in Stone Age, 6; in twelfth/thirteenth centuries, 128–130, *131, 133*
Aidan, 24
Alexander III, King of Scots, 146
Alexius Comnenus, Eastern Roman Emperor, 97
Alfred, King of Wessex, 20, 27, 31, 32–35, 41, 44, 53
Allen, William, 283
Alva, Duke of, 291, 293
Ambrosius Aurelianus, 21
American colonies, 297–299, 339, 394–396, 397–398, 428–430, 438
Anabaptists, 381, 381n
Ancient Custom, 151
Andrew, St., 24
Angles, 20–21, 145
Anglesey, 143
Anglicans, 337, 338, 356–357, 370, 380, 408, 416, 435
Anglo-Saxon Chronicle, 20, 34–35, 65
Anglo-Saxons: achievements of, 48; agriculture of, 39–40, *40;* central government of, 42–44; Christian conversion of, 23–27; code of laws of, 34; Danish wars and, 31–32, 34, 35, 36; education and, 34–35; heptarchy of, 21; invasions of, 4, 21, 22;

Anglo-Saxons *(cont.)*: kingdoms of, 21; local government of, 44–48; location of, 4; and Norman Conquest, 50; political unification of, 27–32; royal succession of, 36, 42–43; social classes in, 37–41
Angoulême family, 99
Angus, Archibald Douglas, Earl of, 280
Anjou, 53, 80, 91, 99, 150
Anne, Queen of England: Catholics and, 339–340; character of, 433–434; English politics and, 437–438; Hanoverian succession and, 438–439; Marlborough-Godolphin coalition during reign of, 434–435; Scottish union and, 440–441, 443; succession of, 417, 420; Treaty of Utrecht and, 438; War of the Spanish Succession and, 435–437
Anne Boleyn, Queen of Henry VIII, 234, 242, 243, 248, 257
Anne Hyde, wife of James, Duke of York (James II), 408
Anne of Bohemia, Queen, wife of Richard II, 181
Anne of Cleves, Queen of Henry VIII, 248
Anselm, Archbishop of Canterbury, 52, 76, 79, 115, 122
Antigua, 396
Antinomians, 381, 381n
Antwerp, 220, 229, 258, 261, 266, 290, 311
Apology of 1604, 342
Apprenticeship, 135, 267
Aquitaine, 91, 92, 99, 106, 150
Arabic learning, 124–125
Archbishops. *See* names of specific archbishops
Architecture: in Elizabethan England, 321–322, *321;* in fourteenth century, 184–185; in seventeenth century, *422,* 424; in twelfth/thirteenth centuries, 120–122, *121*
Argyllshire, 145
Aristocracy. *See* Nobility
Aristotle, 124
Arlington, Henry Bennet, Earl of, 410
Armada. *See* Spanish Armada
Armagnacs, 190
Arminians, 356–357, 359, 360–361, 364–365, 366
Arminius, 337n
Army: Anglo-Saxon, 22, 34; billeting of soldiers in private homes, 359, 360, 361; in Civil War, 377–380; after Civil War, 382–384; of Cnut, 37; under the Commonwealth, 385–386, 387, 389;

Army *(cont.)*: in Dutch War (1652–1654), 397; in fourteenth century, 161–162; New Model Army, 380, 397; for Norman invasion, 55, 57, *57;* under the Protectorate, 392–393. *See also* Knights
Arthur, Duke of Brittany, 99
Arthur, Prince, son of Henry VII, 212, 214, 219
Arthurian legends, 21, 123, 161
Artificers, Statute of, 268, 282
Arts. *See* Architecture; Drama; Literature; Music
Arundel, Richard Fitzalan, Earl of, 180–182
Assertio Septem Sacramentorum, 226
Assize of Clarendon, 86
Assize of *novel disseisin,* 88
Athelings, 38
Athelstan, King of Wessex, 35
Aubrey, John, 421
Audenaarde, Battle of, 437
Augustine, St., Archbishop of Canterbury, 24, 28
Augustine, St., of Hippo, rule of, 117
Austria, 227, 289, 362, 430, 433, 435–437
Avignon, residence of popes, 175, 237
Azores, 298, 308

Bacon, Francis, 317, 341, 345, 352, 421
Bacon, Sir Nicholas, 320
Bacon, Roger, 119, 125
Bailiffs, 46, 129
Ball, John, 171, 178
Balliol, John, 146, 147
Balliol family, 146
Baltimore, George Calvert, 395
Bancroft, Richard, Archbishop of Canterbury, 343
Bank of England, 420, 432
Bannockburn, Battle of, 148, 215
Bantam, Java, 312
Barbados, 396, 398
Barbary Company, 295, 297
Barebones Parliament, 389–391
Barnet, Battle of, 200, 204
Barons: abbeys and, 117; under Edward I, 138, 139, 152; under Edward II, 156–157; in feudal system, 59; under Henry I, 77; under Henry III, 105, 107–108; under John, 99, 100, 102–105; Magna Carta and, 102–105; Norman barons in Ireland, 149; Norman barons in Wales, 143–144; in Norman England, 61–63, 66; representation in Parliament, 154, 155;

Barons *(cont.)*: social and economic life during twelfth/thirteenth centuries, 128–130; under Stephen, 82–83
Barons of the Exchequer, 142
Barrow, Henry, 287
Barrow, Isaac, 421
Barry, Sir Charles, 78
Bastwick, John, 365, 366
Bate Case, 343–344
Bath, 21
Battle-Ax people, 7, 9
Battles. *See* names of specific battles
Bavaria, 435, 436
Bayeux, 51
Beaker folk, 6–9
Beauchamp, Edward Seymour, 274
Beauchamp family. *See* Warwick, Earls of
Beaufort, Cardinal, 197
Beaufort, Henry, 189, 193
Beaufort, John, Earl of Somerset, 189
Beaufort, Thomas, Earl of Dorset, 189
Beaufort family, 195. *See also* Somerset, Dukes of
Beaumaris Castle, 144, *145*
Becket, Thomas, Archbishop of Canterbury, 84, 88–91, *90,* 123, 125, 127
Bede, 20, 27, 28
Bedford, John Russell, Duke of, 193
Belgae, 11. *See also* Celts
Belgium, 293
Benedict Biscop, 26
Benedict, St., 115–118
Benefit of clergy, 237–238
Beorn, nephew of Godwin, Earl of Wessex, 54
Beowulf, 22n
Berkshire, settlement of, 21
Bernicia, settlement of, 21
Bertha, wife of Ethelbert of Kent, 24
Best, Thomas, 398
Bible, *26,* 27, 177, 182, 245, 252, 338, 338n
Bill of attainder, 369
Bill of Rights (1689), 419–420
Bishops: in Anglo-Saxon England, 25, 44; appointment of, 79; Charles I and, 357; Civil War and, 370–371; Edward VI and, 254; feudalism and, 71; opposition to Church of England, 276; Puritans and, 286; response to Wycliffe's teachings, 177; in twelfth/thirteenth centuries, 112, 114
Bishops' Wars, 366–367
Black Death, 163, 164, 169, 170, *170,* 173, 236, 326

Blake Robert, 397
Blenheim, Battle of, 435, 436
Blois, Treaty of, 292
Blount, Elizabeth, 233
Boethius, 35
Bohemia, 260, 289, 351
Boleyn, Anne. *See* Anne Boleyn, Queen of Henry VIII
Boleyn, Sir Thomas, 234
Bolingbroke, Henry St. John, Viscount, 433, 435, 438, 439
Bombay, 398, 408, 409
Bonham Case, 348
Boniface VIII, Pope, 152, 178–179
Boon work, 131
Borough courts, 46
Boroughbridge, Battle of, 157
Boroughs, in Anglo-Saxon England, 46–47. *See also* Towns
Boston, fair at, 132
Bosworth, Battle of, 205, 210
Bothwell, Francis Stewart, Earl of, 334–335
Bothwell, James Hepburn, Earl of, 280
Boudicca, Celtic Queen, 12
Bouvines, battle of, 102
Boyle, Robert, 421, 422
Boyne, Battle of the, 427
Brabant, Duke of, 150
Bracton, Henry de, 126, 140
Brazil, 394, 395, 410
Breakspear, Nicholas, 123
Bretigny, Treaty of, 164, 189
Bretwaldas, 27–28, *29,* 31
Brille, 294
Brinkelow, Henry, 265
Bristol, 23, 135, 223, 378
British Isles, definition of, 1
British West Indies, 428
Britons, 145
Brittany, 11, 20, 47, 99, 163, 210, 213–214, 218
Broadsides, 302
Bronze Age, 7–9
Browne, Robert, 287
Brownists, 380
Bruce, Edward, 149
Bruce family, 146
Bruce, Robert, 146
Bruce, Robert (grandson), 148
Bubonic plague. *See* Plagues
Bucer, Martin, 252
Buckingham, George Villiers, 1st Duke of, 346–348, 352–361

Buckingham, George Villiers, 2nd Duke of, 410, 411–412, 421
Buckingham, Henry Stafford, Duke of, 205
Bullion, 260–261
Burgage tenure, 46
Burgh, Hubert de, 105, 106
Burghley, William Cecil, 273, 302, 313–314. *See also* Salisbury, Robert Cecil, Earl of
Burgundy, 71, 199, 258
Burgundy, Dukes of, 190, 293
Burnell, Robert, 138
Burton, Henry, 365, 366
Bury St. Edmunds, 117

Cabot, John, 223, 225
Cabot, Sebastian, 223
Cadiz, 303, 357, 358
Caen, 51, 52, 72, 163
Caernarvon Castle, 144
Caesar, Julius, 11–12
Calais, 163, 168, 174, 175, 189, 196, 198, 220, 228, 259, 272, 292, 306
Calvin, John, 275, 285
Calvinism, 285–286, 290, 350
Cambridge, fair at, 132
Cambridge University, 127, 238, 252, 286, 314, 421
Camden, William, 316, 317
Campion, Edmund, 284
Canada, 397, 430
Canary Islands, 299, 303, 410
Cannon law, 125–126
Canterbury: archbishopric at, 24, 25, 31, 80, 114; cathedral at, 91, 112, 121; as center of learning, 27, 122, 125; church near, 24; during Roman invasion of Britain, 11; as trade center of Anglo-Saxons, 47; travelers to, 327
Cape Verde Islands, 303
Carberry Hill, 280
Caribbean, 299, 394
Carlos, Don, 280
Carolinas, 428
Carracks, 301–302
Cartae Baronum, 84
Cartagena, South America, 303, 438
Carthusians, 117
Cartwright, Thomas, 286
Carucage, tax, 98
Castellaria, 61
Castlemaine, Barbara Villiers, Lady, 408, 434
Castles, 61, *62*, 129, 144, *145, 201. See also* names of specific castles
Catesby, Robert, 340

Cathedrals, 112, 120–122, *121*
Catherine, daughter of Charles VI, 192
Catherine, daughter of Ferdinand and Isabella, 214, 215
Catherine de Médicis, Queen of France, 278, 292
Catherine Howard, Queen, wife of Henry VIII, 248
Catherine of Aragon, Queen, wife of Henry VIII, 229, 233–235, *235*, 242, 252, 257
Catherine of Braganza, Queen, wife of Charles II, 408–409
Catherine of France, Queen, widow of Henry V, 210
Catherine Parr, Queen, wife of Henry VIII, 248
Catholics: Bill of Rights (1689) and, 419; Charles I and, 358, 365; Charles II and, 411, 414; Charles II as Catholic, 414; church under Henry VIII, 245; before Civil War, 370; after the Commonwealth, 392; doctrine of transubstantiation, 177, 253, 255; Edward VI and, 254; Elizabeth I and, 272, 282–284, 285–286; invasion of England in sixteenth century, 302–303; in Ireland, 309, 379, 387, 388, 427; James I and, 339–340, 346, 350; James II and, 415–417; Mary Queen of Scots and, 274; Mary Tudor and, 255–257, 276; Oxford University and, 416; Popish Plot and, 413; Puritans and, 285–286; Thirty Years' War and, 351–352; Toleration Act (1689) and, 420; traditional Catholicism during fourteenth century, 177
Cavaliers, 370, 384, 386, 393, 400, 405, 406
Caxton, William, 314
Cecil family, 291–292, 320. *See also* Burghley, William Cecil; Salisbury, Robert Cecil, Earl of
Celts: Anglo-Saxon invasions and, 4; defeats of, 20–21, 31, 35; invasions of England, 9–12; La Tène culture, 10–11; location of, 4, 9; Roman conquest of, 11–12, 13; as slaves, 41
Central America, 410
Ceorls. *See* Freemen
Chamberlain, Lord, Office of, 66
Chancellor, Lord, Office of, 66, 78, 138
Chancellor, Richard, 296
Chancery, 43, 107, 138–139
Channel Islands, 387
Chantries, 268
Charlemagne, 28, 31

INDEX

Charles I, King of England: Bishops' Wars and, 366–367; character of, 355–356; Civil War and, 370–371, 374–380; commerce during reign of, 400; finances of, 359, 363–364, 367–368; foreign affairs of, 362; Germany and, 357; during James I's reign, 353–354; Parliament and, 356–361, 367, 368–371, 392; personal rule of, 361–366; Petition of Right against, 359–361; portraits of, *363, 383;* proposed Spanish marriage of, 350, 353; Puritans and, 356, 357, 364–365, 419; Scotland and, 366–367; Short Parliament and, 367; trial and death of, 384–385, *385,* 386, 387, 388; war with France, 358; war with Spain, 353–354, 356–358

Charles II, King of England: Catholicism and, 411, 414; character of, 404–405; church and, 406–408; commerce during reign of, 398, 428; death of, 414; exclusion struggle and, 413–414; foreign affairs of, 408–410, 410–412, 411; music and, 424; Parliament and, 405–406, 411, 412, 413–414; personal government of, 410–412; Popish Plot and, 412, 413; portrait of, *404;* recognition of, 396; Restoration and, 401, 403–408; science and, 421; Scotland and, 388, 440; theater and, 424; view of Prince George of Denmark, 434

Charles IV, King of France, 157
Charles V, King of France, 168
Charles VI, King of France, 188, 190, 192, 193
Charles VII, King of France, 193–194
Charles VIII, King of France, 210, 213, 214, 227
Charles IX, King of France, 278, 292
Charles I, King of Spain, 227
Charles II, King of Spain, 410, 432–433
Charles V, King of Spain and Emperor, 227, 228, 229, 257, 258, 289, 293
Charles, Archduke, 435, 437
Charles, Prince of England, 350
Charles the Bold, 200
Charles the Fat, King of the Franks, 51
Charter of the Forest, 152
Chartered companies, 297
Charters: Anglo-Saxon, 43, 44; in Norman England, 66; of towns, 136
Château Gaillard, castle, 102
Chaucer, Geoffrey, 120, 177, 183–184
Chesapeake Bay colony, 395
Chester, 21, 58
Cheviots, 228

Chichester, 12
Chios, 222
Chippenham, 32
Chirograph, 43
Chivalry, 21, 160–162
Christ Church, Oxford College, 232, 416
Christian IV, King of Denmark, 356, 358, 362
Christianity. *See* Catholics; Church (Church of England); Monasteries; Papacy; and names of other religious groups and churches
Church (Church of England): in Anglo-Saxon England, 23–27, 28, 31, 37, 42; Charles I and, 359, 360–361, 364–365; Charles II and, 411; and Civil War, 370–371, 375, 380–381; concessions made by Stephen, 81; Counter Reformation and, 282–284; and Danes in England, 35; Edward I and, 152; Edward VI and, 256, 257, 275, 276; Elizabeth I and, 276–276; feudalism and, 71; in fourteenth century, 175–180; friars, 118–120; Glorious Revolution and, 419–420; Henry I and, 79–80; Henry II and, 88–91; Henry III and, 106–107; Henry VIII as Defender of the Faith, 258; Henry VIII's establishment of Church of England, 241–245, 275, 276; James I and, 337–340, *338,* 367; James II and, 415–417; John and, 100; Laudian school of churchmen, 356–357; Magna Carta and, 104; Mary Tudor and, 255–259, 275; missionary efforts toward Anglo-Saxons, 23–25; monasteries of, 25–27, 115–18; Puritans and, 284–288; radical Protestantism under Edward VI, 252–255, 276; Restoration and, 406–408; in Roman Britain, 18; in sixteenth century, 236–237; in twelfth/thirteenth centuries, 111–120; view on slavery, 41; William I and, 70–72; William II and, 75; Wolsey and, 232–233. *See also* Religious toleration
Church courts, 81, 89–90, 91, 236, 237–238, 416, 419
Churchill, Winston, 189
Cinque Ports, 84
Cistercians, 117, 121, 134
Civil jury, 88
Civil list, 420
Civil War of 1642–1646: battles of, 375–380; beginning of, 370–371; causes of, 371–373; commerce and, 428; divisions in England during, 374–375
Civil War of 1648, 384

INDEX

Clare, Richard de. *See* Pembroke, Richard de Clare, Earl of
Clarendon, Edward Hyde, Earl of, 371, 393, 403, 406, *407*, 408–410
Clarendon Code, 406–408, 420
Classes. *See* Social classes
Classics, study of, 123, 238–239
"Classis" movement, 287
Claudius, Roman Emperor, 12
Clement V, 179
Clement VII, Pope, 235
Clement VIII, Pope, 340
Clergy, Act for the Submission of, 241, 242
Clericis Laicos, 152
Clifford, Sir Thomas, 410
Cloth and cloth trade, 175, 197, 199, 220, 221, 229, 258, 260, 261–262, 266, 268, 282, 435. *See also* Wool and wool trade
Cluny, monastery of, 71, 125
Cnut, King of England, 36–37, 45, 53, 54
Cobham, Henry Brooke, Lord, 340
Codex Amiatinus, 27
Coinage, 260–261, 281
Coke, Sir Edward, 320, 343, 348, 352, 360
Colchester, 12, 13
Coleman, Edward, 413
Colet, John, 239
Coligny, Gaspard de, 292–293
Cologne, 435
Colonization of America, 297–299, 394–396, 397–398, 428–430, 438, 441, 443
Columba, St., 23–24
Columbus, Christopher, 222–223
Comitatus, 22, 59
Commendams Case, 348
Commendation, 40–41
Commerce: Anglo-French commercial rivalry, 428–430; in Anglo-Saxon England, 31, 46–47; in Bronze Age, 7–8; colonies and, 396–397; custom duties and, 151, 156, 197, 202, 219; in fifteenth century, 201; in fourteenth century, 173–175; Henry VII and, 220–222, 297; Navigation Acts and, 396–397; in Roman Britain, 16–18, *16;* in seventeenth century, 372–373; in sixteenth century, 261–262, 266–267, 290; Spanish War and, 311; tonnage and poundage duties, 360, 361, 369; trading companies and, 311–312, 372, 428; in twelfth/thirteenth centuries, 132, 134; voyages of commercial expansion under Elizabeth I, 295–297. *See also* Cloth and cloth trade; Wool and wool trade

Common law, 85, 125, 142–143, 217, 231–232. *See also* Courts of common law
Common petition, 167–168
Commonwealth (1649–1653), 385–389, 396, 397
Commutation, 132
Company of Cathay, 297
Compton, Henry, bishop of London, 416
Compton, Lady, 346
Compurgation, compurgators, 47, 86
Conciliar courts, 231–232
Confirmation of the Charters, 152, 155
Congregationalists, 287, 370, 381
Congreve, William, 433
Constable, office of, 66
Constance of Brittany, 99
Constitutions of Clarendon, 89
Conventicle Act, 406–407
Convention Parliament, 405–406
Convocation, 197, 202, 241
Conway, Treaty of, 144
Conway Castle, 144
Copernicus, 315
Copyhold, 173
Cornwall, 20, 21, 31, 213, 266, 378
Coronation Oath, 420
Coroner, office of, 98
Corporation Act, 406, 420
Corpus Juris Civilis, 83
Cortez, Hernando, 223
Cotters, 68, 323
Council: under Edward I, 138, 139–140, 139n; under Edward IV, 203; under Henry VII, 216–217. *See also* Privy Council
Council of the North, 247
Council of Trent, 283
Council of Whitby, 25
Counter Reformation, 282–284, 289, 306
Country gentlemen. *See* Gentry
Country party, 412, 432
County courts, 85
Court of chancery, 167, 231, 348, 390–391
Court of Common Pleas, 142
Court of Delegates, 242
Court of Exchequer, 142, 343–344
Court of High Commission, 288, 343, 344, 357, 365, 369, 416
Court of requests, 231
Court of the Green Cloth, 328
Court of the justiciar, 85
Court of the King's Bench, 142
Court of wards, 342, 400
Court party, 412, 432
Courtenay, Lord William, 212

Courtenay, William, Archbishop of Canterbury, 182
Courtney v. Glanvil, 348
Courts of common law, 343, 348, 370, 373, 401
Courts of law: Anglo-Saxon, 44, 45–48, 87; under Charles I, 362, 370; church courts, 81, 89–90, 91, 236, 237–238, 288; courts of piepoudre, 132; due process of law, 104; under Edward I, 140–143, 155; under Elizabeth I, 288; under Henry I, 78–79, 79–80; under Henry II, 84–88; under Henry VII and, 216–218; under Henry VIII, 247–248, 342; under James I, 342, 343–344, 348; judges after Glorious Revolution, 421; Magna Carta and, 103–104; in Norman England, 60, 65–68, 69, 75, 81; papal courts, 79–80; principle of independence to the bench, 348; principle of judicial review, 348; Wolsey and, 231–232. *See also* names of specific courts
Courts of piepoudre, 132
Coventry, 175
Craft guilds, 135
Cranfield, Lionel, 268, 347
Cranmer, Thomas, Archbishop of Canterbury, 252, 253–254, *253,* 259
Crécy, Battle of, 162, 163, *164*
Crete, 222
Crew, Sir Randolph, 359
Criminal courts. *See* Courts of law
Cromwell, Oliver: aptitude for war, 377; Barebones Parliament and, 389–391; contemporary estimates of, 386; death of, 401; dissolution of Parliament, 389; hanging of corpse of, 404; Jews and, 152; as Lord Protector, 392–393; military campaigns of, 378, 380, 384, 387–388, 397–398, 409, 414, 416, 434; portraits of, *390, 391;* religious/political views of, 381–382
Cromwell, Richard, 401
Cromwell, Thomas, 241–242, 243, 244, 246, 247, 248
Crowley, Robert, 265
Crown lands, 202, 218–219, 281
Crusades, 74, 96, 97–98
Cuba, 223
Cunobelinus, Belgic King, 12
Customs duties, 151, 156, 202, 219
Custos Rotulorum, 324

Dacre, Leonard, 291
Danby, Thomas Osborne, Earl of, 412, 413
Danegeld, 36, 43, 45, 64
Danelaw, 32, 35, 36, 45, 64
Danes, 31–32, 34, 35, 36, 51, 64
Daniel, Samuel, 316–317
Darnley, Henry Stewart, 280
David ap Gruffydd, 144, 155
David I, King of Scots, 146
David II, King of Scots, 163
Davis, John, 296
De Donis Conditionalibus, 141
Deane, Richard, 397
Declaration of Indulgence, 411, 416, 417
Declaration of Sports, 339
Decretum (Gratian), 125
Dee, John, 296
Defiance, feudal, 59
Defoe, Daniel, 433
Deira, settlement of, 21
Dekker, Thomas, 317
Demesne, lord's, 69
Denmark, 20, 31–32, 34, 35, 37, 51, 435
Derby, Henry de Ferrers, Earl of, 61
Derbyshire, Norman invasion and, 58
Descartes, René, 421
Desmond, Earl of, 213
Despenser, Hugh, 157
Devereux, Lady Penelope, 317
Devon, 1, 2, 20, 21, 266, 378
Diaz, Bartholomew, 222
Diceto, Ralph de, 126
Diggers, 381, 386
Digges, Sir Dudley, 358
Dioceses, *113,* 114
Domesday Book, 70
Dominic, St., 118
Dominicans, 112, 118–119
Dooms, 31
Dorset, settlement of, 21
Dorset, Thomas Grey, Marquis of, 227
Douai, 283
Douglas, Sir James, 148
Dover, 306, 327
Dover, Treaty of, 411
Drake, 304, 308, 311
Drake, Francis, 295, 299, 300–301, *300,* 303, 357
Drama, 318–319, 424
Drogheda, 215
Druids, 11
Dublin, 215, 427
Dudley, Edmund, 219, 227
Dudley, Guildford, 252
Dudley, John. *See* Northumberland, John Dudley, Duke of

Dudley, Robert. *See* Leicester, Robert Dudley, Earl of
Due process of law, 104
Dunkirk, 409, 438
Dunstan, Archbishop of Canterbury, 36
Durham: Battle of Neville's Cross at, 163; cathedral at, 112, 120–121, 291; county palatine of, 247; as franchise, 140; geographic features of, 1; Norman invasion and, 58; during war with Scotland, 367
Dutch. *See* Holland; Netherlands
Dutch East India Company, 312
Dutch Sea Beggars, 293–294
Dutch Wars, 397, 409, 411, 428
Dutch West India Company, 394
Dyrham, Battle of, 21

Ealdormen, 36, 45, 47
East Anglia, 21, 28, 31, 32, 35, 45, 229
East India Company, 311–312, 394, 397, 398, 400, 428, 432
East Indies, 409
Eastern Association, 377–378
Eastland Company, 297, 429
Ecclesiastical Commission court, 416, 419
Ecclesiastical courts. *See* Church courts
Edgar the Atheling, 54
Edgar the Peaceful, King, 36
Edgehill, Battle of, 377
Edinburgh, 145, 366
Edinburgh, Treaty of, 277–278
Edington, Battle of, 32
Edith, Queen, wife of Henry I, 76
Edmond, King of Sicily, 107
Edmund, Duke of Somerset, 193
Edmund Ironside, 36
Edmund of Abingdon, St., 114
Education: in Anglo-Saxon England, 27, 34–35; in Elizabethan England, 316; rise of universities, 126–128; in sixteenth century, 254; in twelfth/thirteenth centuries, 115–116, 122–123, 126–128
Edward I, King of England: character of, 138; church and, 152; France and, 137, 149–150; government of, 138–143; during Henry III's reign, 108, 109; Ireland and, 148–149; judicial system under, 68, 142–143; knights and, 364; last years of, 152; law under, 140–141; Parliament and, 153–155, *154;* Scotland and, 137, 145–148, 149; subinfeudation prohibited by, 130; taxation under, 150–152, 156; view of kingship, 137; Wales and, 137, 143–144, 149

Edward II, King of England, 146, 148, 156–157, 160, 184
Edward III, King of England: ascension to throne, 160; character of, 160; Chaucer and, 183; children of, 187, 195; chivalry and, 160–162; church and, 175; commerce and, 174; death of, 180; Hundred Years' War and, 163–165; last years of, 168–169; nobles and, 189; Parliament and, 165–168; war with France, 159, 162–165
Edward IV, King of England: character of, 201; claim of throne by, 196; death of, 204–205; finances of, 218; first decade of reign, 199–201; government of, 201–204, 247; relatives of, 212
Edward V, King of England, 205
Edward VI, King of England: birth of, 248; church and, 252–255, 256, 257, 275, 276; finances of, 260; Lord Protector Somerset and, 250–251; minority of, 250; nobility and, 319; Northumberland in power, 251–252; radical Protestantism and, 252–255
Edward, Black Prince, 161, 164, 164n, 168, 180, 183
Edward, Prince of Wales, son of Henry VI, 200
Edward, Prince, son of Edward II, 157
Edward the Confessor, King of England, 37, 50, 53–55, 64, 70, 106, 146
Edward the Elder, King of Wessex, 35
Edward the Martyr, King, 36
Edwin, King of Northumbria, 24, 28
Egbert, King of Wessex, 31
Eleanor, daughter of Simon de Montfort, 144
Eleanor of Aquitaine, Queen, wife of Henry II, 91–92, 93, 99, 100, 150
Eleanor of Provence, Queen, wife of Henry III, 106
Eliot, Sir John, 358, 360
Elizabeth I, Queen of England: attack on Spanish America, 299–301; character of, 270–271; church and, 255, 257, 276–276; colonization during reign of, 297–299; court of, 327–328; decline in political morality and, 312–313; economic reform of, 261, 281–282; foreign relations of, 272, 289–295, 337; France and, 292–293, 311; government of, 272–275; Ireland and, 309–311; maritime enterprise under, 295–302; Mary, Queen of Scots and, 279–281, 290; Netherlands and, 293–295, 303, 311; Parliament and, 329–331;

Elizabeth I, Queen of England *(cont.)*: plots against, 291–292; portrait of, *271;* Privy Council of, 328–329; problems from her reign, 333; Puritans and, 284–288, 331; Scotland and, 292; Spain and, 290–291; Spanish Armada and, 302–307; Spanish War and, 308–311; succession and, 257, 274; voyages of commercial expansion under, 295–297; as woman ruler, 272–275; youth of, 242, 271–272
Elizabeth, Princess, daughter of James I, 350
Elizabeth of York, Queen, wife of Henry VII, 212
Elizabeth Woodville, Queen, wife of Edward IV, 205
Elizabethan England: architecture in, 321–322, *321;* common people in, 323; court at Whitehall Palace, 327–328; decline in political morality, 312–313; drama in, 318–319; gentry in, 320–322; literature in, 315–319; local government in, 323–324; London in, 326–327, *326;* nobility in, 319–320; Parliament in, 329–331; Privy Council in, 328–329; social structure of, 319–326; spirit of the age, 314–315
Ellesmere, Lord Chancellor, 344
Ely, 58
Emma, wife of Ethelred the Unready, 37, 53
Empson, Richard, 219, 227
Enclosures, 264–265, 266, 323
England: definition of, 1; geographic features of, 1–5
English Act of Settlement, 441
English humanists, 238–240
English Revolution, 371
Enzinas, Francisco de, 252
Eorls, 38
Erasmus, 239
Escheat, 60
Essex: in Anglo-Saxon Britain, 21, 28, 31, 44; Peasants' Revolt in, 172; settlement of Angles and Saxons, 21
Essex, Arthur Capel, Earl of, 377, 378–379
Essex, Robert Devereux, 2nd Earl of, 308, 309, 313–314, 317
Etaples, Treaty of, 214
Ethelbald, King of Mercia, 28
Ethelbert, King of Kent, 24, 28
Ethelfleda, Lady of Mercia, 35
Ethelred the Unready, King, 36, 37, 51, 53, 87
Euclid, 124
Euphuism, 317

Eustace of Boulogne, 54
Evelyn, John, 421
Everitt, Alan, 372
Evesham, Battle of, 109
Exchequer, 85, 107, 138–139, 142, 202, 219, 246
Exclusion struggle, 413–414
Exeter, 32, 58, 127

Fagius, Paul, 252
Fairfax, Ferdinand, 378
Fairfax, Sir Thomas, 378, *378*
Fairs, 132
Falaise, 50
Falkirk, Battle of, 148
Fawkes, Guy, 340
Felton, John, 361
Ferdinand I, Emperor of Austria, 289
Ferdinand II, Duke of Styria, Emperor, 351
Ferdinand of Aragon, 214, 223, 227
Fergus I, King of Ireland, 336
Feudal aids, 60
Feudal courts, 60, 68
Feudalism: abolition of, 406; in Anglo-Saxon England, 63–64; "Bastard Feudalism," 199; church officials and, 71; under Henry II, 84; Magna Carta and, 103; in Norman England, 58–64; in Normandy, 51
Fiefs, 59, 60, 61, 68, 70, 71, 79
Field of the Cloth of Gold, 228
Fifth Monarchy Men, 381, 381n, 390
Fine on alienation, 60
Fines, 47, 69, 79, 219
Fisher, John, bishop of Rochester, 243
Fishing, 225, 394, 429
Five Mile Act, 407
Flambard, Rannulf, 75, 76
Flanders, 54, 101–102, 174, 220, 283
Flanders, Count of, 150, 163
Flodden Hill, 228
Folkmoot, 48
Forest laws, 364, 369
Forfeiture, 60
Fortescue, Sir John, 341
Forth, Firth of, 145, 278, 306
Fortresses, in Anglo-Saxon Britain, 34, 46
Fountains, monastery of, 117, 134
Foxe, John, 317
France: architecture in, 121; Charles I's war with, 358; colonies of, 397, 429–430; duchy of Normandy in, 50–53; Edward I and, 137, 149–150; Edward III's war with, 159, 162–165; Edward IV and, 199; Elizabeth I and, 272, 292–293;

France *(cont.):* Henry II and, 91–92, 99; Henry III and, 106, 150; Henry V and, 189–192; Henry VI and, 193–194; Henry VII and, 210, 213–215; Henry VIII's wars with, 227–228, 244; Huguenots in, 289, 290, 292, 293, 358, 362; Hundred Years' War and, 159, 163–165; James I and, 349; John's defeat in, 99, 101–102; Netherlands and, 294; Protestants in, 306; reaction to death of Charles I, 387; religious wars in, 289; Roman invasion of, 11, 12; St. Patrick in, 23; Scotland and, 277, 278, 289; trade and, 132, 221, 223; War of the League of Augsburg, 430–431; war with Holland in seventeenth century, 412; wars with Spain in sixteenth century, 289

Franchises, 140–141, 247
Francis I, King of France, 227, 228, 272, 289
Francis II, King of France, 251, 277, 278
Francis, Duke of Alençon, 292, 294
Francis II, Duke of Brittany, 213–214
Francis of Assisi, St., 118, 177
Franciscans, 112, 118–119
Frankpledge, 47, 68
Franks, 28, 47
Frederick V, Elector of the Palatinate, King of Bohemia, 350, 351, 353
Frederick Barbarossa, German Emperor, 93
Freemen: in Anglo-Saxon England, 37–38, 39–41, 45, 47; in Norman England, 60, 69; in twelfth/thirteenth centuries, 130–131
Friars, 118–120, 177
Frisians, 20, 31
Frobisher, Martin, 296, 304
Fur trade, 428
Fyrd, 34, 39, 45, 55, 57, 64–65, 84

Gama, Vasco da, 222
Gardiner, S. R., 371
Gardiner, Stephen, 256
Gascony, 106, 109, 132, 150, 157, 163, 168, 193–194, 220
Gauden, John, 386
Gaul. *See* Britanny
Gaveston, Peter de, 156
Gentleman, Tobias, 394
Gentry: Civil War and, 374–375; in Elizabethan England, 314, 320–322; enclosures and, 264, 265; Henry VII and, 216; representation in Parliament, 154
Geoffrey, son of Henry II, 93, 99
Geoffrey de Mandeville, 82

Geoffrey of Anjou, 80, 81, 91
George, Duke of Clarence, 202
George, Elector of Hanover, 439
George, Prince of Denmark, 434
Gerald of Wales, 123
Germanic tribes, 20
Germany: Calvinism in, 350; Charles I and, 357; commerce and, 268, 290, 311; Cromwell's interest in, 248; home of Angles, 20; James I and, 349; mines in, 260; Protestantism in, 257, 306; Renaissance in, 238; war in, 351, 362; war with France, 430
Gesiths, 38
Gibraltar, 437, 438
Gilbert, Sir Humphrey, 296, 297–298
Gilbertines, 117
Gildas, 20, 22
Glanville, Rannulf, 125–126
Glastonbury, monastery of, 117
Glendower, Owen, 187–188, 189
Glorious Revolution, 417–421
Gloucester, 13, 21, 65
Gloucester, Gilbert de Clare, Earl of, 128
Gloucester, Richard of Clare, Earl of, 109
Glouchester, Statute of, 141
Goa, 222
Goddard, Jonathan, 421
Godfrey, Sir Edmund Berry, 413
Godolphin, Sidney, 432, 433, 434–435, 437, 438
Godwin, Earl of Wessex, 53–54
Gold, 296, 351
Golden Hind, 301
Good Parliament, 169, 198
Goodwin, Sir Francis, 341
Goodwin v. Fortescue, 342
Goring, George, 374
Gower, John, 183
Grafton, Richard, 316
Grand Alliance, 430, 435
Grand assize, 88
Grand jury, 86–87
Grand Remonstrance, 370
Gratian, 125
Gravelines, Battle of, 306
Great Contract, 344
Great Council, 65–66, 106, 109, 139n, 140, 153, 155
Great Schism, 179, 237
Great Seal of England, 152, 229, 230
Greek culture and learning, 124, 238
Green Ribbon Club, 412
Greene, Robert, 317

Gregory VII, Pope, 63, 71–72, 79
Gregory XIII, Pope, 284
Gregory the Great, 24, 34
Grenville, Sir Richard, 298, 299
Grey, Lady Catherine, 274
Grey, Lady Jane, 252
Grindal, Edmund, Archbishop of Canterbury, 287–288
Grocyn, William, 239
Grosseteste, Robert, 114, 118, 119, 125
Guiana, 395
Guild merchant, 134
Guilds, 46, 134–135, 173, 267–268
Guise, Duke of, 277, 292, 294, 302
Gunpowder Plot, 340, 418
Gustavus Adolphus, King of Sweden, 362
Guthrum, Danish chieftain, 32

Hadrian, abbot of Canterbury, 27
Hadrian, Roman Emperor, 12
Hadrian's Wall, 12
Hainault, Count of, 157
Hakluyt, Richard, 295, 297, 317
Hales, Sir Edward, 416
Hales, John, 265
Halifax, Charles Montagu, 433, 435
Halifax, George Savile, Marquis of, 419
Hallstatt Celts, 10
Hampden, John, 364, 368, 377
Hampden Case, 364, 366
Hampton Court, 229
Hanover, 435
Hanover, House of, 442
Hanoverian succession, 438–439, 441
Hanseatic League, 134, 174, 220, 221–222, 297
Hapsburgs, 227, 257, 362
Harfleur, 191, 192
Harlech Castle, 144
Harley, Robert, 432, 433, 435, 437, 438. *See also* Oxford, Robert Harley, Earl of
Harold, King, son of Cnut, 37
Harold, King, son of Godwin, Earl of Wessex, 53–55, 57, 58
Harold Hardrada, King of Norway, 57
Harrington, James, 371
Harroway, 4
Harthacnut, King of England, 37
Hastings, William, 205
Hastings, Battle of, 50, *57*, 58, 59, 62
Hawkins, John, 290, 299–300, 302, 304, 308
Hein, Piet, 394
Henrietta, sister of Charles II, 411

Henrietta Maria, Queen, wife of Charles I, 354, 356–357, 358, 365
Henry I, King of England: advancement to throne, 76; Church and, 79–80; employment of Abelard of Bath, 124; government of, 77–79; nephew of, 80; personality of, 74; rebellion against, 76–77; scutage and, 62; succession problem of, 80
Henry II, King of England: Abelard of Bath and, 124–125; Angevin Empire of, 91–94, 150; appreciation of the classics, 123; birth of, 80; Church and, 88–91, 117, 123, 125, 127; government of, 83–84, 103, 107, 137; judicial system under, 126, 142; legal reforms of, 84–88, 104; significance of, 83; sons' rebellions against, 93–94; treaty of succession for, 82
Henry III, King of England: Bracton as judge under, 140; church and, 106–107; early years of, 105; France and, 150; historian's connections with, 126; knights and, 364; legal system under, 141, 143; personal rule of, 105–107; Provisions of Oxford, 107–108; Simon de Montfort and, 108–109; Wales and, 144; Westminster Abbey and, 106, 107, 122
Henry IV, King of England, 187–189, 198, 202, 210; as Henry Bolingbroke, 181, 182
Henry V, King of England, 189–192, 193, 210
Henry VI, King of England: capture and death of, 200; collapse of government under, 197–199; minority of, 192–193; relatives of, 210; war in France, 193–194; Wars of the Roses, 194–197
Henry VII, King of England: character of, 209, 281; claim to throne, 210–211; commercial policy of, 220–222, 297; death of, 225, 226; elimination of rivals, 211–213; expansion overseas, 222–223, 225; finance and, 218–220, 229; foreign relations of, 213–215; France and, 210, 213–215; government of, 230, 335; Ireland and, 215; law and order, 216–218, 231; Mary, Queen of Scots as descendent of, 272; overthrow of Richard III, 205; portrait of, *211;* Scotland and, 215; Spain and, 213–215; strengthening of kingship, 213–215; Wolsey as chaplain of, 229
Henry VIII, King of England: character of, 227, *234;* children, 274; church and, 176, 233–240, 242, 244–245, 253, 254, 258, 276; confiscation of monasteries, 265; courts of law under, 342; dissolution of monasteries, 243–244;

Henry VIII, King of England *(cont.)*: divorce from Catherine of Aragon, 257; finances of, 260; government of, 245–248, 250, 329; Ireland and, 309; last years of, 248; local government and, 323; marriage to Catherine, 214; navy and, 295, 301–302; nobility and, 319; Parliament and, 240–243, 329–330; Spain and, 235; wars of, 227–229, 235, 244, 258; wives of, 233–236, 248; Wolsey and, 229–233; as young king, 226–227
Henry I, King of France, 52–53
Henry II, King of France, 272, 277, 289
Henry III, Duke of Anjou, later King of France, 292
Henry IV, King of France, 333, 350
Henry VI, King of France, 193
Henry V, German Emperor, 80
Henry VI, German Emperor, 98
Henry, Prince of Wales, son of James I, 340, 350
Henry, son of Henry II, 93
Henry of Blois, Bishop of Winchester, 80
Henry of Navarre, 293
Henry the Navigator, Prince, 222
Heptarchy, 21, 25
Heralds' College, 321
Hereward the Wake, 58
Heriot, peasant obligation of, 69
Heron, Sir John, 219
Herstomonceaux Castle, *201*
Hexham, 26
Hilda, St., 25–26
Hildebrand. *See* Gregory VII, Pope
Hill, Christopher, 371
Historical writing, 126
Hobbes, Thomas, 371
Holinshed, Raphael, 316
Holland: Charles I and, 356, 358, 362; Charles II and, 410–411; colonies in America, 409, 428; James I and, 349; overseas expansion of, 394, 396, 397; as part of Netherlands, 293–295; Protestants in, 306; Puritans in, 339; reaction to death of Charles I, 387; recognition of Philip of Anjou as king of Spain, 433; rivalry with France, 411; Separatists in, 396; trade and, 312, 394; Treaty of Utrecht and, 438; War of the Spanish Succession, 435; wars with England in seventeenth century, 397, 409, 411, 428; wars with France in seventeenth century, 412, 430. *See also* Netherlands
Holmes, Clive, 372

Holy League, 227
Holyrood, abbey of, 148
Homildon Hill, Battle of, 188
Honor, 61
Hooke, Robert, 421
Hooker, Richard, 317
Hooper, John, 259
Hotham, Sir John, 371
House of Commons. *See* Parliament
House of Lords. *See* Parliament
Housecarls, 37, 55
Hoveden, Roger of, 126
Howard, Catherine. *See* Catherine Howard, Queen, wife of Henry VIII
Howard, Lord Admiral, 304, *304*
Howard, Lord Thomas, 308
Hudson's Bay Company, 428
Hugh of Avalon, 117
Huguenots, 289, 290, 292, 293, 358, 362
Hull, 375, 378
Humanists, 238–240
Humble Petition and Advice, 393
Humphrey, Duke of Gloucester, 192–193
Hundred courts, 46, 48, 60, 65, 67, 68, 87, 140, 141
Hundred Years' War, 159, 163–165, 193–194, 220, 259
Hundreds, 46
Huns, 21
Huntingdon, Henry of, 126

Icknield Way, 4, 6, 21
Impeachment, 167, 169, 369, 410
Impositions, 345
Independence to the bench, principle of, 348
Independents, 370, 379, 380–385, 386, 388, 390, 406, 419
India, 222, 398, 400, 430
Industrial Revolution, 2
Industry: Charles I and, 364; Elizabeth I and, 282; in fourteenth century, 173–175; glass manufacturing, 267; in Roman Britain, 16–18; in seventeenth century, 372–373, 401; in sixteenth century, 261–262, 267; in twelfth/thirteenth centuries, 134–135
Inflation, in sixteenth century, 260–261
Inheritance, rights of, 103
Innocent III, Pope, 99, 100, 105, 118
Inquest of Sheriffs, 84
Inquisition, 283
Instrument of Government, 392
Intercursus Magnus, 221
Intercursus Malus, 221

Investiture compromise, 79
Iona, 23, 24, 26, 31
Ireland: books on, 123; Catholics in, 23–25, 309, 379, 387, 388, 427; Celts in, 4; Counter Reformation and, 284; Edward I and, 148–149; Elizabeth I and, 281, 309–311; English Civil War and, 379, 382; English colonies in, 310–311; English Commonwealth and, 387–388; Henry VII and, 215; Henry VIII and, 309; James I and, 349–350; Mary Tudor and, 309; Norsemen from, 35; revolts of, 281, 370; trade and, 221; William III and, 427–428; Yorkist sympathy of, 211, 212, 213, 215
Iron Age, 10–11
Isabel of Angoulême, Queen, wife of King John, 99, 106
Isabel of Gloucester, Queen, wife of King John, 97, 99n
Isabella, Queen, wife of Edward II, 157, 160
Isabella, Queen, wife of Richard II, 188
Isabella of Castile, 214, 223
Isle of Man, 387
Isle of Wight, 188, 384
Italy, 71, 126, 214, 222, 223, 227, 228, 229, 238, 283, 315, 410, 435
Itinerant justices, 79, 84–86, 98, 140, 142, 155, 199, 218, 325
Ivan the Terrible, 296
Ivo, bishop of Chartres, 79

Jack Cade's Rebellion, 195
Jacobites, 431, 434, 439
Jamaica, 398, 428
James I, King of England, 339–340
James II, King of England: Bill of Rights and, 419; Catholicism of, 411, 413; daughter of, 412, 414; death of, 433, 439; in Ireland, 427, 428, 430; reign of, 415–417; revolution against, 405, 417, 418; Scotland and, 440; supporters during reign of William III, 426, 427, 428, 430, 432; wife of, 408
James VI and I, King of Scotland and England: American colonies and, 395; birth of, 280; character of, 334; commerce during reign of, 400; court of, 268; degeneration in government under, 345–352; foreign affairs of, 336–337, 340, 349–351; judges and, 348; last years of, 353–354; Parliament and, 340–345, 352–353, 354, 349, 350; portrait of, *335;* Puritans and, 337, 337–339; religious settlement of, 337–340, *338;* Scottish rule of, 312, 334–337;

James VI and I, King of Scotland and England *(cont.):* Spain and, 365, 394; Thirty Years' War and, 351–352; Walter Ralegh and, 315, 350–351
James IV, King of Scots, 213, 215, 228
James V, King of Scots, 228, 279
James Edward, the Old Pretender, 417, 433, 438, 439
Jamestown colony, 395
Jane Seymour, Queen, wife of Henry VIII, 248, 251
Jarrow, 26, 27, 31
Java, 222, 312
Jeffreys, George, 416
Jenkinson, Anthony, 296
Jerome, St., 27
Jerusalem, 97
Jesuits, 282, 283, 284, 289, 309, 339, 413, 416
Jews, 151–152
Joan of Arc, 193
Joan of Kent, 180
John, King of England: character of, 98; church and, 100; conflicts with Richard I, 96–97; defeat in France, 101–102; loss of Normandy, 99–100; Magna Carta and, 76, 98, 102–105; as public official, 98–99; rebellion against Henry II, 93, 94; as tyrant, 95
John II, King of France, 164, 168, 177
John, Duke of Bedford, 192
John of Gaunt, Duke of Lancaster, 168, 169, 179, 180, 181, 182, 187, 189, 210
Joint-stock companies, 297
Jones, Inigo, *347*
Joseph Ferdinand, Prince of Bavaria, 433
Journeymen, 135, 173
Judicial review, principle of, 348
Judson, Margaret, 371–372
Jury of accusation, 86–87
Jury trials, 86–88
Justices in eyre, 79
Justices of the peace, 199, 199n, 218, 247–248, 320, 321, 323, 324–326, 362, 416–417
Justiciar, 77, 78
Justiciar's court, 77
Justinian, Roman Emperor, 83, 87, 125
Jutes, 20

Kenneth II, King of Scots, 36
Kenneth MacAlpin, King of Scots, 145
Kent, 21, 24, 31, 32, 44, 172, 213, 229, 258
Kett, Robert, 266

Kett's Rebellion, 251, 265–266
Kildare, Earl of, 213, 215
King James Bible, 338, 338n
King's court of the exchequer, 77
King's courts, 79, 85
King's peace, 42–43, 86
King's writ, 79
Kingship: anarchy under Stephen, 82–83; of Anglo-Saxons, 42–44, 64, 65, 245; Charles I and, 355–356; church's relations with, 237–238; concept of king as holy and sacred ruler, 83, 245; concept of king as legislator, 83, 137; divine right of kings, 336, 355–356; Glorious Revolution and, 421; Henry I and, 77; Henry III and, 108; Henry VII and, 213–215; Henry VIII and, 245–246; James I and, 336, 355; limits of royal authority, 95; Norman monarchy, 64–65; in Normandy, 51; royal birthright to, 83; royal succession of Anglo-Saxon kings, 36, 42–43; social contract theory of, 419–420. *See also* names of specific kings
Kirkstall, monastery of, 117
Knights: under Charles I, 363–364, 369; chivalry and, 160–162; distraint of, 363–364, 369; under Edward I, 138, 152; under Henry II, 84; in Norman England, 59, 60, 61–62; in Normandy, 51; representation in Parliament, 154, 157; tournaments and, 81; in twelfth/thirteenth centuries, 128, 130
Knox, John, 272–273, 277, 279, 280, 335–336
Koran, 125
Kyd, Thomas, 318

La Rochelle, 101, 293, 358, 361, 362
La Tène culture, 10–11
Laborers, Statute of, 170, 195
Lambarde, William, 316, 325
Lancaster, House of, 195, 200, *206*, 210, 212
Lancaster, James, 311–312
Lancaster, Thomas, Earl of, 156–157
Land law, 141
Land ownership, in seventeenth century, 400–401
Landlords, 262–263
Lane, Ralph, 299
Lanfranc, Archbishop of Canterbury, 52, 72, 115, 122
Langland, William, 175, 183
Langley, Edmund, Duke of York, 180, 195
Langton, Stephen, 100, 102, 105

Langton, Walter, 152
Lasco, John à, 252
Latimer, Hugh, 259, 265
Latimer, William, 169
Laud, William, Archbishop of Canterbury, 356–357, 360, 365, 366, 367, 369, 372, 396
Lauderdale, John Maitland, Duke of, 410
Law: Anglo-Saxon, 28, 31, 34, 37, 42–48, 85, 87; cannon law, 125–126; common law, 85, 125, 142–143, 217, 231–232; forest law, 364, 369; under Henry VII, 216–218, 231; judge-made law, 143; land law, 141; reforms of Edward I, 140–141; reforms of Henry II, 84–88, 104; Roman, 83, 85, 87–88, 125–126; statute law, 143; in twelfth/thirteenth centuries, 125–126. *See also* Courts of law
Lay investiture, 79
Le Cateau-Cambrésis, 272
League of Augsburg, 430–431
Leicester, Robert Dudley, Earl of, 274–275, 295, 313, 318
Leighton, Alexander, 365
Leopold, Duke of Austria, 98
Leopold I, Emperor of Austria, 410, 432–433
Levant Company, 297, 429
Levelers, 383, 386, 401
Lever, Thomas, 265
Lewes, Battle of, 108, 109
Lewis IV, German Emperor, 163
Liberties, 247
Lichfield, 21, 31
Liege lords, 62
Lilburne, John, 386
Lily, William, 239
Linacre, William, 239
Lincoln, 13, 47, 122, 127
Lincoln, Battle of, 82
Lincoln, John de la Pole, Earl of, 212, 213
Lincolnshire, 134, 229
Lindisfarne, 24, 26, 27, 31
Lindisfarne Gospels, *26*, 27
Lionel, Duke of Clarence, 187, 195
Literature: Anglo-Saxon period, 20, 22, 34–35; classical literature, 123; in Elizabethan England, 315–319; in fourteenth century, 182–185; in twelfth/thirteenth centuries, 123
Livery and maintenance, 199, 217
Livery companies, 267
Llywelyn ap Gruffydd, Prince of Wales, 144
Local government: in Anglo-Saxon England, 44–48; in Elizabethan England, 323–324;

INDEX

Local government *(cont.)*: Henry II and, 84; Henry VII and, 217; in Norman England, 67–68; in twelfth/thirteenth centuries, 136
Lochleven Castle, 280
Locke, John, 412, 419, 421, 431
Lok, John, 296
Lollards, 177, 189
London: bishopric in, 24; cathedrals in, 239; charter of, 414; Civil War and, 375, 384; commerce and, 47, 221, 261; Danish wars and, 32; in Elizabethan England, 315, 320, 326–327, *326;* Great Fire of, 409; held by Louis of France, 105; Magna Carta and, 104; money market in sixteenth century, 268, *269;* Norman invasion and, 58; plague in seventeenth century, 409; population in twelfth/thirteenth centuries, 135; *Presbyterianism* in, 389; in Roman Britain, *16,* 17, 18; St. Paul's Cathedral in, 102; *theaters* in, 424; Tower of London, 205, 327; Wyatt's Rebellion and, 258
London Bridge, 409
London Company, 395
Longchamp, William, 96
Lord chamberlain, 328
Lord steward, 328
Lords Appellant, 181, 182
Lords lieutenants, 323–324
Lords of the Congregation, 277
Lorraine, Cardinal, 277
Louis VI (the Fat), King of France, 77
Louis VII, King of France, 91, 93
Louis, later King of France as Louis VIII, 105
Louis IX, King of France, 106, 150
Louis XI, King of France, 199
Louis XII, King of France, 227, 228
Louis XIII, King of France, 358, 362
Louis XIV, King of France, 408, 409, 410, 411, 412, 413, 417, 418, 426, 428, 430, 432–433, 435, 437, 438
Lovell, Sir Thomas, 219
Lower classes: in Elizabethan England, 323; in sixteenth century, 259–260
Loyola, Ignatius, 282
Lucy, Richard de, 84
Lusignan, Hugh de, 99
Lusignan family, 99
Luther, Martin, 226, 252–253
Lyly, John, 317
Lyons, Richard, 169

Magdalen College, 416
Magellan, Ferdinand, 223
Magna Carta, 76, 95, 98, 102–105, 107, 108, 142, 151, 152, 419
Maidston, John, 393
Maine, 53, 91, 99, 150
Maitland, John, 336
Maitland, William, 279, 280
Málaga, 437
Malay Archipelago, 222, 311, 312
Malay Peninsula, 312
Malcolm III, King of Scots, 146
Malmesbury, 26, 27
Malmesbury, William of, 126
Malplaquet, Battle of, 437
Manchester, Henry Montague, Earl of, 378, 379
Manhattan, Dutch colony at, 394
Manorial courts, 60, 69
Manors, 69, 171, *203, 243,* 262
Mansfeld, Count Ernst von, 356, 358
Map, Walter, 123
March, Earl of, 187
Marcher lords, 144, 157, 187–188, 247
Mare, Sir Peter de la, 169
Margaret, Duchess of Burgundy, 212, 213
Margaret, "Fair Maid of Norway," 146
Margaret, wife of Malcolm III, 146
Margaret Beaufort, 210, 238
Margaret of Anjou, 193, 196, 199, 200
Margaret Tudor, Queen of Scotland, 215, 219, 228, 280
Marguerite of Valois, 293
Maria Theresa, Queen of France, 410
Marian exiles, 256–257
Marlborough, John Churchill, Earl of, 432, 433, 434–435, 437
Marlborough, Sarah Churchill, Duchess of, 434, 437, 438
Marlowe, Christopher, 318
Marriage: of clergy, 70, 71, 72, 115; under feudalism, 60
Marsh, Adam, 119
Marshal, office of, 66
Marshal, William, Earl of Pembroke, 105
Marston Moor, Battle of, 379
Martin Marprelate libels, 286–287, 288
Martyr, Peter, 252, 253
Marx, Karl, 371
Mary I, Queen of England: Catholicism of, 252, 255–257; character of, 255; as child, 233; church and, 255–257, 258–259, 275; Elizabeth and, 272; Ireland and, 309; nobility and, 319; Parliament and, 258–259; portrait of, *256;* Protestants during reign of, 284; Spanish marriage of, 257–258, 274

Mary II, Queen of England, 412, 414, 417, 418, 420
Mary, Queen of Scots, 251, 272, 274, 277–281, *279*, 290, 291, 303, 312
Mary of Guise, 272, 273, 277
Mary of Modena, 413, 417
Mary Tudor, Queen of France, 228, 252, 274
Maryland, 395, 396
Masham, Mrs. Abigail, 437
Massachusetts Bay Company, 396
Massacre of St. Bartholomew, 292–293
Master of the horse, 328
Matilda, Queen, 80, 81–82, 83, 91, 233
Matilda, wife of William I, 53
Matthias, Emperor, 351
Maximilian, Emperor, 213
Medina del Campo, Treaty of, 214
Medina-Sidonia, Duke of, 303, 306
Melrose, Scotland, abbey of, 26
Melville, Andrew, 336
Mercantilism, 429
Merchant Adventurers of London, 220–221, 261, 266–267, 268, 311, 429
Merchant clothier, 175
Merchants: in Anglo-Saxon England, 46–47; Charles I and, 364; Civil War of 1642–1646, 375; custom duties and, 151; in Elizabethan England, 320; under feudalism in Norman England, 63; in fourteenth century, 174, 175; guilds and, 134–135; Henry VII and, 220; Magna Carta and, 103; in seventeenth century, 372, 401, 429; in sixteenth century, 267–268; voyages of commercial expansion under Elizabeth I, 295–297
Merchants of the staple, 174
Merchet, peasant obligation of, 69
Mercia, 21, 28, 31, 35
Methodists, 408
Methuen Treaty, 435
Mexico, 223, 261, 299–300, 410
Michael the Scot, 125
Middle class: Henry VII and, 216; nonconformity and, 408; representation in Parliament, 154–55
Millenary Petition, 338
Milton, John, 386
Mining, 267
Minorca, 438
Miracle plays, 182–183
Missionaries, 23–25
Model Parliament, 155n, 165
Monasteries: in Anglo-Saxon England, 23–27, 35; church reform and, 71, 72; Monasteries *(cont.)*: dissolution of, 243–244, 265; in fourteenth century, 175, 177–178; Henry I and, 76; king's gifts to, 43; learning and, 25–27; in Normandy, 50, 52; peasants and, 40; plague in, 169; reestablishment of, 36; in sixteenth century, 236; in twelfth/thirteenth centuries, 112, 115–18, *116*, 122; wool trade and, 134

Monck, George, 397, 401
Money market, in sixteenth century, 268, *269*
Monks, 23–27, 35, 52, 53, 71, 100, 115–118, *116*, 126, 244
Monmouth, Geoffrey of, 123
Monmouth, James Scott, Duke of, 414, 415, 418
Monopolies, 311, 352, 364, 372, 401
Mons, 430
Montagu, Edward, 161
Montague, Richard, 357
Monteagle, William Parker, 340
Montfort, Simon de, 108–109, 155
Montrose, James Graham, Marquis of, 379
Moray, James Stewart, Earl of, 279
More, Sir Thomas, 239, *240*, 243
Morley, Daniel of, 125
Morocco, 295, 410
Morrill, J. S., 372
Mortemer, Battle of, 53
Mortimer, Edmund, Earl of March, 188
Mortimer, Roger, 157, 160
Mortimer family, 187, 195
Mortmain, Statute of, 141
Mortuaries Act, 241
Motte, 61, *62*
Mount Badon, Battle of, 21
Mountjoy, Charles Blount, 310
Mountjoy, William Blount, 238
Muscovy Company, 296, 297, 429
Music, in seventeenth century, 422, 424
Muslims, 97, 125, 222
Musters, 324, 325
Mutiny Act, 420
Mystery plays, 268

Namur, 430
Naseby, Battle of, 380, 381
Nash, Thomas, 317
National Covenant, 366
National debt, 432, 443
Navarre, 227
Navigation Acts, 221, 396–397, 409, 428
Navy: Charles I and, 357–358; in Civil War, 375; under the Commonwealth, 387;

INDEX

Navy *(cont.)*: in Dutch War (1652–1654), 397; Elizabeth I and, 302; Henry III and, 301–302; Henry VIII and, 295; James I and, 344; James II and, 415; in seventeenth century, 372, 409, 411; in sixteenth century, 301–302; Spanish Armada and, 304, 306–307; wars with Holland, 409, 411
Neolithic Age, 6
Netherlands: Calvinism in, 290; Elizabeth I and, 281, 303; in fifteenth century, 199–200; independence of, 306; Puritans in, 339; Renaissance in, 238; revolt against Spain, 266, 293–295, 303; Spanish Netherlands, 291, 340, 351, 410, 430–431, 433, 437; trade and, 220–221, 223, 260, 268, 291, 312, 349; War of the Spanish Succession and, 435; war with France in sixteenth century, 311
Neville, Henry, 419
Neville family, 199. *See also* Warwick, Richard Neville, Earl of
Neville's Cross, Battle of, 163
New Custom, 151
New Jersey, 409, 428
New Model Army, 380, 397
New Netherlands, 409
New York, 409, 428
Newburgh, William of, 126
Newbury, Battle of, 379
Newcastle, William Cavendish, Earl of, 378, 379
Newfoundland, 225, 298, 429, 438
Newton, Isaac, 421–422, 433
Nigel, bishop of Ely, 84
Nimwegen, Treaty of, 412
Nobility: Anglo-Saxon, 37–39, 43, 61; appointment of church officials, 71; in armies of fourteenth century, 162; Charles I and, 367; Civil War and, 374–375; in Elizabethan England, 319–320; under feudalism in Norman England, 59–63; Henry VII and, 216; in Normandy, 51; in Parliament, 165–167; sale of peerages, 347
Nombre di Dios, 300–301
Nonconformists, 408, 411, 416, 417
Norfolk, 45, 266
Norfolk, Thomas Howard, Duke of, 291, 292
Norham, 146
Norman Conquest, 37, 55–58, 146
Normandy, 50–53, 59, 65, 77, 80, 81, 99–100, 150, 163, 191, 193
Norris, Sir John, 308
Norsemen. *See* Danes
Northampton, 127, 132, 196

Northampton, Henry Howard, Earl of, 346
Northeast Passage, 296
Northumberland, Henry Percy, Earl of, 340
Northumberland, John Dudley, 251–252, 253–255, 256, 261, 266, 274, 281
Northumberland, Thomas Percy, Earl of, 291
Northumbria, 21, 24, 25, 26, 28, 35, 36, 54, 58, 145
Northwest Ppassage, 296
Norway, 31, 37, 57, 296
Norwich, 47, 135, 175
Notestein, Wallace, 372
Notre Dame Cathedral, 126–127
Nottingham, Charles Howard, Earl of, 344, 347
Nottingham, Thomas Mowbray, Earl of, 180–182
Nova Scotia, 298, 430, 438
Novaya Zemlya, 296

Oates, Titus, 413
Oath of Allegiance, 340
Oath of fealty, 59, 65
Oath of Supremacy, 276
Oath-helpers, 47
Oaths, in Anglo-Saxon Britain, 47
Odo, Bishop of Bayeux, 62
Offa, King of Mercia, 28, 31
Orange, Prince of, 293
Ordeal of battle, 65–66, 86
Ordeal of cold water, 87
Ordeals, 47, 86, 87
Order of the Bath, 216
Order of the Friars Minor, 118
Order of the Garter, 161
Ordinances of 1311, 156, 157
Orkney Island, 145
Orleanists, 190, 192
Orléans, 193
Orleans, Duke of, 190
Ormonde, James Butler, 1st Duke of, 379
Ormuz, 222
Orosius, 35
Oswald, King of Northumbria, 24, 28
Oswy, King of Northumbria, 24, 25, 28
Otto IV, German Emperor, 101–102
Owen, John, 389
Oxford, Robert Harley, Earl of, 439. *See also* Harley, Robert
Oxford University, 114, 125, 127, 179, 189, 229, 232, 238, 239, 252, 314, 365, 413, 416

Pacification of Berwick, 367
Palatinate, 350, 351–352, 356, 362, 418, 430

Panama, 300–301, 308, 441, 443
Papacy: Avignon as papal capital, 175, 179, 237; church reform during eleventh century, 71; Elizabeth I and, 283–284; in fourteenth century, 175, 178–179; Great Schism and, 179, 237; Henry I and, 79–80; Henry VIII and, 242, 245; Holy League and, 227; Innocent III and, 100; Mary Tudor and, 257, 258–259; support of William's invasion of England, 55; William I and, 71–72; Wolsey and, 232–233. *See also* names of specific popes
Papal courts, 79–80
Paris, 51, 126–127, 210, 213
Paris, Matthew, 126
Parishes, 25, 114
Parity, doctrine of, 286
Parker, Matthew, Archbishop of Canterbury, 286, 287
Parliament: under Anne, 438; anticlerical sentiment in, 175–176; Barebones Parliament after the Commonwealth, 389–391; beginnings of, 109, 139n, 140, 153; under Charles I, 356–361, 367, 368–371, 392; under Charles II, 405–406, 411, 412, 413–414; Civil War and, 375, 380–385; under the Commonwealth (1649–1653), 385–389; Convention Parliament, 405–406; destruction by fire of, 78; under Edward I, 153–155, *154;* under Edward II, 157; under Edward III, 165–168; under Edward IV, 202; under Edward VI, 254–255; under Elizabeth I, 275–276, 281–282, 283–284, 329–331; gentry in, 320; after Glorious Revolution, 418–421; Good Parliament, 169, 198; under Henry IV, 188–189, 198; under Henry VI, 197; under Henry VII, 212; under Henry VIII, 246, 329–330; House of Commons in Elizabethan England, 329–331; impeachment proceedings in, 167, 169; under James I, 340–345, 349, 350, 351, 352–353, 354; under James II, 415, 416–417; judicial work of, 167; legislative action of, 167–168; under Mary Tudor, 257, 258–259; Merciless Parliament, 180–181; Model Parliament, 155n, 165; Peasants' Revolt and, 171; under the Protectorate, 392–393; Puritans in, 287; Reformation Parliament, 240–243; Restoration and, 403–404; under Richard II, 180–182, 198; Rump Parliament, 384; Short Parliament, 367; structure of Lords and Commons, 165, 166–167; taxation and, 151, 154, 167;

Parliament *(cont.)*: under William III, 431; Wolsey and, 230–231
Parliamentary privilege, 342
Parma, Alexander Farnese, Duke of, 294, 303–304, 306
Parr, Catherine. *See* Catherine Parr, Queen, wife of Henry VIII
Parry, Sir Thomas, 345
Parsons, Robert, 284
Patents, 352
Patrick, St., 23
Patronage, 313, 346, 431
Paul IV, Pope, 259
Paulinus, Bishop, 24
Pavia, Battle of, 213, 228, 229
Peacham, Edmund, 348
Peasants: in Anglo-Saxon Britain, 37–38, 39–41, 47; Civil War of 1642–1646, 375; definition of, 323n; in Elizabethan England, 323; enclosures and, 264–265; under feudalism in Norman England, 63; in Ireland, 427–428; Kett's Rebellion and, 266; Magna Carta and, 104; after Norman Conquest, 50; in Norman England, 60, 61, 68–69; Peasants' Revolt, 171–173, *172,* 178, 180, 183, 195; revolt in seventeenth century, 415; in sixteenth century, 229, 262; as soldiers, 162; in twelfth/thirteenth centuries, 129, 130–132
Peasants' Revolt, 171–173, *172,* 178, 180, 183, 195
Pecham, John, Archbishop of Canterbury, 119
Pedro the Cruel, King of Castile, 168
Pembroke, Richard de Clare, Earl of, 149
Pembroke, William Herbert, Earl of, 344
Penda, King of Mercia, 28
Penn, William, 398
Pennsylvania, 428
Pepys, Samuel, 421
Percy, Henry, Earl of Northumberland, 188
Percy, Thomas, 340
Percy family, 188, 197
Perrers, Alice, 169
Peru, 223, 261, 300–301
Peter of Blois, 123
Petition of Right, 360, 367
Petre, Edward, 416
Petre, Sir William, 320
Petty, Sir William, 421
Petty, assizes, 88
Petty jury, 87–88
Philip I, King of France, 74
Philip II (Augustus), King of France, 94, 97, 98, 99, 100, 101–102, 105

INDEX

Philip IV, King of France, 150, 178–179
Philip VI, King of France, 163
Philip II, King of Spain, 255, 257–258, 259, 272, 274, 275, 281, 283, 289–290, 293, 294, 296, 303, 308, 309, 312
Philip III, King of Spain, 351
Philip IV, King of Spain, 410
Philip, Archduke, ruler of Netherlands, 221
Philip, Duke of Anjou, 433, 435, 437, 438
Philip, Duke of Burgundy, 193
Philip the bold, 190
Philip the Good, Duke of Burgundy, 192
Philippa of Hainault, Queen of England, 157, 169
Philippines, 410
Philosophy, study of, 123–124, 127
Physicians, College of, 239
Picts, 18, 145
Piers Ploughman, 265
Pilgrimage of Grace, 245
Pilgrims, 339, 396
Pinkie Clough, Battle of, 251
Pinteado, Antonio, 295
Piracy, 21, 31, 35, 51, 290, 400
Pius V, Pope, 283
Pizarro, Francisco, 223
Plagues, 159, 163, 164, 169, 170, *170*, 173, 236, 326, 357, 409
Plantations Act, 429
Pluralities Act, 241
Plymouth, 188
Plymouth colony, 396
Plymouth Company, 395
Poitiers, Battle of, 162, 164
Poitou, 92, 99, 102, 106, 150
Pole, Michael de la, 180–181
Pole, Reginald, 256, 258, 276
Pole, William de la, 193
Political parties. *See* Tories; Whigs
Pollamus, Vallerandus, 252
Poor: in Elizabethan England, 326–327; in seventeenth century, 373, 401
Poor law, 325–326
Pope, Alexander, 433
Popish Plot, 412, 413
Population: of American colonies, 428; in fourteenth century, 169; in seventeenth century, 372–373; of towns during twelfth/thirteenth centuries, 135; in twelfth/thirteenth centuries, 128
Portreeve, 46
Portsmouth, 375
Portugal, 222–223, 296, 297, 303, 311, 398, 429, 435

Poynings, Sir Edward, 215
Praemunire, Statute of, 176, 241
Prayer Book, 254, 255, 266, 276, 287, 366, 367, 406
Predestination, doctrine of, 285, 338
Prerogative courts, 370, 403
Presbyterians, 286–287, 339, 370, 375, 379, 380–385, 386, 388, 389, 401, 406, 440, 441
Presbyteries, 286
Pride, Thomas, 384
Pride's Purge, 384
Priests, 114–115, 178, 236–237, 241–242, 254, 276, 283
Primer seizin, 60
Primogeniture, 59–60
Privateering, 293–294, 409
Privy Council, 246, 258, 268, 273–274, 323, 328–329, 365, 369, 439
Privy Seal, 152, 230
Probate Act, 241
Protectorate (1653–1659), 392–393, 401
Protestant Union, 350, 352
Protestantism. *See* Church (Church of England)
Provisions of Oxford, 107–108, 109, 143, 156
Prussia, 435
Prynne, William, 365, 366
Ptolemy, 124
Puiset, Hugh de, 96
Purcell, Henry, 422, 424
Puritan Revolution, 371, 404
Puritans: beginning of Civil War and, 371–372; Charles I and, 356, 357, 364–365, 419; Civil War and, 386; drama and, 424; Elizabeth I and, 284–288, 313, 315; James I and, 331, 336, 337, 337–339, 342, 346; Massachusetts Bay Company and, 396; reaction abroad to, 387; Restoration and, 405; Strafford and, 367
Purveyance, 152, 152n, 342, 344
Pym, John, 367, 368, 370

Quakers, 381, 381n, 406
Quebec, 430
Quia Emptores, Statute of, 141

Rainolds, John, 339
Ralegh, Sir Walter, 297, 298–299, *298*, 308, 314–315, 340, 350–351, 394
Ramillies, Battle of, 437
Rammekens, 294
Raymond, George, 311
Recusancy Laws, 284
Redwald, King of East Anglia, 24, 28

Reformation, English, 238, 255, 257, 258
Reformation, Scottish, 277–278, 335–336
Reformation Parliament, 240–243
Regnans in Excelsis, 283
Relief, 59–60
Religious toleration, 339–340, 392, 393, 411, 412, 416–417, 419
Renaissance, 122–128, 238–240, 314–315
Repton, 21
Restoration (1660), 393, 401, 403–408, 440
Revocation, Act of, 366
Rhuddlan Castle, 144
Rhuddlan, Statute of, 144
Richard I, King of England, 93, 94, 95–98, 95–98, 102, 141, 146
Richard II, King of England, 149, 172, *172,* 180–182, *181,* 183, 187, 198
Richard III, King of England, 204–205, *204,* 210, 211, 212
Richard, Duke of Gloucester, 203
Richard, Duke of York, 193, 195, 196
Richmond, Henry Fitzroy, Duke of, 227, 233
Ridley, Nicholas, 259
Ridolfi, Roberto di, 291–292
Rievaulx, monastery of, 117, 134
Ripon, 26
Rizzio, David, 280
Roanoke Island, 298–299
Robert, Duke of Normandy, 74–75, 76–77
Robert, Earl of Gloucester, 81–82
Robert, Earl of Leicester, 84
Robert I, King of Scots, 148
Robert of Chester, 125
Robert of Jumièges, Archbishop of Canterbury, 54, 55
Robert the Magnificent, Duke of Normandy, 52
Robsart, Amy, 275
Roches, Peter des, 106
Rochester, 24, 47
Roger, bishop of Salisbury, 77
Roman Britain: commerce and industry in, 16–18, *16;* country life in, 15–16; decline of, 18; Roman invasions of Britain, 11–12; Rome's impact on, 13, 18; towns in, 13, 15
Roman culture, 238
Roman law, 83, 85, 87–88, 125–126
Rooke, George, 437
Root and Branch party, 380
Rouen, 50, 51, 193
Roundheads, 370, 400, 405
Royal Adventurers of England Trading to Africa, 428

Royal African Company, 428
Royal Society, 421, 422
Royalists, 386, 387, 396, 400, 401, 405
Rump Parliament, 384
Rupert, Prince, 377, 379, 421
Russell, Conrad, 372
Russell, William, Lord, 414
Russia, 296, 387
Rye House Plot, 414
Ryswick, Peace of, 431, 432

Sacheverell, Henry, 437–438
Saints. *See* names of specific saints
St. Albans, 12, 117, 126, 230
St. Albans, Battle of, 195
St. Giles's Cathedral, 366
St. Giles's Fair, 132
St. Ives, 132
St. John, Oliver, 381
St. Mary's monastery, 117
St. Paul's Cathedral, 102, 239, 242, 409, *422*
Saladin, King of Egypt and Syria, 97
Salisbury, 122, 350
Salisbury, John of, 123
Salisbury, Robert Cecil, Earl of, 313–314, 341, 343, 344, *344,* 345–346
Salisbury, Roger of, 80, 81
Salisbury Plain, 65
San Juan de Ulúa, 299–300
Sancroft, William, Archbishop of Canterbury, 417
Sanctuary, 238, 241
Santa Cruz, Marquis of, 303
Santo Domingo, 299, 303, 398
Savoy, 435
Saxons, 18, 20–21
Scandinavia. *See* Denmark; Norway; Sweden
Schellenberg, Battle of the, 436
Schleswig, Denmark, 20
Scholasticism, 123–124
Science: in Elizabethan England, 315; in seventeenth century, 421–422; in twelfth/thirteenth centuries, 124–125
Scotland: attack on England during twelfth century, 81; Celts in, 4, 35; Charles I and, 366–367; Charles II and, 410; Christianity in, 23; Civil War and, 379, 383, 384; Commonwealth and, 388–389; connections with Ireland in sixteenth century, 309; cooperation with England, 278; Edward I and, 137, 145–148, 149; Elizabeth I and, 278–281, 292; English conquest of, 388–389; France and, 251, 277, 278, 289; geographic features of, 2–4;

INDEX

Scotland *(cont.)*: Henry VII and, 215; Henry VIII and, 228; Kirk of, 366–367, 441; monasteries in, 26; Parliament of, 366–367, 440, 441; Picts from, 18; Reformation in, 277–278, 335–336; Romans' decision not to conquer, 12; union with England, 342–343, 349, 433, 440–441, 443
Scots, 18, 145
Scrofula, 65
Scutage, 62–63
Security, Act of, 441
Sedgemoor, Battle of, 415
Seekers, 381, 381n
Self-denying Ordinance, 380
Sens, William of, 121
Separatists, 380, 396
Serfs, 68
Settlement, Act of, 420–421
Seymour, Thomas, 271–272
Shaftesbury, Anthony Ashley Cooper, Earl of, 410, 412, 413, 414
Shakespeare, William, 12, 188, 189, 204, 317, 318–319, 325, 424
Sheriffs: in Anglo-Saxon Britain, 45, 47; in Elizabethan England, 323, 324; in fifteenth century, 199; under Henry I, 78–79; under Henry II, 84; under Henry VII, 218; in Norman England, 64, 67–68
Sheriff's tourn, 67
Shetland Islands, 145
Shield money, 62–63
Ship money, 364, 366, 369
Shire courts, 45–46, 67, 75, 87, 140
Shires, 44–48, 65
Short Parliament, 367
Shrewsbury, 155
Shrewsbury, Battle of, 188
Shrewsbury, Charles Talbot, Duke of, 439
Sicily, 107
Sidney, Algernon, 414, 419
Sidney, Sir Philip, 317
Signet, 230, 230n
Silver, 260
Simier, Jean de, 294
Simnel, Lambert, 212, 213, 215
Simony, 70, 71, 72
Six Articles, 243, 245, 254
Skippon, Philip, 379
Slavery, 16, 22, 37–38, 41, 68, 299, 396, 409, 415, 428, 430, 438
Sluys, Battle of, 163
Small Council, 66–67, 77, 139n
Social classes: in Anglo-Saxon Britain, 37–41; Civil War and, 374–375; in Elizabethan England, 319–326; in fourteenth century, 170–173; Henry VII and, 216; in Parliament, 154–155, 165–167; in Roman Britain, 15–16; in seventeenth century, 400–401, 405–406; in twelfth/thirteenth centuries, 128–132. *See also* Barons; Knights; Lower classes; Merchants; Middle class; Nobility; Peasants; Poor
Social contract, 419, 420
Society of Jesus, 282, 283, 284, 289
Solemn League and Covenant, 379, 380, 388
Somers, John, 433, 435
Somerset, 117
Somerset, Edmund Beaufort, Duke of, 195
Somerset, Edmund Seymour, Earl of Hertford, Lord Protector, Duke of, 250–251, 252, 253–254, 260, 265, 266, 271
Somerset, John Beaufort, Duke of, 192, 195, 210
Sophia, Electress Dowager of Hanover, 421
South America, 299, 410. *See also* names of specific countries
Spain: bullion of, 261; Drake's attacks on, 303; Elizabeth I and, 290–291; empire of, 410; Hapsburgs of, 227, 362; Henry VII and, 213–215; Henry VIII's war with, 227, 228–229, 235; Inquisition in, 283; James I and, 340, 349–350, 351, 353, 365, 394; Netherlands' revolt against, 266, 293–295; partition treaties and, 432–433; reaction to death of Charles I, 387; Thirty Years' War and, 351–352; trade and, 220, 221, 297, 311, 349, 429; voyages of discovery overseas, 223; War of the Spanish Succession, 435–437; war with England during sixteenth century), 308–311; war with England under Charles I, 353–354, 356–358; wars with France, 289, 430
Spanish America, 290, 299–301, 303, 349, 397–398, 441
Spanish Armada, 289–290, 295, 302–307, *305*, 308, 344
Spanish Islands, 397–398
Spanish Netherlands, 291, 340, 351, 410, 430–431, 433, 437
Spanish War (1588–1603), 308–311
Spanish West Indies, 397
Spenser, Edmund, 317–318
Spes, Don Guerau de, 291, 292
Spice Islands, 311
Spottiswoode, John, 366
Spurs, Battle of the, 228
Staffordshire, 58

Stamford, fair at, 132
Stamford Bridge, Battle of, 57–58, 199
Staple Act, 429
Star Chamber, 216–217, 219, 231, 246, 288, 329, 369
Statutes of Provisors, 176
Steele, Sir Richard, 433
Steelyard, 221
Steenkerke, Battle of, 430
Stephen, Count of Blois, 80
Stephen, King of England, 80–83, 88, 115
Steward, office of, 66, 129
Stigand, Archbishop of Canterbury, 55
Stirling Castle, 148
Stoke, Battle of, 212
Stone, Lawrence, 371
Stone Age, 5–6
Stone of Scone, 148
Stonehenge, 8–9, *8*
Stourbridge Fair, 132
Stow, John, 316
Strafford, Thomas Wentworth, Earl of, 356, 367–370
Strathclyde, 20, 21, 35, 145
Strickland, Walter, 287
Stuart, House of, 423
Stuart, Lady Arabella, 340
Stukeley, Sir Thomas, 284
Subinfeudation, 61, 130, 141
Subvassals, 61
Succession, Act of, 242–243
Suffolk, Charles Brandon, Duke of, 228, 252, 274
Suffolk, Thomas Howard, Earl of, 344, 347
Sugar, 267, 396, 398, 396
Sumatra, 222, 312
Sunderland, Robert Spencer, Earl of, 416, 438
Supremacy, Act of, 242, 276, 288
Surety, 47
Surrey, Thomas Howard, 1st Earl of, 228
Sussex, 21, 28, 31, 44, 54, 108
Sutton Hoo, 28
Swabians, 20
Sweden, 37, 362, 410–411, 430
Swein, King of Denmark, 36
Swein, son of Godwin, Earl of Wessex, 54
Swift, Jonathan, 433
Switzerland, 257
Swynford, Katherine, 189, 210

Tamworth, 21
Tangier, 408, 409
Tawney, R. H., 371

Taxation: of clergy, 177; under Edward I, 150–152; under Henry VI, 197; in Norman England, 70; Parliament and, 154, 167
Ten Articles, 243
Tenant farmers, 323
Test Act, 411, 413, 415–416, 417, 419, 420
Teutonic tribes, 20
Tewkesbury, Battle of, 200
Theater. *See* Drama
Thegns, 34, 35, 38, 41, 44, 45, 54, 55, 63
Theobald, Archbishop of Canterbury, 89, 123, 125
Theodore of Tarsus, Archbishop of Canterbury, 25, 27
Thérouanne, 228
Thirty Years' War, 351–352, 362
Thomas of Woodstock, Duke of Gloucester, 180–182
Tillières, Count Leveneur de, 334
Tinchebrai, Battle of, 77
Tithes and tithing, 47, 391
Toleration Act (1689), 420, 420n
Tonge, Israel, 413
Tonnage and poundage duties, 360, 361, 369
Tories: Anne and, 434–435, 437–439; Charles II and, 414; James II and, 415–416; in seventeenth century, 412; as social class, 406; William III and, 431–432, 433
Tostig, 54, 57
Toulon, 435
Tournai, 228
Tournaments, 81, 130, 160–161
Tower of London, 205, 327
Towns: in Anglo-Saxon Britain, 46–47; in fourteenth century, 173; industry in, 261–262; in Roman Britain, 13, 15; in twelfth/thirteenth centuries, 135–136
Towton, Battle of, 196
Trade. *See* Commerce
Trading companies, 311–312, 372, 428, 441
Treasons Act, 243
Treasurer, office of, 138
Treaties. *See* names of specific treaties
Tresham, Francis, 340
Trevisa, John of, 182
Trials. *See* Courts of law
Trials for Treason Act, 420
Tribal Hidage, 31
Triennial Act, 369, 403, 420
Triple Alliance, 410–411
Troyes, Treaty of, 192
True Levelers, 386

INDEX

Tudor, Edmund, Earl of Richmond, 210
Tudor, House of, *224*
Tudor, Jasper, Earl of Pembroke, 210
Tudor, Owen, 210
Turkey Company, 297
Turks, 97, 297, 415
Tuscany, 349
Tuscany, Duke of, 303
Tutbury, 291
Tyler, Wat, 172, *172*
Tyrconnel, Hugh Roe O'Donnell, Lord of, 309
Tyrone, Hugh O'Neil, Earl of, 309, 310, 314

Ulster, 23, 309, 310, 364, 370
Uniformity (1548–1549), Act of, 254–255
Uniformity (1559), Act of, 276
Uniformity (1662), Act of, 406
Union of Utrecht, 294
Unitarians, 420
Universities: in Elizabethan England, 315; in Renaissance, 238; in twelfth/thirteenth centuries, 126–128. *See also* names of specific universities, such as Oxford University
University College, 416
Urban II, Pope, 97
Urbanization. *See* Towns
Urn societies, 9
Utrecht, Treaty of, 438

Vacarius, 125
Val-ès-Dunes, Battle of, 52
Vane, Sir Henry the Younger, 381, 405
Varaville, Battle of, 53
Vassals, 59–63, 63, 64, 68, 71
Venables, Robert, 398
Venetian merchants, 222
Venezuela, 351, 395
Venice, 222, 227, 349
Venice Company, 297
Vera Cruz, 438
Vere, Robert de, 180–181
Verneuil, Battle of, 193
Verulamium. *See* St. Albans
Vicomte, 52
Vikings, 31–32, 36, 145. *See also* Danes
Villages, 47, 69, 130. *See also* Towns
Villas, 16
Villeins, 68, 69, 130–132, 171, 173. *See also* Peasants
Virgate, 131
Virginia, 395, 396

Vulgate Bible, 27, 179, 182
Wales: books on, 123; Celts in, 4, 12, 20, 21; Christianity in, 23, 24; Edward I and, 137, 143–144, 149; franchises in, 247; geographic features of, 1–5; Henry IV and, 187–188; Henry VIII and, 247–248; James I and, 344; Norman war against, 54; Roman conquest of, 12
Wallace, William, 148
Waller, Sir William, 379
Wallingford, Treaty of, 82
Walter, Hubert, 97, 98, 100
Walter of Coutances, 96
War of the League of Augsburg, 430–431
War of the Spanish Succession, 435–437
Warbeck, Perkin, 212–213, 214, 220
Wardship, 60
Warham, William, Archbishop of Canterbury, 232
Wars of the Roses, 194–197, *196*, 204, 319
Warwick, Edward, Earl of, 212, 213
Warwick, Richard Neville, Earl of, 197, 198, 199, 200, 202, 204
Warwick, Thomas de Beauchamp, Earl of, 180–182
Waverley, monastery at, 117
Wearmouth, monastery at, 26, 27
Wells, cathedral at, 121–122
Wendover, Roger of, 126
Wentworth, Peter, 287
Wergeld, 38, 39, 41, 45, 47
Wessex, 21, 28, 31, 32, 45
West Indies, 298, 303, 394, 395, 396, 397, 410, 415, 428, 429, 430, 438
West Saxons, 21
Westminster, 65, 76, 81, 84, 85, 88, 139, 142, 229, 369, 429
Westminster Abbey, 53, 106, 107, 122, 167, 205, 216
Westminster Assembly, 380
Westminster Hall, 185
Westminster II Statute, 141
Westmorland, Charles Neville, Earl of, 291
Whig Junto, 432, 435, 437, 438
Whigs: Anne and, 434–435, 437, 438, 439; Charles II and, 414; James II and, 415; in seventeenth century, 412, 414; as social class, 406; William III and, 426, 431–432, 433, 437
Whitby, monastery at, 25
White, John, 299
Whitgift, John, 288
Widow's dower, 63, 103
Wilfrid, Bishop, 26

William I, King of England (William the Conqueror): birth of, 50–51; character of, 51, 52, 53; children of, 80; church and, 70–72, 89, 115; death of, 61; division of possessions among sons, 74–75; Domesday Book and, 70; government of, 64–68, 78, 137; as heir of Edward the Confessor, 50; introduction of feudalism to England, 58–59; James I's view of, 336; local government of, 67–68; as Norman duke, 52–53; Norman invasion of England, 55–58, 146

William II, King of England, 67, 74, 75, 76, 78

William III, King of England, Stadtholder of Holland: character of, 426; death of, 433; as Dutch ruler, 412, 414, 426; English politics and, 431–432; Glorious Revolution and, 417–421; Ireland and, 427–428; partition treaties and, 432–433; Scotland and, 440–441; war with France, 427–431

William I, King of Scots, 93

William II, King, Stadtholder of Netherlands, 387

William, Prince of Orange, 294

William, son of Henry I, 80

Willoughby, Sir High, 296

Wiltshire, 21

Winchelsea, Robert, 152

Winchester, 12, 43, 65, 127, 132

Windmill Hill people, 6, 7

Winstanley, Gerrard, 386–387

Winter, John, 301

Witan, 42, 44, 52, 53, 54, 65

Wite, 47

Witham Abbey, 117

Witnesses, in courts of law, 47

Wolsey, Thomas, Cardinal: as administrator, 226, 230–231, 248; career of, 229; character of, 229–230; church and, 232–233; courts and, 231–232; fall of, 235, 239, 241;

Wolsey, Thomas, Cardinal *(cont.)*: foreign affairs and, 228; Henry VIII's desire for divorce and, 235

Women: in Anglo-Saxon England, 38–39, 63; in Elizabethan England, 323; under feudalism, 60, 63; in fourteenth century, 161; Henry VII and, 217; Magna Carta and, 103; in Norman England, 69; religious orders of, 117; in sixteenth century, 257

Wood, Benjamin, 312

Wool and wool trade, 132, 134, 156, 159, 173–175, 197, 220, 221, 261, 429. *See also* Cloth and cloth trade

Worcester, Battle of, 388, 414

Wren, Sir Christopher, 421, 424, 433

Writ of prohibition, 343

Writ praecipe, 103

Writs, 43

Writs of habeas corpus, 359

Writs of quo warranto, 141

Wyatt's Rebellion, 258, 272

Wych, Richard, 114

Wycliffe, John, 175, 177, 179

Wyndham, Thomas, 295–296

Yeomen, 264, 320, 323

York: abbey at, 117; in Anglo-Saxon Britain, 47; archbishopric at, 31, 72; as center of learning in the Anglo-Saxon period, 27; Christianity in, 26; Civil War in, 379; cloth trade in, 175; geographic features of, 1; Norman invasion and, 57, 58; population during twelfth/thirteenth centuries, 135; reconquest from Danes, 35; Statute of, 157; as Roman town, 13

York, House of, *207*, 210, 211, 212

Yorkists, 195–196

Yorkshire, monastery at, 117, 134

Zeeland, 267, 311